# DEVIANCE AND MEDICALIZATION

**FROM BADNESS TO SICKNESS**

# DEVIANCE AND MEDICALIZATION

## FROM BADNESS TO SICKNESS

**PETER CONRAD**

Brandeis University,
Waltham, Massachusetts

**JOSEPH W. SCHNEIDER**

Drake University,
Des Moines, Iowa

Foreword by **Joseph R. Gusfield**

Illustrated

**The C. V. Mosby Company**

ST. LOUIS • TORONTO • LONDON 1980

Printed in the United States of America

The C. V. Mosby Company
11830 Westline Industrial Drive, St. Louis, Missouri 63141

**Library of Congress Cataloging in Publication Data**

Conrad, Peter, 1945-
Deviance and medicalization: from badness to sickness.

Includes bibliographies and index.
1. Deviant behavior. 2. Social control. 3. Mental illness. 4. Mental health policy. 5. Social ethics.
I. Schneider, Joseph W., 1943- joint author.
II. Title.
HM291.C64 301.6′2 79-20333
ISBN 0-8016-1025-7

GW/M/M 9 8 7 6 5 4 3 2 1 05/D/603

# FOREWORD

The idea of progress is by no means spent. Western societies, and the United States in particular, retain the optimism of the Enlightenment in the belief that in science and technology will be found the means for achieving good and avoiding evil. There is hardly a chapter in the history of the achievements of science as glorious as that of bacteriology's defeat of infectious diseases. Where today is the fear of diphtheria, typhoid, smallpox, or poliomyelitis? The technical apparatus of medicine and its practitioners have been the recipients of that beneficial movement in the eradication of human woes. That such diseases have become the metaphor for many other, perhaps less tractable, woes is the major thought of this volume. Peter Conrad and Joseph Schneider have given a clear and definitive description and analysis of how the "medical model" has become so much of the reality of contemporary public problems. The contribution is both to the general sociological analysis of social problems and to the specific debate and discussion of medicine as a paradigm with which to understand and respond to public problems usually termed "deviance."

During the past two decades, sociology has begun to return to its historic emphasis on the socially shared character of human problems. In a stress on human events as interpreted phenomena rather than objectively and abstractly viewed, this past generation of sociologists has called attention to the necessity for an analysis of public problems to explain the reality of the problem itself. How is it that a particular phenomenon comes to be considered "problematic" and invested with a certain nature? Alcoholism, homosexuality, racial conflict, rebellions, child abuse, and the many situations seen as public problems are not to be "taken for granted." Before they can be explored, their status as problems must be understood. This challenge to the attribution of "deviance" as something clear and unambiguous to the sociologist has been the central note in the loud challenge to past theories and studies of crime, mental health, and the other social problems that make up the content of undergraduate texts. In the writings of influential sociologists such as Howard Becker, Eliot Freidson, Erving Goffman, Thomas Scheff, and others, loosely called "labeling theorists," the approach stressed the ways in which one group used "deviance" to define another. More recently, in the hands of sociologists with a greater interest in the construction of cognitive categories, there is a deeper interest in the ways in which categories are articulated and utilized. Here such sociologists as Aaron Cicourel, Jack Douglas, Harold Garfinkel, and David Sudnow are predominant. Most recently the entire tradition has moved toward an even more historical concern for the development of social problems, as indicated in Malcolm Spector and John Kitsuse's work, *Constructing Social Problems*. As Conrad and Schneider indicate, they agree with these two authors that "the process by which members of groups or societies define a putative condition as a problem . . . is the distinctive subject matter of the sociology of social problems."*

A belief in the multiplicity of ways to conceive the world of nature and of humans and a skepticism about the claims of the medical model to greater validity underlie this signifi-

*Spector, M., and Kitsuse, J. *Constructing social problems*. Menlo Park, Calif.: The Benjamin/Cummings Publishing Co., 1977, p. 415.

cant book. The recent public attention to the mass suicide of the People's Temple at Jonestown, Guyana, is an example of the opposing character of popular thought. After the news of Reverend James Jones and his followers, the media of communication searched out many experts for public guidance and an explanation of how the mass suicide of 900 people could occur. Most often television, radio, newspapers, and magazines turned to psychiatrists, psychologists, and sociologists with the assumption that this bizarre behavior was a sign of sickness, of abnormality. It could only be explained as something that "normal" people could never do.

Such interpretations lost sight of the multifold histories of the normalization of many similar phenomena. The Charge of the Light Brigade or the stubborn refusal of military heroes to surrender, as at the Alamo, seems "normal" to those who have rehearsed such actions as the response to the rules of their societies. The hara-kiri of the traditional Japanese ritual suicide seems understandable to Western minds who have come to know something of Japanese history and culture. In view of the fact that the members of the People's Temple were isolated from continuous outside contacts, imbued with a sense of beleaguerment, and had an authoritarian social organization, the Jonestown mass suicide may be unusual or bizarre, but it can be seen as normalized within that social existence and not a sign of sickness. The Indian suttee is only "sick" to the stranger who fails to recognize the preparation for it in Indian socialization and the difficult life the widow faced if she did not immolate herself on her husband's funeral pyre.

Implicit in all of us who are identified with studying social problems as social constructions is a deep-seated belief in the relativism of fact. There is no "true" problem or "true" solution. Reality, like morality, is subject to explanation and analysis. It is, but it need not be. At least in many of the realms customarily studied by sociologists, not only is "one man's moral turpitude another man's innocent pleasure" but what is fact today and may never have been fact until today may be fiction tomorrow. Science and medicine are not exempt from the relativizing light of social anthropology in the hands of sociologists.

In at least two significant ways this book greatly advances our use of social constructionist perspectives. First, it emphasizes the history of particular problems. Alcoholism, homosexuality, child abuse and child hyperactivity, opiate addiction, and mental disturbance—the specific cases studied here—have not been constant phenomena. They have changed through history and even now are in the process of being as well as having become. This attentiveness to the history of problems is crucial to any understanding of the cultural and social framework within which public problems and public issues are discussed. History is, at least here, also a relativizing device. It gives distance and strangeness to what is otherwise seen as near and familiar. The medicalization of social problems, in each of the cases, is not the culmination of a movement to find a solution to the problems but only another period in which one imputed reality is substituted for another.

There is in this stance a certain ironic mood—a distancing of the observer from the observed. Those being analyzed—the members of the society, official agents, major spokesmen—are caught up in the Enlightenment view of history as evolution toward progress. Science is, in this formulation, outside of history—not itself a target of study. Those doing the analyzing—the sociologists themselves—are not so caught up. They will not give medicine and its claim to authority through science any special consideration or status. They take it as topic rather than resource.

The second aspect of Conrad and Schneider's work that is significant is that they take seriously the perspective that public definitions of public problems are the outcomes and continual objects of claims that interested groups put forth in public arenas. Homosexuality is the clearest instance of how the nature of the problem has been fought about in public places. The appellations of sin, illness, and alternative sexual preference all indicate different ways of "seeing" the phenomena of homosexual relationships. Organizations, groups, and individual persons seek to influence the definition of the problem and the belief in the "facts" about it. Some of their claims receive greater support by the public than others. In 1979, laws concerning homosexuality were objects of elections in several states, and opposing groups debated, discussed, and even fought about these issues.* The same has certainly been the case in other areas of social concern, especially alcoholism, drug addiction, and child abuse. What is essential to Conrad and Schneider's perspective is that these conflicts involve claims to have factual belief as well as moral judgment accepted or rejected. In the eyes of many self-designated "homosexuals," to be seen as "ill" is to be derogated. Hence they struggle to achieve a "normalization" rather than a "sick role." They liken themselves to participants in the black and the civil rights movements and not to the mentally ill and the struggle for institutional facilities.

This focus on a "politics of reality" is part of the importance of *Deviance and Medicalization*. It is essential to the third significant feature of the book and to its special importance: the specific analysis of how the medical model has been used in the social construction of the reality of social problems. Looking at medicine as only another form of constructing social solutions has the consequence of raising questions concerning the adequacy of that model and the possibility of alternatives to it.

Conrad and Schneider have given us a threefold conception of the metaphor of medicine in contemporary public problems. "Sickness" has a cognitive, a moral, and an institutional dimension. To define people who behave "strangely"—homosexuals, opiate addicts, hyperactive children, and child abusers—as "sick people" changes their role in society and their status as deviants. "Illness" puts the object of concern under a different moral light than does "sin" or "preference." It introduces an element of compulsion into the cognitive reality of the phenomenon. As Talcott Parsons suggested, my slipped disc is a legitimate excuse for not giving that lecture today. The "sick" are neither criminal nor morally responsible for their "disease." However, as sick people, they are both obligated and entitled to be helped. Defined as having medical problems, they are fit objects of treatment by medical institutions. They can be cured and helped by a technical knowledge.

It is this shift in moral and institutional settings that has been the occasion for so much of the recent debate about the acceptance or rejection of the medical model in what have been defined, in public arenas and in social studies, as problems of deviance. Conrad and Schneider are adept in describing and analyzing this issue and its development. Solutions to human problems often create new problems in solving initial ones. This has been the case with the use of medicine in the public problems described in this volume. The transformation of problems from ones of badness to ones of sickness has a ring of humanitarian concern. The love of man for man or woman for woman, the wildness of children, or the desire to continually use opiates comes to be seen in neutral, amoral terms. The onus of being "bad people" is cast off when the same phenomena are now viewed as "disease." It makes it less possible for morally upright people to ignore these people's "problems" and makes feasible development of institutional and public facilities for their care.

But in the wake of this change came at least three new issues that raise significant questions concerning the application of the medical metaphor. The concept of compulsive behavior suggests helplessness and loss of control that is itself an unflattering self-portrait to which many object. Better to be thought a sinner, but responsible for myself, than to be a victim of the fates! There is a moral connotation to sickness that underlies the humanitarian perception of the deviant as victim.

There is also another meaning implicit in compulsion, although also contained in the idea of sin. Accepting this concept is an admission of deviance; a way of agreeing with the labelers. One says, "I am thus and so, and I should wish to be otherwise [what I have elsewhere called the "reluctant deviant"]; if I am not bad because I am sick, my supposed affliction is bad." Homosexuality, addiction to opiates, and drinking too much are "deviant" with all the moral connotations that term implies. It is this

*Gusfield, J. California ceremony. *The Nation,* Dec. 9, 1978, *227,* 633-635.

consideration that leads many arrested and drinking drivers to object to the label "alcoholic." In recent years the struggle of homosexuals to shed the label of "sickness" for the status of an accepted alternative form of sex similarly indicates that the medical metaphor is *not* as neutral and as amoral as it seemed in its inception.

These two considerations of the moral status of compulsion are foundations for the second problem of medical metaphors as public issue. With the attribution of disease, the individual is delivered up to a body of institutional experts—psychiatrists, child guidance counselors, physicians, alcohol treatment practitioners, social workers—who seek the person's rehabilitation. In becoming technical objects, the deviants give rise to a new group of control agents and agencies whose power is suspect. The basis of this suspicion is partly the general fear of being powerless and partly the suspicion, much supported by historical outcomes and the social constructionist analysis presented here, that the supposed technical expertise is both shaky as fact and not very successful in its outcomes. The application of social and medical science to the range of issues described has not been salutary.

Last, as Conrad and Schneider emphasize, the effect of medicalizing public problems is their depoliticization. By removing the problems as ones on which honest and reasonable people might differ and in presenting one definition as inherently and "really" preferential, the medicalization of social problems depoliticizes them and diminishes the recognition of differences in moral choices that they represent. Again, the recent movement for homosexual rights or the redefinition of mental illness implied in the works of R. D. Laing and Thomas Szasz have given clear recognition of this. Similarly, the tendency to "blame the victim," in William Ryan's words, carries this conception even further.*

There is another aspect to the depoliticizing effect of medicalization. It puts the responsibility for the problem on individual causes and the solution to social problems on individual treatment. The face-to-face model of the physician-patient is considered the model of how to deal with the cases described in *Deviance and Medicalization*. This psychologizing of social problems leads away from the analyses of the social structure of culture—the socially shared institutions and meanings in the society as elements in the problems. The problems of alcohol use are located in the alcoholic. The alcohol industry, the governmental policies of legal and tax programs, and the structure of work are all ignored. In my current interest in drinking and driving, I have been impressed by the enormous emphasis on drinking and the drinker as causal elements while such institutional aspects as lack of alternate means of transportation are ignored both as causal agents and as possible considerations in providing avenues of solution. Sociological definitions of public problems, unlike psychological ones, raise issues of group interests and moral commitments and move into public and political arenas.

In this analysis of medicalization, where is the sociologist? What does the sociologist bring to the ongoing understanding and even the solution of public problems? I believe that the sociologist brings the stance of the ironist to public phenomena. "The aim of the Ironic statement," writes Hayden White, "is to affirm tacitly the negative of what is on the literal level affirmed positively."* This is exactly what Conrad and Schneider do. They treat the medical model as something strange, not as something that is "taken for granted" as "normal." When a body of thought or a phenomenon is taken as problematic, as something to be explained, its naturalness, its claim to "reality," is called into account. Thus to choose to examine the way in which homosexuality was transformed from sin to sickness or heavy drinking from evil to addiction is to make the medical model itself less than accepted on the strength of its correctness—its greater grasp of the reality of its object. This examination is in the

*Ryan, W. *Blaming the victim*. New York: Vintage Books, 1971.

*White, H. *Metahistory: the historical imagination in nineteenth century Europe*. Baltimore: Johns Hopkins University Press, 1973, p. 37.

classic tradition of the sociologist as exposer of ideology who, in an ironic stance toward human behavior, uncovers what purports to be truth and finds beneath the sheet of universalistic science the particular bed of specific cultures, groups, and human interests.*

The implications of sociological irony for public problems are vastly significant. The intervention of science into human affairs has carried the hope that human problems might be susceptible to solution by technical knowledge and skill as some problems of nature have been. (The tremendous effect of bacterial knowledge is the commanding case in point.) In being skeptical about the source of technical knowledge and the definition of social problems as technical, medical ones, the authors of *Deviance and Medicalization* cannot escape the charge of undermining the authority of the technical treatment and therapy professions. Fortunately, the Socratic hemlock is not available.

On another level, the ironist has also been a moralist of sorts, and the sociologist here follows. In displaying the ways in which the medical metaphor of sickness depoliticizes moral and social conflicts, the sociological analyst brings moral choice into the foreground. The sociologist makes it necessary for the participants in public problems to confront them as issues, as matters of choice, unconstrained by the natural order of things. As long as men and women could believe that some persons were by nature slaves and others free, slavery need not have been faced by slaveholders as a moral choice. The way in which homosexuality is being redefined is indicative of the process by which the transformation from a technical to a nontechnical formulation repoliticizes the issue. As a society, we shall have to decide the moral status of homosexuality if it is not construed as illness. We shall have to decide whose side we are on.

The irony of the sociologist has much in common with the imagination of the artist. Like the artist, the sociologist indicates that there are alternatives to the present. In showing the special character of what purports to be universal, sociology can contribute to public life what the arts contribute to human life—the visions of other realities, other ways of conceptualizing human actions, other possible ways of inventing human institutions.

However, is all a ceaseless and fluid process of multiple realities in which any situation may be defined in any fashion? Is there amidst the skepticism of the sociologist any "realer realities," or are all systems equally possible? The sociologist may dodge the metaphysical difficulties of the ironic stance by claiming finite, although multiple, possibilities in nature. We cannot completely dodge the charge of a cruel Olympianness. Conrad and Schneider, like many of us who affect the sociological disposition, offer no way by which the sufferers can cope with their suffering. Mental illness has indeed undergone a variety of definitions throughout history. How does that realization enable a society or an individual to face the phenomena that the definitions encompass? Are Conrad and Schneider telling us that there is no "mental illness" problem? That any conception of excessive drinking is only the particular construction of a time and a place? What happens to the urgency and exigency of the situation? To be sure, it seems easier to accept this view when the problem is homosexuality, or even opiate addiction, but are we not again in danger of making another metaphor under which to include phenomena whose differences are also significant?

An earlier, more positivistic social science knew where it stood. Less ironic, it sought an engineering solution to known social problems. Convinced that one could find a science for understanding social life and a technology for acting toward it, it possessed a mission, a stand from which to address the society. Can the sociological perspective embodied in this book, as in a good deal of the work of others I have mentioned, including myself, find any such platform, or is our relation to social policy that of the "disinterested observer of the passing scene" whose skepticism and irony lead to understanding, powerlessness, and escape from commitment? Can we only echo Freud's statement? "I have not the courage to rise up before

---

*Brown, R. H. *A poetic for sociology.* Cambridge: Cambridge University Press, 1977.

my fellowmen as a prophet, and I bow to their reproach that I can offer them no consolation: for at bottom that is what they are all demanding—the wildest revolutionaries no less passionately than the most virtuous believers."*

**Joseph R. Gusfield**

---

*Freud, S. *Civilization and its discontents*. New York: W. W. Norton & Co., 1961, p. 92. (Originally published 1930.)

# PREFACE

The subject of this book is the gradual social transformation of deviance designations in American society from "badness" to "sickness." This has been the most profound change in the definition of deviance in the past two centuries. By examining the medicalization (and demedicalization) of deviance in American society, we may also investigate the general sociohistorical processes of defining deviance. Thus this book has a dual focus: it is a historical and sociological inquiry into the changing definitions of deviance and an analysis of the transformation from religious and criminal to medical designations and control of deviance.

Our investigation is both analytical and concrete. We develop a conceptual framework grounded in the labeling-interactionist and conflict approaches to deviance. This directs our attention to an analysis of the changing conceptions of deviance and social control rather than to the behavior of deviance or individual etiology. Moreover, we see the transformation of deviance designations, from moral to medical, as collective and political achievements rather than as inevitable products of the natural evolution of society or the progress of medicine. We therefore pay special attention to the role of the medical profession and its champions in the creation of deviance designations. Since the medicalization of deviance is multifarious and not uniform, we endeavor to paint pictures depicting how and to what extent medicalization is achieved in each instance examined. Within a broad framework (outlined in Chapter 2) each case is permitted to retain its own analytical and historical integrity. In the final two chapters we attempt to draw out commonalities and the general theoretical significance of the cases. Thus the book may be read from beginning to end, or each chapter may be read separately.

This book is intended for students of deviance in the broadest sense. Although we have endeavored to write to make our investigation and analysis available to undergraduate sociology-of-deviance students, we cover territory unfamiliar to many of our colleagues. Sociologists of deviance have only recently come to appreciate the changing definitions of deviance as an important area for study. As will be apparent, we build on the work of both sociologists and historians who have pioneered this territory. Frequently we draw together materials that have not been collected previously, and occasionally we make original scholarly contributions of our own. One objective in writing this book is to provide students with a historical dimension to the study of deviance that has commonly been ignored or glossed over in much previous sociological work.

Finally, this book represents the first major sociological examination and compilation of the medicalization of deviance. It is in part an attempt to set the historical "record" straight and make some order out of unordered "facts," or more precisely, out of facts that have been previously ordered in different ways. Thus our work is neither the first nor the last word on the medicalization of deviance. A great deal more investigation and analysis are necessary, but we believe we have collected much material that will facilitate future research and writing on this topic. Rather than a definitive statement on the medicalization of deviance, we see our book as a good beginning toward greater understanding.

When a 2-year project such as this book is finally completed, there are many people to thank for their support and various contributions. We are grateful to all the people who gave us their intellectual, emotional, and material sustenance, but a few deserve special mention. For their comments on drafts of various chapters, we thank Selden Bacon, Vern Bullough, Karen Conner, Ronald Gold, Meredith Gould, Laud Humphreys, Harry Levine, Kenneth Miller, Michael Radelet, Charles Silverstein, William Sonnenstuhl, and Malcolm Spector. We are grateful to Joseph Gusfield for his appreciation and support of our ideas and for writing the foreword. Our students at Drake and New York Universities deserve thanks for listening to our developing analyses and providing feedback to our arguments and ideas. All are, of course, absolved of responsibility for any omissions and for errors that may appear here.

We thank Laurel Ingram and Sandy Huckstadt for deciphering and typing various chapter drafts. A special debt is owed Dee Malloy, who worked beyond the call of duty to help bring this book to completion, checking references, locating sources, writing for permissions, typing the final draft, and in general being supportive. We thank Carol Kromminga and Claudia Thornton for the tedious but valuable work of indexing.

For allowing us to reprint materials we had published previously, we acknowledge *Social Problems, The Sociology of Health and Illness,* D. C. Heath and Company, Greenwood Press, and Penguin Books.

Finally, we thank Libby and Nancy, the women who share our lives, for their support, love, understanding, and tolerance.

**Peter Conrad**
**Joseph W. Schneider**

# CONTENTS

# DEVIANCE AND MEDICALIZATION

**FROM BADNESS TO SICKNESS**

# 1 DEVIANCE, DEFINITIONS, and the MEDICAL PROFESSION

A slow but steady transformation of deviance has taken place in American society. It has not been a change in behavior as such, but in how behavior is defined. Deviant behaviors that were once defined as immoral, sinful, or criminal have been given medical meanings. Some say that rehabilitation has replaced punishment, but in many cases medical treatments have become a new form of punishment and social control. This transformation is certainly not complete and has not been entirely unidirectional. These changes have not occurred by themselves nor have they been the result of a "natural" evolution of society or the inevitable progress of medicine. The roots of these changes lie deep in our social and cultural heritage, and the process itself can be traced through the workings of specific people, events, ideas, and techniques. We believe that, aside from its technical and intellectual aspects, this change is surely profoundly political in nature with real political consequences. This book presents an analysis of the historical transformation of definitions of deviance from "badness"* to "sickness" and discusses the consequences of these changes. It focuses on the medicalization of deviance in American society.

In this first chapter we introduce our study of deviance. We delineate the two major orientations to deviance and illustrate the interactionist view of deviance with the example of the infamous episode of deviance in 17th-century Salem Village. We discuss the universality and relativity of deviance and define the concept of social control. Because this book focuses on the importance of medicine in the changing definitions of deviance, we offer a capsule analysis of the development and structure of medicine in American society. The criminalization of abortion serves as an example of medical involvement in deviance definitions. Finally, at the end of the chapter we present an overview of the rest of the book.

## SOCIOLOGICAL ORIENTATIONS TO DEVIANCE

There are many ways to study what sociologists call deviance. Even if we limit ourselves to sociological perspectives, there is a great variety of assumptions, definitions, and research methods from which to choose. We believe, however, that there are two general orientations to deviance in sociology that lead in distinct directions and produce different and sometimes conflicting conclusions about what deviance is and how sociologists and others should address it. We call these two orientations the positivist and the interactionist approaches. Others have made similar distinctions using different labels: correctional and appreciative (Matza, 1969), absolutist and relativist (Hills, 1977), scientific and humanistic (Thio, 1978), and objectivist and subjectivist (Goode, 1978). Such labels are merely signposts that summarize content. It is to the substance of these two orientations that we now turn.

The *positivist* approach assumes that deviance is real, that it exists in the objective experi-

---

*Although perhaps a bastardized term, we believe "badness" expresses best the *general* unequivocal morality typical of virtually all traditional major deviance designations, for example, "sin," "crime." Our subtitle, *From Badness to Sickness,* allows us to emphasize precisely the kinds of changes we believe inherent in the medicalization of deviance, that is, a shift from explicit moral judgments of deviants to the implicit and subtle morality of "sickness."

ence of the people who commit deviant acts and those who respond to them. This view of deviance rests on a second important assumption—that deviance is definable in a straightforward manner as behavior not within permissible conformity to social norms. These norms are believed part of a moral or value consensus in society that is both widely known and shared. Positivists devote much of their study of deviance to a search for causes of deviant behavior. In sociology such causes are usually described in terms of some aspect of social and/or cultural environment and one's socialization. Positivists outside sociology typically search for causes in physiology and/or psyche. In medicine, for example, this search is called etiology.* The major questions about deviants the positivist might ask are, Why do they do it? and How can we make them stop?

The *interactionist* orientation to deviance views the morality of society as socially constructed and relative to actors, context, and historical time. Fundamental to this view is the proposition that morality does not just happen; since it is socially constructed, there must be constructors. Morality becomes the product of certain people making claims based on their own particular interests, values, and views of the world. Those who have comparatively more power in a society are typically more able to create and impose their rules and sanctions on the less powerful. In consequence, deviance becomes actions or conditions that are defined as inappropriate to or in violation of certain powerful groups' conventions. Such deviance is believed to be caused not by mysterious forces beyond the individual's control but rather the consequence of particular definitions and rules being applied by members of certain groups to other people and/or situations. The interactionist view assumes that the behaviors called deviant are by and large voluntary and that people exercise some degree of "free will" in their lives. Deviance is then a social definition, and research focuses on how such definitions are constructed, how deviant labels are attached to particular people, and what the consequences are both for those labeled and the authors of such attributions. The major questions about deviants an interactionist might ask are, Who made these deviants? How did they do it? and With what consequences?

This classification, of course, simplifies some complex and contentious theoretical issues. Some of these will be evident in later discussions. General categories such as these necessarily do a certain degree of violence to reality, but we believe this distinction is essentially faithful to broad patterns of sociological theory and research. Finally, we do not mean to suggest that these two orientations are never combined in research on deviance; in fact, some of the best studies have adopted elements of both.

The approach taken in this book is decidedly interactionist. Our main concern is with changing definitions of deviance and the consequences of these changes. The interactionist study of deviance usually focuses on the social processes of defining and labeling deviants in contemporary society. Only rarely have interactionists ventured into history and attempted to use similar assumptions to understand the development of historical definitions of deviance. What makes this book different from most interactionist studies is that we focus explicitly on the sociohistorical development of the definitions of deviance. To the extent we succeed in adding this *historical dimension* to the interactionist study of deviance, we have made a contribution to the development and clarification of the interactionist approach.

This book is a study of deviance, but it is also a study of morality. In the interactionist view the morality of a society—the application of notions of "right" and "wrong"—are relative and socially constructed. There is no absolute morality, although in a world of competing moralities we may prefer some over others because they seem to us more human and life-supporting. Morality and deviance are both products of complex social interaction. In our study of changing definitions of deviance we are also studying changing morality. The individuals and collectivities engaged in defining deviance are at the same time defining morality. Although we mention this several times throughout this text, it might be useful to keep in mind

*It may be helpful to remember throughout this book that the medical model of deviance is essentially a positivist or correctional one.

that this is as much a study of morality as it is a study of deviance.

A word should be said about the term "deviance." We use it in its technical, sociological sense to refer to behavior that is negatively defined or condemned in our society. When we use the term, we do not imply any specific judgment or that we think the behavior is bad or sick. On the contrary, in some cases a considerable disjunction exists between our views and the dominant societal view. We use the term "deviance" to depict how the behavior or activity is generally defined in society.

To introduce our study of deviance and morality, we turn now to an event of 17th-century Massachusetts: the witchcraft phenomenon of Salem Village. Our intention is to illustrate what deviance is and how it is created in a particular social setting.

## WITCHCRAFT IN SALEM VILLAGE

In 1692 in the New England community of Salem Village occurred one of the most remarkable and notorious episodes of deviance production in American history.* In the cold January winter of that year a number of young girls were stricken with a strange malady and began to behave in alarming ways. The first two affected were Betty Parris (age 9) and Abigail Williams (age 11). Betty became forgetful, distracted, and preoccupied. She sometimes would sit staring fixedly at an invisible object and, if interrupted, would scream and begin an incomprehensible babble.

> [Abigail] too was absent-minded . . . and began to make babbling and rasping sounds. . . . She got down on all fours and ran about under the furniture, barking and braying, and sometimes fell into convulsions when she writhed and screamed as if suffering the torments of the damned. (Starkey, 1949, p. 40)†

In addition to the "fits," the victims frequently suffered a temporary loss of hearing and loss of memory and often felt as if they were being choked and suffocated. Vivid and frightening hallucinations tormented and terrified them. Whatever this fearful malady was, it was also contagious. Other girls soon were stricken.

The girls were taken by their parents to physicians who examined them but found no medical problems and were puzzled by this strange behavior. A local physician, however, believed that he understood the problem but that it was out of his realm of expertise. "The evil hand is on them," he announced. The girls were victims of witchcraft.

The Devil was at work in Salem Village. Within a short time half a dozen young girls were stricken. Fears and suspicions mounted. Who, the community leaders asked, were the Devil's accomplices? Who had afflicted these poor children? Ministers from nearby communities were summoned to help Salem Village deal with its emergency. These observers confirmed the community's worst fears: the girls' maladies were real and resulted from supernatural forces.

> "The motions of their fits," wrote the Reverend Deodat Lawson, "are preternatural, both as to the manner, which is so strange as a well person could not screw their body into; and as to the violence also it is preternatural, being much beyond the ordinary force of the same person when they are in their right mind." The Reverend John Hale of Beverly confirmed Lawson's description. "Their arms, necks and backs," he wrote, "were turned this way and that way, and returned back again, so it was impossible for them to do of themselves, and beyond the power of any epileptic fits, or natural disease to effect." (Hansen, 1969, p. 11).

The community leaders and the ministers reached a decision. "The girls must be induced to name their tormenters; the witches must be ferreted out and brought to justice" (Starkey, 1949, p. 45).*

With little urging, the girls named the three witches who were terrorizing them: Tituba, a slave from the West Indies who was acquainted with voodoo and magic; Sarah Good, a pipe-

---

*Our discussion provides only a brief summary of the events at Salem. For more detailed description and analysis, see Marion L. Starkey (1949), Kai T. Erikson (1966, pp. 137-59), Chadwick Hansen (1969), and Paul Boyer and Stephen Nissenbaum (1974).

smoking woman known for her slovenliness and begging and considered neglectful of her children; and Sarah Osborne, a woman of higher standing, but who was negligent in her church attendance and had scandalized the community a year or so earlier by living with a man for a short time before he became her husband (Erikson, 1966). The accused women were all marginal members of the community; in effect, they were outsiders even before the accusations.

The preliminary hearings took place in the meeting house. They were presided over by colony magistrates, who were to ascertain whether enough evidence existed for an actual trial. This was serious business in Salem because the Puritans took literally the biblical injunction "Thou shalt not permit a witch to live." Conviction of witchcraft meant sure death. Certain rules of evidence were agreed on.

> They would accept as proof of guilt the finding of any "teat" or "devil's mark," that is to say any unnatural excrescence on the bodies of the accused. They would accept as ground for suspicion of guilt any mischief following anger between neighbours. And most important of all, they would accept the doctrine that "the devil could not assume the shape of an innocent person in doing mischief to mankind." (Starkey, 1949, p. 53)*

It was this final criterion of evidence that was critical. It simply meant that the Devil could not appear in the form of anyone who was not guilty of witchcraft. This was called "spectral evidence." It enabled hallucinations, dreams, and visions to be accepted in court "as factual proof not of the psychological condition of the accuser but of the behavior of the accused" (Starkey, 1949, p. 54). It was evidence that was impossible to disprove, for if one of the girls accused a person's "specter" or "shade" of haunting them, the accused was left without a defense. It was prima facie evidence for association with the Devil and thus guilt of witchcraft.

The hearings must have been quite a scene. There was a somber excitement in town, and many people packed the meeting house to see the alleged witches examined. The afflicted girls were given a place of honor in front of the hall. When the accused were brought in, the girls began to yell, writhe, and convulse in apparent agony. When questioned, the girls pointed to specters of the accused flying around the room, pinching and tormenting their victims. (Of course, none of the observers could see these specters.) Sarah Good and Sarah Osborne categorically denied their guilt. But when Tituba spoke, a hush settled over the meeting house, for Tituba was confessing to consorting with the Devil. For 3 days she told the astonished court about the "invisible world" of spirits and apparitions with which she had contact. She suggested there were still others in the community with whom she (and the Devil) had consorted. These three women were dispatched to jail to await trial, but the witch-hunt had only begun.

Salem Village was in crisis. Somber excitement was giving way to fearful panic. The Devil was out to take people's souls, and the good God-fearing people of Salem must fight him to the hilt. The afflicted girls were the instruments through which the dastardly witches could be discovered. They performed their witch-finding chores with zeal and gusto. The girls seemed to relish all the attention they received and the power they were given. Within the next 6 months this troop of young girls accused nearly 200 people of consorting with the Devil. Some righteous and upstanding citizens were accused, as well as individuals from distant communities. Farmers, grandmothers, children, even a reverend; if the girls claimed the individual's specter was haunting them, the accused was taken to prison to await a hearing. The community was stunned, but the fear of witchcraft prevailed.

Dozens of the accused were brought to trial, and before the year was out, 19 witches had been executed by hanging, two had died in jail, and one was crushed to death during an interrogation. When the girls began to accuse some of the town's most respected individuals, however, doubts about their infallible judgment began to grow. Toward the year's end people were openly expressing concern about the trials

---

and executions and especially about the validity of "spectral evidence." After the magistrates reversed their earlier decision and decided to disallow spectral evidence, there remained no way other than confession to ascertain guilt in witchcraft. Nearly all those still accused were acquitted. The hundred or so yet residing in jails were released, and the few who had confessed or had been found guilty were granted reprieves. The witchcraft hysteria of Salem Village was over.

Witchcraft as deviance is a fascinating subject to study. Numerous scholars have attempted to understand what happened in Salem Village in 1692. Most agree that the girls' behaviors today would be diagnosed as "hysteria," a psychological disorder rather than a result of witchcraft, and that nearly all the accused were innocent. Several theories have been postulated as to the causes of the witchcraft outbreak. Starkey (1949) suggests that it was a case of mass hysteria caused by Puritan repression and guilt. Erikson (1966) theorizes that the witch trials were an attempt to resolve a "crisis" over the social boundaries of the changing Puritan colony. Hansen (1969) asserts that there were undoubtedly a few practitioners of witchcraft in Salem, and the girls' fear of bewitchment made them hysterical. We need not choose between these theories here because we present the Salem witchcraft example only to illustrate the social construction of deviance rather than to explain the behaviors involved. The example will serve us through the next few pages as we begin to develop our study of deviance.

## UNIVERSALITY AND RELATIVITY OF DEVIANCE

What is deviance? For the moment, let us say simply that deviance consists of those categories of condemnation and negative judgment which are constructed and applied successfully to some members of a social community by others. We intentionally avoid the notion that the essence of deviance is in actors' behaviors; rather, we argue that it is a quality attributed to such persons and behaviors by others. For example, "witchcraft" and all it entailed in 17th-century Salem Village was deviance. We will develop this concept of deviance considerably as we proceed.

Deviance is a universal phenomenon. All societies have definitions of some behaviors or activities as deviant or morally reprehensible. The very notion that a society has social norms or rules ensures the existence of deviance. There can be no deviance without social rules (and, as far as we know, there can be no society without rules and norms, either). As Emile Durkheim (1895/1938) pointed out, deviance is "normal" to society. "Imagine a society of saints," wrote Durkheim,

> a perfect cloister of exemplary individuals. Crimes [or deviance], properly so called, will there be unknown; but faults which appear venial to the layman will create there the same scandal that the ordinary offense does in ordinary consciousnesses. If, then, this society has the power to judge and punish, it will define these acts as criminal [or deviant] and will treat them as such. (pp. 68-69)*

Durkheim touches on many important aspects of deviance in this short passage: deviance is universal, deviance is a social definition, social groups make rules and enforce their definitions on members through judgment and social sanction, deviance is contextual, and defining and sanctioning deviance involves power. Let us consider these one at a time.

1. Deviance is universal, but there are no universal forms of deviance. There are few acts, if any, that are defined as deviance in all societies under all conditions. Incest probably conforms most closely to a universal definition of deviance. Yet different societies consider different activities to be incest: some societies prohibit only brother-sister relations, whereas others consider relations between third cousins to be incestuous. A few societies encourage sexual relationships between parents and children, and in several, siblings may engage freely in all sexual activity until puberty. Premeditated murder is also considered deviant in most societies, but there are societies in which a man who kills an-

* From Durkheim, E. *Rules of the sociological method*. New York: The Free Press, 1938. Copyright 1938 by the University of Chicago. (Originally published, 1895.)

other man for committing adultery with his wife is deemed justified. Even incest and murder are not universally deviant.

Deviance is also relative. Different societies define different activities as deviant. In contemporary American society the young girls of Salem might find their behavior defined as deviant (i.e., hysterical) rather than the behaviors of those they accused of witchcraft. Certain forms of homosexuality were acceptable among the cultural elite in classical Greece, but in America such conduct is condemned and stigmatized. Suicide is considered deviant and ungodly in most of the Christian world, whereas in Imperial Japan it could be an honorable act. The extremely suspicious and treacherous behavior of the Dobu of Melanesia would be labeled ''paranoid'' by modern psychiatric standards, but it would be the accepting and unsuspicious individual who would be a deviant among the Dobu. Ruth Benedict's (1934) notion of ''cultural relativity'' is useful here: each society should be viewed by its own conceptions and standards. What is deviant for a society is relative to that society: witchcraft among the Puritans, hysteria and paranoia in American society.

2. Deviance is a social definition. That is, deviance is not ''given'' in any behavior, act, or status. It must be so defined intentionally by ''significant'' actors in the society or social group. In Erikson's (1966) words, ''Deviance is not a property *inherent in* any particular kind of behavior; it is a property *conferred upon* that behavior by the people who come into direct or indirect contact with it'' (p. 6). Deviance may be seen as a label attached to an act or behavior or as a category by which certain behaviors are defined. Thus deviance is a socially *attributed* condition, and ''deviant'' is an *ascribed* status. Deviance does not inhere in the individual or the behavior; it is a social judgment of that behavior. In short, it is not the act but the definition that makes something deviant.

This view of deviance allows us to separate the *definition* of the behavior and the *behavior* itself. Each may be studied separately. In this light we see deviance as a *system of social categories* constructed for classifying behavior, persons, situations, and things. Puritan society inherited a long tradition of defining certain behaviors as witchcraft (Currie, 1968). Witchcraft, regardless of whether we believe in it, was a generally accepted category for ''deviant'' behavior to the Puritans. In Puritan society there were certain more or less agreed-on criteria for assignment to this deviant category (p. 4, just as we have criteria for applying our contemporary definitions of deviance. As sociologists we may study the origins of witchcraft as a category of deviance, as well as study the ''causes'' of witchcraft behavior. In other words, we may examine the etiology of social definitions of deviance separately from the etiology of the behaviors labeled as deviant. We can ask, for example, how it was that abortion was defined as deviant until recently rather than ask what caused people to have or perform the abortions (we present this example later in this chapter). Again, the definition is separated from the behavior or act. Deviance definitions may change over time. Witchcraft is no longer a relevant type of deviance in American society, but juvenile delinquency, opiate addiction, and child abuse, unknown to the Puritans, are well-accepted contemporary categories of deviance. The approach we take in this book is to analyze the changing definitions of deviance, which may or may not be related to actual changes in ''deviant'' behavior. We develop this further in Chapter 2.

3. Social groups make rules and enforce their definitions on members through judgment and social sanction. Although we view deviance definitions as social categories, in reality they are not separate from their use and application. Definitions do not create themselves: ''social groups create deviance by making the rules whose infraction constitutes deviance, and applying those rules to particular people and labeling them as [deviants]'' (Becker, H. S., 1963, p. 9). The leaders of Salem Village ''created'' deviance by making and enforcing rules whose infraction constituted deviance. (Had they ignored the girls' behavior, the witch trials probably never would have occurred.) Admittedly, most instances of deviance are not nearly as clear examples of the creation and application of rules to produce deviance as the Salem episode, but collective rule making, social

judgment, and the application of sanctions (penalties) are central to all types of deviance. What is important to remember is that "societies" do not make rules and define deviance; people acting collectively do.

4. Deviance is contextual. By this we mean that what is labeled as deviant varies by social context—especially according to such conditions as society, subculture, time, place, who is involved, and who is offended. Willfully taking another's life usually is considered deviant, but not on a battlefield when the victim is defined as the enemy. Marijuana smoking is by law deviant in most states, but in many youth subcultures it would be the nonsmoker who would be defined deviant. Masturbation was defined as a sin and disease in Victorian times but today is considered healthy. Suicide by an 80-year-old man with terminal cancer may be considered by many as justifiable, whereas a suicide attempt by a college student ordinarily is seen as deviant and usually leads to psychiatric treatment. Thus "what" and "who" are "deviant" depends significantly on social context.

5. Defining and sanctioning deviance involves power. In general, powerful people and groups are able to establish and legitimate their morality and definitions of deviance. Those belonging to the more powerful groups in society, in terms of social class, age, race, ethnicity, profession, sex, etc., can enforce their categories of deviance on less powerful groups. It is seldom vice versa. In the witchcraft example the community and religious leaders of Salem Village (all men) were able to implement their categories of deviance on the accused witches (mostly women). Similarly adults make rules children must live by, the middle and upper classes define deviance in the lower classes (perhaps that is one reason why so much deviance is found among the lower classes), and a prestigious profession such as medicine makes rules whose violation is nearly universally termed sickness. We shall discuss the power dimension further in Chapter 2.

In summary, deviance is universal yet widely variable. It is in essence a social judgment and definition and therefore culturally relative. Deviance is socially created by rule making and enforcement, usually by powerful groups over people in less powerful positions.

## SOCIAL CONTROL

Social control is a central and important concept in sociology. Developed by Edward A. Ross (1901) around the turn of the century, the term was used to describe the processes societies developed for regulating themselves. Social control meant social regulation. In the past two decades, however, its common sociological usage has changed. Perhaps dating from the work of Talcott Parsons (1951), social control began to be used in a narrower sense to mean the control of deviance and the promotion of conformity. This is the common usage today, although there are some who call for a return to its original meaning as societal regulation (Janowitz, 1975).

Social control is usually conceptualized as the means by which society secures adherence to social norms; specifically, how it minimizes, eliminates, or normalizes deviant behavior. Even when we limit our discussion of social control to the control of deviance, it is still a broad and complex topic. We introduce here a few dimensions of social control most directly relevant to our argument in this book (for more complete discussions see Pitts, 1968, and Roucek, 1978). Social control operates on both informal and formal levels and through "positive" and "negative" forms. Informal controls include self-controls and relational controls. Self-controls reside within individuals (although their source is external and therefore social) and include internalized norms, beliefs, morals, self-concept, and what is commonly called "conscience." Relational controls are a regular feature of the face-to-face interactions of everyday life. They include such common interactions as ridicule, praise, gossip, smiles, disapproving glances and "dirty looks," mythmaking, group ostracism and support, and essentially any negative or positive sanction for behavior. Informal controls both inhibit individuals from behavior that might be considered deviant and encourage conformity by positive sanction. In most cases these informal controls do not lead to an individual being defined and labeled as deviant, for we are all subject to these controls daily. Formal social control is less ubiquitous in everyday life, but its consequences are usually much more profound and enduring to the individual and society. (Sociologists have studied negative and formal social control far more thoroughly than informal and positive social control, perhaps because the latter are much more difficult to study.) Formal social controls are institutionalized forms of social control. Although they include "the 'official' laws, regulations, and understandings that are supposed to encompass all the members of a group or society" (Buckner, 1971, p. 14), sociologists usually think of formal social control in terms of *institutions* and *agents* of social control. They may be depicted as social control apparatuses that operate, explicitly and implicitly, to secure adherence to a particular set of values and norms, and in this work, to sanction deviance. In our society we usually think of the criminal justice system, with the police, courts, correctional facilities, and auxiliary personnel, as the major institution of social control. Other institutions such as education, welfare, the mass media, and medicine are also frequently depicted as having social control functions.

The greatest social control power comes from having the authority to define certain behaviors, persons, and things. This right to define may reside in an abstract authority such as "the law" or God but is implemented commonly through some institutional force such as the state or church. Such institutions, then (or, perhaps better, the people who represent them), have the mandate to define the problem (e.g., as deviance), designate what type of problem it is, and indicate what should be done about it. In our witchcraft example, representatives of the church (ministers) and the state (magistrates) agreed on the definition of the problem, witchcraft (so, incidentally, did the physician), but it was essentially a theological definition that prevailed (i.e., it was a question of witchcraft, or consorting with the Devil). As we mentioned earlier, a modern psychiatrist might have defined the problem as the young girls' being "hysterical," but there were no psychiatrists with any authority in Salem to challenge the witchcraft definition.

Social control, then, can be seen as the power to have a particular set of definitions of the world realized in both spirit and practice. To the extent that such definitions receive widespread and/or "significant" social support, this power becomes authority and thereby considerably more secure from attack and challenge. This authority, not uncommonly, may become vested in a dominant institution. For example, during the Middle Ages and through the Inquisition the Church had the authority and power to define activities as deviant. With the decline of the Church and the subsequent secularization, the state increasingly gained authority to define deviance. When an institution (e.g., the church, state, medical profession) gains the power and authority to define deviance, that is, to say what kind of a problem something is, the responsibility for dealing with the problem often comes to that institution. In this sense we can say institutions can define their own social control "turf." Representatives of an institution may linguistically stake claims to deviance territory and thus attempt to justify their authority and legitimacy. In areas where an institution's definitions become dominant and accepted, it is capable of defining the territory of its work. The institution and the practitioners within it become designated "experts" in dealing with the problem, or at least stewards of its social control.

It is important to remember that any given "problem" can be viewed by different eyes and thus may be defined and analyzed in different ways. For example, the problems of deviant drinking can be seen as "caused" by sinfulness, moral weakness, psychological disturbance, genetic predisposition, adaptation to stress, or other influences (the problem could also be defined as caused by the promotion and distribution of the liquor industry). What the problem "really" is may be debated and argued; deviant drinking is not obviously one certain type of problem. The right to define a "problem," and thereby locate it within a particular social control turf, is achieved typically through enterprise, strategy, and struggle. We will encounter numerous examples of this throughout the book.

This book examines how increasing forms of deviant behavior have been defined as medical problems and thereby properly under medical social control. We examine how medicine achieved the authority to define problems as ''sickness'' rather than ''badness'' and analyze the consequences of this transformation. We begin this discussion in the next chapter. Before we start this examination, however, it is important to review briefly medicine's rather recent rise to dominance in American society.

## THE MEDICAL PROFESSION AND DEVIANCE IN AMERICA

Since the dominant theme of this book concerns the change in definitions of deviance from badness to sickness and the expansion of medicine as an agent of social control, it is important to have some understanding of the historical development of medical practice and the medical profession. Medicine has not always been the powerful, prestigious, successful, lucrative, and dominant profession we know today. The status of the medical profession is a product of medical politicking as well as therapeutic expertise. This discussion presents a brief overview of the development of the medical profession and its rise to dominance.

### Emergence of the medical profession: up to 1850

In ancient societies, disease was given supernatural explanations, and ''medicine'' was the province of priests or shamans. It was in classical Greece that medicine began to emerge as a separate occupation and develop its own theories, distinct from philosophy or theology. Hippocrates, the great Greek physician who refused to accept supernatural explanations or treatments for disease, developed a theory of the ''natural'' causes of disease and systematized all available medical knowledge. He laid a basis for the development of medicine as a separate body of knowledge. Early Christianity depicted sickness as punishment for sin, engendering new theological explanations and treatments. Christ and his disciples believed in the supernatural causes and cures of disease. This view became institutionalized in the Middle Ages, when the Church dogma dominated theories and practice of medicine and priests were physicians. The Renaissance in Europe brought a renewed interest in ancient Greek medical knowledge. This marked the beginning of a drift toward natural explanations of disease and the emergence of medicine as an occupation separate from the Church (Cartwright, F. F., 1977).

But European medicine developed slowly. The ''humoral theory'' of disease developed by Hippocrates dominated medical theory and practice until well into the 19th century. Medical diagnosis was impressionistic and often inaccurate, depicting conditions in such general terms as ''fevers'' and ''fluxes.'' In the 17th century, physicians relied mainly on three techniques to determine the nature of illness: what the patient said about symptoms; the physician's own observations of signs of illness and the patient's appearance and behavior; and, more rarely, a manual examination of the body (Reiser, 1978, p. 1). Medicine was by no means scientific, and ''medical thought involved unverified doctrines and resulting controversies'' (Shryock, 1960, p. 52). Medical practice was a ''bedside medicine'' that was patient oriented and did not distinguish the illness from the ''sick man'' (Jewson, 1976). It was not until Thomas Sydenham's astute observations in the late 17th century that physicians could begin to distinguish between the patient and the disease. Physicians possessed few treatments that worked regularly, and many of their treatments actually worsened the sufferer's condition. Medicine in colonial America inherited this European stock of medical knowledge.

Colonial American medicine was less developed than its European counterpart. There were no medical schools and few physicians, and because of the vast frontier and sparse population, much medical care was in effect self-help. Most American physicians were educated and trained by apprenticeship; few were university trained. With the exception of surgeons, most were undifferentiated practitioners. Medical practices were limited. Prior to the revolution, physicians did not commonly attend births; midwives, who were not seen as part of the medical establishment, routinely attended birthings (Wertz and Wertz, 1977). William Rothstein (1972) notes that ''American colonial medical practice, like European practice of the period, was characterized by the lack of any substantial body of usable scientific knowledge'' (p. 27). Physicians, both educated and otherwise, tended to treat their patients pragmatically, for medical theory had little to offer. Most colonial physicians practiced medicine only part-time, earning their livelihoods as clergymen, teachers, farmers, or in other occupations. Only in the early 19th century did medicine become a full-time vocation (Rothstein, 1972).

The first half of the 19th century saw important changes in the organization of the medical profession. About 1800, "regular," or educated, physicians convinced state legislatures to pass laws limiting the practice of medicine to practitioners of a certain training and class (prior to this nearly anyone could claim the title "doctor" and practice medicine). These state licensing laws were not particularly effective, largely because of the colonial tradition of medical self-help. They were repealed in most states during the Jacksonian period (1828-1836) because they were thought to be elitist, and the temper of the times called for a more "democratic" medicine.

The repeal of the licensing laws and the fact that most "regular" (i.e., regularly educated) physicians shared and used "a distinctive set of medically invalid therapies, known as 'heroic' therapy," created fertile conditions for the emergence of *medical sects* in the first half of the 19th century (Rothstein, 1972, p. 21). Physicians of the time practiced a "heroic" and invasive form of medicine consisting primarily of such treatments as bloodletting, vomiting, blistering, and purging. This highly interventionist, and sometimes dangerous, form of medicine engendered considerable public opposition and resistance. In this context a number of medical sects emerged, the most important of which were the homeopathic and botanical physicians. These "irregular" medical practitioners practiced less invasive, less dangerous forms of medicine. They each developed a considerable following, since their therapies were probably no less effective than those of regulars practicing heroic medicine. The regulars attempted to exclude them from practice; so the various sects set up their own medical schools and professional societies. This sectarian medicine created a highly *competitive* situation for the regulars (Rothstein, 1972). Medical sectarianism, heroic therapies, and ineffective treatment contributed to the low status and lack of prestige of early 19th-century medicine. At this time, medicine was neither a prestigious occupation nor an important economic activity in American society (Starr, 1977).

The regular physicians were concerned about this situation. Large numbers of regularly trained physicians sought to earn a livelihood by practicing medicine (Rothstein, 1972, p. 3). They were troubled by the poor image of medicine and lack of standards in medical training and practice. No doubt they were also concerned about the competition of the irregular sectarian physicians. A group of regular physicians founded the American Medical Association (AMA) in 1847 "to promote the science and art of medicine and the betterment of public health" (quoted in Coe, 1978, p. 204). The AMA also was to set and enforce standards and ethics of "regular" medical practice and strive for exclusive professional and economic rights to the medical turf.

The AMA was the crux of the regulars' attempt to "professionalize" medicine. As Magali Sarfatti Larson (1977) points out, professions organize to create and control *markets*. Organized professions attempt to regulate and limit the competition, usually by controlling professional education and by limiting licensing. Professionalization is, in this view, "the process by which producers of special services sought to constitute *and control* the market for their expertise" (Larson, 1977, p. xvi). The regular physicians and the AMA set out to consolidate and control the market for medical services. As we shall see in the next two sections, the regulars were successful in professionalization, eliminating competition and creating a medical monopoly.

## Crusading, deviance, and medical monopoly: the case of abortion

The medical profession after the middle of the 19th century was frequently involved in various activities that could be termed social reform. Some of these reforms were directly related to health and illness and medical work; others were peripheral to the manifest medical calling of preventing illness and healing the sick. In these reform movements, physicians became medical crusaders, attempting to influence public morality and behavior. This medical crusading often led physicians squarely into the moral sphere, making them advocates for moral positions that had only peripheral relations to medical practice. Not infrequently these reformers sought to change people's values or to impose a set of particular values on others or, as we shall soon see, to create new categories of social deviance. Throughout this book we will often encounter medical crusaders. We now examine one of the more revealing examples of medical crusading: the criminalization of abortion in American society.*

Most people are under the impression that abortion was always defined as deviant and illegal in America prior to the Supreme Court's landmark decision in 1973. This, however, is not the case. American abortion policy, and the attendant defining of abortion as deviant, were specific products of medical crusading. Prior to the Civil War, abortion was a common and largely legal medical procedure performed by various types of physicians and midwives. A pregnancy was not considered confirmed until the occurrence of a phenomenon called "quickening," the first perception of fetal movement. Common law did not recognize the fetus before quickening in criminal cases, and an unquickened fetus was deemed to have no living soul. Thus most people did not consider termination of pregnancy before quickening to be an especially serious matter, much less murder. Abortion before quickening created no moral or medical problems. Public opinion was indifferent, and for the time it was probably a relatively safe medical procedure. Thus, for all intents and purposes, American women were free to terminate their pregnancies before quickening in the early 19th century. Moreover, it was a procedure relatively free of the moral stigma that was attached to abortion in this century.

After 1840 abortion came increasingly into public view. Abortion clinics were vigorously and openly advertised in newspapers and magazines. The advertisements offered euphemistically couched services for "women's complaints," "menstrual blockage," and "obstructed menses." Most contemporary observers suggested that more and more women were using these services. Prior to 1840 most abortions were performed on the ummarried and desperate of the "poor and unfortunate classes." However, beginning about this time, significantly increasing numbers of middle- and upper-class white, Protestant, native-born women began to use these services. It is likely they either wished to delay childbearing or thought they already had all the children they wanted (Mohr, 1978, pp. 46-47). By 1870 approximately one abortion was performed for every five live births (Mohr, 1978, pp. 79-80).

Beginning in the 1850s, a number of physicians, especially moral crusader Dr. Horatio Robinson Storer, began writing in medical and popular journals and lobbying in state legislatures about the danger and immorality of abortion. They opposed abortion before and after quickening and under Dr. Storer's leadership organized an aggressive national campaign. In 1859 these crusaders convinced the AMA to pass a resolution condemning abortion. Some newspapers, particularly the *New York Times,* joined the antiabortion crusade. Feminists supported the crusade, since they saw abortion as a threat to women's health and part of the oppression of women. Religious leaders, however, by and large avoided the issue of abortion; either they didn't consider it in their province or found it too sticky an issue to discuss. It was the physicians who were the guiding force in the antiabortion crusade. They were instrumental in convincing legislatures to pass state laws, especially between 1866 and 1877, that made abortion a criminal offense.

Why did physicians take the lead in the antiabortion crusade and work so directly to have abortion defined as deviant and illegal? Undoubtedly they believed in the moral "rightness" of their cause. But social historian James Mohr (1978) presents two more subtle and important reasons for the physicians' antiabortion crusading. First, concern was growing among medical people and even among some legislators about the significant drop in birth-

*We rely on James C. Mohr's (1978) fine historical account of the origins and evolution of American abortion policy for data and much of the interpretation in this section.

rates. Many claimed that abortion among married women of the "better classes" was a major contributor to the declining birthrate. These middle- and upper-class men (the physicians and legislators) were aware of the waves of immigrants arriving with large families and were anxious about the decline in production of native American babies. They were deeply afraid they were being betrayed by their own women (Mohr, 1978, p. 169). Implicitly the antiabortion stance was classist and racist; the anxiety was simply that there would not be enough strong, native-born, Protestant stock to save America. This was a persuasive argument in convincing legislators of the need of antiabortion laws.

The second and more direct reason spurring the physicians in the antiabortion crusade was to aid their own nascent professionalization and create a monopoly for regular physicians. As mentioned earlier, the regulars had formed the AMA in 1847 to promote scientific and ethical medicine and combat what they saw as medical quackery. There were, however, no licensing laws to speak of, and many claimed the title "doctor" (e.g., homeopaths, botanical doctors, eclectic physicians). The regular physicians adopted the Hippocratic oath and code of ethics as their standard. Among other things, this oath forbids abortion. Regulars usually did not perform abortions; however, many practitioners of medical sects performed abortions regularly, and some had lucrative practices. Thus for the regular AMA physicians the limitation of abortion became one way of asserting their own professional domination over other medical practitioners. In their crusading these physicians had translated the social goals of cultural and professional dominance into moral and medical language. They lobbied long and hard to convince legislators of the danger and immorality of abortion. By passage of laws making abortion criminal any time during gestation, regular physicians were able to legislate their code of ethics and get the state to employ sanctions against their competitors. This limited these competitors' markets and was a major step toward the regulars' achieving a monopolization of medical practice.

In a relatively short period the antiabortion crusade succeeded in passing legislation that made abortion criminal in every state. A by-product of this was a shift in American public opinion from an indifference to and tolerance of abortion to a hardening of attitudes against what had until then been a fairly common practice. The irony was that abortion as a medical procedure probably was safer at the turn of the 20th century than a century before, but it was defined and seen as more dangerous. By 1900 abortion was not only illegal but deviant and immoral. The physicians' moral crusade had successfully defined abortion as a deviant activity. This definition remained largely unchanged until the 1973 Supreme Court decision, which essentially returned the abortion situation to its pre-1850 condition.

This was not the first nor the last medical venture into the moral world of norm creation and deviance. German physicians in the 18th century proposed development of a "medical police" who would supervise the health and hygiene of the population as well as control activities such as prostitution (Rosen, 1974). Physicians were actively involved in the Temperance and "eugenics" movements of the 19th century. The first legal and involuntary medical sterilizations performed in the United States were on "criminals" by crusading physicians seeking both to curb crime and protect the racial stock (Fink, 1938). The following impassioned defense of such selective and "reformist" sterilization appeared in the *New York Medical Journal* in 1902, written by a surgeon at the Indiana Reformatory:

> It is my judgment, founded on research and observation, that this is the rational means of eradicating from our midst a most dangerous and hurtful class. Too much stress cannot be placed upon the present danger to the race. The public must be made to see that radical methods are necessary. Even radical methods may be made to seem just if they are shown to be rational. In this we have a means which is both rational and sufficient. It remains with you—men of science and skill—to perpetuate a known relief to a weakening race by prevailing upon your legislatures to enact such laws as will restrict marriage and give those in charge of State institutions the authority to render every male sterile who passes its portals, whether it be almshouse, insane asylum, institute for the feebleminded, reformatory, or prison. The medical profession has never failed in an attempt,

and it will not fail in this. (Sharp, 1902, pp. 413-414).

In the 20th century, physicians were central figures in crusades for social hygiene (Burnham, 1972) and birth control (Gordon, 1975). Physicians often saw their scientific and professional values as the values that ought to guide the behavior of others. Frequently they argued for certain positions in the name of science when the issues were actually moral. As John C. Burnham (1972) observes, "Repeatedly the leaders of American medicine sought to impose such values upon others, that is, to exercise social control" (p. 19).

American medicine and physicians have had a long-lived, historic involvement with deviance and social control. Some diseases were considered indistinguishable from deviant behavior; sufferers were treated as both deviant and sick. Physicians perhaps always have had a significant role in the control and treatment of conditions such as leprosy and epilepsy. Leprosy, a long-term degenerative disease that severely and horribly mutilates its victims, was widespread in the 12th and 13th centuries. It was a highly feared disease (although it is *not* very contagious), and its sufferers were stigmatized and treated as deviants because of their frightful appearance. Since no physical cure was known, the only means of dealing with the disease was social. Physicians were the diagnosticians. If the diagnosis was firmly established, the leper was segregated for life.

> He was expelled from human society and deprived of his civil rights; in some places a Requiem was held for him, and thus he was declared dead as far as society was concerned. He lived in a *leprosarium* outside the city walls in the company of other lepers, all of whom were dependent on charity for their sustenance. (Sigerist, 1943, p. 73)

Epilepsy was considered both a disease and a sign of supernatural demonic possession (i.e., deviance) until the 20th century. Surely uncontrolled seizures were a frightening form of deviant behavior, and epileptics were severely stigmatized and frequently segregated (Temkin, 1971). Thus the lines between sickness and deviance sometimes were not clearly drawn: some diseases were considered deviance, and, as we shall demonstrate in upcoming chapters, some deviance became defined as disease. The medical profession would have an increasing role in defining and controlling deviance. This "power" rested at least in part on the growth of medical expertise and professional dominance.

## Growth of medical expertise and professional dominance

Although the general public's dissatisfaction with heroic medicine remained, the image of medicine and what it could accomplish was improving by the middle of the 19th century. There had been a considerable reduction in the incidence and mortality of certain dread diseases. The plague and leprosy had nearly disappeared. Smallpox, malaria, and cholera were less devastating than ever before. These improvements in health engendered optimism and increased people's faith in medical practice. Yet these dramatic "conquests of disease" were by and large *not* the result of new medical knowledge or improved clinical medical practice. Rather, they resulted from changes in social conditions: a rising standard of living, better nutrition and housing, and public health innovations like sanitation. With the lone exception of vaccination for smallpox, the decline of these diseases had nearly nothing to do with clinical medicine (Dubos, 1959; McKeown, 1971). But despite lack of effective treatments, medicine was the beneficiary of much popular credit for improved health.

The regular physicians' image was improved well before they demonstrated any unique effectiveness of practice. The AMA's attacks on irregular medical practice continued. In the 1870s the regulars convinced legislatures to outlaw abortion and in some states to restore licensing laws to restrict medical practice. The AMA was becoming an increasingly powerful and authoritative voice representing regular medical practice.

But the last three decades of the century saw significant "breakthroughs" in medical knowledge and treatment. The scientific medicine of the regular physicians was making new medical advances. Anesthesia and antisepsis made possible great strides in surgical medicine and improvements in hospital care. The bacteriological research of Koch and Pasteur developed the "germ theory of disease," which had important applications in medical practice. It was the accomplishments of surgery and bacteriology that put medicine on a scientific basis (Freidson, 1970a, p. 16). The rise of scientific medicine marked a death knell for medical sectarianism (e.g., the homeopathic physicians eventually joined the regulars). The new laboratory sciences provided a way of testing the theories and practices of various sects, which ultimately led to a single model of medical practice. The well-organized regulars were able to legitimate their form of medical practice and support it with "scientific" evidence.

With the emergence of scientific medicine, a unified paradigm, or model, of medical practice developed. It was based, most fundamentally, on viewing the body as a machine (e.g., organ malfunctioning) and on the germ theory of disease (Kelman, 1977). The "doctrine of specific etiology" became predominant: each disease was caused by a specific germ or agent. Medicine focused solely on the internal environment (the body), largely ignoring the external environment (society) (Dubos, 1959). This paradigm proved fruitful in ensuing years. It is the essence of the "medical model" we discuss in Chapter 2.

The development of scientific medicine accorded regular medicine a convincing advantage in medical practice. It set the stage for the achievement of a medical monopoly by the AMA regulars. As Larson (1977) notes, "Once scientific medicine offered sufficient guarantees of its superior effectiveness in dealing with disease, the state willingly contributed to the creation of a monopoly by means of registration and licensing" (p. 23). The new licensing laws created regular medicine as *a legally enforced monopoly of practice* (Freidson, 1970b, p. 83). They virtually eliminated medical competition.

The medical monopoly was enhanced further by the Flexner Report on medical education in 1910. Under the auspices of the Carnegie Foundation, medical educator Abraham Flexner visited nearly all 160 existing medical schools in the United States. He found the level of medical education poor and recommended the closing of most schools. Flexner urged stricter state laws, rigid standards for medical education, and more rigorous examinations for certification to practice. The enactment of Flexner's recommendations effectively made all nonscientific types of medicine illegal. It created a near total AMA monopoly of medical education in America.

In securing a monopoly, the AMA regulars achieved a unique professional state. Medicine not only monopolized the market for medical services and the training of physicians, it developed an unparalleled "professional dominance." The medical profession was *functionally autonomous* (Freidson, 1970b). Physicians were insulated from external evaluation and were by and large free to regulate their own performance. Medicine could define its own territory and set its own standards. Thus, Eliot Freidson (1970b) notes, "while the profession may not everywhere be free to control the *terms* of its work, it is free to control the *content* of its work" (p. 84).

The domain of medicine has expanded in the past century. This is due partially to the prestige medicine has accrued and its place as the steward of the "sacred" value of life. Medicine has sometimes been called on to repeat its "miracles" and successful treatments on problems that are not biomedical in nature. Yet in other instances the expansion is due to explicit medical crusading or entrepreneurship. This expansion of medicine, especially into the realm of social problems and human behavior, frequently has taken medicine beyond its proven technical competence (Freidson, 1970b). In this book we examine a variety of cases in which personal problems or deviant behaviors become defined as illness and therefore within medical jurisdiction.

The organization of medicine has also expanded and become more complex in this century. In the next section we briefly describe the structure of medical practice in the United States.

## Structure of medical practice

Before we leave our discussion of the medical profession, it is worthwhile to outline some general features of the structure of medical practice that have contributed to the expansion of medical jurisdiction.

The medical sector of society has grown

enormously in the 20th century. It has become the second largest industry in America. There are about 350,000 physicians and over 5 million people employed in the medical field. The "medical industries," including the pharmaceutical, medical technology, and health insurance industries, are among the most profitable in our economy. Yearly drug sales alone are over $4.5 billion. There are more than 7000 hospitals in the United States with 1.5 million beds and 33 million inpatient and 200 million outpatient visits a year (McKinlay, 1976).

The organization of medical practice has changed. Whereas the single physician in "solo practice" was typical in 1900, today physicians are engaged increasingly in large corporate practices or employed by hospitals or other bureaucratic organizations. Medicine in modern society is becoming bureaucratized (Mechanic, 1976). The power in medicine has become diffused, especially since World War II, from the AMA, which represented the individual physician, to include the organizations that represent bureaucratic medicine: the health insurance industry, the medical schools, and the American Hospital Association (Ehrenreich & Ehrenreich, 1970). Using Robert Alford's (1972) conceptualizations, corporate rationalizers have taken much of the power in medicine from the professional monopolists.

Medicine has become both more specialized and more dependent on technology. In 1929 only 25% of American physicians were full-time specialists; by 1969 the proportion had grown to 75% (Reiser, 1978). Great advances were made in medicine, and many were directly related to technology: miracle medicines like penicillin, a myriad of psychoactive drugs, heart and brain surgery, the electrocardiograph, CAT scanners, fetal monitors, kidney dialysis machines, artificial organs, and transplant surgery, to name but a few. The hospital has become the primary medical workshop, a center for technological medicine.

Medicine has made a significant economic expansion. In 1940, medicine claimed about 4% of the American gross national product (GNP); today it claims about 9%, which amounts to more than $150 billion. The causes for this growth are too complex to describe here, but a few factors should be noted. American medicine has always operated on a "fee-for-service" basis, that is, each service rendered is charged and paid for separately. Simply put, in a capitalist medical system, the more services provided, the more fees collected. This not only creates an incentive to provide more services but also to expand these medical services to new markets. The fee-for-service system may encourage unnecessary medical care. There is some evidence, for example, that American medicine performs a considerable amount of "excess" surgery (McCleery et al., 1971); this may also be true for other services. Medicine is one of the few occupations that can create its own demand. Patients may come to physicians, but physicians tell them what procedures they need. The availability of medical technique may also create a demand for itself.

The method by which medical care is paid for has changed greatly in the past half-century. In 1920 nearly all health care was paid for directly by the patient-consumer. Since the 1930s an increasing amount of medical care has been paid for through "third-party" payments, mainly through health insurance and the government. About 75% of the American population is covered by some form of medical insurance (often only for hospital care). Since 1966 the government has been involved directly in financing medical care through Medicare and Medicaid. The availability of a large amount of federal money, with nearly no cost controls or regulation of medical practice, has been a major factor fueling our current medical "cost crisis." But the ascendancy of third-party payments has effected the expansion of medicine in another way: more and more human problems become defined as "medical problems" (sickness) because that is the only way insurance programs will "cover" the costs of services. We will say more about this in Chapter 9.

In sum, the regular physicians developed control of medical practice and a professional dominance with nearly total functional autonomy. Through professionalization and persuasion concerning the superiority of their form of medicine, the medical profession (represented by the AMA) achieved a legally supported monopoly of practice. In short, it cornered the medical market. The medical profession has succeeded in both therapeutic and economic expansion. It has won the almost exclusive right to reign over the kingdom of health and sickness, no matter where it may extend.

## OVERVIEW OF THE BOOK

In this chapter we introduced the sociological study of deviance and social control and offered a brief analysis of the development of the medical profession and practice. We locate our study in the labeling-interactionist sociology of deviance that has emerged in the past two decades. Our emphasis differs from most interactionist work in that we focus on historical construction and change of deviance definitions.

Chapter 2 presents the analytic perspective used for the remainder of the book: the politics of deviance definitions and designations. We also present some introductory thoughts about the medicalization of deviance. Chapters 3 through 8 consist of substantive sociohistorical analyses of the changing definitions of various categories of deviance. Throughout we attempt to focus on people, groups, and organizations as they contend about particular definitions of deviance. Chapter 3 examines the oldest and most widely accepted example of medicalization, the medical model of madness. It traces the events, discoveries, and people involved with the promotion and diffusion of the concept of mental illness. Chapter 4 focuses on the development of the disease concept of alcoholism, highlighting how nonmedical groups can use medical means to their own ends. Chapter 5 examines the fall and rise of opiate addiction as a medical problem, illuminating with particular clarity the political struggles between supporters of criminal and medical definitions of addiction. Chapter 6 reviews the development and legitimation of the designations of juvenile delinquency, hyperkinesis, and child abuse and suggests that children, because of their position in society, are a population at risk for medicalization. Chapter 7 traces the definitions of homosexuality from sin to sickness to life-style, noting the profound moral continuity in definition and social response. The recent demedicalization by the American Psychiatric Association is examined and found more symbolic than real. Chapter 9 (written by Richard Moran) outlines the long search for the ''born criminal'' and the medical treatments used to ''cure'' and control criminals.

The final two chapters present a general analysis and conceptual understanding of the medicalization of deviance. Chapter 10 describes and analyzes three types of medical social control, elaborates on the important social consequences of medicalizing deviance, and examines implications of recent and future social policy on medicalization. Chapter 11 endeavors to present a theoretical statement on the medicalization of deviance, serving both as a summary of what we understand about the process of medicalizing deviance and suggestions about issues those who study the problem need to pursue.

## SUGGESTED READINGS

Erikson, K. T. *Wayward puritans*. New York: John Wiley & Sons, Inc., 1966.
An excellent and highly readable account of deviance among the 17th-century Puritans. Erikson explores the Antinomian controversy, the Quaker invasion, and Salem witchcraft as ''crime waves'' and develops a theory of deviance as boundary marking.

Freidson, E. *Professional dominance*. Chicago: Atherton Press, 1970.
A critical analysis of the social structure of medical practice. Freidson outlines the perquisites and consequences of professional dominance from a sociology-of-work perspective.

Goode, E. *Deviant behavior: an interactionist approach*. Englewood Cliffs, N.J.: Prentice-Hall, Inc., 1978.
A thoughtful and intelligent introduction to the relativist-interactionist approach to the study of deviance. The first eight chapters are especially useful.

Rubington, E., & Weinberg, M. S. *Deviance: the interactionist perspective* (3rd ed.). New York: Macmillan Publishing Co., Inc., 1978.
A well-integrated collection of articles that includes some of the best examples of the interactionist approach to deviance. Either this book or Goode's could profitably be read as a companion to *Deviance and Medicalization*.

Wertz, R. W. & Wertz, D. C. *Lying in: a history of childbirth in America*. New York: The Free Press, 1977.
Traces the definition and treatment of childbirth from a family event to a medical event. This is a well-presented case of the medicalization of a nondeviant activity.

# 2 FROM BADNESS to SICKNESS

## CHANGING DESIGNATIONS of DEVIANCE and SOCIAL CONTROL

This chapter departs from the historical frame that organizes most of this book to present the theoretical perspective we have used in our study of deviance. The perspective serves as a general conceptual framework for the ensuing substantive chapters. The first part of this chapter presents what we call a historical-social constructionist approach to deviance. Ours is a broadly conceived sociology-of-knowledge approach to the construction and change of deviance designations and is rooted in the labeling-interactionist tradition of deviance research. This allows us to focus on how certain activities or behaviors become defined as deviant and how they come to be designated as one particular form of deviance rather than another. We attempt to analyze the factors involved in the changes in dominant deviance designations from moral or legal categories to medical ones, or more simply, from ''badness'' to sickness. This requires a historical view of deviance definitions and designations. The second part of this chapter introduces the general discussion first, of the concepts illness and deviance, and then of the social construction of illness. The final section summarizes the theoretical approach developed in this chapter.

### A HISTORICAL-SOCIAL CONSTRUCTIONIST APPROACH TO DEVIANCE

Since deviance is an attributed designation rather than something inherent in individuals, our approach focuses on the historical, social, and cultural processes whereby individuals, behavior, attitudes, and activities come to be defined as deviant. The power to so define and construct reality is linked intimately to the structure of power in a society at a given historical period. This is another way of saying that historical constructions of deviance are linked closely to the dominant social control institutions in the society. Our perspective emphasizes a dual point of view: the attribution of deviance as a historical, social construction of reality and the activities involved in constructing new deviance definitions or designations for social control. We view religion and the state as social control agents that have lost, or in the case of the state, transferred, some of their control prerogatives in the development of modern societies. Medical science, in particular, typically buoyed by state legitimation, has grown to assume these age-old control functions.

In this section we outline our approach to the study of deviance. Our concern is not so much with deviants per se but with the social processes through which certain forms of behavior are defined collectively as one type of problem or another. In this sense, ours is a sociology of deviance designations or categories. These categories are socially constructed entities, ''neither immutable nor 'given' by the character of external reality'' (Gusfield, 1975; p. 286), that shift and change over time and place. More specifically, our approach focuses on how certain categories of deviant behavior become defined as medical rather than moral problems and how medicine, rather than, for example, the family, church, or state, has become the dominant agent of social control for those so identified. In short, our concern is with how certain forms of deviant behavior have become problems for medical jurisdiction and been designated as sickness rather than badness.

We present our analytical approach here somewhat inductively, tracing its roots from the labeling-interactionist tradition and the sociology of knowledge.

## Deviance as collective action: the labeling-interactionist tradition

As noted in the previous chapter, the labeling-interactionist perspective views deviance as relative to time, place, and audience and as an attribute that is conferred on people by others. This perspective posits that the processes of identifying, defining, and labeling behavior as deviant should be central concerns of the sociology of deviance. The labeling-interactionist approach turns the analysis away from the individual and the "causes" of his or her behavior, which have so long preoccupied the sociologist, to the "societal reaction." Rather than being viewed as an objective condition, deviance is regarded as a social product, produced by the joint action of the "deviant" and various social audiences.

Although the labeling perspective emerged from a symbolic interactionist social psychology, the focus on social process allowed for analysis of a wide range of activities related to deviance production. As Howard Becker (1973) points out, a central tenet of such an interactionist view is that deviance is "collective action." "In its simplest form, the theory insists that we look at all people involved in any episodes of alleged deviance" (p. 183). Edwin Schur (1971) clarifies the essence of this approach:

> Processes of social definition, or labeling, that contribute to deviance outcomes are actually found on at least three levels of social action, and all three require analysis. Such processes—as they occur on the levels of *collective rule-making, interpersonal reactions* and *organizational processing*—all consuitute important concerns of the labeling school. (p. 11).*

Most studies of deviance from a labeling-interactionist perspective have focused on the social psychological and microsociological aspects of deviance: especially the levels of interpersonal reactions (e.g., identification, definition, and contingencies of deviant labeling) and organizational process (e.g., official labeling and its attendant consequences). Thus we have developed considerable knowledge about contingencies in labeling, deviant careers, deviant subcultures, deviant identities, and the effects of stigma.

The "macrosociological" aspects of the labeling perspective have received less attention and consequently are not as developed in the sociological literature. Thus we know considerably less about the "collective definition of deviance" (Davis & Stivers, 1975) than we do about deviance-processing organizations, deviant careers, and stigmatized identities. Certainly this imbalance is not inherent in the labeling perspective itself. There have been a few studies that focus on this collective process of deviance definition and designation. Becker, in his seminal discussion of the Marijuana Tax Act of 1937, which rendered the sales and use of marijuana deviant, developed the concept of moral entrepreneurs to describe those who "lobby" for the creation of social rules. Such works as Kai Erikson's (1966) study of deviance in the Puritan colonies, Anthony Platt's (1969) study of the child-saving movement and the "invention of delinquency," Joseph Gusfield's (1963) analysis of the Women's Christian Temperance Union's crusade for prohibition, Elliot Currie's (1968) analysis of the control of witchcraft in Renaissance Europe, William Chambliss's (1964) study of the origin and change of vagrancy laws, and David Matza's (1966) essay on the disreputable poor are perhaps the classic labeling-interactionist studies that have examined the origin of deviant categories.* Although a few other studies

*Schur, E. *Labeling deviant behavior*. New York: Harper & Row, Publishers, Inc., 1971.

*A few studies that focused on the collective definition of deviance were done before the emergence of the labeling tradition, most significantly Sutherland's (1950) analysis of the diffusion of sexual psychopath laws and Kingsley Davis' (1938) paper on the ideology of the mental hygiene movement (see Chapter 3). Nonsociologists have also explored the collective definition of deviance, such as Thomas Szasz's (1970) essays on mental illness and David Musto's (1973) analysis of the history of opiate addiction in America.

have appeared recently, relatively less attention is still given to how "society" defines an act as deviant.

Sociologists whose work falls within the labeling-interactionist tradition have themselves pointed to this underdeveloped aspect of the perspective. Howard Becker (1973), in his discussion of deviance as collective action, notes that all parties involved in deviance production are fit objects for study.

> At a second level, the interactionist approach shows sociologists that a major element in every aspect of the drama of deviance is the imposition of definitions—of situations, acts, and people—by those powerful enough or sufficiently legitimated to be able to do so. A full understanding requires the thorough study of those definitions and the processes by which they develop and attain legitimacy and taken-for-grantedness. (p. 207)*

Eliot Freidson suggests that sociologists of deviance have recognized only one of the two major sociological tasks in the study of deviance. He points out, as do we, that sociologists have investigated rather thoroughly the etiology of various forms of deviant behavior but largely have "failed to recognize the other task" of studying the etiology of deviance designations. Freidson's (1970a) notions are similar to the perspective we develop here:

> [Sociological researchers] have followed the model of medicine in setting as their task the determination of some stable, objective quality or state of deviance (e.g., criminal behavior) and have sought to determine its etiology. They have failed to recognize the other task of studying the way conceptions of deviance are developed and the consequences of the application of such conceptions to human affairs. . . . *This task does not require explanation of the cause of behavior so much as it requires the explanation of the cause of the meaning attached to the behavior*. (pp. 213, 216, emphasis added)

Since the labeling-interactionist approach argues that deviance is an imputed or attributed condition, a social construction, it makes the study of the imputer or definer as important as the study of those defined as deviant. A fully developed labeling-interactionist perspective must also account for the development and change of deviance designations.

Malcolm Spector and John Kitsuse (1977) recently have taken a similar approach to the study of social problems. In contrast to traditional functionalist and normative approaches to social problems, Spector and Kitsuse suggest that sociologists study the collective activities involved in how certain conditions come to be defined as social problems. They are not concerned with how such social conditions developed but rather with how these alleged conditions came to be seen as social problems. Social problems emerge and are legitimated through the action of various "claims-making" groups in society. Spector and Kitsuse suggest that sociologists need to study the interaction between these claims-makers and responders concerning the definition of social conditions and what ought to be done about them. They see a parallel situation in the study of deviance:

> Central to the subject matter of the sociology of deviance is the processing of the definitions of deviance which may result in the development of informally recognized and enforced categories, as well as the establishment of official categories and populations of deviants. The theoretical problem is to account for how categories of social problems and deviance are produced, and how methods of social control and treatment are institutionally established. (Spector & Kitsuse, 1977, p. 72).*

One final point concerning the labeling-interactionist perspective of deviance is important. Labeling studies have been criticized for being "apolitical" and for avoiding structural considerations in their analysis (e.g., Taylor, I., et al., 1973). By investigating the collective and historical dimensions of the development of deviance categories in a given society, we can begin to examine these structural and political elements involved in defining this or that behavior as deviant: Who defines what as deviant? How does one group manage to have their definition of deviance legitimated? How

---

do deviance designations change as political and economic conditions change? Whose interests do deviance designations serve? The definition of any behavior or action as deviant is essentially a political matter, as Becker (1963, p. 7) has noted. In large part the success of such definitional process is decided by who has the power to legitimate their definitions. Such a perspective must eventually lead to the study of the distribution of power in a society, how those with power are able to effect the production of deviance designations, and whose interests these designations support.*

The labeling-interactionist sociologists, although actually producing few studies on the process of the collective definition of deviance, have developed a framework that allows for study of the macrosociological process of deviance definition. In that this perspective views deviance as an attribution, it allows us to study the etiology of definitions separately from the etiology of behavior. Thus the investigation of the origin, development, and change of deviance designations becomes a central task for the sociology of deviance.

## SOCIAL CONSTRUCTION OF REALITY: A SOCIOLOGY OF KNOWLEDGE

Although the labeling-interactionist perspective presents us with the questions to ask concerning the development of deviance designations, it is a sociology-of-knowledge approach that is necessary to answer them. The sociology of knowledge involves relating "knowledge" or cultural facts to specific social and structural forms in a given society. It sees knowledge as linked intimately to social organization or interaction that can be located in a historical frame. The basic assumption of a sociology-of-knowledge approach is that ideas do not develop in a vacuum but rather are generated and elaborated in a specific social milieu. Using this approach, we view deviance designations as products of the society in which they exist. The task of such an analysis is to investigate, usually in a historical frame, the social sources of these ideas and to trace their development or demise.

A few labeling-interactionist sociologists have pointed clearly in the direction of the sociology of knowledge to aid in this "other task" of sociologists studying deviance, examining how conceptions of deviance are developed (e. g., Goode, 1969). As Freidson (1970a) states,

> The other task is one that is essentially defined by the sociology of knowledge. It is created by the recognition that deviance is not a state as such, so much as an evaluation of the meaning of a state. Its problem for analysis then becomes not the etiology of some state so much as the etiology of the *meaning* of a state. Thus, it asks questions like: How does a state come to be considered deviant? How does it come to be considered one kind of deviance rather than another? . . . What does the imputation of a particular kind of deviance do to the organization of the interaction between interested parties? (pp. 215-216)

The only way to answer such questions about the emergence of dominant deviance designations is to attempt to locate their origins in history and identify the social groups and activities that generate and support them. In this fashion we can begin to understand the meanings we attribute to certain forms of behavior.

There are several different paths we could take toward a sociology-of-knowledge analysis of deviance designations. We have chosen to follow the phenomenological and conflict perspectives. Both view ideas—and in our case, deviance designations—as products of historically locatable social interaction or social organization. But they vary as to where they would ultimately locate the source of the idea and what factors they would take into account in their analysis.

The *phenomenological* perspective views deviance designations as "socially constructed realities," typifications (commonly understood categories or types) that are products of social

*Sociologists with perspectives other than labeling-interactionist may also see the collective definition of deviance as a central sociological concern. As Steven Spitzer (1975) points out in his theoretical discussion of a Marxian approach to the study of deviance, "Most fundamentally, deviance production involves the development of and changes in deviant categories and images" (p. 640). Although Spitzer would call for a class-based analysis of deviance designations, he agrees that such designations should be central in the study of deviance.

interaction and central in our interpreation of the world. "Reality" is defined not as something that exists "out there" for the scientist or anyone else to discover but as a social construction that emerges from and is sustained by social interaction. The social world is thus both interpreted and constructed through the medium of language. Language and language categories provide the ordered meanings by which we experience ourselves and our lives in society. They make the social world (objects, behavior, etc.) meaningful.

Peter Berger and Thomas Luckmann (1966) are perhaps the major proponents of this perspective. They view reality construction as a social process of three stages: externalization, objectivation, and internalization. Externalization is the process by which people construct a cultural product (e.g., the idea that strange behaviors can be caused by a mental illness). Objectivation occurs when cultural products take on an objective reality of their own, independent of the people who created them, and are viewed as part of objective reality (e.g., mental illness causes strange behaviors). Internalization is when people learn the "objective facts" of a culture through socialization and make them part of their own "internal" consciousness (e.g., taking for granted that strange behaviors are caused by mental illness). Objectivation is the institutionalization of the socially produced cultural product; it becomes, then, part of the available stock of knowledge of any society. Language becomes a depository of institutionalized collective "sedimentations" (e.g., mental illness), which we acquire "as cohesive wholes and without reconstructing the original process of formation" (Berger & Luckmann, 1966, p. 69). In a real sense they become part of the taken-for-granted everyday vocabulary of a society. It follows that if reality is socially constructed by human activity, it can be changed by human activity. Indeed, in Berger and Luckmann's view, realities are constantly being constructed and reconstructed in a dialectic process between interacting individuals and their social world qua society.

The *conflict* perspective views deviance designations as the products of social and political conflict, and it defines social control as a political mechanism by which certain groups can dominate others. There are two general schools of deviance conflict theorists, the pluralists and the Marxians. The pluralist conception sees society as made of a variety of competing interest groups in conflict for dominance, status, wealth, and power (e.g., Lofland, 1969; McCaghy, 1976). The Marxian perspective views conflict as a product of the class structure of society and the relation people have to the economic system (e.g., Quinney, 1974; Taylor, I. et al., 1973). For the pluralist, the conflict is most often played out in the conventional arena of institutionalized partisan politics, with different interest groups attempting to legislate their laws or laws that benefit them. The Marxian view sees law as much more a reflection of the interests of a ruling class. In this view, laws and deviance designations are part of the "superstructure," the culture and knowledge of a society, which is determined by the economic "substructure." Dominant or socially "popular" ideas bear the insignia of the ruling economic class and serve to reinforce its interests. A conflict approach sees "the subjective conceptions and definitions of deviance that exist to a given society as ideological products of interest group competition or class conflict" (Orcutt et al., 1977). Deviance designations are produced and influenced more by the powerful and applied more to the powerless.

These two sociologies of knowledge are not fully compatible (nor need they be). For example, Marxians would take issue with the phenomenologists' "social construction of reality" and argue that "reality" is based on the interests and visions of the ruling class rather than emerging out of social interaction. Phenomenologists, on the other hand, would have difficulty with the "hidden forces" (e.g., the economic system or means of production) that Marxians see as determining social life. Important as these differences may be, however, we need not concern ourselves here with such disputes. Although our approach is more phenomenological and pluralist than Marxian, both these approaches are insightful in studying the development and change of deviance designations. The phenomenological perspective sensitizes us to the socially constructed nature of deviance designations—that they emerge from social interaction and that they are humanly constructed and hence can be humanly changed. The conflict perspective sensitizes us to the fact that not all people are equal in their power to construct reality—that deviance designations may serve political interests and that they are created usually through some type of social conflict. We call this conflict the politics of definition.

## Politics of definition

What is considered deviant in a society is a product of a political process of decision making. The behaviors or activities that are deviant in a given society are not self-evident; they are defined by groups with the ability to legitimate and enforce their definitions. As Becker (1963, p. 162) notes, deviance is always a product of enterprise. It is through some type of political process, using "political" in its broad meaning of conflict about power relations, that deviance designations emerge and are legitimated. There are several ways this can occur. An individual or group may champion a cause that this or that behavior should be considered deviant (Blumer, 1971; Mauss, 1975). The antebellum abolitionist movement, antipornography crusades in various communities (Zurcher et al., 1971), the Women's Christian Temperance Union's campaign for Prohibition (Gusfield, 1963), the present-day antiabortion ("right to life") groups, and Anita Bryant's recent crusade against gay rights legislation are examples of this. Such campaigns for deviance designations can be seen as the work of *moral entrepreneurs,* those who crusade for the creation of new rules.*

> The prototype of the rule creator . . . is the crusading reformer. He is interested in the content of rules. The existing rules do not satisfy him because there is some evil which profoundly disturbs him. He feels that nothing can be right in the world until the rules are made to correct it. He operates with an absolute ethic; what he sees is truly and totally evil with no qualification. Any means is justified to do away with it. The crusader is fervent and righteous, often self-righteous. (Becker, 1963, pp. 147-148)*

Becker notes that the claims of most moral crusaders have humanitarian overtones; they truly think that they know what is good both for themselves *and* other people. But the crusader or crusading group is also often a self-interested participant in the deviance-defining process. The crusader (or the group) is not only crusading for a moral change in social rules, but there also may be a hidden agenda which is of equal or greater import and not immediately obvious.

Becker (1963, pp. 135-146) describes the passage of the Marijuana Tax Act of 1937 as an exemplar of moral entrepreneurship. He suggests that there was little public interest in marijuana before a publicity campaign by the Bureau of Narcotics. This campaign, led by Commissioner Henry J. Anslinger, aroused public interest and was followed by Congress passing a law that essentially made marijuana illegal. The marijuana smokers, whoever they were, were unorganized, powerless, and without publicly legitimate grounds for defense. They did not appear at the congressional hearings to oppose the law. The bureau had helped create a new category of deviants, marijuana sellers and users (Becker, 1963; p. 145). Another sociologist, Donald Dickson (1968), a few years later reanalyzed the origin of the Marijuana Tax Act and concluded that Anslinger and the bureau lobbied for its passage for organizational rather than moral reasons. He suggests that the bureau, faced with the threat of a steadily decreasing budget, tried to present itself as essential to the public welfare as a defender against the peril of marijuana.

---

*Becker discusses both rule creators and rule enforcers as moral entrepreneurs, but only the former concern us here. Becker, and some of the other authors of labeling studies we present in this section, did not conceptualize their work in terms of the sociology of knowledge. However, when sociology of knowledge is used as we present it here, these works are clearly within that perspective.

*From Becker, H. S. *Outsiders; studies in the sociology of deviance.* New York: The Free Press of Glencoe, Inc., 1963. Copyright © 1963 by The Free Press of Glencoe.

It attempted to increase its powers and scope of operations by lobbying for the inclusion of marijuana in its jurisdiction. Dickson suggests it was bureaucratic survival and growth rather than moral righteousness that prompted the bureau's efforts in promoting the antimarijuana legislation (the fact that most states already had some type of antimarijuana laws supports his interpretation). In either case, however, it appears that the new deviance designation was a product of enterprise, moral or bureaucratic, and was legitimated through the political process.*

Although the legal process is the most formal and institutionally obvious political avenue by which individuals and groups can influence and promote their definitions of deviance, it is by no means the only one. Moral entrepreneurs and other champions of deviance definitions can operate in any social system that has power and authority to impose definitions of deviance on the behaviors and activities of its members. One could expect to find champions of deviance definitions in schools, factories, bureaucracies, and religious and medical organizations—virtually in any system that has rules and authority. However, in modern industrial society, only law and medicine have the legitimacy to construct and promote deviance categories with wide-ranging application. With medicine this application even transcends social and national boundaries. The labeling of a disease or illness, the medical designation for deviance, is usually considered to have universal application. As Freidson (1970a) points out, the medical profession takes an active role in influencing deviance definitions and designations, discovering new ''illnesses,'' and intervening with ''appropriate'' medical treatment. In these activities the physician can be seen as a moral entrepreneur:

> [Medicine] is active in seeking out illness. The profession does treat the illnesses laymen take to it, but it also seeks to discover illness of which laymen may not even be aware. One of the greatest ambitions of the physician is to discover and describe a ''new'' disease or syndrome and to be immortalized by having his name used to identify the disease. Medicine, then, is oriented to seeking out and finding illness, which is to say that it seeks to create social meanings of illness where that meaning or interpretation was lacking before. And insofar as illness is defined as something bad—to be eradicated or contained—medicine plays the role of what Becker called the ''moral entrepreneur.'' (Friedson, 1970a, p. 252)

Medical work can lead to the creation of new medical norms, whose violation is deviance, or, in the cases we present, new categories of illness. This increases the jurisdiction of medicine or some segment of it and legitimates the medical treatment of sick deviants. Sociological analysis of the 19th-century medical involvement in the definition of madness (Scull, 1975) and the more recent cases of the medical definition of hyperkinesis (Conrad, 1975) and child abuse (Pfohl, 1977) are prime examples of the medical profession's championing of certain definitions of deviance. These examples will be presented in detail in later chapters. Although the ''politics of definition'' may be more obscured in the construction of medical designations than in legal ones, the decision to define certain behaviors, activities, or conditions as deviant still emerges from a political process that produces and subsequently legitimates the imposition of the deviant categories. And, most often, the consequences of medical definitions, especially when they concern human behavior, are also political. The second section of this chapter, which discusses deviance, illness, and medicalization, as well as subsequent chapters, elaborates this point.

**Interests, status, and class in the politics of definition.** Moral entrepreneurship and other championing of deviance definitions are not the only types of politics of definition. Another powerful influence on creating deviance designations is what we call *interest politics:*

---

*A recent reappraisal of the passage of this legislation posits that since most states already had antimarijuana laws, the bureau's publicity campaign was actually rather limited, the public interest was minimal, there was virtually no opposition, and there was no budget increase for the bureau; the act was a symbolic piece of legislation, symbolically reassuring congresspeople and others in what they already commonsensically believed (Galliher & Walker, 1977).

the promotion, directly or indirectly, of definiions of deviance that specifically support and buttress certain class or status interests. This approach aligns neatly with the conflict approach to the sociology of knowledge. In these cases we usually find groups or "power blocs" rather than individual entrepreneurs attempting to create rules that uphold their needs and interests. The deviance designation may become an instrumental or symbolic way in which to achieve ends that are totally unrelated to the deviance or deviance designations themselves. Interest politics may focus on interest groups, status interests, or class interests. Each will be discussed briefly.

Richard Quinney is one of the major conflict sociologists writing on deviance today. His more recent work (Quinney, 1974) assumes a Marxian view, but his earlier work is more pluralistic. In one of these early works Quinney presented a sociological theory of criminal law, in which he outlined an interest group model for the origin and development of law and deviance designations. Building on the work of legal scholar Roscoe Pound, Quinney developed a theory strikingly similar to the early work of Edwin Sutherland. It is based on the pluralist assumptions that society is characterized by diversity, conflict, and change rather than consensus; that law, and therefore deviance definitions, are *created* by interest groups in conflict with one another; and that law usually represents these specific interests rather than all the members of society. Quinney departs from the standard pluralist conception, which sees law as a compromise of diverse societal interests; in his view, law "supports some interests at the expense of others." He proposes four propositions to explain the origin of law through interest group conflict:

1. Law is the creation and interpretation of specialized rules in a politically organized society.
2. Politically organized society is based on an interest structure.
3. The interest structure of politically organized society is characterized by unequal distribution of power and conflict.
4. Law is formulated and administered within the interest structure of a politically organized society. (Quinney, 1969, pp. 20-30)

Quinney sees law as a political instrument used by specific groups to further their own interests; as a tool of those with power to shape the law at the expense of others. Definitions of deviance thus created and/or legitimated through law represent those interests.

But what the interests are, and even whose interests are involved, is not always obvious. Joseph Gusfield (1963) presents us with an interesting example in his analysis of the Women's Christian Temperance Union's crusade for Prohibition. Why would the members of the WCTU, a largely rural, Protestant, middle-class group of women, crusade so fervently for the prohibition of alcohol when problem drinking was not a major concern in their own rural communities? And why did they support only complete prohibition of alcohol use rather than restriction and control? They were moral crusaders for sure, but why engage in a moral crusade against a problem that appeared, at least on the surface, not to affect them?

Gusfield places the Temperance movement and especially the WCTU in a social-historical context to attempt to understand this crusade. The movement gained its strength in the late 19th and early 20th centuries. The United States was changing rapidly from a land dominated by native-born, rural, Protestant farmers and small-townspeople to one increasingly influenced by urban, immigrant, Catholic industrial workers and other urban folk. The drinking of alcohol was part of the everyday life of these urban workers. The rural Protestant culture was beginning to decline in influence; they saw their dominant status as endangered. Gusfield suggests that the Temperance movement for prohibition of alcohol was an instance of *status politics,* with the rural Protestant people trying to legislate their morality and norms. The conflict, according to Gusfield, was one of divergent styles of life, and the issue of alcohol was the symbol of this conflict. Thus he sees the Temperance movement as a "symbolic crusade" to try to maintain status in a changing society. The fact that Temperance advocates were much less concerned with the enforcement of Prohibition legislation than with its passage supports Gusfield's interpretation. The success of the Eighteenth Amendment outlawing alcohol was a public affirmation of their morals; it was clear to all concerned, regardless of enforcement, *whose* law it was (Gusfield, 1967). This analysis depicts how definitions of deviance (e.g., drinking alcohol) can be symbolic representations of one group's struggle against another about issues of morality and style of life.

Karl Marx argued law supports the dominant class's economic interests in society, which in industrial society is that of the bourgeoisie, or the owners of the means of production. It is nearly axiomatic among Marxian theorists that law reflects the interests of the *ruling class*. Sociologist William Chambliss (1964) presents an analysis of the origin and change in the deviance called "vagrancy" that points clearly to the effects of economic changes on law and deviance designations. The first vagrancy statutes emerged in England in the 14th century after the Black Death decimated the labor force. The lack of an adequate supply of labor forced the feudal landowners to pay higher wages for "free" labor and made it more difficult for them to keep serfs on the land. Opportunities for wages were available, and the landowners were hardpressed to keep them from fleeing. Chambliss (1964) concludes that the vagrancy law was to keep serfs from migrating: "There is little question but that these statutes were designed for one express purpose: to force laborers (whether personally free or unfree) to accept employment at a low wage in order to insure the landowner an adequate supply of labor at a price he could afford to pay" (p. 69). By the 16th century the focus of vagrancy laws shifted from a concern with the movement of laborers to a concern with criminal activities. A vagrant became defined in the law as one who "can give no reckoning how he lawfully makes his living." Punishment was severe: public whipping and, for repeated offenses, cutting off an ear. Chambliss points out that this change in vagrancy laws came about when feudalism was crumbling and there was increased emphasis on commerce and industry. This led to an increase in trade, on which English commerce was dependent. Transportation, however, was hazardous, and the traders were frequently attacked and robbed of their goods. The vagrancy law was revived with the changed focus to control persons suspected of being "highwaymen" who preyed on merchants transporting goods. Thus, as the economic structure changed, the law shifted and continued to support the dominant economic class in society—first the landowners, then the merchants.

In summary, the politics of definitions is a process whereby definitions of deviance are socially constructed. In a world where there are multiple "realities" and definitions of behavior, these definitions are constructed through a political process and legitimated in legal statutes, medical vocabulary, or religious doctrine. Although negotiations may occur, more powerful interests in society are better able to implement their version of reality by creating and legitimating deviance definitions that support their interests.

### Politics of deviance designation

The definition of certain behaviors or activities does not necessarily tell us what particular *designation* of deviance will be applied. For example, is the offending conduct a sin, a moral problem, a crime, or a sickness? The particular deviance designation is often a matter of controversy: Is deviant drinking a moral weakness or a disease? Are criminals genetically defective, psychologically abnormal, morally vacuous, or unsocialized brutes?

The professional and popular literatures on deviance are replete with discussions on what constitutes the nature of nearly any form of deviant behavior. Such discussion usually takes the form of an analysis of the etiology and characteristics of the deviant behavior. It is assumed generally that if one could only know the cause and thus the "true" nature of the deviant behavior, one could prevent or, more likely, control it closer to its source. But there is an unacknowledged political dimension to these academic debates. That is the question of who is the appropriate official agent of social control for such deviance. Put another way, in whose turf does the deviance lie? It is when we view discussions of deviance from this angle that such debates descend from the language of intellectual and technical specialization to political battles over turf. If drug addiction and alcoholism are diseases, then the medical profession is the legitimate agent of social control; if they are crimes, then they are in the jurisdiction of the criminal justice system. Needless to say, in a society as complex as ours the jurisdictional lines are not mutually exclusive, and considerable overlap may exist. This, however, does not negate the fact that arguments of etiology may be in essence jurisdictional disputes (this is perhaps clearest in the case of opiate addiction, presented in Chapter 5). As Erich Goode (1969) points out, ''naming'' itself has important political implications: ''By devising a linguistic category with specific connotations, one is designing the armaments for a battle; by having it accepted and used, one has scored a major victory'' (p. 89). In our view, deviance designations are not ipso facto one type of problem or another, and it is similarly not evident which social control agency is most appropriate. Decisions concerning what is the proper deviance *designation* and who is the proper *agent of control* are political questions decided frequently through political contest.

Recent analyses of social problems present an analogous situation. We have already noted that Spector and Kitsuse (1977) suggest that the distinctive focus of the sociology of social problems and deviance should be the social processing of definitions. Sociologists need to focus on the ''claims-making activities'' of the various groups asserting their definitions of deviance and analyze ''how categories of social problems and deviance are produced, and how methods of social control and treatment are institutionally established'' (Spector & Kitsuse, 1977, p. 72). This latter task is analogous to the one we propose here: the examination of ''claims-making'' activities that lead to the establishment of a deviance designation and the appropriate agent of social control. Joseph Gusfield (1975), in his analysis of the appropriate designation and control agent for automobile accidents and deaths attributed to ''drinking-driving,'' suggests we investigate how one agency attains ''ownership'' of a social problem and thus establishes its designation of deviance. For example, why are traffic fatalities and drinking-driving defined as an individual's alcohol problem rather than as a problem in transportation (i.e., getting safely from one place to another)? Although it is usually believed that decisions about proper designations of deviance (i.e., a crime versus a sickness) are made on a rational, even scientific, basis, as social scientists we cannot assume this. The public identity of the problem is not apparent; rather it is constructed through human interaction.

> The ''discovery'' of public facts is a process of social organization. Someone must engage in monitoring, recording, aggregating, analyzing and transmitting the separate and individual events into the public reality of ''auto accidents and deaths.'' At every stage in this process human choices of selection and interpretation operate. Events are given meaning and assumptions and values guide the selection. Public ''facts'' are not like pebbles on the beach, lying in the sun and waiting to be seen. They must instead be picked, polished, shaped and packaged. Finally ready for display they bear the marks of their shapers. (Gusfield, 1975, p. 291)

These facts may be part of claims-making activities of an agency or organization. Spector and Kitsuse (1977) note that their perspective leads them ''to view scientific facts and knowledge about social conditions as products of that organization, not as reflections of the phenomena they purport to explain'' (p. 67). In this view, public ''facts'' about social conditions that render deviance properly in one jurisdiction or another, even those claimed to be scientific ones, are viewed skeptically as ''social constructions'' that may support certain claims of legitimacy.* This perspective is particularly appropriate when ''scientific evidence'' is presented by an agency or organization in support of their deviance designation or to refute the claims of others. In short, such data may become vitally important ammunition in the battle among competing groups and control agencies.

*It is in this light that Goode (1969) notes that ''empirical reality, being staggeringly complex, permits and even *demands* factual selection. We characteristically seek support for our view: contrary opinions and facts are generally avoided. This opens the way for the maintenance of points of view which are contradicted by empirical evidence. And there is invariably a variety of facts to choose from. It is a comparatively simple matter to find what one is looking for in any moderately complex issue'' (p. 87).

Some prestigious claims-makers or organized collectivities have greater power than others to define what is true and false, respectable and disrespectable, normal and abnormal, etc. Howard Becker (1967) suggests there are "hierarchies of credibility" whereby prestigious organizations such as the American Medical Association, the American Bar Association, the Department of Health, Education and Welfare, the Justice Department, and representatives of these organizations have a greater power to define and legitimate reality (and deviance designations) than do other groups. They often use scientific findings selectively to support their particular policies (see, for example, Chapter 5).

**Deviance designations and social change.** Changes in deviance designations have consequences beyond justifying the suitable social control agent:

1. It may change the legitimate "authority" concerning a particular variety of deviant behavior. In the late 17th century, physicians rather than priests or magistrates became the experts on madness.

2. It may change the meaning of behavior. The behavior of restless, disruptive schoolchildren is no longer rebelliousness or willful opposition, but symptomatic of the illness hyperkinesis.

3. It may change the legal status of the deviance. The Harrison Act of 1914 created a new group of criminals—opium peddlers; the 1973 Supreme Court decision made abortion a conventional medical procedure.

4. It may change the contents of a deviance category or the norm itself. Prohibition, the Eighteenth Amendment, altered, at least symbolically, the norm of acceptable drinking behavior—there could be none. With repeal, only certain drinkers were defined as deviant—the underage and the chronic inebriate.

5. It may change the arena where identification and labeling of deviance takes place, as well as the vocabulary used. When homosexual conduct is viewed as a "crime against nature," labeling occurs in judicial processes; when it is defined as an illness, labeling takes place in the psychiatric arena through medical processes.

6. It may produce a change in the mode of intervention. When opiate addicts are defined as criminals, they are given legal punishments; when they are defined as sick, they are given methadone.

7. It may operate as a road sign as to what type of data to collect and on what to focus one's attention. By defining drinking-driving as the "cause" of auto fatalities, we focus on problem characteristics of the individual driver and collect data about him or her, rather than collecting data about the auto industry or analyzing the transportation system. By defining hyperactive children as sick, we turn our attention from the school and the child's situation and focus on the child's physiological characteristics.

8. It may shift the attribution of responsibility. Sinful and criminal deviants are responsible for their behavior; sick deviants are not.

All these changes and others should become apparent in various combinations throughout this book in our examination of changing deviance designations.

When certain types of deviance become accepted and taken for granted as reality, we have something analogous to Thomas Kuhn's concept of paradigm (i.e., a fundamental image of the subject matter). Paradigms structure the way the "faithful" construct and interpret the world. When paradigms change, after a crisis and the emergence of a new paradigm, views of reality change also. According to Kuhn (1970), "though the world does not change with a change in paradigm, the scientist afterwards works in a different world" (p. 121). Different data are collected, the world is seen and interpreted differently, and the new paradigm becomes the dominant manner by which to interpret experience.

We propose that three major paradigms may be identified that have held reign over deviance designations in various historical periods: deviance as sin; deviance as crime; and deviance as sickness. Overlap and competition among these "paradigms" are apparent over time, but they provide, nonetheless, distinct perspectives and images for constructing deviant reality. When a theological world view dominated, deviance was sin; when the nation-states emerged from the decay of feudalism, most deviance became designated as crime; and in our own scientifically oriented world, various forms of deviance are designated increasingly as medical problems. Thus we view the medical paradigm as the ascending paradigm for deviance designations in our postindustrial society.

In a given society a particular paradigm may be dominant. In contemporary American society a tension exists frequently between the legal-crime and medical-sickness paradigms, although opponents can develop comfortable accommodations. Each paradigm has institutional supporters of relatively high status (i.e., lawmakers and judges, medical researchers and physicians). In a world that views science as the ultimate arbiter of reality, deviance designations that can be supported by scientific research are more likely to gain credence. We say "more likely," since the factors in the politics of deviance designation are complex. However, all other things being equal, medical conceptions of deviance are more likely to be proposed in the name of science. When medical designations of deviant reality are in competition with other designations, we may well witness a *hegemony* of medical definitions; that is, a preponderant influence or acceptance of medical authority as the "final" reality and a diminishing of other potential realities. Needless to say, there can be and are challenges to this hegemony, but some see a type of cultural and structural medical hegemony of deviance designations as increasingly apparent in American society (see Illich, 1976; Radelet, 1977a).

We use the approach just outlined in the remainder of this book to study the changing designations of deviance, especially as designations become medical and physicians are involved in treatment and social control. In the next section of this chapter we identify some of the more general issues in "the medicalization of deviance." In all the following substantive chapters (3 to 8), we try to be true to the complexities of the changing definitions and designations of deviance for each particular case. This involves giving attention to such specifics as historical events, relevant settings of conflict and change, attributions of cause, political conflict, social control mechanisms, scientific discoveries, claims-making activities, and negotiation of jurisdictional boundaries. It is important to remember that deviance designations do not change by themselves; social action engaged in by real people or collectivities is necessary to create definitional change. We aim at constructing a historical overview and staying close to the data in each case, rather than trying to fit all cases into a rigid model of medicalization. In a sense, we view each substantive chapter as revealing some aspect of the process of medicalization. In Chapter 10 we attempt to integrate these into a theoretical statement on the medicalization of deviance.

## DEVIANCE, ILLNESS, AND MEDICALIZATION*

Consider the following situations. A woman rides a horse naked through the streets of Denver claiming to be Lady Godiva and after being apprehended by authorities, is taken to a psychiatric hospital and declared to be suffering from a mental illness. A well-known surgeon in a Southwestern city performs a psychosurgical operation on a young man who is prone to violent outbursts. An Atlanta attorney, inclined to drinking sprees, is treated at a hospital clinic for his disease, alcoholism. A child in California brought to a pediatric clinic because of his disruptive behavior in school is labeled hyperactive and is prescribed methylphenidate (Ritalin) for his disorder. A chronically overweight Chicago housewife receives a surgical intestinal bypass operation for her problem of obesity. Scientists at a New England medical center work on a million-dollar federal research grant to discover a heroin-blocking agent as a "cure" for heroin addiction. What do these situations have in common? In all instances medical solutions are being sought for a variety of deviant behaviors or conditions. We call this "the medicalization of deviance" and suggest that these examples illustrate how medical defi-

*The remainder of this chapter is an extended and amended version of "On the Medicalization of Deviance and Social Control" by Conrad, P. In D. Ingleby (Ed.), *Critical psychiatry*. Copyright © 1980 by Peter Conrad. Reprinted by permission of Penguin Books Ltd.

nitions of deviant behavior are becoming more prevalent in modern industrial societies like our own. The historical sources of this medicalization, and the development of medical conceptions and controls for deviant behavior, are the central concerns of our analysis.

Medical practitioners and medical treatment in our society are usually viewed as dedicated to healing the sick and giving comfort to the afflicted. No doubt these are important aspects of medicine. In recent years the jurisdiction of the medical profession has expanded and encompasses many problems that formerly were not defined as medical entities. Ivan Illich (1976) has called this "the medicalization of life." There is much evidence for this general viewpoint—for example, the medicalization of pregnancy and childbirth, contraception, diet, exercise, child development norms—but our concern here is more limited and specific. Our interests focus on the medicalization of deviant behavior: the defining and labeling of deviant behavior as a medical problem, usually an illness, and mandating the medical profession to provide some type of treatment for it. Concomitant with such medicalization is the growing use of medicine as an agent of social control, typically as medical intervention. Medical intervention as social control seeks to limit, modify, regulate, isolate, or eliminate deviant behavior with medical means and in the name of health (Zola, 1972). The remainder of this book examines sociologically the medicalization of deviance and the development of medical social control. It presents an analysis of the transformation of deviance from *badness* to *sickness* and the adoption of the medical model for a number of specific categories of deviant behavior.

Before beginning our introduction to the medicalization process, we discuss two general sociological notions that pertain to the perspective developed here. These are the social construction of illness and the relationship of illness and deviance.

## The social construction of illness

What are disease and illness? On the face of it they seem rather straightforward concepts. A commonsense viewpoint might see disease as something that exists "out there," apart even from the human body, that may enter the body and do harm; ideas of avoiding viruses, germs, and other "diseases" follow from this view. A systematized variant of a commonsense view might be that disease is "a specific destructive process in an organism, with specific causes and specific symptoms" (Webster's New Ideal Dictionary). Sometimes disease is seen simply as a departure from health. Illness, if differentiated from disease, is taken as the condition of being diseased, or more commonly, the state of being sick. Yet, as we will point out, disease and illness are highly complex entities, far more problematic than these commonsense views indicate. It is not our goal here to settle a longstanding academic controversy on the nature of disease and illness, but rather to sensitize the reader to a number of approaches and to some characteristics of illness designations.

A positivist conception of illness is most similar to the commonsense view. Illness is the presence of disease in an organism that inhibits the functioning, or, in Leon Kass's (1975) terms, "well-working" of the physiological organs (in a most inclusive sense) of the organism. This strict and limiting definition includes only malfunctioning organs as diseases. It contains an implicit assumption that there is some norm of functioning or well-working that can be used as a standard and that this normal condition is recognizable by the medical observer. One need only think about the recent medical controversies surrounding tonsillectomies and what constitutes "healthy" or "unhealthy" tonsils to realize that the concept of "well-functioning organs" is itself problematic. Moreover, does such a notion limiting illness and disease to organ malfunctioning include undiscovered diseases or organ changes that may be adaptations to an environment (e.g., the sickle cell trait)? By focusing only on "objective" organ conditions, the medical positivists (at least in theory) limit their concept of disease. It is important to point out that most of the difficulties we call mental illness, especially the so-called functional disorders, do not match this definition at all.

Others have argued that disease and illness are separate entities and can be so analyzed. For example, Abram Feinstein has conceptualized disease

> in purely morphologic, physiologic, and chemical terms. What the physician directly observes in his dialogue [examination] . . . that he terms the *illness* consists of subjective sensations (symptoms) and certain findings (signs). The illness is described as the result of the interaction of the disease with the host or person, emphasis being given to the mechanism by which the disease develops and "produces" or is associated with the illness. (Feinstein, 1967, as summarized and cited in Fabrega & Manning, 1972, p. 95)*

According to this view, disease is a physiological state, and illness is a social state presumably caused by the disease. Although the pathologist sees the disease, the physician sees only signs and symptoms of illness and infers disease. This allows, conceptually at least, for illness without diseases and diseases without illnesses. Such a body/social dichotomy has the advantage of permitting analysis on both the physiological and social levels.

In sharp contrast to the positivist viewpoint is the cultural relativist position: an entity or condition is a disease or illness only if it is recognized and defined as one by the culture. For example, in one South American Indian tribe, dyschromic spirochetosis, a disease characterized by colored spots appearing on the skin, was so common that those who did not have it were regarded as deviant and excluded from marriage (Mechanic, 1968, p. 16). Among the Papago Indians of the American Southwest, obesity has a prevalence of nearly 100%. The Papago do not regard this condition as abnormal; in fact, they often bring babies whose development is normal by Western standards to the medical clinic and ask the physician why their baby is so skinny and sickly. To the Papago, obesity is not an illness; by Western standards nearly all the Papago are ill. Which definition is more valid? René Dubos (1959), an esteemed microbiologist, has argued that the notion that a universal condition exists that is "health" is a mirage and that health and illness are limited by cultural knowledge and adaptations to the environment. Certainly such a relativist stance allows important insight, perhaps especially with what we call mental illness, but it is criticized easily for minimizing the organic-physiological nature of illness and disease. Cultural relativists, however, do sensitize us to the variability in the interpretation and definition of physiological phenomena.

Although all these approaches have some utility and validity in the contexts in which they are used, from a sociological perspective they miss a crucial aspect of illness: they take for granted how something becomes *defined* as an illness in the first place. Illness and disease are human constructions; they do not exist without someone proposing, describing, and recognizing them. There are processes we commonsensically call "disease," but that does not make them a priori diseases. As Peter Sedgwick (1972) points out, "the blight that strikes at corn or potatoes is a *human invention,* for if man wished to cultivate parasites (rather than potatoes or corn) there would be no 'blight,' but simply the necessary foddering of the parasite-crop" (p. 211). An animal may be feebled, have parasites, or be in pain but that in no way means it is suffering from an "illness." As Sedgwick (1972) states,

> Animals do not have diseases either, prior to the presence of man in a meaningful relation with them. A tiger may experience pain or feebleness from a variety of causes. . . . It may be infected by a germ, trodden by an elephant, scratched by another tiger, or subjected to the [aging] process of its own cells. It does not present itself as being *ill* (though it may present itself as being highly distressed or uncomfortable) except in the eyes of a human observer who can discriminate illness from other sources of pain or enfeeblement. Outside the significances that man voluntarily attaches to certain conditions, *there are no illnesses or diseases in nature*. (p. 211)

Another way of saying this is that there are no illnesses in nature, only relationships. There are, of course, naturally occurring events, including infectious viruses, malignant growths, ruptures of tissues, and unusual chromosome constellations, but these are not ipso facto ill-

---

*From "Disease, illness, and deviant careers," by Horatio Fabrega, Jr. and Peter K. Manning, in *Theoretical perspectives on deviance,* edited by Robert A. Scott and Jack D. Douglas, p. 95, © 1972 by Robert A. Scott and Jack D. Douglas, Basic Books, Inc., Publishers, New York.

nesses. Without the social meaning that humans attach to them they do not constitute illness or disease:

> The fracture of a septuagenarian's femur has, within the world of nature, no more significance than the snapping of an autumn leaf from its twig; and the invasion of a human organism by cholera germs carries with it no more the stamp of "illness" than the souring of milk by other forms of bacteria. (Sedgwick, 1972, p. 211)

Thus one could argue that biophysiological phenomena are what we use as a basis to label one condition or another as an illness or disease; the biophysiological phenomena are not in themselves illness or disease. (As we shall see in later chapters, however, a suspicion or hypothesis of biophysiological phenomena may be sufficient to label something as illness.)

Illnesses represent human judgments of conditions that exist in the natural world. They are essentially *social constructions*—products of our own creation. "Illness," as Gusfield (1967) has written, "is a social designation, by no means given by the nature of medical fact" (p. 180). The fact that there is high agreement on what constitutes an illness does not change this. The high degree of consensus on what "objectively" is disease is not independent of the social consensus that constructs these "facts" and renders them "important." For physical illness, the consensus is so extensive and taken for granted that we are inclined to forget that it represents a reality wholly dependent on our collective agreement (Freidson, 1970a, pp. 214-215).

As illnesses are social judgments, they are negative judgments. Can we think of any illness designations that are positive judgments or any illness conditions that are viewed as desirable states? Common sense also tells us that an entity labeled an illness or disease is considered undesirable. In the human world this is as true for tuberculosis* and cancer as it is for mental illness and alcoholism. Biological aberration is neither necessary nor sufficient for something to be labeled an illness: a 7-foot basketball player is outside the normal biological range but not considered ill. Early and late onset of puberty are both biologically deviant conditions, yet only late puberty is viewed as evidence for physiological abnormalities and disorders (Conrad, 1976, p. 69). Nearly all functional mental disorders have no or at best questionable physiological evidence, yet they are defined and treated as diseases. In Western societies most illnesses are assumed to have some biophysiological or organic basis (and most do), but this is not a necessary condition for something to be defined as an illness. Occasionally an undesirable physiological condition such as baldness is not considered an illness. Most physiological conditions found troublesome, however, are defined as illnesses or medical disorders.

As Eliot Freidson (1970a) observes, calling something an illness in human society has consequences *independent* of the effects on the biological condition of the organism:

> When a veterinarian diagnoses a cow's condition as an illness, he does not merely by diagnosis change the cow's behavior: to the cow, illness remains an experienced biophysical state, no more. But when a physician diagnoses a human's condition as illness, he changes the man's behavior by diagnosis: a social state is added to a biophysical state by assigning the meaning of illness to disease. (p. 223)

Think for a moment of the difference in consequences if a person's inability to function is attributed to laziness or to mononucleosis, seizures to demon possession or epilepsy, or drinking habits to moral weakness or alcoholism. Medical diagnosis affects people's behavior, attitudes they take toward themselves, and attitudes others take toward them.

In summary, illness is a social construction based on human judgments of some condition in the world. In some fashion, illness, like beauty (and like deviance), is in the eye of the beholder. Although it is based partly on current cultural conceptions of what disease is, and more often than not in Western society grounded in biophysiological phenomena, this social evaluative process is central rather than peripheral to the concept of illness and disease.

---

*Susan Sontag's (1978) recent characterization of tuberculosis in the 19th century as having an appealing symbolic significance within a small circle of literary and artistic figures appears to be an exception that, when viewed from a more general social perspective, serves to support the rule.

It follows logically that both diagnoses (as systematized classifications) and treatments are founded on these social judgments; they cannot be separated. Just as profound consequences followed from the recognition of microorganisms as agents of "disease," so are there consequences from recognizing illnesses as social judgments. Needless to say, the social construction of illness designations for deviant behaviors is subject to more ambiguity and interpretation than manifestly biophysiological problems. In this light it is understandable that conditions defined as illness reflect the social values and general Weltanschauung of a society.

### Illness and deviance

As Talcott Parsons pointed out in his classic writings on the "sick role," both crime and illness are designations for deviant behavior (Parsons, 1951, pp. 428-479). Parsons conceptualized illness as deviance primarily because of its threat to the stability of a social system through its impact on role performance. Although both crime and illness are violations of norms (social and medical) and can be disruptive to social life, the attributions of cause are different. Deviance considered *willful* tends to be defined as crime; when it is seen as *unwillful* it tends to be defined as illness (see Aubert & Messinger, 1958). Since crime and illness are both designations of deviance, it becomes necessary to distinguish between the two, especially with reference to appropriate mechanisms of social control. It is in this regard that Parsons developed his notion of the sick role.

The social responses to crime and illness are different. Criminals are punished with the goal of altering their behavior in the direction of conventionality; sick people are treated with the goal of altering the conditions that prevent their conventionality. Parsons further argues that there exists for the sick a culturally available "sick role" that serves to conditionally legitimate the deviance of illness and channel the sick into the reintegrating physician-patient relationship. It is this relationship that serves the key social control function of minimizing the disruptiveness of sickness to the group or society. The sick role has four components, two exemptions from normal responsibilities and two new obligations. First, the sick person is exempted from normal responsibilities, at least to the extent necessary to "get well." Second, the individual is not held responsible for his or her condition and cannot be expected to recover by an act of will. Third, the person must recognize that being ill is an inherently undesirable state and must want to recover. Fourth, the sick person is obligated to seek and cooperate with a competent treatment agent (usually a physician).* For sickness, then, medicine is the "appropriate" institution of social control. Both as legitimizer of the sick role and as the expert who strives to return the sick to conventional social roles, the physician functions as a social control agent.

In light of the socially constructed nature of both crime and illness, it should not be surprising to find that there has been a fluidity or drift between designations of crime deviations and illness deviations. One of the major concerns of this book is to explore the factors contributing to the change from moral-criminal definitions of deviance to medical ones, what we call the medicalization of deviance.

## MEDICALIZATION OF DEVIANCE

Conceptions of deviant behavior change, and agencies mandated to control deviance change also. Historically there have been great transformations in the definition of deviance—from religious to state-legal to medical-scientific. Emile Durkheim (1893/1933) noted in *The Division of Labor in Society* that as societies develop from simple to complex, sanctions for deviance change from repressive to restitutive or, put another way, from punishment to treatment or rehabilitation. Along with the change in sanctions and social control agent there is a corresponding change in definition or conceptualization of deviant behavior. For example, certain "extreme" forms of deviant drinking (what is now called alcoholism) have been

*There have been a number of critiques and modifications of the sick role. See, for example, Gordon (1966), Mechanic (1968), Sigler and Osmond (1974), and Parsons (1975).

defined as sin, moral weakness, crime, and most recently illness. Nicholas Kittrie (1971) has called this change the divestment of the criminal justice system and the coming of the therapeutic state. Philip Rieff (1966), in his sociological study of the impact of Freudian thought, terms it the "triumph of the therapeutic."

In modern industrial society there has been a substantial growth in the prestige, dominance, and jurisdiction of the medical profession (Freidson, 1970a). It is only within the last century that physicians have become highly organized, consistently trained, highly paid, and sophisticated in their therapeutic techniques and abilities. Eminent American social scientist Lawrence J. Henderson observed that "somewhere between 1910 and 1912 in this country, a random patient, with a random disease, consulting a doctor chosen at random, had, *for the first time* in the history of mankind, a better than fifty-fifty chance of profiting from the encounter" (quoted in Blumgart, 1964; emphasis added). This observation suggests the poor state of medicine prior to the 20th century. With the apparent success of medicine in controlling communicable diseases (Dubos, 1959), the growth of scientific biomedicine, the regulation of medical education and licensing, and the political organization and lobbying by the American Medical Association, the prestige of the medical profession has increased. The medical profession dominates the organization of health care and has a virtual monopoly on anything that is defined as medical treatment, especially in terms of what constitutes "illness" and what is appropriate medical intervention. As Freidson (1970a) has observed, "The medical profession has first claim to jurisdiction over the label illness and *anything* to which it may be attached, irrespective of its capacity to deal with it effectively" (p. 251). Rieff (1966) contends that the hospital has replaced the church and parliament as the symbolic center of Western society. Although Durkheim did not predict this medicalization, perhaps in part because medicine of his time was not the scientific, prestigious, and dominant profession of today, it is clear that medicine is the central restitutive agent in our society.

The effectiveness of physicians and modern medicine in treating many illnesses has certainly contributed to the authority they are given. This has been especially true in the case of infectious diseases. With the mid–19th-century discovery of the germ theory of disease, a "doctrine of specific etiology" developed (Dubos, 1959). This doctrine implied that each disease had a single, specific, external, and objectively identifiable cause that could be discovered and treated accordingly. The success of this doctrine enhanced the prestige and reputations of medical professionals. However, as Freidson (1970a, p. 83) cautions, the reputations of the medical profession should not be seen only as a result of actual achievement but also as the product of negotiation, persuasion, and impression management by powerful interests involved in health care (recall our discussion of the monopolization of medicine in Chapter 1). This distinction between the reputation and reality of modern medicine is a point we return to in the next chapter in our discussion of how madness became entrenched in medical jurisdiction.

Medical treatments for deviant behavior are heralded frequently as examples of the "progress" typical of modern society, believed to unfold in a linear fashion, leaving beneficial advances in its wake. Medical progress is particularly likely to be seen as holding promise for solutions to age-old human problems. What "progress" is, however, on inspection, is not as clear as it might initially appear. "Progress" is only meaningful in relation to some other point in time and to a specific audience. Progress is a positive evaluation of some change. But social change is not clearly linear and rarely totally beneficial or detrimental. Social change nearly always produces positive and negative effects that are distributed differentially in the affected population (Corzine, 1977). For plantation owners the development of slavery was progress, but for the slaves it was the beginning of oppressive bondage. Perhaps in some respects the medicalization of opiate addiction, deviant drinking, obesity, hyperactivity, madness, and the other behaviors discussed in this book was progress. But changes defined as progress must be viewed as progress for a specific audience; all do not necessarily benefit equally from these changes. And to have a more complete picture, it is important to point out the accompanying problems and consequences created by the alleged progress. When the picture is more complete, change may not appear as clearly to be progress.

## Expansion of medical jurisdiction over deviance

When treatment rather than punishment becomes the preferred sanction for deviance, an increasing amount of behavior is conceptualized in a medical framework as illness. As noted earlier, this is not unexpected, since medicine has always functioned as an agent of social control, especially in attempting to "normalize" illness and return people to their functioning capacity in society. Public health and psychiatry have long been concerned with social behavior and have functioned traditionally as agents of social control (Foucault, 1965; Rosen, 1972). What is significant, however, is the expansion of this sphere where medicine functions in a social control capacity. In the wake of a general humanitarian trend, the success and prestige of modern biomedicine, the technological growth of the 20th century, and the diminution of religion as a viable agent of control, more and more deviant behavior has come into the province of medicine. In short, the particular, dominant designation of deviance has changed; much of what was badness (i.e., sinful or criminal) is now sickness. Although some forms of deviant behavior are more completely medicalized than others (e.g., mental illness), recent research has pointed to a considerable variety of deviance that has been treated within medical jurisdiction: alcoholism, drug addiction, hyperactive children, suicide, obesity, mental retardation, crime, violence, child abuse, and learning problems, as well as several other categories of social deviance. Concomitant with medicalization there has been a change in imputed responsibility for deviance: with badness the deviants were considered responsible for their behavior; with sickness they are not, or at least responsibility is diminished (see Stoll, 1968). The social response to deviance is "therapeutic" rather than punitive. Many have viewed this as "humanitarian and scientific" progress; indeed, it often leads to "humanitarian and scientific" treatment rather than punishment as a response to deviant behavior. As Barbara Wootton (1959) notes:

> Without question . . . in the contemporary attitude towards anti-social behavior, psychiatry [i.e., medicine] and humanitarianism have marched hand in hand. Just because it is so much in keeping with the mental atmosphere of a scientifically-minded age, the medical treatment of social deviants has been a powerful reinforcement of humanitarian impulses; for today the prestige of humane proposals is immensely enhanced if these are expressed in the idiom of medical science. (p. 206)

There are, however, other, more disturbing consequences of medicalizing deviance that will be discussed in later chapters.

A number of broad social factors underlie the medicalization of deviance. As psychiatric critic Thomas Szasz (1974) observes, there has been a major historical shift in the manner in which we view human conduct:

> With the transformation of the religious perspective of man into the scientific, and in particular the psychiatric, which became fully articulated during the nineteenth century, there occurred a radical shift in emphasis away from viewing man as a *responsible agent acting in and on the world* and toward viewing him *as a responsive organism being acted upon* by biological and social "forces." (p. 149)*

This is exemplified by the diffusion of Freudian thought, which since the 1920s has had a significant impact on the treatment of deviance, the distribution of stigma, and the incidence of penal sanctions.

Nicholas Kittrie (1971), focusing on decriminalization, contends that the foundation of the therapeutic state can be found in determinist criminology, that it stems from the *parens patriae* power of the state (the state's right to help those who are unable to help themselves), and that it dates its origin with the development of juvenile justice at the turn of the century. He further suggests that criminal law has failed to deal effectively (e.g., in deterrence) with criminals and deviants, encouraging a use of alter-

*From Szasz, T. *Ceremonial chemistry*. New York: Doubleday & Co., Inc., 1974. Copyright © 1974 by Thomas Szasz.

native methods of control. Others have pointed out that the strength of formal sanctions is declining because of the increase in geographical mobility and the decrease in strength of traditional status groups (e.g., the family) and that medicalization offers a substitute method for controlling deviance (Pitts, 1968). The success of medicine in areas like infectious disease has led to rising expectations of what medicine can accomplish. In modern technological societies, medicine has followed a technological imperative—that the physician is responsible for doing everything possible for the patient—while neglecting such significant issues as the patient's rights and wishes and the impact of biomedical advances on society (Mechanic, 1973). Increasingly sophisticated medical technology has extended the potential of medicine as social control, especially in terms of psychotechnology (Chorover, 1973). Psychotechnology includes a variety of medical and quasimedical treatments or procedures: psychosurgery, psychoactive medications, genetic engineering, disulfiram (Antabuse), and methadone. Medicine is frequently a pragmatic way of dealing with a problem (Gusfield, 1975). Undoubtedly the increasing acceptance and dominance of a scientific world view and the increase in status and power of the medical profession have contributed significantly to the adoption and public acceptance of medical approaches to handling deviant behavior.

## The medical model and "moral neutrality"

The first "victories" over disease by an emerging biomedicine were in the infectious diseases in which specific causal agents—germs—could be identified. An image was created of disease as caused by physiological difficulties located *within* the human body. This was the medical model. It emphasized the internal and biophysiological environment and deemphasized the external and social psychological environment.

There are numerous definitions of "the medical model." In this book we adopt a broad and pragmatic definition: the medical model of deviance locates the source of deviant behavior within the individual, postulating a physiological, constitutional, organic, or, occasionally, psychogenic agent or condition that is assumed to cause the behavioral deviance. The medical model of deviance usually, although not always, mandates intervention by medical personnel with medical means as treatment for the "illness." Alcoholics Anonymous, for example, adopts a rather idiosyncratic version of the medical model—that alcoholism is a chronic disease caused by an "allergy" to alcohol—but actively discourages professional medical intervention. But by and large, adoption of the medical model legitimates and even mandates medical intervention.

The medical model and the associated medical designations are assumed to have a scientific basis and thus are treated as if they were morally neutral (Zola, 1975). They are not considered moral judgments but rational, scientifically verifiable conditions. As pointed out earlier, medical designations *are* social judgments, and the adoption of a medical model of behavior, a political decision. When such medical designations are applied to deviant behavior, they are related directly and intimately to the moral order of society. In 1851 Samuel Cartwright, a well-known Southern physician, published an article in a pretigious medical journal describing the disease "drapetomania," which only affected slaves and whose major symptom was running away from the plantations of their white masters (Cartwright, 1851). Medical texts during the Victorian era routinely described masturbation as a disease or addiction and prescribed mechanical and surgical treatments for its cure (Comfort, 1967; Englehardt, 1974). Recently many political dissidents in the Soviet Union have been designated mentally ill, with diagnoses such as "paranoia with counterrevolutionary delusions" and "manic reformism," and hospitalized for their opposition to the political order (Conrad, 1977). Although these illustrations may appear to be extreme examples, they highlight the fact that all medical designations of deviance are influenced significantly by the moral order of society and thus cannot be considered morally neutral.

## SUMMARY

This chapter has outlined the conceptual framework that informs the remainder of this book. We call it a "historical-social constructionist" approach to deviance. Of the two orientations to deviance noted in Chapter 1, it is clearly interactionist and has its roots in the labeling-interactionist tradition. In addition, it employs a sociology-of-knowledge perspective to examine the emergence and change of definitions and designations of deviance. Rather than focusing on individual deviants and the causes of their behavior, the focus is on the *etiology of definitions* of deviance. In this sense it can be viewed as a sociology of deviance designations. Deviance definitions are treated as products of a political process, as social constructions usually implemented and legitimated by powerful and influential interests and applied to relatively powerless and subordinate groups.

Even after a social definition of deviance becomes accepted or legitimated, it is not evident what particular type of problem it is. Frequently there are intellectual disputes over the causes of the deviant behavior and the appropriate methods of control. These battles about deviance designation (is it sin, crime, or sickness?) and control are battles over turf: Who is the appropriate definer and treater of the deviance? Decisions concerning what is the proper deviance designation and hence the appropriate agent of social control are settled by some type of political conflict.

How one designation rather than another becomes dominant is a central sociological question. In answering this question, sociologists must focus on claims-making activities of the various interest groups involved and examine how one or another attains ownership of a given type of deviance or social problem and thus generates legitimacy for a deviance designation. Seen from this perspective, public facts, even those which wear a "scientific" mantle, are treated as products of the groups or organizations that produce or promote them rather than as accurate reflections of "reality." The adoption of one deviance designation or another has consequences beyond settling a dispute about social control turf; these will become more apparent and will be articulated in subsequent chapters.

When a particular type of deviance designation is accepted and taken for granted, something akin to a paradigm exists. There have been three major deviance paradigms: deviance as sin, deviance as crime, and deviance as sickness. When one paradigm and its adherents become the ultimate arbiter of "reality" in society, we say a hegemony of definitions exists. In Western societies, and American society in particular, anything proposed in the name of science gains great authority. In modern industrial societies, deviance designations have become increasingly medicalized. We call the change in designations from badness to sickness the medicalization of deviance.

Illness, like deviance, is a social construction based on social judgments of some condition in the world. Although based partly on current cultural conceptions of what constitutes disease, and (in Western societies) typically grounded in biophysiological phenomena, the social evaluative process of classifying some condition or event as a disease is central rather than peripheral to the concept of disease and illness. In this fundamental sense a disease designation is a moral judgment, for to define something as a disease or illness is to deem it undesirable.

Sociologists since Parsons have viewed illness and crime as alternate designations for deviance. Deviance that is considered willful is defined as crime; when it is considered unwillful, it tends to be defined as illness. Thus when illness is a designation for deviant behavior, medicine becomes the agent of social control.

Designations of deviance have increasingly shifted from the moral to the medical sphere. With the apparent success of medicine in controlling communicable diseases, the growth of scientific biomedicine, the political organization and lobbying of the American Medical Association, and the profession's control over medical education and licensing, medicine has become a prestigious profession in the 20th century. The medical profession dominates the organization of health care and has a virtual monopoly over anything that is defined as an illness or a "medical" treatment.

Although our portrayals of the social and historical sources of changing deviance designations are painted with a broad brush, and certainly cannot include all the contextual characteristics involved in such complex shifts, clear outlines of the change and development of each deviance designation are delineated. In depicting these individual cases we use a finer brush and give attention to specific detail. Thus we give consideration to historical events, relevant settings of conflict and change, attributions of cause, social control mechanisms, scientific discoveries, and claims-making activities for each case presented in the following six chapters.

## SUGGESTED READINGS

Freidson, E. *Profession of medicine*. New York: Dodd, Mead & Co., 1970.
Considered a seminal and path-breaking sociological analysis of the profession of medicine. Of particular interest is the section on the social construction of illness (pp. 203-331).

Gusfield, J. R. Moral passage: the symbolic process in the public designations of deviance. *Soc. Prob.*, 1967, **15,** 175-188.
Builds on Gusfield's earlier (1963) work on the Temperance movement and analyzes changing public designations of deviant drinking. Although his emphasis is on the symbolic qualities of changing designations, this paper exemplifies the approach outlined in this chapter.

Illich, I. *Medical nemesis*. New York: Pantheon Books, Inc., 1976.
A readable and controversial analysis of the place of medicine in modern society. Illich argues that medicine has become more a threat to health than a healing agent and needs to be dismantled, decentralized, and replaced by various forms of self-help. The section on "social iatrogenesis" is most relevant to medicalization of deviance.

Kittrie, N. N. *The right to be different: deviance and enforced therapy*. Baltimore: Johns Hopkins University Press, 1971.
A superbly documented overview focusing on the legal aspects of medicalization. Kittrie documents the growth of the therapeutic state in relation to the growth of 19th-century deterministic theories, emphasizes lack of legal "safeguards" for deviants, and makes specific recommendations for action.

Parsons, T. *The social system*. New York: The Free Press, 1951.
Parsons' major theoretical treatise. His analysis of "the sick role" (pp. 428-479) is the classical sociological discussion of the relation of crime and illness as deviance designations and medicine as an agent of social control.

# 3 MEDICAL MODEL of MADNESS

## THE EMERGENCE of MENTAL ILLNESS

The roots of the medical conception of madness run deep.* This chapter explores the historical origins of the concept of mental illness, its ascendence and expansion in Western society, and subsequent domination of the medical model of madness in modern times. The concept of madness as an *illness* has a long history in Western culture but has not been always the dominant explanation of madness. We carefully review the historical development of mental illness as it is the exemplar for medical conceptions of deviant behavior. It is literally the original case of medicalized deviance.

All societies seem to recognize certain forms of peculiar and unpredictable behavior as madness. Anthropologists have never discovered that mythical idyllic culture where no idea of madness existed. Cultures define madness differently, however. Grandiose ideas are acceptable among the Kwakiutl, hallucinations among Siberian Eskimos, and fears of persecution among the Dobu; all are seen as symptoms of madness by Western standards. The Yoruba of Nigeria identify 20 separate types of madness, the Iroquois recognized undesirable mental states but did not call them madness, and the Cochiti Pueblos do not distinguish between madness and physical illness at all (Kiev, 1964). The causes of madness are attributed variously to demon possession or spirit intrusion, witchcraft or sorcery, soul loss or devine retribution for taboo violation. What each culture views as the cause of madness is dependent on its world view. In a society with a dominant spiritual or religious world view, one would expect madness to be attributed to some spiritual offense or otherworldly beings. Cultures that have had no contact with Western psychiatry rarely define madness as an illness. It is by no means obvious that madness *is* mental illness or even a medical problem. Indeed, one of the primary purposes of this chapter is to analyze how madness became defined as a medical problem in Western society. The madness-as-illness concept is a product of 2000 years of cultural and social development. We begin our search for roots in biblical Palestine.

### SMITTEN BY MADNESS: ANCIENT PALESTINE

Madness was certainly recognized by the ancient Hebrews. The Bible's Old Testament serves as our best record of the era. For example, Saul's madness is described in detail in the first book of Samuel. He believed, as did most Hebrews of the time, that madness was inflicted by a supernatural power or by an angry deity as punishment for sin. "Among the Hebrews, those presumed to disobey God's commandments and to violate his ordinances were threatened with dire retribution, including the curse of madness" (Rosen, 1968, p. 28). There

*Throughout this chapter we have used a number of different designations to depict mad people (maniacs, lunatics, insane, mental patients, mentally ill), their healers and keepers (mad-doctors, physicians of the insane, medical superintendents, medical psychologists, alienists, psychiatrists), and their institutions (insane asylums, lunatic asylums, madhouses, mental hospitals) in an attempt to capture the appropriate terms of the era. The changing vocabulary of madness is itself symbolic of many of the developments discussed herein.

are several references in the Bible to madness as divine retribution. In Deuteronomy Moses warned his people that if they "will not obey the voice of the Lord your God or be careful to obey all his commandments . . . the Lord will smite you with madness and confusion of mind."

Although the objective criteria for identifying madness among the Hebrews was "the occurrence of impulsive, uncontrolled or unreasonable behavior" (Rosen, 1968, p. 37), not all those who behaved abnormally were defined as mad. The prophets also acted in strange and sometimes bizarre ways, but in the context of their society they were not considered mad. Ezekiel, a sterling example, "was subject to frenzies in which he clapped his hands, stamped his feet, uttered inarticulate cries and shook his sword to and fro" (Rosen, 1968, p. 53). He experienced trances and visions, as well as claiming to speak with God. Medical historian George Rosen (1968) describes clearly some of Ezekiel's peculiar behavior:

> On receiving his prophetic call Ezekiel was commanded by Yahweh to eat papyrus scroll on which were written the words of lamentation and mourning, symbols of the message he was about to deliver. When he did so he had the sensation of eating honey. . . . To forecast the famine and other horrors to which the seige of Jerusalem would lead, Ezekiel rationed his food and drink and prepared it by using for fuel human dung, which was considered unclean. As a sign of the calamities that would befall Jerusalem he cut off his hair and beard using a sword as a razor, then burned one third, destroyed another third, and scattered the remainder to the four winds. . . . To indicate the time during which Israel and Judah respectively would be exiled, he was commanded by Yahweh to lie down for two periods, once on his left side for 390 days . . . and once on his right side for forty days. (p. 44)

Madness and prophecy both were abnormal to the Hebrews. The Hebrew verb "to behave like a prophet" also means "to rave" or "to act like one is beside oneself" (Rosen, 1968, p. 42). Both were attributed to divine intervention and socially ascribed to individuals. Although the mad person and the prophet alike engaged in peculiar and extreme behavior, the prophet's was attributed to divine inspiration and the mad person's to divine retribution. From a sociological viewpoint, there is nothing inherently mad or prophetic in Ezekiel's behavior; the prophecy was attributed by his fellow Hebrews. Prophecy was an explanation available to the Hebrews for certain types of extreme behavior and an available social role for some deviants. It is interesting to speculate where the prophets are today, when we no longer attribute hearing voices to God but to mental illness.

## ROOTS OF THE MEDICAL MODEL: CLASSICAL GREECE AND ROME

The genesis of many of the ideas and conceptions in Western thought can be traced to classical Greece. Perhaps most significant for our discussion, the Greeks introduced an original rational view of nature and humanity. This contrasted sharply with the dominant religious-cosmological views of previous cultures and allowed for the developments of a primitive "science" and a naturalistic medicine. The Romans copied and expanded Greek knowledge, thus preserving it for future civilizations.

Most historians consider modern medicine to have begun with the Greeks. Hippocrates (460-377 BC), called the "Father of Medicine," combined the speculations of the philosophers of medicine who preceded him with detailed bedside observations. He was the first to attempt to explain consistently all diseases on the basis of natural causes. The maintenance of a skeptical insistence on rational knowledge and natural explanations, a pubescent scientific attitude, forms the basis of the Hippocratic tradition of medicine.

The Greeks had two explanations for madness. The cosmological-supernatural explanation—that madness was a possession caused by the gods or inflicted by the spirit underworld—was believed by most of the Greek populace. It made sense, since the mythological gods were considered part of everyday life. The natural-medical explanation, the first elaborated medical explanation in recorded history, which defined madness as a disease with natural causes, seems to have been adopted only by certain segments of the upper classes.

Greek medicine, early in its history, rejected

the supernatural explanation, conceptualizing madness as a disease or the symptom of a disease with the same etiology as somatic diseases (Rosen, 1968, p. 76). The causes of madness were explained by the same general theory of disease used to explain all illness, humoral theory. The *humoral theory,* which held sway in medicine from the time of Hippocrates until well into the 17th century, was deceptively simple in its physiological explanation. The theory postulated the existence of four humors: blood, phlegm, black bile, yellow bile—bodily fluids whose proportion and balance were significant to health. The four humors were thought to enter into the constitution of the body and determine, by their relative proportions, a person's health and temperament. One's disposition and state of mind were determined by the balance of these humors. Madness was looked on as an imbalance of humors, usually as an excess. For example, melancholia or depression was caused by an excess of black bile, which was generated by the liver; a sudden flux of yellow bile from the spleen to the brain would bring on anxiety and produce a "choleric" temperament. The names Hippocrates used to depict madness are still common today: epilepsy, mania (abnormal excitement), melancholia (depression), and paranoia (Zilboorg, 1941, p. 47). Indeed, a residue of this idea of mental health is preserved in our everyday language when we refer to someone as being in a "bad humor."

As treatments follow from etiological or causal explanations, the medical treatments for madness, though relatively uncommon among the Greeks, were attempts to rebalance the humors. Both physical and what we might call psychotherapeutic methods were employed. Physicians recommended rest, a limited diet, and gentle massage, as well as bleeding and cupping. If there was no improvement, nonspecific stimulants such as irritant plasters, purges, vomitives, hot and cold baths, sunbathing and other forms of heating were added to the regimen. When psychological factors were thought to be the cause, mental exercises, games, and recreation were used. Occasionally extreme physical "treatments" were employed: severe physical restraint, violent purges, excessive bleeding, dunking the patient into cold water and even whipping and beating (Rosen, 1968). The Romans practiced a form of "electroshock" treatment by using electric eels applied to the head. Variations on these remedies for madness can be found through modern times.

Not all the Greek intelligentsia accepted fully the medical definition of madness. Socrates, himself later considered a deviant, appears to have been skeptical about the medical notions of madness. With astoundingly profound insight he wrote:

> [Most men] do not call those mad that err in matters that lie outside the knowledge of ordinary people: madness is the name they give to errors in matters of common knowledge. For instance, if a man imagines himself to be so tall as to stoop when he goes through the gateways of the Wall, or so strong as to try to lift houses or perform any other feat that everybody knows to be impossible, they say he's mad. They don't think a slight error implies madness, but just as they call a strong desire love, so they name a great delusion madness. (Quoted in Rosen, 1968, p. 94)

Madness in the Graeco-Roman era was viewed largely as a family problem to be dealt with by kin. People who could not function in society and were not dangerous to others were allowed to wander about and were cared for by family. Eventually some legal restrictions on the insane were enacted: Roman law forbade them to marry, acquire property, and to make or witness a will. Plato may have been influenced by the disease concept of madness. He wrote: "A man . . . either in a state of madness, or when affected by disease, or under the influence of old age, or in a fit of childish wantonness, himself no better than a child" could not be responsible for his crimes "unless he have slain someone, and have within his hands the stain of blood" (quoted in Rosen, 1968, p. 124). Even under these circumstances such a person was to be exiled for a year or have a guardian appointed to care for his other affairs.

Physicians on the whole did not play a large role in the treatment of madness in ancient Greece and Rome. Rosen (1968, p. 135) notes that there is no evidence that medical data or opinion were required to treat manias or *dike paranoias*. The pauper insane who wandered the countryside received no medical care and were ridiculed and stigmatized. Those who could afford it consulted physicians. Most people, however, either because of their belief in the supernatural explanation or because relief could not be obtained any other way, sought religious and magical treatments for madness.

In Greece and later in Rome, competing theories of madness existed side by side. In retrospect, it appears that medical theories were respected by the upper classes and intelligentsia, but supernatural-cosmological theories were the favored explanations of the masses. Greek medicine, by introducing a theory that would remain the major medical explanation for more than 15 centuries, actually laid the foundation for our present conceptions of madness. Roman medicine, influenced heavily by Galen, was more empirical and pragmatic, and expanded and synthesized the knowledge of Greek medicine. After the fall of Rome, the medical definition of madness became subordinate to another supernatural view of madness that arose in the medieval period.

## DOMINANCE OF THE THEOLOGICAL MODEL: THE MIDDLE AGES

The collapse of the Roman Empire in the fifth century produced a general return to supernatural beliefs, mysticism, and mythology. Many historians of the medieval period write as if there were only theological and demonological conceptions of madness, in a psychiatric "dark age."

> On the whole . . . whatever little knowledge the Greeks had established was lost and a tragic decline to an earlier cultural level ensued. The clock was put back a thousand years. For a thousand years the mentally ill were again regarded as possessed by the devil or evil spirits, or considered to be witches or sorcerers who could produce illness in others. (Ackerknecht, 1968, p. 18)*

This is, however, an overstatement. Although theological institutions and theories were certainly dominant, medical conceptions of madness did exist during this period, even if they did not flourish. By the ninth century the medical school at Salerno, building on the Hippocratic as well as other medical traditions, had identified a number of types of mental disorders. They called them stupor, pheresy, epilepsy, hysteria, idiocy, mania, and melancholy. The first four were considered to be physical diseases (Neaman, 1975, p. 14).

The medieval physicians attributed madness to either of two causes, the passions or an imbalance of humors. If the disease was primary, that is, completely caused by physiological conditions, there was little hope for cure. Medieval physicians believed also that two exotic forms of madness, love madness and werewolfism (lycanthropy), were natural in origin and treatable by medical means. Lovesickness was treated as a genuine disease. A medieval physician described its symptoms:

> Their eyes are hollow and do not shed tears and appear to be overflowing with gladness; their eyelids move more rapidly. . . . When they call to recollection the beloved object either from seeing or hearing, and more especially if this suddenly occurs, then the pulse undergoes a change from the disorder of the soul. (Quoted in Neaman, 1975, p. 22)

Medieval physicians never believed that humans were actually changed into werewolves but rather that certain imbalances of humors caused some maniacs to imitate wolves, especially at night.

The therapeutic methods used by medieval physicians were similar to the Greek and Roman treatments, although they added herbal remedies like "lettuces" and "poppies" (opiates). The first psychosurgery appears to be the Byzantine physicians' treatment called "trepanning," or incising of the skull, "to permit compressed atoms of flesh to move apart and thus relieve the pressure on the brain, which they believed was causing these operable cases of insanity" (Neaman, 1975, p. 25).

The medical view was not the dominant conception of madness in medieval times, however. The dominant conception was a theological view based on dogma of the Christian Church. The Church reached its pinnacle of power during this period and was the dominant institution in defining much of human affairs. Theological doctrines pervaded education, law,

---

*From Ackerknecht, E. H. *A short history of psychiatry*. New York: Hafner Press, 1968. Copyright 1968, Hafner Publishing Co.

medicine, and just about everything else. In the theological view, which was based on the biblical tradition, all disease and other misfortune had three principal interpretations. Disease was God's mode of punishment for sin, specifically the sin of faithlessness; it was God's manner of testing an individual's strength, as with Job; or it was a sign warning the individual, and others, that he had better repent. Medieval conceptions of madness to a large degree followed from this. Madness was seen as a *punishment for sin*. Madness was not, as it is commonly thought, depicted as sin itself but was rather caused by and a retribution for sin (Neaman, 1975, pp. 48-50). An interesting consequence of the theological view of madness was that an individual was not held responsible for any behavior committed while mad, but was for the behavior that caused him to be smitten with madness. "The Church reasoned that insanity couldn't be the cause of sin but could be the result of sin" (Neaman, 1975, p. 99).

For centuries the Church was the major institution of social control and the Devil its nemesis. The Devil was powerful and ubiquitous in medieval times. Medical conceptions had to account for this. Some suggested that the Devil could enter the body and upset the humoral balance. Mental diseases were seen as punishments for sin. Both theologians and physicians made clear distinctions between madness and possession. Demonic possession was a spiritual illness, and therefore no medical treatment could cure it; exorcism was more appropriate. Theological and medical views of madness were not competing conceptions of reality; medical views were subordinate to theological ones. Most physicians agreed with the theologians that the first cause of disease was always God or the Devil. This produced a complex intertwining of the medical and theological conceptions of madness and created a delicate division of labor that enabled the two institutions to coexist and divide up the social control turf.

## Witchcraft, witch-hunts, and madness

By the late 13th century enormous social changes were occurring in Europe, producing reactions from the powerful and conservative Church. Feudalism was beginning to crack and crumble; the Gutenberg printing revolution made self-education possible; the dogma and abuses by the Church were being attacked by the precursors of the Reformation; and severe plagues had decimated the population of Europe by nearly half. The dominance and authority of the Church were being threatened and, according to Thomas Szasz (1970), a scapegoat was necessary around which theologian dogmatists could unite.

The most spectacular and devastating Church response was the infamous Inquisition and the organized witch-hunts, which led to the burning, hanging, and drowning of perhaps half a million people accused of being witches and agents of the Devil (Currie, 1968). Mad persons were not considered to be witches and subject to persecution until the 14th century. By the 15th century the Inquisition was a powerful social force, doggedly combating heresy and other deviance. At the peak of this period the *Malleus Maleficarum* (Hammer of Witches) was published in 1487. Written by two Dominican monks, Johan Sprenger and Heinrich Kraemer, and with papal approval, it became the guidebook for the Inquisition. This handbook depicted most dissidents, mad people, deviants, and especially women, as "witches" who had made a compact with the Devil and were then in his employ. Anyone who showed psychological, behavioral, or physical deviation was labeled a witch or a sorcerer. The *Malleus,* which Szasz (1970) calls a diagnostic manual for the witch-hunter, described in detail how to diagnose witches, try them in court, and handle those convicted, usually by burning. The *Malleus* contended that if organic cause could not be determined for a disease, the disease must be caused by witchcraft. Furthermore, if the reader was not convinced by the authors' arguments, it was because he or she, too, was a victim of witchcraft (a 15th-century Catch-22!). A highly misogynic document, the *Malleus* points out: "All witchcraft comes from a carnal lust which in women is insatiable" (quoted in Alexander & Selesnick, 1966, p. 98). For the next 200 years in most of continental Europe, those considered insane were caught in the massive witchcraft net, and theological rationalizations caused many to be burned at the stake.

During the Inquisition period the medical conception of madness was largely muted. There was still an occasional strike for the medical viewpoint. "For example, in Spain the Inquisition as early as 1537 recognized that alleged witches might be insane, and there were several cases on record where such individuals were transferred to hospitals" (Rosen, 1968, p. 12). By the 17th century, physicians were beginning to collect detailed histories of "demonics" and to speak of physiology and pathology in such cases.

Johann Weyer, a German physician, was not the first to espouse the view that the witches were really mentally ill, "but he was [its] most explicit, most forceful and most successful champion" (Ackerknecht, 1968, p. 21). Weyer is considered a central figure in the history of psychiatry because of his methodical attempts to prove that witches were mentally ill and should be treated by physicians. A careful observer and investigator who interviewed both the accusers and the accused, Weyer collected data to support his case that the women persecuted as witches were really mentally sick. His research took 12 years, and in 1563 he published *De Praestigiis Daemonum* (The Deception of Demons), a detailed rebuttal to the *Malleus Maleficarum*. Weyer, in a respectful tone and still maintaining his belief in the existence of witchcraft, argued that the accused were melancholy old women. He wrote, "Those illnesses whose origins are attributed to witches come from natural causes" (quoted in Alexander & Selesnick, 1966, p. 121). This is depicted as a turning point by medical historians—the first stroke of a virtual renaissance, the new search for natural causes of madness. Weyer's immediate impact was not, however, that great. "He did not acquire a true following until almost a century after his death. In the meantime the spirit of the *Malleus Maleficarum* was still alive and active" (Zilboorg, 1941, p. 235).

Medical and psychiatric historians (e.g., Zilboorg, 1941) argue that psychiatry developed as the persecution of witches declined and disappeared. Increasingly, enlightened physicians realized that the alleged heretics were mentally ill. Thomas Szasz rebuts this interpretation and suggests that the deviants were merely redefined and relabeled in medical terms, with medicine replacing the church as the institution of social control. It "happened because of the transformation of a religious ideology into a scientific one: medicine replaced theology; the alienist, the inquisitor; and the insane, the witch" (Szasz, 1970, p. xx).

Szasz (1970) compares theological conceptions of witchcraft with medical conceptions of madness. His comparisons are elaborate and compelling: witchcraft and mental illness are myths "diagnosed" in terms of behavior by a professional diagnostician; they are ascribed statuses based on deviant behavior that are conferred by the powerful on the powerless; witches and mental patients are scapegoats who suffer persecution by society, in one case justified by religion and in the other by medicine; witch trials and sanity trials both lack due process and fail to protect individual rights; and both reinforce the dominant ethic of society. He argues further that institutional psychiatry, the kind practiced in mental hospitals, is a continuance of the Inquisition. It, too, is an institution to control deviants; and mental patients are the "witches" of today. One need not agree completely with Szasz's notion of institutional psychiatry as a replacement for the Inquisition to appreciate the spirit of his analysis. Szasz's argument by analogy is revealing and insightful, and it highlights psychiatry as a social control agent and mental illness as a conception developed to explain certain types of behavior.

The labeling of deviants as witches was possible because an ideology, witchcraft, and a powerful ecclesiastical and secular institution, the Inquisition, had been created and legitimized. This instrument of control had been devised to eradicate dissent and deviance and to protect the established order. The established order was changing, and new conceptions of deviance began to emerge.

## THE EUROPEAN EXPERIENCE: MADNESS BECOMES MENTAL ILLNESS

The Renaissance brought a rediscovery of Greek and Roman art and science, including medicine. While the Graeco-Roman model, based on humoral theory, provided *physicians* with a basic medical conception of madness, it was not the dominant one in society, nor was it the basis for state policies for dealing with madness. In fact, physicians had relatively little to do with madness until the early 19th century.

There are several significant changes that occurred between the 16th and 18th centuries that affected the ascendance of the medical model of madness to its dominant position and the legitimation of physicians as the authorities to treat it. These include the great confinement of lunatics and other deviants; the separation of the able-bodied from the lunatics; the entrance of physicians; and the emergence of a unitary concept of mental illness.

## The great confinement

Before the 17th century, harmless mad people roamed the roads of countryside and town. Although they were occasionally abused and driven from towns, they generally led a free-wandering existence. Responsibility for the mad was with the family and local community; only in rare circumstances were obviously disturbed individuals ''hospitalized'' or formally excluded from the community. Dangerous and criminal mad persons were handled directly by legal procedures. One interesting, although relatively uncommon, innovation was the *Narranschiff* (literally, ''ship of fools''). Ships filled with mad people would sail the rivers and the seas, stopping at various towns to load or unload some of their cargo of lunatics. Prior to the 17th century, madness and folly were not hidden away and were part of everyday life; as Michel Foucault (1965) points out, society's ''debate'' with madness over reality was a public matter.

By the middle of the 17th century the remnants of the feudal order were fading, and a new absolutist, capitalist order was emerging. This was a period of great changes in society; among these was a shift in the treatment of madness and other deviance. In 1656 Hôpital Général was opened in Paris by royal decree. This was not a hospital in the sense we think of hospital; there was no medical treatment and nearly no medical involvement. It was essentially a paupers' prison, constructed to rid the city of idlers and beggars and other socially useless individuals. Mad people, along with criminals, libertines, beggars, vagabonds, prostitutes, the unemployed, and the poor were confined there. At one point it held 1% of the Paris population, about 6000 people. Over the course of its existence, the general hospital combined the characteristics of an asylum, a workhouse, and a hospital. From the outset, social control was a major function of the hospital. With the opening of Hôpital Général, the period of ''the great confinement'' of the poor and the deviant began (Foucault, 1965), and institutions for the deviant and ''socially useless'' emerged in all European countries. Confinement became the new way to deal with deviants.

Hôpital Général and its sister institutions were great moral and social edifices. Confinement was not for medical reasons but as an ''imperative to labor'' to prevent ''mendicancy and idleness as a source of all disorders'' (Foucault, 1965, p. 48). The obligation to work was predominant in these institutions; indeed, through this they served an important function for the new bourgeois society. They provided ''cheap manpower in the periods of full employment and high salaries; and in periods of unemployment, reabsorption of the idle and social protection against agitation and uprising'' (Foucault, 1965, p. 51). It is significant to point out that the emerging capitalist order needed ''willing'' workers, and these institutions served also to ''discipline the work force,'' that is, inculcate people with the value of work and ''proper'' work habits, neither of which could be assumed in the 17th century.

## Separation of the able-bodied from the lunatics

As the importance of a competent labor force increased, it became increasingly necessary to separate the able-bodied poor from the nonable-bodied. After all, how could discipline and good work habits be instilled if lunatics were around disrupting the order of the institution? The 18th century saw a gradual separation of insanity from other forms of dependence and deviance. This gave rise, by the end of the century, to special institutions like the almshouse, the workhouse, the madhouse, and the prison. The mad were separated from other deviants, not for the purposes of special treatment but rather to protect others from the "contagion" of madness (Foucault, 1965) and to impose order and discipline on the hospital and the workhouse. "The presence of the mad [in the institutions] appears as an injustice [not for the mad] but for others" (Foucault, 1965, p. 184). In the early capitalist society, with its highly unstable and fluctuating economy, it became increasingly important to have an able-bodied reserve labor pool who worked in the periods of boom and were institutionalized or controlled in periods of bust. With the rise of industrialism this becomes even more significant (Scull, 1977b).

Lunatics were segregated increasingly into special institutions. The first of these appeared in the 18th century. An extensive "trade in lunacy," private madhouses owned and operated by physicians ("mad-doctors"), developed in England (Parry-Jones, 1972). These madhouses were "frequently a lucrative business dealing with the most acutely disturbed and refractory cases" (Scull, 1977b) and were the precursors to the public asylums that developed a century later. Overall, from a sociological viewpoint, the separation and segregation of the mad from other deviants was accomplished largely for social and economic reasons, not for medical ones.

## Entrance of the physician

As noted earlier, the early institutions for the mad were not medical institutions. Through the 18th century, physicians played a small role in the confinement and provided little treatment. In England it was not until 1774 that a physician's certificate was required for commitment to a madhouse; until then, the judgment of a magistrate was sufficient. It was not apparent to the judicial and political powers or to the potential clientele that physicians had any special expertise in the area of madness. Eighteenth-century physicians did not have any explanatory theories or curative treatments that could have made madness and the madhouse ipso facto their legitimate turf. How did physicians become the keepers of the madhouse and ultimately the legitimate authorities on madness?

Certainly, if physicians could provide useful curative and rehabilitative treatments, then it would be clear why medicine came to dominate the realm of madness. But this does not seem to be the case. Most of the therapies used by the 18th-century physicians were ancient ones: bloodletting, dunking, and purgation were popular treatments. Fear, restraint, starvation, and castration were also used as treatments, as were diets and a few available drugs. New innovations, usually physical treatments, such as the "Darwin chair" (invented by Charles Darwin's grandfather), were introduced. "In this chair the insane were rotated until blood oozed from their mouths, ears and noses, and for years most successful cures were reported as a result of its use" (Ackerknecht, 1968, p. 38). Although this primitive "shock therapy" may have aided a few disordered people, the 18th-century physician's armamentarium and ability to "cure" were limited.

There was, however, considerable optimism concerning the promise of medicine to solve problems of human suffering and pain.

> The intellectual approach to the problems of health gave the illusion that in medicine, as in other social sciences, the Age of Reason would mark the beginning of a new era. In fact, there was justification for the optimism prevailing in medicine during the period of 1750-1800. Leprosy and the plague had all but disappeared from Europe: smallpox, malaria and summer diarrhea had been brought under control. Condorcet envisaged an era when man would be free from disease and old age and death would be indefinitely postponed; Benjamin Franklin made similar predictions. (Dubos, 1959, p. 18)

Undoubtedly some of this optimism was transferred to the physicians who treated madness. Although limited in therapeutic ability, by the end of the 18th century the physician had become essential to the madhouse. Since medical certificates were required for confinement of lunatics, the physician became the gatekeeper of madness, in charge of entry. "The doctor's intervention is not made by virtue of a medical skill or power that he possesses in himself and that would be justified by a body of objective knowledge. It is not as a scientist that *homo medicus* has authority in the asylum, but as wiseman" (Foucault, 1965, p. 217). The physician was not healer of the sick, but guardian of the inept.

Perhaps one of the most dramatic images in the history of the treatment of madness is Philippe Pinel, the great humanitarian director of the French asylums at Bicêtre and Salpêtrière, removing the chains of the mad and liberating them from physical bondage in 1794. In 1801 he wrote a basic text in "psychiatry," *Traité médico-philosophique sur l'aliénation mentale ou la manie* (Treatise on Insanity). Pinel emphasized the role of heredity as the first cause of, and social and psychological factors as contributory to, the development of madness. Pinel presented a classification of mental disease: melancholia, mania, dementia, and idiocy. According to him, these were located in the region of the stomach. Of greatest importance to Pinel were the principles underlying the organization and administration of institutions, beginning with the separation of different types of patients. He rejected chains, used minimum constraints, urged the importance of studying the patient's personality, and believed in the maintenance of constant routine. He stressed the benefits of *moral treatment*, which included kindness, careful coercion, and work therapy. Pinel, and even more especially his favorite student, Esquirol, used careful clinical observation and kept detailed statistics of "cure" rates. Although some have seen this as the "beginning of a new epoch" in the treatment of madness (Ackerknecht, 1968, p. 41), from a more sociological perspective the "asylum [became], in Pinel's hands, an instrument of moral uniformity and social degradation" (Foucault, 1965, p. 208). In Foucault's terms Pinel's asylum was a religious domain without a religion; a moral force for socializing people to values of bourgeois society—obedience, work, and the value of property. While releasing physical restraints, Pinel substituted moral ones.

A contemporary and admirer of Pinel was Englishman William Tuke, a lay Quaker who founded York Retreat. Tuke developed his own brand of moral treatment. His institution, run by lay people, represented an alternative to the ascending medical perspective. Therapy at York Retreat was much more of an educational process, a pragmatic attempt to teach moral values and self-control, to remove obstacles that impeded the "natural" recovery process. "Moral treatment actively sought to transform the lunatic, to remodel him into something approximating the bourgeois ideal of the rational individual" (Scull, 1975, p. 227). The rate of recovery (Tuke never used the word "cure") at York, largely due to humane and kind treatment, was probably better than at most other English madhouses. Andrew Scull (1975) notes that contemporary medical people viewed this as a lay threat to their emerging control of the domain of madness.

Since moral treatment seemed to work, the medical profession had to find a way to accommodate it. Physicians presented the argument that medical and moral treatments were necessary for recovery, and since only physicians had the legitimate authority to dispense medical treatments, they were the natural ones to employ or at least oversee moral treatment also. Since the physicians were relatively organized and the moral treatment people were not, they were successful at convincing Parliament to have their position officially legislated as the dominant one. The mere fact that they had to persuade the legislators is telling.

> The single most effective . . . [argument] would have been to demonstrate that insanity was in fact caused by biophysiological variables. A somatic interpretation could place it beyond dispute within medicine's recognized sphere of competence, and make plausible the assertion that it responded to medicine's conventional remedies for disease. The trouble was that doctors could not show the existence of the necessary physical lesions, and this inconvenient fact was already in the public domain. (Scull, 1975, p. 251)

The fact that those administrating moral treatment were already using a quasimedical vocabulary—"patients," "mental illness," "recovery," "treatment," etc.—probably made it easier. Through testimony, and one suspects lobbying, physicians were able to ensure that they themselves would regulate the madhouses by the enactment of a variety of parliamentary acts (e.g., requiring medical inspection) between 1816 and 1845. This solidified their legal position as the official controllers of madness (Scull, 1975). In a real sense they "captured" madness as their domain, and clarified and extended their "authority in this area, so as to develop an official monopoly of the right to define (mental) health and illness" (Scull, 1975). By 1830 nearly all public mental hospitals had a resident medical director. In Eliot Freidson's (1970b) terms, they had established their professional dominance and autonomy over mental illness. This was a coup for the medical profession, since at this point they had little better to offer in terms of treatments for insanity.

## Emergence of a unitary concept of mental illness

As we pointed out earlier in this chapter, the roots of medical ideas of madness run deep. However, a unitary, popular, and finally dominant concept of mental illness developed only in the late 18th century. It was not an overnight revolution, but rather a gradual development over more than two centuries. A number of factors contributed significantly to its ascendance, including the separation and segregation of the mad (discussed earlier) and the development of the psychiatric profession (to be discussed). It is difficult to point to any single causal agent most responsible for the change.

Both Johann Weyer and the humoral physicians viewed madness as a natural phenomenon with physiological causes, but the concept of madness as *mental illness* was still diffuse and vague. Their theories were esoteric and did not enjoy much popular support. Clearly there was little, if any, empirical evidence to support their medical contentions, and physicians themselves were limited in their curing abilities. Although medical historians (e.g., Ackerknecht, 1968; Alexander & Selesnick, 1966) suggest that with the spread of the Enlightenment, madness could be studied at last on a scientific basis, progress was, to say the least, slow. It is possible, of course, that some of the esoteric medical "knowledge" that increasingly supported a disease concept of madness "trickled down" to the masses over a period of years so that by the late 18th century madness as a mental illness was a dominant concept.

But Theodore Sarbin (1969) offers another interpretation. In the 16th century, with the rediscovery and serious study of the classics, the decline of the Church, and the humanistic thrust of the Renaissance, as well as the rise of science, a concept of *mental illness* slowly emerged. Teresa of Avila provides an interesting example. An outstanding figure of this period, she attempted to save a group of "hysterical" nuns from the Inquisition by arguing that these women were ill and that their behavior could be explained by natural causes. As natural causes she suggested melancholy (as in humoral pathology), weak imagination, or drowsiness. Persons whose behavior could be accounted for by natural causes were not evil, but rather *comas enfermas—as if* they were sick, and thus not fodder for the Inquisition. Hence physicians rather than priests were the experts who should legitimately handle the problem. The social benefits to the nuns of defining them as sick rather than evil are apparent.

Sarbin points out that it was during this period of Western history that the concept of mind came into being. It was used to explain deviant behavior that could not be attributed easily to events external to the person; deviants were seen as behaving as if the "state of mind" was causing the behavior. He suggests that "the 'as if' was dropped, especially when Galenic [Roman] classifications were reintroduced" and accepted uncritically (Sarbin, 1969, p. 13). Thus any bit of peculiar behavior or reports of strange images could be interpreted, like a fever, as a symptom of an underlying disease. "Illness" came to include misconduct and the deviant behavior commonly known as madness, first by its use as a metaphor that was later reified into a "myth," and second as a justification for the medical involvement and authority over madness (Sarbin, 1969; Szasz, 1961, 1970). As Scull (1977b) points out, the emergence of medical "specialists" to deal with madness and the lobbying of physicians buoyed the legitimacy of the mental illness concept:

> The growing power and influence of what was to become the psychiatric profession helped to complete and lend legitimacy to this classification of deviance; transforming a vague cultural view of madness into what now purported to be a formally coherent, scientifically distinguishable entity reflecting and caused by a single underlying pathology [mental illness]. (p. 344) (By permission.)

Regardless of which of these explanations one accepts, two points are clear. First, scientific empirical knowledge of the origin of madness and the physician's ability to "cure" mental disease played at the most a small role in the development of a popular concept of mental illness. Second, by the late 18th century the concept of mental illness was becoming the dominant definition of madness.

Although the mad were institutionalized, certified by physicians, and more and more were considered to be sick, there is little evidence that anything resembling *medical* treatment was carried out. An inspector general of French hospitals and prisons summed up the situation of lunatics in 1785 most succintly:

> Thousands of lunatics are locked up in prison without anyone even thinking of administering the slightest remedy. The half-mad are mingled with those who are totally deranged, those with rage with those who are quiet; some are in chains, while others are free in their prison. Finally, unless nature comes to their aid by curing them, the duration of their misery is life-long, for unfortunately the illness does not improve but only grows worse. (Quoted in Rosen, 1968, p. 151).

It is interesting to note that the disease concept of madness was accepted as public policy even though there was no medical treatment and no "evidence" to support biophysiological theories. As Thomas Kuhn (1970) points out, "scientific revolutions" and associated paradigm changes—in this case from madness to mental illness—may occur for political reasons and not necessarily scientific ones. During this significant period of its ascendance, the mental illness concept is better viewed as an ideology that a scientific achievement.

## THE 19th-CENTURY AMERICAN EXPERIENCE: THE INSTITUTIONALIZATION OF MENTAL ILLNESS

In colonial America, much like contemporary Europe, insanity was seen as a kinship or communal matter. The "harmless" dependent insane were dealt with like other paupers, the well-to-do insane were cared for by their families, and the violent or criminal insane were punished as criminals. Public provision for the dependent insane rarely included medical treatment. Public concern was mostly about the dangerous "lunatick," who was variously found in stocks, pillories, and jails. The colonists "conceived of the family, the church and the network of community relations as important weapons against sin and crime" and madness (Rothman, 1971, p. 16).

The first general hospital in America, Pennsylvania Hospital, was founded by the Quakers in 1756. There were some mad people among the sick persons admitted, although they were confined to the cellar. The treatments employed were the medical treatments for insanity common at the time. "Their scalps were shaved and blistered; they were bled to the point of syncope; purged until the alimentary canal failed to yield anything but mucus, and in intervals, they were chained by the waist or ankle to the cell wall" (Deutsch, 1949, p. 60). It was a local custom for townspeople to come and gaze at the lunatics for a small fee. (This actually continued in some form until 1822.) One suspects that this stigmatized the mad, at the same time providing a warning for those who psychically strayed from the straight and narrow path.

The colonial governor of Virginia became concerned with the treatment of madness and the "case of the poor lunaticks." Beginning in 1766 he appealed regularly to the legislature to construct an asylum so that lunatics need not be confined to the Williamsburg jail. In 1769 the legislature passed an act "to make provision for the Support and Maintenance of Ideots, Lunaticks and other persons of unsound Minds" (Deutsch, 1949, p. 70). In 1773 the Public Hospital for Persons of Insane and Disordered Minds (the Williamsburg Lunatic Asylum),the first hospital exlusively for the insane, was opened in Williamsburg. Insanity was determined by three magistrates, and no provision was made for a medical examination. The Williamsburg Lunatic Asylum was meant to be a last resort. Its primary task was to keep the peace of the community and to constrain the insane from wandering about. This remained the only public lunatic asylum for 50 years.

The confinement of the insane has three sources of *legitimacy* in the Anglo-American political system (Kittrie, 1971). These principles were first developed in English law and were adopted by the colonists and later by the founders of the Republic as the basis of American law. They serve as the legal rationale for involuntary incarceration. The first source of legitimacy is the "police power" of the state to protect the peace and ensure public welfare. This was used with the violent and the "furiously mad." The second source is parens patriae, the principle that the state could assume guardianship of a person who was legally "disabled" and declared incompetent and could control his or her property. The third source is the state's power over the indigent members of the pauper community. This is an extension of the English concept of the Crown's responsibility for the destitute. Most confinement in the 19th century was in the name of parens patriae, with the physician as wiseman and guardian.

Benjamin Rush is widely considered the "Father of American Psychiatry." He was a signer of the Declaration of Independence, a respected reformer, and a well-known physician when he was appointed to Pennsylvania Hospital in 1783. He was firmly convinced that "the patients afflicted by madness should be the first objects of care of the physicians of the Pennsylvania Hospital" (Deutsch, 1949, p. 77). Rush's own theory was that madness was an arterial disease having its primary seat in the brain. Hence his treatments of purgatives, diets, hot and cold showers, and bloodletting were aimed at affecting the circulation of blood. Actually Rush was ambivalent about therapy and punishment, often not clearly distinguishing between them. He believed that physicians had to gain complete control, authority, and power over the mad person. Some of his writings make it apparent that he viewed the insane as wild beasts who needed to be tamed with "wild and terrifying modes of punishment." At other times his writing takes on a flavor of the kindness of moral treatment. Rush's crowning achievement was the publication in 1812 of *Medical Inquiries and Observations Upon the Disease of Mind,* the first American textbook in psychiatry. This was the only American work of its kind for 70 years.

We can also consider Rush as the "Father of the Medicalization of Deviance." He had a rather broad notion of madness. In his autobiography he wrote, "Chagrin, shame, fear, terror, anger, unfit for legal acts, are transient madness. . . . Suicide is madness. . . . Sanity [is an] aptitude to judge things like other men, and regular habits, etc. Insanity [is] a departure from this" (quoted in Szasz, 1970, p. 141). Naturally he viewed physicians as the best judges of insanity. Rush defined a variety of nonconforming and deviant behaviors as medical problems: he depicted lying, drunkenness, crime, and even opposing the Revolution as diseases (the latter he dubbed "revolutiona"). He was an early and active abolitionist, although partly basing his conviction on his belief that blacks had a disease, "Negritude," that was inherited from ancestors with leprosy and had turned their skins dark. Rush saw disease in any behavior not complying with his particular world view. As Szasz (1970) notes, "His eyes thus beheld the world in terms of sickness and health" (p. 140).

## Asylum-building movement: a new "cure" for insanity

During the second quarter of the 19th century a virtual epidemic of state asylum building took place. In 1824 there were two state asylums, but by 1860, 28 of the 33 states had public institutions for the insane, a 14-fold increase. It seems that the asylum was an idea whose time had come; institutionalization became the treatment of choice for insanity. Why did this occur at this time in history? And how does this relate to the medical conception of mental illness?

We first need to examine the perceived causes of madness in early 19th-century America. By the third decade the old order of American society was passing and was rapidly being replaced with a new one. The Jacksonian period (1828-1836) was characterized by an increase in social mobility and political participation, increased religious and intellectual freedom and enthusiasm, and a greater geographical mobility for the population. These changes, according to David Rothman (1971), created a pervasive anxiety in America. It was believed that the old social order was vanishing and that a new, more fluid, potentially chaotic order was taking its place. Students of deviant behavior in this era thought that erosion in the discipline and order of the family was the primary cause of deviant behavior.

Insanity was viewed by physicians, and most explicitly by the medical superintendents of the new institutions, as a biological disease of the brain that was "socially caused" or at least precipitated by social forces. Such factors as lack of discipline, social mobility, disappointed ambition, or economic depression were cited frequently. Although these physicians were convinced that organic lesions existed, they, unlike their European contemporaries, had no interest in biological or anatomical research. The first cause was in the social system, not the body. Insanity was a disease of civilization; any man or woman could succumb to it. Lunatics were not considered a special breed of people. One corollary of these doctrines was that if the source of madness resided in society rather than the individual, then society had a responsibility for these people. Social measures could and should be taken to alleviate and correct the sufferer's condition.

Theories of environmental cause of insanity gave birth to a new belief that insanity was curable. All that was required was to design a proper curative environment to overcome the social order, tensions, and chaos. The needs of the insane could be met by isolating them from the community and developing a model society, which would exemplify the advantages of an orderly, disciplined routine. The physicians of insanity believed they had discovered its cure. This was the invention of the insane asylum (Rothman, 1971).

The 1830s and 1840s was a utopian era in the United States. Isolated "utopian communities" such as the transcendentalist Brook Farm and the Oneida community were founded as models of a more perfect community; the celibate Shakers lived in over a dozen flourishing settlements during this peak period. The asylum movement sprang from similar utopian ideals, endeavoring to create a model society. Those who championed it were believers in asylums as great reforms and vehicles for creating a better society. Now, the reformers said, the asylum would be the curative environment, not merely a prison for the insane.

This was an optimistic time for physicians of the insane. Reports of recovery rates from some of the early asylums were astounding. A report issued by Hartford Retreat in 1827 announced that 21 of 23 new cases of insanity, an amazing 91%, had been cured. The newspapers publicized the report, and this marked the beginning of a curability craze that would last nearly two decades. A "cult of curability" swept the madness world. The "asylum cure" was the rule, not the exception. Reports from medical superintendents of asylums regularly claimed 80% to 90% and even 100% cure rates. It was a virtual contest of figures. Interestingly, these statistics went unchallenged until 1877, when Pliny Earle, an asylum superintendent from Massachusetts, pointed out that the figures were reports of recovery of cases and not persons, and that some of the impressive cure rates represented the ratio of recoveries to patients discharged, not admitted (American Psychiatric Association, 1976). One patient had been discharged 48 times with 48 cures.

The "asylum cure" consisted of (1) removal of the insane from the community, the alleged cause of mental disease; (2) confinement in an institution that was itself separate from the community (leading to the building of asylums with big lawns on the rural fringes); and (3) creation of an order in the asylum to compensate for the fluidity and disorder in society, an American version of moral treatment. As Rothman (1971) points out, the medical superintendents designed their asylums as an attempt to reconstitute the 18th-century virtues they perceived lacking in the changing society:

> They would teach discipline, a sense of limits and a satisfaction with one's position. . . . The psychiatrists . . . conceived of proper individual behavior and social relationships only in terms of a personal respect for authority and tradition and an acceptance of one's station in the ranks of society. In this sense they were trying to re-create in the asylum their own vision of the colonial community. The results, however, were very different. Regimentation, punctuality, and precision became the asylum's basic traits, and these qualities were far more in keeping with an urban, industrial order than a local, agrarian one. (p. 154)

Probably without knowing it, and certainly without intention, the physicians in the asylums were preparing their charges for an impending order, rather than restoring them to past values. In America, as well as Europe, the asylum, though humanizing the treatment of the insane, also became an institution that attempted to instill the discipline necessary for industrial capitalist labor.

The ideas of the asylum and the asylum cure needed proponents to spread the word. Dorothea Dix, an energetic former schoolteacher, was "shocked" by the conditions of the mentally ill kept in almshouses and jails. She was undoubtedly the foremost champion of separate public asylums for the insane. For many years after 1841 she toured the country, visiting institutions and lobbying with legislators for the development of state hospitals. "Her formula was simple and she repeated it everywhere: first assert the curability of insanity, link it directly to proper institutional care, and then quote prevailing medical opinion on rates of recoveries" (Rothman, 1971, p. 132). Her success was remarkable. By 1880 there were 75 state asylums, 32 of which were founded as a direct result of her efforts. She also popularized the medical concept of madness and championed the idea that medical psychologists, as they were called, were the proper restorers of sanity.

In 1844, 13 superintendents of insane asylums organized the Association of Medical Superintendents of American Institutions of the Insane to aid in communication of knowledge and information and set standards for treatment. This organization was the forerunner of the American Psychiatric Association (the name was changed in 1921) and served both as a political force and a professional body. They published the *American Journal of Insanity,* which became the predominant journal in its field. American psychiatry developed very much as administrative psychiatry, and in its early years the association was more interested in asylum architecture, vocational therapy, and cure rates than medical research. Nonetheless, it quickly became the authoritative voice of medical opinion on insanity. The association provided the legitimation of American psychiatry as a medical specialty. "By insisting that special skills and knowledge were required for treating mental illness, psychiatrists were able to justify the exclusion of all other persons having no formal training and instruction in this specialty" (Grob, 1970, p. 312).

By the 1850s the optimism began to wane. Many institutions had never reached the curability rates claimed by others; "incurables" were backlogging and overcrowding asylums, and some Eastern institutions were being flooded with immigrants who were considered by some physicians as "incurable." Many deranged individuals who had resided in almshouses were transferred to asylums. The pressures of rising admissions made moral treatment increasingly difficult. By 1852 the population of Worcester State Lunatic Hospital in Massachusetts had risen to 500 and the physician-patient ratio had dropped significantly (Grob, 1970). Moral treatment, which was possible and to some degree successful, in an asylum of 120 inmates, was impossible in an institution of over 500. Gradually most of the institutions reverted to custodial care and the use of restraints for the "incurables," with the medical directors and legislators rationalizing that it was better than jail. Drugs (e.g., sedatives) and restraints became ends in themselves, not adjuncts to a therapeutic program. Some treatment was available for those recently diagnosed insane, but if they did not recover in a reasonable time, they were deemed incurable and relegated to the custodial section of the asylum. If the hospital could not be justified in terms of numbers of cured, then the easiest way to justify appropriations and the existence of the institution to the legislature was to request funds for providing accommodations and care for the growing number of chronically insane (Grob, 1970). By the late 19th century most asylums were largely custodial enterprises, with medical superintendents serving as gatekeepers and guardians.

With the end of the cult of curability, somatic or physiological pessimism replaced the more optimistic theories of social causation espoused by early asylum superintendents. The disillusionment with the asylum cure and the rise of Darwinian theory gave credence to a new idea—the degeneration hypothesis. This hypothesis stated that there is a degeneration from the normal human type through generations, transmitted by heredity, which deteriorates progressively toward extinction (Ackerknecht, 1968). This rather pessimistic view of mental illness emerged largely in Europe, especially under the influence of Benedict Augustin Morel; but it serves well as an example of the type of medical theories of madness developed at this time. Italian physician Cesare Lombroso proposed his own ideas based on the degeneration hypothesis in his writings on the "born criminal" (see Chapter 8).

In terms of the history of the medical conception of madness, the 19th century was a significant period. In the United States, as in England, madness moved once and for all into medical turf. Alienists (as physicians of the insane were called), with the aid of champions like Dorothea Dix, were able to gain a monopoly over the definition and treatment of madness. All new asylums were run by medical superintendents. Medical men did not have "scientific" evidence of mental disease, nor did their asylum qua hospital offer a medical cure. In fact, both their causes and cures were specifically social. Medicine was embraced as much for its humanitarian "moral treatment" as for any technical expertise. By the time the early optimism of asylum cures had waned, medicine had secured control over the domain of insanity. Again, we point out, this was accomplished without physiological evidence for cause and before the advent of successful "medical" treatments. In America as in Europe, medical dominance of madness was a social and political rather than a scientific achievement.

## THE SCIENCE OF MENTAL DISEASE

The science of mental disease developed in the asylum. The demise of the cult of curability and the constricted morality of the Victorian era supported the pessimism among the physicians of the insane. This pessimism, along with the apparent success of medicine in controlling infectious diseases and an increasing concern about the incurable immigrant insane, led psychiatrists to abandon their environmental approaches and become heavily somatic. Physicians, armed with the microscope, looked increasingly to the brain, spinal cord, and nervous system for the cause of madness. Masturbation was viewed as a cause of insanity, but it was the weakening of the nervous system and the hypothesized organic lesions produced by such "venereal indulgence" that were believed the source of insanity (see Englehardt, 1974).

The somatic approach, with one significant exception, was not particularly fruitful. The discovery of *general paresis,* a type of madness caused by a neurological breakdown in third-stage syphilis, is considered by some as medicine's "greatest triumph in the field of behavior disorders" (White, 1964, p. 16), and by others as providing a rationalization for the disease concept of madness (Szasz, 1976). No doubt it was a great achievement. It followed the discoveries of Pasteur, Koch, and Lister, which had aided in the mastery of other infectious diseases. The "symptom complex" of this disorder was first described by Esquirol as early as 1805, but actual connection with syphilis as a causal agent was not made until 1894 and confirmed through a variety of clinical and microbial studies over the next two decades. When Noguchi and Moore in 1913 found *Treponema pallidum,* the infectious agent of syphilis, in nerve-cell layers of the patient's cortex, any lingering doubts that syphilis was the cause of this type of insanity were erased. Medicine finally had empirical evidence for the cause of at least one type of insanity. This provided "proof" that the medical concept of madness must be correct. If a physiological cause for one type of insanity had been found, then modern medicine would, in time, discover the causes of all mental illness. This was undoubtedly a vindication for the medical model of madness.

Late 19th-century psychiatry took its cues from its more successful sibling, somatic medicine. Alienists or psychiatrists needed only to use more tools of somatic medicine and soon they, too, would be able to discover physiological causes for all mental disease, just as for general paresis. Emil Kraepelin, a German alienist with a gift for observation and synthesis, engaged in detailed studies of "natural histories" of asylum patients. With the publication of *Psychiatrie,* which went through several revisions between 1883 and 1913, Kraepelin changed the classification system of mental illness. His descriptions of the symptom complexes of dementia praecox and manic-depressive psychosis, the two major categories of mental disorder, are still used today. He believed that dementia praecox (literally, early senility) was characterized by progressive deterioration and that manic depression (severe uncontrollable mood swings) tended to improve and recur spontaneously. Kraepelin, fully committed to the medical model, proposed only organic etiologies for mental disorders and viewed them as physical diseases. Eugen Bleuler noted that all dementia patients do not inevitably degenerate, and in 1911 he created a modified and expanded category he called *schizophrenia*. The great concern for classification of mental illness characterizes the development of psychiatry. The official psychiatric diagnostic manual, *Diagnostic and Statistical Manual of Mental Disorders* (American Psychiatric Association, 1968), contains no less than 155 separate classifications of psychiatric disorders, and its latest revision, *DSM-III,* is expected to have twice that many.

## Freud, psychoanalysis, and medicalization

In 1909 Sigmund Freud, a Viennese physician and neurologist, delivered a series of five lectures at Clark University in Worcester, Massachusetts. He presented a theory of the human mind that he had developed over the previous two decades. As a result of Freud's visit and ideas, American psychiatry has never been the same. Freud's theory, which he based largely on his work with neurotic disorders such as hysteria that are rarely seen in the asylum, appears at least on the surface to be a break with the medical concept of mental disease.* He suggested that mental symptoms were intelligible but distorted results of the individual's struggles with internal impulses. He assumed these symptoms arose from conflicts between biogenic drives such as sex and aggression and sociocultural forces. These conflicts usually involved parents, occurred during early childhood, and were repressed into "the unconscious." "He perceived his patients not as examples of brain disease, not victims of hereditary nervous weakness, but as troubled human beings whose strivings, hopes, fears, daydreams, and intimate feelings were mixing them up and destroying their health and happiness" (White, 1964, p. 38). His method of treatment was psychoanalysis, a talking cure based on a series of conversations (an hour daily for several years) in which the patient was encouraged to "free associate," say whatever came to mind, and relive and resolve past conflicts in the safety of the relationship with the therapist. This revelation and catharsis would enable the patient to develop "insight" into his or her difficulties, understand the roots of the "illness," and hopefully have a "corrective emotional experience." Freud was the first to systematically reopen, in Foucault's terms, a dialogue with madness. He gave an entirely new understanding to human problems and substituted a psychogenic explanation for a biogenic determinism.

Freud's break with the medical conception of madness was far from complete. In fact, the Freudian model of madness was grafted onto the existing medical model with little difficulty. Freud was trained as a physician-neurologist and moved slowly from organic and physically determined theories about mental illness to psychological and, to a degree, sociocultural theories of cause. No doubt his training as a physician affected the types of theories and treatments he developed. The people he saw were "patients" and they had "illnesses," albeit psychological ones, which therapy attempted to cure. His theory located the source of problems inside the patients' heads, and his treatment was individualistic. Treatment would occur in the consulting room, with the patient on the couch and the physician present in the room but not in the patient's sight. Freud himself never abandoned the notion that all psychological illness must be attributable ultimately to neurological process and could, like somatic diseases, someday be treated with pills and injections. In

*We are concerned here only with the impact of Freud on the medical conception of madness. The complexities of Freudian personality theory or psychoanalysis are beyond the scope of this chapter, as are the various schisms of his followers and revisionists. For a good introduction, see Freud's *New Introductory Lectures in Psychoanalysis* (1933) or Charles Brenner's *An Elementary Textbook of Psychoanalysis* (1974).

practice, however, because no such treatments were available, his work and practice were carried out on a purely psychological level (Ackerknecht, 1968, p. 93).

Freud and his early followers (e.g., Adler, Jung, Ferenczi) did not deal with the same types of madness that Kraepelin and the other asylum alienists had. Asylum inmates were too disturbed for Freud's theory. Most Freudians were concerned with what are called neurotic disorders such as hysteria, obsessions, compulsions, and phobias that kept people from optimal functioning. Freud did not investigate severely disturbed people suffering the insanity now called psychoses (including schizophrenia and manic depression), until his later years. When he did, he found these disorders inaccessible to psychoanalysis and that these patients lacked "insight" into their difficulties. Only in the 1930s did psychiatrists like Frieda Fromm-Reichmann and Harry Stack Sullivan bring psychoanalysis to the inmates of the asylum.

The effect of Freud on American psychiatry was enormous. The first psychoanalytic institute was founded in New York in 1931, and eventually there were a dozen psychoanalytic centers in major cities. No one could study psychiatry, psychology, or social work without encountering his theories and techniques and those of some of his followers. Psychoanalysts became an elite of the American Psychiatric Association. In fact, psychoanalysis became largely the property of medical psychiatry. Freud had not wanted it that way. "He had 'only unwillingly taken up the profession of medicine'; in fact, Freud had a low opinion of physicians. They were merchants, trading in the mitigation of miseries they scarcely attempted to understand" (Rieff, 1966, p. 83). Freud spoke out several times in his life in support of lay (nonmedical) analysis, but American psychoanalysts created a medical monopoly and trained only physicians.* This further medicalized psychoanalytic theory and therapy.

Freud and his followers both muted and extended the medical model of madness. They muted it by their emphasis on the intrapsychic nature of mental symptoms and psychological illnesses and by their attention to family and childhood experiences. Yet because Freudian theory was grafted onto the existing medical model, it expanded greatly the notions of mental disease. This model of psychological illness included all deviant behavior and emotional problems that were not organic in origin: essentially all human behavior problems but general paresis, senility, and organic brain syndrome. Madness, hysteria, obsessions, compulsions, phobias, anxiety, homosexuality, drunkenness, sexual deviation, chronic misbehavior in children, and delinquency, among others, were all psychological illnesses and subject to medical-psychiatric treatment.

The psychogenic movement, led by Freud and his followers, infused psychiatry with a new sense of optimism, replacing the somatic pessimism of the late 19th century. Freud's theories and techniques for the first time made it possible for physicians to spend their time understanding the patient's psyches, rather than manipulating their bodies or creating moral environments in asylums in which they resided. The Freudian "revolution" was not, however, supported by all psychiatrists. There were, more specifically, somaticists still to be heard from. The somaticism that developed in the 1930s took three forms: "shock" therapies, lobotomies, and genetic theories of mental illness.

## Reappearance of the somaticists

Manfred Sakel, a German physician who had been using insulin to treat morphine addiction, in 1929 noticed some apparent psychological improvement in a patient following a convulsion and coma produced by an accidental overdose of insulin. He extended his research and treatments to schizophrenia and reported some success at reducing overt symptoms. Over the next two decades insulin shock therapy became a common physiological treatment for schizophrenia (Horowitz, W., 1959). Insulin shock had some inherent dangers, was rather expensive and time-consuming, since patients needed continuous nursing care and observation, and yielded unreliable results. In 1938 two Italian physicians, Ugo Cerletti and L. Bini, introduced an "easier" technique, elec-

*Some of the most distinguished psychoanalysts were lay analysts who were trained in Europe: for example, Erik Erikson, Erich Fromm, and Anna Freud.

troconvulsive therapy (ECT), or, simply, electroshock. This technique consists of applying electrodes to the patient's head and passing moderate electrical currents (70 to 130 volts) through the brain for a few seconds. The patient suffers a brief but violent convulsion, loses consciousness, and on reawakening has an amnesia (memory loss) for recent events, which lasts for several weeks or months. Shock treatments are given in a series over a period of weeks. Early medical practitioners of this method advocated it for patients with schizophrenia, but it has not proven particularly useful for this diagnosis. Some recent advocates limit its use to mood disorders such as mania and depression. This crude and violent treatment is used today and remains controversial. There is no accepted explanation of how it works. Some physicians are so zealous about this physiological treatment that they have opened private institutions, referred to by critics as "shock shops," in which they are alleged to administer shock treatments to all their patients. Others see it as a form of psychiatric barbarism (Szasz, 1976).

In 1935 Antonio Egas Moniz, a Portuguese neurologist, introduced the psychosurgery known as prefrontal lobotomy to the psychiatric world. Moniz believed that the fixed ideas and repetitive behavior seen in some mental patients were accompanied by abnormal cellular connections in the brain. His theory suggested that "morbid" thoughts were a result of brain disease and hence the appropriate treatment was brain surgery:

> In accordance with the theory we have developed, one conclusion is derived: to cure these patients we must destroy the more or less fixed arrangements of cellular connections that exist in the brain, and particularly those which are related to the frontal lobes. (Moniz, quoted in Freeman, 1959, p. 1521)

The method that Moniz conceived of as "curative" for this supposed brain damage was lobotomy, a surgical procedure that severed some of the neural connections between the frontal lobes and other parts of the brain. Although immersed in controversy from the start, lobotomy became a common treatment, and advocates such as American neurologist Walter Freeman operated on thousands of institutionalized mental patients. Moniz was awarded the Nobel Prize in 1949 for his work. Supporters claimed cure in a third and improvement in another third of lobotomized patients (Freeman, 1959), but critics claimed the "cure" was worse than the "disease." Many lobotomized patients showed marked irreversible deterioration in personality, difficulty in generalizing and abstract thinking, and an overall passivity, and remained institutionalized; in short, they became "zombies." For this reason, and because of the availability of tranquilizing drugs, by the early 1950s lobotomy fell into disrepute. Up until that time, however, approximately 40,000 to 50,000 such operations were performed in the United States. In the late 1960s a new and more technologically sophisticated variant of psychosurgery emerged, including laser technology and brain implants, and was heralded by some as a treatment for uncontrollable violent outbursts (see Chapter 8).

Psychiatrists and their precursors have long argued that madness runs in families. In this view the question becomes whether it is psychogenically or biogenically caused. The biogenic hereditary theories of the late 19th century rose again with more sophisticated analyses beginning in the 1930s. Franz Kallmann, a German-born American psychiatrist, spurred a new genetic interest in mental illness etiology with the publication of *Genetics of Schizophrenia* in 1938. He became the most influential proponent of the genetic hypothesis. Kallmann (1938) examined the relatives of 1087 mental patients who had been diagnosed schizophrenic. He found that the expectancy of mental illness among relatives was higher than nonrelatives and that it increased with closeness of kinship. Several years later Kallmann (1946) published another study which showed that the concordance of schizophrenia for identical (monozygotic, or one-egg) twins was 86.2% and for nonidentical (dyzygotic, or two-egg) twins 14.7%. He found that a subsample of identical twins who were "reared apart" still showed a 77.6% concordance, whereas those reared together were 91.5% concordant. Comparatively, only about 1% of the population is diagnosed as schizophrenic. Based on his research, and especially the twin studies, Kallmann posited a genetic theory of mental illness.

This research has been amply criticized from

a number of angles, especially methodologically (see Jackson, 1960). First, the psychiatric diagnosis is not reliable. A recent study by David Rosenhan (1973) demonstrates this dramatically. In this study eight sane people presented themselves to the admitting units of a variety of mental hospitals, claiming to hear voices that said "thud," "empty," or "hollow." They did not alter their personal biographies in any other way. All were admitted and each was diagnosed as schizophrenic. Once admitted, they resumed their normal identities, and it took an average of 19 days before they were discharged as "schizophrenia, in remission." Rosenhan (1973) concludes that "we cannot distinguish insanity from sanity" (p. 271). Furthermore, sociologists have pointed out the many pitfalls of using the type of "official" hospital admissions data that Kallmann relied on (see Kitsuse & Cicourel, 1963). Finally, Kallmann minimized the significance of difficult family histories (Coulter, 1973, pp. 15-28), and defined "reared apart" as living apart for only the last 5 years.

No treatments evolved based on the genetic hypothesis, but Kallmann (1959), echoing the eugenicists of an earlier era, warned that society ignored the genetic basis of mental illness at its own peril. Although Kallmann's research is open to different interpretations, his work and similar studies by others lend some "scientific" support to the biogenic hypothesis and reinforce the medical conception of mental illness.

To summarize briefly, the discovery of general paresis symbolized medical vindication for somatic bases of mental illness. Freud and his followers both muted and extended the medical model of madness, whereas Kraepelin and the "new" somaticists attempted to develop scientific theories and data to support medical contentions. The total effect broadened and deepened professional interest in the medical model of human problems and the commitment to medical solutions for them.

## MENTAL ILLNESS AND THE PUBLIC

Though the concept of mental illness was well developed and recognized by the turn of the 20th century, the insane were often still treated severely, and the public did not seem to show any great concern for "the mentally sick." The idea that madness was a sickness like any other sickness did not meet with a great deal of public acceptance.

### Reform and institutionalization

Clifford Beers, a 32-year-old Yale graduate, in 1908 published a book, *A Mind That Found Itself,* detailing his 3 years in mental hospitals. He related his experiences of treatment (which he frequently called torture), his recovery, and his determination to improve the care of the mentally ill. He was outraged that people suffering from mental diseases were so shabbily treated. He set out to awaken the public conscience. The book attracted considerable attention, and Beers began organizing a reform movement.

In 1909 Beers organized The National Committee for Mental Hygiene to implement his ideas. From the beginning Beers had close ties to the medical psychiatric profession; it had been Adolf Meyer, America's foremost psychiatrist, who had suggested the name "mental hygiene." In 1912 Thomas Salmon, another prominent psychiatrist, became the Committee's medical director with Beers as secretary. Medical professionals have always been centrally involved. Twenty of the American Psychiatric Association presidents have been actively involved in the Committee and its successor, the National Association for Mental Health (Mauss, 1975, p. 342).

The goals of the Committee included improving the standard of care and treatment in mental hospitals, encouraging prevention of mental illness, promoting the notion that insanity was curable, supporting research, and to the extent desirable, enlisting government help. The Committee prepared lists of public and private mental institutions and of psychiatrists; compiled a bibliography on nervous and mental diseases; collected and analyzed laws pertaining to the mentally ill; "and started a program of public education, which included an exhibit, and the preparation of four pamphlets, of which they distributed 91,000 copies [in the] first working year" (Ridenour, 1961, p. 19). They cooperated with what is now the American Psychiatric Association in the development of a classification system for mental disease, and along with the federal government, improved the collection of statistics. The Committee became both a reform movement and a public relations agency for psychiatry. Salmon himself perceived psychiatry as "the Cinderella of medicine," indicating its lack of prestige in the medical world and its need for a more positive image. Both the Committee and Beers completely accepted the medical model of madness. In fact, a primary goal was to establish the credibility of an illness interpretation for madness. In the 1950s the National Association of Mental Health, which succeeded the Committee, initiated campaigns with slogans such as "Mental Health is Everybody's Business" and "Fight Mental Illness." They publicized ideas such as "mental illness is an illness like any other illness" and "half of all hospital beds are occupied by mental patients" to further spread the word.

Sociologist Kingsley Davis (1938), in a brilliant analysis of the mental hygiene movement viewpoint, notes that mental hygienists tacitly assume the Protestant open-class society ethic, which is based on personal responsibility and individual achievement. He suggests that the psychological and individualistic view of mental disorder, completely ignoring how social context may affect the human psyche, is a product of the middle-class Protestant ethic biases of its members. The Protestant ethic and the individualism of the medical model are highly compatible.

The psychiatric view of deviance was spreading in the 1920s. The medically inspired "child guidance movement," concerned with juvenile delinquency, extended the illness concept to delinquent and troublesome children (see Chapter 6). Out of this movement a multiprofessional organization, the American Orthopsychiatric Association, was founded by prominent psychiatrist Karl Menninger and 26 others. In late 1923 they sent a letter to their colleagues requesting them to join a new organization of the "representatives of the neuropsychiatric or medical view of crime" (quoted in Ridenour, 1961, p. 39).

The two world wars enhanced the acceptance of psychiatry and led to its institutionalization on a federal level. In 1917 a psychiatric division was established in the Surgeon General's office; the object was to examine recruits for psychiatric difficulties and to treat soldiers with mental problems, especially "shell shock." Psychiatrists participated even more fully in World War II. With William Menninger as head of the psychiatric division, the number of military psychiatrists grew from 35 in late 1941 to 2400 in 1945. The psychiatrists were very busy. Between January, 1942, and June, 1945, an estimated 1,875,000 men (of 15 million) were rejected from the military for alleged psychiatric disabilities (Mechanic, 1969, p. 55) and another 750,000 more were eventually discharged because of mental problems (Ridenour, 1961, p. 60). Undoubtedly these high figures, along with lobbying by the National Committee of Mental Hygiene, contributed to the strong Congressional support in the passage of the 1946 National Mental Health Act. It established a federal mental health agency, the National Institute of Mental Health (NIMH), which began operation in 1949. NIMH would support research and psychiatric training and coordinate a national effort to combat mental illness. Its budget grew steadily: from $9 million in 1950 to $68 million in 1960 to $338 million in 1967 to $502 million in 1978. NIMH was dominated by psychiatrists and thus committed to the medical model of madness from the start.

Mental illness received some media attention in the late 1940s. A spate of newspaper and magazine exposés, in New York's *PM, Reader's Digest, Life,* and other popular media, depicted the overcrowded, decrepit, and inhumane conditions of the state hospitals. A film, *The Snake Pit,* was shown widely, demonstrating powerfully the situation of the mentally ill. These events brought the situation of the mad into the public eye.

## Public acceptance

The public and professional definitions of what constitutes mental disorder are incongruent and probably have always been so. The public has a much narrower conception of what deviant behavior can be attributed to mental illness than do psychiatrists. This has been demonstrated clearly in studies using descriptions of deviant behavior developed by sociologist Shirley Star (1955) (see p. 59). Star had meant these descriptive vignettes to serve as examples of the psychiatric categories of (1) paranoid schizophrenia, (2) simple schizophrenia, (3) anxiety neurosis, (4) alcoholism, (5) compulsive-phobic behavior, and (6) juvenile character disorder. In five different studies randomly selected people were asked to respond whether each of the behavior descriptions was indicative of mental illness. A group of 34 psychiatrists almost unanimously judged *all* these descriptions as illustrating types of mental disorder (Dohrenwend & Chin-Shong, 1967). A look at the results of the various surveys (shown in the right-hand columns, pp. 59-60) indicates that the public has a narrower view of what can be attributed to mental illness than do psychiatrists. There is an incongruity with the medical definitions: only in the first two cases do the majority of people define the behavior as mental illness. It appears that the public does not fully accept the medical model of deviant behavior, although the two "psychoses" are much more commonly seen as mental illness (see p. 59, cases 1 and 2). But the data seem to indicate that public conceptions of mental disorder are changing in the direction of the professional definition. That is, the notion of deviant behavior as mental illness is finding more public acceptance. Whether this is due to the mental health educational efforts, a more educated populace, cultural drift, or some other factors is a matter of speculation.

Since the public conceptions of madness are less medicalized than the psychiatric conceptions, it is not surprising to find that popular attitudes stigmatize the mentally ill. Public conceptions tend to view the mentally ill more as "bad" than as "sick"; according to one landmark study, this is largely because of the public's lack of (psychiatric) information (Nunnally, 1961). The negative stereotype of the "dangerous mental case," although not supported by research evidence, is commonly held (Scheff, 1966). One well-organized and well-financed study of the impact of mental health education in a small Canadian town found public attitudes toward madness extremely difficult to change (Cumming & Cumming, 1957).

It is likely that the trend toward public adoption of the psychiatric viewpoint of deviant behavior has continued. There is also some evidence of a greater tolerance or acceptance of the mentally ill themselves (Halpert, 1970; but see Sarbin and Mancuso, 1970). However, it is also likely that the public still maintains a considerably narrower conception of what constitutes mental illness than does the medical profession. In short, public conceptions remain less medicalized.

### Mental illness and criminal law

It is an old question whether mad people who commit crimes should be held responsible for these acts. Mad persons accused of crimes have been treated in various ways throughout history. For the most part they were treated like any other criminal and subject to criminal law, although there are some historical exceptions. In ancient Israel a mad person "who caused bodily harm to another person could not be held legally responsible" (Rosen, 1968, p. 66); in Greece, under Plato's laws, crimes committed by the mad were subject to certain exemptions (p. 40); and in the 17th century a person who did not know what he was doing any better than "a wild beast" could escape punishment. In our society the law has generally been guided by the principle that without *mens rea* or evil intent, an offender cannot be designated a criminal. This was enunciated most clearly in Anglo-American law in the 1843 case of Daniel M'Naughten. M'Naughten shot and killed Edward Drummond, the private secretary of Sir Edward Peel, believing him to be the Prime Minister. His attorneys used insanity as a defense; medical evidence was presented establishing that M'Naughten was "laboring under an insane delusion" of being hounded by his enemies, including Peel. The jury found him not guilty by reason of insanity. This set the precedent for what became known as the "M'Naughten rule," essentially, that he did not "know right from wrong" at the time the act was committed. This was the major test for the "insanity defense" for more than a century.

In 1954 Judge David L. Bazelon, Chief Justice of the United States for the District of Columbia, enunciated a new criterion for the in-

## RESULTS OF STUDIES USING VIGNETTES IN DEFINING PROBLEM BEHAVIOR

| | Year study was conducted and percentage of respondents that considered the behavior indicative of mental illness | | | | |
|---|---|---|---|---|---|
| | **1950*** | **1951†** | **1960‡** | **1962§** | **1964‖** |
| 1. I'm thinking of a man—let's call him Frank Jones—who is very suspicious; he doesn't trust anybody, and he's sure that everybody is against him. Sometimes he thinks that people he sees on the street are talking about him or following him around. A couple of times now he has beaten up men who didn't even know him. The other night he began to curse his wife terribly; then he hit her and threatened to kill her because, he said, she was working against him, too, just like everyone else. ("Paranoid schizophrenia") | 75% | 69% | 91% | 89% | 90% |
| 2. Now here's a young woman in her twenties, let's call her Betty Smith . . . she has never had a job, and she doesn't seem to want to go out and look for one. She is a very quiet girl, she doesn't talk much to anyone—even her own family, and she acts like she is afraid of people, especially young men her own age. She won't go out with anyone, and whenever someone comes to visit her family, she stays in her own room until they leave. She just stays by herself and daydreams all the time and shows no interest in anything or anybody. ("Simple schizophrenia") | 34% | 36% | 78% | 77% | 67% |
| 3. Here's another kind of man; we can call him George Brown. He has a good job and is doing pretty well at it. Most of the time he gets along all right with people, but he is always very touchy and he always loses his temper quickly if things aren't going his way or if people find fault with him. He worries a lot about little things, and he seems to be moody and unhappy all the time. Everything is going along all right for him, but he can't sleep nights, brooding about the past and worrying about things that *might* go wrong. ("Anxiety neurosis") | 18% | NA¶ | NA | NA | 31% |
| 4. How about Bill Williams? He never seems to be able to hold a job very long because he drinks so much. Whenever he has money in his pocket, he goes on a spree; he stays out till all hours drinking, and never seems to care what happens to his wife and children. Sometimes he feels very bad about the way he treats his family; he begs his wife to forgive him and promises to stop drinking, but he always goes off again. ("Alcoholism") | 29% | 25% | 62% | 63% | 41% |

*Continued.*

*Star (1955), national sample of adults in United States.
†Cumming and Cumming (1957), a Canadian town.
‡Lemkau and Crocetti (1962), Baltimore, Md.
§Meyer (1964), Easton, Md.
‖Dohrenwend and Chin-Shong (1967), a multiethnic cross section in New York City.
¶NA = Not available; vignette not used in study.

## RESULTS OF STUDIES USING VIGNETTES IN DEFINING PROBLEM BEHAVIOR—cont'd

| | 1950* | 1951† | 1960‡ | 1962§ | 1964‖ |
|---|---|---|---|---|---|
| 5. Here's a different sort of girl—let's call her Mary White. She seems happy and cheerful; she's pretty, has a good job, and is engaged to marry a nice young man. She has loads of friends; everybody likes her, and she's always busy and active. However, she just can't leave the house without going back to see whether she left the gas stove lit or not. And she always goes back again just to make sure she locked the door. And one other thing about her: she's afraid to ride up and down in elevators; she just won't go any place where she'd have to ride in an elevator to get there. ("Compulsive-phobic behavior") | 7% | NA | NA | NA | 25% |
| 6. Now, I'd like to describe a 12-year-old boy—Bobby Grey. He's bright enough and in good health, and he comes from a comfortable home. But his father and mother have found out that he's been telling lies for a long time now. He's been stealing things from stores, and taking money from his mother's purse, and he has been playing truant, staying away from school whenever he can. His parents are very upset about the way he acts, but he pays no attention to them. ("Juvenile character disorder") | 16% | NA | NA | NA | 41% |

sanity defense in the case of Monte Durham (*Durham* v. *United States*).

> The rule we now hold is simply that the accused is not criminally responsible if his unlawful act was the product of mental disease or mental defect. We use "disease" in the sense of a condition which is considered capable of improving or deteriorating. We use "defect" in the sense of a condition which is not considered capable of either improving or deteriorating and which may be congenital or the residual effect of a physical or mental disease. (Quoted in Halleck, 1971, pp. 148-149)

This ruling, known as the "Durham rule," institutionalized the psychiatric definitions of mental disease or defect into the legal process. Not only could we have medical experts' testimony (as with the M'Naughten rule), but now the actual medical definitions and diagnoses became in themselves reasons for the insanity defense. Judge Bazelon has continued to be a champion of using psychiatry "to humanize" the legal process (Bazelon, 1974). Nicholas Kittrie (1971), among others, has cautioned us about the consequences of what he calls the "divestment" from the criminal law of much of its traditional jurisdiction, resulting in the removal of blame and responsibility from individuals for certain categories of illegal acts.

Although the Durham rule was subsequently modified (see Bazelon, 1974; Kittrie, 1971, pp. 42-43), and Judge Bazelon himself (1974) has voiced reservations about the nature of psychiatric participation in the legal process, the psychiatric mental illness definition is permanently a part of the legal process and central to the insanity defense.

To sum up briefly, as evidenced by federal legislation, changing public attitudes, and the Durham rule, by the 1950s in the United States there was an increasing public acceptance of the medical model of madness.

## THE THIRD REVOLUTION IN MENTAL HEALTH

In the early 1950s psychiatry in the United States was characterized by a "psychotherapeutic ideology" (Armer & Klerman, 1968), based essentially on the Freudian principles that madness is a result of childhood experiences and rooted in intrapsychic conflicts. Psychotherapy, though not often available in large state mental hospitals, was considered the treatment of choice. There were somatically oriented psychiatrists as well, who maintained a physiological model of madness and whose major forms of treatment were insulin and electroshock therapies. The majority of patients in large, overcrowded state institutions received no treatment at all beyond custodial care and were warehoused on "back wards." By 1955 this all began to change.

## Psychotropic medication

The use of drugs for madness has a long history. Vomitives, purgatives, narcotics, and others were used in the 19th century. The 20th century saw the development of "sedatives" to control problem patients. But it was not until the middle 1950s that drugs became a central part of psychiatric treatment. The impact of the new psychotropic drugs on psychiatry and mental hospitals has been termed by medical historians the third revolution in mental health. (Pinel's contribution is considered the first; psychoanalysis, the second.)

In France in 1952 a newly synthesized drug, chlorpromazine, was developed. It was the first of the psychotropic drugs: chemicals that exert their principal effect on a person's mind, thought, or behavior. They did not sedate in the traditional sense. These drugs, also called phenothiazines or major tranquilizers, were considered antipsychotic drugs because they did not impair consciousness as did sedatives. They enabled, to varying degrees, mad people to function better. The popularity of the drugs took hold slowly but soon spread rapidly, first in Europe and then in the United States.

In May, 1954, the pharmaceutical corporation Smith, Kline & French (SKF) introduced chlorpromazine under the trade name Thorazine in the United States. It was aggressively marketed by a special SKF task force of 50 salespeople, who, armed with promising research reports and testimonies from psychiatrists, set out to convince state legislatures (who were responsible for the then minimal drug budgets for state hospitals) and hospital administrators of the utility of Thorazine. This extensive promotion campaign was highly successful* (Swazey, 1974):

> The drug impact . . . was rapid and profound. Within 8 months Thorazine was given to an estimated two million patients. A stream of professional publications, now totaling over 14,000, began to describe the drug's "revolutionary" impact on mental hospitals. The mass media hailed [it] . . . as a "miracle drug." (p. 160)

Thorazine was soon joined by a sister medication, reserpine (and by 1969, 850 other psychotropic drugs [Swazey, 1974, p. 30]). Under the directorship of Henry Brill, an early and active supporter of pharmacological treatment, New York became the first state mental health system to introduce the drugs en masse. By 1957 the psychiatric response was enthusiastic. Wards became quieter, "delusions" decreased, and institutions ran more smoothly. Perhaps most important, more patients were being discharged from mental hospitals.

A new feeling of optimism permeated the psychiatric world. Because of the dominant "psychotherapeutic ideology," many psychiatrists in the early 1950s embraced drug treatment because they believed with the aid of medications, "now we can really do psychotherapy with the mentally ill." As one prominent psychiatrist noted after reviewing the benefits of chlorpromazine, "thus, many patients who had previously been inaccessible to psychotherapy [could now be reached]" (Overholser, 1956, p. 198; quoted in Swazey, 1974). Mental hospital staffs developed an increased medical orientation in their work. In fact, psychiatrist Jerome Frank (1974) suggests that the greatest effect of the drug revolution was on the staff and not the patients. The staff developed a more optimistic outlook and became more will-

*Within a year Thorazine increased the company's sales volume by a third; and Thorazine was a major component of SKF's phenomenal financial growth, with net sales increasing from $53 million in 1953 to $347 million in 1970 (Swazey, 1974, p. 161). Psychoactive drugs in general have been the most rapidly expanding component of the drug industry's growth. The drug industry has been either the first or second most profitable industry in the United States each of the past 25 years (Goddard, 1973).

ing to interact with the patients. Talk of truly therapeutic rather than custodial hospitals was legion. Within a decade, however, the notions of "really doing psychotherapy" were replaced by the reality that the dispensing of drugs, called chemotherapy, would itself be the major form of treatment for most patients.

There were some critics of drug treatment who argued that drugs only masked the symptoms and did not treat causes; others suggested they were "chemical straightjackets," merely pharmaceutical social control mechanisms. As one recent critic points out, there are important differences between the purposes of medical and psychiatric drug treatments:

> The purpose of medical treatment is to alter the structure and function of the body to influence favorably the course of a physical disease. The purpose of psychiatric treatment is to alter mood, thought and behavior (Leifer, 1969, p. 44).

The critics of drug treatments were a distinct minority, however, and the declining populations of mental hospitals relegated their critique to gadfly status.

By the mid-1950s the psychopharmacological revolution in mental health had been proclaimed. Psychiatrists could now act like "real physicians" and dispense medications for mental ills. The drug treatment itself lent support to beliefs that madness was an illness that could be treated by drugs. A few even viewed it as a cure for mental illness. Drugs qua medications suited perfectly the rhetoric of medicine in the treatment of madness.

## Decline in mental hospital populations

Before 1955 public mental hospitals' populations had been steadily increasing and had quadrupled in the previous half-century (Joint Commission on Mental Illness and Health, 1961, p. 7). Most mental hospitals were large, overcrowded, and custodial; a few, like Pilgrim State Hospital in New York, approached populations of 12,000. The total county and state mental hospital population reached a peak in 1955, with over 558,000 patients residing in such public institutions. In 1956 this trend reversed itself.

Fig. 1 shows clearly the dramatic decline in inpatient populations of county and state mental hospitals since 1955. The inpatient population had dropped to about 174,000 by 1977. Many have pointed out that it was the introduction of drugs, enabling patients to function better and be discharged from hospitals, that was responsible for this decline (e.g., Brill & Patton, 1957, 1962). Some have suggested that social science research on the negative effects of institutionalization (to be discussed shortly) played a significant role. Sociologist Andrew Scull (1977a) argues that economic and fiscal reasons, that is, the expense of state mental hospitals, were predominant factors. All probably contributed to the decline, with the introduction of drugs being most significant. Whatever the explanation, one fact is clear: mental hospital inpatient populations have declined steadily since 1955.

There were other consequences of drug treatment and the decline in inpatient populations. Fewer wards were locked, and mental hospitals became more open institutions. Milieu therapy was introduced. The emptying of hospitals discouraged the building of new ones, and some even closed—14 state hospitals closed between 1970 and 1973 (Scull, 1977a, p. 72). "Aftercare" services increased, since some patients were able to remain in the community "stabilized" on medication. Hospital stays were shorter, but the number of readmissions increased. As we will discuss later, the pharmacological revolution and the decline in inpatient populations encouraged the development of a new social policy, "community mental health."

## Sociological research

The 1950s was the beginning of a growing sociological interest in mental health. Due partly to an increased availability of funding from NIMH and partly to the belief that social factors were significant, if unexplored, elements of madness, sociologists and social psychiatrists began turning their attention to mental health problems. This research focused generally on three subjects: the mental hospital, social epidemiology, and identifying mental illness.

The mental hospital proved a fertile site for sociological research. Between the 1954 publi-

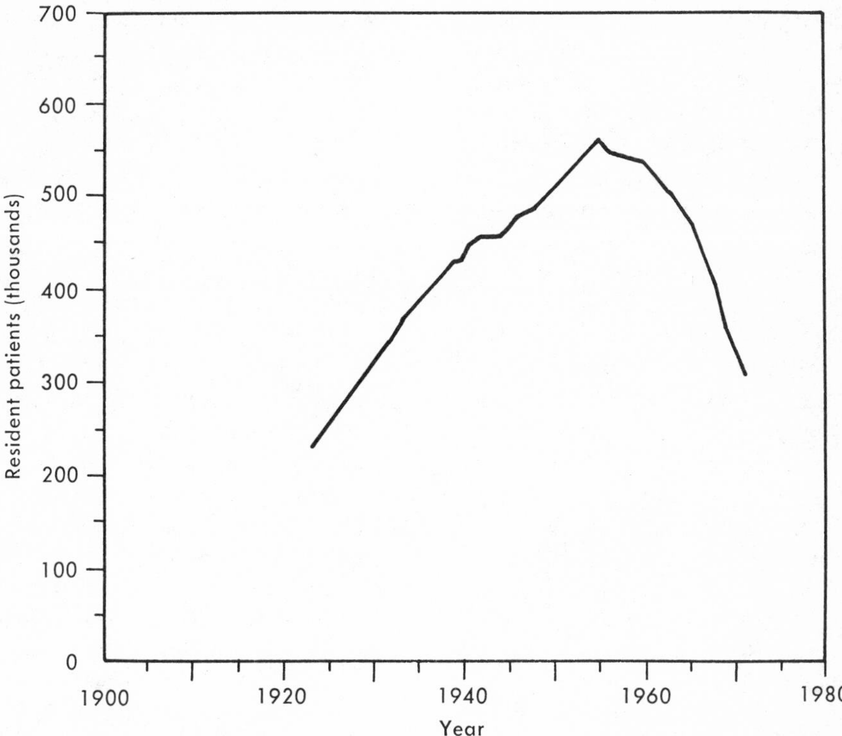


**Fig. 1.** Inpatient populations, state and county mental hospitals. (Courtesy U.S. Department of Health, Education and Welfare, National Institute of Mental Health, Biometry Branch, Washington, D.C.)

cation of *The Mental Hospital* by Alfred A. Stanton and Morris S. Schwartz and the 1964 publication of *Psychiatric Ideologies and Institutions* by Anselm Strauss et al. more than a dozen studies of mental hospitals were conducted (e.g., Belknap, 1956; Caudill, 1958; Dunham & Weinberg, 1960; Goffman, 1961). Nearly all studies used participant observation, with the sociological investigator acquiring first-hand knowledge of the operation and social life of a mental hospital. The most renowned and influential of these is Erving Goffman's *Asylums*. Goffman (1961) spent a year as a participant observer at St. Elizabeth's Hospital in Washington, D.C., a public institution with 7000 patients. Goffman described in vivid detail the underlife of the institution and the social life of the inmates largely from their perspective. He saw the hospital as a "total institution" and found a sharp division between patients and staff, a hospital culture that the patient adapted to, and that patients' responses were institutionalized. Perhaps the latter is most devastating: the hospital "institutionalized" patients to the needs of the hospital organization, engendering patient responses and behavior that were useful in adjusting to the institution but totally detrimental to "getting well" or readjusting to the outside world. Goffman and others discovered that mental hospitals provided little "therapy" and were dangerous to mental health. This marked the beginning of a sociological critique of the medical model of madness.

Sociologists traditionally have pursued the positivist search for social causes of deviant behavior. This has been particularly true in the sociological investigation of madness. The major method of study has been some type of "social epidemiology" in which patterns of incidence and prevalence of mental illness in a population are described. These patterns are then correlated with social factors (e.g., social class, residence, migration, race, sex) that appear to affect the likelihood of mental illness. In the 1930s Chicago sociologists Robert E. L. Faris and H. Warren Dunham (1939) published their classic, *Mental Disorders in Urban Areas*. Examining the "natural areas" of a city, they discovered the highest incidence rates of treated mental disorder to be in the central city. They hypothesized that urban life in the central city, with its isolation and "social disorganization," caused the higher rates of mental illness. Myerson (1941) suggested, in contrast, that perhaps the central city, with its array of rooming houses and its anonymity, attracted people who were already having psychological difficulties. Two decades later social psychiatrist Alexander Leighton and his colleagues, in a series of careful and sophisticated studies (Leighton, A. H., 1959; Leighton, D. C., et al., 1963; Hughes, C. C., et al., 1960) found higher rates of mental symptoms (as defined by psychiatrists) in communities that were more socially "disorganized."

Among the most influential sociological research on madness is *Social Class and Mental Illness,* a study by sociologist August Hollingshead and psychiatrist Frederick Redlich. Hollingshead and Redlich (1958) attempted to collect data on all treated cases of mental illness in New Haven, Connecticut. They surveyed all the clinics, hospitals, and private practitioners in the northeastern United States that might have been used by New Haven residents. Each patient was classified as a member of a social class (designated I through V, with I the highest), based on residence, occupation, and income. The principal finding was that social class varied inversely with diagnosed mental illness, that is, the lower the social class, the higher the rate of mental illness and vice versa. Hollingshead and Redlich also found that individuals in lower classes (IV and V) were more likely to be diagnosed as "psychotic," whereas individuals in higher classes (I and II) were diagnosed more commonly as "neurotic." Furthermore, lower class patients tended to receive custodial care or somatic treatments, and higher class patients were more likely to receive psychotherapy. Class V patients, the lowest social class, had by far the longest periods of hospitalization. In all, they concluded that one's social class position did affect diagnosed mental illness and the type of treatment rendered. Although this study was largely completed before the advent of drug treatment, subsequent studies (e.g., Dohrenwend & Dohrenwend, 1969) have supported many of its conclusions.

Most of the epidemiological studies focused on treated mental illness; it was a much more complex research task to ascertain the amount of *untreated* mental problems. A group of social scientists and psychiatrists devised a method to ascertain the amount of untreated mental symptoms in what has come to be known as the Midtown Manhattan Study (Srole et al., 1962). They interviewed a representative sample of urban residents, using a questionnaire designed to elicit responses concerning behaviors and experiences that psychiatrists might consider symptoms of mental problems. Psychiatrists then rated these questionnaires from zero (no significant symptoms) to six (incapacitating symptoms). Those whose symptoms were rated "marked," "severe," or "incapacitated," the three categories for the most symptoms, were called "impaired." They found a remarkably high 23.4% of their sample to be impaired, 58.1% had mild or moderate symptomatology, and 18.5% were considered well. This high rate of people who were "impaired," at least by psychiatric definitions, was used by some to argue for more psychiatric case finding and expanded treatment facilities.

Another type of sociological research focused on identifying and labeling people as mentally ill. Perhaps the best-known study in this tradition is Thomas Scheff's *Being Mentally Ill,* a major work in the labeling-interactionist approach. Scheff (1966) based his research on data gathered at a state mental hospital and developed a theory of becoming mentally ill. He was not so much interested in etiology of behavior as in the social process by which a person became defined as mentally ill. Scheff shifted the attention from the patient to the defining social audiences (especially psychiatrists) who frequently commit individuals to a mental hospital. He suggested that mental symptoms are "residual deviance" for which we have no other appropriate labels and that they arise from a wide variety of sources. He argued that most deviant acts never come to the attention of psychiatrists; but when they are identified and come to psychiatric attention, they are labeled as mental illness and the individual is cast into the role of mental patient. When in doubt, according to Scheff, psychiatrists are more likely to see and diagnose "illness" than health. In this view the social contingencies that lead to the labeling are more important than the psychiatric symptoms themselves. Scheff suggests that most patients' behaviors are interpreted on the assumption that they are mentally ill (see Rosenhan, 1973), and "appropriate" illness behaviors are reinforced. The patient-physician encounter, then, places the former in the role of mental patient.

"Chronic" mental patients are created by labeling and mental hospital treatment. It is difficult to return to conventional roles in the face of the master status, "ex–mental patient," and this stigma makes "normal" interpersonal relations and employment more difficult. Scheff's work has been the subject of considerable sociological controversy (e.g., Gove, 1970, 1975b; Scheff, 1974). Certainly Scheff's theory only tells part of the story of madness. But it is clear that his work has sensitized us to the fact that it is a profoundly *social* process that defines, identifies, and labels behavior as madness.

Although research by the social epidemiologists essentially accepted medical psychiatric definitions and looked only for "social factors" involved in mental illness causation, their findings served to modify the medical model. Work like Goffman's and Scheff's explicitly challenged the medical model of madness.

## Psychiatric critique

In this chapter we have tended to view psychiatry as a single entity or, perhaps better, as a dual entity with a tension between sociopsychological views and somatophysiological views. Beginning in the 1960s another view developed that we might call the psychiatric critique: psychiatrists who criticized psychiatry and the nature of psychiatric work. The two foremost examples of this minority viewpoint, although different in their critiques, are those of Thomas Szasz and R. D. Laing.

Thomas Szasz (1961, 1963, 1970, 1976), in a number of analytic and polemic pieces, has proposed that "mental illness is a myth," involuntary commitment is persecution in the name of mental health, mental hospitals are prisons for social deviants, and we should be aware of the dangers of the therapeutic state. We have already discussed some of these arguments. Szasz's position is essentially a laissez-faire critique: people ought to be allowed to behave as they wish as long as they do not break the law; if they break the law, they should be treated as criminals. Psychiatry, through the use of involuntary hospitalization, deprives people of their liberty without due process of law. To justify this, psychiatry, specifically institutional psychiatry, has created the myth that the individual is suffering from an illness that needs treatment. Szasz suggests that people have "problems in living," not illnesses, and that if people voluntarily seek help from psychiatrists, contractual psychotherapy may be appropriate. But even then Szasz views individuals as responsible for their behavior; for him, psychotherapy is a "moral dialogue," not treatment for a sick mind.

R. D. Laing's (1960, 1967; Laing and Esterson, 1964) critique comes from a very different angle. Whereas his earlier work is really an extension of psychiatric theory, his later work is quite sociological in nature. Laing's main focus is on the etiology of "schizophrenia." For him madness does not reside within the person, but rather is a response to the life situation in which a person finds himself. The source or cause of the madness is in the family communication system; the mad person is a victim of an oppressive or "sick" family system in which he or she must operate. Far from being illogical or irrational, madness is understandable from the viewpoint of the victim. It may be the only possible response to what Laing terms "a checkmate situation." In this way his theory is similar to Bateson's (1956), which hypothesizes that schizophrenia is the result of "double bind" problems in family communications. Mad people, in Laing's view, are not sick but different; if anything is "sick," it is the environment or social system in which they live. The social system is what needs changing. Short of that, Laing's treatment is to help people go through experiences of madness so they can grow from them. His emphasis on the phenomenological experience of madness still further opens the dialogue with madness that Foucault suggests was closed with the dawn of the age of reason. Laing views mad people as victims who may have a good deal to tell us about the "crazy" society in which we live.

In a sense we can view Szasz as a psychiatric critic from the right and Laing as one from the left. For Szasz, individuals are responsible for their behavior; for Laing, they are victims of an oppressive society. Both, however, reject the medical model assumption that madness is a mental illness and argue that all deviating human behavior is not caused by diseases, mental or otherwise.

To sum up briefly, the psychopharmacological revolution, the decline in mental hospital populations, and the interest in social aspects of mental illness laid a foundation for what appeared to be a major policy change, the development in the 1960s of community mental health centers.

## COMMUNITY MENTAL HEALTH: A BOLD, NEW APPROACH

By 1955, just before the impact of the pharmacological revolution, there was a growing governmental concern with the problem of mental illness. World War II had brought to light a sizable number of individuals with psychiatric problems, public mental hospitals were overcrowded and largely custodial, and there was some disillusionment with psychotherapy as inpatient treatment for mental illness. Congress enacted the 1955 Mental Health Study Act, with an appropriation of more than a million dollars, and established the Joint Commission on Mental Health and Illness.

### Federal action and professional growth

The Joint Commission on Mental Health and Illness, which consisted of representatives from a variety of professional organizations, presented its final report, *Action For Mental Health,* in 1961. This document made sweeping recommendations: no mental hospital should have more than 1000 beds; treatment programs for the acutely ill should be expanded; an emphasis should be placed on prevention; a national recruitment program for mental health personnel on all levels should be established; more funds were needed for training and basic research; mental health expenditures should be doubled in 5 years and tripled in 10; and one community mental health clinic should be established for every 50,000 persons in the population. President Kennedy was receptive to the report, although in his February, 1963, message to Congress and in the legislation he supported, he emphasized the development of comprehensive community mental health centers (CMHC). These centers would enable the mentally ill to be treated in their own communities and returned quickly to a useful place in society. Kennedy declared, "We need a new type of health facility, one which will return mental health care to the mainstream of American medicine" (quoted in Szasz, 1970, p. 319). In October, 1963, Congress passed the Community Mental Health Centers Act, providing financing for construction of facilities; a 1965 bill provided funds for staffing the centers. This was to be a "bold, new approach" in psychiatry, emphasizing prevention and treating the mentally ill swiftly and surely in their own communities.

A number of social conditions made the 1960s ripe for the development of the community mental health center and its professional counterpart, community psychiatry. The American economy was secure and appeared to be growing steadily. There was an incipient concern for the poor, and public "welfare" programs could deliver a certain amount of "outdoor relief." Civil rights activism, and later antiwar activity, was conducive to the development of an activist psychiatry. There was considerable frustration with traditional approaches to treatment in mental hospitals. Sociological and social psychiatric research had demonstrated the importance of social factors in mental illness (although it is questionable whether they had any direct impact on policy; see Roman, 1971). Drug treatment had led to a decline in hospital populations and enabled some individuals to remain in the community. President Kennedy had a personal concern for mental illness, and the notion of the CMHC aligned well with his own notions of "a new frontier."

There was some psychiatric enthusiasm for the new policies. As sociologist Warren Dunham (1976) suggests, in the case of community psychiatry it appears that "ideas followed money." That is, whatever enthusiasm existed in the psychiatric world, it was fueled by the availability of extensive federal funds. In the first 6 years, $477 million was appropriated for construction and staffing grants (Chu & Trotter, 1974, p. 26). The number of psychiatrists grew from 17,047 in 1964 to 22,701 in 1973. Increases of psychiatric nurses, social workers, and paraprofessionals were greater still. By 1973, 540 CMHCs had been funded and 400 were in operation (Robin & Wagenfield, 1977).

## Community psychiatry

The professional arm of the "bold, new approach" was community psychiatry. A somewhat vague and amorphous subspecialty in psychiatry, this was an attempt to turn psychiatric knowledge and techniques to community problems, with a goal of preventing or minimizing mental disorder. Gerald Caplan's (1964) *Principles of Preventive Psychiatry* became the gospel of the community psychiatry movement. Caplan, relying heavily on public health as a model, conceptualized psychiatry as preventing mental illness on three levels. Primary prevention focused on eliminating the causes of mental illness in the community; secondary prevention was aimed at "early identification" of and intervention against mental problems; and tertiary prevention was treatment and rehabilitation efforts that attempted to prevent long-term incapacities. He suggested that psychiatrists should anticipate crises and intervene, providing "anticipatory guidance and emotional inoculation, which help [people] cope with threatening events" in such situations as prenatal clinics, surgical wards, divorce courts, and colleges (Mechanic, 1969, p. 100). Caplan envisioned psychiatrists consulting with legislators and other administrators in an attempt to create a mentally healthy environment. He even suggests that psychiatrists, with the aid of legislators and welfare authorities, can improve the "moral atmosphere" of homes with children of unwed mothers by encouraging these women "to marry and provide them with stable fathers" (Caplan, G., 1964, p. 59). Needless to add, "improvement" in the moral atmospheres is dependent on whose moral view one adopts.

Although Caplan and others who presented similar views were well intentioned in their proposals, a sociologist may find them problematic. Aside from the expansive notions of psychiatric work, which will be discussed shortly, there are problems with the concepts of primary and secondary prevention. In terms of primary prevention, we do not presently have sufficient knowledge about the etiology of mental illness behavior to know how to eliminate it (Roman, 1971, p. 385). Reports of intervention attempts in the anthropological literature are far from promising (e.g., Paul, 1955; Spicer, 1952). Moreover, there are significant ethical issues involved in promoting certain forms of human behavior (e.g., marriage for unwed mothers) in the name of mental health. Secondary prevention, with its early identification, runs a substantial risk of "labeling" what may be transitory life problems (Dohrenwend & Dohrenwend, 1969) and casting the individual into the role of mental patient, thus stabilizing the deviance (see Lemert, 1972). The risks and benefits need to be weighed carefully.

Some conceptions of community psychiatry were less encompassing and expansive than Caplan's. A number of psychiatrists viewed treating individuals in the community as a viable alternative. Demonstration projects established that for many, "home treatment" could be an alternative to hospitalization (Weiner et al., 1967). Researchers showed that nearly three quarters of diagnosed schizophrenics slated for hospital admission could be maintained in the community with medication and regular visits from public health nurses (Pasamanick et al., 1967). Other psychiatrists saw community psychiatry as a means of delivering mental health care to poor and indigent populations. Indeed, the concept of community psychiatry included a range of viewpoints, from inclusive notions of seeing the community itself as patient to narrower views of delivering services to poorly served populations. In general, community psychiatry meant for psychiatrists a shift away from one-to-one relations with patients to new roles as consultants and administrators.

The major role for the community psychiatrist has been administrator of the CMHC. CMHCs are intended to be comprehensive mental health facilities serving a "catchment area" of 75,000 to 200,000 people. They have an interdisciplinary staff, frequently including a contingent of nonprofessionals from the community (Sobey, 1970), and provide a range of services typically including aftercare, home visits, day and night hospitals, outpatient treatment, short-term inpatient treatment, "crisis intervention," consultation to schools and other agencies, and the coordination of a "continuity of care" for their patients. CMHCs almost always are related to mental hospitals and not infrequently located on the mental hospital grounds. The hospitals themselves have endeavored to develop more "therapeutic" environments, mainly through the adoption of "milieu therapy." Milieu therapy, adapted from Maxwell Jones' (1953) work on therapeutic communities, can be viewed as a return to a type of "moral treatment" for madness. It is an attempt to construct a therapeutic environment for recovery, including combining male and female wards, doing away with uniforms, and instituting patient government, ward meetings, therapeutic teams, individual attention, group therapy, and patient involvement in the treatment process. Such innovations, although they have certainly humanized the mental hospital (Cumming & Cumming, 1966), have not been particularly effective in "curing" or even rehabilitating many long-term mental patients. In some hospitals, however, there appears to have been little impact of community psychiatry, and custodial care remains the rule (Fowlkes, 1975).

A major goal of community psychiatry has been to place as many patients as possible "in the community." Increased efforts at "decarceration" have intensified the trend of decreasing mental hospital populations (Scull, 1977a). More patients are admitted on a "voluntary" status, and fewer are committed indefinitely. There has been a continued rise in the number of admissions, but the number of *readmissions* has skyrocketed (Table 1).

**TABLE 1**
ADMISSIONS TO STATE AND COUNTY MEDICAL HOSPITALS*

| Year | Total admissions | First admissions | Readmissions |
|---|---|---|---|
| 1975 | 385,237 | 120,690 | 232,272 |
| 1969 | 367,963 | 163,984 | 173,245 |
| 1957 | 205,041 | 128,124 | 64,823 |
| 1947 | 130,872 | 93,749 | 29,643 |
| 1938 | 106,220 | 79,408 | 21,085 |

* From *Statistical Abstracts* 1940, 1950, 1960 and National Institute of Mental Health, Biometry Branch, Washington, D.C.

The statistics, however, do not tell the whole story. Most mental hospitals have developed a "revolving door" policy, with patients admitted for shorter but more frequent stays. In addition, the psychiatric ward in the general hospital (a community psychiatry innovation) often treats the most "acute" difficulties, and thus many patients never become state hospital statistics. Furthermore, many "chronic" patients simply have been transferred to custodial nursing homes, rather than becoming well-functioning members of the community. Moreover, there is increasing evidence that released patients go "from back wards to back alleys," living meager existences in welfare hotels and receiving little continuity of care (Chu & Trotter, 1974; Kirk & Therrien, 1975). Although more people are remaining in the community, the question increasingly becomes, "Under what conditions?"

Overall, community psychiatry has had mixed results. More individuals are receiving treatment in outpatient facilities and fewer are becoming "institutionalized," a few previously unserved populations are being served, some reforms have taken hold in mental hospitals, hospitalization is shorter, and the team approach has included more nonpsychiatrists in treatment programs. But psychiatrists, perhaps fortunately, have not treated communities; there has been no apparent success in preventing mental illness; difficulties have been encountered in continuity of care; patients have been "dumped" from mental hospitals without the availability of appropriate alternatives; and rehabilitation has been minimal (Kirk & Therrien, 1975). Furthermore, community psychiatry has still other consequences.

## Community psychiatry and the medical model

Community psychiatry represents an attempt by psychiatry to break from the past and originate a bold, new approach. Unfortunately, such breaks are frequently limited by "ideological barriers" (Ryan, 1971b) and existing patterns of organization.

Community psychiatry never relinquished the medical model of mental disorder. For example, the psychiatric focus on the individual remained evident. Patients were still considered to suffer from diseases, qualitatively different from everyday problems in living, and were still "treated" under the aegis of a medical practitioner who typically was director of the CMHC. Although some research prior to "community psychiatry" showed that acceptance of the medical model among psychiatrists varied so that they ranged along a continuum from somatically oriented to socially oriented community psychiatrists (Strauss, A., et al., 1964), research *after* the launching of the community psychiatry movement showed that psychiatrists still tended to favor an organic or individualistic model, rather than a community model (Rogow, 1970). This is not surprising, given the individual orientation of medical education and medical practice and the history of psychiatry.

Small organizational changes were made, especially the training and use of nonprofessionals, but much of the previous organization remained. Because of the psychiatric dominance of the CMHC, the medical model of service and treatment still predominated. Some of the nonprofessionals had been long-time aides in mental hospitals and maintained the institutional viewpoint. Many of the CMHCs were physically tied to the past, since they operated in the shadows of the old state hospital. Such organizational ties made a break from the past extremely difficult.

Most significant to our discussion, however, is that community psychiatry actually expanded the medical model of human problems and the jurisdiction of psychiatry. Dunham (1976) calls it "the widening definition of mental illness." The domain of community psychiatry includes not only traditional mental illness conceptions, but alcoholism, drug addiction, children's school and behavior problems, predelinquency, bad marriages, job losses, and aging. Virtually any human problem could be addressed by community psychiatry and, for the most part, through the lens of the medical model. Psychiatric "case finding," a search for those in need of psychiatric services, is a poignant example:

> The search for "hidden" deviants reflects the dominance of the medical model in psychiatry—namely, the notion that "pathologies" are independent of social norms and can be located by epidemiological methods. A consequence of such procedures may be a large increase in the proportion of the population regarded by psychiatry as "mentally ill." (Roman, 1971, p. 384)*

In short, community psychiatry has broadened the concept of mental illness and expanded the domain of psychiatric intervention in human problems.

One final point: some social scientists (Keniston, 1968; Leifer, 1966; Manning & Zucker, 1976, pp. 61-62) have pointed out the social control aspects of community psychiatry. By defining more people in the jurisdiction of psychiatry and providing treatment for these deviants, psychiatry plays an increased and active role in the maintenance of the social order.

As we have seen throughout this chapter, most reform movements in mental health begin with a high optimism that is eventually institutionalized into business as usual. Largely because of fiscal constraints and an inability to

*Copyright © 1971 by The William Alanson White Psychiatric Foundation, Inc. Reprinted by special permission of The William Alanson White Psychiatric Foundation, Inc., from *Psychiatry* (1971) **34:** 378-390.

fulfill its early and probably excessive expectations, community psychiatry as a social movement lost some of its vigor by the mid-1970s.

## MEDICAL MODEL OF MADNESS IN THE 1970s

This is still the era of community mental health centers, but there are changes occurring in psychiatry and most especially in the medical model of madness.

We have noted a general shift away from the 1960s' concern with searching society or the community for the causes of madness back to a focus on the individual. In actuality community psychiatry never strayed far from the individual, medical model orientation, but the 1970s brought a new concern for individual, especially organic, explanations and treatments of madness. The reasons for this reorientation are complex; it can be explained in part by such factors as a recession-prone economy that contributed to the curtailing of numerous programs, the waning optimism after a decade of community psychiatry, a backlash to the politicization of the 1960s, and a professional attempt to "reintegrate" psychiatry into the mainstream of medicine.

There has been a renewed emphasis on biological and organic models of madness. Biomedical research, especially in the areas of genetics and biochemistry, is capable of measuring increasingly subtle variations between the mentally ill and others. Genetics in particular has captured the imagination of psychiatrists. Many psychiatrists are increasingly convinced of some type of genetic component in manic depression (Rainer, 1974) but are somewhat more equivocal about schizophrenia (Rosenthal, 1974). Most believe that genetic predisposition is a necessary but not sufficient condition for the onset of madness. The use of lithium carbonate, a naturally occurring compound, in controlling the severe mood swings of manic depression has reinforced biomedical conceptions of madness (Fieve, 1970). Drug treatment is still psychiatry's most potent device for making a short-term impact on madness. (It has been discovered that long-term usage of phenothiazine drugs can produce iatrogenic effects such as "tardive dyskinesia," a parkinsonian-like syndrome that leads to loss of muscular control.) There is also a resurgent interest in psychosurgery, although not yet with mental patients (Chavkin, 1976).

One of the most interesting recent events concerning mental illness is the 1975 Supreme Court decision *O'Connor* v. *Donaldson*. Kenneth Donaldson (1976) was involuntarily committed to a Florida state mental hospital in 1957 at age 49. He was never considered to be dangerous. For more than a decade he repeatedly and unsuccessfully tried to secure his own release, particularly through court action. In 1971, after nearly 15 years of custodial care, he was released. Donaldson sued for damages for being involuntarily confined without treatment. A lower court awarded him $38,500 in compensatory and punitive damages. The case was appealed through the judicial system to the Supreme Court. Some supporters had hoped for a ruling that would state that confined patients have "a right to treatment." The Supreme Court's opinion, however, was narrower; nondangerous patients who are capable of surviving outside the institution cannot be confined against their will *without* some treatment. Justice Potter Stewart wrote: "The mere presence of mental illness does not disqualify a person from preferring his home to the comforts of the institution."

The Court did not decide whether a nondangerous, mentally ill person could be confined for the *purpose* of treatment or whether mentally ill persons not considered dangerous to themselves or others have a right to treatment (Miller, K. S., 1976). Although the Court implicitly reaffirmed the medical designation of mental illness, it limited what psychiatrists and others could do about it against a person's will. Some feared the decision would lead fiscally pressed institutions to "dump" thousands of patients. Others acclaimed it as finally giving mad people some rights.

The psychiatric profession has expressed concern over the abuse of the mental illness designation for political ends, especially in the Soviet Union. Considerable evidence has accumulated showing that some Soviet political dissidents, who are sane by Western psychiatric standards, have been declared mentally ill and committed to mental hospitals. This medicalization of dissent serves certain functions for the Soviet state. It permits swift commitment of dissidents without a trial, depoliticizes their dissent by declaring it ravings of madness, and allows for a retraction of statements to be a sign of a "cure." American psychiatrists have decried this as an abuse of psychiatry and a form of psychiatric repression. The Soviet example is an extreme instance of psychiatry as an agent of social control and an explicitly political use of the mental illness designation. It nevertheless underlines the inherent vagueness and malleability of the mental illness concept and the potential, if not yet realized, use of psychiatry for political ends (Conrad, 1977).

One final note about mental illness in the 1970s. It seems likely that some form of National Health Insurance (NHI) will be enacted within the next few years. NHI will probably be a type of expansion of Medicare and Medicaid to the population not covered by these programs, providing payment for many medical services. Treatment for mental illness will be included. It is an interesting question how NHI will affect the medical model of madness. Two general possibilities exist. It may, because payment for service is available for "medical" problems, expand the medical model of mental illness to include previously nonmedical problems. This would enlarge the psychiatric domain and medicalize nearly everything. On the other hand, it may, primarily because of fiscal constraints, encourage the adoption of a narrow traditional definition of mental illness including only schizophrenia, manic depression, and similar disorders. The economic situation and the spirit of Congress make the latter perhaps a more likely possibility.

Overall, in the 1970s, individualistic solutions to human problems abound (Schur, 1976). In mental health this has led to an increased interest in technology—be it drugs, genetics, or behavior technology (behavior modification)—and an intensified emphasis on the medical model of madness.

## SUMMARY

The development of the medical model of madness spans a period of 2000 years. The roots are found in Hippocratic medicine of classical Greece, although there were competing conceptions of the reality of madness among the Greeks. During the medieval period medical conceptions were subordinate and had to accommodate the dogma of the Church. Medical conceptions of madness begin to reemerge partly as a response to the excesses of witchcraft and the decline of the church. Deviants were first confined in the 17th century, establishing the institutionalization of the mad. Physicians entered the institution not as healers but as guardians or wisemen. Medicine, symbolized by Pinel, was a humanitarian reform in the treatment of madness. Psychiatrists or medical psychologists did not have any theories or treatments of madness that would have made madness ipso facto a medical problem. The "capturing" of madness by the medical profession was a social and political achievement rather than a scientific one.

In 19th-century America, the medical superintendents of asylums organized, and with the aid of champions like Dorothea Dix, created a virtual monopoly over the treatment of madness. In the early days they were highly optimistic about the asylum cure, the American version of moral treatment, and scores of asylums were built. By the 1850s social pressures and therapeutic disappointments resulted in custodial care in the asylums. At the dawn of the 20th century the medical profession had a firm dominance over the conception and treatment of madness yet possessed no "successful" medical treatment and no evidence of organic causes of madness.

In the early 20th century the discovery of general paresis reinforced medical conceptions of madness and gave rise to a hope that the organic causes of all mental illness would be similarly discovered. The wide acceptance of Freudian ideas in the first half of this century both muted and expanded the medical model of madness. A psychogenic model was grafted onto the medical model. In the 1930s, with the advent of shock therapy, lobotomies, and genetic theories, somatic conceptions of madness reemerged. By the 1950s, partly through efforts of the mental hygiene movement, public attitudes toward mental illness changed in the direction of medical ones. The public, however, still maintained a narrower view of what constitutes mental illness. The 1954 Durham decision institutionalized the psychiatric concept of madness into the judicial process.

In 1955, because of the introduction of phenothiazine drugs, mental hospital populations began to decline. The diffusion of drug treatments aligned well with medical concepts of madness, since psychiatrists could now give medications for the "illness." The drug revolution, the declining hospital populations, and an increased interest in the social aspects of madness preceded a major change in social policy: the development of community mental health centers. The community mental health movement, and its professional arm, community psychiatry, were an attempt to turn psychiatric concepts to community problems. Although community psychiatry encompassed a range of opinions, in its extreme forms it was the psychiatricization of everything. The 1970s have seen somewhat of a decline in interest in community psychiatry and a resurgence of organic and biomedical theories of madness.

There are a few recurrent themes in our history of the medical concept of madness. Medical theories have located the source of madness in a variety of somatic organs: the humors, the stomach, the nervous system, the brain. Every era seems to have its own reform movements that lead to an increased optimism, which several years later, after the movements fail to live up to their promise, reverts to a pessimistic view of madness. This has often taken the form of a "somatic pessimism," locating the causes of madness in the physiology (e.g., the degeneration hypothesis). Medical involvement with madness, historically speaking, emerges more as a humanitarian reform than as a biomedical accomplishment. It is worth repeating that medical concepts became the dominant conceptions of madness long before there was any evidence that madness had any biophysiological components (and this is still controversial in some circles), and before any medical treatments, other than the nonmedical moral treatment, made any impact on madness. The development of the medical model of madness was a social and political rather than a scientific achievement.

## SUGGESTED READINGS

Alexander, F. G. and Selesnick, S. T. *A history of psychiatry*. New York: New American Library, 1966.

A comprehensive and well-written history by two psychoanalysts. They emphasize theories and therapies, not historic events. Written from the perspective of the development of modern psychiatry.

Foucault, M. *Madness and civilization*. New York: Random House, Inc., 1965.

An interpretive structuralist analysis that traces the conceptions and treatments of madness from 1500 to 1800. Foucault argues we broke the dialogue with madness with the dawn of the age of reason. It is difficult but fascinating reading.

Goffman, E. *Asylums*. New York: Anchor Press, 1961.

A classic sociological study based on participant observation in a mental hospital. A precursor to the labeling-interactionist tradition, Goffman develops his conceptions of the moral careers of mental patients, total institutions, and psychiatry as a tinkering trade.

Rothman, D. *The discovery of the asylum*. Boston: Little, Brown & Co., 1971.

An award-winning social history of the development of institutionalization in 19th-century America. Rothman analyzes the emergence of the asylum as a response to the changing social order in the Jacksonian period.

Szasz, T. *The manufacture of madness*. New York: Harper & Row, Publishers, 1970.

A controversial and provocative analysis of the emergence of institutional psychiatry from the Inquisition and mental illness from witchcraft. Although more polemical than analytic, Szasz's arguments are seminal to the medicalization of deviance.

# 4 ALCOHOLISM

## DRUNKENNESS, INEBRIETY, and the DISEASE CONCEPT

In this chapter we discuss the origins and rise of the idea that repeated alcohol intoxication should be thought of as a sickness rather than a sin or crime. In contrast to the case of mental illness discussed in the previous chapter, the rise for the disease concept of alcoholism illustrates that the process of collective medical definition need not necessarily be sustained primarily by medical personnel. The historical development of medical definitions of deviant drinking involves powerful nonmedical groups, individuals, and organizations whose moral, political, status, and/or professional interests were served by such definitional change. Although physicians were not hapless bystanders in this process, they were not the leading crusaders.

### PHYSIOLOGY OF ALCOHOL: UNCONTESTED APPLICATIONS OF THE MEDICAL MODEL

Unlike mental illness, the medicalization of deviant drinking behavior and opiate use, discussed in Chapter 5, rests importantly on a long-established legitimate medical presence. An absolutely necessary condition of *deviant* drinking is *drinking* itself. Before one can become a "drunkard," "inebriate," or "alcoholic," one somehow has to get the substance ("chemical") alcohol into one's blood. This condition sets deviant drinking and opiate use apart from all the other cases we discuss in this book. That this bears great significance for a legitimate medical presence around "drinking behavior" becomes obvious when one recalls Irving Zola's (1972) remark: "If anything can be shown . . . to effect the inner workings of the body and to a lesser extent the mind (p. 495)," then it may become a legitimate topic for medical study and intervention. The fact that one must put a chemical substance—and one that has been defined as "psychoactive"—inside one's *body* as a prerequisite to deviant drinking immediately established medicine as having at least a prima facie interest and jurisdiction over the causes, consequences, and control of such conduct. This jurisdiction over the physiology of alcohol is what we call the *uncontested* medical model of alcohol. By uncontested we mean that a political status quo based on medical definitions and interventions has been achieved and is supported as legitimate by most parties involved.

For example, no one argues about who should have the legitimate jurisdiction over the definition and treatment of the symptoms of acute intoxication or alcohol poisoning or of the physiological consequences of chronic heavy drinking, (e.g., physical withdrawal symptoms, malnutrition, liver disease). These are identified typically as the physiological, pharmacological, or medical consequences of such drinking (Butz, 1977; Greenberg, 1958; Lieber, 1976; Seixas et al., 1975; U.S. Department of Health, Education and Welfare, 1978). This has been called the "drug centered" perspective on drinking, and it has influenced most conventional as well as scientific work (MacAndrew & Edgerton, 1969; Young, Jock, 1971).

The goal of medical treatment for such conditions is detoxification—regardless of whether for the acutely or chronically intoxicated and whether it occurs in a general hospital or alcohol treatment center. Detoxification aims at mollifying the toxic effects of alcohol on the body. Abstinence is the first and most easily achieved step under such controlled conditions. Depending on the severity of the intoxication, various heroic measures may be instituted if permanent damage or death appears imminent. Short of such interventions, there is actually little that can be done to reverse the intoxicating effects of alcohol, except to allow the liver to metabolize or remove the alcohol from the body.

For the chronically intoxicated, the next step involves attention to the symptoms of *alcohol withdrawal*. The medical concept of physical dependence on alcohol suggests that alcohol has become an integral part of body physiology, that the body has adapted to a particular level of alcohol as a ''normal'' part of its operation. When alcohol is removed from the system, then, physical symptoms ensue in reaction to its absence as a kind of physiological trauma caused by the sudden change. For those whose bodies have become accustomed to alcohol, several hours are usually required for these symptoms to subside. They include moderate-to-violent tremors or shaking, anxiety, nausea, convulsions, hallucinations, and in the most extreme form, *delirium tremens*. Severe alcohol withdrawal can be fatal if the individual does not receive medical attention. Medical treatments at this stage include anticonvulsant and sedative drugs to reduce stress, vitamin supplements, rest, and supportive care.

Once medical control of these short-term effects of severe intoxication is achieved, a variety of less heroic treatments designed to retard or alleviate the more long-term effects of drinking are used. In addition to attention to problems involving gastrointestinal, cardiac, and neurological complications, treatment at this stage often involves psychotherapy, including both individual and group arrangements, use of the so-called therapeutic community, ''reality therapy,'' and various behaviorist techniques. The drug disulfiram, known commonly as Antabuse, is often used in conjunction with such treatment. Antabuse is given typically to outpatient drinkers when they are sober. The drug has no noticeable effect when taken but produces extreme nausea should the individual drink even a small amount of alcohol when it is in effect. This treatment is premised on the behaviorist assumption that drinking under such circumstances will become associated with the negative experience of nausea and gradually will be extinguished (see Chapter 8).

Contributing to the consensus that these are indeed ''medical problems'' is the fact that, in general, such treatments and interventions for intoxication and its effects have ''worked''—physicians have been successful in solving or at least alleviating the problems of intoxication, physical withdrawal, and the pathological conditions associated with long-term heavy drinking. The fact that this uncontested jurisdiction is nonetheless political should not be forgotten. That is, physicians both have been given and have taken control over these problems as part of their expert ''turf.''

From time to time, medical-scientific controversies arise within this generally uncontested jurisdiction that serve to remind us that such control is indeed political. One of the most recent examples is the medical-scientific debate surrounding what is called fetal alcohol syndrome (FAS), or the effects of alcohol consumption by pregnant women on the developing fetus. Such contests also remind us of Thomas Kuhn's (1970) insights on the importance of politics and ideology in scientific work in general. The fact that lay persons as well as scientists consider the conditions we have discussed to be ''obvious'' medical problems means only that such a view has become part of the taken-for-granted wisdom of alcohol. Such ''commonsense'' wisdom is in large part due to the great influence of the natural science, drug-centered, pharmacological paradigm used to ''make sense'' of what alcohol is and what it does to us when we drink it. Although the science of the physiology of alcohol may offer us interesting political questions to pursue, our interest in the medicalization of deviant drinking *behavior* directs our attention to the question of the effects of alcohol on social conduct, or how people behave when they drink. It is this question of alcohol's effects on behavior that provides the arena in which the contested application of the medical model may be defined more clearly.

## ALCOHOL AND BEHAVIOR: THE QUESTION OF CONTROL AND THE BEGINNING OF CONTEST

The consensus of the uncontested medical model of alcohol begins to dissolve when attention shifts from internal and pharmacologic processes to social conduct. By *contested* medical model we mean that the question of "turf," or jurisdiction, has not been settled with any general degree of consensus and that political negotiation continues about whether and to what extent deviant drinking should be defined and treated as a medical problem. At the risk of oversimplification, we argue that the core proposition of these contested medical definitions of alcohol use is that drinking, if done in sufficient quantity and under certain circumstances, causes people in varying degrees to "lose control" over their behavior. This is believed to occur either because of the inherently disinhibiting qualities of the drug itself or because certain people who drink have some genetic or acquired vulnerability to alcohol that predisposes them to lose control over drinking, once begun. The first explanation is often called the "disinhibitor hypothesis" and assumes a universal human vulnerability to alcohol's effects; the second explanation is premised on the existence of some biophysiological flaw in the individual that, when combined with alcohol, produces the disease of inebriety, or alcoholism. This chapter is concerned primarily with the origins and development of this latter idea, but the influence of the disinhibitor proposition has been so widespread in conventional thinking about the effects of drinking that we must first discuss it briefly and the criticisms launched against it. In addition, since it specifically links deviant behavior with drinking, the disinhibitor hypothesis serves to reinforce the medicalization of deviant drinking itself.

### Disinhibitor hypothesis

Conventional lay and scientific wisdom, backed by centuries of tradition (but not necessarily rigorous evidence), holds that because of the physiology and pharmacology of alcohol in the body, certain highly predictable *behavioral* consequences follow inevitably from drinking. Aside from motivation, station in life, or cultural surroundings, it is believed that alcohol, as a result of its chemical action, removes one's inhibitions and lessens the degree of control over behavior. Such conduct is assumed virtually always to be socially undesirable and potentially disruptive—to be, in short, at least rule-breaking and probably deviant behavior. This deviation is believed caused by the drug's indirect and "depressing" effect on the brain, which is generally considered to be the physiological seat of the self.

People, if they drink "enough," are thought to say and do things they would "not normally" say and do. When "under the influence" of alcohol, we are not considered to be our "true" selves. The deviant behavior associated with such drinking is described typically as irrational, bizarre, sometimes antisocial, and primitive, as a working out of some presumed essential and ever-present biological imperative—something that society, for the most part, effectively contains through a variety of social controls. This view of drug taking is what Jock Young (1971, pp. 59-60) has called the "absolutist monolith" and is an extension of the uncontested, physiological-pharmacological view of alcohol into the realm of behavior. Just as the internal "laws" of bodily metabolism regulate the rate at which alcohol is decomposed into its parts, this view assumes that the drug has similar universal effects on the drinker's behavior. It assumes that social and cultural context are by and large irrelevant in understanding what happens to us when we drink.

The popularity of the disinhibitor hypothesis, however, predates the rise of the science of physiology itself. It has long been part of "what everybody knows" about alcohol-influenced behavior. Deviant drinking, in other words, is as old as drinking itself. T. D. Crothers (1903), for example, suggests that as early as 2000 BC the Egyptian government proposed regulations banning drinking among soldiers, who were made ineffective by intoxication. In the famed legal code of Hammurabi, dating from about 1800 BC, we find detailed restrictions on the sale, pricing, and use of alcoholic drink (Harper, 1904). In the 83rd letter of the Roman lawyer-philosopher Seneca (1942), who lived in the first century AD, we find a distinction between "one who is drunk" and a "drunkard": "in [one] case . . . the man who is loaded with wine and has no control over himself; in the other, of a man who is accustomed to get drunk, and is a slave to the habit" (p. 304). This is perhaps the earliest succinct distinction between one who has "lost control" of behavior as a result of *intoxication* and one who has "lost control" because of what came to be called *"alcohol addiction."* We will have considerably more to say about the latter in the rest of this chapter.

In what may well be one of the most colorful statements of the disinhibitor hypothesis, Seneca (1942) in this same letter counsels "good men" against drink:

> How much better it is to arraign drunkenness frankly and expose its vices! . . . if you wish to prove that a good man ought not to get drunk, why work it out by logic? . . . Show how often the drunkard does things which make him blush when he is sober; state that drunkenness is nothing but a condition of insanity purposively assumed. Drunkenness kindles and discloses every kind of vice, and *removes the sense of shame* that veils our evil undertakings. . . . When the strength of wine has become too great and has gained control over the mind, every lurking evil *comes forth* from its hiding-place. Drunkenness does not create vice, it merely *brings it into view;* at such times the lustful man does not wait even for the privacy of a bedroom, but without postponement gives free play to the demands of his passions; at such times the unchaste man proclaims and publishes his malady; at such times your cross-grained fellow *does not restrain* his tongue or his hand. The haughty man increases his arrogance, the ruthless man his cruelty, the slanderer his spitefulness. Every vice is given free play and *comes to the front*. Besides, *we forget who we are*. . . . (p. 306, emphasis added)*

Here we have the unmistakable image of the powerful drug's triumph over the drinker and the antisocial consequences caused by its removal of social and cultural restraints.

Although the disinhibitor hypothesis—in a variety of forms—has been popular in virtually all ages and centuries, it has become part of scientific wisdom only since the rise of the science of physiology and the growth of physiological research in the second quarter of the 20th century. One of the most influential and prestigious proponents during this period was Leon Greenberg, a leading physiologist of alcohol. The following statement by Greenberg (1953) received wide currency in the United States as an absolutely factual description of what happens to our behavior when we drink:

> The most pronounced physiological effect of alcohol is on the brain. . . . A blood concentration of about .05 percent of alcohol . . . depresses the uppermost levels of the brain—the center of inhibitions, restraint and judgment. At this stage the drinker feels that he is sitting on top of the world; he is "a free human being"; many of his normal inhibitions vanish; he takes personal and social liberties as the impulse prompts; he is long-winded and can lick anybody in the country. . . . Contrary to old and popular belief, alcohol does not stimulate the nervous system. The illusion of stimulation results from the removal of inhibitions and restraints. (p. 88)

Finally, Marvin Block, a physician who has been called "perhaps the American Medical Association's leading spokesman on alcoholism" (MacAndrew & Edgerton, 1969), writes of the disinhibiting effect of alcohol in words that parallel those of Seneca almost 2000 years earlier. Block (1965) writes:

> Since alcohol depresses the powers of judgment, drinking may release inhibitions. . . . As far as sexual behavior is concerned, it is well-known that alcohol reduces the inhibitions of individuals and removes the controls. The individual becomes careless and will often do things under the influence of alcohol that he would not do if his judgment were not impaired. Therefore, impairment of the judgment by alcohol may cause sexual behavior that would not occur were he not exposed to the loss of control that alcohol brings about. (pp. 219-220)

Given the commonsense and later professional support of the disinhibitor hypothesis, it is not surprising that challenges have been rather

*Reprinted by permission from *Quarterly Journal of Studies on Alcohol,* Vol. 3, pp. 302-307, 1942, Copyright by Journal of Studies on Alcohol, Inc., New Brunswick, N.J. 08903.

late in coming. Interestingly, these challenges have come most effectively from social scientists who have taken this connection between drink and behavior not as revealed truth but rather as itself a problem for study. Among the most effective critics have been Alfred Lindesmith (1947, 1968), Howard Becker (1953, 1967a), Craig MacAndrew and Robert Edgerton (1969), and Jock Young (1971). We will return to this work in our discussion of addiction later in this chapter, but we may summarize their critique as follows. Although the pharmacological-physiological model of alcohol may tell us something about the effects of alcohol inside the body, it produces faulty conclusions when applied uncritically to drinking (or drug-taking) behavior. The major problem stems from what it ignores—the entire cultural and social realm of meaning and definition. Eschewing a simplistic chemical determinism, these social science critics insist that the effects of drugs on social conduct cannot be understood adequately without considering the questions of, for example, what "drink" means, how drinking is defined, social expectations for "drinking" and even "drunken" behavior, and the appropriate times and places for such conduct. Short of the obviously limiting conditions of unconsciousness and death brought on by a high concentration of alcohol in the blood, a complex set of social meanings influences drinking behavior. Anthropologists, in particular, have provided us with data that demonstrate this in the cross-cultural variety of the impact of alcoholic beverages on behavior (see Cahalan et al., 1969; Everett et al., 1976, Lemert, 1969; MacAndrew & Edgerton, 1969). MacAndrew and Edgerton (1969, pp. 13-82) have addressed this question of the socially constructed and interpreted nature of drinking behavior. They reject the pharmacological-physiological imperative of the disinhibitor hypothesis as itself an inadequate explanation of such conduct and suggest instead the concept of "drunken comportment"—that drunken behavior is a complex combination of physiological effects and individual interpretations of these effects in light of cultural and social contexts; that, in short, drunkenness is in important respects intentional *social* conduct. Sociologist Jacqueline Wiseman (1979) recently has taken this analysis further, arguing that among chronic heavy drinkers even being sober is a carefully orchestrated kind of intentional rather than "natural" comportment.

This social science criticism can be upheld by even the most casual review of our own experience. It is clear that drinking alcohol is not followed by the same behavior in all people—even among those from similar social and cultural situations. It is simply not true that alcohol, even in significant quantities, necessarily and inevitably "causes" drinkers to "lose control" over their behavior. In the face of such variety, and particularly considering the apparent inability of some people to "hold their liquor," a new kind of explanation for drunkenness becomes necessary. Such an explanation, unlike the drug-centered, disinhibitor hypothesis, centers only on those individuals out of all who drink alcohol (the majority of Americans report that they *do* drink some alcohol, but the majority are clearly not deviant drinkers [Cahalan, 1970]) who appear to "lose control" both over their ability to regulate drinking and other conduct as well. The problem, then, becomes one that appears to lie at the intersection of the drug alcohol and the individual drinker. Given the constant nature of the former and the variable nature of the latter, attention is focused particularly on the individual as one who is somehow constitutionally susceptible to the effects of alcohol.

To the extent that such "susceptible" drinkers seem impervious to emotional, rational, and even scientific appeal. we have a "puzzle" that invites solution (MacAndrew, 1969). If there are those "who can't hold their liquor" (MacAndrew & Edgerton, 1969, pp. 13-36), there are, by implication, those who can. As religion was gradually replaced by science, and in particular medical science, as the arbiter of personal problems, the search was begun to discover how deviant drinkers differ from the "normal" drinking population. Deviant drinkers were no longer seen as possessed by threatening spiritual forms but by threatening medical ones; the behavior became evidence of disease rather than of sin or willful malice.

For almost 200 years individuals who evidence patterns of *chronic* and *highly disruptive* intoxication have been identified by medical labels. This is the history of the medicalization of deviant drinking and the rise of the disease concept of alcoholism. With its rise has come a clear example of the political rather than scientific contest that medicalization represents. It is to the origins of this development that we now turn.

## DEVIANT DRINKING AS DISEASE: HISTORICAL FOUNDATIONS*

The first systematic attempts to characterize chronic and disruptive intoxication as a sickness or disease emerge in the last decades of the 18th century in the United States and in England. We will be concerned with tracing the origins and meanings of such characterizations as they developed subsequently in the United States.

### Colonial period

Drinking in the American colonies in the 17th and particularly the 18th century was the norm. Although drunkenness was disapproved, it was far from rare (Keller, 1976; Lender, 1973; Levine, 1978; Paredes, 1976). If there were anything "bad" to be found in drinking, it certainly was not the drink itself. Such prominent Puritan clergy as Increase and Cotton Mather called alcohol a "good creature of God," and churches and drinking houses were often situated close to one another as social centers of the community. Most of the concern and social comment about public drunkenness in the colonies was expressed by a relatively small number of scholarly, aristocratic church leaders who warned against the sin of drunken excess. It is important to note that it was the excess—the responsibility for which rests with the drinker, not the drink—that concerned these church leaders. Such abuse of God's gift was sometimes attributed to the work of the Devil, and punishment for repeated drunkenness was consistent with the dominant institution of social control. Initially it was a clerical admonition, followed by more extreme sanctions such as suspension and, finally, excommunication as the ultimate, although probably infrequently used, religious control. Civil authorities affirmed the church's judgment and meted out various forms of public degradation, fines, ostracism, whippings, and imprisonment* (Lender, 1973).

The colonists, not unlike their ancestors and descendents, made a distinction between being drunk, or intoxicated, and "habitual" drunkenness. The latter not only made the drinker a public spectacle but had unmistakable negative consequences for self, family, and larger community. Historically, it is this pattern of repeated and highly consequential drunkenness that demands explanation. It is like a puzzle for observers that requires solution (MacAndrew, 1969). The particular solutions proposed for such puzzles reflect the dominant interests and ideologies of the time. More specifically, such solutions will also reflect the particular definitions and world view of specialists charged with providing such answers (Holzner, 1972, pp. 122-162). Toward the end of the colonial period, it was not the average citizen but the leading Puritan clergy—bolstered by those more well-placed members of the community who feared the spectre of the hostile, drunken "masses"—who were such specialists and who were most concerned about drunkenness.

The religious heritage of the 17th and 18th centuries defined drinking (and all forms of behavior) as a consequence of the actor's free will. It was assumed that people behaved as they did because of the enjoyment and profit derived and that they avoided things unpleasant and detrimental. Being drunk, according to this hedonistic view, was the result of free choice. This free-will philosophy is also apparent in the roots of classical criminology (see Chapter 8);

---

*The remainder of this chapter is a considerably expanded and altered version of "From deviant drinking to disease: alcoholism as a social accomplishment" (Schneider, 1978). © The Society for the Study of Social Problems.

*These drunkenness laws were not uniformly or consistently enforced in early New England but were likely to vary in their application by individual, context, and governmental unit involved (Lender, 1973). This selective enforcement of such laws has a long and continuing history. Jacqueline Wiseman (1970), in a study of skid row in a modern American city, found a similar pattern of selective and differential enforcement.

people broke laws not by accident but by intent. One of the most eloquent spokesmen for this free-will philosophy was Jonathan Edwards. In his 1754 work, *Freedom of the Will,* he argued:

> It cannot be truly said, according to the ordinary use of the language, that a malicious man . . . cannot hold his hand from striking, or that he is not able to show his neighbor kindness; or that a drunkard, let his appetite be never so strong, cannot keep the cup from his mouth. In the strictest propriety of speech, a man has a thing in his power, if he has it in his choice or at his election. . . . Therefore, in these things, to ascribe a nonperformance to the want of power or ability, is not just. (Quoted in Levine, 1978, p. 150)

Colonial religious thought, however, did allow that those who were repeatedly drunk and incapacitated probably suffered from some kind of moral degeneration. Although the idea that such drunkards might be insane did exist in Europe at about this same time, the prevailing religious and social values of the New World were inhospitable to such a notion (Wilkerson, 1966).

The Puritan free-will doctrine is also at odds with the drug-centered perspective typical of the uncontested medical model of alcohol; indeed, it provides perhaps the clearest example of an explicitly moral paradigm on deviant drinking. It was to give way to a new, decidely medical point of view toward the end of the 18th century. Although both this moral view and the emerging medical views on chronic drunkenness were individualistic, the shift in the "ownership" (Gusfield, 1975) of chronic drinking problems incorporated decidedly new definitions of the drunkard and how he or she should be treated.

## The disease of inebriety and the concept of alcohol addiction

The idea that chronic drunkenness should be considered evidence of a distinct disease entity was first synthesized and championed by none other than Benjamin Rush, the man we have called "the father of the medicalization of deviance." In his *An Inquiry Into the Effects of Ardent Spirits Upon the Body and Mind,* first published in 1785, Rush catalogued bodily and behavioral effects of alcohol and distilled spirits and provided a thorough and systematic clinical picture of intoxication. Appended to the 1790 edition of this classic is what Rush called "A Moral and Physical Thermometer" (Fig. 2) gauging these effects and the decline from temperance to intemperance with the increasing strength of the alcoholic beverage. Most important, Rush argued that those who apparently had "lost control" over their drinking—all of whom presumably were drinkers of distilled alcohol—suffered from the "disease of inebriety." The list of symptoms of "this odious disease" provides insight into the deviant behavior involved: unusual garrulity and silence, a disposition to quarrel, uncommon good humor and insipid simpering or laughing, profane swearing or cursing, disclosing secrets, rudeness, immodesty (especially in women), the "clipping of words" in speaking, fighting, a swelled nose or black eye, and extravagant acts indicating "a temporary fit of madness" (Rush, 1785/1943, pp. 325-336). Rush also enumerated signs of madness linked to inebriety: "singing, hallooing, roaring, imitating the noises of brute animals, jumping, tearing off clothes, dancing naked, breaking glasses and china and dashing other articles of household furniture upon the ground, or floor" (p. 326). This idea that repeated drunkenness and associated deviant behaviors were a form of mental disease was more specifically elaborated at about this same time by Thomas Trotter, an English physician. Trotter's treatise on inebriety was written in 1788 as partial requirement for a medical degree at the University of Edinburgh and was published subsequently in 1804 as *Essay, Medical, Philosophical and Chemical, on Drunkenness.*

The most significant element common to both Rush's and Trotter's descriptions of inebriety was their identification of the connection between drinker and drink as an "addiction" to spiritous or distilled liquors. Rush believed that this addiction developed gradually and was progressive. The initial drinking behavior was not abnormal, but over time, drinking substantial amounts of distilled alcoholic beverages led to the diseased state. This stage was the disease inebriety in which the drinker no longer

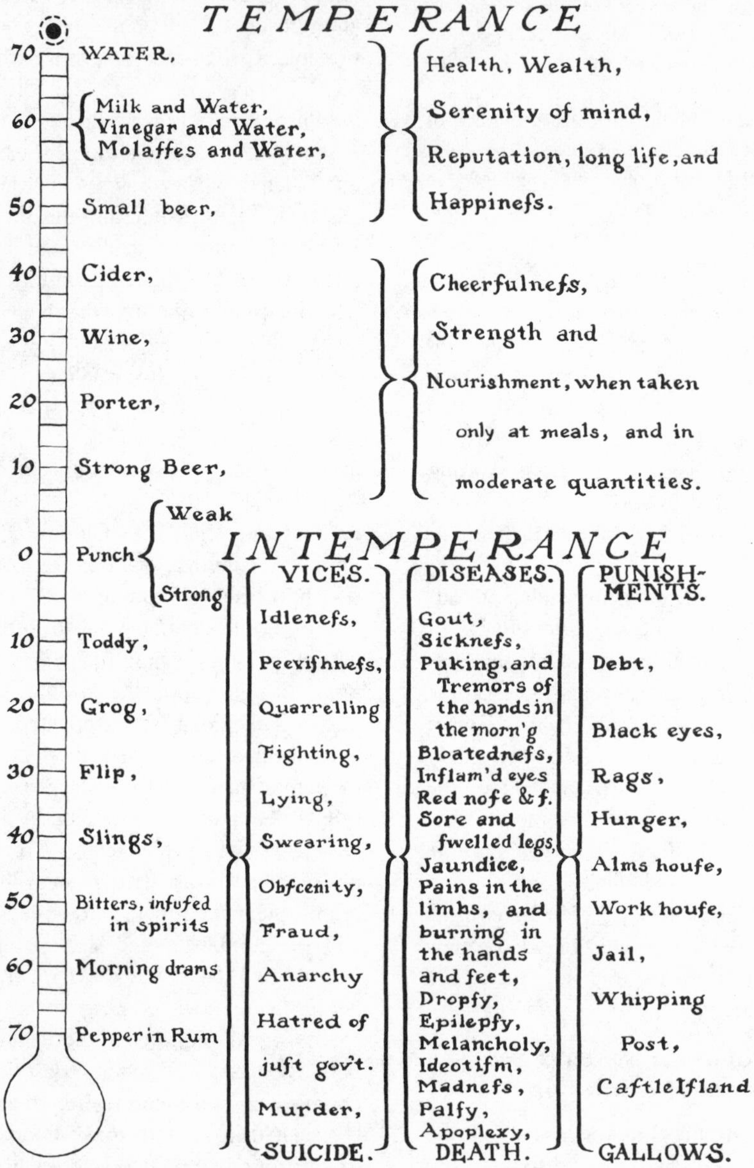


**Fig. 2.** Benjamin Rush's conceptualization of the effects of alcohol and distilled spirits on the body and mind. (From Rush, *An inquiry into the effects of ardent spirits upon the body and mind*, Boston, 1790, Thomas & Andrews.)

had control over drinking itself; in short, the drinker had become addicted. Rush called inebriety a ''disease of the will,'' based on the then popular assumption that one's ''will'' and ''desire'' were quite distinct. It was one's will that became weakened and ultimately debilitated by successive bouts of heavy drinking of spirits. Trotter's view of inebrity was somewhat less philosophical and more psychiatric. He argued specifically that ''the habit of drunkenness is a disease of the mind'' and advised his fellow physicians in their treatment of such persons:

> This disease, I mean the habit of drunkenness, is like some other mental derangements; there is an ascendancy to be gained over the person committed to our care, which, when accomplished, brings him entirely under our control. (Trotter, 1804/1941, pp. 586-587)

Both Rush and Trotter, however, were committed to the notion that the disease of inebriety had physical dimensions that distinguished it from certain more ''purely'' mental conditions. The last words of Rush's title, ''on the body and mind,'' announce this conception of alcohol addiction as both a mental and physiological state. Both these physician-founders of the disease concept of deviant drinking held that the first and foremost step in treatment was abstinence from all alcoholic drink. Incidentally, it is this prescription, along with Rush's general skepticism about the wisdom of drinking distilled spirits, that has led some to identify Rush and his American physician colleagues as the ''physicians' temperance movement'' (Wilkerson, 1966).

Although Rush did not elaborate the specific mechanisms or process through which this ''disease of the will'' developed, his ideas did provide an alternate explanation to the traditional moral account offered by colonial religious leaders. In an attempt to shed new light on the puzzle of habitual drunkenness, Rush and Trotter, along with a few English and European medical colleagues such as John Lettsom, Thomas Sutton, and Magnus Huss (Keller, 1966), adopted a scientific approach. They even avoided the traditional moral language used to describe the connection between drink and drunkard; the notion of ''love'' of drink was supplanted by such physiological-sounding terms as ''craving'' and ''insatiable desire'' (Levine, 1978).

This emerging medical and scientific conceptualization of chronic drunkenness as addiction had important and complicating implications for assigning blame and responsibility for the deviant behaviors often associated with such drinking. If such persons are not willful in their drunkenness, as was previously thought, then to punish them for it and various attendant wrongdoing is contrary to classic notions of justice (Platt, A., & Diamond, 1966). Unclarified, however, was at what point the inebriate becomes irresponsible, or ''loses control.'' Rush was willing to grant that initial drinking was willful but argued that ultimately, through the process of addiction, it became something in which the drinker had no choice. This issue of the determination of responsibility for drunkenness among those identified medically as ''inebriates,'' ''dipsomaniacs,'' and later, ''alcoholics'' remains a point of legal contention (Fingarette, 1970).

Aside from the question of legal responsibility for drinking-associated deviance, this early conception of alcohol addiction was consistent with a developing trend whereby various categories of wrongdoers and deviants were redefined from willful and vicious to helpless and sick. Although such individuals could certainly be incarcerated and punished in the alleged interest of community welfare, more and more they were defined as victims of various illnesses and diseases and subjected to treatment and therapy. This is part of what has been called the ''divestment'' from the criminal justice system of traditional categories of offenders and the rise of the ''therapeutic state'' (Kittrie, 1971; Rieff, 1966; Szasz, 1970). The ideas of Benjamin Rush that common drunkards suffered from a disease that incapacitated their will to avoid drink and that they should therefore be treated as patients rather than criminals represents the symbolic beginning of this divestment process for habitual deviant drinking behavior in America. Paradoxically it was the growing American temperance movement, with its moral theme of abstinence and, ultimately, of prohibition, that popularized the idea that inebriety was indeed a sickness or disease.

## DISEASE CONCEPT AND THE AMERICAN TEMPERANCE MOVEMENT

The definition or identification of chronic intoxication as a disease was attractive to those who urged control and reason—temperance—in drinking behavior (Levine, 1978). Although support of the disease view became less common with the rise of a more specifically prohibitionist stance after about 1870 (Gusfield, 1963), the social movement for temperance drew on and used the developing medical model of alcohol in two important ways.

### An enemy and a weapon: disease and abstinence

First, the clinical descriptions of physiological effects of alcohol and intoxication available toward the end of the 18th century provided temperance reformers with compelling evidence against the use of distilled spirits. As Rush's comments and his ''moral thermometer'' suggest, these ''medical'' descriptions went well beyond physiological effects and included a wide range of deviant behaviors believed to be caused by drink. Such characterizations reiterated the disinhibitor hypothesis and became highly useful grist for the temperance mill. These ''medical facts'' of alcohol were early popularized for temperance purposes by the French-American Quaker reformer, Anthony Benezet (Krout, 1925, pp. 64-66). Benezet became aware of the problems associated with repeated use of distilled spirits through his welfare work with the American Indians. Shocked by what he had seen, Benezet began to take note of similar kinds of behaviors and effects of spirits among his peers. He published his observations in 1774 under the title *The Mighty Destroyer Displayed*. A few years later he distributed a pamphlet that drew together prominent medical opinion of the day on the effects of spirits on the body. Needless to say, the medical consensus was gloomy and thus served temperance interests well in supporting restrictions on strong drink. It was assumed that in the face of such esteemed knowledge on the physical and social perils of distilled alcohol, all rational moderate or temperate drinkers would be dissuaded effectively from excess.

A second important idea the ''temperance physicians'' (Wilkerson, 1966) provided the movement was the very statement that repeated intemperate drinking is itself a disease. The assumption that such behavior is direct evidence of disease rested (and continues to rest) on the belief that no rational person, ''in control'' of his or her will, would continue to drink after learning these facts. This idea, that ''inebriety is a disease,'' became a common theme of temperance literature and speeches until the final decades of the century. It was a widely shared part of the middle-class view of the perils of drinking.

The plausibility of this disease interpretation requires the decline or tempering of the free will argument we discussed earlier, along with an increased acceptance of the idea that people could be compelled to behave in certain ways by forces beyond their control; that, indeed, one's will, or ability to choose, and one's desire were independent (Levine, 1978). Demonic or spirit possession was a competing explanation that had become a less acceptable answer than it once had been. The apparently irrational nature of repeated intoxication, however, remained puzzling. An emerging medical science slowly began to suggest new solutions. Although certainly crude by contemporary standards, medicine attempted to account for suffering and pain in terms of natural laws in an ''objective'' rather than a mystical or transcendental fashion. The puzzle of habitual drunkenness began to be unraveled scientifically. Loss of control over one's body and self was assumed increasingly to be the result of a natural although still obscure disease process. Such an account brought some vague degree of understanding to the behavior itself as well as the ineffectiveness of traditional means of control. Theological and legal interventions had been unsuccessful because they were misguided. The problem was not seated in the soul or the free will, but rather somehow in the body and/or mind.

The identification of inebriety as a disease allowed temperance leaders to draw on a cultural universal. Disease, whatever it is defined technically to be, is undesirable; it should be opposed, controlled, and, if possible, eradicated. By logical extension, all known or suspicioned causes of such conditions should be approached similarly. Probably unintentionally, although Rush was a temperance supporter, the physicians who called inebriety a disease provided the movement with an evil perhaps more universal than sin itself. "Inebriety is a disease" became an important slogan of the temperance movement. "Intemperance," a term whose meaning is sufficiently broad to include even a single instance of intoxication, occasionally replaced inebriety in the slogan. Rush's and other physician's prescription of abstinence as the first and absolutely necessary step in treatment also was turned to temperance use as "the" solution for the problems associated with drinking. As a measure of the movement's appeal, the American Temperance Society reported that only 6 years after being founded in 1826, it could record over half a million people who had signed a public pledge of abstinence from all alcoholic beverages (Krout, 1925, p. 129). The use of the disease slogan and the abstinence prescription by temperance leaders to their own ends is a clear illustration of the rise and acceptance of ideas because of their political and ideological—indeed, their moral—appeal rather than their substantive or technical significance (Christie & Bruun, 1969; Gusfield, 1975).

An important consequence of temperance strategy was that the idea that inebriety is a disease was not evaluated critically as an intellectual or scientific claim during most of the 19th century. As a moral slogan, however, it allowed advocates to pity the sick inebriate who required treatment and support on the one hand and to rail against "Demon Rum," "King Alcohol" and so-called social, or moderate, drinking on the other. Joseph Gusfield (1963) documents the humanitarian factions of the movement that sought to exert an uplifting, ameliorative force in American society, such as the Washingtonian Movement, begun in 1840, and the larger and more powerful Women's Christian Temperance Union, founded in 1874. The temperance stance of sympathy toward the addicted inebriate and the growing demand for control of alcohol that increasingly typified the temperance movement during the 19th century reflected Rush's discussion of inebriety. He agreed that initial drinking was most likely an act of will and that the drinker, consequently, should be held responsible. Once the addictive process had begun, however, Rush believed the drinker could not control whether he or she took a drink or how much was drunk. Alcohol addiction was a condition to which all drinkers of alcohol could in principle fall victim (Levine, 1978). Even social or moderate drinking of spirits was, therefore, considered suspect and foolish.

## Rise of the inebriate asylum and the rush to Prohibition

A fascinating example of the congeniality of these middle-class temperance ideals and the disease concept is found in the rise and proliferation of inebriate asylums—special hospitals for chronic drunkards—during the middle and latter part of the 19th century. Partly as a result of the hostile reception chronic drunkards and severely intoxicated persons received at general hospitals and partly in an attempt to succeed where traditional institutions such as prisons, workhouses, and general and mental hospitals had failed, a small group of concerned physicians established "homes" and asylums. These were special places where inebriates could receive needed physical and, more important, moral care and supervision that temperance supporters believed essential to regenerate and support their defective wills, still believed to be at the heart of the disease itself.

An early plea for such facilities is found in an 1830 report of a committee of the Connecticut Medical Society. The committee concluded that separate institutions for inebriates were necessary, where such persons would

> be subjected to salutary discipline, and needful restraint. Where they shall have no access to intoxicating liquors . . . [and] be constantly and usefully employed. Where they shall not be contaminated by evil associates, and where they shall

> have no opportunity of exerting an unfavorable influence upon others. Where they shall receive whatever medical aid is necessary to restore their debilitated constitutions. . . . Where they shall receive the benefit of moral precepts, correct examples, and such instruction as will induce them permanently to abandon their former vicious courses. . . . Where . . . by an enlightened system of physical and moral treatment, they may be reformed; and whence, if reformed, they may be restored, welcome guests of their families, and useful members of society. (Quoted in Corwin & Cunningham, 1944, pp. 12-13)*

The committee continued, adding that the organization and arrangement of such facility ''must be entirely devoted to the cause of industry and temperance'' and that ''much of [its] success will depend upon the character of the person to whose charge it is entrusted.'' Finally, committee members anticipated some slight legal obstacle that would need to be overcome for this interesting form of medical social control to be realized:

> The only serious objection to the success of such a scheme is that it will require a slight modification of existing laws. Instead of sending a drunkard to a work-house for punishment, we would have him sent to an asylum for reformation; and instead of thirty days' confinement, we would require him to devote at least a year to the great and important work of reformation. (Quoted in Corwin & Cunningham, 1944, p. 13)*

The kind of moral therapy the committee proposed was not original in their 1830 report. We noted in Chapter 3 that persons believed to be insane were regularly subjected to such moral treatment in European and American asylums after the turn of the 19th century. The focus of these treatments was the patients' moral and mental rather than their physical constitutions. The Connecticut committee's reference to the inebriate's ''reform'' signals this image of the kind of disease involved. Finally, as we have argued, such medical treatment is also a clear form of social control. The medical directors of the asylums became the ''keepers'' of inebriety. Not only did the state support commitment to ''medical'' asylums rather than to workhouses but also such ''therapy'' required a much longer ''sentence.'' The prisonlike quality of some of these hospitals is evidenced by the barred windows, locked doors, and searches of patient rooms typical of the New York State Inebriate Asylum at Binghamton, opened in 1858 (Corwin & Cunningham, 1944, pp. 15-16). The New York State institution was the first bona fide special hospital for inebriates, although the famed Washingtonian Home in Boston had been established almost 10 years before, in 1857. The popularity of this medical-moral solution to chronic drunkenness was great, and by 1900 there were more than 50 such special facilities operating in the United States (Wilkerson, 1966, pp. 142-151).

These hospitals for inebriates were, however, not received with universal enthusiasm among either temperance leaders or the medical community. The asylums were even more controversial in those states where laws were passed to divert liquor or general tax revenues to their support (Corwin & Cunningham, 1944; Jellinek, 1960). Temperance leaders toward the latter decades of the century became more and more skeptical about the potentially ''soft'' and tolerant attitudes of asylum officials toward alcohol. It was not until the superintendent-physicians formed an association dedicated specifically to the proposition that inebriety, although a disease, was caused by sinful indulgence in drink that temperance forces adopted a more supportive posture. In response, the National Temperance Society, the coordinator of temperance action, issued its reserved endorsement in 1872, in which their priorities were clear: ''The Temperance press has always regarded drunkenness as a sin and a disease—a sin first, then a disease; and we rejoice that the Inebriate Association are [sic] now on the same platform'' (quoted in Levine, 1978, p. 157).

This same association of physician-superintendents, along with a small number of interested colleagues, began publishing a journal based on the premise that inebriety is a disease. It was called *The Journal of Inebriety,* and the

---

*Reprinted by permission from *Quarterly Journal of Studies on Alcohol,* Vol. 5, pp. 9-85, 1944. Copyright by Journal of Studies on Alcohol, Inc., New Brunswick, N.J. 08903

first issue appeared in 1876, continuing on a limited and precarious basis until 1914. Its approach was distinctly psychiatric and dedicated to promoting the idea that "inebriety is a neurosis and psychosis and that alcohol is both an exciting and contributing cause as well as a symptom of conditions that existed before" (Crothers, 1911). Not surprisingly, the *Journal* contributed to the idea that inebriety is a special kind of mental illness involving alcohol, but the clarity of such formulations barely went beyond that assertion. The question of whether such behavior is a symptom of a psychiatric condition and hence less intrinsically important, or whether it is itself a disease condition continues to divide the medical and treatment communities. The preference of the editors and authors in the *Journal* appears to have been the former. E. M. Jellinek (1960) quotes one of the leading students of this early 20th-century disease concept to illustrate the moral and intellectual confusion surrounding this work:

> I have . . . contended that inebriety is a condition of nervous weakness on which is engrafted a habit. This conception of the condition seems to me to qualify the assertion that inebriety is a disease. While calling it a "disease" we do not by accepting such a definition imply that the inebriate is irresponsible. (p. 5)

Neither the journal nor its parent association received the support of the psychiatric community or medical profession at large. There was a small group of citizens who took an interest in their work, but public opinion ranged from skeptical to negative, particularly about the public financial support and the suspicion that such efforts were attempts to excuse vice and crime (Jellinek, 1960, pp. 2-7).

The medical profession's unenthusiastic reception of these inebriate specialists may be seen as a result of the relatively low scientific quality of their work. We suggest, however, that a good part of this skepticism and hostility was due to political and social considerations. Such analysis focuses our attention on the relatively low stature of psychiatry in the hierarchy of American medicine, the moral stigma attached to working with and in support of heavy drinkers and inebriates, the political controversy surrounding the inebriate hospitals, and the then less-than-revered position of the medical profession in general in the public consciousness. Indeed, many of these considerations provide rare insight into understanding the history and present status of the debate as to whether alcoholism is "really" an illness. Regardless of the scientific quality of the work, these late 19th-century conditions would seem to have precluded both professional and popular acceptance of such ideas. Acceptance of the disease concept turns not on its validity but rather its viability (Spector & Kitsuse, 1977).

By the turn of the century, prohibition advocates had been able to focus attention on legal controls as the only solution to the alcohol problem. The temperance movement became the "antialcohol movement," and the disease concept of inebriety (or alcoholism, as it was then occasionally called) was an issue too technical and esoteric to warrant serious attention. Many of the social, economic, and political changes ushered in with the first decades of the new century made alcohol and its "disinhibiting" effects appear even more threatening to a smoothly running social order, and these dimensions of drinking behavior became most salient. With the passage of the Eighteenth, or Prohibition, Amendment in 1919, drinking, drunkenness, and habitual drunkenness or inebriety did not cease but became illegal for the next 13 years. This symbolic victory of temperance forces (Gusfield, 1963) effectively chilled debate and work on the disease concept for more than a decade.

## POST-PROHIBITION REDISCOVERY: THE YALE CENTER, ALCOHOLICS ANONYMOUS, AND THE JELLINEK FORMULATION

Although there was virtually no organized successful support of the disease concept from the end of the 19th century until after Prohibition (Gusfield, 1975), there was a good deal of interest and development in science and the professionalization of scientific research in American universities (Ben-David, 1971, pp. 139 and 168). At roughly the same time that the moral crusade against alcohol was waning, science and scientific work were becoming established. This was to have a great impact on the kinds of solutions Americans would suggest for a variety of problems. Since after 1933 alcohol was again legal and popular, it was not likely to be defined as the primary source of deviant drinking behavior. Intoxication and drunkenness, when they were deemed disruptive, were problems assigned to civil authorities or the state. But the chronically drunk person remained a puzzle.

In this context, even more than at Rush's time, science and medicine seemed to hold the promise. Three developments, all beginning within a decade after Repeal, provide the foundation on which this renewed medical conceptualization of chronic drunkenness behavior was to rise during the middle years of the 20th century: the Yale research center; the self-help group Alcoholics Anonymous; and a new medical specification of what it means to say "alcoholism is a disease."

## Yale Research Center of Alcohol Studies

The major body coordinating support for scientific work on alcohol problems in the mid-1930s was the Research Council on Problems of Alcohol, established shortly after Repeal (Keller, 1976b). The council was comprised disproportionately of physicians and natural scientists and apparently had grown out of some medical research in progress at Bellevue Hospital in New York City. The group was interested particularly in studying the causes of alcoholism as an important social and personal problem. One member of the committee was Howard Haggard, the physician-director of the Laboratory of Applied Physiology at Yale University. Although the council was unsuccessful in raising significant sums of money for alcohol research, the stature of its individual members did establish such work as scientifically respectable. One grant of financial support, however, was consequential. It was for a review of the scientific literature on the biological effects of alcohol on humans. The council called on E. M. Jellinek, who had been doing research on neuroendocrine schizophrenia, to administer the project.

Haggard and his colleagues at the Yale laboratory were involved in alcohol metabolism and nutritional research—studying the physiological and chemical effects of alcohol on the body. As this work at Yale became increasingly interdisciplinary within the natural sciences, Haggard became convinced that the proper study of such problems required an even more comprehensive approach. He invited Jellinek to come to Yale as director of a multidisciplinary Center of Alcohol Studies. The physiological research at Yale and the broadened approach to alcohol studies were communicated through *The Quarterly Journal of Studies on Alcohol,* founded in 1940 by Haggard. This journal, which in 1975 became *The Journal of Studies on Alcohol,* is perhaps the key international publication on alcohol research, its tenure of continuous publication being second only to *The British Journal of Addiction,* which began publication in 1892 as *The British Journal of Inebriety.* The Yale center, its journal, and the laboratory quickly became the intellectual core of American research on alcohol. The center continued successfully at Yale until 1962, at which time it was moved to Rutgers University in New Jersey, where it remains one of the most prestigious of a small number of such research centers in the world.*

One of the center's most significant early contributions to the idea that alcoholism is a disease was its summer school program, begun in 1943. These annual sessions were organized as educational programs for concerned citizens involved in policy formulation in their local communities throughout the country. A common concern was what to do about "alcoholism" and alcohol-related problems. Robert Straus (1976) and Morris Chafetz and Harold Demone (1962) suggest that the slogan "alcoholism is a disease" was introduced intentionally by center staff at these summer sessions in an

*Robert Straus (1976) provides some fascinating insight into the social and political history leading up to this move. He suggests that the wide publicity the Yale center received in its early days was an embarrassment to that university because of the substance of its work, and that the interdisciplinary quality of the center was perceived as inappropriate in the context of the traditional departmental structure of the university.

attempt to reorient and "de-moralize" local and state government policy and popular thinking about people with drinking problems. This idea was not introduced to stimulate scientific or technical discussions at these summer school sessions. Rather, the school was seen more as providing a good opportunity to disseminate the idea and point out its practical moral and political implications for treatment and cure. Although only a small segment of the total summer program was devoted to the disease question, it was an idea supported by both Haggard and Jellinek and soon became a topic of considerable interest among the lay audience.

The appeal of this idea that alcoholism is a disease requiring treatment rather than a sin or crime calling for punishment must be understood both in terms of the specific history of collective definitions of chronic drunkenness and the politics of medicalization in general. Not only did the idea that chronic drunkenness might be a disease offer a plausible solution to the apparent irrationality of such behavior—a solution which, incidentally, the legalistic approach represented by Prohibition and subsequent drunkenness laws does not address—but also it was morally and politically appealing in the increasingly therapeutic and treatment-oriented context of the American criminal justice system (Kittrie, 1971). Not only would the courts and jails be relieved of a large and growing burden of cases involving alcohol (the most common arrest of all those made by police), but also these and other officials would be freed from the morally objectionable position of righteous indignation and condemnation typical of pre-Prohibition reactions to drunkenness. As the chronic drunkard becomes the "alcoholic," a sick person, those charged with control cease, at least overtly, to be moral crusaders and become humanitarian guardians, responsible for healing and recovery rather than reform. Finally, as Harrison Trice and Paul Roman (1972) suggest, this conception of chronic drunkenness as disease calls forth the development of a virtual "industry" of professional and lay persons charged with the identification, treatment, counseling, and study of such persons. These "alcohologists" (Robinson, 1972; Room, 1972, 1976b) become clearly interested parties in perpetuating and expanding this growing number of organizations, both public and private, dedicated to the diagnosis and treatment of alcoholism.

The Yale center provided the prototype for such diagnosis in 1944 with the establishment of the Yale Plan Clinics (Jellinek, 1943). These clinics were intended as facilities where deviant drinkers could come for help with their drinking problems. The Yale Plan Clinics were established as bona fide interdisciplinary but clearly medical facilities staffed by clinical personnel who could accurately refer patients to the existing treatment facilities in the community. One of the objects of these clinics was to "serve as experimental models for the development of future large-scale procedures." The realization of this goal is seen most clearly in the recent phenomenal rise of the federal bureaucracy established in 1971 to combat "alcohol abuse and alcoholism," The National Institute of Alcohol Abuse and Alcoholism (NIAAA). In a short time NIAAA has developed an annual budget of nearly $170 million, the largest single portion of which goes to local centers for the diagnosis, treatment, and rehabilitation of persons identified as alcoholics. Calling alcoholism "the third greatest health problem in this country," a past director of the Institute, physician Ernest P. Noble, identified bringing "the treatment of alcoholism into the mainstream of our nation's health care delivery system" to be "a central purpose and goal" of NIAAA.

Finally, the Yale center, and especially the early summer sessions, provided a fertile organizational foundation for growth of the National Council on Alcoholism (NCA), a middle-class, voluntary association premised both on the validity and viability of the disease concept (Chafetz & Demone, 1962; Paredes, 1976). The NCA, known initially as the National Committee for Education on Alcoholism, was established in 1944 as a direct result of the efforts of three women: a former alcoholic, a journalist, and a psychiatrist. Mrs. Marty Mann, who had been a member of Alcoholics Anonymous, saw the National Committee as supplementing the work of that organization in terms of public education and organization. In the spring of 1944 these women met with Jellinek, and they decided that the National Committee "plan" should be introduced in the Yale summer school program. At the time of the original incorporation of the National Committee in 1944, its close connection with the Yale center was evidenced by the committee's officers: Dr. Howard Haggard was named president; E. M. Jellinek was chairman of the board; Professor Selden Bacon of Yale was secretary; and Professor Edward Baird, also of Yale, was the committee's legal counsel (Chafetz & Demone, 1962, p. 141). Although the NCA became organizationally independent of the prestigious and influential Yale center in 1950, the association was favorable for the idea that alcoholism is a disease. The extent to which the NCA itself helped to carry this slogan is suggested by Chafetz and Demone (1962):

> NCA then began to search for a formula, something which would translate the basic facts of alcoholism into easily understood and remembered phrases. This resulted in the well known concepts or credo: Alcoholism is a disease and the alcoholic a sick person. The alcoholic can be helped and is worth helping. This is a public health problem and therefore a public responsibility. (p. 142)*

The NCA remains today, through its national office and many local affiliates throughout the United States, perhaps the most forceful nonpublic voice supporting the idea that alcoholism is a disease. In 1972 it published the widely cited and used "Criteria for the Diagnosis of Alcoholism" in *The American Journal of Psychiatry*. These diagnostic criteria, including physiological, behavioral, and psychiatric components, were created by a blue-ribbon committee of physicians organized and supported by the National Council for this task. The promulgation of such medical guidelines obviously is premised on the disease definition of at least certain forms of deviant drinking. They encourage physicians and other clinical health workers to adopt this general definition and the specific guides. Considering the ambiguity and skepticism in medical settings surrounding the notion of alcoholism, such diagnostic criteria provide practical answers to the everyday diagnostic problems clinicians face. It is not surprising that they have been adopted widely.

### Alcoholics Anonymous

A second post-Prohibition development crucially important for the viability of the idea that alcoholism is a disease was the founding and subsequent growth of the self-help organization, Alcoholics Anonymous. AA, as it came to be known, was begun in 1935 by two men, a stockbroker and a physician, who considered themselves among the chronically intoxicated. It was premised on the idea that such individuals could help themselves and others like them to achieve sobriety by developing a supportive, open, frank, and spiritual fellowship committed primarily to that end. The collective and religious nature of the AA program was inherited directly from its early ties with the Oxford Group, a religious movement that flourished briefly during the 1930s and was characterized by "small discussion groups . . . confessions, honesty, talking out of emotional problems, unselfishness, and praying to God as personally conceived" (Trice, 1958). One of the founders of AA, Bill W.* had himself experienced a "spiritual awakening" (Alcoholics Anonymous, 1957, p. 63) through his exposure to an Oxford Group's fellowship. He believed this spiritual experience, in which he submitted himself to a "power greater than myself," was the key to gaining control over drinking and remaining sober.

Bill W., during his many trips to the hospital for emergency treatment of severe intoxication, had been treated by a sympathetic and interested psychiatrist, Dr. W. D. Silkworth. Through the support of Dr. Silkworth and his own observations and reading, Bill W. became convinced that such therapeutic insight could come only after the drinker's life had become virtually devastated and deflated by drink—only after he or she had "hit bottom." Anxious to carry this

*The principles comprising this ideology had been stated earlier by Dwight Anderson (1942), director of public relations for the New York State Medical Society, and subsequently the first public relations director of the NCA.

*Consistent with the tenet of selflessness, anonymity is a fundamental principle espoused and followed by AA members. Only first names are used to identify persons in AA publications, materials, and meetings.

message to others with similar experiences, he engaged in a brief campaign to convert those he believed ready for such insight. After a series of failures to reach his fellow drinkers, Bill W. was given some consequently important advice by his friend Dr. Silkworth (Alcoholics Anonymous, 1957):

> You're having nothing but failure because you are preaching at these alcoholics. You are talking to them about the Oxford Group precepts of being absolutely honest, absolutely pure, absolutely unselfish, and absolutely loving. This is a very big order. Then you top it off by harping on this mysterious spiritual experience of yours. . . . Why don't you turn your strategy the other way around? . . . You've got to deflate these people first. So give them the medical business, and give it to them hard. Pour it right into them about the obsession that condemns them to drink and the physical sensitivity or allergy of the body that condemns them to go mad or die if they keep on drinking. (pp. 67-68)*

Silkworth and Bill W. agreed that only then would the spiritual principles borrowed from the Oxford Groups be effective in giving guidance and strength to gain control over alcohol.

This notion of an obsessive craving for alcohol linked to a physical allergy to this drug became the fundamental proposition on which the AA program developed, both in terms of self-help and education. Many Americans, both lay and professional, see alcoholism through these AA ideas and principles. The themes that alcoholism is a disease and alcoholics are sick people run through all AA publications and speeches. The proposition that this condition rests on an *allergy* to alcohol occupies a central, if sometimes implicit, place in AA ideology. Although medical opinion on this assertion was then skeptical and subsequent research has failed to support it (Jellinek, 1960, pp. 86-88), the idea that chronic drunkenness is a mark of physiological sensitivity rather than moral degeneration was appealing both to such drinkers and those charged with their care. As Dr. Silkworth suggested to Bill W., giving these drinkers "the medical business" was apparently an effective way to prepare them for the spiritual message AA provides. To convince such drinkers that they are sick and, in fact, dying is to impress on them the gravity of their condition, quite aside, it appeared, from any questions of morality. From the first, the only hope for triumph over this disease was to stop drinking forever. Abstinence from all alcoholic beverages became the logical first step in freeing oneself from the devastating effects of the alcohol allergy. The AA slogans, "Once an alcoholic, always an alcoholic" and "One drink away from a drunk," were learned by all members and the general public alike as factual descriptions of alcoholism and alcoholics. Decades of testimonials and impassioned "stories" have cemented this prescription of abstinence firmly at the heart of AA ideology and treatment. It is an absolutely nonnegotiable proposition among AA faithful, including the leaders and founders of the NCA (Mann, 1958).

The physical allergy conception of the disease concept offered an advantage over competing definitions of such drinking behavior as primarily a type of mental illness or psychiatric condition. Although AA ideology agrees that a *compulsion* to drink drives the alcoholic, it rejects the notion that such drinking behavior is merely a manifestation of an underlying psychiatric or mental problem (Cahn, 1970, pp. 139-144; Trice & Roman, 1970). This leads AA members to take a dim view of psychotherapy in the treatment of alcoholism. In addition, AA ideology has generally opposed the use of drugs in treatment, insisting on the importance of the spiritual awakening or experience as an alternate and preferable way for alcoholics to gain control.

The allergy metaphor identifies alcoholism as a bona fide medical or "disease" condition. This in effect legitimizes the medical definition of such drinkers as "sick"; people with allergies are seen as victims who are not held responsible for their conditions. The concept of a purely mental illness or sickness has never held quite the degree of legitimacy or medical stature of physiologically based pathological conditions. Moral stigma and questions of blame and responsibility cling to problems defined primarily or wholly as emotional. Trice and Roman (1970) suggest that a good deal of

---

*From *Alcoholics Anonymous Comes of Age,* copyright © 1957 by Alcoholics Anonymous World Services, Inc. Reprinted by permission of AA World Services, Inc.

the apparent success of AA as a means to sobriety involves the process of removing such stigmatized or negative labels from the drinker and relabeling the person with more socially acceptable identities such as "sick," "repentant," "recovered," and "controlled."

This process of recovery that has come to represent the essence of the AA program was first codified in 1938 and published a year later in the famous book *Alcoholics Anonymous* (1939, pp. 71-72), a compilation of individuals' own life stories of their drinking and how AA helped them stop. It centers around the well-known "twelve steps" toward recovery. Two themes particularly relevant to the AA disease concept are found in the first and third steps. Prior to all else, and derived directly from Bill W.'s spiritual experience and Dr. Silkworth's suggestion, the first step reads: "We admitted we were powerless over alcohol—that our lives had become unmanageable." This is precisely the concept "loss of control," a description of repeated intoxication that has been at the center of the developing disease concept since Rush's writing over 150 years ago. It is, of course, consistent with the conception of alcoholism as a sickness.

The third AA step to recovery requires one to have "made a decision to turn our will and our lives over to the care of God *as we understood Him*." The question of just how religious AA should be has always been somewhat controversial among its members. In an attempt to broaden its appeal to include virtually all spiritual experience, leaders were quick to point out that although the language of these steps sounds traditionally religious, such terms as "God" are to be interpreted loosely and on the basis of the individual's own spiritual biography. Attesting to the scope of this interpretation, John L. Norris (1976), chairman of the board of AA, says:

> This turning over of self direction is akin perhaps to the acceptance of a regimen prescribed by a physician for a disease. The decision is made to accept reality, to stop trying to run things, and to let the "Power greater than ourselves" take over. (p. 740)

This description of the AA role is clearly reminiscent of Parsons' (1951) discussion of the sick role. Norris' suggestion that "God" might be interpreted to be a physician is perhaps not an extreme exaggeration in terms of the latter's control over the legitimacy of sickness and disease designation and admission to treatment.

The success attributed to the AA program in helping drinkers recover from alcoholism has become part of popular wisdom, generally unchallenged even though no comparative, systematically collected empirical evidence appears to be available. The effect of AA programs and ideology on thinking about alcoholism has been humanitarian and educational, and the generally high regard in which it is held in local communities throughout the country serves to reinforce the disease concept implied in its program. This high regard is evidenced by recent research on a sample of physicians. A majority of those agreeing that alcoholism is a disease believed that referring drinkers to AA was the best professional strategy (Jones & Helrich, 1972). An additional interpretation of these results, and one not without support, is that such an attitude serves to free the physician from what is often considered the bothersome responsibility of treating the chronically intoxicated.

### Jellinek formulation

The Yale center and AA contributed importantly to the spread and popularization of the disease concept. It is, however, in the work of E. M. Jellinek, early director of the Yale center, and later in the writing of his associate, Mark Keller, that the disease concept was defined unequivocally as alcohol addiction. The extent to which the assertion that alcoholism is a disease gained scientific credibility at about midcentury probably rests on the work of Jellinek and his associates at Yale. This formulation codified the various meanings of the disease concept as it had developed over the previous century and a half. Its major author, Jellinek, was already a known and established medical researcher before his arrival at Yale. This, coupled with his position as director of that prestigious university's alcohol research center, established his work as prima facie worthy of serious consideration. Short of perhaps Howard Haggard, no one of Jellinek's stature since Rush had chosen to address this question at such length.

Jellinek set out his understanding of what it means to call alcoholism a disease in a series of articles begun shortly after his arrival in New Haven, culminating in a comprehensive and widely cited manuscript, *The Disease Concept of Alcoholism*. In an early paper in 1941 with psychiatrist Karl Bowman as first author, Jellinek resurrected the concept of alcoholism as an addiction to alcohol. A few years later, after persuing data from an AA questionnaire about alcoholics' drinking experiences, Jellinek (1946) constructed his well-known phase progression model of alcoholism. A revision and extension of this paper published in 1952 and titled "The Phases of Alcohol Addiction" had appeared intially under the auspices of the Alcoholism Subcommittee of the World Health Organization (1952), of which Jellinek was an influential and highly regarded member. Virtually all subsequent discussion of the idea that alcoholism is a progressive disease with relatively distinct phases and symptoms of increasing severity rests on this work by Jellinek.

This addictive process was said to occur in four major stages, identified by 43 specific symptoms (Fig. 3): the *prealcoholic* phase, marked by the decided increase of drinking to relieve tension and an increased tolerance to alcohol; the *prodromal* phase, initiated by "alcoholic palimpsests" or blackouts and punctuated by their regularity; the *crucial* phase, wherein loss of control over drinking begins, leading to personally disruptive consequences, rationalizations, nutritional neglect, and diminished sex drive; and, finally, the *chronic* phase, begun by prolonged periods of intoxication, alcoholic psychoses, a decrease in tolerance, obsessive drinking. Although the Criteria Committee of the National Council on Alcoholism (1972) does not cite Jellinek as a specific source of their ideas, their criteria for the diagnoses of alcoholism specifies "early," "middle," and "late" manifestations of the disease in terms of a number of identifiable behavioral symptoms. Physician Max Glatt (1970, 1974) specifically incorporated Jellinek's phases into his own description of alcohol addiction and recovery. He proposed a U-shaped chart, with the base of the U representing the familiar AA view of having to "hit bottom" before starting on the road to "rehabilitation." This chart has become an almost universal tool in alcoholism treatment centers throughout the world to describe the "natural history" of the disease.

That Jellinek "discovered" these phases of alcohol addiction in the AA data is not surpris-

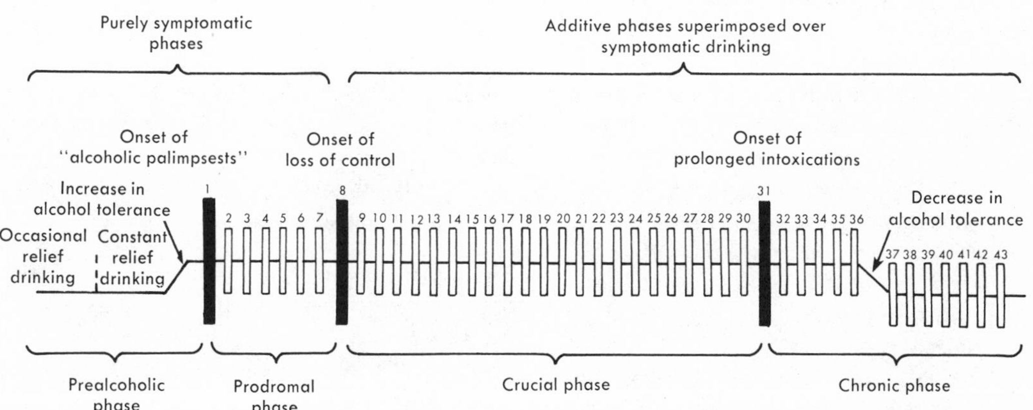


**Fig. 3.** Phases of alcohol addiciton. Large bars denote the onset of major symptoms which initiate phases. Short bars denote the onset of symptoms within a phase. Numbers above bars refer to the identities of the specific symptoms, which may be found in the original Jellinek article. (Reprinted by permission from Jellinek, E. M. Phases of alcohol addiction. *Alcohol*, 1952, *13*, 673-684. Copyright by Journal of Studies on Alcohol, Inc., New Brunswick, N.J. 08903.)

ing. Not unlike the discoveries of hyperactivity and child abuse discussed in Chapter 6. Jellinek's view of alcoholism as a progressive disease with definable phases is in part a product of the way he approached his data. The discovery of such diagnostic categories from a sociology-of-knowledge perspective can be seen as a product of the values, knowledge, and beliefs held by their discoverers. The progressive and increasingly severe phases Jellinek saw in the AA members' responses become then an almost inevitable consequence of the disease-addiction perspective he adopted at the outset.

The concept of disease, particularly when used in clinical settings, conveys an image of process and progression (Fabrega, 1972; Room, 1974). Jellinek's discovery of the phases of increasingly "implicative" drinking in AA members' responses (people already convinced of the disease nature of alcoholism) is reminiscent of Erving Goffman's (1961, p. 145) discussion of the "obvious" mental illness hospital staff sometimes see in case histories constructed for patients already diagnosed as mentally ill.

**Varieties of alcoholism: disease and non-disease types.** Another major purpose of the phase paper was to reiterate and clarify an important distinction central to the alcoholism-as-disease perspective. Drinking that results in problems of living, or "problem drinking," while important in its own right, had to be kept distinct from drinking that is to be called a disease. This distinction is most important to the viability of the disease view: first, because it serves to define the boundaries within which medicine could (and should, according to Jellinek) operate; second, it suggests that forms of deviant drinking not properly seen as diseases should be "managed only on the level of applied sociology, including law enforcement" (Jellinek, 1952). These nondisease forms of drinking behavior are thus defined as moral problems to be met on moral terms. Diseased drinking, suggests Jellinek, is rightfully a medical problem that deserves the serious attention of and treatment by the medical profession and public support for such treatment.

This long-time distinction between people who get drunk and "common drunkards," between someone who is acutely intoxicated and the "dipsomaniac" or "inebriate," between the social drinker who sometimes "goes too far" and the "alcoholic," identifies the latter as qualitatively rather than merely quantitatively different from the former. Alcoholism, then, becomes a particular kind of deviant drinking behavior. As sociologist Selden Bacon (1958) has suggested, "alcoholics don't drink." What Bacon means is that when we speak of alcoholism, inebriety, or chronic drunkenness, we refer to only a relatively small segment of so-called deviant drinking behavior. Disease concept advocates were interested in making a clear distinction between drinking that results in personal and even social problems (e.g., drunk driving. absenteeism on the job, etc.) and drinking that is alcoholic. The first type of drinking problem was believed to be primarily the product of "enough" alcohol—anyone could get drunk and become "disinhibited" or irresponsible. It was, however, the latter set of drinking symptoms—repetitive, highly consequential, impervious to all pleas of both emotion and reason—that was to be given the label "alcoholism." In his phase paper and subsequent work Jellinek sought to reaffirm, once and for all, these important distinctions.

Jellinek argued that there are two subcategories of alcoholics: "alcohol addicts" and "habitual symptomatic excessive drinkers." Although both kinds of drinkers have "underlying psychological or social pathology" that leads to drinking, only the alcohol addict, after a period of years of such drinking, develops a "loss of control" over drinking. Such persons, Jellinek argued, are addicted to alcohol (as evidenced by their loss of control) and are therefore clearly diseased. Jellinek (1952)* attempts to clarify this distinction:

> The disease conception of alcohol addiction does not apply to the excessive drinking, *but solely to the loss of control* which occurs in only one group of alcoholics and then only after many years of excessive drinking. (p. 674, emphasis added)

---

*Quotations from Jellinek (1952) reprinted by permission from *Quarterly Journal of Studies on Alcohol,* Vol. 13, pp. 673-684, 1952. Copyright by Journal of Studies on Alcohol, Inc., New Brunswick, N.J. 08903.

Anxious to separate drinkers who suffer primarily from an underlying psychiatric condition from those whose major affliction is the uncontrolled drinking itself, Jellinek (1952) continues:

> There is no intention to deny that the non-addictive alcoholic is a sick person; but his ailment is not the excessive drinking, but rather the psychological or social difficulties from which alcohol intoxication gives temporary surcease. (p. 674)

The precise nature (''psychopathological'' or a ''physical pathology'') of the addictive process detailed in his phase progression was unclear, but Jellinek (1952) believed that the ''fact that this loss of control does not occur in a large group of excessive drinkers would point toward a predisposing *X* factor in the addictive alcoholics'' (p. 674). Regardless of whether this factor were innate or acquired, such a view defines the source of drinking behavior to be an entity seated in the individual's body and/or mind.

This characterization of the disease of alcoholism as alcohol addiction causing a loss of control over drinking gave a renewed buoyancy to medical definitions of such drinking behavior. Similar to the physical allergy concept at the heart of AA ideology, Jellinek's discussion of addiction and loss of control rest on an assumption that these were, at bottom, physically based phenomena. Walking a careful line between his phychiatric and ''medical'' colleagues, Jellinek (1952) said loss of control means that ''any drinking of alcohol starts a chain reaction which is felt by the drinker as a physical demand for alcohol'' (p. 679). As to what holds the drinker to a pattern of continuing excessive drinking, Jellinek (1952) said that after

> recovery from the intoxication, it is not the loss of control—that is, the physical demand, apparent or real—which leads to a new bout of drinking. . . . The renewal of drinking is set off by the original psychological conflicts or by a simple social situation which involves drinking. (p. 680)

It is not, then, the loss of control that gives rise to new bouts of drinking. Once drinking is started, however, the drinker ''has lost the ability to control the quantity.'' The drinker retains, according to Jellinek, the ability to control whether he will begin to drink in any particular situation. Laying aside the AA emphasis on alcohol's triumph over the drinker's will, Jellinek says that such a notion deludes the addicted alcoholic into believing that it is possible to regain control over drinking by mastering his defective will. ''He is not aware,'' writes Jellinek (1952) ''that he has undergone a process which makes it impossible for him to control his alcohol intake'' (p. 680).

This physiological view of alcohol addiction and loss of control over drinking reflects the dominant, ''official'' view of addiction held at the time Jellinek developed his ideas. It was a conception influenced heavily by the American legal and medical experience with narcotics and opiates (discussed in the following chapter). Basic to this view of addiction were the physiological elements of increased bodily tolerance leading to increased intake (one must take more to get the same physical effects) and the development of a withdrawal syndrome at the end of a period of continued ''heavy'' drinking. The conventional understanding of how this physical inevitability of addiction operated was that the addicted person, somehow knowing automatically that he or she is addicted and must have continued amounts of the drug in question, is driven by this physical inevitability (''compulsion''?) and therefore cannot control his or her drinking. This is a clear example of the drug-centered model of drinking behavior in which the drug is portrayed as the ''cause'' of the deviance or, in this case, the sickness of addiction and loss of control. Ironically, it is the formulation of the disease concept as a physiologically based alcohol addiction that was the fertile soil in which subsequent and successful scientific attacks on these ideas were to grow.

The distinction between the disease and nondisease varieties of alcoholism in terms of addiction became the centerpiece of Jellinek's (1960) major work, *The Disease Concept of Alcoholism,* culminating nearly two decades of research and writing. This work is in some senses paradoxical. It provides an exhaustive and critical review of relevant previous research on the disease question; it contains a more careful classification of types of alcoholism, Jellinek's well-known Greek-letter typology; but it also offers a definition of alcoholism that mollifies considerably any clarifications achieved in other regards. Jellinek (1960), ignoring his own earlier caution against vague and inclusive definitions, calls alcoholism "any use of alcoholic beverages that causes any damage to the individual or the society or both" (p. 35). One could hardly imagine a more inclusive definition. Selden Bacon (1976) has documented such imprecise and careless conceptualization as common to alcohol studies, but it must have been particularly disconcerting for Jellinek's supporters and colleagues that the 20th-century master of the disease concept would have stepped so explicitly into this trap.

Definitional problems aside, Jellinek's (1960) Greek-letter typology of alcoholism did provide a clarifying foundation for future research and debate and an even stronger reiteration of the physical metaphor of addiction. He identified four major types: Alpha, Beta, Gamma, and Delta (pp. 36-39). *Alpha* is the ideal type of symptomatic drinking discussed in his 1952 essay; *Beta* refers specifically to all physical disease conditions resulting from prolonged substantial drinking, what we have called "medical consequences." Jellinek argues that only the *Gamma* and *Delta* types qualify as diseases. These two types share three elements in common: (1) acquired increased tissue tolerance to alcohol, (2) adaptive cell metabolism, and (3) withdrawal symptoms. These three conditions lead to "craving" or physical dependence on alcohol. In addition, Gamma alcoholics display a loss of control over how much is drunk, involving a progression from psychological to physiological dependence. Jellinek identifies this type as most typical of the United States, as causing the greatest personal and social damage, and as the type of alcoholism recognized by AA. Delta alcoholics differ from Gammas in that they show no loss of control over quantity of intake, but rather over the ability to abstain for any significant period of time. As a result, this type of alcoholic, while suffering from the disease of alcoholism, rarely experiences the devastating consequences of Gamma alcoholism and therefore presents a less urgent medical and social problem. Jellinek suggests that this drinking pattern is characteristic of certain European countries, particularly France.

As we noted earlier in this chapter, such disease conditions could not develop without alcohol drinking. Under the disease concept, however, the initial causes of such drinking are not seen as particularly important in understanding the disease entity itself. Stressful or ambivalent social and cultural environments and personal problems deemed important by social scientists* seeking to explain drinking behavior become only background information of little significance in distinguishing the addicted alcoholic from the problem or even "social" drinker. The key explanatory mechanism used to account for the puzzle of the apparently irrational behavior of the alcoholic drinker is the vague, almost mysterious, concept of addiction. Alcoholism (certain varieties, at least) is a disease because it is an addiction. Addiction involves the "loss of control" over drinking (equally mysterious), which is direct evidence of the existence of a disease. It is a person-specific, circular, and medical explanation for a pattern of deviant behavior.

**Challenge and defense: Mark Keller and the post-Jellinek era.** Since Jellinek's death in 1963 the leading advocate for the disease concept has been Mark Keller, a product of the Yale center and long-time associate of Jellinek, who has been influential in editing *The Journal of Studies on Alcohol* since its inception. Keller, widely considered an "expert" on alcohol studies, does not occupy the stature of Jellinek or Haggard. He is not a scientist by training, has no advanced degrees in any special field, is described respectfully by his associates as a "scholar's scholar" (Bacon, 1977), and is noted for his administrative and

*Edwin Lemert (1969) suggests that most traditional sociocultural theories of deviant drinking adopt a "symptomatic" approach. These theories—anomie, status deprivation, anxiety reduction, and ambivalence—define such drinking as a personal symptom of a prior social and cultural disturbance. They share with psychiatry a view of drinking primarily as an indicator of more important underlying problems. See Room (1976a) for a critical review of the highly popular sociological explanation that deviant drinking in the United States is caused by American social and cultural ambivalence about alcohol.

political skills as an archivist of the alcohol literature and a tireless advocate of the disease view.

Keller, like Jellinek, argues that alcoholism is a medical condition, a "psychogenic dependence on or a physiological addiction to" alcohol. The defining characteristic of the condition is "loss of control" over drinking. He translates this latter idea as follows: "whenever an alcoholic starts to drink it is not certain that he will be able to stop at will." The "evidence" for such loss of control is found precisely in the drinker not controlling that which should be controlled:

> The key criterion, for all ill effects, is this: Would the individual be expected to reduce his drinking (or give it up) in order to avoid the injury or its continuance? If the answer is yes, and he does not do so, it is assumed—admitting it is only an assumption—that he cannot, hence that he has "lost control over drinking," that he is addicted to or dependent on alcohol. This inference is the heart of the matter. Without evident or at least reasonably inferred loss of control, there is no foundation for the claim that "alcoholism is a disease," except in the medical dictionary sense of diseases . . . caused by alcohol poisoning. (Keller, 1960, p. 132)*

It is on the basis of such "reasonably inferred loss of control" that the disease status of alcoholism rests. It is not surprising that scientists and physicians have been skeptical of the validity of the idea that alcoholism is a disease, particularly in the hands of Keller.

So important is this loss of control idea to the life of the disease concept that Keller (1972b) wrote a subsequent essay devoted entirely to its defense. This and an even more recent article titled "The Disease Concept of Alcoholism Revisited" (1976a), represent interesting and important attempts to simultaneously align the disease concept with new and critical scientific knowledge and defend it as morally sound. Keller (1972b) avoided what appeared to be the most vulnerable part of Jellinek's formulation, the emphasis on physical dependence as the seat of loss of control over drinking.

By the time Keller wrote his defense of loss of control, the concept "addiction"—with its earlier heavy emphasis on tolerance, increased dose, withdrawal, and harm had been redefined by the World Health Organization (1964, 1969) as "dependence." In place of the earlier opiate-influenced focus on the dangerous "hook" believed inherent in the drug, the new emphasis was given to the user's "perceived need" to continue using the drug (Davies, 1976, p. 61). During this 20-year period, official definitions of the "glue" believed to hold individuals to repeated drug use as physiological had been abandoned (Room, 1973, pp. 1-6), and the link between such drug use and "harm" considerably deemphasized. The anomalous idea of "controlled addiction" or "primary psychological dependence" involving dependence but no deviance (Davies, 1976; Seevers, 1968) had diluted further the importance of physical addiction as the prototype of addiction.

Social scientists, and particularly sociologists Alfred Lindesmith (1947, 1968), Howard Becker (1953; 1967a), and Jock Young (1971), had made convincing arguments that the physical dependence model of addiction is both oversimplified and misleading. They held that an understanding of both the drinker or drug user and the cultural definitions surrounding such use is essential to clarify the origins and nature of addiction. Repeated drug taking is not the automatic consequence of the drug's pharmacological properties but rather a complex process wherein the individual learns to use the drug under particular circumstances. Howard Becker (1967a) argues that such learning is linked to the user's recognition and definition of physical withdrawal:

> One can only be addicted when he experiences physiological withdrawal symptoms, recognizes them as due to a need for drugs, and relieves them by taking another dose. The crucial step of recognition is most likely to occur when the user participates in a culture in which the signs of withdrawal are interpreted for what they are. When a person is ignorant of the nature of withdrawal sickness, and has some other cause to which he can attribute his discomfort . . . he may misinterpret the symptoms and thus escape addiction. . . . (p. 175)

This view emphasizes the importance of meanings and ideas as mediated by the interpretive actor. This, and a variety of less symbolic

---

*From Keller, M. Definition of alcoholism. *Q. J. Stud. Alcohol,* 1960, **21,** 125-134.

learning theory arguments, coupled with the proliferation of the "abuse" of "good" drugs during this 20-year period, provided the intellectual and political context in terms of which Keller's earlier defense of "loss of control" was written. He chose to ignore all such arguments.

Keller proceeded instead to deemphasize Jellinek's focus on the physical dependence typical of the Gamma type of alcoholism. He argues that Jellinek was unduly influenced in such thinking by the AA ideology of an allergic sensitivity to alcohol. Jellinek's idea that when an alcoholic drinks, there is some kind of automatic physiological chain reaction producing craving and an inability to stop drinking is mirrored in the AA slogan "One drink away from a drunk." This idea had been fundamental to the disease concept. Since its early statement in Jellinek's works, however, scientific research to test this proposition had been underway. The accumulating evidence did not support this idea, and Keller had little choice but to acknowledge these results. In summarizing this research, he says: "none of the subjects in these experiments were precipitated into a bout of drinking by the first drink or even by a considerable amount of drink" (Keller, 1972b, p. 156). If alcoholic loss of control is not automatic on drinking, then it must involve mechanisms peculiar to the particular drinker and the drinker's experience. The specific source of loss of control then varies from one drinker to the next. It is, in other words, drinker specific.

Having dethroned physiological reactions to alcohol as the primary form of diseased drinking, Keller (1972b, p. 160) reiterated his 1962 definition of the concept: "if an alcoholic takes a drink, he can never be sure he will be able to stop before he loses control and starts on a bout." The trigger, or, as Keller says, the "cue or signal," that precipitates such loss of control may take any number of divergent forms, and the connection between such cues and drinking found in addiction "is thought of as a form of learned or conditioned response." Alcohol itself, or a "particular blood alcohol level," may even be such a cue. The important thing, argues Keller, is that when such cues are elicited, no amount of rational calculation by the drinker can prevent a bout of drinking. In addition, the drinker is not likely ever to know the precise nature of the critical cues and signals that set off his uncontrolled drinking. This is why abstinence for the alcoholic is the most prudent course; he does not know when or why his drinking may become uncontrolled.

Although Keller suggests that he has clarified the confusion surrounding loss of control and its operation in alcoholism, he has in fact retreated into the circularity and mystery of his previous definitions. Although the drinker is no longer at the mercy of physiological and pharmacological process, Keller has offered even more obscure forces—unknown and almost unknowable cues and signals—that, although they are learned, are beyond the recognition or control of the individual. It is apparent that he has ignored the social science criticisms of the physical dependence model of addiction. This is evident in the language he uses to describe how these cues operate. They "impinge" on the drinker, who is under their "impulse" and "influence" and who requires some "external" circumstances to free him or her from their grip. Although Keller (1972b) cites a variety of well-placed scientific criticisms, he concludes his defense sounding like a traditional advocate of the disease concept: "There comes an occasion when [the drinker] . . . is powerless, when he cannot help drinking. For that is the essence or nature of a drug addiction. And that indeed is why I am sure alcoholism is a disease" (p. 162). Keller warns that critics' assertions that alcoholics may exist who have not lost control "can cause confusion in the public mind, loss of confidence on the part of patients, erroneous jurisprudence, and misdirection of effort by government agencies" (p. 163).

It is this final caveat that is most revealing about the status of the ideas that alcoholism is a disease and alcoholics sick persons. These cautions are not based on evidence or scientific argument but rather on values, ideology, public opinion, politics, and control. In a society that holds persons responsible for behavior that they presumably can control, the viability of the disease concept of alcoholism rests squarely on the assertion that such drinkers lack such control and are therefore to be helped rather than blamed. Keeping this belief alive and well is a job for entrepreneurs and politicians, not scientists. It is toward this end that Keller's efforts are directed.

This is perhaps most clear in Keller's (1976a) latest response to critics, "The Disease Concept of Alcoholism Revisited." In a tone of impatience and disdain for skeptics, buttressed by circular reasoning and argument by analogy (Brandsma, 1977), Keller (1976a) attempts to vanquish foes of the disease concept by a variety of ad hominem arguments attacking the critics' motives:

> It is possible that some people look with envy—unconscious, of course—at those fellows who are having an uproariously good time at everybody else's expense, getting irresponsibly drunk and then demanding to be cared for and coddled—at public cost, yet.
>
> Another motive is apparent in those who, not being M.D.'s, think they know better than doctors how to treat alcoholism. . . . It is understandable that some people would feel uncomfortable—they might even perceive it to be illegal—to be treating a disease without a license to practice medicine. But if only it is not a disease—why, then, they are in business! (p. 1711)*

Not only are such critics of the disease concept misguided and even self-seeking, but they become, at Keller's hands, obstructionist, antimedical, and unhumanitarian. Perhaps worst of all, they are cast ironically into the role of modern-day moral crusaders against alcohol and drinking.

Keller's polemical reaction to critics is curious. Why the emotional and moral tone of his defense? Clearly, challenges to the idea are challenges to established and entrenched groups and interests whose livelihoods depend on the viability of that idea. We have identified some of these groups and interests in this social history of the disease concept. Keller's attempts at "logic" to the contrary, he has become one of the last surviving crusaders on behalf of this idea. He is first a disciple who argues that the disease concept is revealed truth and that skeptics, be they physicians or social scientists, are heretics. Such, of course, is the quality of ideological debate.

*Reprinted by permission from *Journal of Studies on Alcohol,* Vol. 37, pp. 1694-1717, 1976. Copyright by Journal of Studies on Alcohol, Inc., New Brunswick, N.J. 08903.

## IS ALCOHOLISM A DISEASE?

Whether alcoholism is a disease, given our discussion, is both a reasonable and inevitable question. Our historical-constructionist perspective on the medicalization of deviance allows us to conclude that apparently it is, but not because we say so and not in the same sense that Rush, Jellinek, Keller, or AA have drawn such conclusions. Alcoholism is a disease because it has been defined successfully as such, particularly since 1940. The high points of this successful contest have, for the most part, been noted: the rise of the Yale center, the founding and growth of the international organization AA, the active and successful campaigns of the NCA, Jellinek's and Keller's work and the attention it has received, and, finally, the rapid growth of an independent federal bureaucracy, the NIAAA, premised on the ideas that alcoholism is a chronic disease and a major health problem.

We suggested at the beginning of this chapter that an interesting feature of the medicalization of such deviant drinking is that medical personnel and official medical organizations have chosen to remain by and large on the periphery of this contest. Our historical overview, however, does portray some physicians as active supporters of this idea. For example, Rush and his temperance colleagues, the few physicians who operated and supported the inebriate asylums in the late 19th century, Dr. Silkworth who gave AA its allergy concept, and those physicians involved in research and writing at the Yale center during the 1940s and 1950s were central figures in this history. Although some of these physicians had high professional and social prestige, they were few in number and, more often than not, were psychiatrists—practitioners of a specialty of relatively low status in the medical community.

The success of the definitional change that is medicalization must rest ultimately on either passive acceptance (mostly ignoring but not challenging) or official recognition by the established representatives of the medical profession. Prior to 1940 it appears that the disease concept was either ignored or at least not challenged by the American medical establishment, although there were a few physicians who treated the chronically intoxicated seriously as patients. In addition, there were certain moral and social class stigmas associated with repeated intoxication, particularly if it were public. Physicians, since the early 20th century, have occupied a relatively high social class and prestige position in America. They were, in the language of the 1960s, members of the "Establishment"; persons with a good deal invested in the dominant social and economic status quo. Public drunkards or "skid row" types were believed to be just the opposite. They were seen as unable to exert self-control, perhaps the prime middle-class virtue, and were considered irresponsible, lacking self-pride, and without any motivation to mend their ways.

Physicians' belief in this skid row stereotype, along with the personal and social differences between them and their alcoholic patients, were not conducive to establishing the rapport thought so necessary for effective treatment. A review of a series of studies on physicians' attitudes toward alcoholic patients beginning in the mid-1940s (Riley & Marden, 1946; Straus, 1952; Wolf et al., 1965; Corley, 1974; Bischoff, 1976) provides evidence of this skeptical and often hostile stance. Common to all these studies are various descriptions of the alcoholic patient as "weak," "weak-willed," "uncooperative," "troublesome," "hopeless," and a "waste of time." Endorsements of the idea that the alcoholic is a sick person were common, although rarely were such descriptions offered without qualifying negative moral judgments. These findings are paralleled in two studies of attitudes toward the alcoholic in the general population. In a 1961 survey Harold Mulford and Donald Miller (1964) found that although 65% of their sample agreed that the alcoholic was a "sick person," only 24% accepted the sickness view without some kind of moral judgment attached. In a more recent study, Janet Ries (1977) found that alcoholics were defined as "unpredictable" and "responsible" for their behavior. In comparison with the categories "epileptics" and "blind persons," alcoholics elicited the greatest intolerance and the least favorable responses from her respondents. Ries concludes that on the basis of her analysis, "alcoholism is not defined and reacted to 'just like any other illness.'"

In another recent study replicating a 1963 research (Mulford, 1964) on physicians' attitudes toward alcoholics, Harold Bischoff (1976) found that when asked their "personal view" of the alcoholic, only 28% of the 198 physicians sampled described such persons solely as "sick" (as opposed to "morally weak," "weak-willed," "criminal," or other descriptions). When comparing his results to those obtained from a similar sample in the original study, Bischoff found that there had been a decided decline in the popularity of this "sick person" description as the most accurate view of the alcoholic patients (from 45% in 1963). Finally, on the subject of the alcoholic's responsibility for his condition, Bischoff found that 60% of his physician sample believed such persons were "totally" or "mainly" responsible, whereas only 2% said they were "not at all" responsible for their condition.

These attitudes, coupled with the common medical practice of referring detoxified alcoholic patients to nonmedical organizations such as AA, represent something less than enthusiastic support among practicing physicians for the idea that alcoholism is a "real" disease. These definitions and treatment strategies have prevailed for almost four decades in the United States, despite the strength and successes of the alcoholism movement we have described. In light of these and similar findings, it becomes apparent that the "victories" in medical recognition of the disease concept claimed by movement leaders have been perhaps more symbolic than substantive (Gusfield, 1963). The most important symbolic medical recognition is found in the official support given the disease slogan by dominant medical organizations.

### Medical response to the disease concept

One of the most frequent defenses of the proposition that alcoholism is a disease is that the medical profession recognizes it as such.

This argument usually makes reference to official resolutions, committees, or publications of various medical organizations, most notably the AMA. A famous example of this argument was proposed by Jellinek (1960) himself in an attempt to address this definitional problem:

> Physicians know what belongs in their realm . . . a disease is what the medical profession recognizes as such. . . . the medical profession has officially accepted alcoholism as an illness, whether a part of the public likes it or not, and even if a minority of the medical profession is disinclined to accept the idea. (p.12)

Jellinek was content to leave the issue at that and get on with specifying the nature and types of this malady.

The official acceptance to which Jellinek refers has assumed two primary forms: the inclusion of "alcoholism" in the official manuals of medical diagnosis and classification used by the medical profession, and specific AMA resolutions and publications defining alcoholism as a medical problem to which physicians should direct their attention. The three major diagnostic classifications of diseases usually noted in such discussions are the AMA's *Standard Nomenclature of Diseases and Operations* (1961), the *International Classification of Diseases* (ICD) (1968), and their psychiatric counterpart, published by the American Psychiatric Association, *The Diagnostic and Statistical Manual of Mental Disorders* (DSM). These manuals provide the medical community with administratively useful classifications for diagnosis and record keeping. They are organized into sections on the basis of the believed locations of the disease or disorder in the person. All these official publications identify alcoholism as a mental disorder. More specifically, it is a "personality disorder," including, in the ICD and DSM-II, the classification "alcohol addiction." The *Standard Nomenclature* of the AMA (1961, p. 112) does not actually contain the word "alcoholism" but rather uses the classification "000-x641 Alcohol addiction chronic." The ICD (1968, p. 175) and DSM-II (1968, p. 10) manuals do use the word "alcoholism" and subdivide it as follows: "Episodic excessive drinking," "Habitual excessive drinking," "Alcohol addiction," and "Other and unspecified alcoholism." Although this latter classification is somewhat reminiscent of Jellinek's phase progression, the primary identification of alcoholism as a mental disorder is certainly not. Such a definition is also at odds with AA ideology. Although inclusion in these official registers of disease does give credibility to the statement that alcoholism is a disease, it should not be seen as an unbridled endorsement of what we have called the traditional disease concept.

Another commonly cited example of the medical profession's alleged support of the disease concept is the formal resolutions contained in reports of the Board of Trustees of the AMA to its House of Delegates. These statements have originated typically in the Committee on Alcoholism, formed in 1954 under the direction of the AMA Council on Mental Health. The first such resolution from this committee was issued in 1956 and was followed shortly thereafter by a similar statement from the American Hospital Association. It addressed the problem alcoholics face in gaining admission to general hospitals for treatment of drinking-related problems. It is cited commonly as evidence of the medical profession's "recognition" of the disease of alcoholism and is the basis for Jellinek's remarks quoted earlier. The resolution (1956) begins by identifying "excessive drinking" as a "personality disorder" (consistent with the official nomenclature), and goes on to give a vague characterization of alcoholism and the medical profession's responsibility toward it:

> When, in addition to this excessive use, there are certain signs and symptoms of behavioral, personality and physical disorder or of their development, the syndrome of alcoholism is achieved. The intoxication and some of the other possible complications manifested in this syndrome often make treatment difficult. However, alcoholism must be regarded as within the purview of medical practice. The Council on Mental Health, its Committee on Alcoholism, and the profession in general recognizes this syndrome of alcoholism as illness which justifiably should have the attention of physicians. (p. 750)*

*From *J.A.M.A.*, 1956, **162,** 750. Copyright 1956, American Medical Association.

This resolution continues and suggests one reason that some physicians may have been less than enthusiastic about treating alcoholics: hospitals often refuse to admit them as patients. The committee encourages all general "hospital administrators and the staffs . . . [to] look upon alcoholism as a medical problem and to admit patients who are alcoholics to their hospitals for treatment . . ." (p. 750).

Although this resolution is indeed a formal recognition and reaffirmation of alcoholism as a medical problem, it is perhaps most significant in its vagueness about the condition and its treatment. Noticeable by its absence is any mention of "loss of control" or "addiction," either in the quoted segment or anywhere else in the report. It is, of course, this idea that is the heart of the traditional view. In addition, the connection between drinking and the alleged disease is left obscure, the statement asserting only that the "behavioral, personal, and physical disorder" exists "in addition to" drinking. The traditionally important distinction between medical consequences of drinking and some specific disease entity called "alcoholism" is omitted.

A similarly obscure AMA resolution was made a decade later, in 1967. Premised on the assumption that the medical profession could "attack" the "disease of alcoholism" in the same successful fashion used with other diseases, it contains the following statements:

> Resolved, that the American Medical Association identifies alcoholism as a complex disease and as such recognizes that the medical components are medicine's responsibility. . . . Such recognition is not intended to relieve the alcoholic of moral and legal responsibility, as provided by law, for any acts committed when inebriated; nor does this recognition preclude civil arrest and imprisonment, as provided by law, for antisocial acts committed when inebriated. (Quoted in Wilbur, 1969, p. 12)

Two important points about this position should be made. First, the medical profession claims only responsibility for treating the "medical components" (medical consequences?) of alcoholism, the determination of which they as medical experts control. Second, there is a strong moral and legalistic reference to the effect that although alcoholism may be a disease, being a victim of it does not free the sick person from responsibility for deviant behavior committed when sick. Given our discussions of mental illness (Chapter 3) and the history of criminal responsibility (Chapter 8), it is apparent that alcoholism is seen here as a different, less incapacitating kind of sickness.

### Supreme Court and the disease concept

The explicit reference to the legal responsibilities of the alcoholic in the 1967 AMA resolution was no accident. During the decade since the first resolution, three important court decisions were handed down that bore directly on the viability of the disease concept. The first case, *Robinson* v. *California*, in 1962, involved the use of opiates and the issue of whether addiction produces a loss of control that prevents the user from regulating use of the drug in question. Its import for the disease concept is found in the Supreme Court's argument that drug addiction is indeed an illness, a key characteristic of which is loss of control over ingestion of the drug. The Court said it is a violation of the Eighth Amendment to punish a person for displaying the direct symptoms of an illness; that such punishment is indeed "cruel and unusual." Two subsequent cases, both decided in 1966, involved men who had been medically identified as alcoholics. The issue was whether they should be punished for public intoxication. These are the well-known cases of *Driver* v. *Hinnant* and of *Easter* v. *District of Columbia* (Kittrie, 1971, pp. 278-289). In both cases the Court decided in favor of the defendants, arguing that since medical authorities considered alcoholism a disease, one of the defining characteristics of which is uncontrollable intoxication, the sick alcoholic should not be punished as a criminal for such drunkenness. To do so, they argued, is unconstitutional, based on the Eighth Amendment protection. In the *Driver* case, however, the Court made it clear that the decision in no sense exempted alcoholic persons from responsibility for other deviant and unlawful behavior committed while intoxicated; the protection extended only to public intoxication. This, of course, is mirrored in the AMA resolution.

The *Driver* decision addressed specifically the question of how such publicly intoxicated sick persons should be treated. It argued, ''Of course, the alcohol-diseased may by law be kept out of public sight'' and that while confinement in jail is unconstitutional, their ruling did not preclude ''appropriate detention . . . for treatment and rehabilitation so long as he is not marked as a criminal'' (quoted in Kittrie, 1971, p. 281). The *Easter* decision, rendered a few months later, directly affirmed the *Driver* arguments. The immediate effects of this latter decision were to divert arrested alcoholics in Washington, D.C., from the customary jail sentences to medical treatment facilities. To the frustration both of the courts and medical personnel, it became immediately apparent that there simply were neither adequate facilities nor treatments available for this newly created population of ''patients.'' The practical solution of many judges was simply to set such persons free, with neither punishment nor ''treatment.'' Others used long-established civil commitment laws to confine alcoholics in mental hospitals for observation and care. It was generally agreed by both legal and medical authorities that such a situation was undesirable.

A fourth and perhaps most important case decided 2 years after *Driver* and *Easter* signaled judicial dissatisfaction with the consequences of the earlier rulings. In the 1968 case of *Powell* v. *Texas* the Supreme Court was faced with the same issues it had addressed in the *Robinson* decision, only this time it was alcoholism rather than opiate addiction that was to be considered. Contrary to the favorable expectations of alcoholism movement advocates and civil liberties lawyers, in *Powell* the Court decided in a five-to-four vote against the alcoholic defendant. Reacting both to the practical problems created by the previous decisions and the controversy and lack of agreement among medical authorities on ''what it means to say that alcoholism is a disease,'' the *Powell* majority was not convinced by defense arguments. Nicholas Kittrie (1971) highlights the justices' concerns:

> To permit alcoholism as a defense to prohibited conduct, the Supreme Court majority felt, an accused would have to demonstrate a complete lack of fault, by proving both an ''inability to abstain'' from drinking in the first place and a total ''loss of control'' over his conduct once he had commenced to drink. (p. 288)*

In addition, they argued that there were no adequate facilities to provide medical treatment to alcoholics and that to strike down existing practices of incarceration would result in ''thousands of alcoholics . . . roving the streets.'' Finally, the justices were concerned about the possible negative effects of such a ruling on the constitutional doctrine of criminal responsibility. (Bacon, 1969).

The *Powell* case was a decided setback in the progress of the disease concept. Not only did it provide the opportunity for the Supreme Court to evaluate the idea and relevant evidence, it also was the occasion for a number of critical articles in which the disease concept was attacked (see Fingarette, 1970). Perhaps most important, the Court opinion contained a clear criticism of the medical profession, both for the poor state of its knowledge of the nature and cause of alcoholism and for the limited number of medical treatment facilities available for alcoholics. Pressed between the demands of the moral entrepreneurs of the alcoholism movement and the less than laudatory remarks of the Supreme Court, the medical profession had little choice but to accept the challenge, at least at a public and official level.†

This tentative and somewhat uncomfortable nature of medicine's embrace of the disease concept is evidenced in a speech given by the president of the AMA before the 28th International Congress on Alcohol and Alcoholism in 1968. In his remarks President Dwight Wilbur reiterated that alcoholism is a ''disease,'' a

---

*From Kittrie, N. *The right to be different: deviance and enforced therapy*. Baltimore: John Hopkins University Press, 1971. © 1971 by the Johns Hopkins University Press.

†When the NCA's committee of physicians issued their statement on the diagnostic criteria for alcoholism in 1972—attempting to refute the *Powell* opinion regarding the poor state of medical diagnosis—an editorial appeared in the *Journal of the American Medical Association* (1972) proclaiming that ''alcoholism is a disease'' and ''applauding'' the NCA for its action.

"sickness," an "affliction," and an "illness. He cited the AMA's development of a "multifaceted program" on alcoholism that his organization adopted that same year. This program consisted of attempts to encourage and educate physicians to treat alcoholics, to urge general hospitals to admit them, to provide better teaching about alcoholism in medical schools, and to work toward further decriminalization of public drunkenness. Most telling about the position of the medical profession on the alleged disease entity "alcoholism" are his remarks about treatment:

> Physicians who undertake such a job . . . need all the help they can get from organizations that are concerned with this complex and difficult problem. . . . whatever its degree, alcoholism is rarely—probably never—exclusively a medical matter. The physician cannot work alone and have much hope for success. He can only do his part in what must be a team effort. (Wilbur, 1969, p. 15)

This is an uncharacteristically modest position for the medical profession to adopt. Not only is it implied that the physician needs help from nonmedical organizations in treating the alcoholic, but Wilbur (1969) goes on to describe the limited nature of this treatment:

> If medical attention has not been delayed too long, the physician probably can restore the patient's physical health. He might even be able to calm the patient, mentally and emotionally, sometimes just by offering the help. And he can at least contribute to finding the basic cause of the problem that is manifesting itself in alcoholism. . . . (p. 15)

Finally, having laid these modest responsibilities at the physician's door, he argues that the "ultimate" solution to the alcoholic's problem

> may have to come from his religious counselor, his employer, his family, his friends, from social workers or other dedicated people trained to deal with this kind of person. I know of no other medical or health problem in which so many groups and so many individuals outside of the medical profession can contribute so much toward this solution. (p. 15)

As Selden Bacon (1973) has remarked, "That, to put it mildly, is strange medical practice" (p. 23).

## FUTURE OF THE DISEASE CONCEPT OF ALCOHOLISM

The idea that alcoholism, or inebriety, or common drunkenness is a disease indeed has had a long history. Its fortunes as a definition and explanation of repeated intoxication and associated "harm" have risen and fallen in the United States now for almost 200 years. Since 1940 this fortune has been, for the most part, in ascendance. It has become the official political definition of such drinking behavior in our country, as evidenced both by the power of the NIAAA in influencing treatment and research, and by such federal legislation as The Uniform Alcoholism and Intoxication Treatment Act of 1974, which is a congressional endorsement of the assumptions on which the disease concept rests. In addition, private insurance carriers such as Blue Cross and Blue Shield are beginning to cover alcoholism treatment costs, and congressional committees deliberating various national health insurance plans are giving serious consideration to including coverage of such costs.

### A coming crisis?

The advance of this disease model, or paradigm, however, has not been without controversy. We have called it the "contested" medical model of alcohol. Even though this view remains the dominant political and social force in thinking about chronic alcohol problems, we suggest that over the past decade and a half a "crisis" in the viability of the disease paradigm has been developing. Whether this political struggle between disease advocates and a small but growing band of critics will lead to the rise of a new paradigm for chronic intoxication is difficult to predict. We can. however, suggest the nature of this crisis and what its short-range development might entail.

The growing crisis for the disease concept of alcoholism is a product of two developments. First, critics suggest increasingly that although perhaps once a humanitarian and practical strategy, it has now outlived its usefulness. One of the oldest "friends" of the disease view, Selden Bacon (1973)—himself a founder of The National Council on Alcoholism, a colleague of Jellinek, Haggard, and Keller at Yale, and perhaps the premier social scientist of alcohol alive today—has said that the disease concept, although once politically useful, has become an obstruction to progress in alcohol studies and problem solution:

> Twenty-five years ago this belief acted to tear down the walls of avoidance, denial, ignorance, cruelty, and hopelessness. Today, however, I see signs of its being used as a cop-out. For example: "Let's turn the whole problem over to the doctors, it's a disease, isn't it?" This can be seen in efforts of law enforcement agencies to relieve themselves of responsibility. This can be seen in terms of friends, associates, and relatives who can explain away their possible responsibilities by this new magic just as they could escape by such old magics as ideas of lack of will power, of sin, or of biologic inheritance. This means that research shall be medical, that facilities shall be medical. And this, of course, reduces the need for other research, other training, other facilities. In the past we turned over these problems to the churches, to the schools, to legislative sales controls, to policemen and jails. Now it will be medicine's turn, and it looks like a nice new cop-out. (p. 24)*

It is also possible that with the historical loosening of moral prohibitions on a wide variety of behaviors, we no longer need to define the alcoholic drinker as "sick" to adopt a rational and supportive stance in helping individuals cope with such behavior. These and similar arguments undermine the practical and moral appeal of the traditional view, making it appear more of an unncessary ruse than a useful guide to effective action. The functions it was created to serve having been largely met, the need for advocacy is reduced.

A second development that threatens the disease paradigm comes from the accumulation of what Thomas Kuhn (1970) calls anomalous or "difficult" findings that cannot be explained by the traditional, dominant paradigm. The anomalous quality of such evidence is heightened by the existence of the dominant model itself, for it is only in contrast to it that such evidence becomes difficult, embarrassing, and challenging. The accumulation of a growing body of scientific research evidence contrary to the disease concept presents perhaps the most serious threat to its future reign.

This scientific evidence has developed primarily during the last two decades. Paradoxically, this development grew from an attempt by disease advocates, especially Jellinek, to provide a more precise and clear formulation of what it means to say that alcoholism is a disease. As Nils Christie and Kettil Bruun (1969) have argued, one function of the "big, fat words" so common in alcohol studies is to insulate the status quo against critical evaluation and scrutiny. Targets cannot be hit unless they can be seen clearly. Vague and imprecise concepts are particularly disabling of scientific evaluation. Unless the terms and arguments of a theory or point of view can be defined clearly and measured empirically, science can offer little to enlighten debate. Such has been the case for the disease concept.

Once the meanings of the claim that alcoholism is a disease were specified, however, science was put to the task of establishing experiments to test them. It is apparent in retrospect that once such scientific evaluation began, it was only a matter of time before the disease concept was under siege. Coupled with the practical and moral skepticism echoed by Bacon and other critics (Seeley, 1962; Pattison, 1969; Room, 1972; Robinson, D., 1972, 1976; Pattison et al., 1977; Roizen, 1977), these scientific challenges to the validity of disease ideas have become difficult for advocates to ignore. It is ironic that the very vehicle that disease supporters of the 1940s and 1950s chose to launch their argument, medical science, subsequently gave birth to the most serious challenge to its continued existence. To provide an appreciation of the scope and seriousness of this criticism, we review briefly its major elements.

## Scientific claims

First, the proposition that alcoholics have predisposing characteristics that consistently differentiate them from nonalcoholics simply has not been supported by research evidence (Pattison et al., 1977, pp. 61-64). Particularly fruitless has been the search for an "alcoholic personality" that might then be used to explain such drinking behavior. Even disease advocate

Mark Keller (1972a, p. 1147) has remarked that "alcoholics are different in so many ways that it makes no difference." Physician Mansell Pattison, Mark Sobell, and Linda Sobell (1977, p. 62) have reviewed this research and conclude that "except for sharing alcohol problems, all alcoholics are not the same." There appear to be, then, no predisposing systematic distinctions between alcoholics and nonalcoholics, contrary to the disease concept.

A second proposition fundamental to the disease view is Jellinek's idea that alcoholic drinking is a progressive, inexorable process beginning with "implicative" and "symptomatic" drinking and culminating in severe and "chronic" alcoholism. This also has been challenged directly by research evidence. Over two decades ago, Harrison Trice and Richard J. Wahl (1958) found that there was no systematic clustering of symptoms alleged to characterize such phase movement. These and other authors have offered devastating criticisms of Jellinek's 1946 research on which the phase progression hypothesis is based. In an important series of longitudinal studies of American drinking practices, Don Cahalan and his colleagues (Cahalan et al. 1969; Cahalan, 1970; Cahalan & Room, 1974; Clark & Cahalan, 1976) have demonstrated that contrary to the prediction of progressively severe drinking symptoms, a substantial number of young men in their early twenties who reported a variety of serious problems due to drinking turned out, in subsequent interviews several years later, to be "normal" or "social" drinkers. This research has also demonstrated a good deal of moving "in and out" of what might be called "deviant" drinking behavior over the course of an individual drinker's life. The progressiveness inherent in the clinical model of disease appears, then, to be inconsistent with the facts of such deviant drinking behavior.

A third key hypothesis of the disease paradigm is that if a sober, "dried out" alcoholic resumes drinking, he will not be able to choose whether to stop drinking. He will, in effect, "lose control" over drinking because of either some physical sensitivity or unconsciously learned, conditioned response.* We have described the nature of such arguments in some detail and, in Keller's 1960 argument, have pointed out the tautological or circular logic on which this loss-of-control argument rests. The capacity to identify this condition comes primarily from a commitment to the idea that self-injurious behavior is not rational and therefore cannot be willful; that, for example, renewed "binge" drinking among alcoholics must therefore be beyond their control. Having ruled out moral explanations, advocates propose disease as the most plausible account. The scientific hypothesis derivable from this position is that once such drinking begins, it will not be subject to the drinker's will, and he or she will stop only when the body will not allow the continuation of drinking. Pattison et al. (1977) conclude that whether one chooses the physiological or more psychological version of this argument, the scientific evidence has been devastating: "Over the past 15 yeras, an impressive number of studies have robustly demonstrated that even the drinking of chronic, skid-row alcoholics is subject to their precise control under appropriate circumstances" (p. 99). This evidence has accumulated over a broad range of both experimental and natural settings. There appears at this time simply no sound support for "loss of control" as a valid account for patterns of continued drinking among so-called alcoholics.

Finally, even the most inveterate of all disease concept ideas, the absolute necessity of abstinence in the treatment of such drinkers, has come under scientific attack. This core idea has been defended most strongly and con-

*The logically prior question of why an alcoholic resumes drinking was addressed typically in early versions of the disease argument by proposing the existence of a "craving," "irresistible desire," or compulsion to drink. These were believed to be psychological forces that somehow were linked to a mysterious "cell hunger" for alcohol on the physiological level. So controversial and vulnerable were these ideas (Clark, 1975) that even Jellinek urged that they be abandoned in favor of a general social psychological explanation focusing on the drinker and the drinker's environment.

sistently by AA and the NCA followed closely by the federal NIAAA bureaucracy. It is voiced perhaps most clearly in the aphorism ''Once an alcoholic, always an alcoholic.'' Second only to loss of control as a defining quality of alcoholics is the belief that they simply cannot drink. This proposition is perhaps most crucial to the continued viability of the disease view. If it can be shown that alcoholics could become controlled, ''social'' drinkers, then the issue of choice and responsibility reemerge from the humanitarian protection afforded by the sick role. Such data would refute directly the mysterious notions of allergy and physiological sensitivity, and force the psychological, conditioned response version of loss of control into the realm of consciousness—as something we do in fact choose for ourselves. Diseases are not considered to be such phenomena.

The crucial importance of abstinence to the life of the traditional view is evidenced by the typically polemical and emotional reaction of advocates to scientific challenges of this argument. An example is the reaction following David Davies' 1962 research on what happened to alcoholics after they were discharged from medical treatment. Davies innocently reported the finding that some of these people had actually returned to social or normal drinking practices. This finding, rather than being regarded as an interesting and important discovery, was attacked, and Davies' research regaled as invalid and premature (Davies, 1963). It was almost as though one of the faithful had committed an act of heresy rather than simply reporting an objective finding (Pattison et al., 1977, p. 124). A more recent example is the alcohologists' response to the so-called Rand report (Armor et al., 1976). This report was a product of the routine evaluation research that is part of NIAAA-funded research. One, but by no means the only, concern of the report was the finding that some and perhaps a notable number of alcoholics can and do return to controlled drinking. This caused a storm of controversy that shook the disease establishment. The finding and report were denounced by a variety of the faithful, from local AA members to the director of the NIAAA. Ron Roizen (1977) suggests that such findings, quite aside from their scientific or substantive implications, can breed doubt among the many levels of treatment and administrative personnel who comprise the alcoholism establishment. It is a potentially fatal challenge to the orthodox ideology on which this establishment rests.

Given the politically volatile nature of this proposition, it is not surprising to find that alcohol scientists approach its evaluation cautiously. In their general review of research evidence on the disease concept, Pattison et al. (1977, pp. 120-164) are conservative in drawing their conclusions on this question of abstinence. After a review of 74 studies designed to test some aspect of this hypothesis, however, they conclude that it is not supported by existing evidence. Some so-called alcoholics have and will continue to learn to control their drinking. They conclude that this offers a new vista in practical treatment alternatives that historically have been precluded by the dominance of the disease ideology.

Contrary to such optimism, however, we know from Kuhn's analysis of the development of science that entrenched paradigms do not simply crumble in the face of contrary evidence. Although such evidence is probably a necessary component of scientific revolutions, it has to be organized and used as the basis for an attack on the disease concept. Such scientific claims against the disease paradigm must be ''pushed'' or carried by some politically organized group according to a carefully planned strategy in order for them to threaten the disease view. In short, a competing paradigm must emerge that is (1) philosophically appealing, (2) able to incorporate the existing anomalous scientific data as well as the old puzzles the disease concept seemed to solve, and (3) able to draw converts and supporters to it. A glance to the horizon of alcohol studies in the United States reveals no threatening presence of this stature.

The most likely alternative paradigm would seem to focus on the concept of ''problems'' caused by or associated with drinking. In this approach, sick alcoholics become "problem drinkers" whose patterns of drinking behavior are documented carefully in longitudinal or epidemiological studies. The problems approach, not unlike approaches typical of contemporary writing in the sociology of deviance, is less etiological and correctional than the disease paradigm. No underlying disease entity or mechanism is assumed to account for the drinking behavior under study. The first commitment is to a careful description of patterns of actual drinking and associated behaviors as they occur over time. Causes, when they are addressed, are inferred cautiously from empirically established relationships. There is less of a clinical concern with treating individuals and more attention devoted to drinking behavior as an inextricably social and cultural phenomenon—as something that must be understood and influenced in context. The problem paradigm has been reflected most explicitly in the work of Don Cahalan, Walter Clark, Robin Room, Ron Roizen, and their colleagues cited here. These individuals are social scientists associated with the School of Public Health of the University of California at Berkeley. Although their writing and research could provide the basis for a new paradigm in alcohol studies, these social scientists are probably unlikely candidates as vanquishers of the disease concept. They are themselves linked, through research funding and consultation, to the NIAAA establishment.* In addition, they are part of the health "industry." Although their contributions have done, and will continue to do, a good deal for the quality and clarity of our understanding of drinking behavior, they are more likely to effect a reform rather than a revolution in the disease paradigm.

Although the disease concept of alcoholism has been challenged increasingly over the past two decades, it is far from dead. One of Kuhn's greatest insights was to force us to see the extent to which values, ideologies, and vested interests contribute to the inertia of dominant ideas in scientific work. This insight informs our understanding of the disease concept as the dominant paradigm in the study of repeated and negatively consequential intoxication. We have argued that scientists who marshall contradictory evidence must not be seen as the authoritative voice in the debate on the disease status of such behavior. Indeed, they must be seen as only one of a large cast of interested parties in a political and social contest over definitions and social control. Moreover, the medical profession rarely has been in the vanguard of the disease forces. More commonly, physicians have been pulled along by nonmedical interests to provide the necessary legitimation for the latter's claims-making activities. They would seem to occupy a particularly paradoxical position today.

The American medical establishment got on the disease bandwagon not primarily because of science but because of politics. As contradictory scientific evidence accumulates in opposition to the disease view, physicians would appear to have two options. First, and least likely, they could officially repudiate the idea that alcoholism is a disease along with their past endorsements of that idea. This would, in effect, amount to an admission of previous error. More likely, physicians will continue to endorse the "health" approach to such drinking, carefully omitting use of the term "disease." This is part of the "reform" that the problems perspective is already effecting. By jettisoning the vulnerable baggage of "disease," "loss of control," and other "big, fat, words," this reform leaves much of the traditional alcoholism movement undisturbed under the expanding umbrella of medical definitions of deviant behavior. Whether alcoholism will continue to be a "disease" may well be in doubt. We suspect, however, its status as a "medical problem" is secure.

## SUMMARY

The medical model of alcohol and the disease concept of alcoholism add two important dimensions to our understanding of the medicalization of deviance. First, the social definitional quality of medicalization is highlighted by the

*In 1978 these Berkeley social scientists were awarded a large grant from NIAAA to establish one of a handful of new research centers on alcohol use and problems. Robin Room, one of the most effective critics of the disease concept, is the director of this new center.

distinction we draw between the contested and uncontested medical models of alcohol. The uncontested model is organized around questions of what the chemical alcohol is and what it does inside our bodies when we drink. The physiological and medical consequences of sustained drinking are defined for the most part as noncontroversial issues for medical definition and attention. Few would argue that this is a legitimate piece of medical "turf." Our interest focuses more specifically on the contested model of alcohol and particularly on the medicalization of certain forms of deviant drinking behavior. The consensus on these medical definitions and interventions historically has been far from universal.

A second dimension of medicalization this chapter addresses is the authorship and support of such medical constructions. These need not be solely or even primarily the work of medical personnel—although it is important that medicine give such definitions legitimacy by at least a symbolic endorsement. In the case of the disease concept of alcoholism, the major moral and intellectual entrepreneurs have not for the most part been physicians or representatives of the medical profession. Rather, first a "movement" and subsequently an "industry" has grown up around the disease concept, peopled by a variety of interested nonmedical persons and groups.

The uncontested and contested medical models of alcohol often overlap or interpenetrate one another. A good example is the question of alcohol's effects on social behavior. Centuries of carefully selected commonsense as well as expert wisdom has it that when we drink we "lose control" of our conventional selves and our behavior; we become, as the drug accumulates in our bodies, "disinhibited" and "under the influence." We do and say things we would not otherwise do and say. These things are seen typically to involve untoward, rule-breaking, or deviant behavior and are believed to be the inevitable consequence of sufficient drink. All who drink are potentially subject to this uncontrolling influence. Such deviant drinking thus becomes a pharmacological, drug-centered, and medical phenomenon.

This construction has been challenged by a part of the same commonsense and scientific knowledge used to support it. Much cross-cultural and experimental research has failed to document the universally disinhibiting effects of alcohol on behavior. The variety of commonly observed behaviors associated with drinking preclude the validity of this medicalized, drug-centered conception. Being wise, however, to the intransigence of useful ideas, we have seen that this conventional wisdom dies hard, if at all. The idea that drinking-related deviance comes from the drink rather than the drinker is the premise on which most pre–20th-century thinking about the disease concept rests.

That chronic drunkenness should be considered a disease was first stated by Benjamin Rush in a 1785 treatise on the deleterious effects of "ardent spirits" on the body and mind. The drug-centered medical model of alcohol provided the foundation of Rush's argument that inebriety was a disease and the inebriate a sick person needing medical treatment rather than moral scorn. Rush and a few other temperance physicians insisted that all who drink distilled liquor are subject to these overpowering and destroying effects; the wise person should abstain from such drinking completely.

These ideas were to become useful grist for the 19th-century temperance movement. Rather than denying this medical construction, temperance leaders throughout most of the 19th century simply added it to the characterization of "Demon Rum" and "King Alcohol" as the moral poison of American life. Drinking became dangerous medically as well as morally. One interesting manifestation of this moral-medical definition of common drunkenness was the inebriate asylums that grew up during the last half of the century. These special hospitals were intended as places where the sick inebriate could receive physical treatment for his alcohol-related ailments. More important, however, the drinker could be morally rejuvenated. Asylum superintendents walked a precarious line between watchful temperance groups wary of "coddling" drinkers and skeptical medical and popular attitudes toward these facilities. They never received the approval either of the public or medical community, and as the waves of prohibition sentiment grew strong after 1900, asylum personnel and others interested in the disease concept could not withstand the force of history. With passage of the Eighteenth Amendment in 1919, Congress symbolically endorsed the century-long crusade against alcohol by making its production and sale illegal. Between 1920 and 1933, when Prohibition was repealed, no one "owned" or promoted the idea that such drinking behavior should be considered a disease. On repeal, however, a new and promising day for this idea had dawned.

In the decades following the official reappearance of alcohol in America, three important developments gave the disease concept unparalleled vitality: the establishment of a research center on alcohol at prestigious Yale University; the founding and phenomenal growth of the self-help organization AA; and an increasingly clear person-centered statement of what it means to say that alcoholism is a disease, found in the work of Yale center leader, E. M. Jellinek.

The Yale Center of Alcohol Studies, founded in 1940, provided a supportive context in which scientific research and policy questions about alcohol could be pursued. As certain drinking behaviors were defined as important "social problems," the Yale center took the lead in attempting to give humanitarian and progressive direction to public policy on alcohol and alcoholics. Its summer school program provided the impetus for a group of people, some of whom were themselves alcoholics, to formulate an educational and action plan to combat the disease. This plan, including the ideas that alcoholism is a disease and a public health problem, was introduced intentionally in these summer programs at Yale as an enlightened and nonmoral position that community leaders could use to establish a treatment rather than punishment approach to drinkers at the local level. The authors of this plan, along with a collection of Yale faculty, founded what was to become the National Council on Alcoholism. The NCA subsequently became the leading private lobby for the disease concept in the United States.

A second crucial post-Prohibition development of the 1930s was the formation of Alcoholics Anonymous. Premised from the start on the idea that alcoholism is a disease rooted in an allergy to alcohol, AA developed twelve steps by which the sick alcoholic could regain control over drinking. Once recovered, one could remain so only by complete abstinence, a logical consequence of the allergy idea. Although AA remained true to its loose organizational format and principle of anonymity of membership, it has been probably the most influential source of Americans' thinking about deviant drinking.

Finally, the writing of E. M. Jellinek, Yale pioneer and long-time center director, gave focus to what it meant to argue that alcoholism is a disease. Jellinek held that alcoholism is a progressive condition with identifiable stages, that there are important differences between alcoholics and nonalcoholics, that certain forms of alcoholism are bona fide diseases, and that its defining characteristic was the loss of control over drinking. Jellinek's work, although not without problems, provided fellow scientists with a set of propositions on this person-specific form of addiction that they could begin to test. On Jellinek's death, his colleague Mark Keller became the leading advocate of the disease view, reiterating and attempting to clarify some of Jellinek's arguments.

To answer the question of whether alcoholism is a disease, one must refer to the current political status of these ideas. Since 1940, supporters of the disease concept have been successful in sustaining its viability. Recent significant achievements include legal endorsement of its assumptions, the 1970 formation of a $170 million federal bureaucracy, the National Institute on Alcohol Abuse and Alcoholism, premised on the belief that alcoholism is a disease and an important health problem, and a 1974 congressional act that supports decriminalization of public drunkenness and mandates treatment rather than punishment. Finally, the American medical profession has given the symbolic endorsement required for these ideas and definitions to attain legitimacy. In a series of official statements since 1946, the AMA has agreed that this condition is a disease and that its medical aspects should be treated by physicians and medical personnel.

These victories, however, must be seen in a context of recent challenges. Both in terms of practical utility and scientific validity, the disease view has come under attack. Whether these challenges will lead to a "crisis" in the disease paradigm we cannot predict. We suggest, however, that given the entrenched interests behind these ideas, a more likely outcome would be "reform" rather than "revolution." Instead of "disease" it is likely that alcoholism simply will become a "health problem." This subtle redefinition discards the vulnerable baggage "disease" while leaving the traditional definition secure under the ever-expanding umbrella of medicalization.

## SUGGESTED READINGS

Alcoholics Anonymous: *The story of how many thousands of men and women have recovered from alcoholism.* New York: Works Publishing Co., 1939.
Spoken of as "the book" by members of AA. This fascinating work offers as nothing else can the images and values by which AA thrives and, apparently, successfully helps alcoholics recover from their "disease."

Filstead, W. J., Rossi, J. J., and Keller, M. (Eds.). *Alcohol and alcohol problems: new thinking and new directions.* Cambridge, Mass.: Ballinger Publishing Co., 1976.
A high-quality collection of cross-disciplinary discussions of where alcohol research has been and where it might go. It ranges from a historical paper by Mark Keller to an invaluable critique of alcohol concepts by Seldon Bacon, to research in the biology of alcoholism and alcohol problem prevention.

Gusfield, J. *Symbolic crusade: status politics and the American temperance movement.* Urbana, Ill.: University of Illinois Press, 1963.
The best single sociological discussion of the historical foundations of American thought and social action concerning alcohol. Gusfield's analysis, although not of the medical definitions of drinking, parallels our own discussion in that he speaks of temperance as a moral crusade by one set of claims-makers against a set of new values and conduct that they saw as threatening.

Jellinek, E. M. *The disease concept of alcoholism.* New Brunswick, N.J.: Hillhouse Press, 1960.
A must for any student of the disease concept. Jellinek clearly had the greatest 20th-century impact of any single medical model claims-maker on the rise of the disease concept of alcoholism. In this readable book he not only lays out his understanding of what that means but also provides a review of virtually all other important research on alcoholism to the time of his writing.

Pattison, E. M., Sobell, M. B., and Sobell, L. C. *Emerging concepts of alcohol dependence.* New York: Springer-Verlag, 1977.
A recent, critical, and thorough review of the argument that alcoholism is a disease. It is highly readable, well organized, and documented carefully. These authors and other contributors paint a less than optimistic picture for the future of the disease concept as a scientific proposition.

Pittman, D. J., and Snyder, C. R. (Eds.). *Society, culture, and drinking patterns.* New York: John Wiley & Sons, Inc., 1962.
The social science "bible" of research and writing on drinking behavior. Although almost two decades old, it still offers the introductory reader a comprehensive view of how social scientists, as opposed to medical and biological scientists, might approach the study of drinking. These editors are currently considering revising this important book with the same ends and standards in view.

Room, R., Ambivalence as a sociological explanation: the case of cultural explanations of alcohol problems. *Am. Soc. Rev.*, 1976, **42,** 1047-1056.
The most recent and perhaps best critique of the favorite sociological explanation of drinking problems—the ambivalence hypothesis. Not only does the article offer a clear view of the weaknesses of this sociological explanation, but also it provides a good reference section for sociological work on drinking.

# 5 OPIATE ADDICTION

## THE FALL and RISE of MEDICAL INVOLVEMENT

The history of medical involvement with opiate addiction illustrates most clearly the political conflicts involved in the deviance designation battles and the vicissitudes of deviance definitions. This chapter traces a number of clear definitional changes of opiate use: from a time when it was not considered much of a problem, to its definition as a medical problem, through its criminalization, and again to its limited remedicalization. Since our focus is on definitional change and medical involvement, we are interested in drug traffic, criminal activities, legal penalties, or drug subcultures only as they affect medicalization and demedicalization. Our focus is on the politics of deviance designation as seen in actions by Parliament, Congress, the Supreme Court, the medical profession, and government agencies, and on technological discoveries, published research reports, official investigations, and propagandistic appeals.

Opium had no general appeal for the Western world until the middle of the 19th century, and until then its use was not considered much of a social problem or deviant behavior. As background for our discussion of the politics of opiate addiction, we review briefly opiate use prior to the 19th century when opium was used primarily for medicinal purposes and only occasionally as a recreational (i.e., used for pleasure) drug. Before beginning our history of the definition and treatment of opiate addiction, however, it is important to briefly describe opiates, their qualities and physiological effects.

### NATURE OF OPIATES

Opiates are drugs derived from the white juice of certain species of poppy. There is nothing in the chemical nature of opiates that makes them "good" or "bad" drugs. Similar to deviance, it is the social definition that separates the reputable from the disreputable. Heroin and morphine are two opiate drugs that have nearly identical pharmacological compositions and physiological effects, yet one is seen as a "killer" drug and the other a boon to medicine. The largest difference between the two drugs is that one is considered illicit and the other licit. Rather than a drug's chemical nature or biophysiological effects making it licit or illicit, it is who prescribes or who denies the use of the drug that creates the distinction (Horowitz, 1972). Thus a socially defined line has been drawn between licit and illicit drugs, based on some dubious assumptions but having some real consequences.

The physiological effects of opiates are substantial. Opiates have depressant actions on the human body that "include analgesia (relief of pain), sedation (freedom from anxiety, muscular relaxation, decreased motor activity), hypnosis (drowsiness, lethargy), and euphoria (a sense of well-being and contentment)" (Ausubel, 1958, p. 18). Opiates and synthetic opiate-like substances (methadone, meperidine [Demerol]) are the most effective analgesics, or painkillers, known today (Ray, 1978, p. 309). Morphine and heroin are most frequently taken by injection (they can also be "eaten" or "snorted"). After injecting the drug, the user usually feels flushed immediately, experiences a mild itching or tingling, soon becomes relaxed and sleepy, and enters into what can be described as a euphoric state of reverie.

Continued use of opiates gradually produces a physical tolerance, and the dosage must be increased to maintain the same euphoric effect. The body becomes increasingly dependent on the drug for normal functioning. If the drug is not taken, after a number of hours withdrawal symptoms begin. These include, at first, tenseness, restlessness, watery eyes, sweats, and runny nose and, later, chills, gooseflesh, twitching of legs, stomach cramps, and vomiting. They can last from less than a day to nearly a week, depending on a person's "habit." A single dose of the drug will produce relief. Opiate addiction is considered to be based on a physiological dependence on the drug.

We noted in the previous chapter, however, that such "addiction" can exist only when one "experiences physiological withdrawal symptoms, recognizes them as due to the need for drugs, and relieves them by taking another dose" (Becker, 1967a, p. 175). Recognition of the connection between taking the drug and relief of the symptoms appears most important. Some researchers suggest that addiction is characterized by the "hunger" for euphoria (Ausubel, 1958), whereas others (Lindesmith, 1968) posit the avoidance of withdrawal distress as central.

Although there has been little attempt to determine the degree to which individuals are incapacitated by the effects of the opiate drug itself (Horowitz, 1972), it is commonly believed that sustained opiate use and subsequent addiction is in itself harmful to the human body. What little scientific evidence exists in this regard tends to refute this belief. A study completed in 1929 but still cited as authoritative showed "that morphine addiction is not characterized by physiological deterioration or impairment of physical fitness aside from the addiction per se" (Light & Torrance, 1929, quoted in Brecher, 1972, p. 23). This is true for persons addicted as long as 20 years. Other studies have confirmed this. A more recent and often-cited study (Chein et al., 1964) emphasized that opiate addiction does not produce any known organic diseases—such as, for example, those produced by chronic smoking—and its annoying physiological effects (e.g., constipation, sexual impotence) are neither permanent nor disabling. Vincent P. Dole, a long-time and respected researcher of opiates, maintained that "cigarette smoking is unquestionably more damaging to the human body than heroin" (quoted in Brecher, 1972, p. 25). Its effect on the mind seems equally noninjurious; there is no evidence for an increase of mental disorder (psychosis) or decrease of intelligence with opiate addiction. Most studies show that personality does not change from the physiological and psychological addiction itself. In fact, as we shall see later, the most harmful effects of opiate addiction have come from its criminalization and the attendant development of a criminal narcotic underworld rather than from the opiate drugs themselves.

## A MIRACLE DRUG: PRE–19th-CENTURY USE OF OPIATES

The use of opium may be older than alcohol. The Sumerians, an ancient Middle Eastern culture thought to have flourished about 4000 BC, had an ideogram for the poppy plant that meant "joy" or "rejoicing" (Lindesmith, 1965, p. 207). Many writers date the first specific medical use of opium at about 1500 BC based on the Ebers papyrus reference to an opium remedy "to prevent the excessive crying of children" (Ray, 1978, p. 300).

Opium was used by classical Greek physicians as a medicinal agent. Theophrastus, a Greek naturalist and philosopher, recorded what is the earliest undisputed reference to the use of poppy juice (Szasz, 1974, p. 171). Hippocrates, although familiar with opium, cautioned against its use. However, Galen, the last great Greek physician, saw opium as a panacea. In his view, opium cured everything from snakebites to "women's troubles," including "vertigo, deafness, epilepsy, apoplexy, dimness of sight, loss of voice, asthma, coughs of all kinds, spitting of blood, tightness of breath, colic, the iliac poison, jaundice, hardness of the spleen," and sundry other human ills (quoted in Scott, J. M., 1969, p. 111). It is not surprising that Galen, a careful medical observer and a precursor to "scientific" medicine, was so impressed with opium's curing powers; in his time there were few other medical treatments with such powerful effects, especially for pain, coughs, or bowel disorders. Since medical use of opiates was common, there may also have been some recreational use of the drug. Galen commented in his writings on the opium cakes and candies that were sold everywhere in the streets. The Greek knowledge of opium use was lost with the decline of the Roman Empire and did not influence the European use of opium until a thousand years later.

Opium was spread by the Arabs. Perhaps because the Koran forbade wine and other alcohol, but not opium, it was more frequently indulged in by Arabs both as a medicinal and a social drug. Opium was carried east and west by Mohammedan warriors and the merchants that followed them. "In the West, opium was included in the cargoes of spices imported by Venetian merchants in the Middle Ages. It had limited appeal. Opium was one of the products Columbus hoped to bring back from the Indies" (Scott, J. M., 1969, p. 11). Opium was used for medicine and recreation in the Far Eastern countries, and eventually they began cultivating their own poppies. By the 10th century AD, opium was referred to in Chinese medical writings. An Arabian physician, Biruni, composed a pharmacology book shortly after 1000 AD that included what may be the first written description of addiction (Ray, 1978, p. 301).

By the ninth century, opium was used widely in China and the Far East. The Chinese used opium as a medicine, but to a limited degree, and never by smoking it. Smoking opium was only for recreational usage; by the 17th century it was a fairly commonplace and popular activity in some circles. Several emperors' attempts to control opiate use were largely futile, and China remained a world center for recreational opium use until the 20th century.

European travelers to the Orient brought opium back to the West. Paracelsus, a 16th-century Swiss physician who traveled to the East, introduced laudanum, or tincture of opium, into medical practice. He, like Galen before him and others after, thought of opium as a panacea and called it "the stone of immortality." It soon became a staple of European medicine. Thomas Sydenham, an English physician considered the founder of clinical medicine, regarded opium as "one of the most valued medicines in the world [which] does more honor to medicine than any remedy whatsoever" (quoted in Musto, 1973, p. 69). He believed that opium enabled physicians to perform cures that appeared almost miraculous and believed that "without opium, the healing art would cease to exist" (Scott, J. M., 1969, p. 114). In 1762, Thomas Dover, who is thought to have been a student of Sydenham, introduced a prescription for a "diaphoretic powder," which he recommended particularly for the treatment of gout. It became known as Dover's Powder and was the most widely used opium preparation for the next 150 years (Szasz, 1974). Although opium was a mainstay of the medical armamentarium, some 18th-century physicians were cautious and concerned that frequent use could result in habituation.

There is no evidence at all of general addiction in the 17th century, although opium drugs were increasingly prescribed and could be bought without any restriction (Scott, J. M., 1969). Although there had been incidental reports of tolerance to the drug since the Roman period and occasional reports of discomfort on cessation of habitual use that could be relieved by ingesting more opium, no concept of addiction was yet delineated. It was not until the early 18th century that a clear association was made between the discontinuation of regular opium use and the appearance of certain (withdrawal) symptoms. One of the earliest known descriptions, though not defined as addiction, appears in John Jones' 1700 work *The Mysteries of Opium*. He warned that the

> effects of sudden leaving off the use of opium after a long and lavish use thereof [were] great and even intolerable distresses, anxieties, and depressions of spirit, which commonly ended in a most miserable death, attended with strange agonies, unless men return to the use of opium; which soon raises them again, and certainly restores them. (Quoted in Musto, 1973, p. 69)

But this viewpoint was not readily accepted by the medical profession, and the debate over whether opium was addictive and whether only certain people were prone to addiction (e.g., Orientals), raged well into the 19th century.

Prior to the 19th century, then, with the exception of China, opiates were generally limited to medical uses. What came to be called addiction was not considered much of a problem, although certainly many people must have become physically dependent as a result of medical treatment. The great controversies surrounding opium use were not to begin until the 19th century.

## POLITICS OF OPIUM IN THE 19th CENTURY

During the 19th century the definitions and uses of opium began to change. Opium became an important item to trade and was alleged to have been the object of two wars; scientific and medical discoveries made opiates more potent and usable; the usage of opiates increased markedly in the United States, especially in the second half of the century; and opium became the center of increasingly clear political activities. Yet, at the close of the century, opium use was not yet considered a significant problem in American society.

### Recreational use in England and China

The first reports of European recreational use of opium appear in the early 19th century, emanating especially from literary circles. One of the most well-known users was Samuel Taylor Coleridge, who composed his exquisite ''Kubla Khan'' while under the influence of opium. The poet Elizabeth Barret Browning was also addicted to opium. Thomas De Quincy's *Confessions of an English Opium Eater*, in 1823, presented vivid accounts of his experiences with opium and offered a positive view of opium's recreational and aesthetic qualities. He saw opium use as a habit, which must be learned like any other habit, but he also suffered from long and unproductive periods attributed to his habit. These writers and others, sometimes referred to as members of an ''opium cult,'' experimented with drugs and became well-known for their opiate habits, but they were a distinct artistic minority. Their writings and reputations gave a romantic flavor to the image of opiate use, but recreational opiate use in England was actually not widespread in the early 19th century.

In China the situation was different. Chinese use of opium was limited for many years to a select, elite group. After a prohibition edict in 1729, it became necessary to smuggle opium from India. This illegal commerce proved very profitable for all parties (including customs officials); so it was tolerated (Scott, J. M., 1969). This produced a lively international commerce and two ''opium wars.''

The history of the opium wars is a fascinating example of the ravages of Western imperialism, but it is much too long and involved to be told here. However, a few points need to be made to understand how definitions of opiate use were to change in England and subsequently elsewhere. In the late 17th century the port of Canton was finally opened to foreign trade. Tea was a major export, much desired in England. What would be a suitable item of trade? According to J. M. Scott (1969), ''From the first, opium was the only export the Chinese customer took to'' (p. 20). Beginning in the 18th century, European nations traded increasingly in opium as a source of foreign revenue. Opium became a major item of British trade. The British East India Company obtained a monopoly of Indian opium, considered the world's best, and began exporting opium from India to China in 1767. When opium became illegal in China, the British created a complex smuggling network (in which they continually denied involvement). It was a huge and profitable trade. In addition to trading for tea, silks, and silver, the cultivation of opium financed the British colonial administration in India. The Chinese were literally ''force-fed'' opium, and the supply continued to create its own demand (Helmer, 1975). In 1839 a Chinese commissioner arrested opium smugglers and destroyed a considerable amount of opium. This led to a British military reaction and the first opium war (1839-1842). With the second opium war 15 years later, the British extended their distribution of opium in China, and illegal British imports continued. During the latter part of the 19th century, it was estimated that 8 million Chinese were addicted (Kittrie, 1971, p. 216). Although the British received considerable profits from the opium trade, the primary motivation for the wars was to open the potentially huge market of China for international trade in general, not just an opium trade (Ray, 1978, p. 305).

## Medical uses: from a panacea to a problem

In 1806 Frederich W. A. Serturner, a 23-year-old German pharmacist's assistant, extracted a purer alkaloid from raw opium with a potency 10 times greater and named it morphium after the god of sleep. Medical applications for morphine soon became obvious, and it was increasingly substituted for opium in medical practice. In 1831 Serturner was awarded a prize from the French Institute for this medical discovery (Scott, J. M., 1969). A year later other scientists isolated a second important alkaloid called codeine.

The administration of morphine was facilitated greatly by the invention of the hypodermic syringe in 1853. Doses could be controlled, and action was quicker. Physicians thought that injected morphine was not habit-forming (addictive) and used it for a variety of ailments. A standard British medical text, used widely in America, recommended opium for a variety of common medical problems:

> to mitigate pain, to allay spasm, to promote sleep, to relieve nervous restlessness, to produce perspiration and to check profuse mucous discharges from the bronchial tubes and gastrointestinal canal. But experience has proved its value in relieving some diseases in which not one of these indications can be at all times distinctly traced. (Pereira, 1854, quoted in Musto, 1973, p. 70)

But some physicians also warned of the dangers of opium smoking and were able to describe addiction accurately. Physicians believed that "enslavement" to opiates was caused more by the user's weak character than the drug itself and considered the lower classes to be particularly vulnerable to it. They often described a decline in moral character associated with chronic opiate use.

Physicians were so taken with the pain-killing qualities of opiates that they invented a new disease called neuralgia (a term used today in a more restricted sense), for which opium was the treatment. Neuralgia was used "to describe pains, the origin of which is not clearly traceable" (Rothstein, 1972, p. 191). In the United States the Civil War contributed to the spread of opiate use. Morphine injections were given to soldiers to reduce pain and combat dysentery symptoms. So many veterans returned home addicted that it was called the "soldier's disease" (Lindesmith, 1965).

By the end of the Civil War, morphine was commonly used in medical practice. Some physicians considered it safer than opium; moreover, it was easier to ingest, since it could be injected by hypodermic needle. As medical historian David Musto (1973, p. 73) points out, mid–19th-century conventional medical wisdom tended to define opium by its therapeutic qualities, minimizing its dangers, except to the lower classes. It was not until the 1870s that the addictive properties of morphine were recognized and warnings began to appear in the medical literature.

It appears that most addicts of this period were literally recruited into addiction, albeit unintentionally, through the liberal and careless use of opiates in medical treatment (Lindesmith, 1965, p. 129). Occasionally physicians like Oliver Wendell Holmes, Sr., then dean of Harvard Medical School, criticized the ignorance of physicians and blamed them for the prevalence of addiction. In a speech he said, "The constant prescription of opiates by certain physicians . . . has rendered the habitual use of that drug [in the Western states] very prevalent" (quoted in Musto, 1973, p. 4). An 1885 report to the Iowa State Board of Health charged:

> The habit in a vast majority of cases is first formed by the unpardonable carelessness of physicians, who are often fond of using the little syringe, or relieving every ache and pain by the administration of an opiate. (Hull, 1885/1974, p. 39)

But the drug continued to be prescribed freely in the 1890s.

Morphine was not only used for a variety of medical ailments but was touted both as a treatment for opium addiction and alcoholism. Because injection of morphine was thought to be nonhabit-forming, many physicians saw morphine as a cure for addiction to smoking opium and treated their addicted patients accordingly.

Morphine was also heralded as a treatment for chronic drinking problems. In an article entitled "Advantages of Substituting the Morphia Habit for the Incurably Alcoholic," published in 1889 in a medical journal, the physician-author claimed morphine was "less inimical to the healthy life than alcohol" and reported, "After years of experimental trial and observation I arrived at the conclusion that [morphine] is immeasurably the best, or by far the least of the two evils" (quoted in Ray, 1978, p. 307). Many physicians did in fact convert alcoholics to morphine (Brecher, 1972). This strategy of treating one addiction with another occurs with regularity and almost with predictability throughout the history of opiate addiction. Freud, for example, was fascinated with cocaine as a cure for morphine addiction. This game of unwitting "medical substitution" in the treatment of addiction involves the medical profession in a continuing, frustrating, and largely fruitless search for a drug that will cure drug addiction.

Although physicians were partly responsible for recruiting the mid–19th-century addict population, by the latter half of the century another quasimedical industry was increasingly implicated in addiction recruitment. The manufacture of "patent medicines" was a highly successful industry beginning about the time of the Civil War. There were few government regulations, and thus many "soothing syrups" and "tonics" containing opiates were sold as home remedies. Such products as Mrs. Winslow's Soothing Syrup, Hooper's Anodyne, the Infant's Friend, Ayer's Cherry Pectoral, and Godfrey's Cordial were actively promoted by the growing drug industry, sometimes as "cure-alls" but more often for "women's troubles," infant teething, diarrhea, coughs, or pain. Since ingredients did not have to be listed on the label, many users became physically dependent without realizing it. The drug companies also sold guaranteed "drug addiction cures," which were themselves addictive, thus merely transferring the addiction to another drug (Young, James H., 1961). In a nation with a limited level of health care, such potent medicines were popular and, to a degree, useful treatments. They were available at customers' request in every pharmacy and general store. By the turn of the century some concern was voiced about these medicines' addictive qualities, but literally hundreds of thousands of people were already addicted, including many physicians, who had thought themselves immune to addiction (Goode, 1972, p. 164). The availability of a regular supply of drugs allowed these addicted people to lead conventional lives.

## Discovery of addiction as a disease

Physicians in the latter part of the century began to recognize that morphine was addictive, even when injected. Although there were increasing reports in the medical literature, the acceptance of these data by the medical profession was slow. The first documented case of injected morphine addiction was reported in 1864. But in an 1880 questionnaire most physicians still doubted that injections produced addiction (Morgan, 1974). Thomas Szasz (1974, p. 6) notes that the earliest edition of Kraepelin's 1883 psychiatric text made no mention of drug intoxication or addiction at all, while later editions mention "chronic intoxication" and "morphism" but not "addiction" per se. The category of drug addiction did not appear in Bleuler's renowned 1916 *Textbook of Psychiatry*. Warnings of addiction as a result of morphine did not appear in medical texts until about 1900 (Duster, 1970, p. 13).

Although many physicians and psychiatrists denied or ignored the addictive qualities of morphine until nearly the turn of the century, others demonstrated an increasing interest in addiction as a medical problem. These physicians developed both theories and treatments for what they believed increasingly was the disease of opiate addiction. An example is J. B. Mattison's *The Treatment of Opiate Addiction,* published in 1885. The most commonly accepted theories of addiction emphasized its tendency to be inherited:

> Learned journals bristled with confident discussions of "high" and "low" brain centers that governed conduct; of poor nerve endowment, or genetic faults. Social tensions, translated into personal imbalances in weak individuals, were also allegedly high among Americans. . . . (Morgan, 1974, p. 90)

Such ideas, coupled with the belief that lower-class people were susceptible to addiction, led physicians to see addiction more as a problem of ''weak people'' rather than of strong drugs. It was largely the constitution of individuals that made them addictable, not the drug itself. These and similar theories lasted into the 20th century and in fact provided the bases of some of the greatest controversies concerning addiction. By the early 20th century, however, opiates themselves were also indicted by physicians in general as a ''cause'' of addiction. Physicians treated opiate addiction when it appeared in their practice, and were generally optimistic that withdrawal, medical care, and rest would cure addiction.

The late 19th century saw changes in medical practice that made opiates no longer necessarily a panacea. With the discovery of the germ theory of disease, infectious diseases like tuberculosis, caused by germs and bacteria, came to dominate medical practice and became the ''model'' of disease for medical practitioners. Thus, by the end of the century, opiates had few medical uses beyond the relief of pain. They were no longer seen as cure-alls or soothing agents but as a potential medical problem in themselves.

At the close of the 19th century ''many doctors believed that addiction was a disease, to be treated with pragmatic therapy rather than moralism'' (Morgan, 1974, p. 19). Medical theories hypothesized that if opiates changed nerve tissues and cellular activity, then the individual's need for them was uncontrollable. Thus, according to a physician addiction expert of the time, addicts used opiates ''not for social enjoyment but for a physical necessity'' because of alterations in the body's physiology (Mattison, quoted in Morgan, 1974, p. 19). This became an increasingly accepted medical view. By the turn of the 20th century, opiate addiction became defined as a disease and a bona fide medical concern.

In sum, the 19th century saw opium use change from a central medical treatment to an emergent medical problem. Physicians were intimately involved with opiate addiction at all phases: people became addicted through medical and quasimedical treatments; medical discoveries like the hypodermic needle made ingestion easier; and recognition of the ''addiction as a disease'' led to medical treatments. Thus, in a real sense, 19th-century medical practice created the very addiction problem it was treating at the century's close.

## Addicts and addiction in a "dope fiend's paradise"

The late 19th century has been called ''a dope fiend's paradise'' (Brecher, 1972). Almost no federal or state restrictions were in force, opiates were regularly available from physicians and in pharmacies, and no great moral stigma was attached to opiate use or addiction. A wide variety of people were addicted, and obtaining drugs was not much of a problem.

**Yesterday's addicts.** For those of us who are accustomed to thinking of the typical modern-day opiate addict as young, male, urban, lower-class, and a member of a minority group, 19th-century addicts provide a sharp contrast. From all the data we have (which are somewhat limited by today's research standards), it appears that the typical 19th-century addict was middle-aged, female, rural, middle-class, and white. The only exceptions were the opium-smoking Chinese immigrants who were limited to the West Coast. An 1872 Massachusetts Board of Health Survey found many women and small-town residents among opiate users (Oliver, 1872/1974). A Chicago study in 1880 reported that the model age of addicts was 30 to 50, and only 12 of 235 addicts were ''colored.'' This study further suggested it was ''among the middle class that we find the great majority who are today opium eaters'' (Earle, 1880/1974, p. 56). The Iowa Board of Health survey noted ''the age at which the habit is most common is fifty and sixty'' (Hull, 1885/1974). It has been estimated that 60% to 75% of the addicts were women, perhaps as a result of the ''widespread medical custom of prescribing opiates for menstrual and menopausal discomforts, and the many proprietary opiates advertised for female troubles'' (Brecher, 1972, p. 17). Another probable factor was the strong negative sanctions against alcohol drinking by women.

Most addicts purchased their drugs at the

local pharmacy. An 1880 Boston researcher found that of "10,200 recipes taken in 34 drugstores, I found 1,481 recipes which prescribed some preparation of opium. . . . [In addition] I learned that proprietary or 'patent' medicines which have the largest sales were those containing opiates" (Eaton, 1880/1974, p. 182).

The number of addicts during this period was probably greater than at any other time in American history. Estimates by recent researchers range from 250,000 (Musto, 1973) to a prevalence eight times greater than today (Duster, 1970). There is no doubt that opiate addiction was widespread, perhaps encompassing "no less than 1% of the population" (Ray, 1978, p. 308). Yet, despite such a high prevalence of addiction, it was not considered especially deviant or a major social problem. This was partly because addicts could easily obtain their drugs and were thus able to function normally in society. This was facilitated by a different public definition of opiate addiction than exists today in the United States; by 1920 this public definition had changed, drugs were no longer easily available, the addict population shifted drastically, and addiction became a major social problem.

## Entrepreneurs and the morality of opium: the creation of an evil

Public moral definitions of behavior do not change by themselves. Moral entrepreneurs, interest groups, and other claims-makers work to legitimate their versions of morality. Sometimes this politics of definition making is obscure. In the case of opiate addiction, however, the arenas of conflict are public, and the definitional politicking is fairly clear. In the 19th century we encounter moral entrepreneurship and interest group politicking in the British Parliament's "great debate" over the opium trade. In the next century we see the conflict expanded to an international arena (and especially dramatically in the United States).

In the first half of the century the "opium question," to the extent there was one, was not a particularly pressing moral issue for Europeans (although it certainly was to the Chinese). There were few voices questioning the British opium trade. A few missionaries who had been to China began to suggest the opium trade might have deleterious effects on the Chinese people. Missionary W. H. Medheurst reported in 1840 in his book, *China,* that nearly 3 million people were demoralized by the opium habit, their bodies debilitated, their families ruined, and their life expectancies reduced by 10 years (Inglis, 1975). One of the first times the issue was publicly raised was in an 1842 lead article in *The Times* denouncing the trade. A few voices condemned the trade in ensuing years, but the great debate did not become really heated for nearly three decades.

The major adversaries in the debate about opium were the opium interests and the antiopium crusaders. The opium interests were those who profited economically from the trade: the merchants, the traffickers, the Indian colonial government, and, to a degree, the British government itself. The British government had considerable vested interest in the trade: an estimated 10% to 14% of the British-controlled Indian government's revenues came from the opium trade (Johnson, B. D., 1975). The antiopium groups included some moral reformers and missionaries who organized themselves into a variety of antiopium organizations. Predominant among these groups were the Society for the Suppression of the Opium Trade (SSOT) and the Anti-Opium Society. The intensity of the debate developed slowly; in the first years when the issue was raised in Parliament, defenders of the trade argued that its "evils" had been greatly exaggerated. But controversy grew, and over the years the sheer number of words exchanged, both in and out of Parliament, was enormous. Scores of books, articles, letters, and pamphlets appeared extolling one position or another; the Anti-Opium Society's journal, *The Friend of China,* financed in its beginning in 1875 by four wealthy Quakers, eventually reached 32 bound volumes. The antiopiumists attempted to persuade both the public and Parliament of the justice of their cause.

The issues were fairly clear for both sides, and the same arguments were repeated over and over. The pro-opium interests argued that there was a demand for the product—opium—and the Chinese people wanted it, "free" trade should not be hampered, the revenues were important to (Britain's) economic stability, and the drug was not dangerous and its "evils" were exaggerated. The antiopium crusaders claimed that the trade had been forced on China and she had been consistently hostile to it, the market for opium had been created by the supply, it was immoral to trade this addicting and dangerous drug that leads inevitably to destruction and demoralization of people, and self-interested profits from this immoral vice were immoral (Johnson, B. D., 1975; Scott, J. M., 1969).

Both sides drew on medical evidence to support their claims, usually concerning the effects of the drug. Pro-opium interests quoted medical figures such as George Birdwood:

> I hold [opium] to be absolutely harmless. I do not place it simply in the same category with even tobacco smoking . . . but I mean that opium smoking, in itself, is as harmless as smoking willow bark, or inhaling the smoke of a peat fire, or vapour of boiling water. . . . I hold opium smoking, in short, to be a strictly harmless indulgence, like any other smoking, and the essence of its pleasure to be not in the opium in itself so much as the smoking of it. If something else were put into the pipe instead of opium, that something else would gradually become just as popular as opium, although it might not incidentally prove so beneficial. (Quoted in Scott, J. M., 1969, p. 99)

Antiopium crusaders would also quote well-known physicians such as D. W. Osgood, a medical missionary:

> Rich and poor find that the continual use of opium [smoking] interferes with digestion, diminishing the secretions of the alimentary canal, producing constipation, loss of appetite and the usual discomfiture of dyspepsia. In nearly every case there is difficulty in breathing, and in many chronic bronchitis and asthma. The smoker becomes anemic and impotent. (Quoted in Scott, J. M., 1969, pp. 99-100)

Sometimes these medical claims became explicitly moralistic. Physician D. W. Moore, an opium supporter, suggested "that in ancient times the Chinese were a very drunken people" and if opium had not been introduced into China, alcohol use would be more of a problem. Other physicians argued vehemently for the evil nature of the drug (Scott, J. M., 1969). An extension of the controversy, whether certain individuals were more addictable than others (already heard in the United States), was also debated. Predictably, some physicians and others suggested it was not the drug but the Chinese moral constitution that was the cause of any degeneration from opium. Antiopium forces directly countered this argument with increasing evidence to suit the needs of its position. Although medical people can be moral entrepreneurs in their own right, nonmedical interest groups frequently select medical evidence to support their particular claims.

Although opium had been mentioned in Parliament before 1870, it was not until that year that a motion to condemn the opium trade was introduced. It was soundly defeated. After a period of decreased public interest and several defeats, antiopium crusaders managed to persuade Parliament to pass a motion in 1891 stating "that the system by which Indian opium revenue is raised is morally indefensible" (Scott, J. M., 1969, p. 107). The motion, however, never became a resolution; so it remained merely a symbolic moral stand, with no practical political implications.

Under the direction of Prime Minister William Gladstone, a royal commission was assigned to study the problem. The commission was screened and picked by authorities in India; so a critical report could hardly be expected. The Royal Commission on Opium published a massive seven-volume, 2500-page report in 1895. The commission's major conclusions were that the dangers of opium had been exaggerated and were no worse than those resulting from the excess use of alcohol, that a limitation of production was created by the monopoly in India, and that if it was unsatisfactory to China, it was their responsibility to prohibit importation. It also pointed out that India's opium was the world's best and that India's economy could not afford to lose the revenue from opium production (Scott, J. M., 1969, pp. 107-108). In short, opium was an important economic venture, and associated dangers were considered minimal.

The ensuing years were difficult ones for the antiopium movement. Numerous pamphlets and books attempted to refute the commission and discredit the report. The main thrust of the opposition to the report was an 1895 pamphlet by Joshua Rowntree, "The Opium Habit in the East: A Study of the Evidence Given to the Royal Commission on Opium." Rowntree showed conflicts of opinion and manipulation of evidence in the commission report. He pointed out, for example, that although 49 out of 52 missionaries from China had given evidence that condemned opium, the report had quoted only the views of two of the three who had been less critical (Inglis, 1975, p. 92). Within 10 years the report was discredited, and today scholars generally agree that the commission had "whitewashed the opium problem and rubber-stamped the opium monopoly and trade" (Johnson, B. D., 1975, p. 315). Parliament did pass an antiopium trade bill in 1906, but the trade did not end finally until 1913.

In their efforts to end the opium trade with China, the antiopium crusaders also changed public opinion about the drug and the definitions of opium use. *Opium addiction became an "evil."* Their arguments about the immoral and detrimental nature of opium use still echo in today's society. As sociologist Bruce D. Johnson (1976) points out,

> The main legacy of the British anti-opium movement to modern times was the institutionalization of anti-opium, but scientifically dubious, beliefs that opiates cause almost immediate and life-long addiction, cause physical and moral harm to the user, cause crime, prostitution, gambling, etc. (p. 21)

## American attitudes toward opiate addiction: from empathy to anxiety

There was some ambivalence in the 19th-century American attitude toward opiate addiction. Because of their medical use and medical connotation, some favorable images of opiates were available. Addiction was not considered a major social problem, and there was no public moral devaluation of addicts, but as people became aware of the addictive qualities of opiates, the seeds of public concern began to germinate. Nineteenth-century addicts, however, generally aroused sympathy and were people to be pitied rather than scorned.

As suggested, physicians were partly responsible for these attitudes. They had been largely indifferent to addiction and tended to treat it with "pragmatic therapy rather than moralism." Now that the addictive potential of the drugs became better known, they viewed opiate addiction rather matter-of-factly. It was a disease to be treated like any other disease; addicts were just "poor victims."

This was not necessarily the dominant public attitude. In some circles opium was viewed as immoral—a vice akin to dancing, smoking, theatergoing, gambling, or sexual promiscuity (Brecher, 1972). Narcotics were seen as making an individual a "slave," robbing the addict of free will. The popular stereotype of the addict was an individual who "lacked both proper inhibitions and the stimuli of individual responsibility" (Morgan, 1974, p. 22). Late 19th-century Americans were beginning to view opiate use as a "will-weakening vice" that they believed people of strong will could stop if only they tried hard enough. Addiction was loathed, but "because of the connection between medical therapy and addiction, the drug addict was viewed as a helpless victim, an unfortunate sick person in need of medical attention" (Goode, 1972, p. 189). Acquaintances felt somewhat sorry for the addict's dependence on medication but did not disvalue the addict or his role. As we shall soon see, this all changed by the 1920s.

Although addiction was imbued with negative values, there does not seem to have been the same hard-nosed public support for banning opium as existed in the later stages of the temperance movement. This may be partly because the public considered opiates a medical concern and because addiction was not viewed as a problem for society, whereas alcohol was. Nevertheless, these negative public views tended to undercut the more benign medical position on opium. Most people developed a basic fear of drug addiction (Musto, 1973), a view which was increasingly promoted in the media and through other channels of propaganda.

A concern developed among the public and medical profession alike that addiction could weaken the key to America's strength: its young and its middle class. After 1865 some anxiety began to be voiced that women and the young may be particularly vulnerable to addiction (they were likely candidates to have weak constitutions), and many middle-class, respectable citizens were addicted. In 1902 a physician wrote, "morphism is one of the most serious addictions among active brain workers, professional businessmen, teachers, and persons having large responsibilities" (quoted in Morgan, 1974, p. 14). It was especially worrisome, since as long as the drug supply was maintained, it was difficult to detect an addict.

But much of the concern with addiction came from the association in the public eye of addiction, opium-smoking dens, and Chinese immigrants. "By the 1870s the press reported often on opium smoking, the first form of addiction to attain wide public notoriety" (Morgan, 1974, p. 5). The anti-Chinese sentiment in the United States became intimately tied to a fledgling antiopium sentiment. The 19th-century press was silent on morphine medication and its addicting effects, despite the vastly larger number of morphine addicts than opium smokers. Newspapers depended on advertising that included opium products, and "did not want to alienate the advertisers, because they were a major source of revenue" (Duster, 1970, p. 8). Thus the American view of opiate addiction began to turn on anti-Chinese sentiments.

### First prohibition of smoking opium

The amount of smoking opium imported into the United States increased markedly after 1860. The largest consumers were Chinese immigrants who had brought their opium habits with them when they were recruited and imported as cheap labor to build the railroads. One antiopium crusader estimated in 1900 that 35% of the Chinese immigrant population smoked opium with some degree of regularity (Hamilton Wright, in Helmer, 1975). This estimate may be too high, but even if there were only half or a third as many opium smokers, the number was substantial. Anti-Chinese sentiments ran high, especially on the West Coast, since the Chinese were seen taking jobs from Americans and undercutting the American labor market. This culminated in the Chinese Exclusion Act of 1882, which suspended Chinese immigration.

Many Chinese immigrant laborers migrated to San Francisco. This engendered increased hostility, based partly on racial prejudices and partly on their willingness to accept employment at low wages. In 1875 the city passed an ordinance prohibiting opium smoking in the dens of San Francisco. This was not a health ordinance but rather a clear-cut attempt to regulate the life-style of a minority. It was the first of a number of racist laws aimed at restricting the Chinese use of opium. Prohibition pushed opium smoking underground. In the ensuing years several states passed anti–opium-smoking laws, but they were relatively ineffective. In 1887 Congress passed a law prohibiting opium importing by the Chinese, and in 1890 it limited opium manufacture to American citizens. Even with these local, state, and federal efforts the amount of smoking opium legally imported in the United States continued to rise steadily. By 1909 legal importing of opium had risen sevenfold in 50 years. It was in that same year that importation of smoking opium was prohibited altogether (Morgan, 1974).

These laws were futile attempts to control opium smoking. They failed, as have other prohibitionary laws since, largely because opium smoking is a "crime without a complaint." Since the laws were aimed at private transactions between willing sellers and willing buyers, there was no individual complainant to bring these "transgressions" to the attention of the authorities. Such laws also have other unintended effects such as creating an illegal underground and converting smokers to more hazardous but available substances.

### Discovery of heroin

In 1898 the German Bayer Laboratory, a major pharmaceutical company, introduced a new morphine derivative that had been discovered two decades earlier. This new drug was three times as potent as morphine and was marketed as a nonaddicting substitute for morphine or codeine. It was named heroin for these "heroic" properties. Physicians writing in medical journals described it as a nonaddicting drug. A paper in the *Boston Medical and Surgical Journal* asserted that "there was no danger of acquiring a habit" (cited in Szasz, 1974, p. 179). The *New York Medical Journal* (Manges, 1900) dismissed its addiction problems as minimal:

> Habituation has been noted in a small percentage . . . of the cases. . . . All observers agreed, however, that none of the patients suffer in any way from this habituation, and that none of the symptoms which are so characteristic of chronic morphinism have ever been observed. On the other hand, a large number of the reports refer to the fact that the same dose may be used for a long time without any habituation. (Quoted in Ray, 1978, p. 308)

Heroin was a popular drug, easy to administer, and available without prescription (Duster, 1970). Users frequently injected it with hypodermic needles readily acquired by mail from the Sears catalogue.

In its early years heroin was lauded as a cure for opiate addiction. This, however, turned out to be another case of wishful thinking and the "medical substitution game" as reports of heroin addiction began to appear in the medical literature. Within 5 years of its introduction to the market it was abundantly clear that heroin was at least as addictive as morphine, and warnings appeared in the medical journals (Pettey, 1902-1903, cited in Duster, 1970).

Following the reports of heroin's addictive qualities, the medical profession declared that heroin had no value for medical treatment and called for a curtailment of its use in cough syrups and other remedies. With this medical repudiation, heroin was divorced from any respectability and legitimacy. Unlike morphine and codeine, it had no medical definitions; it was a drug that had only "recreational" uses and thus became quickly imbued with far greater negative connotations than either of its sister drugs. Muckraking exposés of addiction appeared in the popular press, which depicted heroin as the most threatening drug in history. It was portrayed as having special appeals and dangers for youth (Morgan, 1974). Stripped of its medical respectability, heroin became defined as a drug with no redeeming value, a view which remains prominent today.

In sum, the late 19th century saw an increased public concern with addiction. Yet addiction certainly was not considered a major social problem, and little of the moral opprobrium we associate with addiction and addicts was apparent; addiction was a medical problem, a disease, and addicts engendered sympathy. With the connection of opium use to the prevalent anti-Chinese sentiment and the divorce of heroin from any medical connotations, we see the beginnings of a definitional transformation and a hardening of the public view that became clear in the first two decades of the 20th century.

## CRIMINALIZATION AND DEMEDICALIZATION

The definition of opiate addiction and the treatment of opiate addicts shifted radically in the first two decades of the 20th century. By the middle of the 1920s, opiates were prohibited, addicts were seen as "dope fiends," and a criminal subculture emerged. Many of these changes in the definition and treatment of opiate addiction remain in force today, although there has been a reemergence of medical definitions. International developments around the turn of the century significantly affected a changing American opium policy.

### A quest for international control and the United States' response

Shortly after the turn of the century the United States government seemed suddenly to emerge on the international scene as a driving moral force championing world-wide control of "evil" opiates. Although the United States took a strong and righteous moral stand, it was not a selfless one. In fact, the State Department's leadership in the antinarcotics movement "originated with one of the peaks of American imperialism, the seizure of the Philippine Islands from Spain and the drive for a share of the China market" (Musto, 1973, p. 24).

The United States annexed the Philippines from Spain after the Spanish-American War in 1898. The Philippines had an established government opium monopoly, and the United States Philippine Commission soon created a special committee to study "the opium problem." The committee consisted of the Commissioner of Public Health for the Philippines, a Filipino physician, and an Episcopal bishop named Charles Henry Brent. Reverend Brent eventually became a leading international crusader in the antiopium movement. The committee reported in 1904, after an extensive investigation of opium in the Far East. Their conclusions were exactly the opposite of those presented by the Royal Commission on Opium a decade earlier (Taylor, A., 1969). The committee's report stated that opium was an evil influence, and it proposed governmental control of opiates and the gradual decrease of individual opium rations toward the eventual goal of prohibition except for medical purposes. Hospital cures and the teachings of the evils of opium also should be made available.

> The report's authors considered it in accord with contemporary medical opinion selected, no doubt, to make their point: the craving for opium is irrepressible and a habitué gradually increases his intake until systematic intoxication leads to moral and physical degradation. (Musto, 1973, p. 27)

The American response was even more drastic than the report's recommendations. In 1905 Congress ordered an immediate opiate prohibition for Filipinos except for medical purposes. After 3 years prohibition would include non-Filipinos. This report and legislation were significant because these prohibitionary measures became more or less a model for future antiopium legislation. In all cases prohibitionary legislation carried the conditional phrase ''except for medical purposes.'' The closing off of other legal sources increased the medicalization of opiate addiction and brought more addicts under medical jurisdiction.

China initiated legislation in 1906 to end all opium production in 10 years. Britain agreed to reduce Indian opium exports to China in proportion with her own reductions in cultivation and imports from other countries (Scott, J. M., 1969). American missionaries played a significant role in promoting an antiopium movement and inducing the United States to become involved. For missionaries like Bishop Brent, opium was a moral issue ''and transactions in the drug . . . a social vice—a crime'' (Taylor, A., 1969, p. 37). He believed opium was ruining lives in many countries and could only be controlled with some international agreement. He wrote a letter to President Theodore Roosevelt articulating his views and calling for some international concerted action. In 1906 President Roosevelt suggested convening an international opium conference. The United States wanted to expand her interests in China and thus offered aid to the Chinese in dealing with their opium problems. American policymakers hoped this might predispose China to adopt a position favorable to United States' trade interests (Platt, J. J., & Labate, 1976).

**Two international conferences.** The United States, spearheading the new international conference convened in 1909, was in the rather embarrassing position of having *no* federal legislation limiting opium use. But in 1909, just as the conference was beginning, Congress passed legislation prohibiting the importation of smoking opium to the United States.

The Shanghai Opium Commission convened in 1909 with 13 nations attending. The American delegation consisted of Hamilton Wright, a physician and enthusiastic antiopium crusader; Charles Tenney, an expert on China and a strong antiopium advocate; and Bishop Brent, who acted as chairman. The United States proposed a prohibition of opium except for medical and scientific purposes; other nations were interested but not enthusiastic. The commission had no real power and was thus limited to making recommendations. There was general agreement that some controls were needed, but no way to implement them was outlined. The commission's recommendations provided an impetus and support for subsequent American legislation (Platt, J. J., & Labate, 1976). The main result of the conference was to focus political attention to the opium problem.

A second conference was called for 1912. Attempts in Congress to pass an opium-control bill before the second conference failed. The principal interest group involved in defeating the legislation was the drug industry, which would not accept the severe restrictions proposed (Musto, 1973). The International Conference on Opium at the Hague recommended governmental limitation on importing opium for nonmedical purposes and governmental licensing for all persons engaged in all phases of the production and distribution of opiates. No administrative mechanisms were created to carry out the recommendations, however, and it took the better part of two decades to finally create some international controls on opium manufacture and distribution.

Although these international conferences did not directly affect the medicalization of opiate addiction in the United States, they had important indirect ramifications. First, they were the prelude and impetus for the legislation that prohibited nonmedical opiate manufacture and sale in the United States. Second, by restricting opiate supplies to medical purposes, they forced opiate addicts to rely increasingly on physicians as their suppliers of the drug.

## Harrison Act: the criminalization of addiction

The early 20th century was a "progressive era" in the United States, resulting in the increased governmental regulation of industry and commerce. Domestic concern about drugs was increasing. In response to the crusading of Dr. Harvey W. Wiley and the "muckraking" journalism that exposed the patent medicine industry, Congress in 1906 passed the Pure Food and Drug Act. This law required that medicines containing opiates (and certain other drugs) have their contents clearly labeled. It appears that some addicts subsequently discontinued their use of opiate preparations. Following the Flexner Report in 1910, which was a devastating indictment of the quality of medical education, the medical profession itself began to exert tighter regulation on medical training and thus on who could become a physician. The temperance movement had become prohibitionist and by the end of the second decade succeeded in winning such an amendment to the Constitution.

**Passage of the Harrison Act.** From 1885 to the commencing of the first international conference on opium, many states passed laws against opiate use, usually opium smoking. The first comprehensive narcotics law, the Boylan Act, was passed in 1914 by the New York state legislature. But with the exception of the 1909 law on smoking opium, no federal legislation on opiates existed until the Harrison Act.

Dr. Hamilton Wright and a few others, mostly missionaries and physicians, were largely responsible for "discovering" the domestic "drug problem" (Reasons, 1974). In reaction to the agreements of the second international opium conference, a bill restricting the manufacture and distribution of narcotics was introduced in Congress. Representative Francis Burton Harrison agreed to shepherd this legislation through the House of Representatives. He appeared not to have a particular interest in the specific philosophy of the legislation so much as in its political viability (Musto, 1973, p. 54). Among the champions of the bill was Secretary of State William Jennings Bryan, a long-time prohibitionist and supporter of missionary activities. He urged prompt passage of the law to fulfill the United States' obligations under the new international treaty.

The various components of the drug and pharmaceutical industry were still opposed to a very restrictive bill. The AMA at this time supported the restrictive legislation. The Harrison bill, which incorporated numerous compromises of interested parties, was introduced in 1913. The Harrison bill's supporters had little to say about the evils of opiate addiction in the United States (Brecher, 1972, p. 49). Debate centered more on the necessity of meeting our international obligations than on the morality or health hazards of opiate addiction, and the bill passed the House easily. More than a year later the Senate passed a version with amendments lobbied for by special interest groups. On December 14, 1914, the Harrison Act was passed, and it was signed by the president 3 days later. The American government had vindicated its moralistic international promises: opiates and other narcotics would be brought under federal control.

On the face of it, the Harrison Act did not seem to be a prohibition law. Its official and cumbersome title suggests its function as a *control* law by tax and registration:

> An Act to provide for the registration of, with the collectors of internal revenue, and to impose a special tax upon all persons who produce, import, manufacture, compound, deal in, dispense, sell, distribute, or give away opium or coca leaves, their salts, derivatives, or preparations, and for other purposes.

Physicians, pharmacists, and manufacturers dealing in opiates would be licensed. Addicts were not mentioned (Lindesmith, 1965). The act had three major provisions: (1) Through registration and licensing it gave the government precise knowledge of legal traffic; (2) it required all parties to pay a tax, therefore placing the responsibility for enforcement on the Bureau of Internal Revenue of the Treasury Department; and (3) it limited the purchase of narcotics (except for a few exempt small amounts) to those prescribed by physicians for legitimate medical use. Thus physicians retained control over opiates and their distribution. The *intent* of the bill appears to have been to place opiates and addicts completely in the hands of the medical profession (Duster, 1970) and to achieve a controlled and orderly marketing of opiates. This is not, however, what happened.

**Interpreting and implementing the Harrison Act.** Although the Harrison Act was intended to be a law aimed at the regulation, control, and record-keeping of opiates, it was neither interpreted nor implemented in that light. Rather, through a campaign by the Treasury Department and a series of Supreme Court decisions, the Harrison Act became increasingly interpreted as mandating the complete prohibition of nonmedical opiate use and the criminalization of addicts. How did this occur?

The Harrison Act's provision that permitted the medical prescription of opiates if prescribed in "good faith" in "the legitimate practice of medicine" left physicians as the only legal suppliers of opiates. Thus the medical profession, somewhat unwittingly, obtained a legal monopoly over the treatment and maintenance of addiction. Many law-abiding addicts suddenly came to physicians' offices for their drugs. It seems that only a minority of physicians actually dealt with addicts. Some physicians developed methods of "treating" addiction, and a few operated medical sanitaria specifically designed for curing addiction. A small subgroup of physicians, uncomplimentarily called "opium doctors," organized their entire practices around prescribing opiate substances to patient-addicts. Many opium doctors saw hundreds of patients daily, perhaps only for the few minutes it took to write a prescription, and when the law allowed, they dispensed opiates. The public outcry against these physicians was minimal, perhaps because the public believed that since the addict was under a physician's care, there was little reason for concern. Most physicians, however, were reluctant to maintain addicts and did not include them in their practice. As Musto (1973) points out:

> The rare physician who before 1919 favored the maintenance of addicts pleaded with his associates to cooperate, but the practitioner's interest in doing so, either initially or as anti-narcotic legislation gained ground, appeared to be rather small. (p. 92)

Thus it does not appear that physicians, as a whole or as an organization, favored the maintenance of opiate addicts. On the other hand, it is clear that they did favor the *medical control* of opiates, largely through physician prescription. From their viewpoint, so long as physicians controlled the substances, the problems of abuse and addiction would be minimized.

The Treasury Department did not see it that way. They became concerned about addicts who went to the physicians and the physicians who prescribed them drugs. The Treasury Department interpreted the Harrison Act in terms of a moral principle—that taking narcotics for other than bona fide medical purposes was harmful and should be prevented (Musto, 1973). Possession of narcotics received from unregistered sources, according to the Treasury Department's interpretation, would be in itself a violation of the Act. Increasingly, specific Treasury Department regulations narrowed and eventually forbade opiate maintenance. Physicians and druggists who prescribed opiates freely were harassed and prosecuted. The Treasury Department adopted a dual strategy of disseminating (mis)information to the public about the narcotics problem and "degenerate" addicts and instigating court proceedings against physicians who maintained addicts. They launched a major attack against the medical profession through court cases. Although the medical profession was coming under attack for dereliction of duties in prescribing drugs indiscriminately, physicians continued to prescribe opiates based on the "legitimate medical practices" clause (Reasons, 1974). The conflict would be settled in the Supreme Court.

**Supreme Court support of the criminal designation of addiction.** The Supreme Court handed down a series of decisions between 1915 and 1922 that effectively demedicalized addiction and upheld a criminal definition. In 1915 in *United States* v. *Jin Fuey Moy* the Court ruled that possession of narcotics by unregistered persons was essentially a crime. This decision literally forced addicts to go to physicians as their only legal source of drugs. Subsequent decisions further limited both the physicians' and the addicts' options. The central issue became what constituted "legitimate medical use." In 1919 the Court ruled in *Webb et al.* v. *United States* that prescribing drugs for an addict "not in the course of professional treatment in the attempted cure of the habit, but being issued for the purpose of providing the user with morphine sufficient to keep him comfortable by maintaining his customary use" was *not* in the realm of legitimate medical practice. Thus medical opiate maintenance became illegal. The Court decisions of *Jin Fuey Moy* v. *United States* in 1920 and *United States* v. *Behrman* in 1922 further narrowed the medical prerogative of prescribing opiates. In the latter case physicians were effectively denied the right to prescribe opiates to treat and cure addicts (Lindesmith, 1965). These decisions made outpatient treatment of addiction impossible. The Court softened its view considerably by 1925 in the *Lindner* v. *United States* decision by deeming that "addicts are diseased and proper subjects for [medical] treatment," but it was too late. By that time physicians had largely adopted the dominant moral-criminal definition of addiction and had all but abandoned medical treatment of addicts.

But why did this dramatic shift in the definition occur when it did? Clearly the Treasury Department championed the criminal definition of addiction and claimed the addict as within its legitimate social control turf. Their use of judicial decisions, rather than legislative action, circumvented the strong medical and pharmaceutical congressional lobbies (Reasons, 1974). The medical profession had only a limited interest in addiction per se, and focused its concern on the physicians' prerogative to practice medicine in a manner they saw fit. Only a few physicians actually championed the medical model of addiction. Musto (1973) suggests that the political atmosphere changed between 1915 and 1919, as did the public's and the Treasury Department's views of narcotics use:

> What had been a respectable viewpoint by 1915, although not the dominant attitude of the public—the value of addict maintenance by physicians and others—by 1919 and 1920 had come to seem a great danger and folly. Advocacy for maintenance was repressed as strongly as socialism. (p. 32)

By the time America entered World War I, drug addiction was not only viewed as immoral because it wasted people's lives but was also perceived as a threat to the national war effort. It was seen as sapping the nation's energies. In 1919 the Palmer raids against Bolsheviks and anarchists took place, and Prohibition was ratified. Opiate maintenance could not be defended any more than alcoholism. It is not surprising that the Supreme Court decisions reflected an increasing concern with controlling "degeneracy" and deviance. Thus the Court's decision to oppose opiate maintenance, as Musto (1973) points out, could be broadly interpreted as a strike against activities that weaken a nation.*

**Narcotics clinics: the medical swan song.** In 1918-1919 the Special Narcotic Committee of the Treasury Department was convened to attempt to close the loopholes revealed by several court decisions. The committee produced a report, "Traffic in Narcotics," which contained their analysis and recommendations. It presented unreliable and very inflated statistics regarding the scope of the addiction prob-

*Although sociologists like Richard Quinney (1974a, p. 97) and John Helmer (1975) present Marxian analyses of the passage of the Harrison Act, theories postulating class and power struggles or minority oppression do not adequately explain this complex phenomenon. Scotty Embree (1978) presents a plausible economic analysis but lacks data to support her argument.

lem (it estimated that there were about a million addicts at that time) and presented an optimistic view of the "cure" rates of addiction. The report defined opiate addiction as having aspects of a disease—the addiction that resulted from continued use of opiates and the addicts' subsequent use of the drug to remain "normal"—but also depicted addicts as weak creatures, lacking morality, who would resort to crime when deprived of the drug. The committee believed that an addict could not discontinue drug use without intervention and thus recommended the provision of medical care. However, it did not specify which of the medical approaches would be most suitable. By the time the report was released, the Supreme Court had already handed down its decisions narrowing medical discretion in the treatment of addiction (Musto, 1973).

Although the Treasury Department considered medical treatment a necessary step in addiction control, the United States Public Health Service did not see it that way. The Public Health Service, the major government branch of medicine, stepped out of the opiate treatment picture after 1919 and "excused itself from claiming knowledge of how to cure addicts and drew the conclusion that the nation should rely on legal enforcement to control narcotic supply" (Musto, 1973, p. 146). The Treasury Department, frustrated in its attempts to control addiction through enforcement, sought medical help and urged the establishment of local municipal narcotics clinics.

Between 1919 and 1920 about 44 narcotics clinics opened in scattered cities across America. They varied in size and organization, but all adopted a medical approach to treating drug addiction. From their start, most clinics used an outpatient or ambulatory maintenance approach to addiction. The goal, ideally, would be to "cure" the addicts. In some clinics this involved medical treatment and follow-up care, but in others it amounted to merely giving out drugs to those who registered and requested them. Although the clinics were always deemed to be a temporary measure, it appears that federal officials quickly became disenchanted with their operation. The Narcotics Division of the Treasury Department (newly created as a semi-autonomous section of the Prohibition Unit) adopted a view that addiction maintenance was only tolerable for medical reasons. A battle with these federal agents ensued over who should have legitimate control over this turf, and many physicians, pharmacists, and even clinic personnel were arrested.

The operation of the clinics was uneven; some, like the Shreveport, Louisiana, clinic may have been successful in treating addicts, controlling the spread of addiction, and limiting the development of a criminal drug underworld. On the other hand, the New York City clinic, probably the largest in the country, was run poorly and distributed drugs rather indiscriminately. The Treasury Department focused its attack on the clinics in New York: it conducted an investigation and, with the aid of muckraking journalists, discredited narcotics clinics as a means of dealing with drug problems. By 1923 all the clinics were closed. The Treasury Department distorted evidence (which actually was mixed) to brand the clinics and the medical approach to addiction as untenable and a total failure (Lindesmith, 1965).

The clinics received considerable bad press, and this contributed to an increased public concern about addiction. The AMA in 1925 took a firm position against ambulatory treatment of addicts, suggesting that institutionalization was the only alternative. The AMA passed a resolution calling on federal and state governments "to exert their full powers and authority to put an end to all manner of so-called ambulatory methods of treatment" (quoted in Schur, 1965, p. 159). The narcotics clinics were the swan song of the medical approach to addiction; with their demise, physicians by and large abandoned treatment of opiate addicts. The closing of the clinics marks the end of the medical era: the medical approach to addiction was no longer a viable competing definition of reality. All concerned seemed to agree that addiction was a criminal problem.

There seem to be several reasons why physicians relinquished their jurisdiction over opiate addiction. First, the medical profession's support of opiate maintenance had been based more on a belief in the physician's prerogative to control medical treatment and a distaste of government interference in medical practice than on any real commitment to the morality or efficacy of maintenance treatment. Few physicians were heavily invested in treating addicts, and physicians still retained control of opiates for ''medical uses'' (minus heroin, whose manufacture for any purpose was prohibited in 1924). Second, by the 1920s most physicians no longer believed addiction was a disease (Musto, 1973, p. 83), and their optimism for achieving a cure was waning. Third, the medical profession also may have had enough of the Treasury Department's harassment. One study estimated that in the 25 years following the Harrison Act, 25,000 physicians were arrested on narcotics charges and 3000 actually served prison sentences (cited in Goode, 1972, p. 191). Thousands more had their licenses revoked. The state had effectively recalled the medical profession's license to treat opiate addiction.

In sum, the medical profession relinquished its turf of opiate addiction. The Narcotics Division of the Treasury Department had successfully challenged medicine and staked out addiction as within its legitimate and exclusive jurisdiction. As such, the Narcotics Division's entrepreneurship had created an entire new category of criminals, ''drug addicts,'' and manufactured a social problem where there had been none before. As Erich Goode (1972) points out, the result of this was

> the dramatic emergence of a new criminal class of addicts—*a criminal class that had not existed previously*. The link between addiction and crime—the view that the addict was by definition a criminal—was forged. The law itself created a new class of criminals. (p. 194)

The social definition of opiate addiction as a criminal problem became a self-fulfilling prophecy.

## REIGN OF THE CRIMINAL DESIGNATION

In the wake of the Harrison Act and the subsequent Court decisions that ''clarified'' it, the problem of opiate addiction was securely on the Narcotics Division's turf. But there were some unanticipated consequences of taking a criminal approach to addiction. Although in the short run a punitive approach may have reduced the number of addicts, several long-run consequences actually created new and more difficult narcotics-related problems (Goode, 1972). Cutting off the legal medical supply of drugs left addicts with two choices: they could give up their habits and suffer greatly from withdrawal or turn to an expanding illegal network to procure their drugs. The prohibition of opiates thus contributed to the creation of an addict subculture, an underworld where addicts could find protection and connections. Erich Goode (1972, p. 196) suggests that this subculture has been central in the ''recruitment'' of new addicts. Moreover, the prohibition of opiates made narcotics a highly profitable commodity, and an entire criminal industry developed to market them. The drugs' illegality and subsequent scarcity inflated their price and made it nearly impossible for addicts to work at conventional jobs to support their habits. Many addicts therefore had to turn to crime as the only way to finance their addiction.

There is undoubtedly a relationship between addiction and crime; the important question is, however, what is the nature of this relationship? Many addicts resort to burglary and other property crimes to pay the inflated prices of black-market drugs. In places where drugs are cheaply available, addicts are no more criminal than nonaddicts. Thus the Narcotics Division's prohibition of opiates amplified any opiate problems that may have existed previously by setting conditions that gave rise to an addict subculture and forcing addicts into a world of crime to maintain their addiction.

Along with the change in the definition and designation of addiction, a shift occurred in the population of addicts and in the moral condemnation of addiction. Troy Duster (1970, pp. 20-23) argues that certain social categories are more easily morally condemned than others. As the population of addicts became typified by the young, lower-class black male, rather than the middle-aged, middle-class white female, American's moral hostility increased proportionately. The Harrison Act did not create the strong moral judgments about heroin use per se but pushed addiction into an arena populated by the lower classes and the crime underworld, groups about which strong moral feelings already existed. As the addict population shifted, the image of the addict changed from a sick to a contemptible deviant.

### Addiction becomes a "criminal menace"

The change of the addict's image did not happen by chance. The Narcotics Division had institutionalized its definition of addiction as national policy and through "educational" efforts changed the "image of the addict . . . from ailment to evil" (Reasons, 1975, p. 19). Its "success" was rewarded by increased budgets (Dickson, 1968) and by its being established in 1930 as a separate organization, the Federal Bureau of Narcotics (FBN). Henry J. Anslinger, a former Prohibition official, was named to head the new bureau. He came to have an enormous effect on national drug policy for three decades. Anslinger viewed opiate addiction as a clearly criminal problem and the addict as a moral degenerate. The FBN's propagandistic activities were central in creating and popularizing the myth of the addict as a degenerate, violent "dope fiend" who is out to convert others to drugs (Lindesmith, 1940). Here was the source for the belief that heroin itself "caused" crime and violence. In the late 1930s the FBN, under Anslinger's leadership, expanded its turf to include jurisdiction over marijuana use (Becker, H. S., 1963).

The period before World War II saw little medical attention to addiction and nearly no claims-making activity. A few widely scattered physicians took issue with the criminal approach to addiction. Dr. Charles E. Terry's and Muriel Pellens' (1928) massive work, *The Opium Problem,* presented data at variance with FBN reports (Lindesmith, 1965). Dr. Henry Smith's 1939 book, *Drug Addicts Are Human Beings: The Story of Our Billion Dollar Drug Racket,* indicted government officials for intimate involvement in creating the drug problem. But such critiques were few, and the criminal definition of addiction became taken for granted.

Large numbers of addicts were imprisoned under the Harrison Act's provisions. The Justice Department became concerned with finding some alternative to traditional imprisonment, since addicts had become the largest class of offenders in prisons (Musto, 1973, p. 204). A bill was introduced in Congress that called for the establishment of Federal Narcotics Farms (later called hospitals); essentially these would be separate prisons run by the Public Health Service. Hospital-farms were opened in Lexington, Kentucky, in 1935 and in Fort Worth, Texas, in 1938. Run as prisons, they provided segregation and limited medical treatment. Although Anslinger reported that 64% of addicts treated at Lexington never returned for treatment (Anslinger & Tompkins, 1953, p. 24), the "cure" rate was actually low. Anslinger's figures included only those who returned to Lexington; most addicts relapsed and went to prison or other hospitals. More rigorous studies suggest that the Lexington success rate (as evidenced by nonprison abstinence from narcotics for several years) was a meager 2%, and at best, 7% (Hunt, G. H., and Odorhoff, 1962; Vaillant, 1965). Perhaps the most significant contribution of the hospital-farms was as research centers and training grounds for future National Institute of Mental Health (NIMH) people, who were disillusioned with the FBN and the criminal approach to addiction (Musto, 1973). They provided an institutionalized setting for the ferment over medical approaches that would reemerge in the 1950s.

World War II interrupted the international heroin traffic, and as a result the addict population in the United States may well have declined (McCoy, 1973). For a short time, this minimized the FBN's problems with smuggling and addiction. At the war's end there were only 20,000 known addicts in the United States (Goode, 1972, p. 196). Few challenged the criminal definition of addiction (an exception was sociologist Alfred Lindesmith, discussed later).

By the 1950s heroin addiction was associated increasingly with ghetto life and organized crime; public attention was again drawn to the alleged "criminal menace" of addiction, especially as it threatened teenagers and schoolchildren. The Kefauver Committee on Crime, in a series of televised hearings, focused public attention on narcotics problems. Popular magazines like *Newsweek, Life,* and *Reader's Digest* published articles on the drug evil with such alluring titles as "New York Wakes Up to 15,000 Heroin Addicts" and "Children in Peril," based largely on information from Anslinger and the FBN. Anslinger recommended that Congress pass laws with tougher penalties to combat the addiction "menace." In the McCarthy era the narcotics problem was linked with communism and deemed an agent of subversion, corruption (Reasons, 1975), and a threat to the American way.

Congress responded by passing two laws that strengthened and extended the criminal approach. The Boggs Amendment of 1951 called for mandatory sentences for narcotics violations, with no suspended sentence or parole for repeated offenders, and made prosecution of users and peddlers easier. The Narcotic Control Act of 1956 extended the Boggs law, eliminating parole for all but first offenders, and "combined the threat of death with mandatory minimum sentences for the first conviction" (Musto, 1973, p. 242). Numerous states modeled their own laws after these, and a few enacted legislation making addiction per se a crime. The penalties for drug offenses were more severe than for crimes like armed robbery and burglary (Lindesmith, 1965). These "get tough" laws reinforced the criminal definition of addiction. They represent the high-water mark of the FBN's philosophy, which had emerged more than 30 years before—that if penalties were made severe enough and enforced effectively, addiction would disappear. This, however, has not been the case.

## Why narcotics laws have failed

The criminal approach has failed to eliminate or even effectively control addiction. The number of addicts and the amount of illegal opiate trade have increased substantially in the past 25 years. The 1960s saw addiction spread to middle-class communities and college campuses and become a major problem in the armed forces. Why has the criminal approach failed?

Several factors underlie this failure. First, there has been and continues to be a demand for chemical substances that relieve pain, alter human consciousness, and provide recreation and distraction from mundane experiences. Explanations that hypothesize psychological or physiological predispositions or "addictive personalities" miss the point; drugs are attractive to a large variety of people (witness the popular use of cigarettes, alcohol, and marijuana). Although social circumstances like oppression, the availability of drugs, and cultural meanings of drug-taking may increase or decrease the demand, such a demand exists in most societies. Second, opiates *are* drugs with addicting properties (Brecher, 1972, pp. 61-89). There is a great deal of evidence that demonstrates the difficulty of terminating opiate use. Relapse rates are high no matter what method of treatment or punishment is used. Rehabilitation has been largely a failure—prison has served to perpetuate drug use—and addicts return frequently to the same environment with the same problems that engendered addiction in the first place. Third, the black-market sales of heroin and other drugs have created a huge illegal industry. This industry is an international and highly profitable one and at times has been nearly monopolistic in its control of the market (Chambliss, 1977). Government attempts to control the industry, usually through efforts at curtailing "smuggling," have served to decrease supply and thus maintain high prices. This has not, however, reduced effectively the use of opiates and other drugs in American society. Fourth, the very laws that made opiates illegal ironically gave rise to a criminal underworld that has nurtured the spread of drug use. The addict subculture, which emerged in response to the criminalization of opiates, became a means by which information and drugs could be disseminated. Finally, despite the failure of criminal sanctions, certain groups in society, particularly the FBN and other law-enforcement agencies, continued to promote the punitive approach to the drug problem. Politicking in legislatures, misleading publications and research (Lindesmith, 1965, p. 121), and increased budgets for control and enforcement, along with a general acceptance of punitive sanctions for lower-class and minority deviants, kept the criminal approach dominant.

In sum, the 1950s saw the criminal definition reach a peak. But criticism was mounting that the harsh, punitive approach was not stemming the tide of addiction. It had not "worked." Murmurings of a reemergence of a medical definition of addiction could be heard.

## REEMERGENCE OF MEDICAL DESIGNATIONS OF ADDICTION

By the mid-1950s a small chorus of voices could be heard criticizing the punitive approach to addiction and calling for alternatives. Perhaps the premier and most articulate voice was that of sociologist Alfred R. Lindesmith.

Lindesmith, in a series of papers and most specifically in his 1947 book, *Opiate Addiction,* developed a sociological explanation of addiction that contradicted the conventional popular and medical wisdom that addiction was caused by the euphoria drugs produced. Lindesmith concluded, on the basis of extensive, in-depth interviews with a large variety of addicts, that opiate addiction (i.e., the continued use of opiates) was not caused by the search for euphoria but by the usage of drugs to alleviate withdrawal distress. In Lindesmith's (1968) words:

> Addiction occurs only when opiates are used to alleviate withdrawal distress, after such distress has been properly understood or interpreted. . . . If the individual fails to conceive of his distress as withdrawal distress brought about by the absence of opiates, he does not become addicted, but, if he does, addiction is quickly and permanently established through further use of the drug. (p. 191)*

This explanation emphasizes the importance of the cognitive element in addiction: the individual's *interpretation* of the biological events associated with drug use and disuse are central to becoming addicted. According to Lindesmith, those who experience withdrawal symptoms and do not connect them to the ingestion of the drugs (e.g., who view them as a result of a disease) escape addiction. Thus in Lindesmith's model of addiction the fear of withdrawal distress creates the "craving" for drugs.*

In a final section of *Opiate Addiction* Lindesmith criticized the criminal approach for failing to deal adequately with the problem of addiction. He proposed that the law-enforcement approach be limited to controlling illegal narcotics traffic and that the addict be handled as a medical rather than criminal problem. This could be accomplished by reinterpreting the Harrison Act to recapture its original intent and by changing laws so "prescription of drugs to addicts by a physician is defined as being within the field of medicine" (Lindesmith, 1968, p. 234). He pointed to the British system (discussed later) as a model of successful medical control of addiction.

The middle 1950s saw segments of the medical profession begin to reassert publicly their claims that addicts are a medical problem. The Committee of Public Health of the prestigious New York Academy of Medicine asserted in a 1955 report:

> There should be a change in attitude toward the addict. He is a sick person, not a criminal. That he may commit criminal acts to maintain his drug supply is recognized; but it is unjust to consider him as a criminal simply because he uses narcotic drugs. (New York Academy of Medicine, 1955/1966, p. 188)

The report further maintained that to eradicate drug addiction, the profit must be taken out of drug traffic. To facilitate this, the committee proposed a federally controlled medical dispensary-clinic system whereby addicts could receive drugs at low cost. The goal of the clinics would be to persuade addicts to undergo withdrawal. If addicts could not be persuaded "de-

---



*Lindesmith's theory has been criticized by researchers who posit more drug-centered, physiological models of addiction (e.g., Ausubel, 1958; Duster, 1970, pp. 59-60). In a recent study, McAuliffe and Gordon (1974) attempted to test Lindesmith's withdrawal-versus-euphoria hypothesis and claimed their findings refuted his theory. In a reply Lindesmith (1975) points out that these findings, although valid in their own right, do not refute his theory.

spite all efforts'' and were ''resistant to undertaking therapy,'' minimum doses of drugs should be legally and cheaply supplied. The central thesis of the report was that addicts would be under medical supervision. A year later, in 1956, psychiatrist Marie Nyswander, who had treated addicts at the Lexington narcotic hospital and in private practice, published *The Addict as Patient*. She argued for accepting addicts as patients, not criminals, and suggested that opiate maintenance might be the only feasible solution because none of the treatments worked well.

The most controversial and influential document claiming addiction as a medical problem was a report by the Joint Committee of the American Bar Association and the American Medical Association on Narcotic Drugs. The joint committee consisted of six well-respected members of these associations, including Rufus King, a lawyer well-known for his writings on narcotics. The Interim Report, published in 1958 in limited edition for use by the professional associations, made a number of recommendations: (1) The laws on narcotics need review, (2) qualified physicians should be allowed to dispense narcotics, and (3) medical treatment in outpatient facilities should be tried on a controlled experimental basis. The thrust of the report was that a strict law-enforcement approach had not provided an answer to the addiction problem.

The FBN reacted sharply to the ABA-AMA report. Their domain of drug addiction threatened, the FBN retorted with a caustic rebuttal that amounted to ''largely a vehement attack on the 'un-American' ABA-AMA committee members, the sources cited in the report, and the Supreme Court'' (Reasons, 1975; p. 33). When the report was about to be published by the Indiana University Press, FBN chief Anslinger sent a narcotics agent to Indiana University to ''investigate'' it (Lindesmith, 1965, p. 246). The report was published in 1961 as *Drug Addiction: Crime or Disease?*

## Support for a medical designation

In 1962 the Supreme Court struck down a California statute that had defined addiction as a punishable crime. In this significant decision, *Robinson* v. *California,* the Court reaffirmed the long-dormant Lindner decision of 1925 that accepted addiction as a disease. The decision compared addiction to other diseases:

> It is unlikely that any State at this moment in history would attempt to make it a criminal offense for a person to be mentally ill, or a leper, or to be afflicted with venereal disease. . . . a law which made a criminal offense of such a disease would doubtless be universally thought to be an infliction of cruel and unusual punishment. (Quoted in Kittrie, 1971, p. 239)

The decision proposed that rather than punishing addicts, states should compel them to undergo treatment, presumably under civil commitment statutes. Although *Robinson* did not affect laws on possession, sales, or other narcotics offenses or make a therapeutic approach imperative (Kittrie, 1971, p. 240), it added considerable legitimacy to the supporters of the medical approach.

Change in the definition and treatment of addiction was definitely in the air. In 1963 the Presidential Comission on Narcotics and Drug Abuse Report called for (1) the relaxation of mandatory sentences, (2) an increase in appropriations for research, (3) dismantling of the FBN and transfer of its functions to the Department of Health, Education and Welfare and the Justice Department, and (4) reinstituting the medical profession as the authority on what constituted legitimate medical treatment of addiction (Platt, J. J., and Labate, 1976, p. 28). Almost as if to mark a change in eras of drug control, FBN Commissioner Anslinger, the author and staunchest defender of the punitive approach to addiction, retired in 1962.

The late 1950s, then, saw a slight shift in the definition of addiction. Perhaps in response to the punitive peak reached by the Boggs law and the Narcotics Control Act of 1956, a small group of claims-makers and supporters of medical definitions of addiction began to challenge dominant criminal definitions. Addicts were increasingly portrayed as sick rather than evil. It is unclear exactly why this challenge occurred at this point, but certain factors seemed to support definitional change. There had never been an unbending consensus in organizations like the AMA and the ABA that addicts were dangerous and pathological criminals (Rock,

1977). The apparent failure of punitive addiction control and the increased isolation of the FBN from other professional viewpoints made the time ripe for a challenge. The province and status of psychiatry was growing as a result of the pharmacological revolution that began in 1955. This may have ignited new hopes in medical approaches to deviance control. And by the early 1960s President Kennedy's "bold, new approach" in mental health treatment could easily be expanded to include addiction.

This is not to say that criminal designations of addiction disappeared. Rather, claims-makers were promoting a medical designation of addiction that would challenge, and ultimately coexist with, law-enforcement agencies' criminal approach. It sometimes appeared that champions of the medical approach supported it more as a strategy for citicizing the dominant punitive approach than out of a deep belief in the morality and efficiency of medical interventions. Although they had no proven "answers" to propose as addiction policy, the critics often pointed to the success of the British system of heroin maintenance as a medical approach worthy of emulation.

## EXCURSUS: THE BRITISH EXPERIENCE

American champions of medical designations for addiction point frequently to the British experience as an exemplar of the utility and success of a medical approach. The British approach designates addiction as a sickness and treats the addict almost entirely as a medical concern. Treatment of addicts resides with medical practitioners and consists, in general, of supplying opiates to addicts under medical supervision. We will briefly explore the development and operation of the British approach to addiction.

Great Britain responded to the international conferences of the early 20th century in a manner similar to the United States; in 1920, Parliament enacted the Dangerous Drug Act, which, like the Harrison Act, was intended to limit opiate distribution to medical channels. But, as in the United States, a dispute over jurisdiction developed, and an interpretation of the law was necessary. The Ministry of Health appointed a committee, headed by Sir Humphrey Rolleston, "to resolve what appeared to be a conflict of views between physicians, who were in fact caring for addicts, and law enforcement bodies, which thought the 1920 statutes prohibited this" (Lindesmith, 1965, pp. 167-168). The Rolleston Committee issued a report in 1926 that was favorable to the physicians. Although eschewing the supplying of drugs "solely for the gratification of addiction," the report stated:

> morphine or heroin may properly be administered to addicts in the following circumstances, namely (a) where patients are under treatment by the gradual withdrawal method with a view to cure, (b) where it has been demonstrated, after a prolonged attempt at cure, that the use of the drug cannot be safely discontinued entirely, on account of the severity of the withdrawal symptoms produced, (c) where it has been similarly demonstrated that the patient, while capable of leading a useful and relatively normal life when a certain minimum dose is regularly administered, becomes incapable of this when the drug is entirely discontinued. (Quoted in Schur, 1962, p. 76)

In effect, this ruling gave physicians final authority in dealing with addiction and defined "treatment" as regularly providing drugs for addicts. Thus the British never took the American route of trying to keep drugs away from addicts.

For the first four decades of the medical approach to addiction, an addict could go to any physician and receive a prescription for opiates; physicians voluntarily notified the Home Office of their addict-patients. This approach worked well; in 1935 there were only 700 known addicts in Britain; by 1950, the number had dropped to about 300 (Brecher, 1972, p. 121). Even if a small number were unknown to officials (which is likely), the British still appeared to have the addiction problem well controlled. Furthermore, no black market of drugs had developed, there was virtually no drug-related crime (since addicts did not need to resort to crime to support their habits), and many addicts were still employed and leading productive lives. It is little wonder that American champions of the medical approach held up the British system as a model (e.g., Lindesmith, 1947; Joint Committee of the American Bar Association and the American Medical Association, 1961).

Anslinger and the FBN, as well as other supporters of the law-enforcement approach, tried continually to discredit the British program. Much of the FBN critique is contradictory. At various times Anslinger depicted the British approach as a "nonsystem," and, incredibly, as the same as the American approach (after all, according to his reasoning, they both included laws against opiate traffic and nonmedical opiate use). FBN officials charged that the British statistics were phony or at best unreliable and that the British approach worked in Britain because it was an island and the British character was less addiction prone. When the number of addicts rose sharply in the early 1960s, FBN officials announced that the British approach was simply a failure (Brecher, 1972, Lindesmith, 1965).

When a committee to evaluate the British policy toward addiction met in 1961 under the direction of Sir Russell Brain, it reported that the system was working well, and no alterations in policy were necessary. But by July, 1964, the situation had changed sufficiently for the committee to be reconvened (Scull, 1972).

Beginning in the early 1960s, the number of opiate addicts in Great Britain rose sharply (Table 2). By the mid-1960s, the number of new addicts was increasing at a rate that doubled the addict population every 16 months. Black markets could be found in Soho and Picadilly (May, 1971). When the Brain Committee reconvened, there was serious concern that the British system was indeed breaking down.

The Brain Committee reported in 1965. They attributed the rise in opiate addicts mainly to a few irresponsible physicians who were overprescribing drugs to addicts, and to addicts who peddled these excesses on the street, creating a "gray market." Other factors, not specifically noted by the committee, also undoubtedly had contributed to the increased addiction. In the early 1960s a small group of Canadian and American addicts had migrated to England to escape repressive drug laws and

**TABLE 2**
NUMBER OF KNOWN ADDICTS IN GREAT BRITAIN*

| Year | Number of known addicts | Year | Number of known addicts |
|---|---|---|---|
| 1945 | 367 | 1968 | 2782 |
| 1950 | 306 | 1969 | 2881 |
| 1955 | 335 | 1970 | 2661 |
| 1960 | 437 | 1971 | 2762 |
| 1961 | 470 | 1972 | 2934 |
| 1962 | 532 | 1973 | 3021 |
| 1963 | 635 | 1974 | 3254 |
| 1964 | 753 | 1975 | 3427 |
| 1965 | 927 | 1976 | 3480 |
| 1966 | 1349 | 1977 | 3611 |
| 1967 | 1729 | | |

*"Throughput" figures calculated from data from the Statistical Division of the Home Office.

take advantage of the availability of high-quality, low-cost legal heroin (Brecher, 1972, p. 123). A new pattern of drug use also was discernible among British youth. The rise of a teenage subculture with favorable attitudes toward drug experimentation created for the first time a potential market for opiate-type substances (Scull, 1972). The public's demand for punitive action and a delay in responding to the changed climate further exacerbated the situation.

The Brain Committee's second report reaffirmed the medical approach to addiction: "The addict should be regarded as a sick person, he should be treated as such and not as a criminal, provided that he does not resort to criminal acts" (quoted in May, 1971, p. 348). The committee did, however, recommend a number of changes, which finally went into effect in 1968. These included: (1) that all addicts should be "notified" (reported) to the Home Office, (2) special treatment clinics should be established, and (3) prescription of heroin and cocaine should be limited to physicians at these clinics (other physicians could still prescribe morphine or methadone). These simple measures seemed to be effective, since the number of new addicts began to decrease markedly after 1968 (May, 1971) and the total addict population increased at a slower rate and appears to be relatively stabilized (Table 2).* Although some addicts who obtain their drugs from illicit sources never come to "official" attention, the British addict population never approached the estimated 150,000 to 250,000 Americans addicted during the same time period. (In relative terms, the United States has about 10 times the number of opiate addicts as Britain.) American proponents of the law-enforcement approach to addiction had written a premature obituary, for the British had at least slowed the increasing spiral of addiction.

There is no evidence, however, that British physicians had any better success at "curing" addiction than had their American counterparts in the narcotics clinics in the early 20th century. For a variety of reasons, many already mentioned, heroin maintenance never had substantial official support in the United States. Americans seem to want to "cure" by compulsion or a forced cure, whereas the British do not (Lindesmith, 1965, p. 169). However, there never were any "cures" that were very successful. But when methadone maintenance was discovered in the early 1960s, many Americans thought they had found that elusive cure for heroin addiction, and it was embraced accordingly.

## METHADONE AND THE REMEDICALIZATION OF OPIATE ADDICTION

Methadone is a synthetic opiate-like drug that possesses many of the same qualities of opiates, including addictiveness and analgesic action. Methadone was developed by a German chemist and first used by physicians as an analgesic in medical treatment when opium was scarce during the second World War. After the war a governmental team investigating Nazi drug companies brought methadone to this country. Beginning in the late 1940s, E. J. Lilly Pharmaceutical Company marketed it as cough medicine. However, the main use for methadone was in the detoxification of opiate addicts.

Many hospitals, following procedures that were developed at the Lexington research center, used methadone to "detoxify" opiate addicts. The procedure was simple. Under medical supervision addict-patients had their addiction transferred from morphine or heroin to methadone. Then, over a period of about 10 days, the daily dose of methadone was progressively reduced until it reached a zero level. This procedure was intended to minimize the suffering of withdrawal and was a common practice by the early 1960s. In a sense, the medical involvement in these detoxification procedures occasioned the return of medical practitioners to the treatment of opiate addiction. Until the discovery of "methadone maintenance" in the mid-1960s, however, physicians nearly always exited from the treatment process after withdrawal was accomplished.

Methadone maintenance as a treatment for addiction was discovered accidentally by two medical researchers, Vincent Dole and Marie Nyswander. Dole, a specialist in metabolic disease, became interested in heroin addiction through his research on obesity. This research led him to conclude that relapses among some obese patients were due to metabolic, biochemical causes, rather than simply a lack of "willpower" (Brecher, 1972, p. 135). Nyswander, a psychiatrist with considerable experience treating addiction and addicts at Lexington and in New York City storefronts, became Dole's associate for his heroin research. She was a long-time advocate of a medical approach to addiction, as evidenced by her book, *The Drug Addict as Patient* (1956). Together, at Rockefeller University, they began research on the metabolics of heroin addiction. In October, 1963, they placed two addicts on high doses of methadone to compare morphine and methadone metabolism. Much to their surprise, when the addict-patients were on high doses of methadone, unexpected changes in their behavior and activity began to occur. Nyswander

*The actual number of addicts receiving medical treatment at any one time is smaller. For example, according to the Home Office, 1879 addict-patients were receiving drugs from physicians on January 1, 1977.

reported, "The older addict began to paint industriously and his paintings were good. The younger addict started urging us to let him get his high school equivalency diploma" (Hentoff, 1969, p. 114). Both were allowed to live and attend school outside the hospital while being maintained on methadone. They became, apparently, effectively functioning human beings—and were essentially "cured" of their cravings for heroin. The researchers soon replicated these results with four additional "hard-core" addicts. Thus, by accident, Dole and Nyswander discovered that methadone could be used as a maintenance drug that enabled addicts to engage in conventional pursuits.

Dole and Nyswander published a series of articles reporting the results of their work with methadone maintenance and proposing a theory of how it worked. The first article (Dole & Nyswander, 1965) reported striking improvements in employment, education, and family reconciliation for 22 patients receiving methadone maintenance. According to the report, all the addict-patients had many previous treatment experiences and had been unable to remain drug free after withdrawal; they had been treatment "failures." On methadone the craving for heroin appeared to be suppressed. Dole and Nyswander (1965) concluded:

> This medication appears to have two useful effects: (1) relief of narcotic hunger, and (2) induction of sufficient tolerance to block the euphoric effect of an average illegal dose of [heroin]. With medication and a comprehensive program of rehabilitation, patients have shown marked improvement; they have returned to school, obtained jobs, and became reconciled with their families. Medical and psychometric tests have disclosed no signs of toxicity, apart from constipation. Methadone treatment needs careful medical supervision and many social services. In our opinion, both the medication and the supporting program are essential. (p. 646)*

In another early report (Dole & Nyswander, 1966) they claimed that methadone "blocked" the euphoric action of heroin, and they described it as an "antinarcotic drug." Dole and Nyswander (1967) developed a theory conceptualizing opiate addiction as a metabolic disease, with methadone as part of its "cure." Their theory was that opiate addiction created a permanent biochemical change in the physiology—hence methadone maintenance can be seen as necessary to the life of the addict. Methadone stabilized the physiology of an addict much as insulin stabilized the diabetic. These scientific reports and the results from early demonstration projects and evaluations provided ammunition for the supporters of the medical approach in the battle over the designation and treatment of addiction. Between 1963 and 1971, in the wake of a heroin "epidemic," methadone maintenance went from an esoteric accidential finding to a dominant position in public policy.

### "Heroin epidemic" and available treatment

The 1960s saw an increased public concern with "the drug problem," especially heroin addiction. The number of heroin users increased dramatically; estimates ranged from 150,000 to 500,000 addicts. By the end of the decade, writers in both the professional (DuPont, 1971) and popular (*Newsweek*, July 5, 1971) media were declaring a virtual "heroin addiction epidemic" in America. (It is interesting to note that in the 1960s the problem was designated in quasimedical terms as a drug "epidemic," whereas in the 1930s it had been a drug "menace.") Not only was heroin use increasing, but it was no longer confined to the ghettos. Middle-class youth were experimenting with drugs—at first, marijuana and hallucinogens, and later, opiates and other drugs. Newspapers reported high rates of heroin addiction among soldiers in Vietnam. "Drug abuse" no longer was limited to poorer and minority elements of society; law-enforcement agencies and legislatures were showing great concern about the drug epidemic. Rising crime rates were attributed to drug-related offenses. President Nixon declared drug abuse to be "public enemy number one" and "the most

---

*From *J.A.M.A.*, 1965, **193**, 646-650. Copyright 1965, American Medical Association.

serious threat this nation has ever faced'' (Dumont, 1972).*

The *Robinson* Supreme Court decision in 1962 had vindicated the medical approach and essentially mandated civil commitment and some type of treatment, rather than only imprisonment, for addicts. But the two major forms of treatment available at the time, ''detoxification'' and therapeutic communities, were not actually medical programs. Detoxification programs, as mentioned earlier, involved physicians only in the early stages of treatment. Beyond that, civil commitment involved some loose rehabilitation programs, but as Lindesmith (1965, p. 292) points out, they functioned largely to segregate the addict and, being compulsory, were implicitly a punitive measure. Little rehabilitation, much less treatment, was accomplished.

The first and best-known ''therapeutic community'' for addicts was Synanon. It was founded in 1958 in California by Charles E. Dederich, a talented former AA devotee and businessman. Synanon emphasized withdrawal from drugs without medical help, as well as residential treatment, availability of 24-hour-a-day care, and abstinence from drugs. The core of the treatment was daily seminars and leaderless groups that met three evenings a week to ''release hostilities'' (Yablonsky, 1967). Synanon members, however, defined their approach as educational rather than therapeutic. As Dederich himself said, ''We don't presuppose sickness so much as stupidity. . . . Our starting point is not a hospital but rather a school'' (quoted in Yablonsky, 1967, p. 387). Synanon was basically a self-help lay-run program that eschewed the medical approach to addiction. It had some success getting and keeping addicts drug free, especially when members remained in the Synanon community and its related businesses for life. But if addicts left Synanon, the relapse rate was well over 90% (Brecher, 1972, p. 78). Many therapeutic communities based on the Synanon model or some variation of it began during the 1960s. A few used methadone detoxification, and several had physicians associated with the program, but nearly all rejected the medical approach to addiction.

The detoxification and therapeutic community approaches were limited. Detoxification had no program and little proven success; therapeutic communities had modest success and limited appeal to addicts, and, being by necessity small, could take few addicts. A 1971 congressional committee recommended a ''Manhattan Project'' to develop ''a drug which will effectively treat, prevent or cure heroin addiction. . . .'' (quoted in Nelkin, 1973, p. 141). With the ''heroin epidemic'' a problem of great public concern, the drug control turf was fertile for a drug program that ''worked.''

## Adoption of methadone maintenance as public policy

The publication in medical journals of impressive research results reporting a new treatment for an old social problem does not in itself create or change public policy. Some individuals or groups must become the champions of this particular treatment approach and convince those with the authority and resources to implement it of its viability before it is used as a solution to the problem. Often this process takes many years or even decades. But the immediate and urgent nature of ''the drug problem'' in the late 1960s compressed the process. Only 6 years after Dole and Nyswander's (1965) first publication, methadone maintenance had become public policy.

The champions of methadone maintenance had to overcome some entrenched resistance to

*The late 1960s and early 1970s revealed a definite and distinct cleavage between the ''Establishment'' and the antiwar youth culture. Students and other youth were engaged in the most severe anti-Establishment activities in three decades. Closely associated with the youth culture was drug use. Although many young people used ''soft'' drugs such as marijuana, the ''Establishment'' often did not distinguish between drugs in enforcing laws. Thus President Nixon's proclamation of drug abuse as ''public enemy number one'' may have had a more generalized meaning. In a symbolic frame, drug abuse could be viewed as a symbol of protesting youth. One might suggest that the protesting youth were really ''public enemy number one,'' and President Nixon could focus on ''drug abuse'' as a symbolic vehicle for discrediting alienated protestors and controlling deviants.

any maintenance approach. For nearly 50 years the official policy toward opiate addiction advocated abstinence; all punitive and treatment programs viewed a drug-free state as the only legitimate rehabilitative goal. As recently as 1963, a joint statement by the AMA and the National Academy of Sciences reaffirmed the 1920s position on maintenance: "Continued administration of narcotic drugs solely for the maintenance of dependence is not a bona fide attempt at cure nor is it ethical treatment except in . . . unusual circumstances" (quoted in Miller, R., 1974, p. 173). The Bureau of Narcotics and Dangerous Drugs (the BNDD, a reorganized and renamed FBN), the major law-enforcement agency for drug abuse, maintained an official stance until 1970 that methadone maintenance was illegal under the Harrison Act (Nelkin, 1973). There was considerable resistance to medicalization among law-enforcement agencies. Administrators and clients in therapeutic community drug programs were vocal in denouncing any maintenance approach as a sham because it failed to get addicts off narcotics.

New York City has the nation's largest heroin addiction problem. It has been estimated that between a fourth and a half the American addict population resides there. It was fertile ground for experimental programs to control addiction. In 1965, Dr. Dole went to New York City's commissioner of hospitals, Dr. Ray Trussell, with his early research results. He hoped to obtain the use of six hospital beds to expand his methadone research. Dr. Trussell was impressed with the preliminary findings and arranged for more than $1 million to implement the Dole and Nyswander program in New York City (Brecher, 1972, p. 138). Until this time the study and treatment of narcotics addiction had been solely in the domain of the Public Health Service, especially at the Lexington hospital. The BNDD, which opposed any maintenance program and saw its turf threatened, apparently "put pressure on the associate hospitals to shadow people, to obtain records, to seize methadone prescriptions and to threaten the pharmacist who filled the prescriptions" (Etzioni & Remp, 1973, p. 44). But with reports and evaluations of "success" the program grew rapidly. By 1970 New York City had 42 methadone maintenance centers with nearly 3500 patients (Brecher, 1972, p. 140).

Reports of "success" permeated the scientific and popular media. Perhaps the strongest scientific legitimation came from a series of independent evaluations of the Dole and Nyswander program carried out by Francis Gearing of the Columbia University School of Public Health. Gearing, a respected researcher, presented positive and optimistic evaluations of methadone maintenance to the First National Conference on Methadone Treatment in 1968 and in succeeding conferences over the next several years. These national conferences became a showcase for research on methadone. The *Journal of the American Medical Association* published results from this first evaluation in late 1968. The major conclusions were impressive:

1. Of the 871 patients admitted to the program, 86% remained in treatment.
2. For patients who remained in the program at least 3 months, rates of employment improved from a pretreatment 28% to 45% after 5 months and a rather amazing 85% after 24 months.
3. There was a notable decrease in criminal arrests among the patients.
4. None of the patients became readdicted to heroin.*

Although some methodological criticisms of the study were voiced, the overall thrust was clear: methadone maintenance "worked" to reduce crime, keep people off heroin, and get them reemployed. Subsequent reports by Gearing and his colleagues, as well as somewhat less glowing reports from other programs, confirmed these conclusions (Miller, R., 1974). Gearing's evaluations became "evidence" that advocates used to promote methadone

*Most subsequent studies of methadone maintenance adopted these criteria for evaluation of a program's effectiveness in treating addiction: (1) the retention of clients in the program; (2) the number of clients employed; and (3) the reduction of criminal activity, usually measured in terms of arrest rates. Other criteria are also used, most frequently abuse of other drugs, often measured by chemical tests of the patient's urine.

maintenance. These reports of the "success" of treatment, in the hands of professional and political claims-makers, stimulated the spread of methadone treatment and softened resistance by critics and opponents.*

Any new and successful treatment for opiate addiction would have been big news in the late 1960s; so methadone maintenance received substantial coverage in the news media. The popular press, however, presented methadone in a rather misleading fashion. This was at least in part because of the presentation by Dole and Nyswander. For instance, Dole referred to his program in a *New York Times* article as the substitution of "pain-killing methadone" for "crippling heroin." Press reports regularly avoided referring to methadone as a narcotic, thus creating an image that it was a cure for heroin (Etzioni & Remp, 1973). It is likely that much of the public was ready to see methadone as a solution to the heroin epidemic. The public and policymakers alike would increasingly view methadone maintenance as "the answer" to the problem of opiate abuse.

**Nixon Administration as a champion of methadone maintenance.** President Nixon and his administration became both direct and indirect supporters of methadone maintenance (Epstein, 1977). It was under the Nixon Administration that methadone maintenance became a central part of public drug policy. With the Administration's "law and order" stance against "crime in the streets," drug abuse could become public enemy number one. Physician Jerome Jaffe, a successful director of state drug programs in Illinois and an advocate of a "multimodal" approach to addiction, became the administration's special consultant on drug abuse. Jaffe soon became the head of the new Special Action Office for Drug Abuse Problems (SAODAP), which would be the coordinating agency for drug policy. Under his direction SAODAP became a strong advocate for methadone treatment. In 1969 Jaffe said, "If I had a limited number of dollars to spread around Chicago . . . we would be expanding our methadone program without any question" (quoted in Moss, 1977, p. 141). What seemed to impress the Administration most was the decline in criminal activity among addicts on methadone. The obsession with lowering crime statistics focused the Administration on drug programs that would reduce heroin use and especially "drug-related crime" (Epstein, 1977). Methadone maintenance seemed the most promising.

Opposition to methadone was waning. The FDA and BNDD in June, 1970, formally defined methadone for maintenance as an investigational new drug (IND)—literally, a research drug. Methadone maintenance "was viewed as a research technique which showed 'promise' in management and rehabilitation but also had significant potential for abuse" (Miller, R., 1974, p. 175). Later that year, following a cautious AMA statement approving methadone maintenance, the BNDD announced a limited acceptance of methadone treatment. The opposition had retreated, but remained cautious and gave only limited approval to methadone treatment. These cautions contrasted with the White House's embracing of methadone treatment. The Administration wanted to extend drug treatment, consisting mainly of methadone maintenance, to the entire population of heroin users in America (Moss, 1977).

President Nixon's recommendation to Congress had authorized SAODAP to spend about $1 billion in its first 3 years. The agency would be directly under White House supervision. Under Jaffe's direction the new agency's favorite approach to opiate addiction was methadone maintenance (Stevenson, no date). Some of the reasons for the Administration's enthusiasm for this approach are clear. In a time of national concern with drugs and crime and with an election year upcoming in 1972 (Epstein, 1977), it appeared as a relatively simple

---

*In addition to its apparent "success" as a treatment, methadone was easy to administer and was regularly depicted as having numerous distinct treatment advantages. First, it was addicting, so the patient could not stop taking it. Second, it could be given orally and produced no euphoric "highs." Third, it was fairly long-acting; thus treatment could be organized on an outpaitent basis, with the patient returning every 1 to 2 days. Fourth, patients could be "stabilized," so that the drug did not need to be continually increased. Finally, it created a "blockage" of other opiate highs.

**TABLE 3**
ESTIMATED RELATIVE COSTS OF DRUG PROGRAMS PER ADDICT PER YEAR (IN 1971 DOLLARS)*

| Program | Cost |
|---|---|
| NIMH civil commitment | $10,000 to $12,000 |
| Prison | $8000 |
| Therapeutic communities | $4400 (plus welfare) |
| Methadone maintenance | $2000 (plus welfare) |

*From *Methadone maintenance: a technological fix* by D. Nelkin, 1973, New York: George Braziller, Inc.

technological solution to a perplexing problem. Although a large amount of federal money was allocated to the "war on drugs," the cost per addict was low enough to appeal to the fiscally conservative Administration (Table 3). Undoubtedly, redefining the problem as a medical one and placing addicts in the jurisdiction of medically run clinics appealed to the medically oriented leadership of SAODAP. From less than three dozen programs with several thousand addicts in 1970, methadone maintenance programs were begun by private physicians, hospitals, and mental health centers*; although sometimes they received support from law-enforcement agencies, they were clearly under medical jurisdiction. By 1974, the peak year for methadone treatment, approximately 80,000 addicts were involved. To coin a phrase, there had been a virtual counterepidemic of methadone programs.

In sum, the Nixon Administration, taken with the early impressive results of methadone maintenance, became its prime champion. By creating a separate agency to coordinate drug policy, some entrenched resistance could be circumvented and the Administration's war against heroin could be fought with double barrels: the BNDD continuing its law-enforcement approach, with SAODAP becoming a proponent for methadone maintenance. In the early 1970s it appeared that with the success of methadone maintenance the "medical substitution game" might finally have found a winner.

*Some of the private methadone maintenance programs proved to be lucrative and profitable ventures. Between 1970 and 1974, 24 private methadone clinics began in New York City alone. Investigations by City Councilman Carter Burden and the newspaper *The Village Voice* reported the programs totaled between $2 and $3 million in profits per year (Smith, 1978). Entrepreneurship and profitability undoubtedly contributed to methadone maintenance's rapid spread.

## Methadone revisionists

Methadone maintenance became a popular and common treatment for addiction. In 1973 methadone was formally labeled by the FDA as a "treatment" drug. Comprehensive reviews by the editors of *Consumer Reports* (Brecher, 1972) and by social scientists (e.g., Miller, R., 1974) were generally approving and optimistic about methadone maintenance. But methadone's critics, who had been overshadowed by the reports of success and the methadone bandwagon, began to reemerge.

The first critique concerned the "diversion" of methadone into black markets. As early as 1973 there were reports of methadone diversion from clinics and clinic patients to the street and to drug users; a methadone black market had been created. Many clinics resorted to a "no take home" policy (Miller, R., 1974), and in 1973 new regulations went into effect that attempted to control methadone diversion. These policies appear to have had little success. Methadone became the most easily obtainable street drug in New York City and popular with addicts because it gave "good highs" (Agar, 1977; Agar & Stephens, 1975). Methadone diversion also created new addicts, as well as being regular fare for those already addicted. Many street users "shot" methadone (rather than taking it orally), and these reported methadone "highs" dealt the myth of the "heroin blockade" a severe blow.

Reports and papers presented at the Fourth and Fifth National Methadone Maintenance Conferences in 1972 and 1973 revealed many discrepant findings and raised important questions about methadone maintenance. A paper by Avram Goldstein, director of the Addiction Research Laboratory at Stanford, cast doubt on Dole and Nyswander's metabolic theory of addiction. Other reports presented data that questioned the high retention figures of methadone maintenance programs. Considerable skepticism was evident as to whether abstinence was a realistic goal of methadone treatment. Reports of serious problems with the street use of methadone were presented (Moss, 1977). Although few people probably read these technical reports, an article published in *The Public Interest* by journalist Edward Jay Epstein (1974) made many of these "revisionist" findings more widely available. This article, cited frequently by methadone critics, attacked the claims made by methadone proponents. After reviewing much of the methadone research, Epstein concluded that (1) methadone does not by itself reduce crime, (2) it does not block addicts against heroin (many still used heroin), and (3) there was no evidence that heroin addiction was a "metabolic disease" as Dole and Nyswander hypothesized. This article raised doubts more publicly than before about the efficacy of methadone maintenance and gave the antimethadone view some exposure.*

Critics also voiced concern about the fact that methadone was more addictive than heroin. Why should the government and the medical profession support the use of an addictive drug? Supporters of drug abstinence saw it merely as another substitution and a worse addiction. Dr. Peter Bourne, who for a time was head of SAODAP, saw it differently: "The fact that methadone is addicting is essential to allow therapy to occur . . . it develops a trust between the patients and the doctor" (quoted in Stevenson, no date, p. 5). In response to increasing criticism of methadone's effectiveness, one critic reports that some methadone proponents shifted their claims to view the addiction of maintenance as a "chemical parole." The methadone addiction, in this view, had the latent function of forcing addicts to report to the clinic for methadone several times weekly, where they would come into contact with physicians and counselors in rehabilitative programs (Epstein, 1977).

> [Proponents of methadone maintenance] stated that all the responsible doctors and social scientists involved in the program viewed methadone simply as a lure to entice addicts into treatment programs where the real "rehabilitative effort" could take place. (Epstein, 1977, p. 286)

Critics seized on this as using methadone overtly as a social control mechanism and not as a treatment drug.

Rather suddenly during 1974, methadone maintenance began to lose favor as federal public policy. It is unlikely that this was a direct result of scientific evaluations, since many of them were published after 1974. Several factors seem to have led to a reversal of policy. Generally, methadone maintenance had not made the major dent in crime statistics that the pre-election Nixon Administration had hoped for. The heroin epidemic may have tapered off by itself by this time. More specifically, a report by the Drug Enforcement Agency (the successor of the BNDD, which never fully supported methadone maintenance) reported a sharp rise in methadone-related deaths and a relatively high arrest rate among methadone users and suggested that "methadone is partially replacing heroin as the drug of abuse" (quoted in Epstein, 1977, p. 248). Such reports may have made the Administration uneasy. One analyst suggests that in the Administration's policy statement, "Federal Strategy for Drug Abuse and Drug Prevention 1974," "it appears to be the government's intention to expand drug-free treatment programs over the next 2 years, while allowing methadone maintenance programs to shrink away" (Moss, 1977, p. 150). President Nixon and his White House staff began to disassociate themselves from the funding of methadone programs. The White House officially divorced itself from SAODAP, the agency the President had created to oversee drug treatment; SAODAP was moved to the Department of Health, Education and Welfare, where it merged into another federal agency (National Institute for Drug Abuse) (Epstein, 1977, p. 249). Thus, as the Nixon Administration extricated itself from the drug treatment business,

*Other critiques, especially of Gearing's studies, appeared also in the psychiatric (e.g., Maddox & Bowden, 1972) and sociological (e.g., Waldorf, 1973) literatures.

methadone maintenance lost its chief source of financial support.

Methadone maintenance programs, however, have not withered away. Only their expansion seems to have been curtailed. Methadone programs seem to have stabilized at about 80,000 addict patients, estimated to be about 15% of the addict population (DeLong, J. V., 1975). Scientific reports continue to point out the flaws in early evaluations of methadone maintenance's "success," to question the validity of data used in evaluations, and to present a more limited view of its treatment efficacy.*

*Validity problems include "the shrinking sample," the unreliability of patient self-reports, and, most critically, the criteria for measurement of "success" (Cohen, M., et al., 1976). Major criteria used in evaluating the programs were retention, employment, number of arrests, and drug abuse. These revisionist studies found problems with the measurement of all of these. The "shrinking sample," counting only those who remained in the program for a specific period rather than the entire cohort admitted to the program, inflated retention rates (Cohen, M., et al., 1976; Newman, 1976). As many as three fifths of the patients terminated by the end of the second year (Kleinman et al., 1977). Improved rates of employment may not have represented the "success" of treatment. This criterion of evaluation was bound to improve, since programs were often self-selective—an individual had to remain employed to remain in it. One 5-year study showed that employment improved for the two fifths of the original cohort who remained in the program for 2 years but not for others (Kleinman et al., 1977). These figures were further complicated by reliance on patients' self-reports and lack of differentiation between full- and part-time employment (Cohen, M., et al., 1976). The reduction of criminal behavior was also less than first reported. The only real decline linked clearly to the availability of a heroin substitute was in drug-related arrests. According to one study, prosocial changes were limited almost exclusively to the 23% who remained in the program for more than 3 years. Overall, the results of the studies depicted methadone maintenance as providing "modest help for a few" (Kleinman & Lukoff, 1975). It appears to be most successful with older addicts who volunteer for the program and are motivated to remain in it for several years. In fairness to Dole and Nyswander, they always pointed out the need for supportive counseling and rehabilitation. Their small program provided this; most of the later programs were much larger and focused more on dispensing and controlling the methadone.

Dole and Nyswander themselves have concluded that their early projections were overly optimistic but cite administrative regulations and errors as causes of methadone maintenance's loss of effectiveness. With the incredibly rapid expansion of programs that quickly grew too large and were placed under the jurisdiction of a government monopoly that imposed too many arbitrary controls, they suggest that "the treatment programs have lost their ability to attract and rehabilitate addicts." (Dole & Nyswander, 1976, p. 211). Yet methadone maintenance remains far less expensive on a per patient basis than other treatments and has proved to be no *less* successful. Thus approximately 800 methadone clinics were in operation in 1977 at the cost of 50 million federal dollars (*Newsweek,* Feb. 7, 1977, p. 29). Some hold out hope that longer lasting heroin substitutes (for example, LAAM) will alleviate some of the problems of methadone maintenance (Blaine & Renault, 1976). Others see the narcotic "antagonists" (that block opiate "highs"), such as naltrexone, as having great potential for successful treatment (Lex & Meyer, 1977), although they may bring problems similar to those in methadone treatment (Goldstein, 1976). Some consideration has been given to long-acting narcotic antagonists that could be implanted under the skin (Willette, 1976). A few have suggested medically controlled heroin maintenance. Even with the recent disenchantment with methadone maintenance, medical approaches to opiate addiction are alive and well.

### A final note on methadone and medicalization

Methadone was a medical technological discovery that received extravagant early reports of success. Its promotion by the medical profession was limited mostly to the relatively few individuals engaged in methadone research or treatment programs. The adoption of methadone maintenance by the Nixon Administration as a way of combating the heroin epidemic and an attempt to reduce crime statistics was its greatest boost. In fact, from the original Dole and Nyswander project to the creation of SAODAP, it was politicians and government administrators who were methadone's strongest champions.*

In its early days methadone was seen as a panacea. However, as in similar previous rounds of "the medical substitution game," methadone was soon found not to be "the answer" to opiate addiction and to engender new problems. Presently it remains one of several types of treatment available for opiate addiction.

From the perspective of this book, the development of methadone maintenance offers some significant insights into the process of medicalization. After a dormant period of over 40 years, a medical approach to addiction reemerged in the 1960s. The introduction of methadone maintenance vindicated the medical approach and reengaged the medical profession in the treatment of addicts. But it would be a mistake to view this as the medical profession's attempt to expand medical jurisdiction; on the contrary, the rapid rise and diffusion of methadone maintenance was accomplished with only minor contributions by the medical profession. There were few specific medical entrepreneurs for methadone outside governmental agencies. Medical interest perhaps was limited, since most physicians did not regularly come in contact with opiate addicts and because they had no access to highly regulated methadone. On a theoretical level, no well-developed disease concept of opiate addiction was generated to justify medical intervention (as had occurred with alcoholism). On a practical level, few physicians wanted to deal with addicts.

The waxing and waning of methadone maintenance was largely a political matter handled by politicians and governmental administrators. This is no different from the Harrison Act's demedicalization of opiate addiction. The adoption of a medical approach was a political decision in a most conventional sense: it was a policy adopted by an elected administration to meet its own ends and was supported through legislative process. The medical profession's mandate to treat addiction was directly dependent on the government's policies; the adoption of methadone maintenance placed medicine in the service of the government. With noncriminal deviance, medical professional dominance is an important factor determining medicalization. However, in matters related to criminal law, treatment by the medical profession is accomplished at the determination of the state, with medicine functioning as a social control agent for the state. Thus the medicalization of opiate addiction highlights the connections between medical and legal social control networks, something we will explore further in Chapters 9 and 10.

The criminal approach to deviance, however, has not been abandoned. Law-enforcement agencies continue to prosecute addicts for drug-related activities. The emergence of methadone maintenance and the medical control of addiction created some tensions between medical and criminal jurisdictions. For the most part, in recent years an uneasy alliance has been forged between the law-enforcement and medical systems, with functional cooperation on a local level (Lidz & Walker, 1977). We are left with a hybrid criminal-medical designation of addiction: opiate addiction is still criminalized, but addicts are deemed suitable for medical treatment.

*Heroin addiction becoming more a middle-class rather than only a lower-class phenomenon seems to have made medicalization a more likely and more acceptable policy. High prevalence of deviance among the middle class (e.g., alcoholism, hyperactivity) increases the likelihood of medicalization and medical sanctions.

## SUMMARY

The history of medical involvement with opiate addiction is long and marked with overt political conflict. A number of definitional changes are apparent: from a time when it was not considered a problem, to its definition as a medical problem, to its criminalization, and again to its remedicalization.

Opiates are powerful analgesic drugs. Continued use creates a physiological dependence; when the drug is discontinued, withdrawal symptoms commence. Opiate addiction stems from a recognized physiological dependence on the drug. To the best of our knowledge, physical dependence on opiates is in itself not particularly harmful to the human body.

The use of opium is at least 3000 years old. Prior to the 19th century it was used largely as a medical agent. There is little evidence of extensive recreational usage, except in China. After it was brought to the West by travelers, it became an important remedy in European medicine. There was little concern about addiction, and it was not considered much of a problem.

Definitions and uses of opium changed during the 19th century. Imperialistic British policies forced an opium trade on China. The supply created its own demand, and millions of Chinese were addicted to smoking opium. Two "opium wars" were fought to ensure the profitable British trade.

Innovations and medical use facilitated the spread of opium. Purer forms of opiates were isolated (morphine and codeine), the hypodermic syringe was invented, and the medical use of morphine during the Civil War created so many addicts that addiction was called the "soldier's disease." In fact, nearly all the 19th century addicts were recruited through some medical channels: many physicians used opiates with little regard to addiction, and a growing patent medicine industry promoted nostrums that contained opiates. Tens of thousands unwittingly became physiologically dependent. Unproven medical beliefs that only "weak" individuals could become addicted and that injected morphine could cure opium addiction contributed to this dependence. The latter is the first instance of what we call the "medical substitution game." By the close of the 19th century, medical practice had changed and opiates had fewer medical uses. Addiction was considered a diaease, to be treated by pragmatic medical intervention. In a real sense, 19th-century medical practice had created the very problem it was treating at the century's close.

The typical 19th-century American addict was middle-aged, female, rural, middle-class, and white; she had become addicted either by her physicians's treatments or from her use of patent medicines. More addicts probably existed at this time than any other, but it still was not considered a major social problem.

Moral entrepreneurship and interest-group politicking both created addiction as a social problem and changed its definition. The "great debate" about the opium trade in the British Parliament lasted several decades; it pitted the antiopium crusaders against the opium interests. Millions of words were exchanged. Both sides summoned medical evidence to support their claims. After numerous defeats, the antiopium forces won a Parliamentary victory in 1906. The definitions of opium addiction were changing: it was now considered immoral and an evil.

In late 19th-century America, addicts aroused sympathy and pity, but addiction was seen increasingly as will weakening and immoral. The first American opiate prohibition attempted to control opium smoking by Chinese immigrants. Heroin was discovered and at first viewed as a cure for morphine addiction. It was, however, soon defined as devoid of medical uses and a drug with no redeeming value. The American views of opiate addiction turned in a negative direction on the axis of anti-Chinese sentiment and fears of heroin.

After banning opium in the newly acquired Philippines, the United States, under the leadership of several moral entrepreneurs, spearheaded two international conferences on controlling opium. As a domestic response, the Harrison Act was passed. It was originally intended to limit and regulate the marketing of opiates, giving physicians control of opiates and placing addicts completely in medical hands. But the Treasury Department defined taking opiates for nontherapeutic purposes as harmful and criminal. A battle over criminal and medical jurisdiction began, with the Supreme Court supporting the Treasury Department's definition, making medical treatment of addiction impossible. After a short-lived era of narcotics clinics, the medical profession gave up all claims to treatment of addiction. Opiate addiction had been demedicalized.

Opiate addiction remained securely as the FBN's turf for over three decades. But there were consequences of criminalizing addiction: an addict subculture emerged, a criminal drug underworld was created, the image of the addict as dope fiend was promoted, the population of addicts changed, and addicts began to fill the prisons. Only a tiny percent of addicts were rehabilitated. In the 1950s the criminal approach reached a high-water mark with increased penalties for narcotics offenses. But the criminal approach had failed to stem the increasing tide of addiction.

By the mid-1950s, a small chorus of voices, including some medical professionals, began criticizing the punitive approach and calling for medical alternatives. They pointed to the British system of heroin maintenance as a model. The FBN attempted to discredit these critics. But the long-silent champions of medical definitions would be heard; their viewpoint was echoed by a Supreme Court decision and a presidential commission.

The discovery of methadone maintenance was the vehicle for the remedicalization of opiate addiction. In light of early reports of success, supporters viewed it as a panacea. In response to the "heroin epidemic" and in an attempt to reduce crime statistics, the Nixon Administration embraced methadone for its use in the "war" on drugs. Medical methadone programs grew rapidly. Soon it became clear that the success of methadone maintenance had been overstated, and the Administration withdrew its support. Overall, the introduction of methadone maintenance vindicated the medical approach and reengaged the medical profession in the treatment of addicts. But since the medical profession's mandate to treat addiction is dependent on (and accomplished at the determination of) the state, medicine functions as a social control agent in the former's behalf. The uneasy alliance between the law-enforcement and medical systems has created a hybrid criminal-medical designation of addiction.

## SUGGESTED READINGS

Brecher, E. M. *Licit and illicit drugs*. Boston: Little, Brown & Co., 1972.

The best readily available single source on the history of drugs. It also includes an intelligent evaluation of drug effects. Since it is written by the editors of *Consumer Reports,* it contains no sociological analysis.

Duster, T. *The legislation of morality*. New York: The Free Press, 1970.

A readable analysis of the changing definition of addiction. Duster focuses on how legislation contributed to the creation of a negative moral judgment of addiction.

Lindesmith, A. *The addict and the law*. New York: Vintage Books, Inc., 1965.

An outstanding sociological analysis of the creation of American drug policy. Highly critical of the criminal approach, Lindesmith calls for the development of a truly medical approach to addiction.

Musto, D. *The American disease*. New Haven, Conn.: Yale University Press, 1973.

The most complete historical analysis of the definition and treatment of opiates in America. Written by a medical historian, it includes a good analysis of medical involvement.

Nelkin, D. *Methadone maintenance: a technological fix*. New York: George Braziller, Inc., 1973.

Analyzes the technological, social, and political factors involved in the development of methadone maintenance. Nelkin critically evaluates methadone as a technological solution to a complex social problem.

# 6 CHILDREN and MEDICALIZATION

## DELINQUENCY, HYPERACTIVITY, and CHILD ABUSE

Children are a special group of people in our society: they are considered innocent, dependent, and, because of their immaturity, not wholly responsible for their deviant behaviors. Many deviant behaviors by children, and some behaviors that victimize them, have come under medical jurisdiction in American society. This medicalization of childhood deviance has occurred in part because of the status of children in society and the types of attention and reaction we are able to give to childhood problems. To better understand this special status of children, we first briefly review "the discovery of childhood," focusing on the development of the modern conception of "child." We then present discussions of the expansion of medical jurisdiction to encompass three types of deviance related to children: delinquency, hyperactivity, and child abuse. Finally, we discuss the status of children and their "risk" for medicalization.

### DISCOVERY OF CHILDHOOD

"Childhood" has not always been a separate and distinct stage in the life cycle. Clearly, infants and children have always aged chronologically and, to a degree, biologically the same way, but "childhood" as a special period or stage does not exist in nature. Childhood is a social construction, an invention of the postmedieval period. Childhood, with its special rights and privileges, is no more than a few hundred years old.

Through the latter parts of the Middle Ages, children, soon after weaning, interacted, labored, and played with adults in everyday life. The child was viewed as a small version of an adult. For example, children in medieval paintings were depicted as miniature adults, little people with all the dress and features of adults (Ariès, 1962). Children were largely ignored or exploited until a century or two after the Middle Ages and were not considered of particular importance. Infanticide was a regular, if subterranean, form of birth control (Harris, 1977; Langner, 1974). Abandonment of children was a common practice (de Mause, 1974).

This indifference to children (Empey, 1978) is more understandable given the facts of child mortality, or death rate. As late as the 17th century, from one half to two thirds of all children died before the age of twenty (Empey, 1978, p. 32). Into the 18th century the odds were two or three to one against a child living to age 5 (Kessen, 1965, cited in Empey, 1978, p. 44). Under such conditions, with the child's great vulnerability and small survival rate, people could not afford to invest a substantial amount of time and energy or become attached to children: the prospects of return were not good. Those who did survive were often boarded out, as young as at the age of 7, to become apprentices or serve in the homes of other people (Ariès, 1962).

Childhood was not discovered at any one specific time. Rather, it was a by-product of the Enlightenment, gradually emerging over two to three centuries. As symbolic of its discovery,

Phillipe Ariès (1962) points out that well-to-do persons in the 16th and 17th centuries began to commission individual portraits of their children and show them in special outfits designed for children. These children for the first time resemble our conception of a child, rather than a miniature adult. Children were increasingly seen as having special characteristics and "on account of [their] sweetness, simplicity and drollery, became a source of amusement and relaxation for the adult" (Ariès, 1962, p. 129).

The two major attributes characterizing this new view of children were innocence and dependence. Although Christian moralists long had emphasized the innocent natures of children (de Mause, 1974), they were paid little attention until the 16th century. The idea that children are "innocent" and because of this innocence and sweetness need to be protected from the harsh and sinful world has its roots in the discovery of childhood (Empey, 1978, p. 8). "The idea of childish innocence," Ariès (1962) notes,

> resulted in two kinds of attitude and behaviour towards childhood: firstly, safeguarding it against pollution by life, and particularly by the sexuality tolerated if not approved of among adults; and secondly, strengthening it by developing character and reason. (p. 119)

Children were also increasingly seen as dependent beings who needed careful guidance and direction. For the child's proper development "he must be stringently safeguarded, both physically and morally, he must receive a carefully structured and special education, and, only after long years of preparation, will he be properly prepared for adulthood" (Empey, 1978, pp. 50-51). For a child to live in the adult world "he had to be subjected to a special treatment, a sort of quarantine, before he was allowed to join the adults" (Ariès, 1962, p. 412). During this developmentally segregated childhood, children would be subject to a moral education based on five principles. First, children must be closely watched, under constant supervision, and never left alone.Second, children should not be pampered and must learn strict discipline early in life. Third, children must practice modesty and decency. Fourth, children should be brought up to work diligently. Fifth, children were to respect and obey authority (Ariès, 1962, pp. 114-118; Empey, 1978, pp. 54-55). From these, the modern notion of childhood as a special period of dependence had been created.

The sources of this change were both general and specific. Although the infant mortality rate did not change greatly until after the 19th century, children were becoming more important in families. Industrialization and urbanization created the nuclear family, and this drew more energy and attention to children and individual needs. At first, "coddling" of children became common in the family circle as children became a center of family amusement. The principles and admonitions of a small group of champions of children's morality warned, however, of the dangers of "coddling" as opposed to disciplining children. These reformers, including moralists, educators, and clergy, supported child-rearing philosophies that emphasized psychological control and moral solicitude, in the name of benefiting the child (Ariès, 1962, pp. 330-412; Empey, 1978, pp. 51-68). These ideas prevailed, and children came to be seen "as fragile creatures of God who needed to be both safeguarded and reformed" (Ariès, 1962, p. 133). Eventually this led to the creation of special institutions to educate children; soon much child-rearing would be taken over by schools. Thus the modern conceptions of childhood were forged: children were innocent and dependent but corruptible and needed guidance and discipline. With the discovery of childhood the behavior and activities of children became worthy of attention in their own right.

## ORIGINS OF JUVENILE DELINQUENCY

As we have pointed out throughout this book, new deviance designations do not emerge by themselves but are products of collective enterprise and claims-making activities. The "invention" of juvenile delinquency, as Anthony Platt (1969) terms it, is one such example. Unlike most of the other forms of deviance we discuss, delinquency never became a manifest medical problem, and the medical professions' involvement with it was never more than peripheral. Yet the definition and treatment of delinquency shares many attributes with the therapeutic-clinical approach; in fact, those who crusaded for delinquency prevention adopted a medical rather than a punitive model of deviance. It is these aspects of a quasimedical approach that we emphasize here, giving special attention to the early medical analogies for delinquency and the subsequent developments of the juvenile court and child-guidance movement.

## Childhood deviance into the 19th century

Many children's behaviors now considered deviant have a long history of being seen as common and conventional children's behavior. As late as the 17th century, children engaged in behaviors that today would be defined as delinquency: most learned and used obscene language regularly, many freely engaged in a variety of sexual activities, some drank regularly in taverns, and few ever went to school (Empey, 1978, p. 71). These behaviors, although not condoned, were largely tolerated. Today these children could well be labeled delinquent. Why has this occurred? One might suggest that children engage in more deviant behaviors now or that today there are more troublesome children around. However, there is little evidence to support this contention. On the other hand, there have been clear changes in how these behaviors have come to be defined. The discovery of childhood and the subsequent changes in the perception of children focused increased attention on children's behavior and welfare. Through the efforts of reformers and child-saving crusaders, the definition and treatment of children's behavior changed. Certain behaviors became defined as delinquent.

This is not to say that no childhood deviance was condemned or punished in pre–17th–century society. Children have always "misbehaved," and social groups have always endeavored to control this deviance. But this control was, until the 19th century, largely informal. Families, the local community, and the church took care of troublesome children. Only in severe cases were the formal mechanisms of state or civil authority called on. The early American colonists, for example, equated crime with sin and did not consider sinners rehabilitable; their deviance demanded retribution and punishment, which was swift and usually severe.

But even before the 17th century, children were sometimes differentiated from adults. Societal response to children's deviance often turned on whether a child could be held *responsible* for criminal or deviant behavior. The Code of Hammurabi, the earliest-known code of laws, took specific note of children's duties to parents and prescribed punishments for violations. Age became an important factor in defining responsibility for children's behavior. Roman law defined children under 7 as incapable of *mens rea* (criminal intent) and therefore not responsible for criminal behavior. From the age of 7 to about puberty children's responsibility could be determined by the courts. If a child were deemed responsible, he or she was subject to adult laws and courts (Short, 1968). Common law in England and informal practice in Europe and America did not hold children criminally responsible for their acts below the age of 7, but beyond that, the laws were open to interpretation and permitted severe punishments by courts, parents, and apprentice masters (Empey, 1978, p. 42). Thus prior to the 19th century children received some special considerations under the law, but they were limited.

## Child-savers and the house of refuge

As a result of the Enlightenment and the emerging ideas of individualistic and collective progress, the colonial practice of equating crime and sin lost favor, and the idea that the causes of deviant behavior were "inborn tendencies" and "the work of the devil" became less popular. By the early 19th century the causes of deviance were increasingly found in the environment. Urbanization and industrialization and the breakdown of the traditional social order were depicted as causing individual deviant behavior. With childhood recognized as a unique stage of development in the early

19th century, attention was paid to the plight of children in their own right. The Jacksonian reformers, among the first interested in saving children from "ruin," located the sources of crime and delinquency in society. An inadequate family upbringing and the spread of vice through the community were believed especially important in leading children astray. Parental neglect was deemed the primary cause of deviant behavior, with the debilitating influences of the environment, such as taverns and houses of prostitution, seen as contributory (Rothman, 1971, pp. 76-78).

As we argued in Chapter 3, early 19th-century reformers viewed the "asylum" as the cure for all social ills and deviant behavior. If the breakdown of social order was the cause of deviance, then a well-ordered environment would be its solution. This was also true with childhood deviance. Delinquency and pauperism were subjects of considerable concern in the 19th century. They were seen as closely related; a delinquent was a potential pauper (Finestone, 1976b). In 1823 the Society for the Prevention of Pauperism reorganized itself as the Society for the Reformation of Juvenile Delinquents. This middle- and upper-class group of "gentlemen reformers" saw delinquency as a problem of the individual. Armed with the best of intentions, their goal was to reach the delinquent early, before he (or she) was too tainted by environmental influences, and provide a "correct" environment that would lead to a responsible adulthood. The vehicle for this was "the house of refuge."

The first house of refuge opened in New York City in 1825, followed soon by many others in various Eastern cities. The champions of these child-saving institutions were confident that the incarceration of the juvenile offender, the wandering street urchin, the child of impoverished parents, and the disobedient child, could be nothing but beneficial for the child. They shared the intense faith of the asylum superintendents (see Chapter 3) "in the rehabilitative powers of a carefully designed environment and were certain that properly structured institutions would not only comfort the homeless but reform the delinquent" (Rothman, 1971, p. 206). The child would be subjected to an ordered and disciplined model routine, and in the words of a fund-raising appeal from the Philadelphia House of Refuge, would be "shielded from the temptations of a sinful world" (quoted in Rothman, 1971, p. 210). The house of refuge would be a "superparent" (Empey, 1978) restituting what reformers perceived as the loss of a tightly knit community and the laxity of family structure.

Superparent is an apt metaphor for such institutions. The state's jurisdiction over these children was based on the concept of "parens patriae," a term derived from the English concept of the King's role as father of the country, giving the state power to protect the rights of these children and, if need be, assume the parental role. The houses of refuge would act in loco parentis, in place of parents, to transform socially dependent and deviant children into responsible adults, not with punishment but through treatment (Kittrie, 1971, p. 3). The reformatory superintendents endeavored to replace parental authority and substitute their own. In an attempt to bring the child under as full control as possible, they frequently insisted parents transfer to them their legal rights on the child's admission (Rothman, 1971, p. 221).

The well-ordered family was also the model of reformatory organization. The institution's goal was to reform each individual child. Contact with the outside world and outsiders' contact with the children were minimized. The children were subject to a carefully regulated and organized schedule, with an extraordinary emphasis on obedience and authority. Discipline for the benefit of the child could not be too absolute. Although the family was the ideal model, historian David Rothman (1971, p. 235) suggests that "a military tone seems to have pervaded these institutions." The organization and routines more resembled an army camp than a family.

By the 1850s some of the optimism had faded. The reformatories were overcrowded, and the population of delinquents had changed. More foreign-born and children from the "dangerous classes," deemed less suited for reform, were being sent to the reformatories (Rothman, 1971, p. 261). New theories stressing the powerful influences of heredity on deviant behavior dimmed the belief in the viability of social reform. After the Civil War a new generation of reformers criticized the harsh discipline and prisonlike atmosphere of these institutions. In fact, the reformatories had become increasingly custodial and in actuality much like "youth prisons." But even when they could not reform, they found community support because at least they functioned as a benevolent method of keeping child offenders off the streets.

With the development of the houses of refuge, the die was cast for the creation and treatment of juvenile delinquency. Children were a separate and dependent class of people who needed both protection and reform. The state could intervene with delinquent or potentially delinquent children deemed in need and "treat" them in the children's own best interests. While the reformatories lost some favor as a vehicle for reform, a new group of child-saving crusaders proposed changes that led to the creation of another type of superparent to treat deviant children, the juvenile court.

## Child-savers and the ideology of child welfare*

The post–Civil War period saw the emergence of a new and regenerated child-saving movement. This movement, essentially composed of two separate though overlapping threads of reform, developed a particular ideology of child welfare that was eventually institutionalized in the juvenile court system.

The first thread of reform came from within the existing system. Numerous penal specialists and institutional superintendents became champions of penal reform, urging the revamping of the reformatory structure and organization. They proposed reforms, including a "simpler, more natural" life in the country for delinquents, a reorganization of the institution into a smaller "cottage system" with a resident family, and the training of youth in agricultural and industrial trades. As Anthony Platt (1969) notes, the penal reformers advocated nonurban, middle-class values for these children yet taught lower-class skills. Although undoubtedly sincerely concerned with their charges and the welfare of children in general, these child-savers had a turf to protect, the reformatory, and thus aimed their reforms at modifying the existing system.

The second group of child-savers was outside the system. They were charitable and philanthropic crusaders, largely women, who saw child-saving as an ethical and humanitarian calling. Their interest was in saving not just deviant children but all less fortunate children from the afflictions of rapid urbanization. Their child-saving activity gained legitimacy partly because it was taken to be a natural extension of their female role as "caretakers" and "experts" in the welfare of children. They argued that women should be involved in child-saving because they were "the better half" (Filene, 1974), morally superior and endowed with a temperament that was better suited for work with delinquents. Women as nurturers, it was argued, would have a "civilizing" effect on child penology. Many of these crusaders, however, were also feminists. The child-saving movement gave feminists a cause that had broad-based support in society and gave women an acceptable public role at a time when few such roles were available. Most of the child-saving women, such as Louise Bowen and Jane Addams, were from rural and middle-class origins, and they promoted a middle-class orientation toward delinquents. Although the child-savers' interests included removing children from almshouses, private institutions, and jails, their major impact was not on the jails or reformatories (Platt, 1969, p. 99). Their legacy stems from their expansion of child-saving activities to all children in need and the particular view of child welfare they espoused.

The late 19th-century child-savers embraced and promoted a particular "ideology of child welfare," the assumptions of which were ultimately institutionalized in the juvenile court. Their ideology was an amalgam of ideas drawn from available theories of deviance and de-

*The material in this section comes largely from Platt (1969). Since we select only elements of his intriguing analysis that bear directly on children and medicalization, the reader is encouraged to consult that volume for a more complete picture of the child-saving movement.

pendence of the period and was displayed in their child-saving claims. As David Matza (1964) points out, nearly all theories of delinquency are positivistic and deterministic, assuming that psychological, social or biological "forces" rather than some type of "will" determines the behavior of the child. He suggests that students of delinquency, including perhaps especially these child-savers, have developed an "ideology of child welfare." Because juvenile delinquency is seen always in a deterministic framework, Matza (1964) argues that

> statements reinforcing the delinquents' conception of irresponsibility are an integral part of the ideology of child welfare shared by social work, psychoanalysis and criminology. This ideology presents a causal theory of delinquency which, when it attributes fault, directs it to parent, community, society, or even to victims of crime. (p. 95).

This ideology, nascent and undeveloped before the 19th century, took a particular form in the hands of these reformers, a form that outlined the contours of the juvenile court.

If the earlier child-savers of the house of refuge era borrowed their rhetoric from social theories of environmental causation, the new child-savers borrowed their ideal from medicine. Since the child-savers were concerned with humanitarian benefit and the welfare of the child rather than punishment, the medical therapeutic analogy was fitting. Taking their cues from physicians who had pioneered positivist criminology (Platt, 1969, p. 29), and perhaps impressed with the successes of medical work in the late 19th century, the child-savers updated social origin theories with the new ideas of biological determinism and borrowed the medical "imagery of pathology, infection, and immunization" (Platt, 1969, p. 18)* as their strategy for handling delinquency. Even if, as popular theories suggested, heredity and biology played a role in causing deviant behavior (some child-savers challenged this with their own theories of urban slums, disorganized families, and moral decay), most believed early and proper social intervention could prevent or reform delinquency. One aspect of the ideology, echoing Lombroso, was a faith that delinquents could be identified, treated, and changed. "Crime, like disease, was revealed 'in the face, the voice, the person and the carriage,' so that a skillful and properly trained diagnostician could arrest criminal tendencies" (Platt, 1969, p. 30). In these cases medical intervention could be a preventive measure. But it was the medical model and vocabulary, rather than medical intervention, that became the hallmark of juvenile delinquency treatment. Delinquency could be prevented by therapeutic intervention.

In sum, the child-savers made relatively minor reforms in the reformatories themselves. But they made a lasting impact on the definition and treatment of delinquency in three more significant matters. First, they extended public concern for the general welfare of children (as dependent individuals) rather than focusing attention on specific types of behavior engaged in by deviant children. This, as Platt (1969, p. 99) observes, extended governmental control "over a whole range of activities that had been previously ignored or dealt with informally." Second, they developed a particular ideology of child welfare, based on the medical model of prevention and treatment. Third, they managed to institutionalize most of their reforms in the creation of the juvenile court.

## Juvenile court

The "success" of the child-saving movement was the juvenile court. The first legislation establishing a juvenile court was passed in 1899 in Illinois. A result of many years of concern by child-saving and other humanitarian groups, the legislation created a special children's court and established a new type of legal machinery for handling juveniles outside the adult criminal justice system.

The mandate of the juvenile court was broad—the welfare of children under 16 who were in some kind of trouble. Based on the traditional parens patriae concept, the court would "regulate the treatment and control of dependent, neglected and delinquent children"

---

*Quotations from Platt (1969) on pp. 150 to 152 from Platt, A., *The child savers: the invention of delinquency*. Chicago: University of Chicago Press, 1969, Copyright 1969 by University of Chicago Press.

(Platt, 1969, p. 134). The juvenile court could gain guardianship over the child, not as a criminal but as a ward of the state. A child could be brought into the jurisdiction of the court for three types of problems: (1) for criminal offenses (similar to adults); (2) for being neglected by parents or guardians; and (3) for "status" offenses—offenses that came under legal control only because of the juvenile's age, including drinking, truancy, incorrigibility, running away, begging, and being "in danger of immorality." Both neglect and status offenses, neither of which would bring adults into the purview of the law, emphasized the court's claim over the dependent status of children.* And, as Platt (1969) points out, the status offenses reflected the child-savers' "concern" with the behavior of the poor, since "they were primarily attributable to children of lower-class migrant and immigrant families" (p. 139).

Although the legislation did not invent delinquency out of whole cloth (cf. Hagan & Leon, 1977), it expanded and consolidated the state's control over youthful activities and institutionalized the dependent status of children (Platt, 1969). Many states shortly thereafter passed juvenile justice legislation; by 1928 all but two states had adopted a juvenile court system, and by 1932 there were 600 juvenile courts in the United States (Platt, 1969, p. 10).

The creation of the juvenile court actually punctuated and institutionalized a change that had been occurring for more than a century. The colonists had blamed deviant children for their innate depravity. By the late 19th century, Americans largely externalized blame by defining conduct as socially or biologically determined and sought "treatment," not retribution, for deviance (Empey, 1978, p. 93). To accomplish this, the juvenile court was established with a separate judge, a special court, confidential records, and informal sessions. As mentioned, the court not only dealt with lawbreakers but also with neglected and dependent children. Prior to the creation of the juvenile court, the "sick" (mentally ill) and the "bad" (criminal) were more or less separate categories (see Chapter 3). The juvenile court blurred those distinctions for children, however, by developing a mechanism that was "to operate in the interest and protection of the child with the intent to understand the development of disturbing behavior" (Rafferty, 1977, p. 273). It was not important to establish whether the child was "bad" (i.e., guilty or innocent), because legally the child was seen as incapacitated (Kittrie, 1971, p. 106) and dependent, but to ascertain what could be done in the child's best interest to save him or her from a criminal career. Like medicine and unlike law, the etiology and development of the problem or difficulty was a central concern. The focus was on the child's background and environment rather than on the offense.

Although the juvenile court did not exactly adopt the rhetoric of medicine, it borrowed a number of medical assumptions. It adopted the medical model ideal of early diagnosis and preventive treatment. The court's procedures were quasimedical, with private hearings, secret records, and an emphasis on therapeutic intervention with "predelinquents." The judge was depicted as a "doctor-counselor" and based his decisions "largely on social history reports by probation officers" (Sanders, 1976, p. 183).

> The role model for the juvenile court judges was doctor-counselor rather than lawyer. "Judicial therapists" were expected to establish one-to-one relationships with "delinquents" in the same way a country doctor might give his time and attention to a favorite patient. The courtroom was arranged like a clinic and the vocabulary of the participants was largely composed of medical metaphors. (Platt, 1969, p. 142)

Like medical treatment, the court's intervention was assumed to be "good" and for the benefit of the child. An emphasis on "due process" of law—formal charges, legal coun-

*The juvenile court's jurisdiction over children was sweeping and comprehensive. The 1899 Illinois law "made it possible for a youth to be held in detention or sent to a state training school if he was destitute; or if he was homeless, abandoned, or dependent; or if he had improper parental care; or if he was begging or receiving alms; or if he was living in a house of ill-fame or with any vicious or disreputable person; or if he was in an unfit place" (Lerman, 1977, p. 286).

sel, adversary proceedings, etc.—was seen as unnecessary and actually detrimental to the child's welfare. Critics have pointed out, however, that although the juvenile court was viewed as a therapeutic institution, children were sometimes denied their civil rights and treated arbitrarily in the name of "clinical treatment" and "moral development" (Kittrie, 1971; Platt, 1974, p. 372).

The limitations of the court's capacity to cause therapeutic change soon became apparent. Well-meaning judges, probation officers, and reformatory personnel found that many children's problems were beyond their abilities.

> Many cases proved to be beyond the skills and resources of probation officers; a substantial volume of juvenile recidivism persisted despite all efforts at treatment and control. The psychological sciences were drawn upon to provide resources to deal with violators. (Finestone, 1976b, p. 8)*

From the juvenile court, with its jurisdiction over dependent children, its emphasis on early diagnosis and treatment, its ideal of therapeutic intervention for the individual child, and its rhetoric of medical analogies, it was only a small step to actual medical intervention. The "psychological sciences" and medical-psychiatric expertise were brought to the juvenile court system by William Healy and the supporters of the guild guidance movement.

## William Healy, court clinics, and the child guidance movement

Soon after juvenile courts began, it became evident to some people involved in delinquency work that many children had severe problems and that more professional expertise was necessary. Social welfare pioneer Jane Addams "recalled that at last it was apparent that many of these children were psychopathic cases and they and other borderline cases needed more skilled care than the most devoted probation officer would give them" (Hawes, 1971, p. 171). Ten years after the original legislation, clinical expertise was brought to the juvenile court.

In the early 1900s Dr. William Healy, a rather remarkable Chicago psychiatrist, began what would be a life-long study of the causes and treatment of juvenile delinquency. In 1909, with the financial support of philanthropist Mrs. W. F. Dummer, the Juvenile Psychopathic Institute of Chicago was founded. The Institute was established with a twofold purpose: first and foremost, to engage in the scientific study of delinquency and delinquency prevention, especially its psychological and psychiatric aspects; and second, to serve as a clinical resource for the Chicago Juvenile Court. Healy, on the recommendation of reknowned psychologist William James, was named its first director (Finestone, 1976b). The institute under Healy's direction would endeavor to carry out the child-saving goal of understanding delinquency.

Healy was both a researcher and a clinician. His first major piece of research, *The Individual Delinquent,* was published in 1915. Healy analyzed 1000 case histories of repeated juvenile offenders in an attempt to understand juvenile delinquent behavior. He included physiological, developmental, social, and psychological case histories of individual delinquents (Rafferty, 1977). He tested popular theories, such as Lombroso's physiological stigmata theory (see Chapter 8) and found them wanting. He held that existing causal theories of delinquency were inadequate and that delinquency could be understood only by analyzing individual cases. He wanted to develop a better theory, but he eschewed simplification. "Such statements as 'crime is a disease,'" Healy (1917) wrote, "appear dubiously cheap in light of our experience" (quoted in Finestone, 1976b, p. 55). Although Healy did not appreciate fully the sociological and social psychological aspects of delinquency, beyond seeing the family as influential, his work was provocative and led to a cross-fertilization between the behavioral and social sciences. Many of Healy's initiatives were later pursued by Clifford W. Shaw from a sociological perspective (Finestone, 1976b, p. 19), and Shaw, in turn,

---

*Quotations from Finestone (1976b) on pp. 152 to 153 taken from *Victims of change: juvenile delinquents in American society* by Harold Finestone and used with the permission of the publisher, Greenwood Press, Inc., Westport, Conn.

appears to have persuaded Healy to consider sociological demographic analysis.

Healy also influenced delinquency treatment as a clinician. He was a leader in developing clinical psychiatric procedures for diagnosing and treating emotionally disturbed children (Finestone, 1976b, p. 75). Healy's perspective as a clinician influenced his scientific work. He insisted on the intensive study of the individual as a necessary prerequisite to understanding delinquent behavior and strove to make his scientific work have clinical applications. "Altogether our task has not been so much [to] gather material for generalizations," Healy (1917) wrote, "as ascertainment of the methods and facts which will help towards the making of practical diagnoses and prognoses" (p. 4) (quoted in Finestone, 1976b: 55).

Healy was influenced by psychoanalysis, especially the work of the Austrian August Aichorn, and in the 1930s introduced a psychoanalytic perspective to the study and treatment of delinquency. Psychoanalytic concepts had a significant impact on the delinquency field. In this framework, delinquents were seen as "acting out" underlying psychic conflicts and "antisocial impulses." Healy's research increasingly centered on family life as the origin of the psychic conflicts that were the basis of delinquent behavior. In a study comparing delinquents and nondelinquents, conducted with his colleague and wife, Augusta Bronner, Healy (1936) concluded that the delinquent child "had never had affectional identification with the one who seemed to him a good parent" (p. 10) and found "the origins of delinquency in every case unquestionably to represent the expression of [internal and external] desires and urges which were otherwise unsatisfied" (p. 2). The psychoanalytic viewpoint, focusing on intrapsychic conflicts, aligned well with the ideology of child welfare and had a swift and profound influence on the diagnosis and treatment of juvenile delinquency.

The Juvenile Psychopathic Institute became an exemplar for juvenile court clinics that sprouted up in a number of major cities. Healy himself moved to Boston in 1919 to head the Judge Baker Foundation (Clinic). Although the clinics had originally been created as adjuncts to the court, they soon broadened their mission. The clinics expanded their domain in an attempt to reach potential delinquents earlier and also to serve middle-class children. They became known as "child guidance clinics." The clinics were interdisciplinary, with psychiatrists, psychologists, and social workers working together as a treatment "team."

Professional psychiatric groups promoted the clinics as the first line of defense against delinquency. The National Committee for Mental Hygiene (see Chapter 3) established a new Division on the Prevention of Delinquency in 1922. Dr. Karl Menninger and a number of other prominent psychiatrists founded the multiprofessional American Orthopsychiatric Association in 1924 to study and promote "the neuropsychiatric or medical view of crime" (Ridenour, 1961, p. 39). It became a major vehicle for developing ideas of preventive psychiatry, and prevention of delinquency was a principal theme (Finch & Green, 1977, p. 161). Appropriately, William Healy served as the organization's first president. In the late 1920s the development of children's clinics became the focus of a social movement, sometimes called "the child guidance movement." Between 1927 and 1932, with the support of millions of dollars from philanthropic sources such as the Commonwealth Fund, 27 cities set up child guidance clinics and hundreds more established some type of part-time service (Ridenour, 1961, p. 38). The child guidance clinics institutionalized the psychiatric approach to delinquency.

Healy always remained true to his belief in the complexity of juvenile delinquency. By the mid-1930s, while still seeing child guidance as a valid and essential approach, Healy became aware of its inherent limitations for the prevention of delinquency.

> Aside from the individuals who became delinquent mainly because of inner conflicts and frustrations, it is plainly discernable that in the complex of factors which make for delinquency there are many social elements, deprivations and pressures that cannot possibly be bettered by clinic effort alone. (Healy, 1934, p. 14, quoted in Finestone, 1976b, p. 123)

Healy brought both scientific study and clinical practice to the treatment of delinquency. Although a physician and psychiatrist by training, Healy was more psychological than medical in his approach. His legacy and that of his followers was the dominance of the clinical approach to delinquency prevention and treatment.* Although sociological studies of urban life (Shaw & McKay, 1942), gangs and gang subcultures (Thrasher, 1927/1936; Cohen, A., 1955), and opportunity structures (Cloward & Ohlin, 1960) subsequently challenged and modified the purely clinical-individual approaches Healy espoused, the child guidance clinics served as front-line troops in delinquency prevention for many decades.

## Medical-clinical model of delinquency today

Despite the spread of child guidance clinics, juvenile delinquency showed no signs of abating. The medical-clinical approach to delinquency was strongly challenged by sociological research in the 1950s and 1960s. Sociological studies clearly demonstrated the prominence of sociocultural and socioeconomic aspects of delinquency (see Gibbons, 1976, pp. 89-141), giving rise to a variety of experiments in social intervention and delinquency prevention, including diversion from the juvenile court. But the severest challenge to the "therapeutic" powers of the court was mounted by the legal profession. The lawyers charged that juveniles were denied "due process" and constitutional and legal protections and that the juvenile court had great potential for unfairness and arbitrariness. Through a series of Supreme Court decisions, some of the original, informal procedures of the juvenile court's therapeutic superparent approach were deemed unconstitutional. These decisions by a Supreme Court concerned with offenders' rights—*Kent* v. *United States,* 1966; *in re Gault,* 1967; and *in re Winship,* 1970—extended adult safeguards to the juvenile court, giving delinquents legal rights and protections and providing some degree of due process.* These decisions limited the juvenile court's power to intercede on behalf of delinquent children and eroded the "therapeutic ideal" of court intervention.†

Although the medical model of the juvenile court appears to be waning, other innovations appear to have expanded therapeutic-medical intervention with deviant children. In early 1967 Congress passed the Early and Periodic Screening, Diagnosis and Treatment Program (EPSDT) as part of the Medicaid package. The bill, although not aimed at delinquent children, mandates screening for physical, mental, psychological, and behavioral deviations of eligible children. It calls for

> such early and periodic screening and diagnosis of individuals who are eligible under the plan or are under the age of 21 to ascertain their physical or mental defects, and such health care, treatment, and other measures to correct or ameliorate defects and chronic conditions discovered thereby as may be mandated by the Secretary (Title XIX, Section 105 [a] [4] [B]).

This modern-day medical child-saving venture, passed surely with the good intentions of extending medical and psychiatric treatment to lower class children, may well increase the medicalization of children's deviance. As psychiatrist Lee Coleman (1978, p. 67) notes, the "EPSDT and similar schemes [of screening and intervention] *require* diagnosis of medical or quasi-medical disorders" for services to be

*There was some tension as well as cooperation between the juvenile courts and the child guidance clinics. The courts, although therapeutic and preventive in orientation, were also legalistic and justice oriented and did not accept completely the psychiatric approach to delinquency.

**Kent* v. *United States,* 1966, said that juveniles were entitled to a hearing, legal representation, and other rights in the instance of waiver to a criminal court. The landmark *in re Gault,* 1967, decision ruled that juveniles must be given such legal protections as the right to counsel, notice of charge, confrontation, and the right to cross-examine. The *in re Winship,* 1970, decision stated the juvenile court was obliged to apply the same standard of evidence as in the adult criminal court.

†The New York state legislature recently passed a bill that would allow some juveniles to be tried for murder and other crimes in adult courts. Although this bill still must be constitutionally tested, it exemplifies a legislative "backlash" against a perceived "soft" and coddling treatment of juveniles.

rendered. Coleman suggests that such programs reinforce the medical model of deviance and encourage the creation of medical diagnoses of behavior problems so that the child may be "covered" under the program.

EPSDT, unlike the juvenile court or the child guidance movement, was not a product of the lobbying of child-saving groups or the claims-making of professional psychiatrists. It was, rather, promoted by the federal bureaucracy and the educational establishment (Schrag & Divoky, 1975). With massive screening programs like EPSDT, it is possible to establish early diagnosis and intervention with deviant children to an extent beyond the dreams of the 19th-century child-savers. We do not suggest any sinister intentions in the passage of EPSDT legislation—on the contrary, its passage at the peak of 1960s liberalism suggests the opposite—but rather point out that this program greatly expanded the potential of medical control of children's deviance. While it has not yet, to our knowledge, been used widely to identify delinquent children, it demonstrates the federal government's faith in medical interventions and controls. But the potential for the medicalization of delinquent behavior remains, as exemplified by the Hutschnecker plan described later in this chapter.

In sum, today's juvenile court relies less on the therapeutic-medical analogy, but certain forms of children's deviant behavior have become defined as medical problems and shifted into medical jurisdiction. A classic example is hyperkinesis.

## DISCOVERY OF HYPERKINESIS*

We now turn to a theoretical review and analysis of the development of hyperkinesis as a medical diagnosis. We describe the diagnosis, review the pertinent literature relevant to its development, and present a sociological analysis of its discovery.

*This section slightly amended and extended from Conrad, Peter, *Identifying hyperactive children: the medicalization of deviant behavior:* (Lexington, Mass.: Lexington Books, D. C. Heath and Company, Copyright 1976, D. C. Heath and Company), and from Conrad, P. *Social Prob.*, 1975, **23**,12-21 (Oct.).

### Medical diagnosis of hyperkinesis

*Hyperkinesis*, a behavior disorder, is prevalent in an estimated 3% to 10% of the elementary school population.* It is a particularly good example for investigating the process of the medicalization of children's deviance, since it is a relatively recent phenomenon as a medical diagnostic category. Only in the past two decades has it been available as a recognized diagnostic category, and perhaps only in about the most recent decade did it begin to receive widespread notice and medical popularity. However, as shown below, the roots of the diagnosis and treatment of this disorder are found earlier.

Hyperkinesis is also known as minimal brain dysfunction (MBD), hyperactive syndrome, hyperkinetic disorder of childhood, and several other diagnostic designations. Although occasionally the symptoms emphasized vary a little from category to category, and the presumed etiology frequently varies by diagnosis, the behaviors that are considered symptomatic of each are, in general, similar and overlap considerably.† Typical symptom patterns for diagnosing the disorder include extreme excess of motor activity (hyperactivity), short attention span (the child flits from activity to activity), restlessness, fidgetiness, often wildly oscillating mood swings (the child is fine one day, a

*Until recently there has been no methodologically sound community-wide epidemiological research on hyperkinesis. Most of the estimates vary between 3% and 5% of the elementary school populations, but there have been estimates as high as 20% (Huessy, 1973). It is likely that between 250,000 and 500,000 children have been identified as hyperkinetic. A recent careful community study in California (Lambert et al., 1978) suggests that epidemiology varies by social system and who is diagnosing the disorder. A strict medical diagnosis yields less than 2% of schoolchildren as hyperactive, whereas a school system count is over 12%.

†The U.S. Public Health Service report (Clements, 1966) included 38 terms that were used to describe or distinguish the conditions that it labeled MBD. Although the literature attempts to differentiate MBD, hyperkinesis, hyperactive syndrome, and several other diagnostic labels, it is our belief that in practice they are almost interchangeable—especially in terms of treatment.

terror the next), clumsiness, aggressive-like behavior, impulsivity, the inability to sit still in school and comply with rules, a low frustration level, sleeping problems, and delayed acquisition of speech (Stewart, 1970; Stewart et al., 1966; Wender, 1971).

Most of these indications or symptoms for the disorder probably would be considered deviant behaviors, although it is usually defined as a physiological disorder found in children (with a prevalence six times as great among boys). Since we are more concerned with the sociological process than with the specific diagnostic criteria, we use the term "hyperkinesis" as representative of all the daignostic categories of this disorder. This term is more descriptive and less assumptive of etiology than "minimal brain dysfunction" and more medically appropriate than the popular description "hyperactivity." In the remainder of this chapter hyperkinesis and hyperactivity are used interchangeably.

## Discovery of hyperkinesis

In developing an analysis of the discovery of hyperkinesis it is useful to distinguish what might be called *clinical factors* (events directly related to the diagnosis and treatment of hyperkinesis) from *social factors* (factors that are not directly related to hyperkinesis but are relevant). Clinical and social factors do, of course, overlap, but such an analytic distinction will be useful in our discussion.

**Clinical factors.** In 1937 Charles Bradley (1937) observed that recently discovered amphetamine drugs had a spectacular effect in altering the behavior in a number of schoolchildren who exhibited behavior disorders or learning problems. Fifteen of the 30 children he treated actually became more subdued in their behavior. Bradley termed the effect of this medication "paradoxical," since he expected that amphetamines would stimulate the children as they stimulated adults. After the medication was discontinued, the children's behavior returned to premedication level.

Although there was a scattering of reports in the medical literature in the next two decades on the utility of stimulant medications with "childhood behavior disorders" (mostly by Bradley and his associates), the next significant contribution was the work of A. A. Strauss and his associates (Strauss, A. A. & Lehtinen, 1947). Building on prior research, they reported that they found certain behavior (including hyperkinetic behaviors) in postencephalitic children suffering from what they called minimal brain injury. This was the first time that these behaviors (similar to those found in children reported by Bradley and others) were found to be caused by this new organic distinction of minimal brain injury (or damage).

This disorder still remained unnamed or at least went by a variety of names (usually simply "childhood behavior disorder") and did not exist as a specific diagnostic category until Maurice W. Laufer and his associates described it as the "hyperkinetic impulse disorder" in 1957. On finding that "the salient characteristics of the behavior pattern . . . are strikingly similar to those with clear-cut organic causation," they went on to describe a disorder *with no clear-cut history or evidence for organicity*. They also presented a case for the possible organic etiology of the disorder (Laufer et al., 1957).

In an attempt to clarify the ambiguity and confusion in terminology and symptomatology in diagnosing children's behavior and learning disorders, a task force sponsored by the U.S. Public Health Service and the National Association for Crippled Children and Adults presented a report in 1966. From over three dozen diagnoses, they agreed on the term "minimal brain dysfunction" (MBD) as an overriding diagnosis that would include hyperkinesis and other disorders (Clements, 1966).* Since this time, MBD has been the primary formal diagnosis or label, although many others still remain in use.

In the middle 1950s a new drug, methylphenidate (Ritalin), was synthesized. This drug

---

*The report stated, "The term minimal brain dysfunction will be reserved for the child whose symptomatology appears in one or more specific areas of brain function, but in mild, borderline or subclinical form, without reducing overall intellectual functioning to the subnormal ranges" (Clements, 1966, p. 9).

is a stimulant that has many qualities of amphetamines without some of the more undesirable side effects. In 1961 it was approved by the FDA for use with children. Since that time a large body of research has been published on the use of Ritalin in the treatment of childhood behavior disorders. This medication became increasingly considered the "treatment of choice" (along with the older amphetamine, dextroamphetamine $50_4$ [Dexedrine] and the more recent addition, pemoline [Cyclert]) for children with hyperkinesis.

There has been a virtual flood of papers and research published since the early 1960s. The vast majority is medical research concerned with etiology, diagnosis, and treatment of hyperkinesis (see Cole, Sherwood, 1975; Delong, A. R., 1972; Grinspoon & Singer, 1973). By far the largest number of these publications (perhaps as many as three fourths of them) are concerned with drug treatment of the disorder. There has been increasing publicity of the disorder in the mass media as well. A perusal of the citations in the *Reader's Guide to Periodical Literature* showed no articles on hyperkinesis before 1967, one each in 1968 and 1969, and a total of 40 for 1970 through 1974 (a mean of eight per year) (Table 4).

Hyperkinesis has become the most common child psychiatric problem (Gross & Wilson, 1974, p. 142); special clinics have been established to treat hyperkinetic children, and substantial amounts of federal research monies have been invested in etiological and treatment research. Furthermore, outside the medical profession, teachers have developed a working clinical knowledge of hyperkinesis' symptoms and treatment (Robin & Bosco, 1973), and as articles appear regularly in mass circulation magazines and newspapers, parents often come to clinics with knowledge of this diagnosis. Hyperkinesis is no longer the relatively esoteric diagnostic category it may have been 20 years ago; it is now a well-known clinical disorder.

**Social factors.** The social factors affecting the discovery of hyperkinesis can be divided into three areas: (1) the pharmaceutical revolution, (2) trends in medical practice, and (3) government action.

**TABLE 4**
ARTICLES ON HYPERACTIVITY IN THE POPULAR AND EDUCATIONAL MEDIA, 1966-1974*

| Year | Number of articles in popular media | Number of articles in educational media |
|---|---|---|
| 1974 | 12 | 16 |
| 1973 | 7 | 20 |
| 1972 | 4 | 10 |
| 1971 | 11 | 23 |
| 1970 | 6 | 7 |
| 1969 | 1† | 5 |
| 1968 | 1 | 1‡ |
| 1967 | 0 | 0 |
| 1966 | 0 | 0 |

*Reprinted by permission of the publisher, from Peter Conrad, *Identifying hyperactive children: the medicalization of deviant behavior* (Lexington, Mass.: Lexington Books, D. C. Heath & Co., Copyright 1976. D. C. Heath & Co.). Information from *Reader's Guide to Periodical Literature,* 1965-1975, and *Educational Index,* 1965-1975.
†Prior to 1970, articles on hyperactivity were listed in the *Reader's Guide to Periodical Literature* under "problem children."
‡Prior to 1969, articles were listed in the *Educational Index* under "activity level."

The pharmaceutical revolution. Since the 1930s the pharmaceutical industry has been synthesizing and manufacturing a large number of psychoactive drugs; this has been part of a virtual revolution in drug making and drug taking in America (Silverman & Lee, 1974).

Psychoactive drugs are agents that affect the central nervous system. Benzedrine (amphetamine $SO_4$), Ritalin, and Dexedrine are all synthesized psychoactive stimulants that were indicated for narcolepsy, appetite control (as "diet pills"), mild depression, fatigue, and, more recently, MBD. These drugs, which have all been used with hyperkinetic children, are only three of the hundreds of psychoactive drugs that have been synthesized since the 1930s.

Until the 1960s there was little or no promotion and advertisement of any of these medications for use with childhood disorders.* It was at this time that two major pharmaceutical firms (Smith, Kline & French, manufacturer of Dexedrine, and CIBA, manufacturer of Ritalin) began to advertise increasingly in medical journals, through direct mailing, and the "detail men" who call on physicians. Most of this advertising and promotion of the pharmaceutical treatment of hyperkinesis was limited to the medical sphere, but some of the promotion was targeted for the educational sector also (Hentoff, 1972). This promotion was probably significant in disseminating information concerning the diagnosis and treatment of this newly discovered disorder.†

Trends in medical practice. Two recent trends in medical practice have affected the increase in the diagnosis and treatment of hyperkinesis. Probably the most significant is what has been called "the great pharmaceutical revolution" in mental health: the use of psychoactive medications (especially phenothiazines) for the treatment of persons who are mentally ill. Since 1955 the increasing use of these medications has made psychopharmacology an integral part of treatment for mental disorders. It has also undoubtedly increased the confidence of the medical profession in the pharmaceutical approach to mental and behavioral problems.

In the past decade there also has been burgeoning interest in child mental health and psychiatry. It has been argued that children's mental health was generally ignored or at least given a second-class position until recent years (e.g., see Task Force of Children Out of School, 1972). It is likely that this increased interest in child psychiatric problems is related to the discovery of hyperkinesis in children; if one does not look for a disorder or has no way of conceptualizing it, it is likely that it will remain unidentified or undiagnosed or even considered outside the purview of medical attention.

Government action. Since the publication of the U.S. Public Health Service report on MBD there have been at least two significant governmental reports concerned with the issue of treating schoolchildren with stimulant medications for behavior disorders. Both of these inquiries came either directly or indirectly as a response to the national publicity created by the *Washington Post* report in 1970 that 5% to 10% of the 62,000 grammar schoolchildren in Omaha, Nebraska, were being treated with "behavior modification drugs to improve deportment and increase learning potential" (quoted in Grinspoon & Singer, 1973). Although the figures were later found to be a little exaggerated, they nevertheless spurred a congressional investigation (U.S. House Committee on Government Operations, 1970) and a conference sponsored by the Office of Child Development (1971) on the use of stimulant drugs in the treatment of behaviorally disturbed schoolchildren.

The Congressional Subcommittee on Privacy chaired by Congressman Cornelius E. Gallagher held hearings on the issue of prescribing drugs for hyperactive schoolchildren. In general, the committee showed great concern with the facility in which the medication was prescribed; more specifically, that some children at least were receiving drugs from general practitioners whose primary diagnosis consisted of teachers' and parents' reports that the child was doing poorly in school. There was also a concern with the absence of follow-up studies on the long-term effects of treatment.

The Department of Health, Education and Welfare committee was a rather hastily convened group of professionals (the majority being physicians), many of whom already had commitments to drug treatment for children's behavior problems. They recommended that only physicians make the diagnosis and prescribe treatment, that the pharmaceutical companies promote the treatment of the disorder only through medical channels, that parents not

---

*Part of this may have to do with the AMA's change in policy in accepting more pharmaceutical advertising in the late 1950s. Probably more specifically involved was the FDA approval of the use of Ritalin for children in 1961. It is interesting to note that until 1970 Ritalin was advertised for treatment of "functional behavior problems in children." Since then, because of an FDA order, it has only been promoted for treatment of MBD.

†The drug industry spends fully 25% of its budget on promotion and advertising; so it is likely to be effective. See James Coleman et al. (1966) for the role of the detail men and how physicians rely on them for information.

be coerced to accept any particular treatment, and that long-term follow-up research be done. This report served as blue-ribbon approval for treating hyperkinesis with psychoactive medications.

## A sociological analysis

Three issues are discussed in this section: how children's deviant behavior became conceptualized as a medical problem, why this occurred when it did, and what the present status is of hyperkinesis as a medical problem.

A primary question that this analysis addresses is how deviant behavior became conceptualized as a medical problem. It is assumed that before the discovery of hyperkinesis this type of behavior was defined as disruptive, disobedient, rebellious, antisocial, or deviant (perhaps even the label "emotionally disturbed" was sometimes used when it was in vogue in the 1960s) and was usually handled in the context of the family or the school or, in extreme cases, the child guidance clinic. How, then, did this constellation of deviant behaviors become a medical disorder?

What stands out to a sociologist is that the treatment was available long before the disorder that was being treated was clearly conceptualized. It was 20 years after Bradley's discovery of the "paradoxical effect" of stimulants on certain deviant children that Maurice W. Laufer named the disorder and described its characteristic symptoms (behaviors). In terms of the sociological study of deviance this is most interesting. The social control mechanism (in this case, pharmacological treatment) preceded the label (hyperkinesis) by 20 years. This presents an interesting problem for a sociological perspective: Do medical labels appear when medical social control mechanisms are available? In this case, an extremely cynical reading of the history of the development of medical control might be that the label was invented to facilitate the use of a particular social control mechanism, in this case psychoactive drugs.* In our society, only the medical profession has the mandate to use drugs to modify human behavior in others (although to a certain extent, within the limits of legality and availability, we can do it ourselves), so that to justify the treatment, there had to be a medical label. In other words, for medical social control mechanisms to operate, deviance must be conceptualized in medical terms.

A second question that we can address is why this type of deviance became defined as a medical problem when it did. Why did the label "hyperkinesis" (and its treatment with psychoactive medications) become so popular in the 1960s and 1970s? In the first place, only in the late 1950s were both the diagnostic label and the pharmaceutical treatment available. Second, the pharmaceutical revolution in mental health and the increased interest in child psychiatry provided a favorable background for the dissemination of knowledge about this new disorder. The latter, in fact, probably made the medical profession more likely to consider behavior problems in children within their clinical jurisdiction.

There were, however, agents outside the medical profession that were significant in "promoting" hyperkinesis as a disorder that was within the medical framework. These agents might be conceptualized in Howard Becker's terms as "moral entrepreneurs," those who crusade for creation and enforcement of the rules whose violation constitutes deviance (Becker, 1963).* In this case the moral entrepreneurs were the pharmaceutical companies and the Association for Children with Learning Disabilities.

The pharmaceutical companies spent a great amount of time and money promoting stimulant medications for this new disorder. After the middle 1960s it is nearly impossible to read a medical journal or the free "throw-away" magazines without seeing some elaborate ad-

*We do not necessarily endorse such an extreme view, but it is a possible interpretation of the evidence.

*Eliot Freidson (1970a) also notes the medical professional role as moral entrepreneur in this process: "The profession does treat the illnesses laymen take to it, but it also seeks to discover illness of which the laymen may not even be aware. One of the greatest ambitions of the physician is to discover and describe a 'new' disease or syndrome . . ." (p. 252).

vertising for either Ritalin or Dexedrine. These advertisements explain the utility of treating hyperkinesis (or any of the other labels that are used such as MBD) and urge the physician to diagnose and treat hyperkinetic children. The advertisements may run from one to six pages. They often advise physicians that "the hyperkinetic syndrome" exists as "a distinct medical entity" and that the "syndrome is readily diagnosed through patient histories and psychometric testing" and "has been classified by an expert panel" of the Department of Health, Education and Welfare as MBD. These same pharmaceutical firms also supply sophisticated packets of "diagnostic and treatment" information on hyperkinesis to physicians, pay for professional conferences on the subject, and support research in the identification and treatment of the disorder. Clearly these corporations have a vested interest in the labeling and treatment of hyperkinesis; it was reported that CIBA realized $13 million profit from Ritalin alone in 1971, which was 15% of its total gross profits (Charles, 1971; Hentoff, 1972).

The other moral entrepreneur, less powerful than the pharmaceutical companies but nevertheless influential, was the Association for Children with Learning Disabilities. Although its focus is not specifically on hyperkinetic children, it does include it in its conception of learning disabilities, along with aphasia, reading problems such as dyslexia, and perceptual motor problems. Founded in the early 1960s by parents and professionals, it has functioned much like the National Association for Mental Health does for mental illness: promoting conferences, sponsoring legislation, and providing social support. One of its main functions has been to disseminate information concerning this relatively new area in education—learning disabilities; although the organization does have a more educational than medical perspective, most of its literature indicates that at least with hyperkinesis it has adopted the medical model and the medical approach to the problem. It has sensitized teachers and schools to the conception of hyperkinesis as a medical problem.

The medical model of hyperactive behavior (and associated treatment with medications) has become well accepted in our society. Physicians, parents, teachers, and children have, for a variety of reasons, come to accept this conception of deviant behavior. Physicians find treatment to be relatively simple (medication) and the results sometimes spectacular. Hyperkinesis minimizes parents' guilt by emphasizing "it's not their fault, it's an organic problem" and allows for nonpunitive management or control of deviance. Medication often makes a child less disruptive in the classroom and sometimes facilitates learning. There are, however, some other, perhaps more subtle, consequences of such medicalization of deviant behavior, which we discuss in Chapter 9.

In recent years a few studies on the sociological aspects of hyperactivity have been reported. Most of this work takes a skeptical view of hyperactivity. Some have argued that hyperactivity as a medical disorder is a myth (Schmitt, 1975) and is merely a form of medical child control (Schrag & Divoky, 1975). Other research has pointed out that physicians' diagnosis of hyperactivity is based primarily on observed *behavior* and reports from teachers and school (Conrad, 1976, pp. 51-70; Kenny et al., 1971; Sandoval et al., 1976), and some children are defined as hyperactive in one social system and not in another (Conrad, 1976, pp. 77-85; Lambert et al., 1978). But these "critiques" of the medical model of hyperactive behavior remain largely outside the mainstream of medical practice.

In another sense the definition of hyperactivity may be expanding. It has been suggested that girls who suffer from the disorder are hypoactive rather than hyperactive (Huessy, 1967). Their symptoms are daydreaming and "spacing out" in school. Some researchers have postulated that hyperactive children may develop into juvenile delinquents (Berman & Siegal, 1976); that hyperactivity may be the precursor to adult sociopathy, alcoholism, and hysteria (Cantwell, 1975). A few have claimed to discover adults with the hyperactive syndrome (Mann, H. & Greenspan, 1976). The diagnosis of hyperactivity appears to be slowly expanding beyond school-aged children to adolescents and adults.

In sum, the discovery of hyperkinesis brings up most clearly the question of whether the development of new medical mechanisms of social control (stimulant drugs) leads to the emergence of new categories or designations of deviance and the expansion of medical jurisdiction. From the example of hyperkinesis, and to a lesser extent methadone, as discussed in Chapter 5, the answer appears to be a tentative "yes."

## CHILD ABUSE AS A MEDICAL PROBLEM

The physical maltreatment of children has become a recognized problem only in the last century. "Child abuse" has become a medical problem only in the past two decades. This is not to say that children did not suffer willful harm resulting in injury or death prior to the last century; they certainly did. The history of child maltreatment, neglect, and physical injury is a long one, but it is only in the past two decades that child abuse became clearly defined as a social and medical problem. This section traces that development.

### Historical notes on the maltreatment of children

As noted earlier in this chapter, children were not regarded highly or treated as "little darlings" until the most recent centuries. The degree of neglect and maltreatment varies from society to society, but for nearly every society some evidence exists for what we would today call child abuse. The physical abuse of children can be divided into two general types: infanticide and abandonment, and discipline and punishment.

Infanticide, the killing of a newborn or infant with the consent of the parents, was regularly practiced in many societies. Until the most recent centuries, it was a common and effective means of population control. This, along with the inability of individual families to support the child, illegitimate births, and, in some cultures, ritualistic sacrifice (Radbill, 1968, pp. 6-7) are usually cited as causes of infanticide. For virtually all recorded history, except among Judeo-Christian societies, infanticide has been an acceptable procedure for disposing of not only deformed or sickly infants but any newborns who might strain the resources of the family or the community (Langner, 1974). Recent historical studies of "sex ratios" (comparing the number of adult males to females) suggest that infanticide, especially of females, was not uncommon in Europe as late as the 16th century, despite its Judeo-Christian definition as murder (Harris, 1977). Death was commonly attributed to "overlaying"—accidental suffocation caused by a mother's rolling over on her infant in bed. Married women so accused merely had to appear as a penitent in church; unwed mothers were often labeled witches and put to death (Harris, 1977).

A much more widespread form of child maltreatment in Western society was abandonment. Foundling hospitals, institutions for abandoned children, first were organized in the 18th century. Apparently they were busy places. "In France, admissions rose from 40,000 a year in 1784 to 138,000 in 1822. By 1830 there were 270 revolving boxes [in which one could place infants] in use throughout France, with 336,247 infants legally abandoned from 1824 to 1833" (Harris, 1977, p. 120). Most of these infants died in the first year of life. The first foundling hospital in the United States was established as the New York Foundling Asylum in 1869 in an attempt to curb the high rate of infant abandonment and subsequent death. In 1873, 1392 foundlings were left there (Radbill, 1968, p. 10). As late as 1892, 200 foundlings and 100 dead infants were found on the streets of New York City (Fontana, 1966, p. 236). This was probably only a small portion of the abandoned and abused children, those who for some reason came to the attention of social and medical authorities.

The other major historic form of child maltreatment could be defined broadly as "child discipline." Child-rearing methods in Western society were often austere and severe; harsh punishments inflicted by parents and other adult authorities were commonplace, in fact, normative. Parents had total sovereignty over their children. In colonial times physical punishments in the name of discipline rarely could be viewed as too harsh. The whipping and birching of children was the prerogative of parents, teachers, and the courts. Indeed, corporal punishment was the regular disciplinary fare. The dictum "spare the rod and spoil the child" captured the child-rearing spirit. And there was little a child could do about it. There was general agreement that this was simply the way it was. "It was always taken for granted that parents and guardians had every right to treat their children as they saw fit" (Radbill, 1968, p. 4). No doubt, serious injuries frequently occurred, but no one called them "child abuse," nor were they, short of murder, restricted by society.

Through the 19th century, then, infanticide and abandonment were prevalent, and severe punishment was the norm of childhood discipline. Yet these were generally taken for granted as part of the lot of the child's life. Even when "child protection" emerged as a cause, the concern was largely children who were neglected, not physically abused.

## Child protection

Among the first forms of "child protection" were the houses of refuge discussed earlier in this chapter. They frequently took charge of neglected or even abandoned juveniles. But these institutions dealt mostly with older children. Younger children were shipped to orphanages or left to their own devices. Not until the foundling homes did infants and very young children have an institution specifically mandated for their care. Again, these were for neglected or abandoned children. There was literally no societal response to physically maltreated children. The first organization with the explicit purpose of "protecting" and caring for physically mistreated children was the New York Society for the Prevention of Cruelty to Children (SPCC).

The founding of the SPCC is an interesting story, and it highlights the lack of a social definition of physical child abuse as a social problem. In the early 1870s a 9-year-old child named Mary Ellen was being severely mistreated by her foster parents. Concerned church workers brought her to various agencies who refused to intervene, primarily because they viewed the right of parents to chastise their children as absolute, and there was no law under which they could intervene to protect the child. Finally, Mary Ellen was brought to the American Society for the Prevention of Cruelty to *Animals,* who took her case and was able to have Mary Ellen removed from her home. Ironically, the ASPCA was able to intervene because Mary Ellen was a member of the animal kingdom, and thus could be included under the laws which protected animals from human cruelty (Radbill, 1968, p. 13). As an outgrowth of significant journalistic publicity, the Society for the Prevention of Cruelty to Children was established. This was soon followed by legislation that extended some protections to children. The SPCC, however, rarely concerned itself with the maltreatment of children in their "natural" families, concentrating much of its effort on children mistreated by their employers or foster parents (Pfohl, 1977, p. 312). Natural parents were not considered to abuse their children; their sovereignty over child rearing remained nearly absolute.

By the beginning of the 20th century the juvenile court gained jurisdiction over dependent and delinquent children. As mentioned earlier, the juvenile court's concern was the prevention of delinquency; thus its focus was on neglected children who were viewed as potential delinquents rather than on the protection of physically abused children from their parents or guardians. Both the juvenile courts and the SPCC often advocated the removal of neglected children from their homes, a perspective that clashed with the emerging social work and child guidance professions. These new "helping professions" sought, at least ideally, to strengthen the family (for a critical analysis of this, see Lasch, 1977). The 1909 White House Conference on Children supported this emerging viewpoint, declaring that poverty was not a sufficient reason for removing children from their homes and calling for social services and financial aid to bolster the home environment (Pfohl, 1977, p. 313). Parents' physical abuse of children was not yet defined as a particularly "important" kind of deviance.

Stephen Pfohl (1977) points out that most of the measures up to this time were essentially "society-saving" rather than "child-saving." Although the child was the focus of concern, the object was to save society from the long-term burdens and hardships of dependent or delinquent juveniles who would grow up to be dependent or criminal adults, rather than to save the child from abusive parents. Parents were ignored as a source of deviant behavior or as an object of sanction, reform, or treatment. The victim of abuse, not the perpetrator, was considered the problem.

Specific medical intervention in child maltreatment, beyond marginal involvement with the foundling hospitals, was limited. To the extent that physicians treated the casualties of child maltreatment, they were involved, but they were treating specific *physical injuries* in children, not cases of "child abuse." In fact, many physicians did not consider abuse to exist (Pfohl, 1977). It took certain organized interests in medicine to discover child abuse as a medical problem.

## Medical involvement and the discovery of child abuse

Undoubtedly physicians treated countless children's physical injuries sustained at the hands of their parents or guardians. But these injuries were treated only as specific medical pathological conditions (a broken bone, a burn, a skull fracture), and the source of the injury was overlooked, ignored, or simply unknown. This is not to suggest that physicians were derelict in their medical duty; many factors kept physicians (and others) from "seeing" the injuries as results of parental abuse.

Medical practice frequently treats symptoms rather than causes; child trauma was no different. Pfohl (1977, p. 13) suggests four barriers that kept physicians from recognizing the injuries as child abuse. First, many doctors were simply unaware that "abuse" could be a diagnosis; no clear diagnostic label was available. Second, physicians may have been psychologically unwilling to believe parents would inflict such injuries on children. Third, physicians were concerned that reporting such maltreatment would violate the norm of medical confidentiality and create the possibility of legal liability from the violation. Finally, many doctors were reluctant to become involved in a time-consuming criminal justice process that would also take the consequences of their diagnosis out of their hands. There is, of course, no reason to assume that physicians should be any different from the society at large in granting parents' nearly complete prerogative in raising and disciplining their children.

The first medical recognition of what is now called child abuse appeared in an 1888 paper on acute periosteal swelling in infants by a Dr. S. West (Solomon, 1963, p. 774). It was not, however, until 75 years later that child abuse became a bona fide medical entity.

Articles leading to the medical discovery of "child abuse," nearly all based on x-ray studies by pediatric radiologists, appeared in medical journals over a number of years. John Caffey (1946) reported a frequent association of subdural hematoma (a hemorrhage between the brain membranes usually caused by trauma) and abnormal changes in the long bones revealed in x-ray pictures. Other researchers clearly defined the traumatic nature of the injuries and even suggested they resulted from "parental conduct" (Silverman. 1953). Woolley and Evans (1955) were the first to suggest specifically that these traumas might be willfully inflicted, the product of "indifference, immaturity and irresponsibility of parents." What had been considered as "unspecific trauma" was redefined as "misconduct and deliberate injury" (Caffey, 1957). Reports filtered into the media, and an increase in public concern for abused children began to develop (Radbill. 1968, p. 16).

Probably the key work in defining and legitimizing child abuse as a medical problem was Kempe and associates' 1962 paper published in the *Journal of the American Medical Association* (Kempe et al., 1962). The appearance of the article "The Battered Child Syndrome" in the most prestigious and widely read medical journal, complete with an editorial underlining the medical seriousness of the problem, gave visibility and legitimacy to battered children as a significant medical problem. Kempe and his associates described the clinical manifestations, psychiatric aspects, techniques of evaluation, radiologic features, and management of physically abused children and their families. They described a "syndrome" with characteristics that included the victims being usually under 3 years of age and neglected, having traumatic injuries especially to the head and long bones, and having parents who often themselves had been battered as children and who denied the abuse of their own child. They exhorted physicians to find and report such cases to proper authorities:

> The principal concern of the physician should be to make a correct diagnosis so that he can institute proper therapy and make certain that a similar event will not occur again. He should report possible willful trauma to the police department or any special children's protective service that operates in the community. (Kempe et al., 1962, p. 247)*

With the publication of this article in a widely read journal, physicians could now more easily "recognize" child abuse when they encountered maltreated, injured children. The label "battered child syndrome" gave physicians both a measure and a legitimacy for medical intervention.†

The central figures in the discovery of "child abuse" were pediatric radiologists, whose research reports, published in a variety of professional journals for over a decade and a half, demonstrates an increasing willingness to "see" and define child abuse as a distinct medical entity. Why pediatric radiologists? Why not emergency room physicians, who frequently saw injured children, or surgeons or internists who treated their injuries? Sociologist Stephen Pfohl (1977) presents a suggestive analysis. Clearly, hospital physicians, especially those in emergency rooms, encountered abused children more directly than radiologists; should not they have discovered it first? Pfohl points out that the four obstacles listed earlier for physicians kept the direct caretaking physicians from seeing injury as "child abuse." The pediatric radiologists, on the other hand, had a certain distance from the abused children and their families. This reduced or eliminated some of the obstacles that kept the clinicians from discovering "child abuse." All the radiologists involved in the discovery were researchers in children's x rays; they could see the radiological remnants of injury in black-and-white x rays but little of the bloody assault itself. The distance also minimized the radiologists' concern with confidentiality or violating the physician-patient relationship. They had less connection with parents; thus it may have been easier for them to hypothesize parental fault. These factors neutralized many of the obstacles that kept other physicians from attributing child injury to parental abuse.

Pfohl (1977) posits further that the status of pediatric radiology in the medical profession contributed to pediatric radiologists' discovering child abuse. Pediatric radiology is a relatively marginal and low-prestige specialty within organized medicine. It has few of the characteristics of more esteemed specialties such as surgery and internal medicine: it has no face-to-face clinical interaction, is research oriented with virtually no patient relations, and has little of the life-and-death "risk and responsibility" of the high-prestige specialties. Pfohl suggests that the discovery of "child abuse" as a viable medical entity was an opportunity for pediatric radiologists to achieve some prestige in the medical community. "Child abuse" linked the radiologists to the critical medical tasks of patient diagnosis; it enabled pediatric radiologists to publish their research in prestigious medical journals, including the *Journal of the American Medical Association,* where pediatric radiological research reports rarely appeared; and it facilitated the development of medical coalitions with more prestigious segments of medicine such as pediatrics and psychodynamically oriented psychiatry. Most of all, it gave pediatric radiology and its allied specialties the opportunity to discover a bona fide medical diagnosis, "the battered child syndrome." In all, Pfohl points out that it was the distance from the abuse and injury and the opportunity for advancement within the organized medical community that led these medical professionals to discover and define child abuse as a medical problem. Once it was conceptualized and discovered in the professional medical community, it found many champions in wider society. The "battered child" became a national concern.

Following the 1962 report describing the battered child syndrome (Kempe et al., 1962), both professional journals and the popular me-

---

*From *J.A.M.A.*, 1962, **181,** 17-24. Copyright 1962, American Medical Association.

†As Gelles (1975) points out, "The Kempe article made physicians and medical practitioners aware of the problem of child abuse, but none of this was new to other agencies, which had for years been trying to cope with the problem of abused children" (p. 369).

dia carried an increasing number of articles on battered children. Mass circulation magazines popularized the "syndrome" with such provocative titles as "Cry Rises From Beaten Babies," "Parents Who Beat Their Children," and "Terror Struck Children," all heralding the discovery of a new and terrible type of deviant behavior and medical problem (cited in Pfohl, 1977, p. 320).

The professional journals, echoed by the popular media, essentially presented a "psychopathological" model of child abuse. It became widely accepted that "the parent who abuses his or her child suffers from some psychological disease which must be cured in order to prevent further abuse" (Gelles, 1973, p. 611). The abusive parent became a psychomedical problem; it was tacitly assumed "anyone who would abuse his child was sick" (Gelles, 1973, p. 612). The cause of abuse was located in the pathological psyche or in the socialization experience of the parent. Sometimes abusers were considered to have a mental disorder; frequently they were assumed to have distinctive characterological traits typical of a psychopathic personality. Clearly, the psychopathological-medical model of child abuse focused directly on the "sick" individual abuser; however, as with much medicalized deviance, focusing on the "clinical condition" of the parent allowed the sociocultural aspects of child abuse to be ignored.

In sum, "child abuse" was discovered and defined by pediatric radiologists. In a sense they functioned as a professional interest group, promoting child abuse as a medical entity. Probably because of the tragic and critical nature of battered children, they met with little resistance inside or outside the medical profession. Indeed, discovering child abuse may have served as a vehicle for status gain within organized medicine and for professional collaboration with higher status specialties (Pfohl, 1977). Defining child abuse as a bona fide medical entity, the battered child syndrome, legitimized medical intervention with physically abused children. Moreover, by pairing deviance with sickness, the professional autonomy of medicine was assured (Pfohl, 1977). By designating abuse as illness, parents of maltreated children were for the first time clearly implicated; child abusers were suffering from a psychopathological "sickness" that needed treatment. Medical practitioners had discovered the problem, but it was through the legislatures that it was diffused and institutionalized as a sanctionable form of deviant behavior.

## Child abuse as a medical and social problem

As we have suggested in previous discussions, publication of scientific or professional articles, even in prestigious medical journals, does not assure the recognition or acceptance of a particular deviance designation. Child abuse needed its champions and moral entrepreneurs to bring the problem to public attention and to carry the antiabuse banner in legislatures.

It was not a difficult banner to carry. No one is for child abuse. In fact, in the early 1960s a "child abuse–reporting movement" emerged, promoting rapid passage of state laws on child abuse reporting.* The only question was what type of laws would be passed. Would they be oriented toward "treatment" or "punishment" of the abuser? The supporters of the treatment orientation were most active. Social welfare organizations such as the Children's Division of the American Humane Association, the Public Welfare Association, and the Child Welfare League, called for research on abuse and lobbied for "treatment based" (i.e., not punitive) legislation (Pfohl, 1977, pp. 319-320). The Children's Bureau of the Department of Health, Education and Welfare in 1963 proposed model legislation on reporting cases of physically abused children (Silver et al., 1967). Medical interests, of course, supported child abuse legislation, although organizations were divided about whether reporting should be

*Actually, prosecution of child abuse did not require new legislation: murder, assault and battery, even when committed by parents, are punishable crimes in every state. Moreover, existing laws specifically forbade "cruelty to children" (Paulsen, 1966, p. 42). The new laws, however, mandated reporting of abuse and "treatment." The "punishment" laws had been enforced in only the most severe cases; supporters of the new laws hoped to increase reporting and intervention and to help the child and family.

mandatory: the American Medical Association wanted physicians to be allowed discretion in reporting, the American Academy of Pediatrics supported mandatory reporting (Paulsen, 1966, p. 46). Legislative committees concerned with abuse legislation were nearly always chaired by a physician, usually a pediatrician associated with academic medicine (Pfohl, 1977); so undoubtedly medical positions were well represented.

Some nonmedical interests challenged the treatment of abusers as "sick." Several law-enforcement groups argued that the abuse of children was a crime and abusers should be treated as criminals. Yet, as Pfohl (1977) notes, "nearly all legal scholars endorsed treatment rather than punishment to manage abusers" (p. 320). Disagreement existed among the legal profession as well about whether the reports should be mandatory and to whom the reports should be made (Pfohl, 1977). All agreed, however, that reporters of abuse must be granted immunity.

A major issue in the passage of legislation was whether the reporting of child abuse should be mandatory and, if so, for whom. The focus increasingly became that it should be mandatory for physicians to report abuse either to law-enforcement or child welfare agencies, depending on the state.

> The argument for focusing on the reporting by physicians is very strong. Doctors face special confidentiality problems arising from the physician-patient relationship and are concerned about the threat of legal action. Actually, the chief aim of legislation is to uncover cases which only medical skill can detect in the course of a medical examination and a review of the medical history. (Paulsen, 1966, p. 46)

Focusing on physicians as reporters is not without precedent: physicians were already required to report venereal disease and gunshot wounds to various government agencies. The reporting mandate to the physician drew child abuse further into medical jurisdiction.

Diffusion of child abuse laws was rapid, and laws were passed easily in most state legislatures. In 3 years (1963 to 1965), 47 of 50 states had passed child abuse reporting laws (DeFrancis, 1966). Although the laws varied, most made reporting mandatory and designated the county or state department of welfare to handle the reports and cases. The intent of the child abuse reporting laws was primarily to protect the child, although they were premised on the notion that a crime had been committed and action might be taken against the parents (Bain, 1963). In some states the results of legislation were dramatic. In Florida, for example, the passage of new statutes, buttressed by a media campaign and a 24-hour WATS line, led to a phenomenal increase of reported cases from 17 to 19,120 in a single year (Nagi, 1977).

But not all physicians readily "saw" the "battered child syndrome" or were aware of what they should do about it. Based on a survey of over 200 physicians most likely to be in contact with abused children—pediatricians, general practitioners, and emergency room physicians—Silver et al. (1967) concluded, "A strikingly high percentage of the physicians suggested a lack of awareness of the battered child syndrome or a lack of knowledge about community procedures" (p. 67).

## Social scientists' views of child abuse

Social scientists, with different training, intellectual frameworks, and tasks than physicians, often present a variant view of a medical phenomenon or at least point to social variables that are glossed over by a clinical viewpoint. Richard J. Gelles and David H. Gil are social scientists who have cast a critical eye on the medical-illness view of child abuse. Their basic critique is that the medical model of abuse, focusing nearly exclusively on the abuser and the abuser's characterological makeup, is limited and neglects the social context of child abuse. They see child abuse as a multidimensional, rather than singular, phenomenon. The focus of each analysis is somewhat different. Gelles suggests that social and sociological factors need to be taken into account in ascertaining cause of individual child abuse, and, while Gil agrees, he maintains the causes of child abuse are rooted in our culture and social structure.

Gelles (1973) criticizes the psychopathological model of child abuse as narrow and inconsistent. He argues that by locating the causes of child abuse in a single variable, the mental abnormality of the parent, we ignore other equally important causal variables. He proposes a more sociological approach to child abuse that includes overlooked variables such as the social characteristics of abusive parents and their children as well as the situational or contextual properties of the act(s) of child abuse (Gelles, 1973). After reviewing previous studies, Gelles notes, for instance, that the lower and working classes tend to be overrepresented among child abusers, that abusers are often female (unusual in violent crimes), and that social stresses such as unemployment or unwanted pregnancies may play important causal roles in child abuse. He further suggests we investigate the social process by which individuals are designated and labeled as abusers, with specific attention to how the label is differentially applied (Gelles, 1975).

Whereas Gelles essentially maintains an individual focus on the abuser, Gil (1970, 1971, 1975) sees child abuse as a symptom of a greater malady. Basing his analysis on a nationwide epidemiological survey of child abuse, he suggests that the incidence of the classic "battered child syndrome" is actually relatively infrequent (6000 to 7000 cases a year) and argues for a more sociocultural approach to child abuse. In the nationwide survey he found a greater incidence of child abuse in families subject to social stress: lower class families, broken families, and families with four or more children (Gil, 1970).* To Gil, child abuse is not an isolated phenomenon; he finds its roots in the sociocultural configuration of our society. He maintains that violence against children is rooted deeply in our theories and practices of child rearing. He locates the "causes" of child abuse both in our culture, especially in our approval of the use of force in adult-child relations, and in our social structure, most particularly in the existence of poverty. Moreover, Gil argues that "child abuse" is far more pervasive and subtle than the medical-clinical conception, which focuses only on severe physical maltreatment, would lead us to believe. He claims that far more children are victims of societal forms of "child abuse" such as malnutrition, poverty, poor education and medical services, and physical abuse in schools and other child caretaking institutions (Gil, 1971). Thus, he calls for the application of a four-part "public health model of preventive intervention to physical abuse with children" (p. 392): (1) the outlawing of corporal punishment in institutions, (2) elimination of poverty, (3) education for family life and comprehensive family planning, including the availability of abortion, and (4) the availability of high-quality, neighborhood social and medical services. This could be called a social-structural approach to child abuse prevention.

We have presented these social scientific critiques in some detail not only because they point up the limitations of a purely medical-clinical approach to child abuse but also because they present alternative models as well. Gelles (1973) summarizes succinctly the significance of a sociological viewpoint on child abuse:

> When a patient is diagnosed as sick, the treatment which is administered to him is designed to cure his illness. Consequently, when a child abuser is diagnosed as a psychopath, the treatment which is given him is designed to cure his disease and prevent future episodes which result from that disease. . . . So far, treatment of psychopathic disorders of abusive parents tends to be of limited effectiveness . . . one reason may be that the [treatment] strategies are based on an erroneous diagnosis of the problem. . . . [It] is now necessary to stop thinking of child abuse as having a single cause: the mental aberrations of the parents. (p. 620)*

But sociological approaches, although they may be more comprehensive and focus more on

*So many writers and analysts have claimed that child abuse occurs nearly equally in all classes that a "myth of classlessness" can be said to exist. Leroy H. Pelton (1978) notes that nearly all studies show a significantly higher incidence of child abuse in the lower class. He argues that this relationship is real, rather than being an artifact of selective public scrutiny and reporting. Viewing child abuse as a classless phenomenon supports the medical model of abuse; it is seen as a "disease" that can strike anyone regardless of social class. This glosses over the possibility that child abuse is a result of structured class-based social stresses. It focuses attention on causes in the individual, not in the social structure, thus supporting intervention with the abuser rather than the society.

*Reprinted, with permission, from the *American Journal of Orthopsychiatry*: copyright 1973 by the American Orthopsychiatric Association, Inc.

"root" causes of abuse, are largely disregarded by those who have to deal with more practical tasks at hand: reporting abuse, protecting children, and treating abusers.

## Changes in the definitions of what constitutes child abuse

Child abuse has been institutionalized as a social problem, the abuser defined as a psychopathological deviant, and the "battered child syndrome" established as a legitimate medical problem. Like hyperkinesis, child abuse has become a well-known form of deviance. Millions of federal dollars have been authorized for research and treatment. In 1973, Congress passed The Child Abuse Prevention and Treatment Act. This legislation created The National Center of Child Abuse and Neglect to function as a clearinghouse for child abuse research and information and earmarked $85 million for treatment of abuse. Included in the act was a definition of child abuse that was more comprehensive than the previous medical definition:

> Child abuse and neglect means the physical or mental injury, sexual abuse, negligent treatment, or maltreatment of a child under the age of eighteen by a person who is responsible for the child's welfare under circumstances which indicate that the child's health or welfare is harmed or threatened thereby. . . . (Cited in Gelles, 1975, p. 365)

This legislation officially expanded the definition of child abuse beyond physically battered children. But what constitutes "mental injury," "negligent treatment," "harm," or "threat" is not clear. How do we know when we have a mental injury? What is a threat? What is harm and according to whom? In our judgment it is problematic to expand the definition of child abuse without expanding significantly the levels of prevention and intervention. As long as intervention (and prevention) remains only at the clinical-medical and child welfare agency level, such a comprehensive definition serves only to expand the clinical domain. And this seems to have occurred. In 1972, only 60,000 alleged incidents of child abuse were brought to official attention in the United States; by 1976 the number was more than half a million (Newsweek, Oct. 10, 1977, p. 112). Although the agency's director calls child abuse an "epidemic," it is more likely that the recent publicity has encouraged more people to speak out about it. Still, undoubtedly the pool of potential cases of "child abuse" is large; a recent study (Gelles et al., 1977) estimated that between 1.4 and 1.9 million children were vulnerable to physical injury from violence in 1975. The expanded definition has created a larger net for defining mistreatment of children as deviance. A more comprehensive approach to intervention, such as suggested by Gil, seems also to be necessary if we are not simply to treat the casualties of child maltreatment.

Yet not all signs point to an expansion in the definition of child abuse. The Supreme Court has recently defined some violence toward children as acceptable and as not constituting child abuse. In a 1977 case of two students who had been beaten with a wooden paddle by school officials (*Ingraham* v. *Wright et al.*), the Court ruled that school spankings, no matter how harsh, did not violate the constitution's ban on cruel and unusual punishment. According to Gil (1975), however, this type of decision encourages child abuse:

> when schools and other child care settings employ practices that are not conducive to optimal child development, e.g., corporal punishment and other demeaning and threatening, negative disciplinary measures, they convey a subtle message to parents—namely that such methods are appropriate, as they are sanctioned by educational authorities and "experts." . . . Whenever corporal punishment in child rearing is sanctioned, and even subtly encouraged by society, incidents of serious child abuse are bound to happen, either as a result of deliberate, systematic and conscious effort on the part of the perpetrators, or under conditions of loss of self control. (pp. 348 and 352)*

In sum, child abuse has found a place among medical maladies in our society. Since the medicalization of child abuse, physicians have acted as significant "protectors" of children. Yet intervention has not moved far beyond the

---

*Reprinted, with permission, from the *American Journal of Orthopsychiatry*: copyright 1975 by the American Orthopsychiatric Association, Inc.

medical-clinical approach, and child abuse is still defined as only an individual's problem.

## CHILDREN AS A POPULATION "AT RISK" FOR MEDICALIZATION*

As we discussed earlier in this chapter, the discovery of childhood led to a differentiation and separation of children from adults. Childhood became a distinct period in the life cycle, and children became a separate class of people with distinctive characteristics, rights, and obligations. Children were defined as "fragile creatures . . . who needed to be both safeguarded and reformed" (Ariès, 1962, p. 133). Children were unlike adults and needed special attention. Among the most significant characteristics of this depiction of children was that they were innocent and dependent.

The innocence of children manifested itself in defining children as in need of protection from the harsh and sinful world. They required guidance and discipline to grow up into responsible adults. Childhood became a special period of dependence, "a sort of quarantine, before [children were] allowed to join the world of adults" (Ariès, 1962, p. 412). In fact, children became a separate, dependent class of people. Parents had full sovereignty over this dependency; and if they faltered, the state via parens patriae assumed parental control and responsibility. Closely aligned with and as a consequence of viewing children as innocent and dependent, children were defined as people who were not fully responsible for their behavior. This led to their exemption from certain types of criminal prosecution. In short, by being relegated to a special status in society, children became a special class of people: innocent, dependent, and not fully responsible for their actions.

Children are also a relatively powerless group in society. They are powerless because they are physically weaker, socially unorganized, politically disenfranchised, and economically dependent. Children are most susceptible to the rules and sanctions of more powerful people (adults), even if such direction is carried out in "the best interests of the child." They are on the short end of the archetypal paternalistic relationship.

Over about the past century there has been an erosion of parents' control of child rearing and discipline (Lasch, 1977). In part this is a result of the increase in geographical mobility, exponential growth of communications, and a general decline in strength of traditional status groups such as the family and Church. But, more specifically, institutional forces such as public schools, the juvenile court, and the child guidance movement and cultural forces such as Dr. Spock's baby books, more permissive child rearing, and television have eroded parents' authority and control. Their sovereignty over child rearing has been considerably modified. In place of this parental authority a variety of extrafamily "resources" have emerged: schoolteachers, day-care specialists, child experts, guidance counselors, welfare workers, and pediatricians, among others. Medicine, in the form of the family physician, pediatrician, or medical clinic, has become a significant family resource and a source of "authority." As David Mechanic (1973) notes, "As medicine has developed, it has increasingly taken over the functions of care provided by the family and close associates . . ." (p. 16).

The combination of defining children as innocent, dependent, and nonresponsible people and the diminution of authority in the family have made deviant children a population at risk for medicalization. Let us explore this assertion a little further, both theoretically and in particular examples.

As Talcott Parsons (1951) pointed out nearly three decades ago, when deviance is seen as willful, it tends to be defined as a crime; when it is seen as unwillful, it tends to be defined as sickness. In our society, because of the way children are defined and the status ascribed to them, they are much less likely to have their behavior defined as willful. It is much more likely that they will be seen as not responsible for their behavior or, literally, as incapacitated or not fully competent human beings. To come full circle, when individuals are not considered to be responsible for their behavior, they are

* We present this section in lieu of a summary in this chapter.

considered "sick."* This is not to imply the absurdity that children are sick all the time but to point out that when children's behavior is deviant, it is more likely to be designated as an illness or dysfunction. The status of "child" affects how the behavior will be defined. Consider the example of hyperactivity. Imagine that instead of a child in a classroom being identified as hyperactive, it is a worker in a factory or a salesman in an automobile showroom. Would they be referred to a physician for their deviant behaviors? Would a physician diagnose them as hyperactive and prescribe stimulant medications for them on the basis of reports of a boss, a spouse, or a parent? How much is the identification and definition of hyperactivity a function of the dependent and relatively powerless status of the child?

The dependent status of children increases the propensity of arousing a protective response in society: for example, the houses of refuge, foundling hospitals, orphanages, juvenile court, child labor laws, and child abuse laws. The medical ideal, perhaps most clearly demonstrated in public health but also visible in clinical practice, is an ideal of prevention. In this sense, medicine, too, is a protective institution. The child-protective response of society aligns with the protective-preventive response of medicine. It encourages medical "child protection" in the name of health. Moreover, in a democratic society early "diagnosis" and intervention "in the best interests of the child" is more easily justified by medical-therapeutic intervention than with legal or civil intervention. Thus we have a medical-protective response with child abuse but not spouse abuse. The adult battering of other adult family members has not been defined as a medical problem (see Martin, 1976; Steinmetz & Straus, 1974).

An extreme example of potential vulnerability of children to medicalization was a plan designed by a physician named Arnold Hutschnecker. In a memo submitted by way of a presidential advisor to the Department of Health, Education and Welfare in early 1970, Dr. Hutschnecker proposed the massive administration of psychological tests to schoolchildren between the ages of 6 and 8 to detect potential mental disturbances or tendencies toward violent or antisocial behavior. According to what the tests showed, children identified as having "delinquent tendencies" would receive "corrective treatments"—in day-care centers for the young, counseling for older children, and special camps for incorrigible deviants. After someone at the Department of Health, Education and Welfare leaked the plan to the press, both medical and governmental officials disavowed support of it. Dr. Hutschnecker was surprised at the negative response: "My premise is that we vaccinate children to prevent physical disease, why not provide psychological tests and treatment to prevent the problems of crime?" (quoted in *Newsweek*, April 20, 1970, p. 76).

In sum, the definition and status of children has facilitated and encouraged the expansion of medical jurisdiction to encompass more types of children's behavior.* Although in part a protective response, medicalization also includes the identification and treatment of behaviors that would not be defined as medical maladies in adults.

## SUGGESTED READINGS

Ariès, P. *Centuries of childhood.* New York: Vintage Books, Inc., 1962.
An accessible and by now classic analysis of the development of the modern image of children. Using a variety of cultural and historical data, Ariès weaves a fascinating theory of the discovery of childhood.

Conrad, P. *Identifying hyperactive children: the medicalization of deviant behavior.* Lexington, Mass.: D. C. Heath & Co., 1976.
Uses the labeling-interactionist frame and participant observation at a medical diagnostic clinic to investigate parents' and physicians' constructions of the medical entity of hyperactivity. Of special

*This may in part explain why Matza (1964) found all theories of juvenile delinquency to be deterministic. If children are not considered responsible for their behavior, it must be determined by external or internal "forces."

*Normal child development has also become codified in medical terms; deviances from these developmental norms are defined as disorders such as learning or developmental disabilities.

interest is Chapter 6, "Uncertainty and Medical Diagnosis: The Social Construction of Hyperactivity."

Empey, L. T. *American delinquency: its meaning and construction*. Homewood, Ill.: Dorsey Press, 1978.

Approaches juvenile delinquency from a perspective that complements ours. This is a comprehensive and readable text and a fine resource for students of deviance.

Gil, D. G. *Violence against children*. Cambridge, Mass.: Harvard University Press, 1970.

A provocative book and, if taken seriously, a profound challenge to the medicalization of child abuse. In addition to reporting a nationwide epidemiological study of child abuse, Gil argues persuasively for a sociocultural rather than medical approach to the problem.

Platt, A. *The child savers*. Chicago: University of Chicago Press, 1969.

An excellent study of how middle-class champions defined lower class deviance. Combining a labeling and class analysis, Platt traces the "invention of delinquency" to the work of 19th-century child-savers.

# 7 HOMOSEXUALITY

## FROM SIN to SICKNESS to LIFE-STYLE

The subject of this chapter is the medicalization and demedicalization of homosexual or same-sex sexual conduct (hereafter, simply "same-sex conduct"). We place this discussion toward the end of our case examples because it allows us to reiterate several of the key themes of our medicalization argument as well as providing a clear illustration of demedicalization of deviance—a topic to which we have thus far only alluded.

The origin and rise of the medical definitions of same-sex conduct and those who engage in it provide us with a clear-cut example of the historical complementarity and continuity of religious, legal, and medical definitions and explanations of deviance. It also demonstrates how these three institutions of social control typically reinforce each other in the general moral definitions and prescriptions they champion. In addition, the medicalization of same-sex conduct portrays physicians as moral entrepreneurs for sickness definitions of "undesirable" conduct and persons. Finally, the case of homosexuality allows us to address the process of demedicalization and to raise important questions about the possible consequences of removing medical (and in a sense, protective) definitions from certain kinds of behavior within an essentially disapproving moral universe.

### MORAL FOUNDATIONS: THE SIN AGAINST NATURE

It is, of course, too simple to claim that homosexual conduct has been always and everywhere despised and prohibited. At the same time, it is essentially accurate to argue that at least in the West, the overwhelming pattern has been one of disapproval if not condemnation (Bullough, 1976, 1977). This is true not only for same-sex conduct but for virtually all sexual behavior; indeed, Western culture has been called "sex negative" (Churchill, 1967).

Social historian Vern Bullough (1976, p. ix), in his exhaustive *Sexual Variance in Society and History,* concludes that although the particular forms of these judgments have changed, the essential morality has not. From its origins as primarily a religious transgression, a sin, same-sex conduct had become by the end of the medieval period, a matter for state control, a crime, and ultimately was redefined in modern society as a sickness.

Some historical evidence suggests that even before it became a sin, same-sex conduct was disapproved because it might interfere with fulfilling one's reproductive responsibility to the community. This included ensuring oneself of care during old age, continuing the family line, and the proper performance of ritual responsibilities (Bullough, 1976). In the Mesopotamian culture of the Tigris-Euphrates valley, dated about 3000 BC, anal intercourse was apparently common (involving both male-male and male-female partners). This tolerance, however, depended on such activities neither precluding progeny nor being exploitive.

The connection between heterosexual reproduction and species-community survival became a kind of practical standard against which other forms of sexual as well as nonsexual conduct might be judged. This biological premise for attitudes toward homosexuality (and other forms of nonprocreative sex) is one important foundation for the common reference to such behavior as "unnatural," with heterosexual, especially reproductive, sex being "natural." It is clear that such a distinction represents the same kind of social construction process we have discussed throughout this book. Nevertheless, this natural-unnatural designation has been taken generally as both a biological and moral absolute throughout human history and has profoundly influenced social definitions of and actions toward same-sex behavior.

## Ancient origins: The Persians and Hebrews

By the time the Persians conquered the Egyptians and established their culture about the sixth century BC, negative attitudes toward nonprocreative sex outside marriage were common. The Persians, influenced by Zoroastrian religious doctrines, believed that although sexual activity should not be forbidden (eliminating vital progeny), it harbored great potential for social disruption if not carefully controlled and channeled toward "higher" virtues. Doctrines of divine preordination and prescription became superimposed on evolutionary arguments supporting heterosexual conduct as the norm. The Persians believed that male sperm or "seed" had particularly unique and wondrous generative powers (an idea that continued to influence thinking on sex for centuries). To "waste" or "spill" it voluntarily outside the nurturing body of a woman was repudiation of a divine gift. To do so in homosexual conduct was to mock both "Nature" and its creator. It was, in short, an abomination assuring damnation.

The Hebrews were by far the most influential of the ancient Middle Eastern peoples in shaping Western attitudes toward sex. They were a male-centered society (which was typical of that and subsequent historical periods). Women enjoyed perhaps certain marital (including sexual) and family prerogatives, but outside their roles as wives and mothers they received little attention. Marriage was expected of everyone who had reached puberty, and remarriage on the death of a spouse was assumed. Children, and especially males, were important assurance of social and religious continuity.

Sexual liaisons between women were regarded as considerably less significant than those involving men. Doctrines of male supremacy in procreation made what women might do together irrelevant to the reproductive potential of the community. This indifference toward female same-sex conduct is reflected not only in historical records of the ancients but for all societies. Although we speak of homosexual conduct in this chapter, both the historical and contemporary writing on homosexuality concentrates overwhelmingly on males. Regardless of the reasons, same-sex conduct among women simply has not engendered the same social reaction as similar conduct among men.* As long as women's behavior did not interfere with carrying, bearing, and rearing children, it received comparatively little attention.

Condemnation of such behavior among males, however, has been rarely ambiguous. Vern Bullough (1976, p. 82) locates the first specific biblical prohibition in Leviticus 18:22, dating probably from before the seventh century BC: "Thou shalt not lie with mankind, as with womankind: it is abomination"; and later: "If a man also lie with mankind, as he lieth with a woman, both of them have committed an abomination: they shall surely be put to death; and their blood shall be upon them" (Leviticus 21:13). This bibilical prophecy was to be interpreted subsequently as a religious sanction for capital punishment and torture.

By far the most influential of all biblical stories used to condemn homosexual conduct is the Old Testament story of Sodom, from which comes the term "sodomy." According to Genesis 19:1-11, God vows to destroy Sodom and several other cities because of the sins of their inhabitants. Abraham pleads with God to spare the innocent who would perish unjustly. God sends two angels into Sodom to determine the true state of affairs. The angels (presumably male figures) are met by Abraham's nephew, Lot, who invites them to his house. During their stay, the men of the city assemble outside and call on Lot to present his

*It is important to remember that those who made male same-sex conduct so important a transgression—a sin, a crime, and later a sickness—were themselves males. This dearth of information on lesbians has only recently begun to give way to popularly available works and public discussion of the topic.

guests to them so that they might "know them." Lot refuses but offers to present his daughters instead. The crowd, however, persists and is struck blind by the visiting angels. The next morning Lot and his family are led from Sodom, after which God destroys it by fire.

The common interpretation is that the foremost sin of the Sodomites was homosexual conduct and that such behavior brings damnation and destruction both to those who pursue it and those who tolerate it. The irony of this interpretation is that the Sodom story contains no specific references to homosexual acts. Indeed, the sins for which the city was destroyed are specified as wickedness, inhospitality, pride, slothfulness, and "abomination"—interpreted most accurately as idolatry rather than same-sex conduct (Bailey, 1955, pp. 9-10). The linguistic justification for the homosexual interpretation turns on the two meanings of the Hebrew word *yādha* (to know). Beyond its conventional usage, meaning to become acquainted with, the word also can be used to mean "to have sexual knowledge of" or sexual relations with. Presuming that both the angels and those outside Lot's house were males, selecting the latter usage implies that the Sodomites were interested in homosexual acts. Such an interpretation, however, would have to be chosen *against* the conventional and more likely one. Given the historic popularity of the homosexual interpretation, it is important to speculate on its source.

Biblical scholar Derrick Bailey (1955, pp. 9-28) and historian Vern Bullough (1976, pp. 82-85) review the historical record carefully and conclude that such interpretation was added by the ancient Hebrews some considerable time after the original story was written, probably some time around the first century AD. The story, as elaborated and used by the Jews of this period, may be in large part a reaction against the rise of paganism and Greek culture. Bailey (1955) argues that Sodom became a "symbol for every wickedness which offended the devout Jewish spirit—pride, inhospitality, adultery, forgetfulness of God and ingratitude for his blessings" (p. 27). As the ancient Hebrews felt more threatened by the expansion of Greek culture, the content of this symbol changed to reflect that which they found most heinous in the Hellenic world. The homosexual interpretation has become so entrenched that it is accepted uncritically not only by Christians and Jews but also by generations of historians, philosophers, and scholars. It has become, in effect, part of the revealed wisdom of the West, providing an almost unimpeachable condemnation of same-sex conduct.

## Contributions of the Greeks

The actual prevalence of homosexual conduct in ancient Greece is impossible to determine, the distinction between Greek values and practice forever obscure. There is, however, evidence sufficient to conclude that certain forms of such behavior were institutionalized firmly in Greek culture and practice, and to speculate with some confidence that certain kinds of same-sex liaisons between males were common, particularly between the eighth and second centuries BC (Dover, 1978). This acceptance derived from two cultural ideals: male superiority and an ideal of love that was believed to uplift the human spirit and strengthen community solidarity. To the extent that practice approximated these ideals, the Greeks believed such sexual conduct was neither unnatural nor bad.

Greek culture and social life were penetrated by testimonies to the superiority of the male and his diverse potential for moral, physical, and intellectual perfection. The phallus symbolized strength, power, and wisdom and was believed to possess special religious properties that could nullify evil (Licht, 1932/1963, p. 369; Vanggaard, 1972, pp. 59-62). The Greek ideal of physical and spiritual beauty was male rather than female, and the nude youth in athletic contest occupied a central and frequent place in art (Dover, 1978) and writing. Greek mythology and lyric poetry provide important insights into cultural values and contain many references not only to the male's exalted position but to heroic figures who championed and excelled in homosexual love. Women were defined as bound naturally to their childbearing functions (except for prostitutes, whose sexuality was for male pleasure) and were considered neither worthy nor capable of serious male companionship (Symonds, 1931, pp. 85-87).

Although sensuous and particularly sexual pleasures were important and desirable, the cultural foundations of Greek homosexuality appear in fact to rest primarily on a spiritual rather than a physical level. Sexual relationships between males were idealized to the extent that they were an expression of this more noble bond. The most important example of the institutionalization of these ideas is the Greek system of education.

At the core of this system was the ideal of *paiderasty,* the Greek term meaning the love of boys. This "love" was the complex, spiritual-emotional bond just described rather than simply physical stimulation and orgasm. It was precisely this kind of relationship between an adult male and a pubescent boy, in which the former took virtually total personal and social responsibility for the youth and his development, that was the homosexuality approved most by the Greeks. This student-teacher, beloved-lover bond drew heavily on the processes of emulation and admiration on the one hand, and example and mentorship on the other. The responsibility of this tutelage was believed most directly beneficial for the youth, but, in addition, it was to motivate the adult to high levels of moral, intellectual, and physical performance. The social and personal benefits of this reciprocal pederastic relationship were praised, perhaps most eloquently by Plato in his *Symposium* (178C-179B).

The Greeks were not, however, insensitive to the existence of less spiritual forms of same-sex conduct. It must be remembered that the pederastic ideal was just that, an ideal. As such, the Greeks took pains to distinguish it from less lofty sexual activity. This latter, "deviant" kind of homosexual relationship was considered more purely sexual and less spiritual. The one was for "pleasure," the other "beauty"; one an "involuntary sickness," the other healthy; one "virile," the other "effeminate"; one Greek, the other barbarous (Symonds, 1931, p. 16).

Homosexual sex was socially approved only when embedded in a complex set of personally and socially redeeming norms. The development of manly social and military skills and responsibilities, including marriage, heterosexual life-style, and procreation on completing this education period (at about age 19), were its primary aims. Later, when these men became established and respected, they were expected to select a free youth of the community, pursue him, and repeat the process (Lacey, 1968).*

Outside these socially and personally enhancing contexts, boy love and homosexual conduct were officially disapproved (although probably not uncommon). Sexual assault of young boys still in primary school was against the law. Male (as well as female) prostitution was disapproved. Sexual relationships between adult males were not encouraged, and it was thought degrading for a male much beyond his teens to play the passive role in anal intercourse. Although the Greeks institutionalized a positive attitude toward sensual pleasure in human relationships, they also imposed controls against homosexual conduct they believed threatening to the family and larger social fabric.

One particular form of such deviant homosexual conduct is identified as "effeminate." The approved sexuality was called "virile." Plato described an idealized form of love consistent with typically "masculine" rather than "feminine" pursuits. "Effeminate" homosexuality apparently refers to males, in their sexual conduct, acting or assuming the culturally prescribed role of the female. There is some evidence to suggest that such men—and women who "acted" sexually like men—were thought to be "unnatural" and, in fact, suffering from a disease or sickness. Aristotle, for example, proposed a prescientific explanation of this sexual deviance based on the premise that accumulated semen in the genital or anal areas predisposes men to pursue either the active or passive role, respectively. The "natural" or normal male was believed to experi-

*Sappho, the legendary sixth century BC queen of the island of Lesbos, was said to be a lover of young women. There are no records of her being reviled for this preference, which was, as in Greece, a spiritual as well as physical attraction (Bullough, 1976, pp. 111-112).

ence variation in the relative concentration of semen in these areas over his lifetime. Effeminate males, however,

> are unnaturally constituted; for though male, they are in a condition in which this part of them is necessarily incapacitated. Now incapacity may involve either complete destruction or else perversion; the former, however, is impossible, for it would involve a man becoming a woman. They must therefore become perverted and aim at something other than the discharge of semen. The result is that they suffer from unsatisfied desires, like women . . . . (Aristotle, *Problemata:* 879B-880A)*

The following medical explanation of effeminacy in males offered by the Greek physician Soranus during the second century AD expands Aristotle's proposition:

> People find it hard to believe that effeminate men or pathics . . . really exist. The fact is that, although the practices of such persons are unnatural to human beings, lust overcomes modesty and puts to shameful use parts intended for other functions. That is, in the case of certain individuals, there is no limit to their desire and no hope of satisfying it; and they cannot be content with their own lot, the lot which divine providence had marked out for them. . . . They even adopt the dress, walk and other characteristics of women. Now this condition is different from a bodily disease; it is rather *an affliction of a diseased mind.* (Quoted in Bullough, 1976, p. 143, emphasis added)

Such persons were ''perverted'' because of a physiological and/or mental disablement. These may well be the earliest medical explanations for deviant homosexual conduct. The ''puzzle'' that these accounts were intended to solve was not so much the fact of same-sex conduct but rather the ''perversion'' represented by men who wanted to be or act like women. This simply did not ''make sense''; thus the source of sense, the mind, must be troubled.

This distinction between ''natural'' and ''unnatural'' homosexual conduct became irrelevant in Rome. Indeed, the rarefied spiritual and philosophical distinctions that supported Greek pederasty were lost on the Romans, for they regarded such conduct as a shameful aspect of Greek life. Pederasty was not an institutionalized part of either the educational or military systems, and although Roman fighting units were pervaded by a strong sense of companionship and loyalty, this did not include intimate fraternization. Homosexual conduct between both men and women probably occurred, but the Romans either gave official and legal disapproval or chose to ignore it. Their sexual ideal was staunchly heterosexual.

## FROM SIN TO CRIME: EARLY CHRISTIANITY AND THE MIDDLE AGES

By the time Roman influence began to wane, a new asceticism was being reflected in a variety of religious and civil prohibitions. In the ensuing centuries of the Middle Ages the ''naturalness'' of heterosexual reproductive sex within marriage was reaffirmed with a vengeance. At the hands of clerics such as the fifth-century figure St. Augustine, Western Christianity defined sex of any sort as base at best. The ''goodness'' of marital sex was contingent on conception—the promise of progeny redeeming an essentially lustful act. ''Unnatural'' sexual urges were clearly beyond the bounds of membership in the official Christian community—even though actual practice and this ideal, from Rome to 16th-century England, were rarely aligned.

Christian fathers and sympathetic rulers often cited homosexual conduct throughout this period as posing a serious threat to community welfare. Harsh prohibitions and formal civil penalties for the guilty resulted. Celibacy and chastity, particularly in Western Europe, became the ideal and most spiritually pure state. This remained largely unchallenged until Martin Luther's 16th-century reforms held out heterosexual marriage as an even greater good. It was this general cultural prescription of asceticism, control, and the denial of pleasure that became the centerpiece of developing Christianity and particularly its Western Catholic and Protestant forms.

Specific New Testament references to homosexual acts, although few in number, leave no doubt as to their moral status in

---

*From Aristotle. *The works of Aristotle* (Vol. VII). W. D. Ross (Ed.), E. S. Forster (trans.). Oxford, Clarendon Press, 1927. By permission of Oxford University Press.

Christendom. In I Corinthians (6:9-10), the "effeminate," along with "fornicators," "idolators," "adulterers," and "abusers of themselves with mankind," were precluded from heaven. Two other references to homosexuality, one from I Timothy (1:9-10) and the other from St. Paul's letter to the Romans (1:26-27), offer equally clear judgments: "the law is not made for the righteous man, but for the lawless and disobedient, for the ungodly and for sinners, for the unholy and the profane . . . for *them that defile themselves with mankind* . . . (emphasis added)." And

> For this cause God gave them up into vile affections: for even their women did change the natural use into that which is against nature:
> And likewise also the men, leaving the natural use of women, burned in their lust one toward another; men with men working that which is unseemly, and receiving in themselves that recompense of their error which was meet.

Other New Testament passages are sometimes interpreted as condemnations of homosexual conduct, but their terms are ambiguous (e.g., "shameful," "abomination," "unnatural," and additional references to the "sin of Sodom"). There is, however, no unimpeachable evidence to support such claims (Bailey, 1955, pp. 29-63); most likely, they reflect the same hostility to and fear of Hellenic and pagan practices revealed in the Old Testament.

Part of this confusion derives from the difficulty the Christian fathers faced in deciding just what was and was not in accord with nature and God's plan. Given St. Augustine's narrow definition of natural sex, the "sin against nature" variously included anal intercourse, masturbation, bestiality (sex with animals), mouth-genital contact involving either sex, and even heterosexual intercourse in positions other than face-to-face with the man on top. St. Thomas Aquinas attempted to clarify this somewhat in the 13th century. He insisted that a distinction was necessary between same-sex and cross-sex sins. In effect, Aquinas argued that homosexual "unnatural" sex was more heinous than heterosexual "unnatural" sex, such as fornication and adultery (Bullough, 1976, pp. 380-381). These confusions about the precise nature and moral seriousness of "unnatural" sex during the medieval period were enshrined in what came to be known as canon, or Church, law.

This separate system of rules and punishments emerges from the penitential writings of English and Welsh clerics about the sixth century. These penitentials were practical manuals by which clergy-confessors could determine proper penance for people's sins. Explicit attention was given to sexual transgressions. Such writings offer insight into how the early Western Church judged homosexual acts. Interestingly, although there is great variety in seriousness and penance, there is little distinction made between so-called natural and unnatural sexual sins. Fornication and adultery (and other heterosexual sins) and sodomy, including fellatio, kissing, and interfemoral intercourse, were often regarded as of roughly equal seriousness (Bailey, 1955, pp. 100-110). In short, canon law incorporated a good deal of ambiguity not only about the moral seriousness of such conduct but indeed about what such conduct actually entailed.

This confusion was later translated into civil statutes when the vague "sin against nature" became the equally vague but more consequential "crime against nature." This developing criminalization of same-sex conduct throughout the medieval period culminated in the 1533 English statute, enacted under the reign of Henry VIII, making the "crime against nature" a capital offense. It was through this statute, along with its subsequent versions, that the moral condemnation of such behavior common in the Middle Ages came to exert such an important influence on Western social and legal definitions (Gigeroff, 1968, pp. 1-7).

Church punishments, however, were directed toward spiritual renewal rather than corporal sanctions. Variously long periods of atonement including prayer, self-imposed isolation, special diet, and introspection were common. The ultimate punishment was excommunication, banishing the nonrepentant sinner to eternal damnation. There is apparently no evidence that the medieval Church ever executed anyone for anything—including homosexual acts. What did happen, and particularly during the

11th and 12th centuries, is that the accused would be tried by the ecclesiastical court and, if found guilty, turned over to the state for proper secular punishment. In effect, this involved the state as a kind of henchman for the Church. We do not suggest that the state necessarily occupied a subservient position here, but rather that, particularly after the 11th century, these two institutions were rarely in conflict on questions of sexual morality. Increasingly, so-called unnatural sexual sins became transgressions against the state. This criminalization of homosexual conduct in the West may be seen as the continuation of a precedent established centuries earlier among the Eastern faithful in Rome and Constantinople.

One of the most dramatic examples of such political-religious cooperation is the Inquisition of the 13th and early 14th centuries. Threatened by what appeared to be a veritable wave of heresy and revolt inspired by the forces of darkness, Pope Gregory in 1233 appointed an order of clerics as official detectives in behalf of the Roman Catholic Church to rout out heretics and bring these sinners either to God or destruction. Charges of unnatural, and specifically homosexual, acts were sometimes included in accusations against such persons. Some historians suggest (Bullough, 1976; Lea, 1911; Lerner, 1972) that a good many of the accusations brought during this period were motivated by both politics and personality rather than religion alone. Once the spiritual status of an individual or group was brought into question, charges of sexual deviance often were added on the slimmest of evidence. Perhaps the most famous case is that of the Knights Templars and their Grand Master, Jacques de Molay.

A final example of this medieval criminalization is the Italian sodomy courts, established in Florence and Venice during the first half of the 15th century. A public office, the *Ufficiali de notte,* was created in 1432 with the avowed purpose of purging the city of sodomy. Vern Bullough (1976) describes the peculiar justice of this institution:

> officials set up boxes *(tamburi)* in various prominent locations around the city and encouraged citizens to drop anonymous accusations in these drums. Over a period of 70 years for which records are extant, there were often several hundred accusations in one year. . . . The accused were brought before the officials, testimony was given, and a verdict was rendered. (p. 417)

Florentine convents and their environs were the objects of particular attention by these officials, suggesting that the medieval concern with "unnatural" sex was not limited to males, although discussion and edict focused primarily on them. Among the most celebrated of the accused in Florence was Leonardo da Vinci in 1746 (Vallentin, 1938, pp. 35-39).

By the end of the 16th century in the West the Church seemed to be losing some of its moral dominance. This did not, however, herald a change in the content of official morality but only a shift to and consolidation of civil or state control. The power of the Church bureaucracy was thereby lessened, but its moral precepts about sex—control, the "natural-unnatural" dichotomy, and the key importance of reproductive sexuality—were preserved intact in the new secular regulations of the 17th and 18th centuries. For example, Elizabeth I attempted to supersede the Church of England and appease Puritan critics in 1558 by establishing the Court of the High Commission to punish sexual offenses that threatened orderly married life. Unsatisfied with this capitulation, Puritan reformers persevered until in 1650 under the leadership of Oliver Cromwell, Parliament passed the Act of May 1, which, among other things, reiterated the 1553 decree that sodomy was an offense punishable by death (Bullough, 1976, p. 464). That these legal judgments were not merely idle threats is seen from official records of the 17th century that indicate several persons were in fact executed for (probably open or public) homosexual conduct (Bingham, 1971).

At about this same time, there was an increase in popular, and particularly upper-class, interest in sex. The late 17th and 18th centuries were a time of rapid social, political, and intellectual ferment. What had once appeared to be universal standards of right and wrong conduct were gradually recognized by some as relative to social and cultural locale. It was indeed the Age of Enlightenment—a time of questioning, discussing, and pursuing answers according to the tenets of reason and examination of the empirical world rather than on the basis of tradition alone, and sex was a topic included for study. Guided by reason into a new age of tolerance and investigation, it was a time (as are all) wedded inextricably to its past. Paradoxically it was the leading force of this rationalism and tolerance—science—that was to provide the new form for the old sexual morality.

## NEW MORAL CONSENSUS: SIN BECOMES SICKNESS

### Medicine and moral continuity in the 18th century

The Enlightenment affected sexual attitudes and behavior in important ways. Increasingly the Church had to contend with secular authority; a growing popular interest in sex and sexuality is evidenced in literary and pornographic materials and more specifically in the numerous and highly popular sex manuals available, most notably those bearing the name of the great philosopher, Aristotle*; there was probably also an increase in the incidence of variant sexual practice, although it remained largely covert, and systematic documentation is impossible. London and Paris sported brothels supplying homosexual favors for pay (Bullough, 1976, p. 480). This tolerance toward sexual variety even received the official sanction of the French government under Napoleon in the famed but short-lived 1810 criminal statutes bearing his name. The Napoleonic Code decriminalized homosexual conduct between consenting adults in private.

We must not, however, overstate the scope of Enlightenment tolerance or the extent to which traditional moral principles—particularly regarding sex—were swept aside. This new beacon of tolerance on the continent was only a faint glimmer in England. English thought and laws on deviant sexual conduct—those most influential in America—continued until the latter half of the 19th century to define homosexual acts as inherently detestable crimes punishable, at least in principle, by death. Sexual "excess"—indeed, excess of any sort—was soundly disapproved as beyond reason and order. The particular forms of sexual behavior that came to be defined as excessive were inevitably those which had been morally disapproved. Deviant sex, including of course homosexual conduct, was therefore clearly excessive.

The new theories of health and illness that emerged in the 18th century made this distrust of moral excess their scientific centerpiece. Early in that century and throughout the next, a handful of physicians and their popularizers promoted conceptions of health and illness that viewed the body as a closed system of vital nervous energy. Health was defined vaguely in terms of nervous system stability, balance, and equilibrium, which, in turn, were thought to be products of the individual's integration with (read "conformity to") the larger moral and social environment. To the extent that one's activities in the latter realm were "healthy," that is, morally proper, internal physiological and nervous system function would follow accordingly. Conversely, activities that made repeated, unusual, and "unhealthy" (immoral) demands on one's body would lead inevitably to its depletion, debility, wasting, and disease (Rosenberg, 1977). Thus immorality, as evidenced by social behavior, was believed causal of sickness and disease.

Sexual behavior became immediately a focus for such explanation. As had been clear for centuries, sexual orgasm expends energy and is followed by a period that might be described as mild fatigue. These observations, coupled with the new medical theories, yielded the conclusion that too much sexual activity, and particularly deviant sexual activity, could be detrimental to one's health (see Graham, 1834/1837, p. 49).

Proponents of these theories were not, of course, prepared to prescribe abstinence. Arguments that sex was a natural part of life had become too firmly entrenched. In addition, some medical theories warned that retention

*Otho Beall (1963) has analyzed these enormously popular works and concludes that virtually none of them were faithful either in letter or spirit to Aristotle's work. Although his name lent them credibility and moral legitimacy, Beall concludes they were clearly products of 17th-century thought.

of ''seed'' in the male could itself be harmful to health. The solution was to recommend a course of careful moderation. This reflected clearly the traditional moral heritage of Christianity. Procreative sex, judiciously pursued, was somehow believed to be less debilitating to one's nerves than sex for its own sake. It followed that those forms of sexual activity which had been and continued to be sins—including homosexual conduct—were even more threatening.

Sexual activity, and most particularly deviant sex, became medicalized precisely at the time in history when religious prohibitions were becoming less dominant. Medicine, although only beginning to emerge as an efficacious technology, became a new system of social control for sexual behavior (Bullough, 1976; Bullough & Bullough, 1977; Comfort, 1967; Haller & Haller, 1974; Smith-Rosenberg, 1978). Although ''badness'' thereby became ''sickness,'' the moral principles on which this translation were based remained essentially unchanged.

## Masturbation and threatened manhood: a crusade in defense of moral health

The rallying point for this medicalization of variant sexual activity in the 18th and particularly 19th centuries was masturbation, variously called ''onanism'' (after the biblical story of the sin of Onan), the ''solitary vice,'' ''secret sin,'' ''self-pollution,'' and ''self-abuse.'' Throughout this period, and particularly during the Victorian era in America, masturbation was defined by both medical and popular writers as a major cause of physical and particularly mental illness. One especially threatening consequence was feared to be a ''morbid interest'' in others of one's own sex. These claims against masturbation became so foreboding and consensual among the rising middle class that today's historians of sexuality have named the period the ''age of masturbatory insanity'' (Bullough, 1976; Comfort,1967; Englehardt, 1974).

By the middle of the 19th century, middle-class champions of purity and the Christian life (Pivar, 1973) began organizing a crusade to save the youth of America from the physical and moral consequences of improper sexual activities; a prime focus of these guardians of social and political stability was the male youth, the ''hope for tomorrow.'' Although homosexual conduct was mentioned only rarely, its existence and alleged link to masturbation and sexual excess were used to nuture a widespread fear that the one indulgence would lead inevitably to the other.

The warriors in this battle consisted mainly of middle-aged, middle-class medical men and popular medical writers of the mid-19th century (Smith-Rosenberg, 1978). Their audience was the postpubescent-to-young adult male of the middle class, as the titles of some of these works attest: *The Young Man's Guide* (Alcott, 1833), *Lectures to Young Men on Chastity* (Graham, 1834/1837), and *Hints to Young Men on the True Relations of the Sexes* (Ware, 1850/1879). An important theme in this writing was that masturbation could easily lead to homosexual experimentation and subsequent involvement. Carroll Smith-Rosenberg (1978) suggests that given the middle-class restrictions on public speech about sex, masturbation may have been a ''code'' for unexpressed concerns about homosexuality.* This fear is seen in veiled references to ''threatened masculinity'' (and occasionally, femininity), expressed typically in conjunction with discussions of chronic masturbation (Fowler, 1857, p. 28). The portrait of the youthful devotee of sexual indulgence was a person who is

> timid, afraid of his own shadow, uncertain . . . nor will he walk erect or dignified as if conscious of his manhood and lofty in his aspirations, but will talk with a diminutive, cringing, sycophantic, inferior, mean, self-debased manner. . . . This secret practice has impaired both his physical and mental manhood, and thereby effaced the nobleness and efficiency of the masculine and deteriorated his soul. . . . (Quoted in Smith-Rosenberg, 1978, p. S226)

---

*Bullough and Voght (1973) show that ''onanism'' and ''the secret sin'' were terms used often to include a variety of deviant sexual practices, and specifically same-sex conduct. Physician James Foster Scott, (1908, p. 419) offers a particularly clear example of this expansive usage.

The parallel between this description and the effeminate homosexual stereotype that was yet to emerge is apparent. Indeed, the chronic masturbator is depicted in the writings of these moral crusaders as representing the antithesis of what we now call traditional male sex role characteristics.

The setting most commonly believed to encourage masturbation and such "unnatural" same-sex liaisons during the latter part of the 19th century was the English public or boarding school. It was in such sexually homogeneous settings that boys, thrown together and freed from moral guidance, were thought most vulnerable to such practices. The mechanism whereby masturbation and same-sex conduct develop was somewhat vague, but it was spoken of in a kind of contagion model. Older, more experienced boys were believed to induct the younger, innocent but interested boys (see Graham, 1834/1837). These schools were sometimes scandalized by allegations and stories of homosexual conduct between the youthful residents and between school personnel and those under their charge (Bullough & Bullough, 1978).

## CONSOLIDATING THE MEDICAL MODEL: THE INVENTION OF HOMOSEXUALITY

### Hereditary predisposition

By the turn of the century the idea that "immoral" behavior might make people sick was losing support among both popular and medical audiences. Subsequent research on the physiology of human sexuality has, of course, undermined these notions completely.* As physicians turned away from masturbation as the primary cause of sexual deviance, they turned increasingly toward the principles of heredity and evolution. These ideas had gained wide currency among the American middle and upper classes of the latter 19th century in the form of social Darwinism. Physicians who addressed the "problem" of same-sex conduct proposed that it was the product of a hereditary predisposition, "taint," or congenital "degeneration" in the central nervous system. Sexual deviance was somehow produced by the operation of physiological mechanisms largely impervious to environmental influence, although masturbation, reading "dirty books," and association with those already accustomed to such practices were still thought unwise, if not dangerous, to one's sexual normality. Even in cases where such behavior appeared to be acquired, it was explained commonly as due to the hereditary weakness of the individuals in question; they did not have the constitutional stamina sufficient to withstand environmental pressures.

One of the early representatives of this general view was French physician Paul Moreau, who in 1887 proposed that same-sex conduct was the consequence of a perverted genital sense, a "sixth sense" to accompany the traditional ones of sight, hearing, smell, touch, and taste. Just as the person born blind or deaf may be described as having an impaired sense of sight or hearing, homosexuals were, according to Moreau, afflicted with an impaired sense of sexuality. Physician Cesare Lombroso, the father of scientific criminology, offered an explanation of such conduct that incorporates both acquired and inherited hypotheses. According to Lombroso, "sexual perverts" were the inevitable products of a physical and moral constitution typical of an earlier, more primitive evolutionary period. They were, in effect, "survivals" of less moral civilizations that had since become extinct. Such persons were born "morally insane" and could benefit neither from penal sanction nor specific medical treatments. The only reasonable solution was confinement. Lombroso believed these people should be treated kindly and not blamed, but that all necessary steps—including sterilization—should be taken to prevent them from perpetuating their kind and "infecting" others (Bullough, 1977, p. 32).

*William Masters and Virginia Johnson (1966, p. 210), in their pathbreaking research on human sexuality, however, report that a significant number of men expressed concern about the possibility that excessive masturbation might affect their mental functioning. Twenty-six percent of a 1970 United States sample of adults said they believed masturbation was "wrong" (Levitt & Klassen, 1974, p. 30).

## Criminalization and medicalization

The late 19th century was also a time of renewed criminalization of same-sex conduct in Germany, England, and the United States. In the late 1860s in Germany, the Second Reich proposed a considerably more harsh penal code against men found guilty of mutual sexual activity. This particular section of the code was called "Paragraph 175" (Lauritsen & Thorstad, 1974). When sodomy was removed from the list of capital offenses in England in 1861, prosecutions of same-sex conduct increased. With less harsh penalties, convictions were more common (Bullough, 1976, p. 569). Data from the United States Census Office document a dramatic increase in the number of persons in American prisons for "crimes against nature." Between 1880 and 1890 (Katz, 1976, pp. 37, 39) this number more than tripled while the increase in population was only about 25%. Crusades against female prostitution in England and the United States produced, ironically, movements for legislation against homosexual conduct. In the late 1880s in London, middle-class crusaders interested in stamping out "white slavery"—the recruitment of naive young girls into prostitution—produced a law prohibiting "gross indecency" between "male persons" in both private and public places.* In 1909 the Chicago Vice Commission, formed originally to study prostitution, reported on what its members believed to be the alarming number of "sex perverts" in the city and the existence of an underground community, including public meeting places and special symbols whose meanings only insiders understood. Calls for legal control followed, and several states formulated harsh and restrictive laws (Bullough, 1976, pp. 570-571, 578, 609).

This simultaneous medicalization and criminalization of same-sex conduct may appear contradictory; we have suggested that these two historical processes represent the rise to dominance of different institutions of social control. It is important, however, to remember that religion, law, and medicine are all systems of morality. The rise of one in any particular historical period is not necessarily accompanied by the decline of another. In fact, as the preceding discussions attest, they are commonly superimposed on and concurrent with one another.

Such is the case with same-sex conduct. In fact, the rise of legal-criminal definitions toward the end of the 19th century may well have stimulated medicalization. The logic of this argument derives from the therapeutic alternative that medical definitions and interventions represent over more punitive, legal mechanisms of control. As same-sex conduct was attributed to biological-genetic roots, blame was lifted from the actors' wills and relocated in their biology and heredity. The concept of free choice and its attendant responsibility was believed applicable only in persons whose wills were healthy and mature. If same-sex conduct were the consequence of hereditary or congenital degeneration, such persons became less likely candidates, as Kittrie (1971) has argued, for criminalization.

In the face of movements toward increased prosecution and arrest in late 19th-century England and America, medical definitions and interventions offered a particularly viable intellectual and philosophical alternative. It is probable that this criminalization, given the growing promise of medicine, produced a strong supportive climate for medicalization of same-sex conduct.* Indeed, it appears that it was precisely at this time that homosexuality as a medical diagnosis began to emerge.

---

*It was not a child molester that became the most celebrated victim of this law but rather the noted English author Oscar Wilde.

*We speculate that this was particularly true for male homosexual conduct. It appears that the late 19th-and early 20th-century repressive laws against such behavior were aimed primarily, if not exclusively, at men rather than women. This may well have contributed to a greater medical interest in and subsequent medicalization of such conduct among men. American physicians at the turn of the century were perhaps primed to concentrate on problems of male rather than female sexuality, given the crusade against male masturbation. Virtually all those charged under the new laws were males. Physicians may simply have assumed that men were most commonly afflicted with this condition. Finally, those "criminals" which physicians defended as "patients" were in fact men.

## Homosexuality as a medical pathology

The term "homosexuality" was invented in 1869 by Hungarian physician K. M. Benkert, who wrote (presumably for his own protection) under the pseudonym of Kertbeny (Lauritsen & Thorstad, 1974). He argued against the growing legal repression of same-sex conduct and the harsh punishments contained in the Prussian legal code, Paragraph 175. Such treatment, he insisted, was both unjust and ineffective inasmuch as homosexuality was congenital rather than acquired. He described the condition, homosexuality, as follows:

> In addition to the normal sexual urge in man and woman, Nature in her sovereign mood had endowed at birth certain male and female individuals with the homosexual urge, thus placing them in a sexual bondage which renders them physically and psychically incapable—even with the best intention—of normal erection. This urge creates in advance a direct horror of the opposite [sex] and the victim of this passion finds it impossible to suppress the feeling which individuals of his own sex exercise upon him. (Quoted in Hirschfeld, 1936a, p. 322)

It was not, as some normals feared, a contagious or communicable disease. Quarantine and confinement were unnecessary, except in those cases involving bodily threats to others.

In the same year, Berlin psychiatrist Karl von Westphal published a case history of a young woman he examined in a local asylum. The woman reported a fondness for boys' games when growing up, liked to dress as a boy, professed strong physical and emotional attractions for certain other women, and said that she had been successful in realizing these desires on a number of occasions. She indicated virtually no sexual interest in men. The patient expressed anxiety and sorrow over this condition and "wished to be free of it." Westphal reported that the woman appeared to be a physically normal female, evidenced no delusions or hallucinations, and displayed no notable peculiarities other than her sexual desires and activities (Shaw, J. C., & Ferris, 1883). He concluded that the problem was congenital, did not necessarily indicate insanity, and should not be considered a vice, since it was not a consciously chosen preference. He called the condition "contrary sexual feelings." Westphal's treatment of this case is important in that it gave a certain degree of medical legitimacy to the topic. Several similar cases were contributed to European medical literature over the next decade.

In 1883 American physicians J. C. Shaw and G. N. Ferris published an important article in *The Journal of Nervous and Mental Disease* entitled "Perverted Sexual Instinct." Shaw and Ferris, stimulated by a patient who had come to the former for help, reviewed all the published medical cases of this condition they could find. Most of these were in German or French, and their review introduced to their American colleagues an area of medical study neither common nor understood widely in this country. The moral tone of the review is decidedly more neutral than the earlier medical writings on masturbation, but there is no doubt that the authors considered the condition undesirable, describing it as "a most interesting pathological sexual phenomenon" typified by "abnormal desires."

The most important physician-psychiatrist whose cases Shaw and Ferris discussed is the late 19th-century German student of deviant sexuality, Richard von Krafft-Ebing. More than any other physician of the period, Krafft-Ebing established same-sex conduct and the mental states from which it was presumed to flow as a physiologically based psychiatric pathology. His most influential work, *Psychopathia Sexualis,* was published first in 1886 and contained many case histories of various "sexual abnormalities." Written primarily for his medical colleagues, the work enjoyed an enormous success and ran into many printings and editions. Each successive edition seemed to include more case histories of sexual pathology collected from associates, his own practice, and police and court records. By the 11th edition, published in 1894, they numbered over 200 in all (Bullough, 1977). Krafft-Ebing's book became the definitive source of descriptive material on sexual variety and may well continue to be "the most comprehensive collection of case histories of sexual deviation available" (Van Den Haag, 1965, p. 12). A gauge of this popularity with medical and subsequently lay audiences (much to the author's chagrin) is that it is still in print today.

Krafft-Ebing has been called a pivotal and transitional figure between 19th- and 20th-century medical study of sexuality (Bullough, 1976; Robinson, P., 1976). The 19th-century face of his work is seen in his allegiance to a Victorian moral code that defined heterosexual procreative sex as a standard. Sexual acts and intimate emotional attachments between members of the same sex were considered unequivocally abnormal in Krafft-Ebing's work. In addition, although he gave greatest causal emphasis to a "hereditary taint," a congenital weakness of the nervous system, he agreed that repeated masturbation and sexual excesses of various types could excite or precipitate this condition. In all cases of "sexual inversion," however, physicians were instructed to presume the existence of a constitutional susceptibility. Krafft-Ebing regarded sex as the most powerful and potentially devastating force with which human beings had to cope; to overcome the desires of sexual lust required a vigilant fight.

At the same time, however, he previsions a 20th-century approach to variant sexuality in his willingness to address it openly and directly. This was not, as we have noted, common at the first publication of *Psychopathia Sexualis,* and some of his medical colleagues chided him for what they considered unnecessary frankness on such morally detestable practices (Bullough, 1976, p. 643). He brought attention to what had been up to then, at least in the West, a submerged and dark corner of human experience. Aside from whether he approved or disapproved of such behaviors (and he did disapprove), his work effectively broke this Western, Christian, and middle-class conspiracy of silence about unconventional sexual behavior. At minimum, he enlightened both medical and lay audiences to the incredible variety of sexual expression of which human beings are capable. Having done so, there was no denying this diversity; thereafter it had at least to be recognized.

He is also a specifically pivotal figure in the medicalization of homosexuality. In the face of late 19th-century criminalization of variant sexual practices, physicians (e.g., Benkert and, more significantly, Krafft-Ebing) were called on often to give expert testimony. The latter testified that homosexuals could not change the direction or the expression of their sexual desires and that such persons were sick and therefore should be treated therapeutically rather than punitively. He called not for sympathy but understanding. Finally, Krafft-Ebing's case histories and analyses contributed to the emergence of homosexuality as a medical entity and the homosexual as a distinctive kind of person.

As we have argued, a medical case history is not constructed in an intellectual vacuum. Rather, it is usually developed by clinicians attempting to solve people's "problems" within the context of the medical model. The accumulation of case histories around the diagnostic labels "invert," "sexual pervert," and "homosexual" gradually gave support to the notion that these names represent a disease entity, a "thing" people can "have" or "get" (Cassell, 1976). As medical consensus around such diagnoses grew, it also became part of the popular, lay understandings about what the condition "is" and what "kinds of people" the afflicted "are." Krafft-Ebing presented the typical features of this condition:

> Congenital absence of sexual feeling toward the opposite sex. . . . This defect occurs in a physically completely differentiated sexual type and normal development of the sexual organs. [There is] absence of the psychical qualities corresponding to the anatomical sexual type, but [rather] the feelings, thoughts, and actions of a perverted sexual instinct. Abnormally early appearance of sexual desire. Painful consciousness of the perverted sexual desire. Sexual desire toward the same sex. . . . There are symptoms of a morbid excitability of the sexual desires, together with an irritable weakness of the nervous symptoms. . . . The perverse sexual impulse is abnormally intense and rules all thought and sensation. The love of such individuals is excessive even to adoration, and is often followed by sorrow, melancholy, and jealousy. People afflicted with this abnormality frequently possess an instinctive power to recognize one another. (Quoted in Shaw, J. C., & Ferris, 1883, pp. 203-204)

Although perhaps not as dramatic as some of the discoveries of medical science earlier in the century, the accumulating case histories of "such persons" gave credence to the proposition that another medical mystery was being solved, another battle about to be won. It is in terms of the repeated images of pathology, pain, anguish, and the bizarre contained in these case histories that homosexuality and the homosexual emerged as medical entities in the 20th century.

## RISE OF THE PSYCHIATRIC PERSPECTIVE

### Contribution of Freud

We pointed out in Chapter 3 that the work of Sigmund Freud revolutionized the way medicine and psychiatry in particular defined and treated a broad range of patient problems. That was certainly true for homosexuality, although his work on this topic defies simple classification. For our purposes, Freud's most significant contributions are paradoxical: he explained homosexuality by a general theory of sexuality that rejected the notions of congenital etiology and hereditary degeneration; this explanation, in effect, "normalized" homoerotic desires by making them part of "normal" sexual development and a "latent" dimension of heterosexuality; he argued that homosexuality is not best understood as a disease, yet his work strengthened considerably medical dominance over the definition and treatment of this "condition." In short, Freud expanded and clarified the medical definition of homosexuality, but it became a considerably different condition than had been described before.

First, Freud embedded his discussion of homosexuality in a more general theory of psychosexual development that eschewed both biological and environmental determinism—the two common explanatory contenders to that date. He argued that adult sexuality was a complex product of the dynamic tension between physiological sexual desires—the "libido," or sexual appetite—on the one hand and social and cultural prescriptions and proscriptions on the other. A distinctive feature of Freud's theory was that the most crucial period for adult sexuality was childhood. All people were believed born with a "polymorphous perverse" sexual capacity that included the potential for stimulation by and attraction to same-sex others. Indeed, Freud posited that as children we all pass through a stage of sexual "latency" during which these homoerotic desires and attachments are perfectly normal yet largely covert. He characterized such sexuality as "infantile." As children pass through puberty, however, they typically transfer their sexual attentions to peers of the opposite sex and thereafter pursue the goal of heterosexual reproductive sexuality. This was "mature" and "complete" sexual development in the Freudian scheme. It was not, however, the product of any predisposition other than that imposed by cultural rules and socialization. Such cultural influences were usually effective in "making" heterosexuals, but Freud argued that all "normal" adults retained the "latent" remnants of their homosexual desire. These were "repressed" into the unconscious mind from which they were then expressed in "sublimated" or disguised forms consistent with conventional sexual standards (e.g., same-sex "best friends," poker clubs, sports).

Homosexual adults were described as persons who had not fully completed this sexual development or who had "regressed" to an immature stage. They were depicted as casualties of the various "complexes" and conflicts typical of the Freudian childhood. Among the most important of these is the Oedipus complex wherein children, during puberty, must manage socially prohibited and threatening incestuous desires for opposite-sex parents. Difficulties in relationships with one or both parents almost always assume great importance in Freudian discussions of homosexual conduct. Whereas the sexually mature adult weathers these traumas on the way to heterosexuality, the homosexual's attention to same-sex others represents an inappropriate and immature solution to such crises. Although clearly undesirable, homosexuality under Freud became intimately linked with the sexually "normal."

As part of his criticism of past congenital explanations, Freud attempted to counter the negative image of homosexuals conveyed by the notion of "hereditary degeneration." He insisted that

> inversion is found in people who otherwise show no marked deviation from the normal. It is found also

in people whose mental capacities are not disturbed, who on the contrary are distinguished by especially high intellectual development and ethical culture. (Freud, 1905/1938, p. 556)*

Neither was homosexuality a monolith; homosexuals were not all alike. There were, for example, the "absolutely inverted" (exclusively homosexual in feelings and action), those whose sexual object choice could be either male or female (the "psychosexually hermaphroditic"), and the "occasionally inverted," who engaged in same-sex conduct because of environmental isolation or limited access to cross-sex others (those we might call "situational homosexuals"). Freud reported that inverts' feelings about their "condition" ranged from matter-of-fact defense and demands for equal treatment to a consuming struggle against what was seen as a "morbid compulsion."

Linked closely to the proposition of "polymorphus perverse" sexuality was Freud's idea of a universal biological predisposition to bisexuality. He believed that people were not simply "masculine" *or* "feminine," but that *both* men and women displayed such qualities and characteristics:

there is no pure masculinity or femininity either in the biological or psychological sense. On the contrary, every individual person shows a mixture of his own biological sex characteristics with the biological traits of the other sex and a union of activity and passivity; this is the case whether these psychological characteristic features depend on biological elements or whether they are independent of them. (Freud, 1905/1938, p. 613)

This confounded further the traditional simplicity that depicted "normal" heterosexuality as clearly distinct from "sick" homosexuality. If the subjects and objects of sexual attraction were themselves blurred, how could one be sure which behaviors and feelings were normal and which perverse? Indeed, the very notion that there were physical and psychological dimensions of sexuality that could be distinct and contrary opened up an entirely new realm of study and debate.*

In 1935, Freud unwittingly made one of his most famous statements on the nature of homosexuality. In a letter to a mother who had written to him regarding her son, Freud (1935/1960) summarized the major themes in his writing on the subject:

I gather from your letter that your son is a homosexual. I am more impressed by the fact that you do not mention this term yourself in your information about him. May I question you, why you avoid it? *Homosexuality is assuredly no advantage but it is nothing to be ashamed of, no vice, no degradation, it cannot be classified as an illness*; we consider it to be a variation of the sexual function produced by a certain arrest of sexual development. Many highly respectable individuals of ancient and modern times have been homosexuals, several of the greatest men among them. . . . It is a great injustice to persecute homosexuality as a crime and cruelty too. . . .(pp. 423-424, emphasis added)

We must reiterate. Freud here argues that homosexuality is a *variation* rather than a deviation; it is not something particularly "bad" but rather something that is merely "different." One would search long for such an unequivocally nonjudgmental statement on this topic among physicians before, during, or after Freud.† His letter continues by addressing the question of "cure." It reflects an early pessimism about what psychiatric intervention can and indeed should attempt (see also Freud 1920/1959):

By asking me if I can help, you mean, I suppose, if I can abolish homosexuality and make normal

*Quotation from Freud (1905/1938) reprinted by permission of Gioia Bernheim and Edmund Brill.

*Robert Stoller (1968) suggests that Freud's distinction between biological and psychic sexuality represents the origins of the idea of gender as distinct from sex as a physiological condition. Although this idea existed prior to Freud's specification of it, the location of homosexuality as primarily a problem of gender identity rather than genetic or physiological predisposition became the official psychiatric as well as popular position in subsequent decades.

†The paradoxical nature of Freud's ideas on homosexuality are evident, however, in a recent argument by Stephen Mitchell (1978). He asserts that the concept of pathology is itself inherent in the very theory and therapy that Freud proposed: psychoanalysis.

heterosexuality take its place. The answer is, in a general way, we cannot promise to achieve it. In a certain number of cases we succeed in developing the blighted germs of heterosexual tendencies which are present in every homosexual, in the majority of cases it is no more possible. It is a question of the quality and of the age of the individual. The result of treatment cannot be predicted. (p. 424)

What Freud says here about the effectiveness of psychiatric treatment that attempts to "cure" homosexuality could be taken as a summary of the history of such treatments in the 20th century. It is indeed probable that this lack of a successful medical technology for solving the "problem" of homosexuality was a major factor giving support to its demedicalization. Finally, Freud previsions what psychiatric treatment might best aim for in persons presenting problems associated with same-sex conduct:

What analysis [*meaning psychoanalysis*] can do for your son runs in a different line. If he is unhappy, neurotic, torn by conflicts, inhibited in his social life, analysis may bring him harmony, peace of mind, full efficiency, *whether he remains a homosexual or gets changed*. . . . (p. 424, emphasis added)

Rather than aiming primarily for a "cure," with its implicit image of sickness, medical intervention might best facilitate the individual's life as that of one whose sexuality represents a variation rather than a moral blemish.

## Sacrificing Freud:* the reestablishment of pathology and the promise of cure

One important consequence of Freud's work for the medicalization of homosexual conduct was that it was established first and foremost as a psychiatric condition and psychiatrists became the medical experts—the new "priests" in charge of its diagnosis and treatment. The therapeutic had triumphed over the religious and legal as the official language to define and explain homosexual conduct and, more to the point, those who engaged in it. Although such conduct was still "criminal" in the United States and England, enforcement was uneven and seemed to occur primarily as a result of complaints in the name of "common decency" and "protection." Its intellectual boundaries as a category for medical attention had expanded decidely; homosexuality was not only a question of what one was or did but also of what one thought—including unconscious desires only the trained psychiatrist could identify.

Freud's reasoned caution regarding therapy was compromised in subsequent psychiatric writing on homosexuality. Indeed, considering some of the medical interventions during and after Freud's time, such as hormone therapy, aversive conditioning using electric shock and drugs, electroshock therapy, lobotomy, and "therapeutic castration" (Katz, 1976, pp. 129-207), psychoanalysis must be considered relatively benign. These "treatments" or attempts to control homosexuals were premised in all cases on a vision of this condition as a considerably more serious problem than Freud proposed. His equivocal position on the disease status of homosexuality and homosexual conduct and his pessimism about medical cures were supplanted by a growing consensus in American psychiatry that the condition is a serious psychopathology, that it in all cases produces anguish and unhappiness for those so afflicted, that it is clearly abnormal (not a variant of normal sexuality), and that, like all diseases, it should and could be cured.* The kinds of violent medical interventions noted were probably linked in a reciprocal way to the reservoir of revulsion that was the general cultural inheritance regarding same-sex conduct in the West. There was, in other words, considerable nonmedical support for such medical practices and ideas, which in turn reinforced popular thought on the subject.

*We are indebted to Christopher Lasch (1976) for this heading. It captures not only what happened to Freud's more general theory but also the fate of his proposition that homosexuality is not necessarily pathological.

*The Freudian analysis of homosexuality—albeit in a variety of altered formulations—was pursued most specifically after Freud by Adler, Bleuler, Coriat, Ferenczi, Jekels, Jones, Ortvay, Sadger, and Senf. See Ellis (1936, pp. 305-306) and Bullough (1977) for brief synopses of and reference to some of this work. See Freud (1914) for a more general discussion of the history of the psychoanalytic movement.

These nonmedical definitions sometimes took precedence over the more "humanitarian" stance of medicine, and medical rhetoric was used sometimes in the service of other institutions of social control. One of the clearest examples is the American armed forces during and after World War II. The military bureaucracy during the war provided not only an arena for wholesale psychiatric and psychological screening but also a set of circumstances in which the "problem" of homosexuality received considerably increased attention. In their review of sexual behavior and the military law Louis J. West and Albert Glass (1965) conclude that homosexual conduct is the area of sexuality of primary concern to military officials. During World War II such persons were classified as "psychopathic" and received a dishonorable or "blue" discharge. Military psychiatrists typically provided the official diagnosis on which this action was taken. Soon after the war, official military policy toward homosexuality hardened, and its boundaries expanded. In addition to their mental problems, homosexuals became "security risks," "threats to morale," and highly "unreliable." So concerned with the threat of homosexuality were the American government and military after 1947 that they moved to discharge not only those who had engaged knowingly in such conduct but also those "who exhibit, profess, or admit *homosexual tendencies* or associate with known homosexuals" (Williams and Weinberg, 1971, p. 28, emphasis added). Psychiatrists reluctantly became involved in what could be called an official campaign to separate such persons from service; although they protested what they considered overly punitive policies, their claims had little impact until the late 1950s (see West et al., 1958).* Medical definitions of homosexual pathology were used in the name of politics and ideology (Menninger, 1967, pp. 451-562; Szasz, 1965).

The congenital explanation of homosexuality, although challenged by the growing power of psychoanalytic psychiatry, was given new life in the late 1930s and again in 1952 in the work of Franz J. Kallmann (see Chapter 3). Extending a perspective developed in earlier work on the genetics of schizophrenia, Kallmann (1952) reported the results of a study of 85 twins, 40 monozygotic (products of a single fertilized ovum) and 45 dizygotic (two fertilized ova) pairs. The sets of monozygotic twins were all homosexual, and Kallmann reported this pattern had developed independently of each other's socialization, cooperation, or knowledge. Half the dizygotic twins were homosexual, but the co-twins showed no disproportionate signs of overt homosexuality. Kallmann concluded that this evidence supported the importance of genetic factors in the origin and development of homosexuality.

Kallmann's findings and conclusions have been cited and debated widely. Subsequent research (Sawyer, 1954; Paré, 1956; Money et al., 1957; Hampson & Hampson, 1961) has, however, raised serious questions that both undermine Kallmann's conclusions and cast doubt on the genetic explanation itself. Although the hope for a genetic etiology of homosexuality continues to be nourished in certain medical-scientific circles (Evans, 1973; and see *Behavior Today,* Nov. 15, 1976), it remains a theory with highly inconclusive empirical support. It was, in any event, rejected and hence not "owned" by the psychoanalytic psychiatrists who had become by midcentury the experts on homosexuality.

Most influential in supporting the pathology-treatment definition of homosexuality have been practicing clinical psychiatrists who have adopted various psychodynamic versions of the Freudian scheme. Among the most influential American advocates (and there have been many) are Edmund Bergler, Irving Bieber, and Charles Socarides.*

**Edmund Bergler.†** Bergler, a psychoana-

*The failure of these military psychiatrists to successfully exert professional dominance and authority on this question provides a specific example of the larger proposition that in the face of the state the power of medicine is tentative and conditional.

*An additional candidate might be Albert Ellis (1965).

† Pages 189 to 190 contain selections from *Homosexuality: disease or way of life?* by Edmund Bergler, M.D. Copyright © 1956 by Edmund Bergler. Reprinted with the permission of Hill and Wang (now a division of Farrar, Straus & Giroux, Inc.).

lytic psychiatrist trained at the University of Vienna who subsequently established a private practice in New York City, held that homosexuality is a mental disease characterized by "oral regression," masochism, and (in males) an irrational fear of women. Lesbian relationships were believed distortions of the mother-child bond, wherein one woman becomes self-destructively dependent on the other, parent-figure partner. All such persons manifest "trademark" unconscious characteristics, according to Bergler (1956, p. 15).

Bergler's published work on homosexuality began with a few articles in the early 1940s and culminated in several major works roughly a decade later. He framed the essential question in a 1956 book, *Homosexuality: Disease or Way of Life?* His answer was unequivocally the former. He was one of medicine's most vocal critics of the famous Kinsey studies of male homosexual conduct published in 1948. Bergler (1948) challenged Kinesy's generalization that one out of every three adult males in America had had a homosexual experience after adolescence. He believed the popular dissemination of such alleged "findings" was a cause of a new population of "statistically induced homosexuals"—those "borderline" cases swayed to full membership by this picture of supposed incidence. He rejected the concept of "bisexuality" as a "flattering description of the homosexual who is at times capable of mechanical heterosexual activity"; he insisted that "every 'bisexual' . . . is a true homosexual" who uses this label as an "alibi" (Bergler, 1956, p. 8). Finally, although he agreed that heterosexuality was no assurance of mental health, healthy heterosexuals do exist. There are, Bergler (1956, p. 9) insisted, "no healthy homosexuals."

On the basis of "30 years" of clinical practice. Bergler (1956, pp. 16-28) provided the following picture of the typical homosexual:

1. Such persons are "injustice collectors" and "psychic masochists" who strive for "defeat, humiliation, and rejection" because of their early failure to master the oral stage of psychodynamic development; they are "regressed personalities."

2. Male homosexuals* are terrified of women and flee from them to other men.

3. They typically "obliterate" the personalities of their love objects—sex is impersonal and contempt-ridden.

4. "The typical homosexual is perpetually on the prowl," and the constant "cruising" for sex partners represents the masochistic desire to be caught and punished.

5. Homosexual relationships are often "camouflaged" as "husband-wife" bonds, with one member attempting to escape into the argument of "biological femininity" to account for his effeminate ways.

6. These persons are characterized by "an unfounded megalomaniacal conviction" that they are superior persons and the false belief that "at bottom everybody has some homosexual inclinations."

7. Despite an outward flippancy and casual air, all homosexuals suffer from a "deep inner depression." "Scratch a homosexual and you find a depressed neurotic." This outward veneer is characterized also by an "exaggerated and free-flowing malice," which, under psychiatric gaze, becomes "pseudo" or irrational aggression.

8. All homosexuals experience a deep sense of guilt from their "perversion," which "denotes infantile sex encountered in an adult . . . leading to orgasm. In short, a disease."

9. Irrational and violent jealousy as a masochistic mechanism is common.

10. "Unreliability, ranging from a trace to a pronounced trend, is the rule and not the exception among homosexuals" and is often justified by the rationalization that "I've suffered so much."

The components of this portrait become common themes in subsequent psychoanalytic work.

Summarizing his professional experience with homosexuals, Bergler (1956) asserts that although he has "no bias" against them, "if I

*Bergler (1956, pp. 261-290) discusses female homosexuality in a separate section of his book. His description and alleged origins of the condition in women are, however, essentially the same as those offered for men.

were asked what kind of person the homosexual is, I would say: 'Homosexuals are essentially disagreeable people, *regardless of their pleasant or unpleasant outward manner*' " (emphasis added). Although they ought not be held accountable for their condition, their personalities are

> a mixture of superciliousness, fake aggression, and whimpering. . . . they are subservient when confronted with a stronger person, merciless when in power, unscrupulous about trampling on a weaker person. *The only language their unconscious understands is brute force*. . . . you seldom find an intact ego (what is popularly called "a correct person") among them. (pp. 28-29, emphasis added)

One is struck immediately by the similarity between these remarks and the traditional moral judgments about same-sex conduct we have reviewed. Bergler's writing is perhaps one of the best examples of how thinly guised by the rhetoric and professional status of medicine this traditional hostility can be. It is clearly grist for the nonmedical mill of hostility toward such conduct and persons.

In an article titled "What Every Physician Should Know About Homosexuality" Bergler offers some advice to his psychiatrist colleagues. Facing on the one hand growing numbers of homosexuals claiming to be "normal" and on the other another group of heterosexuals demanding harsh punishments, what, Bergler asks, is the "poor psychiatrist . . . caught in the middle and attacked by both sides. . . " to do? His prescriptions are insightful: professional and public education that homosexuality is a neurotic and severely damaging, yet curable, disease and not "just a way of life"; encouraging outpatient services for treatment; opposition to and reversal of the "conspiracy of silence" maintained by the media; "publicity" that will assure homosexuals and "potential homosexuals" that there is no "glamour" in "being different"; and assistance to "horrified parents" in handling the problem of homosexuality in the family (Bergler, 1956, p. 690). The psychiatrist should, according to Bergler, become an activist on behalf of the medical "truth" about this disease and its cure.

**Irving Bieber et al.** The most ambitious psychoanalytic defense of the pathological status of homosexuality has come from Irving Bieber and his associates in *Homosexuality: A Psychoanalytic Study*, published in 1962. Much more reserved in its moral tone than Bergler's writing, it is based on a systematic study of 106 male homosexual patients under psychoanalysis and a comparison group of 100 heterosexuals also under psychiatric care, but not for homosexuality. The research was the product of a committee formed in 1952 within the Society of Medical Psychoanalysts. Bieber was the founding chair of the nine-person group, initiated specifically to pursue the study of homosexuality. Eight of its members were psychoanalysts, and they were joined later by a clinical psychologist. Data were collected by sending questionnaires to the members of the society asking them to complete one for each of the male homosexuals currently in their care and for a comparable number of their other, nonhomosexual, male patients. Analysis of the data was in terms of relationships between patients and parents, psychosexual development, so-called latent homosexuality, and treatment.

The Bieber report provides a review of previous psychoanalytic work on homosexuality since Freud, as well as research premised on hereditary theories. It identifies several opponents to the view that homosexuality is a pathological condition: the Wolfenden Report from England, Kinsey's research, the anthropological studies of Ford and Beach, and the psychiatric evidence of Hooker, and Chang and Block (Bieber et al., 1962, pp. 3-18). The committee concludes this review, however, with the following terse remark: "All *psychoanalytic* theories assume that adult homosexuality is psychopathological and assign differing weights to constitutional and experiential determinants" (Bieber et al., 1962, p. 18, emphasis in original). The determinants of this pathology are rooted in childhood and the family.

The research of Bieber et al. has been cited widely and the subject of several medical forums and popular discussions (Beiber, 1964). It is taken typically among sympathetic physicians as a major empirical support for the disease view. Briefly, the conclusions of this research are as follows: heterosexuality is the "biologic norm" from which homosexuality represents a pathological deviation; it is the result of "hidden but incapacitating fears of the opposite sex"; these specific fears include anticipated threats to the male genitals, aversion to female genitals, and anxiety about actual or anticipated heterosexual conduct. As a result, sexual gratification is sought in members of one's own sex. Homosexuality is not a "variant of 'normal' sexual behavior" and is not the product of universal "latent" homosexual desires. Homosexuality frequently flows from pathological "close, binding, and possessive" relationships between boys and their mothers and from "detached and hostile" fathers. In fact, "a constructive, supportive, warmly related father *precludes* the possibility of a homosexual son." The consequences of these early relationships are subsequently supported in peer and play groups in a kind of self-fulfilling cycle, leading the young man into supportive groups of other similarly disturbed individuals (Bieber et al., 1962, pp. 303-319). The committee members held, however, that therapeutic evidence (37% of the 106 homosexuals under analysis became "exclusively heterosexual") is optimistic, particularly if (as Bergler recommended) patients were carefully selected.* One of the important criteria for success is that the patient is "motivated to become heterosexual." Bieber and his colleagues urged psychiatrists to strive for a cure (heterosexuality) rather than an "adjustment" (the "happy" homosexual) in their treatment of these patients.

**Charles Socarides.** A third important psychoanalytic advocate of the disease view of homosexuality at midcentury is Charles Socarides. A student of homosexuality and other "perversions" for more than two decades, Socarides began publishing professional discussions of the former in the early 1960s. He was instrumental in initiating discussion of homosexuality in 1958 at the first panel held on the topic by the American Psychoanalytic Association and subsequently was a major participant in various interdisciplinary and medical study groups on homosexuality that supported the disease view (New York Academy of Medicine, 1964; Socarides et al., 1973). He subsequently became one of the staunchest defenders of the definition of homosexuality as a serious medical pathology and, along with Bieber, the premier medical "expert" on this topic.*

Socarides' major contribution to this view of homosexuality appears to be primarily as a compiler of previous psychoanalytic theory and research, an experienced clinician, and a vocal defender of the pathology perspective. His major work, *The Overt Homosexual* (1968), offers a literature review and critique, case histories, and the elaboration and extension of selected themes from the psychoanalytic tradition. Much of what we have discussed from Bergler and Beiber is reiterated by Socarides: homosexuality is a form of mental illness with "pre-Oedipal" origins; it is an infantile and regressed or fixated form of sexuality based on profound fears and/or hostilities to one or both parents, and reflects a "pathological family constellation"; it is aggressive, self-destructive, and typified by paranoid feelings, a "masquerade of life" in which the actors are "tormented" individuals. Socarides (1968, p. 91) reiterates his own version of the traditional psychiatric distinction between "true" or "obligatory" homosexuality and situational, "utilitarian" or "episodic" homosexuality. It is only the former, wherein perversion arises from childhood trauma and conflict, that should be the subject of medical and psychoanalytic intervention. The latter, presumably less diseased type of homosexual, is so by choice, stemming from motivations of "power, gain, protection, security, vengeance, or specialized sensations" or the temporary unavailability of a partner of the opposite sex. Socarides (1968, p. 216) calls psychoanalysis the "treatment of choice" for homosexuality, provided the patient expresses a degree of guilt for uncon-

*One of the most widely cited psychodynamic discussions of interest is Lawrence Hatterer's (1971) *Changing Homosexuality in the Male*.

*Dr. Socarides has asked that, in conjunction with our discussion of his work, we point out that, to quote his correspondence, he has "never been against the decriminalization of homosexual acts occurring between consenting adults" and that he "was in the vanguard of promoting this, even before 'gay rights' became an issue in this country." He cites the 1973 Task Force Report of the New York County District Branch, American Psychiatric Association (Socarides et al., 1973) as a reference.

scious wishes and comes to therapy voluntarily.*

In 1970 Socarides published an article titled "Homosexuality and Medicine" in *The Journal of the American Medical Association*. He challenges what he and others perceive as a spreading and grievous misperception of homosexuality on the part of some in the medical profession, certain lay groups defending the "normality" of the condition, and many homosexuals themselves. It is a call to action and a defense of expert medical authority. He begins by asserting that homosexuality is publicly abhorrent and that "the majority of the public" favors legal punishment for such conduct, even if private.† At the core of the confusion about homosexuality is the fact that some have lost sight, or refuse to recognize, that it is first and foremost a "medical problem." In unmistakably turf-defending remarks, Socarides‡ (1970) writes: "Only in the consultation room does the homosexual reveal himself and his world. No other data, statistics, or statements can be accepted as setting forth the true nature of homosexuality" (p. 1199). The well-meaning but "unqualified" defender of homosexual normality is "misguided" because of the absence of clinically trained medical insight necessary to "discern the deep underlying . . . disorder" homosexuality represents. Rather than their being subjected to harsh punishments based on a moral-criminal model, Socarides insists such true homosexuals be helped by medical treatment. Although he supports decriminalization, Socarides believes that without simultaneous medicalization such measures are dangerous. Such legislation should always include unequivocal statements that homosexuality is an emotional illness that "may cause such grave disruption to the . . . individual that all meaningful relationships in life are damaged from the outset and peculiarly susceptible to breakdown and destruction" (1970, p. 1201).

He ends his almost impassioned plea for medical control with some cautions and encouragements to fellow physicians:

> We practice today in the atmosphere of a sweeping sexual revolution. Together with the mainstream heterosexual revolt has come the announcement that a homosexual revolution is also in progress and that homosexuality should be granted total acceptance as a valid form of sexual functioning, different from but equal to heterosexuality. Such acceptance . . . is naive, not to say grounded in ignorance. (p. 1202)

That such "fantasies" have been accepted as truth is evidenced by the following ominous example:

> colleges can be pressured to charter homosexual groups on campus with all the privileges of other scholastic and social organizations, thereby lending tacit approval. The implications of such trends are profound. (p. 1202)

He closes, however, optimistically, buoyed by the invincible armor of medical science:

> The whole issue of homosexuality must be transformed into one more scientific challenge to medicine which has time and again been able to alleviate the plaguing illnesses of man. With this respected leadership on the part of the physician, we will see a surge of support for the study and treatment of the disorder by all the techniques and knowledge available through the great resources and medical talent of the United States. (p. 1202)

The battle lines drawn and the call to arms made, only the ignorant, the ill, and the malevolent can fail to join the fight.

A final piece of evidence for the dominant status of the pathology definition of homosexuality comes from the official classification of psychiatric disorders of The American Psychiatric Association, its *Diagnostic and Statistical Manual of Mental Disorders* (DSM), and its parent document, the World Health Organization's *International Classification of Disease* (ICD). These manuals, and particularly the former, represent the professionally approved

*The sense in which any such therapy for homosexuality is "voluntary" is of course clouded considerably by the widely negative cultural definitions that attach to such conduct and persons. The choice here is rather clearly not free of strong predisposition in favor of treatment.

†A 1970 survey of the United States adult population found that approximately 59% of the representative sample thought that "homosexuality is a social corruption that can cause the downfall of a civilization" (Levitt & Klassen, 1974, p. 34).

‡Quotation from Socarides from *J.A.M.A.*, 1970, **1**, 1199-1202. Copyright 1970, American Medical Association.

diagnostic labels for virtually all mental disorders with which American psychiatrists are concerned. It is, so to speak, the "blue book" of mental illness and not only serves for statistical and operational classification but also provides the official list of what is and what is not considered a psychiatric condition. By reviewing the place of homosexuality in this manual, we can determine the extent of professional organizational support for the notion that it is a bona fide mental illness.

The first edition of DSM was published by The American Psychiatric Association in 1952 and was patterned after ICD-6, the sixth edition of the *International Classification*. This and subsequent editions are the work of a special committee within the association called the Committee on Nomenclature and Statistics. In DSM-I the diagnostic label "homosexuality" is identified as one of several forms of "sexual deviation" and falls under the more general psychiatric category "Sociopathic Personality Disturbance." The more clinically distinct and medically significant conditions are assigned individual numbers according to a systematic scheme. In DSM-I, homosexuality was one of many unnumbered conditions under this larger sociopathic umbrella.

The second edition of DSM was published in 1968 and is a reflection of ICD-8. In DSM-II, homosexuality assumed new significance as a medical pathology. Under the major category "Personality Disorders and Certain Other Non-Psychotic Mental Disorders" (301-304), and specifically under "Sexual Deviation" (302), we find "Homosexuality" (302.0) (American Psychiatric Association, 1968, p. 10). In a section of the manual on definitions of terms, no specific definition of homosexuality is offered beyond that for "sexual deviations": "This category [302] is for individuals whose sexual interests are directed primarily toward objects other than people of the opposite sex. . . . It is not appropriate for individuals who perform deviant sexual acts because normal sexual objects are not available to them" (American Psychiatric Association, 1968, p. 44). This reaffirms the important distinction in the psychoanalytic literature between "true" homosexuals and homosexuality and those who, for a variety of "normal" reasons, engage in homosexual conduct. According to both DSM-I and DSM-II, as well as the manuals of the World Health Organization, homosexuality is a mental disorder, a psychopathology. A 1970 survey of public attitudes toward homosexuality found that about 62% of American adults agreed, calling it a "sickness that can be cured" (Levitt & Klassen, 1974).

## DEMEDICALIZATION: THE CONTINUING HISTORY OF A CHALLENGE

As is apparent from this book, the history of the medicalization of deviance is both longer and more "rich" in detail that that of demedicalization. That this discussion comes as the final section of this last historical chapter reflects both what has been—and probably will continue to be—the growing dominance of medical definitions of and interventions in "social problems" and "deviant behavior" in American society. Although we have discussed specific criticisms of medical definitions and practice (e.g., "mental illness," "addiction," "alcoholism"), it appears that only in the case of homosexuality do we find a clear challenge to basic assumptions of the medical model itself.*

The origins of this challenge derive, paradoxically, from the very expansion of medicine at about the turn of the 20th century into various behavior problems. Most turn-of-the-century physicians saw homosexuality, although a sickness and no cause for blame, as a congenital (inborn) pathology. A small but respected number of physicians, in the face of legal repression and criminalization, pressed for a slight variation on this theme: although homosexual preference was probably congenital, it was not pathological. It was understood best not as a deviation but rather as a *variation* from

*Although the Harrison Act and subsequent court decisions did effectively "demedicalize" opiate addiction, this condition was never defined clearly as a medical disorder (i.e., it was the subject of no well-regarded medical theory or treatment), and there were few champions for such medical definition.

typical sexuality, produced by *natural* forces. They strived to separate heritability of the "condition" from pathology. Being inborn, homosexual preference could not be a product of will. We have noted throughout this book that the notion of disease or pathology is implicit particularly in the clinical model of medicine. Although these turn-of-the-century medical reformers wished to leave the moral protection provided by congenitality undisturbed, they challenged the moral proposition of pathology. This is, we believe, the origin of what later was to become a growing challenge to the medical model itself.

In about 100 years' time, from the closing decades of the last century in Germany to the early 1970s in the United States, we have witnessed this growing (although not linear) attack on negative definitions of homosexual conduct and preference. The church and state both have been arenas for such challenges. In the latter half of the 20th century, medicine remained not only steadfastly opposed to "normalization" but in fact, as we have shown, advocated an even stronger sickness view. It is not surprising, then, to find psychiatry as the prime target of such attacks. As we will show, the most successful battle was fought in 1973-1974, but the war had been declared a century before. These first salvos, however, could hardly be considered grave, since they came from a friendly source: other physicians.

## The armor of pioneering defense: "nature," knowledge, and medicine

The earliest physician-proponent of the view that homosexuality was not pathological was the Hungarian Benkert, whom we identified earlier as the inventor of the term "homosexuality." He spoke out publicly as early as 1869 against the growing Prussian repression of males found guilty of homosexual acts. In an open letter to state jurists, he criticized imprisonment and fines for such persons as not only a contradiction of the most basic principles of human justice but scientific knowledge as well. He named a long list of important historical figures who were homosexuals as evidence of its nonpathological nature (Lauritsen & Thorstad, 1974).

An important nonphysician advocate of this congenital-variation argument was German jurist Karl Heinrich Ulrichs, himself a homosexual, who authored a wide range of polemical, analytic, and theoretical discussions on the topic for over a decade beginning in 1864. Most significantly, he proposed a congenital theory that homosexuals, or "Urnings" as he called them, were persons whose physical sex simply did not correspond with their own sexual instinct. Urnings were men who had a "feminine soul enclosed in a male body"; later medical writers adapted this to a "female brain in a male body." They were a "third sex" midway between males and females. Ulrichs insisted that the condition was not pathological and that legal repression was both unfair and irrational (Bullough, 1976; Symonds, 1931). His ideas were widely influential in medical circles, and many physicians (e.g., Krafft-Ebing) cited his work.

The most consequential medical defender of the period was German physician Magnus Hirschfeld. Hirschfeld (1936b, p. 318) theorized that the "sexual urge, normal and abnormal, is the result of a certain inborn goal-striving constitution, influenced by the glands of secretion." He reiterated Ulrich's notion that homosexuals were "sexual intermediates." Like Benkert and Ulrichs before him, Hirschfeld vigorously opposed legal and moral persecution of homosexuals and argued that the cool wisdom of science be used to direct a more just and socially useful policy. He often testified in trials involving sex crimes and is credited with "saving" many from prison and even death. Hirschfeld founded what might be called the first homosexual civil rights organization in 1897, the Scientific Humanitarian Committee. This body, whose motto was "Justice through Science," published an annual *Yearbook for Intermediate Sexual Types* that contained a wide variety of information about homosexuality and other forms of variant sex. The committee's goals were (1) to influence legislatures to repeal the repressive Paragraph 175 of the German Penal Code; (2) public education about homosexuality; and (3) "interesting the homosexual himself in the struggle for his rights" (Lauritsen & Thorstad, 1974, p. 11). Aside from his reputation as a scientist,

Hirschfeld—and the committee itself—was known widely as devoted to political action. The most vigorous example was a 25-year campaign that gained wide medical and popular support to repeal Paragraph 175. Signed by more than 6000 leading figures of the day, it was finally presented to the Reichstag in 1922, from where it never emerged. The rise of Nazism in Germany signaled an even greater repression, and the movement for homosexual normalization was brought to a standstill during this period.

Hirschfeld put great stock in the assumption that knowledge was the key to progressive and humane attitudes toward homosexuals and sexuality in general. He conducted what was the first nonclinical study of sexual attitudes and practices in which he sent questionnaires to over 10,000 men and women (Hirschfeld, 1936b, p. 318). The diversity of the responses convinced him even more firmly that the metaphors of sickness and pathology were, more often than not, inappropriate descriptions of sexually variant behavior and caused him to question whether, indeed, there was even something that could be defined unequivocally as sexually "normal." Hirschfeld founded the Institute for Sexual Science in Berlin in 1918, which, until it was destroyed by the Nazis in 1933, was a world center for information and study of sex.

All Hirschfeld's colleagues in the Scientific Humanitarian Committee did not agree with his etiological theory of homosexuality. One of the most vocal critics, Benedict Friedländer, established a splinter group in 1907 called The Community of the Special. Friedländer rejected Hirschfeld's theory of the biological origins of homosexuality, and considered it "degrading and beggardly . . . pleading for sympathy" (quoted in Lauritsen & Thorstad, 1974, p. 50). He cited anthropological evidence to support a more culturally relative view of sexual practice in opposition to what he saw as the prison of biological determinism proposed by Hirschfeld and others. The involvement of medical authorities as experts on homosexuality offended Friedländer, and he warned that congenital arguments brought with them more than a protection from political oppression: to be biologically "different" from the majority precluded equality. Friedländer's fear was indeed realized during roughly this same period. When medical treatments for homosexuality proved repeatedly unsuccessful, the congenital theory was used as the foundation for the pessimistic notion of "hereditary degeneration." Treatment based on this view tended toward confinement and control. This concept came to assume major explanatory significance in the work of Krafft-Ebing and other physicians supporting the pathology view.

The last major turn-of-the-century challenger to medical pathology (with the exception of Freud) was English physician Henry Havelock Ellis, described as the first truly modern thinker on sexuality in the 20th century (Robinson, 1976). Ellis sought first and foremost to describe sexuality rather than to judge it. He was confident that homosexuality or "sexual inversion" was a congenital, inherited condition, and although he admitted the possibility of "exciting" environmental events, he rejected the weight placed on such experiences by Freud and psychoanalysis. His medical training is reflected in the taken-for-granted descriptions of inversion as "unfortunate," "abnormal," and an "anomaly." Ellis insisted, however, that it was not itself a "morbid" condition, except insofar as social hostility could render it so. He found the doctrine of organic bisexuality a plausible but crude explanation of the emergence of homosexuality. It would give way ultimately, he believed, to a more precise hormonal theory. True inversion was not amenable to medical treatment aimed at cure. The physician served best as a counselor who encouraged patients toward restraint and self-discipline in a negatively predisposed social world. It was "outside the province of the physician to recommend his inverted patients to live according to their homosexual impulses. . . ." (Ellis, 1936, p. 1936, p. 342).*

Ellis appreciated the influence of context and intellectual-political predisposition in the definition of inversion. After enumerating various such definitions ranging from vice to

*Quotations from Ellis (1936) by permission of the Society of Authors as the literary representative of Havelock Ellis.

benefit, and from disease to "sport," Ellis (1936) concludes insightfully:

> There is probably an element of truth in more than one of these views. Very widely divergent views of sexual inversion are largely justified by the position and attitude of the investigator. It is natural that the police-official should find that his cases are largely mere examples of disgusting vice and crime. It is natural that the asylum superintendent should find that we are chiefly dealing with a form of insanity. It is equally natural that the sexual invert himself should find that he and his inverted friends are not so very unlike ordinary persons. We have to recognize the influence of professional and personal bias and the influence of environment. (p. 302)

He might have added that physicians are also predisposed to "discover" inversion as a condition emerging from the body and that that is itself an additional kind of "bias"—but such comment would have perhaps dulled the intended theme of moral tolerance for "natural abnormalities" that he hoped to convey.

Like his medical colleagues, Ellis used the case history to present data on the condition of sexual inversion. Unlike virtually all other such medical case histories, however, Ellis chose to display people who, quite aside from their homosexuality, were generally healthy, happy, successful, intelligent, and sensitive human beings rather than the tortured and neurotic figures that emerged from Krafft-Ebing's work. The people Ellis described were not, on the average, consumed with the goal of "cure," that is, of becoming heterosexual, and they defended their moral character as equal—if not superior—to that of so-called normals. Ellis pointed out that the generally positive picture of the inverts in his cases was probably due to the fact that none of them had come from police files or psychiatrists' offices. They were drawn, in effect, from that "other" population of homosexuals who rarely if ever become known to the variety of "experts" charged with their control. This contrast served to emphasize the highly selective and unrepresentative nature of the clinical case history as the basis for knowledge about larger populations.

These early medical apologists for homosexuality were important advocates of social and political reform. Their argument that homosexuality was a congenital condition, however, was used by opponents as the basis for increased legal and medical controls. Ellis himself recognized this problem, although he attempted to mitigate the evaluations inherent in such medical terminology. "All . . . organic variations," he noted, "are abnormalities" (Ellis, 1936, p. 318). The argument that homosexuals are organic anomalies but not pathological simply did not win the favor of those in charge of official legal and medical definitions. As medicine expanded its boundaries to include a variety of deviant behaviors, the optimistic hopes of these sympathetic reformers were sacrificed (just as were Freud's ideas on pathology) in the name of "treatment," "cure," and the "protection" of "normal" society.

## Spreading skepticism: social change and social science research

Physicians were not the only ones speaking about homosexuality in the early decades of the 20th century, although their voices were the loudest and increasingly most respected. Gradually, literary figures and historians not only raised questions about homosexual civil rights but also presented images of such persons that questioned the tenets of pathology and congenitality. Paul Brandt in Germany, Edward Carpenter and John Symonds in England, and Irenaeus Stevenson (also known as Xavier Mayne) in the United States addressed homosexuality sympathetically in their work (Bullough, 1976, pp. 643-644; 1977).

Public as well as professional interest in sexuality increased dramatically in the first third of the century, and a series of social changes created a growing awareness that sexual activity need not always be linked to procreation. Vern Bullough (1977) suggests the following as providing particularly important arenas in which this independence could be seen and debated: developments and applications of contraceptive techniques and ideology; serious scientific, and gradually popular, study and appreciation of the virtually ignored sexual interests and capacities of women; even more dramatic scientific discoveries about the nature and control of venereal disease (syphilis, in particular); and an appreciation of the ominous implications of overpopulation. In light of this, Bullough suggests the stage was set historically for more serious consideration and tolerance of alternatives to traditional sexual values and activities.

**The Kinsey studies.** It was against the background of these developments that Alfred C. Kinsey and associates Wardell Pomeroy, Clyde Martin, and, later, Paul Gebhard, published their monumental and sensational studies of sexual behavior in America. The first volume, *Sexual Behavior in the Human Male,* appeared in 1948, followed 5 years later in 1953 by *Sexual Behavior in the Human Female*. These publications have had (and in many regards, continue to have) an enormous impact on what Americans think about sex. Although similar research had been conducted before Kinsey,* nothing of its scope or detail had been attempted. Kinsey and associates collected data from 16,392 men and women through an interview and survey (statistical analysis was done on only 11,240—5300 males and 5940 females). Although Kinsey was criticized subsequently because his sample was not completely representative of the American adult population (Cochran et al., 1954), never before had so many people provided so much information about their sexual lives outside the clinic or the church. Even the authors of these studies were unprepared for the incredible variation in and incidence of sexual practice that they found. Indeed, this theme of the infinite variety in human sexual response became central to their work. Kinsey (1948, pp. 638-639) argued that the traditional categories "heterosexual," "homosexual," and "bisexual" were but synthetic mental constructs that covered an infinite variety of actual behavior.

Kinsey was first and foremost a scientist committed to painstakingly careful description and classification. He believed that there was an unbridgeable gap between statements of fact and statements of value. He was particularly disdainful of the traditional medical categories "normal," "abnormal," and "pathological" and their effects on scientific understanding:

> Nothing has done more to block the free investigation of sexual behavior than the almost universal acceptance, even among scientists, of certain aspects of that behavior as normal, and of other aspects of that behavior as abnormal . . . and the ready acceptance of those distinctions among scientific men may provide the basis for one of the severest criticisms . . . of the scientific quality of nineteenth and early twentieth century scientists. *This is first of all a report on what people do, which raises no question of what they should do, or what kinds of people do it.* (Kinsey et al., 1948, p. 7, emphasis added)*

It is this nonjudgmental spirit of the Kinsey research that was such a dramatic break not only from Freud and other psychoanalysts but even from his predecessor Ellis. The medical heritage of pathology was simply inappropriate to understand the variation in social behavior:

> The term "abnormal" is applied in medical pathology to conditions which interfere with the physical well-being of a living body. In a social sense, the term might apply to sexual activities which cause social maladjustment. Such an application, however, involves subjective determinations of what is good personal living, or good social adjustment; and these things are not as readily determined. . . . It is not possible to insist that any departure from the sexual mores . . . always, or even usually, involves a neurosis or psychosis, for the case histories abundantly demonstrate that most individuals who engage in taboo activities make satisfactory social adjustments. (Kinsey et al., 1948, p. 201)

Kinsey and his colleagues spoke with confidence, for they had thousands of ostensibly "healthy," functioning, sexual "deviants" to support them.

---

*See Kinsey et al. (1948, pp. 21-34) for a review and evaluation of previous studies on sexual practices and attitudes.

*Paul Robinson (1976) points out that Kinsey did labor under a few preconceptions, some of which were clear (e.g., a commitment to tolerance, the norm of biologic naturalism, and science itself) and others that were less so (e.g., Kinsey occasionally displays his own preference for the heterosexual norm).

The Kinsey research addressed a variety of sexual activities, but the data and conclusions about homosexual conduct were among the most consequential (their discussions of masturbation and female sexuality might follow in a close second and third place). They rejected the mysterious psychic processes and sexual "identities" that were the stock-in-trade of psychiatry: homosexual conduct is any physical sexual contact that involves a person of the same sex (Kinsey et al., 1948, pp. 615-617). To their own admitted surprise, they found such behavior considerably more common than they had expected. On the basis of the white male sample, Kinsey (1948, pp. 650-651) concluded that 37% of the adult male population of the United States had "some overt homosexual experience to the point of orgasm between adolescence and old age"; that 50% of the males who were still unmarried at age 35 had had such experience; and that 4% of the white adult male population is "exclusively homosexual throughout their lives." That means, Kinsey (1948, p. 623) interpreted, more than one male in every three that one passes on the street has had an adult homosexual experience. Predictably, the incidence data for women were lower: 13% had had such an adult experience to orgasm; 26% still single at age 45 reported a homosexual orgasm, and less than 3% of the women were exclusively homosexual throughout their lives (Kinsey et al., 1953, p. 487). The immediate effect of these data was, of course, to hail such conduct as a fact of sexual life; quite aside from cultural ideals, homosexual behavior clearly was not rare.

Having documented such incidence, Kinsey offered what he considered to be the only legitimate explanation: it was a perfectly natural phenomenon. Human beings possess, like their mammalian relatives, the biological capacity for sexual stimulation. The particular source of that stimulation (e.g., male, female, animal, self) in no way precludes and is biologically independent of that capacity. The fact that we develop strongly held ideas about the proper nature of this source of stimulation is a testimony not to nature but to culture and social values. Through learning cultural proscriptions, we effectively come to deny the suitability of certain of these sources. Kinsey's data showed that this cultural learning and socialization was not foolproof. Contrary to age-old social norms, a significant number of people, and apparently without dire psychological consequences, had engaged in a variety of such forbidden, homosexual conduct.

Following directly from this explanation was one of Kinsey's most startling conclusions about homosexuality: it simply did not exist. There were only homosexual acts and homosexual relationships; as an "identity" or a disease entity—as a "thing" independent of those who constructed it as a category—it did not exist (Kinsey et al., 1948, pp. 616-617). It was (in particular) a medical artifact rather than either a congenital or psychic condition of the human species. It followed directly that if homosexuality did not exist either in people's heads or bodies, it certainly could not be a problem for explanation, unless such explanation would be of its origins and rise as a diagnosis or of social and cultural reactions to the conduct involved. What did exist was same-sex behavior, which one could attempt to explain.* Kinsey summarized what he and his colleagues (1953) believed to be the most important factors in such an explanation:

> (1) the basic physiological capacity of every mammal to respond to any sufficent stimulus; (2) the accident which leads an individual into his or her first sexual experience with a person of the same sex; (3) the conditioning effects of such experience; and (4) the indirect but powerful conditioning which the opinions of other persons and social codes may have on an individual's decision to accept or reject this type of sexual contact. (p. 447)

In short, homosexual conduct was learned and therefore a question of "choice" (Kinsey et al.,

---

*Kinsey himself, however, had difficulty avoiding usage of the terms "homosexuality" and "homosexual" as typifications of individuals. His well-known seven-point continuum ranging from "exclusively heterosexual" to "exclusively homosexual" (Kinsey et al., 1948, pp. 636-641) also contributes to what he elsewhere tried to avoid—the characterization of persons as types of sexual beings rather than reserving the use of such terms as adjectives to describe behaviors.

1948, p. 661). The fact that we are called on to provide an "explanation" of it is more a reflection of these larger social and cultural constraints than a testimony to its inherent pathological nature.

The conclusions of the Kinsey research did not stand alone. By midcentury a growing body of social science research took up the challenge to the traditional morality of medicine. Support was gathering for the proposition that sexual behavior on the one hand, and the way people choose to construe or define it on the other, are independent questions. Anthropological research, in particular by Devereaux (1937/1963), Ford and Beach (1951), Malinowski (1932, 1955), and Margaret Mead (1949), demonstrated that homosexual conduct both was more common than had been suspected and, in some cases, was an institutionalized part of social life. It became clear that such behavior was "bad," "criminal," or "sick" only when judged so by certain sets of cultural or dominant subcultural values and norms.

In 1956 clinical psychologist Evelyn Hooker (1956, 1957) directly addressed the question of the psychological normality of homosexuals compared to heterosexuals. Using results from psychological tests and life histories, a panel of psychiatrists was unable to distinguish the homosexuals from the heterosexual controls in terms of their emotional health. Hooker concluded tentatively that homosexuality may be "within the normal range psychologically" of human sexual behavior. Chang and Block (1960) drew similar conclusions using scores from a self-acceptance inventory. They concluded that homosexuals were not suffering a psychiatric pathology.*

The 1950s also witnessed the famous Wolfenden Report in England. The report was presented to Parliament in 1957 as the result of a special committee called to investigate homosexual "offenses" and prostitution. After meeting for over 2 months, hearing over 200 "expert" witnesses, and considering the extant scientific research, the committee concluded that "legislation which covers . . . [homosexual acts in private between consenting adults] goes beyond the proper sphere of the law's concern" (Wolfenden Report, 1963, p. 43). The committee added, significantly, that whatever homosexuality might be, it most probably is not a disease and that it fails to meet standard medical criteria for such designation (Wolfenden Report, 1963, p. 31). Although the essence of the committee report was not adopted officially for about 13 years,* its moral tone signified and contributed to a gradual redefinition of such conduct and how it should be regarded by the state. At about this same time, the progressive American Law Institute issued its Model Penal Code that recommended similar decriminalization of private consensual adult homosexual conduct.

The seeds of a new, more tolerant, and popular rather than expert-controlled definition of homosexual conduct had been sown and were growing in America. They were about to emerge into the sunlight and fresh air of public view in the form of a political movement that demanded not only respect and equality before the law but also an official repudiation of what its advocates saw increasingly as the last barrier to normalization: the medical argument that *to be* a "homosexual" is itself a pathological condition. It is to the origins and development of this political movement that we now turn.

## Rise of gay liberation: Homosexuality as identity and life-style

The rise of "gay liberation" as a cultural theme and social movement in the United States similar to the struggles waged by women and blacks may have been inevitable. Al-

*This tradition of social science research on homosexuality has been extended significantly by recent work from The Institute for Sex Research (source of the Kinsey studies). Weinberg and Williams (1974) and Bell and Weinberg (1978) draw on an enormous amount of observation and interview data to nullify the simplistic assumptions inherent in traditional medical descriptions and explanations of such behavior and its authors.

*Decriminalization of private consensual homosexual acts between adults became law in England on July 21, 1967. See Alex Gigeroff (1968, pp. 82-95) for a detailed recapitulation of the political life of this committee recommendation and the debate that surrounded it.

though larger "enabling" social change must not be ignored, the seeds of this social and political protest derive most probably from the particular contradiction of democratic ideology and actual experience found in this country.

The irony of social movements is often such: the preconditions for their emergence derive from the segregating, isolating, and discrediting definitions and treatment persons face from the majority and those who steer its "official" morality. For homosexuals, this "differentness," a sense of depravity, rejection, and inferiority ascribed by centuries of righteous, law-abiding, and "healthy" heterosexuals, had produced covert enclaves of people who were, at least intellectually, ready to challenge these ideas and their guardians. This challenge and an attempt to redefine homosexuality and homosexuals is what "gay liberation" in America has been about. What had been historically a moral "cancer," homosexuality, was to become at the hands of a largely self-interested minority something natural, worthwhile, and good. The stigma of the old meanings surrounding "homosexual" had to be removed and a new, more positive definition substituted. Under these circumstances, homosexuals would gradually become "gay" and "proud" and public (see Dank, 1971).

Underlying this transformation, however—and this is perhaps the center of the irony involved—is the assertion that indeed there *are* homosexuals and there *is* something called "homosexuality"—the entity on which most traditional moral opprobrium rested. But it has become an entity morally transformed. Leaders of movement organizations, supported by a much larger population of sympathetic others, have deemphasized questions of etiology. They argue that, short of academic and rarefied scientific debates about sexuality in general, there is no particular importance in searching for the cause of something that is good. Although the question of cause may remain important at the individual, biographic level, redefinition has turned attention to what homosexuality is. It has become a "sexual preference," an "identity" (or "role" [McIntosh, 1968]), and a "life-style."

Such formulations capture and reflect the popular philosophy of personal freedom, choice, and introspection: "Do your own thing"; "I'm OK, you're OK." Indeed, "being" a homosexual, rather than one who simply engages in Kinsey's "homosexual acts," has become the core of an identity that is both source and consequence of the political challenge gay liberation represents. As sociologists have long suggested (see Goffman, 1963; Becker, 1973), and more recently demonstrated specifically for "homosexuals" (Warren & Johnson, 1972; Warren, 1974; Weinberg, T. S., 1977; Ponse, 1978), identity and community are inextricably linked. The "healthy homosexual" (see Weinberg, G., 1972), just as the morally flawed one we have discussed, is a *social* construction, a product of concerted and conscious political activity. We will now discuss the origins and development of that activity.

**Origins of the "homophile movement."** The first groups of self-proclaimed homosexuals in America were small, secret, and self-help oriented. They used euphemistic names to protect their real purposes. Although some of these existed in the United States before 1945, they were short-lived. Between 1945 and 1950 several organizations dedicated to helping people arrested for homosexual conduct were founded that provided counsel and support. The membership of these service organizations was not exclusively homosexual but included various professional and religious persons committed to helping those in need. A social-recreational group of homosexuals (something then considered dangerous) existed in New York beginning in 1945. It was called The Veterans Benevolent Association, had a total membership of about 75, and lasted for roughly 9 years. The West Coast witnessed similar developments, the first being the "Friendship Circle" in 1947. This group consisted of a few women who circulated a mimeographed paper called *Vice Versa* in the Los Angeles area. A somewhat larger and more diverse organization, The Knights of the Clock, formed in 1949 and was committed both to homosexual and black equal rights (Humphreys, 1972).

The early 1950s might be called the beginning of "homosexual consciousness." In 1950 five men established The Mattachine Foundation in Los Angeles. They chose the name "Mattachine" in reference to medieval court jesters who spoke the truth to the royalty of the court from behind masks that protected their identities (Humphreys, 1972). Such secrecy was indeed important, for it was the period of the Cold War, anti-Communism, and Senator Joseph McCarthy. Persons who engaged in homosexual acts were considered serious security risks by the government and prime targets for Communist manipulation. The House Un-American Activities Committee scrutinized carefully the past records of those suspected of such conduct.

Internal dissension about issues of national "loyalty" fractured the Mattachine Foundation. In 1953 it gave birth to the Mattachine Society and a smaller group that became organized around publication of a magazine called *One*. This magazine subsequently developed a rather wide and successful national circulation. The Mattachine Society began publishing its own journal, *The Mattachine Review,* in 1955, and a few chapters were established in larger cities across the country. In 1955 the Daughters of Bilitis was founded by eight women in San Francisco. Organized to serve the interests of lesbians, the DOB (its popular acronym) grew slowly and privately, supportive but independent of male-dominated homosexual organizations. Soon, DOB began publishing *The Ladder,* a magazine of information and support for lesbian women by lesbian women. The magazine and the organization, even more so perhaps than The Mattachine Society, were successful beyond their founders' most optimistic expectations (Martin & Lyon, 1972).

These and similar kinds of activities throughout the United States became characterized as the "homophile" (meaning love of same) movement. The first popular (although somewhat apologetic) attempt to describe the conditions faced by homosexuals in the United States was published in 1951, *The Homosexual in America: A Subjective Approach,* by Donald Webster Cory (pseudonym of Edward Sagarin who later became a sociologist-expert on homosexuality and sexual deviance). Psychologist Evelyn Hooker (1967) and sociologists John Gagnon and William Simon (1967) contributed additional detailed portraits of the "homosexual community." Edwin Schur (1965), in his highly popular and influential *Crimes Without Victims,* argued forcefully that the criminalization of homosexual conduct in America led not only to personal tragedies but also to police corruption and a general lack of respect for the law. The topic of homosexuality was becoming an increasingly salient one among the American middle class.

Representatives of established religious denominations such as the Episcopal and Unitarian churches lent their support to the movement for respect and equal rights for the homosexual. The Council on Religion and the Homosexual was formed in San Francisco in 1965, and by the end of the decade some of these religious leaders became the strongest external advocates of legal and social reform (Bullough, 1976; Martin & Lyon, 1972). Organizations concentrating on legal assistance and reform, such as Philadelphia's Homosexual Law Reform Society, Los Angeles' Homosexual Information Center, and New York's Council on Equality for the Homosexual (Teal, 1971, p. 44), began at about this same time. Local, self-interested groups of homosexuals patterned after those in California and New York emerged in many of the middle-sized to larger cities across the country, and a nationally circulated newspaper for the gay community, *The Advocate,* began publication in 1967. Even a special religious organization, the Metropolitan Community Church (MCC), was founded in 1968 by a young fundamentalist minister in Los Angeles. A diverse, loosely-knit social movement for homosexual rights and respect was growing. The first national coordinating organization, The North American Council of Homophile Organizations (NACHO), was established in 1964, and The Society for Individual Rights (SIR) was formed in 1966 by Mattachine members in California impatient with the cautious strategies of the parent body. SIR began publishing a newsletter called *Vector* that carried analysis and criticism of treatment of homosexuals in American society (Humphreys, 1972).

As the 1960s drew to a close, the first chapter in the story of gay liberation in the United States had been written. It was a period of important organizational and identity-forming work by homosexuals in their own behalf. Although the homophile movement, not unlike most social movements, was by no means without internal dissension (see Humphreys, 1972; Teal, 1971), there was agreement at least on a highly positive, new definition of what it meant to be a homosexual. Franklin Kameny (1969), a respected leader in the movement, captures the essence of this new socially constructed identity:

> it is time to open the closet door and let in the fresh air and the sunshine; it is time to doff and to discard the secrecy, the disguise, and the camouflage; it is time to hold up your heads and to look the world squarely in the eye as the homosexuals that you are, confident of your equality, confident in the knowledge that as objects of prejudice and victims of discrimination you are right and they are wrong, and confident of the rightness of what you are and of the goodness of what you do; it is time to live your homosexuality fully, joyously, openly, and proudly, assured that morally, socially, physically, psychologically, emotionally, and in every other way: *Gay is good*. It is. (p. 145)*

The change from "homosexual" to "gay" in Kameny's passage is instructive. It represents a larger change in meaning and definition that was taking place. "Gay" was used increasingly to refer to a total life-style and a way of thinking about oneself and others (Teal, 1971, p. 44). Not unlike the change in usage from "Negro" to "black," and from "lady" to "woman," "gay" was intended to deemphasize the one-dimensional image imposed by traditional and particularly medical definitions. In many regards, "homosexual" could be seen as itself an oppressive term that grew out of a need to defend rather than assert one's human rights. It was the eve of a new, considerably less deferential, and more militant struggle for normalization. Although this mood did not begin suddenly at the end of the decade, one particular event is cited frequently as the dramatic crucible in which this new militancy was forged: the "Stonewall rebellion" in New York's Greenwich Village.

**Politics of confrontation.** The Stonewall Inn was a small gay bar on Christopher Street off Sheridan Square in Greenwich Village, sometimes called the "Mecca" for homosexuals on the East Coast. On June 27, 1969, police conducted a raid on the Stonewall premised on alleged liquor code violations. It was generally believed in the gay community that such raids were in fact to harass and frighten homosexuals (Teal, 1971). The typical scenario was for the management to be arrested, liquor confiscated, and the patrons unceremoniously and sometimes violently ushered out. Also typical was the patrons' passive cooperation. The reaction of those in the Stonewall that night was dramatically different. They, quite literally, fought back in the face of what they perceived as unfair, corrupt, and inhumane treatment. In a battle of fists, rocks, bottles, fire, and even a parking meter used as a battering ram, homosexuals forced police to barricade themselves inside the bar until reinforcements arrived. It was a resistance for which police were clearly unprepared. Over the course of the next several nights, street demonstrations and some violence between police and homosexual protesters and their allies filled Sheridan Square. To the cheers of "Gay Power!" a new, aggressive, politically attuned, and youthful homosexual presence in America was born.

Two highly influential organizations grew out of the Stonewall experience: the Gay Liberation Front (GLF) and the Gay Activist Alliance (GAA). The GLF was organized about a month after Stonewall; it was avowedly militant and politically radical to revolutionary. Its aims were to "liberate" not only homosexuals but all "oppressed" people suffering under the dominance of the "capitalist state." Many of the members of GLF were veterans of the sometimes violent student antiwar movement of the 1960s. They argued that the condition of homosexuals in American society was part of a general exploitive relationship between American economic and political interests and "the people." They insisted that only by drawing the

*Franklin E. Kameny, "Gay is good," *The same sex: an appraisal of homosexuality,* ed. Ralph W. Weltge (New York: The Pilgrim Press, 1969), p. 145. 

various groups supporting "people's liberation" together—gay people, black people, prisoners, women, third-world people—could true freedom be won. The revolutionary themes in GLF speeches and pamphlets were clear (see Teal, 1971).

The GAA was born about 5 months later, and although billing itself as "militant," its leaders and members pursued a course devoted to nonviolent confrontation and working "within the system" for political and social change. It was devoted exclusively and solely to the realization of complete and equal homosexual civil rights in American society. Open to anyone sympathetic to this goal and structured around an active committee system, GAA's constitution delineated the specific rights these "liberated homosexual activists" demanded:

> The right to our own feelings. . . . to feel attracted to the beauty of members of our own sex and to embrace those feelings as truly our own, free from any question or challenge whatsoever by any other person, institution, or moral authority. The right to love. . . . to express our feelings in action . . . provided only that the action be freely chosen by all the persons concerned. The right to our own bodies. . . . to treat and express our bodies as we will, to nurture them, to display them, to embellish them . . . independent of any external control whatsoever. The right to be persons. . . . freely to express our own individuality under the governance of laws justly made and executed, and to be the bearers of social and political rights . . . guaranteed by the Constitution of the United States and the Bill of Rights . . . and grounded in the fact of our common humanity. (Quoted in Teal, 1971, p. 126)

Avowedly more liberal in philosophy than the GLF and dedicated to a single issue, GAA was to become the more popular and probably more influential of these two organizations. Both quickly became established in California and Chicago. Within a year's time five new newspapers emerged to reflect and extend this new sense of consciousness and community: *Gay, Gay Power!, Come Out!, Gay Sunshine,* and *Gay Flames* (Teal, 1971). By 1972, over 1000 local gay organizations existed throughout the United States.

This new homosexual presence in America was based on the slogans of "Gay Pride" and "Gay Power" and was a product and reflection of the activist political climate of the late 1960s. It was celebrated on the first anniversary of the Stonewall confrontation by a public parade in New York, from Sheridan Square to Central Park, in which several thousand homosexuals and their supporters participated. The event became institutionalized as Gay Pride Day, and by 1971 it had attracted an estimated 5000 to 10,000 people in New York City (Humphreys, 1972). It was a celebration but also a public statement that the new definition of homosexuality—at least according to these participants—was here to stay.

Evidence that this new presence was being recognized and endorsed outside the gay community began to accumulate soon after Stonewall. In September, 1969, the American Sociological Association adopted a resolution condemning discrimination against persons on account of sexual preference (Teal, 1971). The American Library Association formed a Task Force on Homosexuality in 1970 to formulate a change in library classification to remove the topic of homosexuality from its then current location under "Sexual Perversion." This change followed shortly thereafter (Spector & Kitsuse, 1977). New college courses on homosexuality were being offered in a variety of disciplines across the country (Humphreys, 1972), and the National Institute of Mental Health had at about this same time called a special task force of experts, chaired by Evelyn Hooker, to investigate and reevaluate existing knowledge and research on homosexuality (National Institute of Mental Health, 1972). By the end of 1971, five states—Colorado, Connecticut, Idaho, Illinois, Oregon—had passed laws to decriminalize private consensual homosexual acts between adults. In its December 31, 1971, issue, *Life* magazine, a chronicle of popular taste in America, devoted 10 pages to pictures and a story titled "Homosexuals in Revolt."

An important component of the new definition—that gay is good and healthy—was in direct conflict with the official medical view and the vocal public statements of a handful of active psychiatric opponents. Given the development of what appeared to be a trend away from such thinking coupled with the confrontation strategy of GAA, it was only a matter of time before this important bastion of traditional morality would be attacked.

## Official death of pathology: the American Psychiatric Association decision on homosexuality

**Challenging professional control.** With effective challenges to traditional religious and legal definitions of homosexual conduct underway, gay activists began to focus attention on the "helping" professions—those who for so long had attempted to "cure" this illness. Pursuing its dramatic strategy of public confrontation, or "zapping" as it came to be called, gay activists "liberated" (a movement term meaning to disrupt and reconstitute in "more appropriate" form) a session of formal papers at the annual meeting of the American Psychiatric Association on May 14, 1970, in San Francisco (Teal, 1971). The particular target of this attack was a presentation on "aversion therapy," a popular form of behavior control used in the clinical treatment of homosexuals. This treatment in effect punishes emotional responses toward same-sex others (typically, with electric shock) and rewards positive responses toward opposite-sex others. In a later session at the same meeting, a gay activist shouted from the audience at Irving Bieber and his colleagues:

> You are the pigs who make it possible for the cops to beat homosexuals: they call us queer; you—so politely—call us sick. But it's the same thing. You make possible the beatings and rapes in prisons, you are implicated in the torturous cures perpetrated on desperate homosexuals. (Quoted in Teal, 1971, p. 295)

This initial challenge to the medical establishment view of homosexuality was clearly not to be on its own "rational," scientific terms.

Similar confrontations were staged that year at meetings of the American Medical Association against Dr. Charles Socarides, a nurses' seminar on the East Coast, the national convention of American psychologists held in Los Angeles, and a conference on behavior modification (Teal, 1971). Donn Teal, in his book *The Gay Militants*, gives a detailed account of the closing of the "liberated" session at this last conference. A gay activist addressed the behaviorists, pointing up the significance of what had happened:

> large meetings such as the one you have had here today happen in Los Angeles each year. Most of them come and go and nobody but the families of those involved know that they came . . . [but] we noticed you—and the Associated Press and United Press noticed you, and this little episode that we had with you this morning is going out on the wires right now, and everybody in the country is being told that psychologists and homosexuals were *talking* together and we think that's news. I would like to thank . . . the kind people who had the good sense to send the police away. It would have been . . . inconvenient for us to have been in jail this weekend, but we were prepared to do so. . . . We would, in turn, have charged you with disturbing our peace, as you have disturbed our peace lo these many years. Because we cannot and will not allow it to be disturbed any more. This is the unique thing that the Gay Liberation Front does. We no longer apologize because we have nothing to apologize for. When we say "We're Gay and We're Proud," we *mean* it. We *are* proud! (Quoted in Teal, 1971, p. 300)

These challenges continued and were focused on the major spokesmen of the pathology view: psychiatrists Bieber and Socarides and their supporters.

As a result of the 1970 American Psychiatric Association (APA) confrontation, five homosexual activists were invited to participate in the panel "Life-Styles of Nonpatient Homosexuals" at the annual meeting the following year in Washington, D.C. Coordinated by Kent Robinson, a Baltimore psychiatrist, the panel consisted of Frank Kameny of the Washington Mattachine Society; Jack Baker, newly-elected (and homosexual) president of the student body at the University of Minnesota; Larry Littlejohn, past president of the Society for Individual Rights (SIR); Lilli Vencenz, active in lesbian organizations on the East Coast; and Del Martin, a founder of the Daughters of Bilitis and representing the Council on Religion and the Homosexual (Martin & Lyon, 1972, p. 249). In addition to the panel, which as expected produced stinging denunciations of the pathology and cure doctrines, gay activists made their presence known in a discussion of a paper by Dr. Bieber, a seizure of the podium by Kameny at a general session at which time he outlined the implications for homosexuals of the disease view, and an attack on a company advertising and selling its aversion therapy technology (Martin, 1971).

**Dissent from within the psychiatric establishment.** Dissent to the illness view did not come from gay liberationists alone. Significantly, some psychiatrists themselves were beginning to challenge the views of Bieber, Socarides, and others. Highly respected and influential psychiatrist Judd Marmor had edited a scholarly collection of scientific writings in 1965 called *Sexual Inversion*. The volume contained some classic works on homosexuality and represented the full range of scientific opinion. In his editorial remarks Marmor (1965) wrote the following:

> we must conclude that there is nothing inherently "unnatural" about life experiences that predispose an individual to a preference for homosexual object-relations *except insofar as this preference represents a socially condemned form of behavior in our culture and consequently carries with it certain sanctions and handicaps*. . . . In a very basic sense, therefore, our psychiatric approach to the problem of homosexuality is conditioned by whether we come to it as pure scientists or as practical clinicians. The scientist must approach his data nonevaluatively; homosexual behavior and heterosexual behavior are merely different areas on a broad spectrum of human sexual behavior. . . . The clinical psychiatrist, on the other hand, is by the very nature of his work, deeply involved in concepts of health and disease, normality and abnormality. These concepts, however, are not absolutes, particularly in the area of social behavior. (pp. 16-17, emphasis in original)*

Marmor argues, in effect, that what homosexuality "is" depends primarily on cultural and social context. To the clinician in Western society, therefore, it becomes immediately an undesirable condition at variance with the healthy norm of heterosexuality; that is, it is a pathology.

A considerably more harsh and irreverent critic of psychiatric diagnosis and intervention in homosexuals' lives is Thomas Szasz. In his 1970 *The Manufacture of Madness,* Szasz repudiates such psychiatric diagnosis as a self-serving facade for social control:

> In stubbornly insisting that the homosexual is sick, the psychiatrist is merely pleading to be accepted as a physician. . . . psychiatric opinion about homosexuals is not a scientific proposition but a medical prejudice. (pp. 173-174)

He continues, using the metaphor of the Inquisition to represent the parallel between psychiatrists and inquisitors on the one hand and patients and heretics on the other, suggesting that the disease view will not be relinquished without a struggle: "For an inquisitor to have maintained that witches were not heretics and that their souls required no special effort at salvation would have amounted to asserting that there was no need for witchhunters. . . ." (1970, p. 176). Seymour Halleck (1971), in his critique of psychiatry, *The Politics of Therapy,* enumerates the injustice done by the "myth" that homosexuality is a disease:

> Psychiatrists insist that homosexuality should be treated as an illness [footnote to Socarides (1968)] yet there is no convincing evidence that the homosexual differs in any profound biological or psychological manner from the heterosexual. . . . there . . . is no justification, even in terms of social expediency, for thinking of consenting adult homosexuality as an illness. . . . This behavior should be considered a problem only if the homosexual wants to see it as a problem. (pp. 107-108)

Finally, psychiatrist Richard Green (1972) concludes his carefully reasoned scientific evaluation regarding the illness status of homosexuality:

> What I question . . . is the given state of "knowledge" that homosexuality is by definition a "disorder," a "disease," or an "illness" . . . that orgasms between males and females are by definition better than between females and females or males and males, that the components comprising the major factor, "love," are by definition superior between males and females to between males and males or females and females. I am not convinced we have the data by which to base these judgments. I question them because they are not proved. (p. 95)

These and other professional writings of the

---

*From *Sexual inversion: the multiple roots of homosexuality*, edited by Judd Marmor, pp. 16-17, © 1965 by Basic Books, Inc., Publishers, New York.

late 1960s and 1970s make it clear that psychiatric opinion on the question of homosexuality was considerably more diverse than the pathology advocates' work suggested. This disenchantment within psychiatry, coupled with (and likely in part as a response to) gay activists' confrontations and a growing public awareness of homosexuals' experiences with psychiatry (see Hoffman, 1968; Miller, M., 1971; Weinberg, G., 1972), set the historical and political stage for the official repudiation that was near at hand.

After the 1971 meetings of the American Psychiatric Association, vice-president Judd Marmor began to raise informally the question of dropping the diagnosis of homosexuality as a psychiatric condition from the *Diagnostic and Statistical Manual*. The 1972 annual meetings of the association brought a dramatic event: a gay psychiatrist, masked to protect his identity, spoke at a session on homosexuality. That fall two important developments began that were aimed directly at removing homosexuality from the APA nomenclature (Spector, 1977).

**Politics of official nomenclature.** The Social Concerns Committee of the Massachusetts Psychiatric Society, a committee that routinely had been considering such issues as drugs, the war in Vietnam, and abortion met to consider the question of homosexuality. Dr. Richard Pillard, a counselor of homosexuals who had just recently announced his own homosexuality to colleagues (Brown, 1976, p. 205), urged the committee to adopt a statement in strong support of homosexual civil rights that, in addition, stipulated: "Homosexuality per se should not be considered an illness and APA nomenclature on this subject should therefore be altered" (Spector, 1977, p. 54). The Massachusetts Society approved the committee's resolution early in 1973, as did a regional association, clearing the way for its appearance before all regional representatives at the national meeting in May. At that time a controversy about wording arose, and the resolution was withdrawn for more work. Sponsors, however, discovered a simultaneous but independent development aimed in the same direction.

Robert Spitzer, psychiatrist-member of the APA Committee on Nomenclature and Statistics, had attended a Fall, 1972, meeting of behavior therapists at which a session was disrupted and "liberated" by members of the Gay Activist Alliance, including a man named Ronald Gold. As the result of an encounter with Gold after the meeting, Spitzer began a series of discussions that culminated in a presentation to nomenclature committee members by a contingent of gay activists, including Gold, in February, 1973. It is important to note that this presentation was tailored for its audience: it was based on a careful and thorough review of existing medical and scientific research and writing; it was sensitive—even empathetic—to the increased 20th-century demand on psychiatry to solve a broad range of personal problems (the medicalization of personal troubles as well as deviance), and it was offered in a polite but critical manner (see Silverstein, 1976). In what must have been a rather embarrassing situation for the APA committee members, GAA representative and psychologist Charles Silverstein (1976) catalogued the flaws in scientific methodology of most past medical research. The psychiatric disease theories simply had not been supported by systematic evidence, and treatment technologies, ranging from standard psychotherapy to aversive conditioning* (see Chapter 8), had not been evaluated critically. In a plea couched in the language of reason and science itself, Silverstein (1976) concluded:

> I suppose what we are saying is that you must choose between the undocumented theories [and treatments] that have unjustly harmed a great number of people, and which continue to harm them, or the controlled scientific studies cited here and in our previous report to you. It is no sin to have made an error in the past, but surely you will mock the principles of scientific research upon which the diagnostic system is based if you turn your backs on the only objective evidence we have. (pp. 157-158)

These gay claims-makers were playing sophisticated politics. By deciding to use not their own but rather their opponents' rules, that is, reason, science, and data, they risked being

*Gerald Davison and G. Terence Wilson (1973) found in a 1971 study that among behavior therapists (who in general are not physicians), some form of aversion therapy was the most preferred technique in attempting to change "homosexuals in the direction of heterosexuality."

challenged as amateurs in a professional world. The fact that their strategy was successful can be understood, we think, as a result of two conditions that characterized psychiatric definition and treatment of homosexuals at the time.

First, the scientific evidence for psychiatric disease theories was indeed sketchy and inconsistent. With the focus on this fundamental criterion of scientific evaluation and judgment—evidence—the challengers knew their psychiatric audience would have to listen. When they pointed out the morally based nature of the medical diagnosis of homosexuality, this imbalance between facts and values became painfully clear. Second, although they did not address it specifically, we believe that an important key to the successful challenge to psychiatric diagnosis was the lack of any notably effective treatment. Although the disease proponents we discussed along with others had cited various "cure" rates as "significant," rarely did such rates approach or exceed 50% of those treated. Psychiatrists were, compared to their medical colleagues, relatively ineffective in solving the problem of homosexuality, even when it was presented to them by guilt-ridden, unhappy patients. Gay activists knew this, if only intuitively, and their keen political judgment is seen in the brand of politics they chose to play with APA officials. It was the politics of science. Their strategy is a good example of how the medicalization of deviance is political in both an obvious sense (e.g., lobbying, "log rolling," the use of influence) and in a more subtle, "expert" sense (e.g., adherence to the rules of scientific evidence, winning the approval of an audience of scientific peers, and success in the practical task of solving people's problems). The ultimate success of gay critics may have been much more in doubt if the challenge could have been launched only on the former, more "crass" political plane.* But their comments had been directed to and heard by medical ears and, apparently, taken to heart. After the nomenclature committee meeting, chairman Henry Brill reportedly agreed that indeed some change seemed in order (Spector, 1977).

At the 1973 APA meetings in May, Spitzer organized a panel addressed specifically to the question "Should homosexuality be in the APA nomenclature?" Participants, in addition to Spitzer as presider, were three psychiatrists sympathetic to the removal of the diagnosis: Robert Stoller, Judd Marmor, and Richard Green. Representing the disease view were Bieber and Socarides. The only nonphysician was Ronald Gold, representing himself as well as other gay people. The presentations by Stoller, Marmor, and Green were strongly in favor of a changed classification. They were scholarly, intellectual, and premised on the legitimacy of scientific argument and evidence. Marmor held that the "pathology" of the homosexual qua homosexual came down to its contradiction of a culturally preferred pattern: heterosexuality. Homosexuality in the absence of bona fide mental disturbance was best conceived as a "life-style," and psychiatric diagnosis of it as a treatable illness "puts psychiatry clearly in the role of an agent of *cultural control* rather than of a branch of the healing arts" (Marmor, 1973, p. 1209, emphasis added). The papers by Bieber and Socarides were predictable. They gave unequivocal support to homosexual civil rights but held steadfastly to their earlier interpretations. They, too, appealed to evidence, objectivity, and research. Activist Gold captured the theme of his presentation in its title: "Stop It, You're Making Me Sick!" Gold said that his only "illness" had come from what psychiatrists had told him about "the way I love" and from social elaborations and amplifications of those dour medical judgments. Gold (1973, p. 1211) says. "It is amazing how I could have kept on believing this nonsense about homosexuality when so little of it had anything to do with my life," and that "the worst thing [about a psychiatric diagnosis] is that gay people believe it." In spite of this, he described himself and many other homosexuals as happy and healthy people due, in no small part, to the gay liberation movement. He encouraged those

*We speculate that if there were some highly effective medical technology by which the deviance of homosexuality could be changed into heterosexuality, gay activists would have been forced into a contest of much less specialized and influence-dominated politics that they probably would have lost. In addition, they would have been faced with the popular conclusion that if physicians could cure it, homosexuality must then be a disease.

psychiatrists who opposed the disease view to be as vocal and outspoken as its supporters.

In November, 1973, these papers appeared in the APA's *American Journal of Psychiatry*. In the interim Spitzer had written a statement of his own that was also published. Although he was sympathetic to gay activists' and others' calls for change, Spitzer (1973, pp. 1214-1216) was not a crusader and did not himself hold the view that homosexuality is as "normal" as heterosexuality. Neither was he prepared to endorse the "life-style" view of Marmor. Instead, Spitzer chose to define homosexuality as "an irregular form of sexual behavior" and stated that, as such, it should not be considered a psychiatric diagnosis. He proposed instead the term "sexual orientation disturbance" to refer to such persons who are "troubled by or dissatisfied with their homosexual feelings or behavior." He believed that the proposed change would help mitigate the charge of some psychiatrist-critics that psychiatrists were "acting as agents of social control" and that the diagnosis itself had been the basis for the abridgement of homosexual civil rights. Steering a course of appeasement, Spitzer closed by insisting that the proposed change would in no way repudiate "the dedicated psychiatrists and psychoanalysts who have devoted themselves to understanding and treating those homosexuals who have been unhappy with their lot." They could now simply help those same "troubled" people under his proposed new diagnosis.

When the APA Board of Trustees met in December, 1973, to consider the nomenclature committee's resolution (essentially Spitzer's position), they voted to adopt it with slight but important modifications, the most significant being that they simply deleted Spitzer's word "irregular" in describing homosexuality. The final text of the approved change of DSM-II read as follows:

> This category is for individuals whose sexual interests are directed primarily toward people of the same sex and who are either disturbed by, in conflict with, or wish to change their sexual orientation. This diagnostic category is distinguished from homosexuality which by itself does not necessarily constitute a psychiatric disorder. Homosexuality per se is one form of sexual behavior and, like other forms of sexual behavior which are not by themselves psychiatric disorders, is not listed in this nomenclature of mental disorder. . . . (Quoted in Spector, 1977, p. 53)

The new diagnosis was to be Spitzer's "Sexual Orientation Disturbance (Homosexuality)" and would replace line 302.0 "Homosexuality" in the official diagnostic manual of the association.* Gay activists hailed the decision as a "major step" in the right direction, but opponents Bieber and Socarides had been working actively in opposition to the change and were prepared to continue the struggle.

In the spring of 1973, Bieber had formed a committee of psychiatric colleagues sympathetic to the illness view. He criticized the nomenclature committee for addressing a topic on which none of its members were "experts." His committee also denounced a report issued by the National Institute of Mental Health Task Force on Homosexuality (1972) on the same grounds. Pathology proponent Socarides responded to the trustees' decision with a petition-supported demand that it be subjected to a referendum of the entire association membership. This relatively rare event (it had been used just once before involving a position statement on the war in Vietnam) was newsworthy and brought a good deal of embarrassing publicity to psychiatrists across the country. Perhaps never before had it been made so clear that disease is first and foremost what the medical profession says it is (Freidson, 1970a). The public had a rare opportunity to witness the politics of disease designation in action.

Three months of political campaigning by both sides followed. A letter, drafted by Spitzer and Gold and paid for by the newly formed National Gay Task Force (NGTF), was sent to all APA members. It endorsed the proposed DSM change, opposed the Bieber-Socarides view, and was signed by all candidates for APA offices. The referendum was part of the regular election held in April, 1974. Slightly more than

---

*Robert Spitzer was chosen to direct the preparation of DSM-III, scheduled for publication in 1980. In this newest version, "Sexual Orientation Disturbance" apparently has been changed to "Homosexual-Conflict Disorder" (Goleman, 1978).

58% of the 18,000 APA membership voted. Of those, 58% favored the trustees' proposed change, 38% opposed it, and 4% had no opinion (Hite, 1974). At this same election, Judd Marmor, proponent of the life-style view of homosexuality, was elected association president. The National Gay Task Force, a newly formed and middle-class movement organization, publicly endorsed the outcome as "strengthening our position all around" and urged that this new medical position on homosexuality be used to fight for complete human rights for gay men and women. At least officially, preferred same-sex conduct was by itself no longer to be considered an illness. It was a political victory that had indeed been a long time coming.

### Beyond sickness, what?

Although these events must be regarded as still recent and their significance therefore difficult to judge, we comment on what this official change might mean for the social control of "homosexuality" and "homosexuals" in American society. First of all, and somewhat counterintuitively, it could be argued that the APA decision does not represent demedicalization as much as a more careful and therefore more secure specification of legitimate medical turf. As Thomas Szasz (1977) has suggested, the decision was made after all on APA terms—it was the activists that spoke "scientese" to psychiatrists; who were *invited by* psychiatrists to speak. A gay psychologist, Brad Wilson, wrote and another gay psychologist, Charles Silverstein, presented to the nomenclature committee the scientific case for changing the diagnosis. The decision was hailed as a "victory," a "major step" by gay leaders. But Szasz (1977) argues, "I think the homosexual community is making a big mistake by hailing the APA's new stance . . . as a real forward step in civil liberties. It's nothing of the sort. It's just another case of co-optation" (p. 37). Critic Szasz (as well as Socarides [1976] himself) believes that the decision was intended to get homosexual activists off psychiatrists' backs. In fact, he continues, "they have merely relented on where they draw the boundaries around homosexuality" (Szasz, 1977, p. 37). This is, of course, true. The new diagnosis for DSM-III is to be "Homosexual-Conflict Disorder" (Goleman, 1978). There is no comparable "Heterosexual-Conflict Disorder" diagnosis, and it was never suggested seriously that being unhappy with one's sexuality—*except* if it is homosexual sexuality—might be a psychiatric diagnosis, a sickness. The boundaries of medical social control thus have not been erased, but rather more unequivocally drawn.* The proposed "tonic" for such illness remains becoming heterosexual, that is, sexually normal.† And were the members so inclined, nothing in the APA decision precludes a reversal at some later time; they retain final control over official medical definitions and interventions while at the same time receiving praise from liberal humanitarians and gays for their "sensible" action.

One wonders also how widespread is the popular support for the decision among American psychiatrists. In a recent survey of 2500 psychiatrists, 69% said that they usually considered homosexuality a "pathological adaptation" rather than a "normal variation" (Lief, 1977). In contrast to the optimism of Bieber and Socarides, only 3% of this sample of psychiatrists said that "in most cases" homosexual patients could become heterosexual through treatment. Harold Lief (1977, p. 111) provides three possible interpretations: first, the APA vote was cast in the name of homosexual civil

---

*A common response to the referendum by psychiatrists, including those who supported the change, was that now they and their colleagues could be more effective in helping homosexuals who really "need" and "want" help. Socarides is reported to have said that one good thing about the decision was that more psychiatrists were aware of the problem of homosexuality and might therefore be more willing to treat it rather than ignoring it as they had often done in the past (Hite, 1974).

†Treatment has now become the central theme of the professional debate over homosexuality. Not surprisingly, Bieber (1976) and Socarides (1976) counsel cure (heterosexuality), whereas a new set of opponents are considerably more skeptical (see Begelman, 1977; Coleman, E., 1978; Davison, 1976; Freund, 1977; Halleck, 1976; Silverstein, 1977). Even the recently published and widely reported research on homosexuality by Masters and Johnson (1979), although giving unequivocal support to the nonpathological nature of homosexuality, devotes almost half of its pages to the question of treatment for "dysfunctional" and "dissatisfied" homosexual men and women.

rights rather than medical substance; second, those responding to the survey are an unrepresentative group of psychiatrists; and finally, "psychiatrists' opinions on the matter have changed since 1974."

Despite claims that the APA decision would bring dramatic improvements in the social and legal status of homosexuals, we suggest that although there are notable signs of more permissive attitudes, these changes have been less than dramatic. Although the data are as yet limited, certain information and events may be noted. Sociologists Kenneth Nyberg and Jon Alston (1976) reviewed public attitudes toward homosexual behavior in a 1974 representative sample of United States adults. They found that 72% of their sample said that such conduct was "always wrong."* Based on comparable data from a 1960 study, they conclude that negative attitudes toward homosexuality and homosexuals have remained essentially unchanged despite the increased public awareness and official redefinitions that occurred during that period. Norval Glenn and Charles Weaver (1979) compared national attitudes toward homosexual relationships between adults from four surveys between 1973 and 1977. In none of the surveys did the percent saying homosexual relations are "always wrong" drop below 75%. Glenn and Weaver (1979) conclude that "there is no indication in the data that a majority of American adults are likely to consider homosexual relations to be morally acceptable in the near future" (p. 115). Journalist Grace Lichtenstein (1977) reports the result of a July, 1977, United States Gallup poll of adults in which 43% said "homosexual relationships between consenting adults should not be legal." Fifty-six percent of the respondents said they believed homosexuals should have equal job rights, but for the occupations of teachers and clergy, this dropped to 27% and 36%, respectively. Finally, Lichtenstein reports that 53% of the sample believed that homosexuals cannot be good Christians or Jews. In 1976 the United States Supreme Court allowed to stand a Virginia court ruling based on an 18th-century law prohibiting "crimes against nature" (Kittrie, 1976). The case involved an adult male homosexual couple who argued that the law and its enforcement against them was an unconstitutional invasion of privacy. Refusing even to hear the legal arguments of the contending parties, the justices indicated that the state's protection of privacy simply does not extend to such persons and conduct. There are only 23 states that have statutes specifically decriminalizing consenting adult homosexual conduct in private.

Entertainer and religious crusader Anita Bryant has been catapulted into the national consciousness in her drive against the moral "threat" of homosexuality. Aiming her initial 1977 crusade against a Dade County, Florida, regulation prohibiting housing discrimination on the basis of sexual preference, Bryant has led and/or inspired similar successful campaigns against gay people in St. Paul, Minnesota; Wichita, Kansas; and Eugene, Oregon, and again in Miami under the banner "Save Our Children." In 1978, the city council of New York City defeated, for the seventh time in as many years, a gay rights amendment (*The Advocate*, Dec. 13, 1978). Such campaigns appeal to ancient fears and ignorance about same-sex conduct while glossing their inherent violence with the patina of "Christian love"; Bryant says, for example, "I love homosexuals, but I hate their sin." Such "hardening" (if in fact they were ever "soft") of attitudes toward homosexuals was epitomized in the 1978 California elections by the Briggs Initiative, or "Proposition 6." John Briggs, a conservative state senator, introduced a bill that would have prohibited any public, self-defined homosexual from holding a position in the public school system. Until Californians began to realize that the Briggs Initiative was a scandalous infringement of freedom of speech (school personnel supporting homosexual rights and freedom of sexual preference were also threatened) and saw virtually every public figure across the entire political spectrum oppose it, they apparently thought Proposition 6 might well be a good idea. As late as August before the November election, a Field Company poll

*The degree of this negative judgment decreased rather dramatically with increased education of respondents, their being of Jewish or no religious preference, and among young, urban respondents (Nyberg & Alston, 1976).

showed approximately 60% of Californians in support of the Briggs legislation (*The Advocate*, Nov. 15, 1978). In the end, although it was defeated, 42% of California voters agreed with John Briggs. These events can hardly be said to represent a widespread popular acceptance of homosexuals as "healthy," nonthreatening people.

It is, of course, true that the APA decision has made "homosexual" and "sick" no longer "per se" (as the APA text reads) synonymous. It is public knowledge that psychiatrists, as represented by their major professional association, have voted the disease of homosexuality out of existence. Since physicians remain very much in charge of what and who is "sick," groups challenging unequal legal and social practices can cite the authoritative APA decision in their defense. A new set of sympathetic psychiatric "experts" on homosexuality have emerged from the APA struggle while those defeated appear to be losing their popular as well as professional appeal (see Spector, 1977). These new leaders can be expected to say that homosexuality is "not necessarily" an illness, but that only certain kinds of homosexuality fall within official medical jurisdiction—the types that causes people "conflict." Finally, it appears that more homosexuals are "coming out," perhaps encouraged by what the psychiatrists have done. *The Advocate* (Aug. 9, 1978) reported that "literally hundreds of thousands" marched, rallied, and celebrated during the annual Gay Pride Week in 1978. New York City mayor Edward Koch (a long-time defender of gay rights) issued an official proclamation of these events in that city. Even the APA has recognized its gay members. Begun in 1977, the Task Force on Gay, Lesbian and Bisexual Issues of the APA was an official part of the APA meetings in 1978 (*The Advocate*, Sept. 6, 1978).

We must ask, however, what gay people have "won" in this alleged victory of demedicalization. What does it imply for an increasingly visible minority (the gay movement urged homosexuals to "Come Out!") that had been considered widely as sick *and* criminal *and* immoral to be declared no longer "sick"? We suggest that it leaves such persons still "immoral," "bad," or "wrong." There are, as we and others have pointed out, certain protections in being considered "sick" that simply do not extend to the categories "criminal" or "sinner"—although the latter offers some hope for the repentant. Our historical review shows that one of the greatest "buffers" between homosexuals and state control at the turn of the 20th century was physicians willing to argue that such persons suffered a disease over which they had no control. In a social and cultural environment where same-sex conduct and its authors are fundamentally disapproved—where moral judgments are made against them—a medical diagnosis, albeit itself oppressive, provides nevertheless an official or Establishment protection against hostile crusaders and an insensitive state. In short, if a behavior is demedicalized but not vindicated (absolved of immorality), it becomes more vulnerable to moral attack. As our discussions suggest, medicalization has apparently increased in the face of political and moral repression of same-sex conduct; it may well be that as medical definitions are detached from such still "unnatural" behavior, openly gay people may face political controls that arise from the ballot box and legislatures rather than the clinic. As Edward Sagarin (1976) suggests, the personal "costs" of becoming a public homosexual may indeed be high. Some of the events of the late 1970s would appear at least to make this interpretation plausible. The image of the wise and knowing physician treating the personal casualties of this "new era" as patients suffering "Homosexual-Conflict Disorder" is one that brims with bitter irony and paradox. We hope it remains only an image.

## SUMMARY

The moral prohibitions against homosexual conduct are age-old. We have argued that this moral continuity has remained largely intact for over 2000 years, although its particular forms have changed to reflect historical shifts in dominant institutions of social control. First, such behavior was sinful, then criminal, and then for about the last 100 years, a sickness. Only recently has this latter designation been challenged by a movement striving for yet another definition, that of "life-style" or personal choice. We have attempted to trace the history of this medicalization and challenges to it.

Although religious proscriptions against same-sex conduct date from the sixth century BC, its foremost spiritual opponents were the ancient Hebrews and early Christians. Much of what is "sex negative" about Western culture may be traced rightfully to the ideals and values espoused by these groups. All sexual conduct was defined against the only fully approved standard: heterosexual procreative intercourse. Homosexual conduct was clearly far off the mark. It was "unnatural" because it contravened God's obvious intent; it was sinful because it was pleasure for pleasure's sake. It was, in short, a grievous wrong and has remained so throughout Christendom.

Canon law forbade same-sex conduct, and gradually as the Church and state became intertwined, the force of the latter was placed behind such norms. Throughout the Middle Ages such behavior became a "crime against nature" as well as a sin. The state, in effect, gave these religious rules "teeth" and provided the machinery for controlling such behavior in the name of these values. As early as 1533 Henry VIII of England decreed such offenses to be capital and prescribed the supreme penalty. This tradition of harsh legal punishment for "crimes against nature"—a category that remained only vaguely specified—became the official inheritance of the West.

The 18th century witnessed the rise of a third system for defining and controlling same-sex conduct: medicine. Crude by modern standards, medical theories proposed that one's physical and mental health were intertwined intimately with one's morality. Sinful, and particularly sexually sinful, behavior became not only wrong but also unhealthy. The moral strain from knowingly engaging in immoral conduct made such conduct doubly taxing. Throughout the latter part of the 18th century and particularly in 19th-century Victorian America, the symbol of this dangerous sexual excess was masturbation. Masturbation was believed to cause all manner of physical and mental ailments, including insanity, if practiced habitually. One of the dangers of such activity among young men was that it could lead them into "the filthy congress with one another." In other words, masturbation could lead to homosexual experimentation and a life of ruin, disease, and vice. A flood of popular medical pamphlets emerged toward the middle of the 19th century that offered "advice for the young" and their parents on how to curb this grave threat to manhood and national destiny.

By the end of the 19th century a more careful medical formulation of the causes of same-sex conduct had been fashioned out of the popular hereditary ideas of the age. "Homosexuality," a term invented by a Hungarian physician in 1869, was believed to be the product of a congenital, hereditary weakness, a "degeneration" of the nervous system that could be neither remedied nor reversed. Although such persons should not be punished for this pathology, they should most certainly be prevented from reproducing their kind. Increasingly, physicians became the experts on same-sex conduct to whom others deferred. They portrayed such persons as sad and tortured victims of a "trick" of nature. Among the most influential of these empathetic but not sympathetic apologists was forensic psychiatrist Richard von Krafft-Ebing.

The medical model of homosexuality was given new intellectual vitality in the 20th-century writings of Sigmund Freud. Freud opposed the congenital explanations of the 19th century and proposed instead a psychogenic theory based on the sexual experiences and relationships of childhood. Freud believed that homosexuality was the product of an incomplete or arrested psychosexual development involving unresolved conflict between parents and child. Most important for our purposes, Freud deemphasized the pathological quality of homosexual preference and conduct. Although he agreed it was "no advantage," he insisted it was not a disease. His many followers in psychoanalysis chose, by and large, to ignore this conclusion and fashioned a set of medical definitions and explanations that reemphasized pathology and urged cure, which, of course, meant heterosexuality.

Among the most vocal and influential advocates of this pathology-cure view in the middle of the 20th century have been Edmund Bergler, Irving Bieber, and Charles Socarides, all clinical psychoanalytic psychiatrists. Although all urged "humane" and "just" treatment for homosexuals, they described them as "injustice collectors," "psychic masochists," living a "masquerade of life," and "handicapped." They voiced their positions in both scholarly and popular media and were legitimated by the official support of the American Psychiatric Association.

Resistance to the medical concept of pathology began almost as soon as homosexuality was invented as a medical diagnosis at the end of the 19th century. A small number of physicians argued that although it was true that the condition was inborn, it was incorrect to call it pathological. It was rather best seen as simply a natural variation. German physician Magnus Hirschfeld and English physician Havelock Ellis made perhaps the most influential scientific arguments on behalf of this view. It was not until after World War II, however, that significant opposition to the medical pathology view began to arise. Foremost among this opposition was publication of the Kinsey studies in the United States. Not only had Kinsey and his colleagues found much more adult homosexual conduct than they or others expected, they argued that the medical notions of "natural"/"unnatural" and "pathology" were simply inappropriate to describe same-sex conduct. It was merely a reflection of a natural and universal human capacity. A growing number of social science studies and social changes that encouraged appreciation of sexuality as an end in itself combined with Kinsey's research to create a new climate of nonmedical interest and discussion around same-sex behavior.

At about this same time, and no doubt in response to the stigma and repression we have discussed, homosexuals began to form self-help and support organizations. In 1950 the Mattachine Society was founded in California, followed 5 years later by the Daughters of Bilitis. This was the beginning of the "homophile movement"—for dignity, equality, and civil rights. Buoyed by similar movements of the 1960s, gay liberation was born. By the end of the decade, new, more militant groups of homosexuals pursued strategies of confrontation and challenge. Among their foremost targets was the oppressive medical model of pathology and medical treatment. Members of the Gay Activists Alliance and Gay Liberation Front demanded that these physicians remove the label of sickness from their lives; they were "gay, happy, and proud." After 4 years of confrontation and dialogue the American Psychiatric Association voted in 1974 to remove homosexuality "per se" from its diagnostic manual. In its place they would put "Sexual Orientation Disturbance (Homosexual)" to refer only to those homosexuals who were unhappy with their sexuality. An old disease had been laid to rest, but a new disorder had been created.

The APA vote might well be seen as a victory for gay people and as an instance of demedicalization. There are, however, persistent questions that remain several years after this event. First, homosexuality is still mentioned in the APA diagnostic manual; so the sense in which demedicalization has occurred is somewhat unclear. Although the decision was hailed as a blow for civil rights, the official political situation for openly gay people in America has not improved dramatically. And although there are new experts to speak for the nonpathological nature of same-sex preference, the removal of the protective cover of the sick role leaves the status of such conduct and persons in doubt. If it is not a sickness, then what is homosexuality? Whatever else it may be, we suggest it is still considered "wrong" or "deviant" by a sizable proportion of the population. Self-interested advocates of the life-style view are left to defend their position in a political world where they enjoy only limited resources. The possibility that the old definitions of such conduct and persons might reemerge and be championed by powerful opponents should not be ignored.

## SUGGESTED READINGS

Bullough, V. *Sexual variation in society and history*. New York: John Wiley & Sons, Inc., 1976.
A detailed, encyclopedic historical discussion of "variant" sexuality from the origins of human societies to the present. Although various forms of such sexuality are discussed, most attention is paid to homosexuality. It is an invaluable resource.

Levine, M. P. (Ed.). *Gay men: the sociology of male homosexuality*. New York: Harper & Row, Publishers, Inc., 1979.

A collection of recent sociological writing and research on male homosexuality. Although it does not address the issue of medicalization at length, it provides a well-organized review of some of the best sociological work on the topic.

Marmor, J. (Ed.). *Homosexual behavior: a modern reappraisal*. New York: Basic Books, Inc., 1979.
An updated version of the important 1965 book also edited by Marmor. It is a collection of articles from a wide variety of disciplines and professions and is intended to review the state of our present knowledge about homosexuality and indicate directions for future research.

Teal, D. *The gay militants*. New York: Stein & Day Publishers, 1971.
A useful and highly detailed picture of the origins and development of the most militant phase of the gay rights movement as it developed in the late 1960s and early 1970s. Long quotations from movement people and publications provide the clear sense of ethos and direction of activist gays during this time. Unfortunately, it is out of print.

Weinberg, M. S., & Bell, A. P. *Homosexuality: an annotated bibliography*. New York: Harper & Row, Publishers, Inc. 1968.
Over 1200 bibliographic entries with brief, concise descriptions of content and findings. Although slightly dated, this is a valuable resource.

Wolf, D. G. *The lesbian community*. Berkeley: University of California Press, 1979.
An ethnographic study of a lesbian-feminist community on the West Coast. In addition to interesting insights about the contours and history of this community, the book provides an up-to-date bibliography of important writings on lesbians in America.

# 8 MEDICINE and CRIME

## THE SEARCH for the BORN CRIMINAL and the MEDICAL CONTROL of CRIMINALITY

**Richard Moran**

INTRODUCTORY NOTE

Medical and biological approaches to crime came into prominence in the middle-to-late 19th century and continue to have their advocates today. In this chapter Richard Moran traces the historical development of the medical and criminological search for the "born criminal." While the early theories have been soundly discredited, Moran finds contemporary biomedical theories of "criminal types" strikingly similar, although much more technologically sophisticated. He explores the emergence of medical and "therapeutic" methods used to "treat" and control criminality, including various forms of biotechnology, behavior modification, and mind control. Although his discussion goes beyond explicitly medical controls to include various psychological technologies, we believe the latter are also examples of the medicalization of deviance and social control. Most significantly, he discusses the therapeutic or rehabilitative ideal in the treatment of criminals and recognizes the potential for its ascendance in the future. This chapter serves, in effect, as a transition from our historical perspective of the past five chapters to the more conceptual analyses of the final two.

P. C. and J. W. S.

In *A Clockwork Orange*, Anthony Burgess' futuristic novel, Alex, an ultraviolent criminal, had been given a life sentence for rape and murder. To obtain his release from prison, he agreed to "reclamation treatment," a program designed to rehabilitate him in less than 2 weeks. The prison warden opposed the new "Ludovico Technique," which was said to "turn the bad into the good." He believed in "an eye for an eye" and thought that the new treatment was unduly soft on criminals. But the orders had come from above, and he was powerless to resist them.

The aim of the new technique was to impel a person toward the good by turning his natural inclination for evil against itself. Each time the subject intended to behave criminally he would become severely ill. The only way he could regain a feeling of well-being was to change his behavior. In this way, the criminal would be turned into the perfect citizen—the person who *must* obey the law: the perfect Christian—the person who *must* turn the other cheek. Even the thought of killing a fly would make him sick to his stomach. Speaking through the prison chaplain, a weak and lonely figure, Burgess drew the moral and ethical problem presented by the new therapy. In the following passage the chaplain is addressing Alex (also known as 6655321) just prior to the reclamation treatment:

> It may not be nice to be good, little 6655321. It may be horrible to be good. And when I say that to you I realize how self-contradictory that sounds. I know

□Expanded version of an article published in *Contemporary Crises*, 1978, *2*, 335-357, reprinted with permission of Elsevier Scientific Publishing Co., Amsterdam.

I shall have many sleepless nights about this. What does God want? Does God want goodness or the choice of goodness? Is a man who chooses the bad perhaps in some way better than a man who has the good imposed upon him? Deep and hard questions, little 6655321. But all I want to say to you now is this: if at any time in the future you look back to these times and remember me, the lowest and humblest of all God's servitors, do not, I pray, think evil of me in your heart, thinking me in any way involved in what is now about to happen to you. And now, talking of praying, I realize sadly that there will be little point in praying for you. You are passing now to a region where you will be beyond the reach of the power of prayer. A terrible terrible thing to consider. And yet, in a sense, in choosing to be deprived of the ability to make an ethical choice, you have in a sense really chosen the good. So I shall like to think. So, God help us all, 6655321, I shall like to think. (Burgess, 1963, pp. 97-98)*

Hence Alex, deprived of the ability to make moral choices, ceased to remain a person. Some may argue that what happened to him was merely the consequence of his choice to commit a crime, that he got what he deserved. But it was much more than that. Government functionaries, who cared little for the "subtleties" of ethical questions, had used these so-called therapeutic techniques for political purposes. As Dr. Brodsky, the chief technician, said in response to the chaplain's complaint about Alex's loss of moral choice: "We are not concerned with motives, with higher ethics. We are concerned only with cutting down crime. . . ." To which the minister of interior added: "And . . . with relieving the ghastly congestion in our prisons" (Burgess, 1963, p. 128). In the process of appealing to the public's fear of crime and violence to win reelection, they turned Alex, and by extension an entire society, into "a clockwork orange"—something mechanical that only appears organic.

*A *clockwork orange,* by Anthony Burgess. Copyright © 1962 by Anthony Burgess. Copyright © 1963 by W. W. Norton & Co., Inc. With the permission of W. W. Norton & Co., Inc.

## THE THERAPEUTIC IDEAL AND THE SEARCH FOR THE BORN CRIMINAL

The notion that the state should function in a parental and therapeutic role probably originated in the English common law concept of *parens patriae*. The king, through his chancellor, the keeper of the King's conscience, was responsible for the care and protection of all those unable to look after themselves because of physical or mental infirmities. The king's law included sanctions against behavior that offended the public welfare and morals, as well as behavior that directly harmed individuals. In 17th- and 18th-century England, both the criminal and the pauper were subject to the law; those convicted of a crime were sent to prison, and those found to be paupers were sent to the workhouse (Kittrie, 1971, p. 357).

The *parens patriae* power of the state remained relatively unchallenged until the epoch-making work of an untrained Italian jurist, Cesare di Beccaria. In July, 1764, Beccaria published an essay, *Trattato dei delitti e delle pene* (Essay on Crime and Punishment), in which he made an extraordinary plea for the reform of European criminal law. So devastating was the 26-year-old Beccaria's challenge to the existing criminal justice system that he decided to publish his now-famous essay anonymously (Paolucci, 1963, pp ix-xi). In *Trattato dei delitti e delle pene* Beccaria, relying heavily on the work of the French rationalists Montesquieu, Rousseau, and Voltaire, proposed equal application of the law and the development of procedural safeguards. Although the Church of Rome denounced Beccaria for sacrilege and heresy, and officials in Milan accused him of sedition, his essay was an immediate success. Its tightly reasoned arguments and its commonsense approach to the administration of criminal justice engendered enormous public support. Beccaria believed that an individual could determine his own destiny through reason and knowledge and that the desire to avoid pain and pursue pleasure was the strongest motivational force (Monachesi, 1955). Beccaria's Classical School of

Criminology was concerned with the legal concept of crime and punishment, not the study of the criminal as a biological or social type. Placed against a background of a rampantly abusive and blatantly arbitrary application of the criminal law, equal protection and the limitation of penal sanctions to punish overt actions, rather than to enforce public standards of morals and virtue, became the wave of progress for the next century.

Becarria's dream was never to be fully realized. Biological explanations of crime and human behavior that had been popular since antiquity began to reassert themselves. Physiognomy, the pseudoscience that judged a person's character by the structure and appearance of his face, was perhaps the first "scientific" attempt to understand human behavior in terms of biology. It can be traced to Aristotle's (1809) *History of Animals of Aristotle and A Treatise of Physiognomy*. Aristotle argued that a person who had facial features resembling an animal's, also had the temperament commonly associated with that animal. For example, if a person resembled an owl, he was wise; if he resembled a bulldog, he was tenacious; if he resembled a weasel, he was sneaky. At the end of the 18th century John Caspar Lavater developed this concept to its fullest. He believed that the mind and body were interdependent and that the nature of a person's soul was written on his face. Lavater (1804) produced a detailed map of the human face, relating various shapes and structures to personality and character traits. Today physiognomy is no longer given any scientific credence—it is mostly practiced by fortunetellers at carnivals—but the notion the "face mirrors the soul" is still held to, at some level, by a significant portion of the American population (Dion, 1972).

At the beginning of the 19th century Franz Joseph Gall and John Caspar Spurzheim published a two-volume work on the new science of phrenology.* Gall and Spurzheim theorized that the brain controlled mental capacity and temperament, and by measuring the shape and contour of the skull, it was possible to index the various mental characteristics of an individual. Gall originally catalogued 26 psychological characteristics (Spurzheim expanded this to 35) that made up the emotional and intellectual portions of the brain. The emotional, or lower, propensities, such as combativeness, amativeness, and destructiveness, were dominated by the higher intellectual faculties of friendship, veneration, and firmness. Crime and violent behavior occurred, however, when one of the lower propensities, through an imbalance of forces, came to dominate the personality, for example, the domination of amativeness led to rape, and the domination of destructiveness led to arson (Fink, 1938, pp. 1-19).

*For a description of Spurzheim's and Gall's work, see Fink (1938).

## Lombroso and the emergence of a biological criminology

Although phrenology enjoyed a tremendous popularity in scholarly circles during the early part of the 19th century, by the middle of the century it had been eclipsed by psychiatry. The search for the "born criminal" received a major push, however, with the work of Cesare Lombroso.* In 1864, while working as a physician in the Italian Army, Lombroso observed that many of the disruptive soldiers were tattooed. He wrote: "From the beginning I was struck by a characteristic that distinguished the honest soldier from his vicious comrade: the extent to which the latter was tattooed and the indecency of the designs that covered his body" (quoted in Lombroso-Ferrero, 1972, p. xii). Drawing on contemporary scientific theories, Lombroso believed that physical characteristics could be correlated with inward psychological traits. Therefore he concluded that tattoos reflected the "primitive nature" of the troublesome soliders. Lombroso was so stimulated by his initial observations that he later conducted a thorough anthropometric study of convicts in Italian prisons. These early studies led him to conclude that the criminal could be distinguished from the non-

*For a description of the intellectual antecedents of Lombroso's work, see Gina Lombroso-Ferrero (1972, pp. v-xx).

criminal by certain physical characteristics, which he called stigmata:

> deviation in head size . . . asymmetry of the face; excessive dimensions of the jaw and cheek bones; eye defects and peculiarities; ears of unusual size, or occasionally very small, or standing out from the head as do those of a chimpanzee; nose twisted, upturned, or flattened in thieves, or aquiline or beak-like in murderers, or with a tip rising like a peal from swollen nostrils; lips fleshy . . . excessive length of arms, supernumerary fingers and toes; imbalance of the hemispheres of the brain (asymmetry of cranium). (Quoted in Wolfgang, 1960, p. 181)

Because Lombroso believed that these stigmata closely resembled the characteristics of primitive people, he theorized that the criminal was a biological throwback, an atavistic being unable to avoid criminality in a modern world. His theory of *atavism* was given apparent support when in 1876, while working in the forensic laboratory at the University of Pavia, Lombroso performed a postmortem examination on a famous Italian bandit named Vilella. On completion of the examination Lombroso reported finding a peculiar depression at the base of the skull, which he named, because of its location, the *median occipital fossa*. This depression was ordinarily found in the lower animals, being most developed in birds. In recalling the effect this examination had on his subsequent understanding of criminals, Lombroso wrote:

> This was not merely an idea, but a revelation. At the sight of that skull, I seemed to see all of a sudden, lighted up as a vast plain under a flaming sky, the problem of the nature of the criminal—an atavistic being who reproduces in his person the ferocious instincts of primitive humanity and the inferior animals. (Quoted in Wolfgang, 1960, p. 184)

With the publication of *L'Uomo delinquente* (Criminal Man) in 1876 Lombroso succeeded in shifting attention away from the criminal law and toward the scientific study of the individual offender. The criminal became identified as a "subspecies" or "type" distinct from rational man, destined or born to be a criminal.

The search for the born criminal was taken up the following year by Robert L. Dugdale, an Englishman who as a child had immigrated to America. In 1877 he published his famous study, *The Jukes: A Study in Crime, Pauperism, and Heredity* in which he traced the genealogy of a so-called degenerate family. While inspecting the county jail system for the state of New York in 1874, Dugdale noticed that many of the prisoners were blood relatives. On inquiring, he learned of a particular family (whom he called the Jukes) that seemed to have an unusual number of criminals, paupers, and degenerates. Dugdale traced the origin of this family back 150 years. Regarding their history, he wrote:

> Between the years 1720 and 1740 was born a man who shall herein be called Max. He was a descendant of the early Dutch settlers, and lived much as the backwoodsmen upon our frontiers now do. He is described as "a hunter and a fisher, a hard drinker, jolly and companionable, averse to steady toil," working hard by spurts and idling by turns, becoming blind in his old age, and entailing his blindness upon his children and grandchildren. He had numerous progeny, some of them almost certainly illegitimate. (Dugdale, 1910, p. 14)

By 1874 Max Juke had approximately 1200 progeny, but only 709 could be fully traced. More than 25% (180) had been paupers, receiving state welfare benefits for a cumulative total of over 800 years. At least 140 of the Jukes were convicted of crimes. Of these, 60 were thieves, 7 murderers, 50 prostitutes (40 had venereal disease and were believed to have infected 440 persons), and 30 had been prosecuted for bastardy (Dugdale, 1910, p. 68).

From his study of the Jukes Dugdale concluded that although "hereditary criminality," "hereditary pauperism," and "hereditary degeneracy" existed and were transmitted from one generation to another, they were by no means beyond the ability of the environment to modify and ultimately eliminate. And since "vigor" was what separated the criminal from the pauper, hereditary crime was more amenable to environmental manipulation than hereditary pauperism. Despite Dugdale's emphasis on the role of the environment, the thrust of his study seemed to demonstrate that crime was inherited, and it was widely interpreted as such. Much to his chagrin, Dugdale's Jukes lent considerable support to the eugenics movement, which wanted to eliminate "undesirable stock" before they inflicted further economic and moral hardships on the country.

In 1913 Charles Buckman Goring, physician of His Majesty's Prisons, published *The English Convict,* a biometric study of more than 3000 British prisoners. Although he stressed the biological aspects of criminal behavior, Goring took particular issue with Lombroso's concept of the "born criminal." Goring believed that criminals differed in degree but not in kind from the general population. This view led him to postulate the existence of a "criminal diathesis" of "a constitutional proclivity either mental, moral, or physical, present to some degree in all men, but so potent in some as to determine for them, eventually, the fate of imprisonment" (1913, p. 26). In his exhaustive 12-year study Goring compared his convicts to control groups of Cambridge and Oxford students, University of London professors, and British Royal Engineers (soldiers), among others. He found that the prisoners did not differ strikingly from the controls: they showed no evidence of the physical stigmata associated with the Lombrosian criminal type. Such differences as did appear could be attributed to social class and occupational choices. Goring found, however, that his prisoners' heads were slightly narrower than those of the soldiers. He also found that prisoner's (90% of whom were property offenders) were shorter in stature and lighter in weight than the general population, except violent offenders who were taller and more muscular (p. 175).

Goring took these differences in physique to indicate that the criminal population was physically inferior. He attempted to explain the criminal's "inferior" physique by postulating that the physically weak would have less chance of avoiding the law by escaping apprehension. In addition, he argued that the sons of criminals would inherit the "diminutive stature" of their fathers. "In the course of generation this would lead to an inbred physical differentiation of the criminal classes" (1913, p. 200). In relation to "mental" characteristics, Goring found that offenders convicted of fraud were egotistic, and those convicted of violence had bad tempers. It was with respect to intelligence, however, that criminals were most easily distinguished from non-criminals. With the exception of those convicted of fraud, the criminal population was decidely inferior in intelligence. Goring concluded his study by stating that "in every class and occupation of life it is feeble mind and the inferior forms of physique which tend to be selected for a criminal career" (p. 268).

Johannes Lange approached the question of the inheritance of crime by studying the criminality of twins. In 1929 he published *Crime as Destiny.* With the cooperation of the Bavarian Ministry of Justice, Lange located 30 pairs of twins, at least one of whom was in prison. In his sample Lange had 13 monozygotic pairs (single-egg), or identical twins, and 17 dizygotic pairs (double-egg), or fraternal twins. If heredity did not play a role in criminality, Lange theorized, then a comparison of identical and fraternal twins should reveal no difference in their criminal behavior. If, however, identical twins were found in prison together more often than fraternal twins, this would indicate that crime was inherited. Furthermore, if not all the fraternal twins were imprisoned, then a three-way comparison among identical twins, fraternal twins, and ordinary siblings would yield a measure of the relative importance of heredity and environment in producing criminal behavior (Lange, 1931, pp. 38-48).

Lange's findings seemed to confirm the heredity hypothesis. Of the 13 identical twins, Lange found in 10 cases that they were in prison together. For the 17 fraternal twins, the other twin had been imprisoned in only two cases. These data led Lange (1931, p. 41) to conclude that "as far as crime is concerned, monozygotic twins on the whole react in a definitely similar manner, dizygotic twins behave quite differently"; that, in short, "innate tendencies play a preponderant part" in the causes of crime. This conclusion was apparently further confirmed by the fact that both fraternal twins were only slightly more likely to be criminals than ordinary siblings. Since fraternal twins would probably have a greater uniformity of social environment (if crime was predominantly influenced by environment), and one of the twins was already in prison, it would be expected that the other would be in prison as well.

Twenty-six years after Goring had repudiated Lombroso's doctrine of a criminal type, Ernest A. Hooton, a Harvard physical anthropologist, published *The American Criminal* (1939). Hooton introduced his 12-year-long study of 13,873 male prisoners in 10 states with an attack on Goring's work, charging that it was based on unscientific research methodology. According to Hooton (1939, p. 17), Goring had distorted "the results of his investigation to conformity with his bias" and so he had not, in fact, repudiated Lombroso. Hooton argued that the criminal population was biologically inferior and that crime and antisocial behavior were almost exclusively caused by physical and racial factors.

Much of Hooton's work was devoted to explaining racial differences. He believed that the reason races differed in criminality was that they differed psychologically, and psychological differences were the result of physical or racial differences. For example, after dividing Caucasians into nine racial types, he concluded that the Pure Nordic type is "an easy leader in forgery and fraud, a strong second in burglary and larceny, and last or next to last in all crimes against persons" (Hooton, 1939, p. 249). The dark-haired, round-headed, Alpine type ranked first in robbery, whereas the East Baltic type (Russians and Polish-Austrians) "takes first place in burglary and larceny, and is notably low in offenses against the person, except rape." Among the Old American type, sex offenders contain "a majority of shrivelled runts, perveted in body as in mind, and manifesting the drooling lasciviousness of senile decay" (Hooton, 1939, p. 374). Both Negroids (blacks with "white" blood) and Negroes "commit a great deal of homicide, they are parsimonious in sex offenses, and perpetuate a modest amount of robbery. . . ." As is true with Old American criminals, black murderers tended to be "bigger and brawnier," whereas thieves were smaller, and bootleggers were "bulky, square-jawed, thick-necked, and broad faced" (Hooton, 1939, pp. 385-386).

As most textbooks in criminology have pointed out, professional reviews of *The American Criminal* were extremely critical. Although Hooton's 107 different anthropometric characteristics were properly measured, they did not provide an adequate basis from which to theorize. Hooton failed to establish an independent measure of the "inferiority" or "superiority" of any of the traits he examined. He simply took those traits which were more often found in the prison population and labeled them inferior. He then used this measure of inferiority to explain criminality—an elementary research error, and one not easily overlooked by professional critics. For example, Edwin Sutherland (1939a) launched an immediate attack on Hooton's methodology, charging that *The American Criminal* "proves nothing and leaves the controversy [over the role of heredity] just where it was twenty years ago." Yet, Harvard University Press published a condensed version of the massive three-volume work for public consumption entitled *Crime and the Man*. Hooton's lively style and the book's amusing illustrations caught the public's imagination, and his "scientific" confirmation of popular prejudices against blacks and the lower classes added greatly to its success.

In 1940 Hooton's colleague at Harvard, William H. Sheldon (with S. S. Stevens and W. B. Tucker) published *The Varieties of Human Physique*. Building on the work of the German psychiatrist Ernst Kretschmer, Sheldon sought to chart the assumed relationship between the human physique and personality and ability. Like Kretschmer, Sheldon believed that people could be placed in one of three general categories according to body type. The three categories were the endomorph, the mesomorph, and the ectomorph. According to Sheldon et al. (1940), the endomorph had a "relative predominance of soft roundness through the . . . body"; the mesomorph had a "relative predominance of muscle, bone, and connective tissue"; and the ectomorph was characterized by a "predominance of linearity and fragility." Each type had an accompanying temperament. The endomorph was viscerotonic, that is, he was "characterized . . . by a general relaxation of the body. . . . He loves comfort, soft furniture, a soft bed.'' He was an extrovert with a ''fondness for fine food.'' On the other hand, the mesomorph was somatotonic, that is, ''energetic . . . a person addicted to exercise and relatively immune to fatigue.'' He was often loud and aggressive, meeting adversity with direct action. Finally, the ectomorph was cerebrotonic, that is, an introvert. He kept his problems to himself and was unable to relax and ''let go.'' He often suffered from ''allergies, skin trouble, chronic fatigue, and insomnia. . . . He is not at home in social gatherings and he shrinks from crowds'' (p. 236).

In his later work, *Varieties of Delinquent Youth,* Sheldon (1949) attempted to relate these body types and accompanying temperaments to delinquent behavior. He studied the somatotypes of 200 juveniles at the Hayden Goodwill Institute, a rehabilitation center for delinquents in South Boston, Massachusetts. From extensive testing of the boys, Sheldon (1949, p. 294) developed an ''index of delinquency.'' The index included such measures as IQ insufficiency, medical problems, psychotic problems, psychoneurotic traits, cerebrophobic delinquency (alcoholism and drug use), gynandrophrenic delinquency (homosexuality), and primary criminality (legal delinquency). Sheldon quantified those factors according to degree. A composite score indicated a juvenile's scale of shortcomings or delinquency potential. Sheldon (1949, pp. 107-108) related these scores back to the young boys' physiques; since both differed markedly from college males, he drew the dubious conclusion that delinquency was inherited through the inheritance of predisposing physiques and temperaments.

Sheldon's work led to a long progression of prediction studies designed to identify potential delinquents at an early age. Eleanor and Sheldon Glueck (see Wolfgang et al., 1975) devoted a lifetime to unraveling the meaning of prediction tables. Although they were the most frequently quoted authors during the years 1945 to 1972, the utility of their work has not been demonstrated. Today there is general agreement that criminality cannot be predicted with any reasonable degree of accuracy. The search continues, however, for a prediction table that works, and criminologists are not intellectually free from the legacy of the early attempts to ''weed out'' the delinquent before he (for it is usually boys that most people have been worried about) becomes an adult criminal.

Although criminology has moved far beyond such fledgling biological theories, the biomedical approach itself has evidenced a marked resilience as researchers continue to search for the so-called criminal type. During the past century the classical notion of ''let the punishment fit the crime'' gave way to the positive notion of ''let the punishment fit the criminal.'' Instead of concentrating on the development of a system of criminal justice in which the arbitrary powers of the courts could be substituted for ''the proper quantum of punishment . . . meted out for each quantum of crime'' (Geis & Bloch, 1967, p. 86), criminologists have searched for the causes of crime in the environment or in the criminal's biological endowment. The control and prevention of crime has been sought in social welfare programs, often aimed at the detection, treatment, and rehabilitation of offenders, both real and potential.

During the last 100 years the biomedical understanding of crime has defined criminal deviation more and more in terms of illness. With the absence of moral guilt, the definition of the criminal offender has changed from someone who has *done* bad (morally guilty conduct) to someone who *is* bad or defective. Hence the offender must be treated rather than punished. Yet, as Nicholas Kittrie (1971) has written: ''As more groups of people are exempted from the criminal law because they are too sick . . . to posses a mens rea [what he calls ''divestment''], the less effective the criminal law is in providing society with protection . . .'' (p. 35). To protect the state from those ''dangerously ill,'' it was necessary that the civil and administrative systems of removal be expanded. Because these systems, like the juvenile court, are supposedly operated for the ''good'' of the individual as well as the welfare of the state, the ordinary safeguards built into the criminal law were considered inappropriate. The rights to counsel, jury trial, and protection against hearsay and illegally obtained evidence were not included. Crime became viewed as a medical or scientific problem, in which the state employs medical experts to control crime. This Kittrie (1971) has called "the rise of the therapeutic state." Crime, rather than being primarily a question of morality or politics, becomes a problem to be solved by applying the allegedly neutral technology of medical practice.

## DANGER OF THERAPEUTIC TYRANNY

The gradual transformation of crime into illness opened up new possibilities for prevention and control. With medical science and technology acting for the state in the *parens patriae* (parental) role, seeking not to discipline through punishment but to rehabilitate or remake through treatment, the individual offender can be handled more in harmony with the requirements of social defense. The new therapeutic solutions to the age-old problem of crime were superior to social condemnation and penal retribution as tools of social control and coercive conformity. In a nontotalitarian state, political, social, moral, and religious values have served to moderate the operation and goals of the criminal justice system through the recognition of individual rights. The rise of the therapeutic ideal made the "major point of confrontation between the *parens patriae* power [of the state] and the rights of individuals . . . less visible" (Kittrie, 1971, p. 303). The fact that crime is a by-product of the conflict between those who make and enforce laws and those whose behavior violates such laws will become further obscured by an overriding concern for the "health" and "cure" of the law violators. Concern for health, especially community health, might justify governmental intervention and the employment of coercive corrective measures. As Thomas Szasz (1963) notes:

> Health values are . . . treated differently than ordinary moral, political, or religious values. . . . The American people approve of the right of the government to compel people to be vaccinated against smallpox, for the unvaccinated person is a potential danger to the community. (p. 5)

On the surface the therapeutic solution may appear to offer a more humane approach to the problem of crime. However, a brief look at penal history reveals that it was under the banner of humanitarian concerns that involuntary sterilization of the mentally ill, the mentally defective, the epileptic, the sex offender, the "degenerates," the syphilitic, and the so-called hereditary criminal were undertaken. Lobotomy, electric shock, and preventive incarceration of the "dangerous classes" were likewise practiced as preferable penal substitutes (Kittrie, 1971, p. 314). In an important and widely cited paper, Edwin Sutherland (1950) recognized the punitive and capricious nature of sexual psychopath laws, arguing that persons were often incarcerated for life in security hospitals under vague and futile mental health statutes. The danger of a therapeutic tyranny lies in the complete obfuscation and circumnavigation of the political, social, moral, and religious conflicts that characterize a nontotalitarian state. In place of this diversity a monolithic health standard by which to judge human deviation is offered. Just as the criminal law reflects clearly the values and interests of certain dominant groups in society, the emerging therapeutic state can be expected to protect the standards of "appropriate" or "normal" conduct and values of these same dominant groups.

To conceive of crime in medical terms is to depoliticize and remove moral judgment from the behavior in question. Much as the label "crime" allows no attention to the social environment, "sickness" removes the offending act and actor even farther from any political and ethical context. Under this definition, crime becomes a question of the individual's ability to "adjust" ultimately to the status quo. Maladjustment (crime) signifies illness; successful adjustment or conformity signifies health, and rehabilitation means readjustment. With the employment of the health-illness metaphor, a person becomes accountable for who he *is,* rather than responsible for what he *did:* "criminal" becomes an *identity* rather than a *behavior*. This was precisely the goal of Carl Schmitt, Nazi Germany's leading constitutional lawyer, when he proposed the theory of a priori culpability. According to Schmitt, a criminal was not necessarily one who committed an illegal act, but one whose character and personality rendered him a criminal (Schwab, 1970). Under a therapeutic approach to crime the criminal law in Nazi Germany became little more than a tool for political coercion and oppression. As Stephen Schafer (1974) has observed:

> This approach attempted to find what was called the "normative type" of criminal, and the penal consequences of his responsibility would be decided by the deviation of his personality—and not his actions—from the ideologically saturated and politically interpreted norm. Capital punishment under this concept would not necessarily be inflicted on a person who actually committed a murder, but on any individual who, in view of his total personality, should be regarded as a "murderer type," regardless of whether he committed a homicide or not. (p. 23)*

The danger of therapeutic tyranny lies in the fact that under a purely therapeutic approach to crime, health standards and regulations can become little more than tools for political coercion and oppression. For example, the Nazi leaders apparently believed it necessary to first define political opponents as mentally ill before ordering their extermination. Psychiatric experts diagnosed political offenders and members of racial minorities as "inveterate German haters" and dispatched them to killing centers (Alexander, L., 1949). This was, of course, merely part of a larger policy of exterminating all those who were deemed physically or mentally unfit.

## A CENTURY OF BIOMEDICAL RESEARCH

The therapeutic approach to the problem of crime has met with limited success. Although it allowed the state to expand its control of behavior by extending its *parens patriae* power over juveniles, "defective delinquents," "sexually dangerous persons," and others ostensibly in need of care, the therapeutic approach failed to prove an effective means of rehabilitation. In fact, the current disillusionment with the therapeutic or rehabilitative ideal in corrections can be explained largely by its failure to "correct" the criminal. When evaluated in terms of recidivism, the rehabilitative approach has been an unquestionable failure. In the past several years, however, advancements in medical science and rapid technological developments generated by the aerospace program and the war in Vietnam have increased greatly the state's potential capacity to prevent crime and remake the criminal.

The development of biomedical techniques to control crime is still in the experimental stage. Once such techniques become available for large-scale application, however, it is probable that the rehabilitative idea in corrections will reassert itself. The current antirehabilitation forces are sure to raise their voices in protest, and the "nothing works, lock 'em up" people are certain to become more adamant. Both groups will be silenced, however, by the pragmatists, who, in pointing to the capability of biotechnics to "correct" the criminal, will argue, "but it works."

Since an exhaustive account of current biomedical research might require several volumes, it is perhaps best for our purposes to select a few areas that are particularly significant. A sociological and scientific critique will be presented, although no real attempt to weigh or evaluate the relevant biomedical and biotechnological evidence will be undertaken. Instead, they will be described as a way of calling attention to the capacity and skill the medical profession possesses for the modification of our biosystem and to the technological capability of the state to monitor and alter human behavior. Current biomedical and biotechnological research will be examined.

The century-old belief in the efficacy of the therapeutic ideal has created a new branch of science called behavioral medicine. Fundamentally this discipline involves the movement of the medical practitioner into the diagnosis, prediction, and control of actions formerly considered to be social and behavioral problems. Just as Philadelphia physician Benjamin Rush entered into the care and treatment of the mentally ill with reckless abandon in the 18th century (Baines & Teeters, 1943, p. 759), today's medical practitioners are similarly moving into the field of crime with the correspond-

*From Schafer, S. *The political criminal*. New York: Macmillan Publishing Co., Inc., 1974. Copyright 1974 by The Free Press. A division of Macmillan Publishing Co., Inc.

ing overshadowing or ousting of the sociologically and philosophically oriented. This medicalization of problem behavior, as has been argued, has gained tremendous public and governmental support.

In attempting to explain why biological explanations of crime were so enthusiastically met at the turn of the 19th century, Lindesmith and Levin (1937) pointed to their ideological efficacy:

> For more than a century before criminal anthropology came into existence society's responsibility had been recognized and embodied in the legislation of all civilized countries. It may be that the theory of the born criminal offers a convenient rationalization of the failure of preventive effort and an escape from the implications of the dangerous doctrine that crime is an essential product of our social organization. (p. 670)*

These comments are equally applicable today. By encouraging the view that the problem of crime is rooted in the biological makeup of the individual criminal, the biomedical explanation of human behavior—currently embodied in the work of the sociobiologists—has provided a scientific rationalization for the failure of the ameliorative programs of the 1960s. Not only were the War on Poverty and the crime-prevention programs it spawned destined to fail, but, as some have argued, it was a cruel trick to play on people who, because of their biological limitaitons, could never hope to "measure up."

In addition, medicine was a prestigious mantle under which to introduce new theories and programs of intervention. For many years the public has assumed that coincident with the recognition of crime as illness there would come obvious cures. Like the problem of polio in children, medical science would solve the problem of crime in the criminal; it would be only a matter of time and money.

## Psychosurgery and the control of violence

In 1890 Gottlieb Burckhardt performed the first modern brain operation for the purpose of modifying human behavior. In the insane asylum at Préfargier, Switzerland, Dr. Burckhardt removed a small section of the brains of six dangerous and psychotic patients to render them harmless to themselves and others (Chorover, 1974a). Burckhardt claimed success for his new surgical technique, but ethical questions raised by his colleagues forced him to discontinue his operations.

Psychosurgery apparently disappeared as a medical procedure until 1935, when two Portuguese physicians, Antonio Egas Moniz and Almeida Lima, inspired by the work on chimpanzees by Americans Jacobsen and Fulton, performed 20 prefrontal lobotomies in less than a 3-month period (Chorover, 1974b). A year later Walter Freeman and James W. Watts introduced psychosurgery into the United States. The two Americans developed the technique of cutting the frontal lobes of the brain by inserting an ice pick–like surgical instrument through the eye socket. Freeman and Watts' technique was termed a success, since it reduced the operation's mortality rate to 1.7% and markedly limited the debilitating effects associated with earlier surgical procedures (Kittrie, 1971).

The medical profession gradually began to accept brain surgery as a possible treatment for psychosis and severe depression. By the early 1950s more than 50,000 people had been subject to irreversible destructive brain lesions to relieve symptoms thought to be associated with mental illness. The introduction of new behavior-modifying drugs into mental hospitals and penal institutions in the middle 1950s, however, greatly reduced the amount of psychosurgery. Today neurosurgeons perform fewer than 600 lobotomies a year (Breggin, 1973b).

During the past 5 years, both scientific and ethical pressure have been directed toward the goal of establishing a moratorium on all psychosurgery, especially on prisoners, mental patients, and children under 10 years of age. In response to public and congressional criticism, the National Commission for the Protection of Human Subjects of Biomedical and Behavioral Research was created. The commission's charge was to recommend policies outlining under what conditions, if any, psychosurgery was permissible. According

*From Lindesmith, A., & Levin, Y. *Am. J. Sociol.* 1937, *42*, Copyright 1937 by The University of Chicago.

to Barbara Culliton (1976), writing in the prestigious journal *Science,* most members of Congress were against such brain operations: "And it is probably fair to say that several, perhaps most, of the 11 members of the Commission approach their study of psychosurgery with a negative bias" (p. 299). Yet the commission adopted a report that encouraged the Department of Health, Education and Welfare to support further research. Apparently impressed by the increased efficacy of recent surgical techniques in which only selected areas of the brain tissue are destroyed, the commission took the position that recent advancements in the science of brain surgery had reduced the ethical problems normally introduced by such a procedure. In sum, the commission argued that it was ethical to destroy a portion of a person's brain (1) if it is effective, (2) if it serves the advancement of science, (3) if the patient has been chosen for the right reasons (his own good), and (4) if there is informed consent.

Although psychosurgery has been known for almost a century, it was not until the late 1960s that it became openly advocated as a technique to quiet political protest and racial unrest in America. In 1970, physicians Vernon Mark and Frank Ervin published *Violence and the Brain,* in which they theorized that an undetermined number of recurringly violent people are suffering from undiagnosed brain damage. Probably a minor form of epilepsy that cannot be detected by ordinary neurological examinations, this damage keeps the brain's deep limbic structures volatile and ready to erupt at minor provocations. Although little evidence is offered to support their theory, the notion of a disordered temporal region in the brain being responsible for violent fits of rage in a few individuals is certainly feasible and worthy of further research. When the authors apply their theory to social phenomena and begin to advocate a government-supported program of detection and surgical intervention, a problem arises, and one with obvious political appeal. For example, in 1967, Mark, Ervin, and a third colleague, Sweet (1967), wrote to the *Journal of the American Medical Association* concerning the more "subtle" causes of urban riots, that is, brain dysfunctions in the rioters:

> It is important to realize that only a small number of the millions of slum dwellers have taken part in the riots, and that only a sub-fraction of these rioters have indulged in arson, sniping, and assault. Yet, if slum conditions alone determined and initiated riots, why are the vast majority of slum dwellers able to resist the temptations of unrestrained violence? Is there something peculiar about the violent slum dweller that differentiates him from his peaceful neighbor? (p. 895)*

According to Mark, Sweet, and Ervin, the "real lesson" of the urban riots was the need to "pinpoint, diagnose, and treat those with low violence thresholds before they contribute to further tragedies." They called for "early warning tests" to screen the violence-prone from the normal population.

> The human species now dominates the earth. Our greatest danger no longer comes from famine or communicable diseases. Our greatest danger lies in ourselves and in our violent fellow humans. In order to reverse the trend of human violence, we must set certain basic standards of behavior (e.g., "golden rule" or "Ten Commandments") that any individual with a normal brain can follow. In addition, we need to find some way to detect those individuals with brain abnormalities who are unlikely to be able to follow those standards. In other words, we need to develop an "early warning test" of limbic brain function to detect those humans who have a low threshold for impulsive violence, and we need better and more effective methods of treating them once we have found out who they are. *Violence is a public health problem,* and the major thrust of any program dealing with violence must be toward its prevention—a goal that will make a better and safer world for all of us (Mark & Ervin, 1970, p. 160, emphasis added).

Apparently the view that violence is a public health problem is gaining recognition. The research reported in *Violence and the Brain* was supported by grants from the Department of Health, Education and Welfare (The National Cancer Institute, The Social and Rehabilitation Service, The National Institute of Mental Health), the U.S. Public Health Service, and the Dreyfus Foundation; in short, the mental health establishment (Mark & Ervin, 1970). Since 1970 the Neuro-Research Foundation,

*From *J.A.M.A.,* 1967, *201,* 895. Copyright 1967, American Medical Association.

which is devoted to the "diagnosis and treatment of persons with poor control of violent impulses" (Mark, Ervin and Sweet are its trustees), has received a half million dollars to do the kind of research proposed in Mark and Ervin's book (Breggin, 1973a).

### The XYY chromosome carrier

In 1965 Patricia A. Jacobs and her colleagues at the Western General Hospital in Edinburgh published their findings on 197 mentally abnormal inmates in a prison hospital in Scotland. Their work brought into prominence the theory of a relationship between the XYY karyotype and crime. Although all the institutionalized inmates were described as "dangerously violent," only seven of the male inmates examined were found to be of the XYY chromosomal constitution. The 3.5% was considered highly significant because the general population is thought to contain only 1.3 XYYs out of every 1000 live births (Jacobs et al., 1965).

The Y chromosome was theorized to possess an elevated aggressiveness potential, whereas the X chromosome was thought to contain a high gentleness component. Consequently, the addition of an extra Y chromosome presents a double dose of aggressiveness. The XYY male was considered a "double male," who is by virtue of his chromosomal constitution doubly aggressive. In a carefully worded statement, Jacobs et al. concluded that the presence of an extra Y chromosome appeared to increase the chances of an individual being institutionalized.

Research has described such XYY males as being unusually tall (Jacobs et al., 1965) and mentally dull (IQ between 80 and 95) and having facial acne, abnormal electroencephalographic recordings, and a relatively high occurrence of epilepsy. Disorders of the teeth such as discolored enamel and malocclusion have also been reported (Amir & Berman, 1970). Mary Tefler has described the outward XYY symptoms as the following:

> extremely tall stature, long limbs with strikingly long arm span, facial acne, mild mental retardation, severe mental illness (including psychosis), and aggressive, anti-social behavior involving a long history of arrests, frequently beginning at an early age. (Quoted in Fox, Richard, 1971, p. 62)

The physical stigmata thought to be associated with the XYY chromosome carrier were not cited merely for their intrinsic interest. As will become evident, these observations are important to a historical critique of present biological understandings of crime and the types of intervention programs they suggest.

The growing relationship between the mental health and law enforcement establishments is demonstrated in the work of Lawrence Razavi, a cytogeneticist from Massachusetts General Hospital, whom Mark and Ervin acknowledge for significant help in preparing the text and bibliography for their chapter "Genetic Brain Disease." Razavi was the principal investigator for a 1-year, $79,000 Law Enforcement Assistance Act (LEAA) grant to study whether dermatoglyphics (i.e., fingerprints, palm prints and footprints) can be correlated with abnormal chromosome constitution (XXY, XYY) and violent behavior in prisoners (Hunt, J., 1973). The scientific rationale for such an investigation is the fact that the skin and brain originate from the same embryological source, the ectoderm. There is evidence among carriers of Down's syndrome that a unique and identifiable palm print is associated with an abnormal chromosomal constitution and mental retardation. Hence screening dermatoglyphics may be a way of detecting abnormal genetic constitutions. The LEAA was interested in Razavi's work because "screening via fingerprints offers a cheap and efficient method to establish the incidence of chromosome aberration" (Hunt, J., 1973, p. 4).

### The Lombrosian recapitulation

These current investigations are reminiscent of the work of Cesare Lombroso. Although the techniques and methods available today are superior to the anthropometric methods available to Lombroso, current belief in the "born criminal" does not differ markedly. Mark and Ervin's diseased amygdala has its Lombrosian counterpart in the *median-occipital fossa*. Mark and Ervin (1970, p. 108) contend that because artificial electrical stimulation of the amygdala initiates rage and aggression in human patients, those with a malfunctioning amygdala have a "low threshold for impulsive violence." Both theorists point to epilepsy as a cause of crime. Lombroso believed that epilepsy was the "bond that unites . . . the moral imbecile [the insane criminal] and the born criminal in the same natural family" (Wolfgang, 1960, p. 188). Mark and Ervin (1970, p. 65) believe that temporal lobe epilepsy is "causally related to poor impulse control and violent behavior." Dr. Razavi's dermatoglyphics are similar to the anatomical measurements that characterized the works of Gall, Goring, Hooton, Sheldon, Spurzheim, and others. Jacobs' and Tefler's work invites comparison with the physical stigmata of Lombroso.

All three approaches are theoretically close to the so-called bad genes studies at about the turn of the 19th century, inasmuch as they postulate an inherited or genetic predisposition to crime and violence. Dugdale's *The Jukes*, published in 1877, and *The Kallikak Family* by Henry H. Goddard, published in 1912, are perhaps the two most famous examples. In his report Goddard argued that feeble-mindedness, not criminality, is inherited, but the feeble-minded are well-fitted by nature to commit crime. Similarly. the "new Lombrosians" believe that many criminals are biologically predisposed to crime and violence and that modern scientific technology can provide the means for their identification. This "sign" of criminality, contrary to Lombrosian theory, is not engraved on their countenances, but rather is outlined in their fingerprints, footprints, and palm prints, or in the temporal lobe region of their brains, or in the constitution of their sex chromosomes. Science can thus tell the good people from the bad, but more sophisticated instruments than the naked eye are required.

In a sense, all theories of criminal behavior contain the assumptions from which programs of social control and defense may emerge. Medical understandings ordinarily give rise to biomedical programs of intervention. For example, Lombroso's disciple Raffaele Garofalo grounded his suggestions to combat crime in social Darwinism. His emphasis on the biological deficiency of the criminal resulted in a policy of punishment and treatment that made eliminating the criminal of primary importance.

> In nature, through the processes of natural selection, the penalty for lack of adaptation is elimination. The true criminal by the absence or deficiency of the basic altruistic sentiments similarly demonstrates his "unfitness" or lack of adaptation to his social environment. Elimination from the social circle is thus the penalty indicated. In this way, the social power will effect the artifical selection similar to that which nature effects by the death of individuals inassimilable to the particular conditions of the environment in which they are born or to which they have been removed. Herein the state will be simply following the example of nature. (Allen, 1960, p. 265)

Similarly, Ernest Hooton (1939) contended that prisoners showed a definite physical inferiority that makes it necessary that the "criminal stock" be eliminated. Only by sterilizing these "defective types" and breeding a better race is it possible to check the growth of criminality. Charles Goring (1913) believed that the "real cure" for crime lay in the regulation of the reproduction of those traits associated with the criminal diathesis, namely, feeble-mindedness, epilepsy, insanity, and defective social instinct.

In this tradition Mark and Ervin (1970) called for the establishment of a prison hospital in which to study the sociobiology of violent persons. They write:

> In our view, the best way to go about gathering the information we so desperately need about violence is to start with a sociobiological study of violent persons. This study must be aimed at (1) establishing the physical and social causes for such behavior; (2) developing reliable early-warning tests for violence; (3) assessing presently available methods of treatment, including medical and surgical therapies; and (4) establishing community facilities to help violent persons—facilities that also might be used for medical and sociological studies.
>
> Two kinds of facilities are necessary for any such investigation. One is a place to house the individuals being studied; the other is a medical center staffed with specialists in the field of neurology, psychiatry, neurosurgery, psychology, and genetics. Of necessity, these two institutions should co-exist—as they do *not* today—and must be set up so that the safety of the community is not jeopardized by the violent patients. This means a building with a particular kind of physical construction, and a staff of physicians, nurses, and attendants who are capable of dealing with the violent behavior of the inmates.

> Ideally, this kind of study would be made on two groups: Individuals self-referred to the general hospital because of inability to control destructive impulses; and individuals who appear before the courts who have committed violent anti-social acts. (pp. 156-157)

Likewise, the XYY chromosome theory has given rise to newly proposed programs of early warning and corrective thearapy. For example, in 1970 Dr. Arnold Hutschnecker, one of President Nixon's personal medical advisors, proposed a massive program of chromosomal screening and psychological testing for every 6-year-old in the country. The policy was aimed at detecting evidence of criminal potential. He suggested that "hard-core 6-year-olds" be sent to "therapeutic" camps where they could learn to be "good social animals." The White House sent the plan to Elliott Richardson, Secretary of Health, Education and Welfare (HEW), for consideration and polishing. HEW turned down the proposal because it was not feasible to implement on a national scale at that time (Hunt, J, 1973).

In 1968 Stanley Walzer, a psychiatrist at the Harvard Medical School, and a colleague, Park Gerald, a geneticist at the Boston Hospital for Women, began karyotyping the sex chromosomes of all newborn male infants. Their tagging of the newborn males continued until June 20, 1975, when public pressure brought to bear by the Boston-based organization Science for the People and the Washington-based Children's Defense Fund forced the curtailment of the screening portion of the study. Walzer and Gerald, however, plan to continue the psychological testing and behavioral analysis. For the next 20 years researchers will visit the homes of the so-called affected children two or three times a year to record the parents' detailed descriptions of their son's behavior and to administer a series of psychological tests to these children. In addition, teachers will be asked to complete a questionnaire concerning the child's sexual and aggressive behavior (Roblin, 1975).

The project is distinguished by the fact that it combines scientific research with a program of therapeutic intervention. Parents will be informed if their child carries a sex chromosome abnormality, and they will be counseled on how to treat behavioral problems (Roblin, 1975). This procedure will undercut the experimental validity of the study, rendering its research findings almost meaningless. Even if a higher incidence of violence and sexual deviance is found among the XYY and XXY individuals, there would be no way of telling whether it was caused by a chromosome aberration or if it was merely the result of self-fulfilling prophecy.

## BEHAVIOR MODIFICATION

In 1913 American psychologist John B. Watson published "Psychology as the Behaviorist Views It," in which he argued that human behavior occurs in response to stimuli from the environment, conditioned over a period of time. Watson believed that since behavior was the result of external stimuli, it could be predicted and controlled without reference to internal mental states or processes. In the early 20th century, professional psychology was exclusively the study of consciousness, with the method of introspection its primary tool. Watson asserted, however, that a knowledge of such subjective states was not necessary for an adequate understanding of human behavior. He urged psychologists to redefine their discipline as the study of overt behavior, with exclusive attention devoted to the examination of observable acts.

As the first explicit statement of the doctrine of behaviorism, Watson's work attracted considerable attention. In 1920 he founded the behaviorist school of psychology and began work on a number of important experiments, the best-known of which were on an 11-month-old baby he called "Little Albert." While the child was amusing himself, Watson introduced a white rat into his play space. Little Albert's "natural" response was to pick up the rat and cuddle it. After Little Albert had played several times with the rat, Watson began to aversely condition him. Each time the infant was allowed to see the rat, Watson made a loud and frightening noise. Soon the child came to associate the awful noise with the appearance of the rat and would cry when the animal appeared. In this experiment Watson (1930) believed that he had demonstrated the new principles of *conditioning*.

In Russia, Ivan Pavlov, a contemporary of Watson, developed what became known as classical conditioning. In a number of famous experiments on dogs, Pavlov showed that not only voluntary responses like Little Albert's, but involuntary responses as well, could be conditioned. Pavlov began by observing that dogs would salivate when food was placed in their mouths. He called food an *unconditioned* (natural) stimulus that elicited the *unconditioned* (natural) response of salivation. Pavlov found that when the bell was rung before the dogs were given food, eventually the sound of the bell alone would evoke salivation. In Pavlovian terms, the originally "neutral" stimulus of the bell became a "conditioned" stimulus that elicited the "conditioned" response of salivation (Pavlov, 1927).

Beginning in the 1930s, Burrhus Frederick Skinner, an American psychologist, introduced the theory of *operant conditioning*. The central concept of operant conditioning is that of the "reinforcer." In its most common form, a reinforcer or reward is given to the subject each time he produces the desired behavior. The reinforcer is made *contingent* on the correct response. The response is known as the *operant*. The person must "operate" on his environment to receive the reinforcement. Operant conditioning is based on the premise that behavior which is reinforced tends to be repeated, whereas behavior that is not reinforced tends to be eliminated (Skinner, 1953).

Skinner's early experiments involved conditioning pigeons to move through a maze and to press various levers. As a reward, or reinforcer, the birds would receive food. After the behavior was conditioned, the pigeons continued to perform the task even when the food was not forthcoming. Skinner soon learned that the reinforcer need not be given after each successful task completion. Intermittent rewards were sufficient to maintain the behavior. Concerning the application of this principle to human behavior, Skinner (1953) has written:

> The efficacy of such schedules in generating high rates has long been known to the proprietors of gambling establishments. Slot machines, roulette wheels, dice cages, horse races, and so on pay off on a schedule of variable-ratio reinforcement. . . . The pathological gambler exemplifies the result. Like the pigeon with its five responses per second for many hours, he is the victim of an unpredictable contingency of reinforcement. The long-term net gain or loss is almost irrelevant in accounting for the effectiveness of this schedule. (p. 104)*

Skinner extended his experiments to the higher animals, eventually eliciting from them almost any behavior he desired. Taking his cue from Watson's notorious statement "Give me the baby, and I'll make it climb and use its hands in constructing buildings. . . . I'll make it a thief, a gunman, or a dope fiend. The possibilities . . . are almost endless," Skinner decided to apply his techniques to the socialization of children. He constructed the famous "Skinner box," or baby tender. So strong was his belief in the efficacy of the baby tender for bringing up children that he committed his daughter to it for most of her early years. Skinner's success with his daughter was more limited than his success with his pigeons. She was reported to have been rebellious in school and to have experienced considerable emotional difficulties during adolescence (Bowart, 1978).

Programs of behavior modification have become a significant part of the biomedical control of crime and social deviance. Although behaviorism denies that crime is caused by psychological or physiological problems, it treats socially unacceptable behavior much as a physician treats the symptoms of a disease he cannot cure. It has been integrated into the therapeutic framework and becomes part of the biomedical armamentarium. Short of "cure," the alleviation of the outward and debilitating symptoms of a disease is considered an important function of medicine (see Chapter 9).

Behavior modification differs in a number of significant ways from traditional psychologically based therapies. In the latter, behavior is considered symptomatic of underlying causes (e.g., feelings or emotions). It is these causes which must be treated if the behavior is to be successfully altered. In contrast, behavior modification does not concern itself with uncon-

---

*From Skinner, B. F. *Science and human behavior*. New York: Macmillan Publishing Co., Inc., 1953. 

scious motivations. Actions, not feelings, are important. Consequently, changes in behavior need not involve expensive and time-consuming congnitive exchanges with a therapist. Since behavior is the result of conditioned responses to environmental stimuli, understanding human behavior merely requires an evaluation of the individual's response to the environment, and changing behavior necessitates manipulation of the stimulus and/or response. In *Beyond Freedom and Dignity,* Skinner has illustrated the fundamental difference between behaviorism and the more traditional forms of psychology. The italicized phrases in parentheses represent the behaviorists' way of looking at human behavior.

> He lacks assurances or feels insecure or is unsure of himself *(his behavior is weak and inappropriate);* he is dissatisfied or discouraged *(he is seldom reinforced, and as a result his behavior undergoes extinction);* he is frustrated *(extinction is accompanied by emotional responses);* he feels uneasy or anxious *(his behavior frequently has unavoidable aversive consequences which have emotional effects);* there is nothing he wants to do or enjoys doing well, he has no feeling of crastsmanship, no sense of leading a purposeful life, no sense of accomplishment *(he is rarely reinforced for doing anything);* he feels guilty or ashamed *(he has previously been punished for idleness or failure, which now evokes emotional responses);* he is disappointed in himself or disgusted with himself *(he is no longer reinforced by the admiration of others, and the extinction which follows has emotional effects);* he becomes hypochondriacal *(he concludes that he is ill)* or neurotic *(he engages in a variety of ineffective modes of escape);* and he experiences an identity crises *(he does not recognize the person he once called "I").* (Skinner, 1971, pp. 146-147)

Recently behaviorist principles have been employed in "therapeutic" settings to modify or alter human behavior. This type of therapy is known as behavior modification. The term itself often encompasses all techniques used to change or control behavior. In a 1974 investigation of federal involvement in behavior modification programs, the U.S. Senate Subcommittee on Constitutional Rights (1974) stated that the common features were:

> each employs methods that depend upon the direct and systematic manipulation by one individual of the personality of another through the use of consciously applied psychological, medical and other technological methods. *Because it is not based upon the reasoned exchange of information, behavior modification is not a traditional learning process.* Analogous to a surgeon operating to remove a tumor, the behavior therapist attempts to remove an undesirable aspect of an individual's behavior through direct intervention into the latter individual's thought processes. The aim of behavior modification is to restructure personality and the methods range from gold-star-type awards to psychosurgery. The objective of behavior modification, whatever its form, is that the individual will no longer act in a manner previously determined to be unacceptable. (p. 1, emphasis added)

The Senate subcommittee's definition includes techniques that are not generally considered applications of the principles of conditioning, such as psychosurgery, chemotherapy, and electrode implantation. These techniques, which involve physiological changes, will be discussed in the following section. This section will employ the more limited definition of behavior modification used by the U.S. Senate Subcommittee (1974): "The systematic application of psychological and social principles to bring about desired changes, or to prevent development of, certain 'problematic' behavior and responses" (p. 1).

### Positive reinforcement

Positive reinforcement is the most commonly used technique of behavior modification. In an effort to increase the occurrence of a desired behavior, positive reinforcements, or rewards, are given each time the behavior occurs naturally. For example, Bednar et al. (1970) used money to reinforce or improve reading skills among delinquent boys. Hayes et al. (1975) paid inmates of a federal prison money and privileges to pick up litter. Marked pieces of litter were exchanged for money. Not surprisingly, Hayes found that there was less litter in areas where the inmates were paid to clean up than in areas in which they were not. Most behavior modifiers agree that money is the most effective positive reinforcer. Social reinforcers such as praise, smiles, or offers of friendship can often be rendered ineffective by the individual's peer group who apply the same reinforcers to the undesired behavior.

**Token economies.** The token economy is a clinical outgrowth of operant conditioning. Based on the priciple that behavior is strengthened or weakened by its consequences, token economies shape behavior by controlling the environmental feedback that a person receives. Several conditions define the token economy in total institutions, where they have been used extensively. First, institutional authorities designate desired behaviors through a process of value judgments and identification of the program's goals. In a prison or juvenile home, desired behaviors might include cooperativeness and a no-troublemaking attitude. Second, a medium of exchange must exist (known as the secondary reinforcer), such as money, tokens, beads, or performance points. The individual is rewarded for conforming to desired behaviors by earning a certain number of tokens. Loss of tokens occurs for behavior that is contrary to those desired by authorities. This general, or secondary, reinforcer is used because a specific reward system would require a knowledge of each individual's prized privileges. The token system operates in a manner similar to that of a market economy, where the token is a medium for obtaining a privilege or benefit chosen and therefore prized, by the individual. The third condition that must exist to define a token economy is access by individuals to privileges, commodities, and benefits (known as primary reinforcers) for which they can trade the tokens they have earned (see Kazdin & Bootzen, 1972).

Achievement Place is a residential center located within the Lawrence, Kansas, community that provides a program of behavior modification for predelinquent boys through the use of a token economy. The residents of Achievement Place are boys who have a history of troublemaking but have not as yet been adjudicated delinquents. The goals of the program include the modification of undesirable and antisocial behavior in conjunction with the development of "new and appropriate forms." On arrival at Achievement Place the boys enter a highly structured token economy in which specific desired behaviors such as class attendance, improved grades, and reduced unpleasant contact with the police are rewarded by privileges and increased self-control over their time. Through the acquisition of tokens the boys can "earn" their way out of the token system and return to their parents' or foster parents' home. The parents, who are schooled in the techniques of behavior modification while the boy is away, closely monitor his progress, with the help of individuals from the juvenile center. Should the boy regress, he can reenter the residential facility. In time, theoretically, the boys will be weaned from the token system, and the parents will be able to rely on more natural reinforcers such as parental, academic, and peer approval plus an occasional ice cream cone (Milan & McKee, 1974).

**Tier systems.** Like a token economy, the tier system seeks to motivate the individual to work his way through the system by earning more and more privileges. In a tier system each participant is initially assigned to the bottom tier where his privileges and obligations to behave properly are at the lowest level. The participant can move to a higher tier only by performing the behavior expected by the authorities. Each successive tier carries with it greater privileges, but it also requires more stringent behavior. Completion of the program requires the participant to fulfill the requirements of the highest tier, and it is possible to lose ground by being put back for inappropriate behavior (U.S. Senate Subcommittee on Constitutional Rights, 1974, p. 267).

The most controversial tier system has been the Special Treatment and Rehabilitation Training (START) program begun in 1972 at the Medical Center for Federal Prisoners in Springfield, Missouri. START, as described by the U.S. Bureau of Prisons, was intended to "promote change" in "disruptive" offenders' behavior toward the goal of allowing *them* greater control (U.S. Senate Subcommittee on Constitutional Rights, 1974, p. 263). The program was based explicitly on the principles of operant conditioning proposed by Skinner.

In its final form START combined a tier system with a token economy. Difficult-to-manage prisoners were selected from the segregation units of several federal penitentiaries and administratively transferred into the program. The tier system had eight levels, with movement to higher levels contingent on earning "good days," determined by assessing the individual's performance in the three major subgoals of the program: (1) personal hygiene, (2) work performance, and (3) social interaction with others. These subgoals were measured by a 12-item checklist, which included:

> Willingness to participate; neat and clean appearance; accepted a "no" or other reasonable response when making requests; made requests in a non-abusive manner; settled differences without fighting, wrestling, striking, or other overt, physically aggressive acts toward another person. (U.S. Senate Subcommittee on Constitutional Rights, 1974, p. 267)

Level one of the program consisted of confinement in a solitary cell with 1 hour of daily exercise and two showers per week. A good day could be earned by fulfilling 9 of the 12 criteria on the checklist; 20 good days were necessary to move to the second level. At level two the inmate was expected to maintain level one behavior plus pursue education and treatment goals. He was also expected to work cleaning the START unit. Twenty-five good days were necessary to move to level three. At the third and subsequent levels, behavior requirements were more stringent (11 and then all of the 12 criteria have to be met to earn a good day). Once the inmate had accumulated 195 good days and had demonstrated himself to be a cooperative prisoner, he had "earned" his way out of the START unit (U.S. Senate Subcommittee on Constitutional Rights, 1974, p. 266).

In a follow-up study of START participants, Scheckenbach (1974) found that of the 19 inmates who began the program, only 10 completed it. Of these, three were eventually released from prison and "adjusted" to the community, three were living in prison outside of segregation, and four were back in segregation units. These figures compare favorably with the nine prisoners who did not complete the program. Of these, only one was out of segregation, two had committed additional offenses in prison, and six were still in segregation. The fact that more than 60% of those inmates who completed START were no longer in segregation seemed to indicate a limited success. V. S. Johnson (1977), however, has pointed out that "comparison of those who completed the START program with those who did not is hardly an acceptable experimental design" (p. 419). The total START group would have to be compared with a control group of prisoners in segregation to yield statistically significant results.

The START program was controversial from its inception. In a criticism similar to others of token economies and tier systems (see Johnson, V. S., 1977), Richard Singer (1977) found that START

> neither focused on the original offense . . . nor sought to enhance [the prisoner's] chances for return to the outside world; instead START was explicitly designed to make the prisoner more 'adaptable' to the *general prison environment*. (p. 35)

The methods used to encourage START prisoners to conform have been criticized as arbitrary and coercive. The program actually used punishment and aversive conditioning rather than positive reinforcement. The prisoners received fewer privileges than they had in segregation units and, at the lowest levels, existed in abysmal conditions. In addition, advancement came to be contingent not solely on behavior but largely on the subjective assessments and "whims" of prison personnel. Like so many other "therapeutic" programs, START rapidly degenerated into an excuse to use sensory deprivation and other punitive measures on "unruly" inmates. When in 1974 the Supreme Court ruled that the selection procedure was unconstitutional because it violated the right to due process, START was stopped.

### Negative reinforcement

A second major form of behavior modification is negative reinforcement. As with positive reinforcement, this form uses operant conditioning to increase the incidence of desired behavior. Escape training and avoidance learning are the two major techniques. Escape training uses an aversive stimulus that is applied continuously until the subject performs the desired behavior. In avoidance learning, a person can learn a response that enables him to avoid a negative stimulus. For example, in Somers prison in Connecticut, child molesters were shown pictures of children and adults in sexually suggestive poses. When a picture of a child was flashed on the screen, the inmate could request to have the picture changed. If he did not within 3 seconds, he received a "harmless but painful" electric current close to the genitals. The inmates received no shock when viewing the adult pictures. After several months the inmate should have "repress [ed] completely the ability to think of children as sex objects" (Cockerham, 1975, p. 78). In addition, sexual relations with a man or a woman were reinforced. In the words of psychologist Roger Wolfe: "It doesn't really matter which as long as it's an adult" (quoted in Cockerham, 1975, p. 80).

The effectiveness of avoidance learning in treating child molesters has not been empirically verified. Such programs must be considered experimental and therefore require higher standards of informed consent. The American Civil Liberties Union (ACLU) has claimed that the Connecticut program is coercive. Even though inmates can decline to participate, they are aware that such a decision would be looked on with extreme disfavor by the state's Board of Parole (Cockerham, 1975, p. 80). The side effects of this type of therapy remain unknown. The ACLU is concerned about its possible consequences. Will the former child molester become a child murderer when he seeks relief from the pain associated with seeing a half-clothed child? Will the patient or his physician be criminally responsible? Will this conditioning produce a phobia as in the case of a former male homosexual who became nauseated every time he had to shake hands with another man? Watson's Little Albert was conditioned to the point where he reacted to all fur-bearing animals with equal terror.

**Punishment.** Punishment is the oldest known form of behavior modification. Although negative reinforcement and punishment are often equated, they are not, strictly speaking, the same technique. Negative reinforcement involves removing an unpleasant stimulus to encourage the continuation of a desired behavior, whereas punishment seeks to stop an undesired behavior through the application of a negative reinforcer (positive punishment) or by removing a positive reinforcer (negative punishment). For example, a disobedient child can be punished by being spanked (positive punishment) or by having his allowance withheld (negative punishment).

Evaluation of behavioral changes in the light of positive punishment has posed ethical questions. Researchers are limited by the amount of pain they can inflict on subjects in a laboratory setting. Most clinical studies are fraught with difficulties in identifying the effects of positive punishment on the studied behavior. Consequently, no conclusive results have been obtained. Instead, the advocates of positive punishment have relied on theoretical works for substantiation of their views. For example, in 1944, Estes explained the effects of punishment on behavior in terms of operant conditioning. He said that the effect of punishment was to evoke emotional reactions that were conditioned in a classical manner to environmental stimuli during the punishment. He further held that later exposure to a similar situation would inhibit the punishment response.

From what little empirical evidence exists, this theory would not seem to be validated. Corporal punishment, a positive punishment, was used in both schools and prisons until the 20th century with little success. In 1845 in a 250-pupil school near Boston, 65½ whippings on the average occurred each day. In the same year, 400 Massachusetts schools were broken up by disruptions. Today, corporal punishment is seldom used, and the behavior of the children is no worse (Andenaes, 1968). Until recently, flogging, mutilation, branding, and other physical punishments were used in American prisons. A study by Caldwell (1974) of public whipping in Delaware between 1900 and 1942 found that 62% of those offenders whipped were later reconvicted. In comparison, 65% of those sent to prison were reconvicted, and only 35% of those paroled were reconvicted. Allowing for the fact that those paroled were probably the least serious offenders, positive punishment (corporal punishment) was not more effective than negative punishment (imprisonment) in reforming offenders.

**Aversive conditioning.** From a learning theory perspective the primary problem with punishment is the time lag between the occurrence of the unacceptable behavior and the application of punishment. This delay reduces the effectiveness of punishment as a means of correcting behavior. Aversive conditioning has allowed researchers to eliminate the lag between the behavior and its punishment. In aversive conditioning an actual or proxy stimulus for a targeted behavior is paired with a stimulus that elicits a noxious, unconditioned response. Based on the principles of classical conditioning, the central objective is to develop in the patient a conditioned, unpleasant reaction to the undesired behavior. Electric shocks and drugs are most frequently used to evoke the unconditioned response.

Shock therapy has been most commonly used to "treat" sex offenders. Schwitzgebel (1971) identified 26 studies dealing with the use of aversive conditioning on this group, most of which used shock therapy. As in the Somers prison project discussed previously, shock therapy usually involved showing the offender sexually stimulating pictures followed by the administration of a shock. Unlike avoidance therapy, the inmate-patient does not have the option to avoid the shock by requesting that the picture be changed. In aversive conditioning there is no such option. This procedure has also been used in the treatment of alcoholism, sadism, fetishism, and transvestism (Schwitzgebel, 1971). Recently, offenders convicted of property crimes such as bank robbery and shoplifting have also been subject to shock therapy, with limited success (Singer, 1977).

Perhaps the most notorious form of aversive conditioning has been that which uses drugs. A commonly used drug is succinylcholine chloride, also called Anectine. Within 30 to 40 seconds of being injected with this drug, a person experiences paralysis of the diaphragm and cardiovascular system, creating a sensation that has been compared with death, drowning, and suffocation (Sage, 1974). While in this paralyzed state, the patient is told that his condition is the consequence of the behavior that preceded the injection. For example, in the treatment of alcoholism, the drug is injected just after the patient takes a drink. This pairing causes the dying sensation to be associated with drinking. Emetics (nausea-producing drugs) have also been used to modify behavior, most usually with alcoholics, narcotics addicts, and sexual offenders (Schwitzgebel, 1971). The patient is given an emetic such as apomorphine and just before vomiting, he is required to look at alcohol, sexually suggestive pictures, or other stimuli.

The success of this treatment is difficult to evaluate. It is especially hard to devise carefully constructed control groups against which to test its effectiveness vis à vis other therapies. In several studies dealing with alcoholics, aversive conditioning using emetics seems to have been as ineffective as psychotherapy. In other research the techniques have increased rather than decreased the frequency of the targeted behavior. A general problem is that aversive conditioning often appears to decrease but not eliminate the behavior. The patient often requires frequent "refresher" treatments and also appears to benefit greatly from other forms of therapy (Schwitzgebel, 1971). As with other behavior modification methods, aversive conditioning can produce a wide variety of side effects, including extreme anxiety, skeletal fractures, and destruction of brain tissue (Sage, 1974).

Aversive conditioning methods have been used on inmates without their consent, frequently to punish rather than rehabilitate. At Atascadero State Hospital in California, Anectine was used on black militants as well as other inmate-patients whose behavior was found to be "uncooperative" or "disruptive." At Atascadero, electroconvulsive shock therapy (ECT) was employed "not for medical reasons, but as a punishment for violation of ward rules" (Jackson, 1973, p. 44). Similar uses of aversive conditioning methods have been fully documented at other so-called therapeutic institutions, including Vacaville Rehabilitation Center in California and the Iowa Security Medical Facility (Jackson, 1973; Singer, 1977). At Vacaville, in 1971, fluphenazine dihydrochloride (Prolixin), a highly potent behavior-modifying drug, was administered to 1093 of the 1400 inmates (Jackson, 1973) for ostensibly therapeutic reasons. The side effects of Prolixin, as listed by the manufacturer, include "nausea . . . the induction of a catatonic state . . . blurred vision . . . liver damage . . . impotency . . . hypotension severe enough to cause fatal cardiac arrest. . ." (Singer, 1977, p. 35).

A number of court cases have ruled that the use of behavior modification methods without consent of the individual involved is unconstitutional because it violates the Eighth Amendment protection against cruel and unusual punishment (Singer, 1977). In 1973, a Michigan court ruled (*Kaimowitz* v. *The Michigan Department of Mental Health*) that the inherently coercive nature of mental hospitals made it impossible for a mental patient to give truly voluntary consent to experimental procedures (Singer, 1977). Since the Detroit decision the trend has been toward outlawing nonconsensual experimental programs in total institutions. However, given past experiences, it seems reasonable to assume that such programs will not be eliminated. (As one researcher told me, "If the government stops funding behavior modification programs we'll just call them by a different name.") Prisoners will probably continue to be coerced into signing consent forms, if only by the promise of early release. It must be remembered that the constitutionality of behavior modification programs themselves has never been ruled on. Rulings have only concerned their application in a closed institution and only because these techniques are currently considered experimental.

If the behavior modifiers solve the problem of correcting the criminal, they will have created a more vexing problem. What kind of ex-offender will be produced? Is the juvenile who learns to manipulate his token economy any more "moral" for his experience? Has he become a "better" person or simply more clever at getting the environment to serve his own ends? As Bedau (1975) has aptly noted:

> It has been said by some doctors closely associated with the use of these techniques that they will transform a person into a "model citizen," a "responsible, well-adjusted citizen." One is inclined to doubt whether Locke, Rousseau, Kant, Jefferson, and Mill would have agreed that these techniques can have such results. (p. 662)

## BIOTECHNOLOGY

Behavior modification can never be completely successful in controlling crime, either because reinforcers that work in a laboratory setting may differ from those in the community or because the effects of the treatment are often reversible. Researchers have attempted to solve these problems by simulating the "real world" in the laboratory or by bringing the patient in for periodic "refresher" treatments. These strategies have met with limited success. Because biotechnology allows technicians to monitor and control the patient while he lives in the community, it appears more promising in controlling potential offenders.

Essentially, biotechnology involves the implantation of electrodes into the brain through a hole or holes in the skull. The brain is then stimulated electrically until the unwanted behavior is elicited. Once the unwanted behavior is located (e.g., fits of rage, depression, euphoria), that area of the brain is coagulated with electricity. The goal is a carefully titrated lobotomy that blunts the emotional responsiveness associated with the unwanted behavior without otherwise incapacitating the individual. Although the technology is highly sophisticated, the method rests on the dubious, outdated theory that behavioral problems can be reduced to foci of disordered brain tissue (Breggin, 1973b). Regardless of its theoretical validity, the technological capability to blunt the emotions and thereby control or eliminate the unwanted behavior appears impressive.

It is not difficult to imagine the potential for political manipulation of such advances in mind control. Physician José M. R. Delgado (1969), former professor of physiology at Yale University, has outlined a nationwide program of mind control in his book, *Physical Control of the Mind: Toward a Psychocivilized Society:*

> National agencies should be created in order to coordinate plans, budgets, and actions just as NASA in the United States had directed public interest and technology, launching the country into the adventures and accomplishments of outer space. (p. 259)*
>
> The mass media must be mobilized for this purpose, and preparation of entertaining and informative programs should be encouraged and promoted by the neurobehavioral institutes. (p. 262)

---

*Specified excerpts from *Physical control of the mind: toward a psychocivilized society* by José M. R. Delgado, M.D. Vol. 41 of World Perspectives Series, Planned and Edited by Ruth Nanda Anshen. Copyright © 1969 by José M. R. Delgado. Reprinted by permission of Harper & Row, Publishers, Inc.

Delgado is currently working on direct control of the brain by computer. He points out that one can open garage doors from a distance, adjust a television set without leaving one's seat, and direct orbiting spacecraft from earth. Why not remote control of humans by computers?

> A two-way radio communication system could be established between the brain of a subject and a computer. Certain types of neuronal activity related to behavioral disturbances such as anxiety, depression, or rage could be recognized in order to trigger stimulation of specific inhibitory structures. The delivery of brain stimulation on demand to correct cerebral dysfunctions represents a new approach to therapeutic feedback. While it is speculative, it is within the realm of possibility, according to present knowledge and projected methodology. (p. 200)

The direct political potential for the control of society by those who program such computers becomes explicit when Delgado describes experiments conducted on monkeys. By using computerized remote control techniques, he has been able both to stimulate the followers to revolt against and overthrow the leaders, and to activate the leaders to be more aggressive in punishing the followers.

If Delgado's proposal for an educational program to instill respect for physical control of the mind proves successful, the "afflicted" person may come to participate voluntarily in a "therapeutic" program of mind control. Robert G. Heath (1963), in his article "Electrical Self-Stimulation of the Brain of Man," describes experiments that involve individuals who wear self-stimulation units. Such units allow people to voluntarily and selectively control their own emotional response and behavior. His experiments involve research into the pleasure and pain centers of the brain. He postulates that many mentally ill persons suffer from "inappropriate anxiety." The cure is "instantaneous replacement of irrelevant anxiety with positive pleasure feelings" (Heath, 1970, p. 87), voluntarily activated by the patient. Heath, in a recent presidential address to the Society for Biological Psychiatry, contended, for example, that drug addiction is a problem of a neurological defect in the addict's pleasure center. Psychosurgery critic Peter R. Breggin (1973b) comments on Heath's address:

> He becomes quite specific . . . when he talks about drug addiction. Is the root of the problem poverty and racism, since drug addiction around the world and in America is overwhelmingly a problem of the poor? No, it's not that. Is the new phenomenon of drug addiction among the middle class youth related to the disaffection of youth from the society? No. Does it relate to the tremendous profits made by criminal groups from promoting drugs among the poor? No. What then is the problem of drug addiction, according to Dr. Heath? Drug addiction, he says, is an attempt at self-medication for pleasure in people who have a neurologic defect in their pleasure centers. His cure then is corrective surgery or a better, more efficient pleasure producing compound. (p. E1609)

Heath's suggestion of electrical self-stimulation is in concert with the recent shift in penal practice to community-based treatment programs. These programs extend treatment and counseling to offenders during a temporary or conditional release from the institution. The treatment of criminal offenders in the community, however, presents the problem of a potential escape and increased risk to the community. This problem has plagued these programs since they were first inaugurated. The public has somehow required a 100% success rate.

In recent years there has been considerable research conducted on telemetry as a means of solving the 100% problem. A prototype monitoring system called an "electronic rehabilitation system" has been developed. This new electronic system is capable of continual monitoring of a parolee's location, voice, blood pressure, brain waves, and even penile erection. R. K. Schwitzgebel (1968) has described the system:

> As presently designed the electronic rehabilitation system is capable of monitoring the geographical location of a subject in an urban setting up to 24 hours. The subject wears two small units approximately 6 inches by 3 inches by 1 inch in size, weighing about 2 pounds. As the wearer walks through a prescribed monitored area, his transmitter activates various repeater stations which re-transmit his signal, with a special location code, to the base station. The repeater stations are so located that at least one is always activated by the wearer's transmitter.
>
> This prototype system as now used extends only a few blocks during street use and covers the inside

of one large building. The primary purpose of this system is to demonstrate the feasibility of larger, more complete systems and gather some preliminary data. Through the use of carefully placed repeater stations in each block, the system is theoretically duplicable such that large geographical areas may be covered with a large number of subjects each transmitting a unique signal. The range of the system and the specificity with which a person can be located depend largely upon the number of repeater stations used. (p. 99)

It is conceivable that in the near future all parolees, as well as those who have had their sentences suspended, might come under the guardianship of an electronic rehabilitation system. Preventive measures could be taken to render any parole violation or further criminality impossible. Hidden cameras could clandestinely watch the business district of our urban centers, as is already the case in Smyrna, Delaware; San José, California; Hoboken, New Jersey; and Mount Vernon, New York (Garth, 1974). Citizens could be licensed to carry miniature radio transmitters, which, when worn as a watch, pendant, or belt buckle, could signal the wearer's location, in the event of an attack, to a central communication unit operated by security police (LEAA, 1974). This alert system is currently being tested in public housing projects with plans for 5000 to 10,000 devices to be in operation within a year. Vandalism, arson, and robbery in public schools could be reduced by adapting the public address system for use in audio monitoring, and by installing closed-circuit television to patrol corridors, classrooms, and lavatories, as in the Alexandria, Virginia, school district (LEAA, 1975).

The ease with which the 100% problem can be adapted to include clandestine surveillance in public places of the entire population is apparent. If the public's fear of falling victim to crimes of violence continues to grow, it might be all too willing to trade its right to privacy for increased security. Witness the ease with which metal detectors, body searches, and baggage inspections were introduced into our nation's airports. The public's fear of hijacking took precedence over its desire for privacy. An individual's chance of being in a bank during a robbery is approximately 100 times greater than his chance of being hijacked at the airport. Because of the fear of hijacking but not bank robbery, the individual gladly undergoes a search by airport authorities who, because they are not public police, hold broader powers of search and seizure.

Nicholas Kittrie (1971) has used the analogy of astronauts who will some day live and work in orbiting stations to illustrate the point that if the environment is viewed as hostile enough, people will come to depend on constant surveillance for their security:

Recently a man was placed on the moon. Plans are being made for the establishment of a space station where men could live and work in orbit around the earth. In these hostile environments, it is essential that the men involved be under constant environmental, physical, and mental surveillance, for one error or miscalculation could endanger not only the individual but the entire miniature society. The men who are involved in this work must be able not only to cope with the hostile environment but literally to thrive under the constant watchfulness of some controlling authority. That men are undertaking such tasks under such constant scrutiny suggests—although the analogy is not exact—that man might adapt himself to live under the conditions of total surveillance that must prevail in a therapeutic society. (p. 351)

In a perceptive footnote to the above, Kittrie added:

In a telecast from Apollo 10, Ground Control at Houston used the epigram, "Big Brother is Watching" to describe its source of information about the space craft. One of the astronauts replied, "And we're glad he is!" (p. 351)

## CIA and mind control

In the late 1940s and early 1950s the CIA launched a 25-year covert project to develop techniques of mind control. The project involved the "research and development of chemical, biological, and radiological materials capable of employment in clandestine operations to control human behavior."* The multimillion dollar project was a closely guarded

*From an unpublished memorandum from the CIA Inspector Gerneral to the CIA Director, July 26, 1963, communicated privately to me.

secret; neither Congress nor the executive branch knew of its existence. Because of possible political and diplomatic repercussions, the agency channeled its funds through private medical research foundations. In all, the CIA sponsored behavior control experiments by 185 privately employed scientists at 80 different institutions (Horrock, 1977a).

Project CHATTER, the initial mind control program, was begun by the U.S. Navy in 1947. At that time CIA officials believed that some American prisoners of war in North Korea had been brainwashed. Project CHATTER was designed to test "truth drugs" for use in interrogations by rendering an individual "subservient to an imposed will or control" (*The New York Times*, 1977, p. 16), and to develop a drug that would prevent CIA agents from being brainwashed (Szulc, 1977). The project included the laboratory testing of substances such as *Anabasis aphylla*, scopolamine, and mescaline "in order to determine their speech-inducing qualities" (Church Committee, 1976, p. 387). During the Korean War the project grew enormously, but for reasons that remain unclear it terminated in 1953.

In 1950 Project BLUEBIRD/ARTICHOKE was added to the CIA's programs of mind control. Like Project CHATTER, its objectives were to prevent the "extraction of information" from agency personnel and the development of "special interrogation techniques" involving hypnosis and chemical and biological agents. The CIA has claimed that the original research was necessary to defend its agents against Soviet and Chinese techniques of brainwashing. By August, 1951, however (when BLUEBIRD was renamed ARTICHOKE), the agency, with its research on inducing people to perform acts against their will, was clearly looking to the development of offensive capabilities (Church Committee, 1976).

Projects MKULTRA and MKDELTA (MKDELTA was the name given to MKULTRA abroad) were the broadest and most comprehensive of the CIA programs to alter human behavior through the use of chemical and biological agents. Such techniques as electric shock, radiation, and psychosurgery were employed to control human behavior (Horrock, 1977b). In addition, the Smithsonian Institution was used as a cover to fund a study of the possible use of migratory birds in germ warfare. The National Institute of Mental Health conducted a study of the effects of hallucinogenic drugs at its rehabilitation center in Lexington, Kentucky. In the initial phase of the study, only volunteer inmates who were rewarded with the drug of their addiction were experimented on. By the final stages of the study, however, LSD was being administered surreptitiously to unwitting human subjects, the details of which have been outlined in the Church Committee Report (1976).

There is little question that the CIA was interested in the political uses of biomedical research. The agency conducted medical experimentation that often violated the Nuremburg code of ethics. In its drugging of unwitting patrons of bars in New York and San Francisco, the LSD experiments on prisoners at federal penitentiaries, and the knockout drug testing on unknowing terminal cancer patients, the agency evidenced a fundamental disregard for the value of human life. Two American citizens died as a direct result of these programs, thousands had their constitutional rights violated, and an undetermined number suffered permanent debilitations (Church Committee, 1976).

Although there is little available evidence that the CIA used its mind control techniques against internal political opponents, the recent history of the agency would suggest that this is a definite possibility. Yet it must be remembered that the search within the scientific community to find biomedical causes and biotechnological controls of human behavior is essentially independent of CIA involvement. If the CIA has, in fact, terminated its mind control experiments, there is reason to believe that biomedical research will continue to be supported by private and governmental agencies. Some of the main proponents of large-scale mind control (e.g., Mark and Ervin and Delgado) apparently conducted their research and promoted its use to control "target" populations without CIA monies. Similarly, Dr. Robert Heath, who has often advocated the wide-scale application of his research on the pleasure centers of the brain, refused CIA funding for a project to study its pain centers. One suspects that funding for such research in the future will be only too easy to find.

## SUMMARY AND IMPLICATIONS

We have examined the origins and proliferation of the therapeutic ideal, selected research in biomedics, behavior modification, biotechnics, and associated programs of crime control. It has been noted that the Italian physician Cesare Lombroso laid the scientific foundation for the development of biomedics in criminology, thereby making possible the extension of the state's *parens patriae* power over those exhibiting aberrant behavior. If the past is an accurate indicator of the future, it is not difficult to chart the course of biomedical research in criminology.

Currently there is widespread dissatisfaction with the rehabilitative ideal. Some writers (e.g., Kittrie, 1971; and Lewis, 1953) view rehabilitation as essentially coercive and believe that under its guise the state has been able to extend its punitive powers. Others (e.g., Norval Morris, 1974) maintain that rehabilitation does not work, that the "noble lie" should be abandoned, and that people should be locked up as punishment. The combined criticism of these two groups has all but killed the rehabilitative ideal in corrections. In the process of pursuing their divergent assault, the antirehabilitation group has managed to extend constitutional rights to mental patients and juveniles. The so-called nothing works, lock 'em up faction, exemplified by Robert Martinson et al. (1975) and James Q. Wilson (1975), has supported passage of death penalty statutes in many states, introducing programs to crack down on career offenders, and instituting mandatory minimum sentences.

Yet it would be a mistake to conclude that the rehabilitative ideal is completely dead or that its effects will be short-lived. Although some procedural safeguards such as due process and equal protection under law have been introduced into the mental health and juvenile justice systems, with the single exception of juvenile status offenses, none has challenged the state's right to intervene in noncriminal matters (Klapmuts, 1972). In fact, the introduction of procedural safeguards may make the violation of substantive rights more politically acceptable. In the case of juvenile diversion the net effect has been to increase the web of state control over juveniles, not to lessen it (Morris, 1974). In addition, juvenile diversionary programs have begun to erode the fundamental principle on which the criminal law is founded—innocent until proven guilty. Under those programs, juveniles are often diverted into the mental health system for treatment without a judicial determination of their guilt or innocence.

As stated previously, the antirehabilitation forces have been successful in demonstrating the moral bankruptcy of an ideal that failed to rehabilitate criminals or cure mental patients. The main thrust of their criticism has been that it is immoral to tinker with the "whole" person, that the law should concern itself only with the person's criminal behavior, not his values, attitudes, or personality (American Friends Service Committee, 1971). This is a tenable philosophy, but it is only palatable to policymakers when it is coupled with the fact that rehabilitation has not worked. Today it simply is not practical to attempt to rehabilitate criminals.

There is a growing conservatism in the nation, which is reflected in the research and writings of those who study crime. Policymakers have lost interest in attempting to alleviate the underlying causes of crime. Instead they now demand short-term, prophylactic methods of crime prevention. Sociologists, who for the most part are hesitant about giving simple answers to a problem as complex as crime prevention, have not responded to this new demand. Consequently, policymakers have turned to those whose transient knowledge of criminology makes them more able to deliver the "easy" answer.

At the moment, policymakers are looking toward political scientists and economists for cost-effective answers. Once biomedics and biotechnological control of crime has been demonstrated to be effective and practical, it is probable that the rehabilitative ideal, or something close to it, will reassert itself. This reemerging ideal may not be known as rehabilitation, it may be called habilitation or simply correction, but behind it will probably be a biomedical model of causality and a biotechnological program of control. The antirehabilitation forces will undoubtedly protest, but without evidence of rehabilitative failure to support their moral argument, they will not exert much influence. The "nothing works, lock 'em up" people can be expected to embrace the new methods as the first really effective means society has developed to protect its citizens against criminal trespassers.

For over 100 years the rehabilitative ideal has been the companion of biomedical research. At first glance the "new pragmatism" in corrections may appear to threaten the role of biomedical research in criminology. Classical criminology, with its roots in Bentham's utilitarianism, is generally viewed as opposed to the rehabilitative ideal. There is, however, a point of intersection of purpose. Both purport to have the "greater good" as their aim. The rehabilitative ideal, which emphasizes the patient's good and presents its arguments in terms of morality, humanity, and therapy, still depends heavily on its practical utility. The classical approach, which emphasizes the protection of society, presents its arguments in terms of utility, practicality, and justice. Both agree that the state should pursue the "greater good" and that this means developing a mechanism to control aberrant behavior. The point of disagreement is on which strategy to employ in the control of crime. Bentham's Panopticon Prison or Inspection House is no more nor less humane than Mark and Ervin's prison hospital. The question is which approach is more effective in controlling crime. According to the New Pragmatists, this is the only question.

## SUGGESTED READINGS

Fink, A. E. *Causes of crime: biological theories in the United States, 1800-1915*. Philadelphia: University of Pennsylvania Press, 1938.

A comprehensive and detailed discussion of late 19th- and early 20th-century theories of crime causation in the United States. Not only is it fascinating reading, but it makes clear how important the medical point of view was during that period in providing explanations and treatments for various forms of criminal conduct.

Fox, R. G. The XYY offender: a modern myth? *J. Crim. Law Criminol. Police Sci.*, 1971, *62* (1), 59-73.

A clear review and critique of the research and methodology surrounding the XYY hypothesis. Fox traces the history of the proposition and concludes that the data simply do not support this most recent form of the biological explanation of crime.

Mannheim, H. *Pioneers in criminology*. Chicago: Quadrangle/The New York Times Book Co., Inc., 1960.

A fine compilation of key pieces of work from the founders of the science of criminology. This convenient source book allows the reader to see the fundamental differences between classical and positivist schools of criminology discussed in this chapter.

Sutherland, E. H. Book reviews of *Crime and the Man* and *The American Criminal: An Anthropological Study*, Vol. 1, by Ernest Hooton. *J. Crim. Law Criminol.*, 1939, *29*, 911-914.

Reviews of Hooton's book. Sutherland draws carefully and clearly the line between a sociological and biological-medical view of crime; they provide a good opportunity to see the contrast between these two highly divergent ways of considering such conduct.

U.S. Senate Committee on the Judiciary, Subcommittee on Constitutional Rights. *Individual rights and the federal role in behavior modification*. 93rd Congress, end session. Washington, D.C.: U.S. Government Printing Office, 1974.

A thorough and objective review of the ethical and civil rights issues posed by the development of behavior modification technology to control deviant (and other) behavior. It details the nature of such technology and its various applications.

# 9 MEDICINE as an INSTITUTION of SOCIAL CONTROL

## CONSEQUENCES for SOCIETY

In the final two chapters we leave behind the specific cases and focus on some general features of the medicalization of deviance. These are important chapters, for together they outline the sources and consequences of medicalizing deviance in American society. Chapter 9 examines medicine as an institution of social control, and Chapter 10 offers a statement of what a theory of medicalization of deviance might look like, based on the cases presented in earlier chapters. We attempt, in essence, to provide a more succinct sociological analysis of the medicalization of deviance.

In our society we want to believe in medicine, as we want to believe in religion and our country; it wards off collective fears and reduces public anxieties (see Edelman, 1977). In significant ways medicine, especially psychiatry, has replaced religion as the most powerful extralegal institution of social control. Physicians have been endowed with some of the charisma of shamans. In the 20th century the medical model of deviance has ascended with the glitter of a rising star, expanding medicine's social control functions. In earlier substantive chapters we focused on the changing definitions and designations of deviance, frequently alluding to medical social control. In this chapter we focus directly on medicine as an agent of social control. First, we illustrate the range and varieties of medical social control. Next, we analyze the consequences of the medicalization of deviance and social control. Finally, we examine some significant social policy questions pertaining to medicine and medicalization in American society.

### TYPES OF MEDICAL SOCIAL CONTROL

Medicine was first conceptualized as an agent of social control by Talcott Parsons (1951) in his seminal essay on the "sick role" (see Chapter 2). Eliot Freidson (1970a) and Irving Zola (1972) have elucidated the jurisdictional mandate the medical profession has over anything that can be labeled an illness, regardless of its ability to deal with it effectively. The boundaries of medicine are elastic and increasingly expansive (Ehrenreich & Ehrenreich, 1975), and some analysts have expressed concern at the increasing medicalization of life (Illich, 1976). Although medical social control has been conceptualized in several ways, including professional control

□ This chapter is an adapted, amended, and extended discussion from Conrad, P. Types of social control. *Soc. Health & Illness,* 1979, *1,* 1-12, by permission of Routledge & Kegan Paul Ltd.; and Conrad, P., The discovery of hyperkinesis. *Social Problems,* 1975, *23,* 12-21. Portions of this chapter also taken from "Medicine" by Conrad, P., and Schneider, J., in *Social control for the 1980s: a handbook for order in a democratic society* edited by Joseph S. Roucek, 1978, pp. 346-358, and used with the permission of the publisher, Greenwood Press, Inc., Westport, Conn., and our forthcoming article in *Contemporary Crises,* reprinted by permission of Elsevier Scientific Publishing Co., Amsterdam.

of colleagues (Freidson, 1975) and control of the micropolitics of physician-patient interaction (Waitzkin & Stoeckle, 1976), the focus here is narrower. Our concern, as is evident throughout this book, is with the medical control of deviant behavior, an aspect of the medicalization of deviance (Conrad, 1975; Pitts, 1968). Thus by medical social control we mean the ways in which medicine functions (wittingly or unwittingly) to secure adherence to social norms—specifically, by using medical means to minimize, eliminate, or normalize deviant behavior. This section illustrates and catalogues the broad range of medical controls of deviance and in so doing conceptualizes three major "ideal types" of medical social control.

On the most abstract level medical social control is the acceptance of a medical perspective as the dominant definition of certain phenomena. When medical prespectives of problems and their solutions become dominant, they diminish competing definitions. This is particularly true of problems related to bodily functioning and in areas where medical technology can demonstrate effectiveness (e.g., immunization, contraception, antibacterial drugs) and is increasingly the case for behavioral and social problems (Mechanic, 1973). This underlies the construction of medical norms (e.g., the definition of what is healthy) and the "enforcement" of both medical and social norms. Medical social control also includes medical advice, counsel, and information that are part of the general stock of knowledge: for example, a well-balanced diet is important, cigarette smoking causes cancer, being overweight increases health risks, exercising regularly is healthy, teeth should be brushed regularly. Such directives, even when unheeded, serve as road signs for desirable behavior. At a more concrete level, medical social control is enacted through professional medical intervention, qua medical treatment (although it may include some types of self-treatment such as self-medication or medically oriented self-help groups). This intervention aims at returning sick individuals to compliance with health norms and to their conventional social roles, adjusting them to new (e.g., impaired) roles, or, short of these, making individuals more comfortable with their condition (see Freidson, 1970a; Parsons, 1951). Medical social control of deviant behavior is usually a variant of medical intervention that seeks to eliminate, modify, isolate, or regulate behavior socially defined as deviant, with medical means and in the name of health.

Traditionally, psychiatry and public health have served as the clearest examples of medical control. Psychiatry's social control functions with mental illness, especially in terms of institutionalization, have been described clearly (e.g., Miller, K. S., 1976; Szasz, 1970). Recently it has been argued that psychotherapy, because it reinforces dominant values and adjusts people to their life situations, is an agent of social control and a supporter of the status quo (Halleck, 1971; Hurvitz, 1973). Public health's mandate, the control and elimination of conditions and diseases that are deemed a threat to the health of a community, is more diffuse. It operates as a control agent by setting and enforcing certain "health" standards in the home, workplace, and community (e.g., food, water, sanitation) and by identifying, preventing, treating, and, if necessary, isolating persons with communicable diseases (Rosen, 1972). A clear example of the latter is the detection of venereal disease. Indeed, public health has exerted considerable coercive power in attempting to prevent the spread of infectious disease.

There are a number of types of medical control of deviance. The most common forms of medical social control include medicalizing deviant behavior—that is, defining the behavior as an illness or a symptom of an illness or underlying disease—and subsequent direct medical intervention. This medical social control takes three general forms: medical technology, medical collaboration, and medical ideology.

## Medical technology

The growth of specialized medicine and the concomitant development of medical technology has produced an armamentarium of medical controls. Psychotechnologies, which include various forms of medical and behavioral technologies (Chorover, 1973), are the most common means of medical control of deviance.

Since the emergence of phenothiazine medications in the early 1950s for the treatment and control of mental disorder, there has been a virtual explosion in the development and use of psychoactive medications to control behavioral deviance: tranquilizers such as chlordiazepoxide (Librium) and diazepam (Valium) for anxiety, nervousness, and general malaise; stimulant medications for hyperactive children; amphetamines for overeating and obesity; disulfiram (Antabuse) for alcoholism; methadone for heroin, and many others.* These pharmaceutical discoveries, aggressively promoted by a highly profitable and powerful drug industry (Goddard, 1973), often become the treatment of choice for deviant behavior. They are easily administered under professional medical control, quite potent in their effects (i.e., controlling, modifying, and even eliminating behavior), and are generally less expensive than other medical treatments and controls (e.g., hospitalization, altering environments, long-term psychotherapy).

Psychosurgery, surgical procedures meant to correct certain "brain dysfunctions" presumed to cause deviant behavior, was developed in the early 1930s as prefrontal lobotomy, and has been used as a treatment for mental illness. But psychosurgery fell into disrepute in the early 1950s because the "side effects" (general passivity, difficulty with abstract thinking) were deemed too undesirable, and many patients remained institutionalized in spite of such treatments. Furthermore, new psychoactive medications were becoming available to control the mentally ill. By the middle 1950s, however, approximately 40,000 to 50,000 such operations were performed in the United States (Freeman, 1959). In the late 1960s a new and technologically more sophisticated variant of psychosurgery (including laser technology and brain implants) emerged and was heralded by some as a treatment for uncontrollable violent outbursts (Delgado, 1969; Mark & Ervin, 1970). Although psychosurgery for violence has been criticized from both within as well as outside the medical profession (Chorover, 1974b), and relatively few such operations have been performed, in 1976 a blue-ribbon national commission reporting to the Department of Health, Education and Welfare endorsed the use of psychosurgery as having "potential merit" and judged its risks "not excessive." This may encourage an increased use of this form of medical control.*

Behavior modification, a psychotechnology based on B.F. Skinner's and other behaviorists' learning theories, has been adopted by some medical professionals as a treatment modality. A variety of types and variations of behavior modification exist (e.g., token economies, tier systems, positive reinforcement schedules, aversive conditioning). While they are not medical technologies per se, they have been used by physicians for the treatment of mental illness, mental retardation, homosexuality, violence, hyperactive children, autism, phobias, alcoholism, drug addiction, eating problems, and other disorders. An irony of the medical use of behavior modification is that behaviorism explicitly denies the medical model (that behavior is a symptom of illness) and adopts an environmental, albeit still individual, solution to the problem. This has not, however, hindered its adoption by medical professionals.

Human genetics is one of the most exciting and rapidly expanding areas of medical knowledge. Genetic screening and genetic counseling are becoming more commonplace. Genetic causes are proposed for such a variety of human problems as alcoholism, hyperactivity, learning disabilities, schizophrenia, manic-depressive psychosis, homosexuality, and mental retardation. At this time, apart from specific genetic disorders such as pheylketonuria (PKU) and certain forms of retardation,

*Another pharmaceutical innovation, birth control pills, also functions as a medical control; in this case, the control of reproduction. There is little doubt that "the pill" has played a significant part in the sexual revolution since the 1960s and the redefinition of what constitutes sexual deviance.

*A number of other surgical interventions for deviance have been developed in recent years. Surgery for "gender dysphoria" (transsexuality) and "intestinal by-pass" operations for obesity are both examples of surgical intervention for deviance. The legalization of abortions has also medicalized and legitimated an activity that was formerly deviant and brought it under medical-surgical control.

genetic explanations tend to be general theories (i.e., at best positing "predispositions"), with only minimal empirical support, and are not at the level at which medical intervention occurs. The most well-publicized genetic theory of deviant behavior is that an XYY chromosome arrangement is a determinant factor in "criminal tendencies." Although this XYY research has been criticized severely (e.g., Fox, 1971), the controversy surrounding it may be a harbinger of things to come. Genetic anomalies may be discovered to have a correlation with deviant behavior and may become a causal explanation for this behavior. Medical control, in the form of genetic counseling (Sorenson, 1974), may discourage parents from having offspring with a high risk (e.g., 25%) of genetic impairment. Clearly the potentials for medical control go far beyond present use; one could imagine the possibility of licensing selected parents (with proper genes) to have children, and further manipulating gene arrangements to produce or eliminate certain traits.

### Medical collaboration

Medicine acts not only as an independent agent of social control (as above), but frequently medical collaboration with other authorities serves social control functions. Such collaboration includes roles as information provider, gatekeeper, institutional agent, and technician. These interdependent medical control functions highlight the extent to which medicine is interwoven in the fabric of society. Historically, medical personnel have reported information on gunshot wounds and venereal disease to state authorities. More recently this has included reporting "child abuse" to child welfare or law enforcement agencies (Pfohl, 1977).

The medical profession is the official designator of the "sick role." This imbues the physician with authority to define particular kinds of deviance as illness and exempt the patient from certain role obligations. These are general gatekeeping and social control tasks. In some instances the physician functions as a specific gatekeeper for special exemptions from conventional norms; here the exemptions are authorized because of illness, disease, or disability. A classic example is the so-called insanity defense in certain crime cases. Other more commonplace examples include competency to stand trial, medical deferment from the draft or a medical discharge from the military; requiring physicians' notes to legitimize missing an examination or excessive absences in school, and, before abortion was legalized, obtaining two psychiatrists' letters testifying to the therapeutic necessity of the abortion. Halleck (1971) has called this "the power of medical excuse." In a slightly different vein, but still forms of gatekeeping and medical excuse, are medical examinations for disability or workman's compensation benefits. Medical reports required for insurance coverage and employment or medical certification of an epileptic as seizure free to obtain a driver's license are also gatekeeping activities.

Physicians in total institutions have one of two roles. In some institutions, such as schools for the retarded or mental hospitals, they are usually the administrative authority; in others, such as in the military or prisons, they are employees of the administration. In total institutions, medicine's role as an agent of social control (for the institution) is more apparent. In both the military and prisons, physicians have the power to confer the sick role and to offer medical excuse for deviance (see Daniels, 1969; Waitzkin & Waterman, 1974). For example, discharges and sick call are available medical designations for deviant behavior. Since physicians are both hired and paid by the institution, it is difficult for them to be fully an agent of the patient, engendering built-in role strains. An extreme example is in wartime when the physician's mandate is to return the soldier to combat duty as soon as possible. Under some circumstances physicians act as direct agents of control by prescribing medications to control unruly or disorderly inmates or to help a "neurotic" adjust to the conditions of a total institution. In such cases "captive professionals" (Daniels, 1969) are more likely to become the agent of the institution than the agent of the individual patient (Szasz, 1965; see also Menninger, 1967).

Under rather rare circumstances physicians may become "mere technicians," applying the sanctions of another authority who purchases their medical skills. An extreme example would be the behavior of the experimental and death physicians in Nazi Germany. A less heinous but nevertheless ominous example is provided by physicians who perform court-ordered sterilizations (Kittrie, 1971). Perhaps one could imagine sometime in the future, if the death penalty becomes commonplace again, physicians administering drugs as the "humanitarian" and painless executioners.*

### Medical ideology

Medical ideology is a type of social control that involves defining a behavior or condition as an illness primarily because of the social and ideological benefits accrued by conceptualizing it in medical terms. These effects of medical ideology may benefit the individual, the dominant interests in the society, or both. They exist independently of any organic basis for illness or any available treatment. Howard Waitzkin and Barbara Waterman (1974) call one latent function of medicalization "secondary gain," arguing that assumption of the sick role can fulfill personality and individual needs (e.g., gaining nurturance or attention) or legitimize personal failure (Shuval & Antonovsky, 1973).† One of the most important functions of the disease model of alcoholism and to a lesser extent drug addiction is the secondary gain of removing blame from, and constructing a shield against condemnation of, individuals for their deviant behavior. Alcoholics Anonymous, a nonmedical quasireligious self-help organization, adopted a variant of the medical model of alcoholism independent of the medical profession. One suspects the secondary gain serves their purposes well.

*It is worth noting that in the recent Gary Gilmore execution a physician was involved; he designated the spot where the heartbeat was loudest and measured vital signs during the execution ceremony. A few states have actually passed death penalty legislation specifying injection of a lethal drug as the means of execution.

†Although Waitzkin and Waterman suggest that such secondary gain functions are latent (i.e., unintended and unrecognized), the cases we have discussed here show that such "gains" are often intentionally pursued.

Disease designations can support dominant social interests and institutions. A poignant example is prominent 19th-century New Orleans physician S. W. Cartwright's antebellum conceptualization of the disease drapetomania, a condition that affected only slaves. Its major symptom was running away from their masters (Cartwright, S. W., 1851). Medical conceptions and controls often support dominant social values and morality: the 19th-century Victorian conceptualization of the illness of and addiction to masturbation and the medical treatments developed to control this disease make chilling reading in the 1970s (Comfort, 1967; Englehardt, 1974). The recent Soviet labeling of political dissidents as mentally ill is another example of the manipulation of illness designations to support dominant political and social institutions (Conrad, 1977). These examples highlight the sociopolitical nature of illness designations in general (Zola, 1975).

In sum, medicine as an institution of social control has a number of faces. The three types of medical social control discussed here do not necessarily exist as discrete entities but are found in combination with one another. For example, court-ordered sterilizations or medical prescribing of drugs to unruly nursing home patients combines both technological and collaborative aspects of medical control; legitimating disability status includes both ideological and collaborative aspects of medical control; and treating Soviet dissidents with drugs for their mental illness combines all three aspects of medical social control. It is clear that the enormous expansion of medicine in the past 50 years has increased the number of possible ways in which problems could be medicalized beyond those discussed in earlier chapters. In the next section we point out some of the consequences of this medicalization.

## SOCIAL CONSEQUENCES OF MEDICALIZING DEVIANCE

Jesse Pitts (1968), one of the first sociologists to give attention to the medicalization of deviance, suggests that "medicalization is one of the most effective means of social control and that it is destined to become the main mode of *formal* social control'' (p. 391, emphasis in original).* Although his bold prediction is far-reaching (and, in light of recent developments, perhaps a bit premature), his analysis of a decade ago was curiously optimistic and uncritical of the effects and consequences of medicalization. Nonsociologists, especially psychiatric critic Thomas Szasz (1961, 1963, 1970, 1974) and legal scholar Nicholas Kittrie (1971), are much more critical in their evaluations of the ramifications of medicalization. Szasz's critiques are polemical and attack the medical, especially psychiatric, definitions and treatments for deviant behavior. Szasz's analyses, although path breaking, insightful, and suggestive, have not been presented in a particularly systematic form. Both he and Kittire tend to focus on the effects of medicalization on individual civil liberties and judicial processes rather than on social consequences. Their writings, however, reveal that both are aware of sociological consequences.

In this section we discuss some of the more significant consequences and ramifications of defining deviant behavior as a medical problem. We must remind the reader that we are examining the *social* consequences of medicalizing deviance, which can be analyzed separately from the validity of medical definitions or diagnoses, the effectiveness of medical regimens, or their individual consequences. These variously ''latent'' consequences inhere in medicalization itself and occur *regardless* of how efficacious the particular medical treatment or social control mechanism. As will be apparent, our sociological analysis has left us skeptical of the social benefits of medical social control. We separate the consequences into the ''brighter'' and ''darker'' sides of medicalization. The ''brighter'' side will be presented first.

## Brighter side

The brighter side of medicalization includes the positive or beneficial qualities that are attributed to medicalization. We review briefly the accepted socially progressive aspects of medicalizing deviance. They are separated more for clarity of presentation than for any intrinsic separation in consequence.

First, medicalization is related to a longtime *humanitarian* trend in the conception and control of deviance. For example, alcoholism is no longer considered a sin or even a moral weakness; it is now a disease. Alcoholics are no longer arrested in many places for ''public drunkenness''; they are now somehow ''treated,'' if only to be dried out for a time. Medical treatment for the alcoholic can be seen as a more humanitarian means of social control. It is not retributive or punitive, but at least ideally, therapeutic. Troy Duster (1970, p. 10) suggests that medical definitions increase tolerance and compassion for human problems and they ''have now been reinterpreted in an almost nonmoral fashion.'' (We doubt this, but leave the morality issue for a later discussion.) Medicine and humanitarianism historically developed concurrently and, as some have observed, the use of medical language and evidence increases the prestige of human proposals and enhances their acceptance (Wootton, 1959; Zola, 1975). Medical definitions are imbued with the prestige of the medical profession and are considered the ''scientific'' and humane way of viewing a problem. (Concerning the actual scientific basis for medical definitions, recall our discussion of the disease concept of alcoholism in Chapter 4.) This is especially true if an apparently ''successful'' treatment for controlling the behavior is available, as with hyperkinesis.

Second, medicalization allows for the extension of the *sick role* to those labeled as deviants (see Chapter 2 for our discussion of the sick role). Many of the perceived benefits of the medicalization of deviance stem from the assignment of the sick role. Some have suggested that this is the most significant element of adopting the medical model of deviant behavior (Sigler & Osmond, 1974). By defining deviant behavior as an illness or a result of illness, one is absolved of responsibility for one's behavior. It diminishes or *removes blame* from the individual for deviant actions. Alco-

*From Pitts, J. Social control: the concept. In D. Sills (Ed.), *International encyclopedia of social sciences* (Vol. 14). New York: Macmillan Publishing Co., Inc., 1968. Copyright 1968 by Crowell Collier and Macmillan, Inc.

holics are no longer held responsible for their uncontrolled drinking, and perhaps hyperactive children are no longer the classroom's "bad boys" but children with a medical disorder. There is some clear secondary gain here for the individual. The label "sick" is free of the moral opprobrium and implied culpability of "criminal" or "sinner." The designation of sickness also may reduce guilt for drinkers and their families and for hyperactive children and their parents. Similarly, it may result in reduced stigma for the deviant. It allows for the development of more acceptable accounts of deviance: a recent film depicted a child witnessing her father's helpless drunken stupor; her mother remarked, "It's okay. Daddy's just sick."*

The sick role allows for the "conditional legitimation" of a certain amount of deviance, so long as the individual fulfills the obligations of the sick role.† As Renée Fox (1977) notes:

> The fact that the exemptions of sickness have been extended to people with a widening arc of attitudes, experiences and behaviors in American society means primarily that what is regarded as "conditionally legitimated deviance" has increased. . . . So long as [the deviant] does not abandon himself to illness or eagerly embrace it, but works actively on his own or with medical professionals to improve his condition, he is considered to be responding appropriately, even admirably, to an unfortunate occurrence. Under these conditions, illness is accepted as legitimate deviance. (p. 15)‡

The deviant, in essence, is medically excused for the deviation. But, as Talcott Parsons (1972) has pointed out, "the conditional legitimation is bought at a 'price,' namely, the recognition that illness itself is an undesirable state, to be recovered from as expeditiously as possible" (p. 108). Thus the medical excuse for deviance is only valid when the patient-deviant accepts the medical perspective of the inherent undesirability of his or her sick behavior and submits to a subordinate relationship with an official agent of control (the physician) toward changing it. This, of course, negates any threat the deviant may pose to society's normative structure, for such deviants do not challenge the norm; by accepting deviance as sickness and social control as "treatment," the deviant underscores the validity of the violated norm.

Third, the medical model can be viewed as portraying an *optimistic* outcome for the deviant.* Pitts (1968) notes, "the possibility that a patient may be exploited is somewhat minimized by therapeutic ideology, which creates an optimistic bias concerning the patient's fate" (p. 391).† The therapeutic ideology, accepted in some form by all branches of medicine, suggests that a problem (e.g., deviant behavior) can be changed or alleviated if only the proper treatment is discovered and administered. Defining deviant behavior as an illness may also mobilize hope in the individual patient that with proper treatment a "cure" is possible (Frank, J., 1974). Clearly this could have beneficial results and even become a self-fulfilling prophecy. Although the medical model is interpreted frequently as optimistic about individual change, under some circumstances it may lend itself to pessimistic interpretations. The attribution of physiological cause coupled with the lack of effective treatment engendered a somatic pessimism in the

---

*It should be noted, however, that little empirical evidence exists for reduced stigmatization. Derek Phillips' (1963) research suggests that people seeking medical help for their personal problems are highly at risk for rejection and stigmatization. Certain illnesses carry their own stigma. Leprosy, epilepsy, and mental illness are all stigmatized illnesses (Gussow & Tracy, 1968); Susan Sontag (1978) proposes that cancer is highly stigmatized in American society. We need further research on the stigma-reducing properties of medical designations of deviance; it is by no means an automatic result of medicalization.

†On the other hand, Paul Roman and Harrison Trice (1968, p. 248) contend that the sick role of alcoholic may actually reinforce deviant behavior by removing responsibility for deviant drinking behavior.

‡Reprinted by permission of *Daedalus*, Journal of the American Academy of Arts and Sciences, Boston, Mass. Spring 1977, *Doing better and feeling worse: health in the United States*.

*For a contrasting viewpoint, see Rotenberg's (1978) work, discussed in the next chapter.

†From Pitts, J. Social control: the concept. In D. Sills (Ed.), *International encyclopedia of social sciences* (Vol. 14). New York: Macmillan Publishing Co., Inc., 1968. Copyright 1968 by Crowell Collier and Macmillan, Inc.

late 19th-century conception of madness (see Chapter 3).

Fourth, medicalization lends the *prestige of the medical profession* to deviance designations and treatments. The medical profession is the most prestigious and dominant profession in American society (Freidson, 1970a). As just noted, medical definitions of deviance become imbued with the prestige of the medical profession and are construed to be the "scientific" way of viewing a problem. The medical mantle of science may serve to deflect definitional challenges. This is especially true if an apparently "successful" treatment for controlling the behavior is available. Medicalization places the problem in the hands of healing physicians. "The therapeutic value of professional dominance, from the patient's point of view, is that it becomes the *doctor's* problem" (Ehrenreich & Ehrenreich, 1975, p. 156, emphasis in original). Physicians are assumed to be beneficent and honorable. "The medical and paramedical professions," Pitts (1968) contends, "especially in the United States, are probably more immune to corruption than are the judicial and parajudicial professions and relatively immune to political pressure" (p. 391).*

Fifth, medical social control is more *flexible* and often more *efficient* than judicial and legal controls. The impact of the flexibility of medicine is most profound on the "deviance of everyday life," since it allows "social pressures on deviance [to] increase without boxing the deviant into as rigid a category as 'criminal'" (Pitts, 1968, p. 391).* Medical controls are adjustable to fit the needs of the individual patient, rather than being a response to the deviant act itself. It may be more efficient (and less expensive) to control opiate addiction with methadone maintenance than with long prison terms or mental hospitalization. The behavior of disruptive hyperactive children, who have been immune to all parental and teacher sanctions, may dramatically improve after treatment with medications. Medical controls circumvent complicated legal and judicial procedures and may be applied more informally. This can have a considerable effect on social control structures. For example, it has been noted that defining alcoholism as a disease would reduce arrest rates in some areas up to 50%.

In sum, the social benefits of medicalization include the creation of humanitarian and nonpunitive sanctions; the extension of the sick role to some deviants; a reduction of individual responsibility, blame, and possibly stigma for deviance; an optimistic therapeutic ideology; care and treatment rendered by a prestigious medical profession; and the availability of a more flexible and often more efficient means of social control.

## Darker side

There is, however, another side to the medicalization of deviant behavior. Although it may often seem entirely humanitarian to conceptualize deviance as sickness as opposed to badness, it is not that simple. There is a "darker" side to the medicalization of deviance. In some senses these might be considered as the more clearly latent aspects of medicalization. In an earlier work Conrad (1975) elucidated four consequences of medicalizing deviance; building on that work, we expand our analysis to seven. Six are discussed here; the seventh is described separately in the next section.

**Dislocation of responsibility.** As we have seen, defining behavior as a medical problem removes or profoundly diminishes responsibility from the individual. Although affixing responsibility is always complex, medicalization produces confusion and ambiguity about who is responsible. Responsibility is separated from social action; it is located in the nether world of biophysiology or psyche. Although this takes the individual officially "off the hook," its excuse is only a partial one. The individual, the putative deviant, and the undesirable conduct are still associated. Aside from where such conduct is "seated," the sick deviant is the medium of its expression.

*From Pitts, J. Social control: the concept. In D. Sills (Ed.), *International encyclopedia of social sciences* (Vol. 14). New York: Macmillan Publishing Co., Inc., 1968. Copyright 1968 by Crowell Collier and Macmillan, Inc.

With the removal of responsibility also comes the lowering of status. A dual-class citizenship is created: those who are deemed responsible for their actions and those who are not. The not-completely-responsible sick are placed in a position of dependence on the fully responsible nonsick (Parsons, 1975, p. 108). Kittrie (1971, p. 347) notes in this regard that more than half the American population is no longer subject to the sanctions of criminal law. Such persons, among others, become true "second-class citizens."

**Assumption of the moral neutrality of medicine.** Cloaked in the mantle of science, medicine and medical practice are assumed to be objective and value free. But this profoundly misrepresents reality. The very nature of medical practice involves value judgment. To call something a disease is to deem it undesirable. Medicine is influenced by the moral order of society—witness the diagnosis and treatment of masturbation as a disease in Victorian times—yet medical language of disease and treatment is assumed to be morally neutral. It is not, and the very technological-scientific vocabulary of medicine that defines disease obfuscates this fact.

Defining deviance as disease allows behavior to keep its negative judgment, but medical language veils the political and moral nature of this decision in the guise of scientific fact. There was little public clamor for moral definitions of homosexuality as long as it remained defined an illness, but soon after the disease designation was removed, moral crusaders (e.g., Anita Bryant) launched public campaigns condemning the immorality of homosexuality. One only needs to scratch the surface of medical designations for deviant behavior to find overtly moral judgments.

Thus, as Zola (1975) points out, defining a problem as within medical jurisdiction

> is not morally neutral precisely because in establishing its relevance as a key dimension for action, the moral issue is prevented from being squarely faced and occasionally from even being raised. By the acceptance of a specific behavior as an undesirable state the issue becomes not whether to treat an individual problem but how and when. (p. 86)*

Defining deviance as a medical phenomenon involves moral enterprise.

**Domination of expert control.** The medical profession is made up of experts; it has a monopoly on anything that can be conceptualized as an illness. Because of the way the medical profession is organized and the mandate it has from society, decisions related to medical diagnoses and treatment are controlled almost completely by medical professionals.

Conditions that enter the medical domain are not ipso facto medical problems, whether we speak of alcoholism, hyperactivity, or drug addiction. When a problem is defined as medical, it is removed from the public realm, where there can be discussion by ordinary people, and put on a plane where only medical people can discuss it. As Janice Reynolds (1973) succinctly states,

> The increasing acceptance, especially among the more educated segments of our populace, of technical solutions—solutions administered by disinterested and morally neutral experts—results in the withdrawal of more and more areas of human experience from the realm of public discussion. For when drunkenness, juvenile delinquency, sub par performance and extreme political beliefs are seen as symptoms of an underlying illness or biological defect the merits and drawbacks of such behavior or beliefs need not be evaluated. (pp. 220-221)†

The public may have their own conceptions of deviant behavior, but those of the experts are usually dominant. Medical definitions have a high likelihood for dominance and hegemony: they are often taken as the last scientific word. The language of medical experts increases mystification and decreases the accessibility of public debate.

**Medical social control.** Defining deviant

---

*Reprinted with permission from Pergamon Press, Ltd.

†From "The medical institution: the death and disease-producing appendage" by Janice M. Reynolds, first published in *American society: a critical analysis* edited by Larry T. Reynolds and James M. Henslin. Copyright © 1973 by Longman Inc. Reprinted by permission of Longman.

behavior as a medical problem allows certain things to be done that could not otherwise be considered; for example, the body may be cut open or psychoactive medications given. As we elaborated above, this treatment can be a form of social control.

In regard to drug treatment, Henry Lennard (1971) observes: "Psychoactive drugs, especially those legally prescribed, tend to restrain individuals from behavior and experience that are not complementary with the requirements of the dominant value system" (p. 57). These forms of medical social control presume a prior definition of deviance as a medical problem. Psychosurgery on an individual prone to violent outbursts requires a diagnosis that something is wrong with his brain or nervous system. Similarly, prescribing drugs to restless, overactive, and disruptive schoolchildren requires a diagnosis of hyperkinesis. These forms of social control, what Stephan Chorover (1973) has called "psychotechnology," are powerful and often efficient means of controlling deviance. These relatively new and increasingly popular forms of medical control could not be used without the prior medicalization of deviant behavior. As is suggested from the discovery of hyperkinesis and to a lesser extent the development of methadone treatment of opiate addiction, if a mechanism of medical social control seems useful, then the deviant behavior it modifies will be given a medical label or diagnosis. We imply no overt malevolence on the part of the medical profession; rather, it is part of a larger process, of which the medical profession is only a part. The larger process might be called the individualization of social problems.

**Individualization of social problems.** The medicalization of deviance is part of a larger phenomenon that is prevalent in our society: the individualization of social problems. We tend to look for causes and solutions to complex social problems in the individual rather than in the social system. William Ryan (1971a) has identified this process as "blaming the victim": seeing the causes of the problem in individuals (who are usually of low status) rather than as endemic to the society. We seek to change the "victim" rather than the society. The medical practice of diagnosing an illness in an individual lends itself to the individualization of social problems. Rather than seeing certain deviant behaviors as symptomatic of social conditions, the medical perspective focuses on the individual, diagnosing and treating the illness itself and generally ignoring the social situation.

Hyperkinesis serves as a good example of this. Both the school and parents are concerned with the child's behavior; the child is difficult at home and disruptive in school. No punishments or rewards seem consistently effective in modifying the behavior, and both parents and school are at their wits' end. A medical evaluation is suggested. The diagnosis of hyperkinetic behavior leads to prescribing stimulant medications. The child's behavior seems to become more socially acceptable, reducing problems in school and home. Treatment is considered a medical success.

But there is an alternative perspective. By focusing on the symptoms and defining them as hyperkinesis, we ignore the possibility that the behavior is not an illness but an adaptation to a social situation. It diverts our attention from the family or school and from seriously entertaining the idea that the "problem" could be in the structure of the social system. By giving medications, we are essentially supporting the existing social and political arrangements in that it becomes a "symptom" of an individual disease rather than a possible "comment" on the nature of the present situation. Although the individualization of social problems aligns well with the individualistic ethic of American culture, medical intervention against deviance makes medicine a de facto agent of dominant social and political interests.

**Depoliticization of deviant behavior.** Depoliticization of deviant behavior is a result of both the process of medicalization and the individualization of social problems. Probably one of the clearest recent examples of such depoliticization occurred when political dissidents in the Soviet Union were decared mentally ill and confined to mental hospitals (Conrad, 1977). This strategy served to neutralize the meaning of political protest and dissent, rendering it (officially, at least) symptomatic of mental illness.

The medicalization of deviant behavior depoliticizes deviance in the same manner. By defining the overactive, restless, and disruptive child as hyperkinetic, we ignore the meaning of the behavior in the context of the social system. If we focused our analysis on the school system, we might see the child's behavior as a protest against some aspect of the school or classroom situation, rather than symptomatic of an individual neurological disorder. Similar examples could be drawn of the opiate addict in the ghetto, the alcoholic in the workplace, and others. Medicalizing deviant behavior precludes us from recognizing it as a possible intentional repudiation of existing political arrangements.

There are other related consequences of the medicalization of deviance beyond the six discussed. The medical ideal of early intervention may lead to early labeling and secondary deviance (see Lemert, 1972). The "medical decision rule," which approximates "when in doubt, treat," is nearly the converse of the legal dictum "innocent until proven guilty" and may unnecessarily enlarge the population of deviants (Scheff, 1963). Certain constitutional safeguards of the judicial system that protect individuals' rights are neutralized or by-passed by medicalization (Kittrie, 1971). Social control in the name of benevolence is at once insidious and difficult to confront. Although these are all significant, we wish to expand on still another consequence of considerable social importance, the exclusion of evil.

## Exclusion of evil

Evil has been excluded from the imagery of modern human problems. We are uncomfortable with notions of evil; we regard them as primitive and nonhumanitarian, as residues from a theological era.* Medicalization contributes to the exclusion of concepts of evil in our society. Clearly medicalization is not the sole cause of the exclusion of evil, but it shrouds conditions, events, and people and prevents them from being confronted as evil. The roots of the exclusion of evil are in the Enlightenment, the diminution of religious imagery of sin, the rise of determinist theories of human behavior, and the doctrine of cultural relativity. Social scientists as well have excluded the concept of evil from their analytic discourses (Wolff, 1969; for exceptions, see Becker, E., 1975, and Lyman, 1978).

Although we cannot here presume to identify the forms of evil in modern times, we would like to sensitize the reader to how medical definitions of deviance serve to further exclude evil from our view. It can be argued that regardless of what we construe as evil (e.g., destruction, pain, alienation, exploitation, oppression), there are at least two general types of evil: evil intent and evil consequence. Evil intent is similar to the legal concept mens rea, literally, "evil mind." Some evil is intended by a specific line of action. Evil consequence is, on the other hand, the result of action. No intent or motive to do evil is necessary for evil consequence to prevail; on the contrary, it often resembles the platitude "the road to hell is paved with good intentions." In either case medicalization dilutes or obstructs us from seeing evil. Sickness gives us a vocabulary of motive (Mills, 1940) that obliterates evil intent. And although it does not automatically render evil consequences good, the allegation that they were products of a "sick" mind or body relegates them to a status similar to that of "accidents."

For example, Hitler orchestrated the greatest mass genocide in modern history, yet some have reduced his motivation for the destruction of the Jews (and others) to a personal pathological condition. To them and to many of us, Hitler was sick. But this portrays the horror of the Holocaust as a product of individual pathology; as Thomas Szasz frequently points out, it prevents us from seeing and confronting man's inhumanity to man. Are Son of Sam, Charles Manson, the assassins of King and the Kennedys, the Richard Nixon of Watergate, Libya's Muammar Kaddafi, or the all-to-common child beater sick? Although many may

*Writing in the early 1970s, Kittrie (1971) noted, "Ours is increasingly becoming a society that views punishment as a primitive and vindictive tool and is therefore loath to punish" (p. 347). Some recent scholarship in penology and the controversy about the death penalty has slightly modified this trend.

well be troubled, we argue that there is little to be gained by deploying such a medical vocabulary of motives.* It only hinders us from comprehending the human element in the decisions we make, the social structures we create, and the actions we take. Hannah Arendt (1963), in her exemplary study of the banality of evil, contends that Nazi war criminal Adolph Eichmann, rather than being sick, was "terribly, terrifyingly normal."

Susan Sontag (1978) has suggested that on a cultural level, we use the metaphor of illness to speak of various kinds of evil. Cancer, in particular, provides such a metaphor: we depict slums and pornography shops as "cancers" in our cities; J. Edgar Hoover's favorite metaphor for communism was "a cancer in our midst"; and Nixon's administration was deemed "cancerous," rotting from within. In our secular culture, where powerful religious connotations of sin and evil have been obscured, cancer (and for that matter, illness in general) is one of the few available images of unmitigated evil and wickedness. As Sontag (1978) observes:

> But how to be . . . [moral] in the late twentieth century? How, when . . . we have a sense of evil but no longer the religious or philosophical language to talk intelligently about evil. Trying to comprehend "radical" or "absolute" evil, we search for adequate metaphors. But the modern disease metaphors are all cheap shots . . . Only in the most limited sense is any historical event or problem like an illness. It is invariably an encouragement to simplify what is complex. . . . (p. 85)

Thus we suggest that the medicalization of social problems detracts from our capability to see and confront the evils that face our world.

In sum, the "darker" side of the medicalization of deviance has profound consequences for the putative or alleged deviant and society. We now turn to some policy implications of medicalization.

---

*We *do not* suggest that these individuals or any other deviants discussed in this book are or should be considered evil. We only wish to point out that medicalization on a societal level contributes to the exclusion of evil. To the extent that evil exists, we would argue that social structures and specific social conditions are the most significant cause of evil.

## MEDICALIZATION OF DEVIANCE AND SOCIAL POLICY

"Social policy" may be characterized as an institutionalized definition of a problem and its solutions. There are many routes for developing social policy in a complex society, but, as John McKnight (1977) contends, "There is no greater power than the right to define the question" (p. 85). The definition and designation of the problem itself may be the key to the development of social policy. Problem definitions often take on a life of their own; they tend to resist change and become the accepted manner of defining reality (see Caplan, N., & Nelson, 1973). In a complex society, social policy is only rarely implemented as a direct and self-conscious master plan, as, for example, occurred with the development of community mental health centers (see Chapter 3). It is far more common for social policies to evolve from the particular definitions and solutions that emerge from various political processes. Individual policies in diverse parts of society may conflict, impinge on, and modify one another. The overall social policy even may be residual to the political process. The medicalization of deviance never has been a formalized social policy; as we have demonstrated throughout this book, it has emerged from various combinations of turf battles, court decisions, scientific innovations, political expediences, medical entrepreneurship, and other influences. The medicalization of deviance has become in effect a de facto social policy.

In this discussion we explore briefly how some changes and trends in medicine and criminal justice as well as the recent "punitive backlash" may affect the future course of the medicalization of deviance.

### Criminal justice: decriminalization, decarceration, and the therapeutic state

Over the past two decades the percent of officially defined deviants institutionalized in prisons or mental hospitals has decreased. There has been a parallel growth in "community-based" programs for social control. Although this "decarceration" has been most dramatic with the mentally ill, substantial deinstitutionalization has occurred in prison populations and with juvenile delinquents and opiate addicts as well (see Scull, 1977a). Many deviants who until recently would have been institutionalized are being "treated" or maintained in community programs—for example, probation, work release, and community correctional programs for criminal offenders; counseling, vocational, or residential programs as diversion from juvenile court for delinquents; and methadone maintenance or therapeutic community programs in lieu of prison for opiate addicts.

This emerging social policy of decarceration has already affected medicalization. Assuming that the amount of deviance and number of deviants a society recognizes remains generally constant (see Erikson, 1966), a change in policy in one social control agency affects other social control agents. Thus decarceration of institutionalized deviants will lead to the deployment of other forms of social control. Because medical social control is one of the main types of social control deployed in the community, decarceration increases medicalization. Since the *Robinson* Supreme Court decision and the discovery of methadone maintenance the control of opiate addicts has shifted dramatically from the criminal justice system to the medical system. Control of some criminal offenders may be subtly transferred from the correctional system to the mental health system; one recent study found an increase in the number of males with prior police records admitted to psychiatric facilities and suggested this may be an indication of a medicalization of criminal behavior (Melick, Steadman, & Cocozza, 1979). There is also some evidence that probation officers, in their quest for professional status, adopt a medical model in their treatment of offenders (Chalfant, 1977). Although some observers have suggested that the apparent decarceration of mental patients from mental hospitals and the rise of community mental health facilities has at least partially demedicalized madness (see Chapter 3), this is an inaccurate interpretation. Moreover, the extent of decarceration has been exaggerated; many of the former or would-be mental patients are located in other institutions, especially nursing homes (Redlich & Kellert, 1978). Here they remain under medical or quasimedical control. In short, decarceration appears to increase the medicalization of deviance.

Decriminalization also affects medicalization. Decriminalization means that a certain activity is no longer considered to be a criminal offense. But even when criminal sanctions are removed, the act may still maintain its definition as deviance. In this case, other noncriminal sanctions may emerge. Alcohol use and deviant drinking provide a useful example. We noted in our discussion of the definition of deviant drinking (Chapter 4) that the disease model of alcoholism did not begin its rise to prominence until after the repeal of Prohibition, that is, after alcohol use in general was decriminalized. More specifically, we can examine the response to the decriminalization of "public drunkenness" in the 1960s. A recent study has shown that although alcohol and drug psychoses comprised only 4.7% of the mental health population (inpatient and outpatient) in 1950, in 1975 "alcoholism accounted for 46 percent of state hospital patients" and became the largest diagnostic category in mental hospitals (Redlich & Kellert, 1978, p. 26). It is likely that the combination of the declining populations in state mental hospitals and the decriminalization of "public drunkenness" (e.g., police now bring drunks to the mental hospital instead of the drunk tank) is in part reflected in this enormous increase of alcoholics in the mental health system.

Medicalization allows for the decriminalization of certain activities (e.g., public drunkenness, some types of drug use) because (1) they remain defined as deviant (sick) and are not vindicated and (2) an alternative form of social control is available (medicine). If an act is decriminalized and also demedicalized (e.g., homosexuality), there may well be a backlash and a call for recriminalization or at least reaffirmation of its deviant status rather than a vindication. We postulate that if an act is decriminalized and yet not vindicated (i.e., still remains defined as deviant), its control may be transferred from the criminal justice to the medical system.*

In the 1960s and early 1970s considerable concern was voiced in some quarters concerning the "social policy" that was leading to the divestment of criminal justice and the rise of the therapeutic state (Kittrie, 1971; Leifer, 1969; Szasz, 1963). As pointed out in Chapter 8, there has been some retreat from the "rehabilitative ideal" in criminal justice. On the other hand, both decarceration and decriminalization have increased medicalization. Thus we would conclude that although the "therapeutic state" is not becoming the dominant social policy as its earlier critics feared, neither is it showing signs of abating. We would suggest that to the extent that decarceration and decriminalization remain social policies, medicalization of deviance can be expected to increase.

## Trends in medicine and medicalization

The medicalization of deviance has been influenced by changes in the medical profession and in social policy regarding medical care. The prestige of medicine has been growing since the turn of the century. Medical practice has become increasingly specialized; whereas only 20% of physicians were specialists in 1940, by the early 1970s nearly 80% considered themselves specialists (Twaddle & Hessler, 1977, p. 175). This is in part the result of the increasingly technological nature of medicine. The number of personnel employed in the medical sector has increased considerably since the Second World War. But the most spectacular growth has been in the cost and investment in medical care in the past three decades.

In 1950 the expenditures for medical care comprised 4.6% of the Gross National Product (GNP); by 1976 they accounted for 8.3%, for a total of over $130 billion spent on medical care. Since 1963 health expenditures have risen more than 10% yearly, while the rest of the economy has grown by 6% to 7%. In other words, medicine is the fastest expanding part of the service sector and one of the most expansive segments of our economy. In one sense we might see these increasing expenditures themselves as an index of increasing medicalization. But more likely, the increasing economic resources allocated to medical care create a substantial pool of money to draw from, thereby increasing the resources available for medical solutions to human problems. It should be noted, however, that the inflation of medical costs could ultimately become a factor in decreasing the medicalization of deviance, simply because medical solutions have become too costly.

Much of the rising cost of medical care has been attributed to the growth in third-party payments (i.e., when medical care is paid not by the patient or the provider of the care but by a third party). The major source of third-party payments has been Blue Cross and Blue Shield and the health insurance industry, and, since the enactment of Medicare and Medicaid in 1965, also the federal government. More than 51% of medical costs was paid directly by the patient in 1966; by 1975 this figure had dipped to less than 33% (Coe, 1978, p. 387). The largest increase in third-party payments has been the amount paid by the federal government; in 1975, 27.7% of medical costs was borne by the federal government, and this is expected to continue to increase. What this all means for the medicalization of deviance is that "third parties" are increasingly deciding what is appropriate medical care and what is not. For example, if medical insurance or Medicaid will pay for certain types of treatment, then the problem is more likely to be medicalized. Although the medical profession certainly has influence in this area, this removes the control of medicalization from medical hands and places it into the hands of the third-party payers. Although 90% of America's Blue Cross plans provide some hospital coverage for alcoholism, less than 10% of the cost of treatment is currently covered by private insurance and

*The decriminalization of abortion has led to its complete medicalization. It is interesting to speculate whether the decriminalization of marijuana, gambling, and prostitution would lead to medicalization. It is likely that with marijuana and gambling, "compulsive" and excessive indulgence would be defined as "sick"; with prostitution, medical certification might be required, as is presently the case in several European countries.

health-care protection programs (*Behavior Today,* June 21, 1976). Although many physicians consider obesity to be a bona fide medical condition, virtually no health insurers will pay for intestinal by-pass operations as a treatment for obesity. Clearly, changes in policies by third-party payers can drastically affect the types or amount of deviance medicalized.

Until about the past two decades, the dominant organization of medical practice was private, solo practice. There has been a growing bureaucratization of medical practice. The hospital rather than the private office is becoming the center for health care delivery. These large modern hospitals are both a result of, and an inducement for, the practice of highly specialized and technological medicine. Hospitals have their own organizational priorities of sustaining a smoothly running bureaucracy, maximizing profitable services, justifying technological equipment, and maintaining the patient-bed load at near full capacity. Although bureaucratic organizations reduce medical professional power, the institutional structure of the hospital is better suited to function as an agent of social control than the singular office practice. Hospital medicine can be practiced at a high biotechnological level, is less client dependent (because of third-party payments), has less personal involvement, and is more responsive to demands of other institutions, especially the state, on whom it is increasingly dependent for financial support.

For many years American medicine was considered to be suffering from a shortage of physicians. In the 1960s federal programs to expand medical schools increased greatly the number of physicians being trained. We have just begun to experience the effects of the rising number of physicians. Between 1970 and 1990 we can expect an 80% increase in the number of physicians—from about 325,000 to almost 600,000. And if present population and medical trends continue, as we expect they will, by 1990 there will be one physician for every 420 people in the United States and an even greater enlargement in the number of nurses and allied health workers (U.S. Department of Health, Education and Welfare, 1974).

One result of the growing number of medical personnel could be an increase in the number of problems that become defined as medical problems (after all, we have all these highly trained professionals to treat them). Although the greater number of physicians could result in better delivery of medical services, it could also increase medicalization as new physicians attempt to develop new areas of medical turf as old ones become saturated. David Mechanic (1974, p. 50) suggests, for instance, that for "family practice" to become a viable discipline in medicine, family practitioners would have to develop a "scientific and investigatory stance" toward common family practice problems such as "alcoholism, drug abuse, difficulties in sexual development, failure to conform to medical regimen and the like." The potential for the expansion of the medical domain here is great.

But there are also some countertrends in medicine. There is an emphasis on both self-care and individual responsibility for health (see Knowles, 1977). Health is becoming defined as more of a personal responsibility. As Zola (1972) observes, "At the same time the label 'illness' is being used to attribute 'diminished responsibility' to a whole host of phenomena, the issue of 'personal responsibility' seems to be re-emerging in medicine itself" (p. 491). Increased personal responsibility for sickness could cause the responsibility for the behavior to return to the individual. For instance, alcoholics would be deemed responsible for deviant drinking, obese people for their deviant bodies, and opiate addicts for their habits. This could ultimately spur some demedicalization.*

But the most important social policy affecting the future of medicalization hinges on the notion of a "right to adequate health care" and

---

*Reneé Fox (1977, pp. 19-21) contends that the recent trends of viewing patients as consumers, the emergence of physician extenders such as nurse practitioners and physicians' assistants, and "the increased insistence on patients' rights, self-therapy, mutual aid, community medical services and care by non-physician health professionals" constitute evidence for demedicalization. We think Fox is mistaken. *Demedicalization does not occur until a problem is no longer defined in medical terms and medical treatments are no longer seen as directly relevant to its solution.* Fox confuses deprofessionalization with demedicalization.

the development of a National Health Insurance (NHI) program. The proposal of an NHI program has become a significant political issue. In the past decade dozens of bills advocating different NHI plans have been submitted to various congressional committees. No specific NHI plan as yet has emerged as the most probable candidate for passage, but there is a high likelihood that some type of NHI plan will be enacted within the next decade. Because of the recent fiscal crunch and the strong lobbying of powerful vested interests (e.g., the health insurance industry, the medical profession, the hospital associations), it is unlikely that it will be an NHI program providing comprehensive coverage. More likely, NHI will not alter the present structure of the medical system and will resemble present insurance programs (although with increased public accountability); it will be at least partly federally financed and extend insurance coverage to all Americans. Regardless of which NHI bill is enacted, it will have an effect on medicalization. What the effect will be, however, is uncertain. There are at least three possible scenarios.

SCENARIO ONE: Because the cost of paying for treatment is high and deemed prohibitive, fewer deviant behaviors are defined as medical problems. Perhaps alcoholism, marital problems, drug addiction, psychosurgery, and treatment for obesity will be excluded from NHI coverage.

SCENARIO TWO: Because NHI will pay for the treatment of anything defined as a medical problem, more deviance becomes medicalized. Gambling, divorce, boredom, narcissism, and lethargy will be defined as illnesses and treated medically.

SCENARIO THREE: Individuals are not considered responsible for their illnesses; so activities that are seen as leading to medical problems become defined as deviant. Smoking, eating poorly, getting insufficient exercise, or eschewing seat belts all will be defined as deviant. Certain medical problems could be excluded from NHI coverage because they are deemed to be willfully caused (i.e., "badness").

This final scenario takes us full circle, as we would develop the notion of "sickness as sin."* Scenarios two and three would further the convergence of illness and deviance. At this point, it is difficult to predict which, if any, of these scenarios might result from the enactment of NHI.

*Paradoxically this could also encourage demedicalization, for the medical model then becomes less functional in removing the culpability for deviance.

## Punitive backlash

Since about 1970 there has been a "backlash" against the increasing "liberalization" of the treatment of deviance and the Supreme Court decisions that have granted criminal suspects and offenders greater "rights." This public reaction, coming mostly from the more conservative sectors of society, generally calls for more strict treatment of deviants and a return to more punitive sanctions.

This "punitive backlash" takes many forms. In 1973 New York passed a "get tough" law with mandatory prison sentences for drug dealers. Other legislative attempts have been made to impose mandatory minimum sentences on offenders. There is considerable public clamor for the return of the death penalty. A current New York state law has allowed juveniles between ages 13 and 15 to be tried as adults for some offenses. The antiabortion crusade has made inroads into the availability of abortions and is aiming for the recriminalization of abortion. Recently antihomosexuality crusades have appeared from Florida to Oregon, defeating antidiscrimination referenda and limiting the rights of homosexuals.

This swell of public reaction may be in part a response to the therapeutic ideology and the perceived "coddling" of deviants. Should this backlash and other recent public reactions such as California's Proposition 13 taxpayer revolt continue to gather strength and grow in popularity, they well may force a retreat from the medicalization of deviance.

## Some social policy recommendations

Our examination of the medicalization of deviance in American society has led us to some conclusions related to social policy. In this discussion we briefly outline some social policy recommendations.

1. The medicalization of deviance needs to be recognized as a de facto social policy. Recognized as such, issues like those pointed to in this chapter could be raised and debated. It is

important that public discussion by physicians, politicians, and lay persons alike be encouraged and facilitated. In recognition of the salience of medicalization and its consequences, perhaps "medicalization impact statements" should be required of social policy proposals affecting medicalization. For example, it is important to weigh the impact of NHI on medicalization.

2. Research is needed on the extent of medicalization, its benefits, and its costs. This includes research into the efficacy, the financial and social costs, and the extent of actual medicalization. We need continued research into the politics of medicalization and further investigation into the areas of medicalized deviance covered in this book as well as those not covered, such as the medicalization of suicide, old age and senility, obesity, abortion, and mental retardation. We need to compare these with uncontested medical problems that were at one time defined as deviance, such as epilepsy and leprosy. Close attention needs to be given to the efficacy, costs, and benefits for each type of medicalization. Hopefully such knowledge and understanding will better guide social policy decisions concerning medicalization.

3. Medicalization removes the constitutional safeguards of the judicial process (see Kittrie, 1971). Because of this, it is important to create some type of medical due process or redress for putative deviants who are the objects of therapeutic interventions. Since this type of due process would probably be resisted by the medical profession and labeled antitherapeutic, we propose the development of some type of "counterpower" to medical social control. This could take the form of patient or deviant advocates, intervention review organizations, or even a Nader-type watchdog group. This would help ensure that individual rights were not circumvented in the name of health.

4. It is our belief that we need to develop social policies toward deviance that hold people *accountable* for their actions but do *not blame* them. This is a delicate but possible balance. One proposal is bypassing such slippery concepts as responsibility and guilt, substituting an assumption of human fallibility combined with accountability for human action. As Kittrie (1971) suggests,

> Every person who lives in a society is accountable to it for his anti-social behavior. Society, in return, may seek to curb his future misdeeds, not as a punishment for the improper exercise of free will but as a remedy for his human failings.

Although the notions of guilt, moral responsibility, and accountability are profound philosophical (and political) questions that cannot begin to be addressed here, we believe they must be directly discussed and reevaluated, since many people's lives are profoundly affected by them.

Presently our society's only "no blame" model for deviant behavior is the medical model. We need to develop new models of deviance that do not assume ultimate individual moral responsibility and yet do not define those who are not considered responsible as "sick." Presently the only alternative to the criminal-responsibility model is the medical-no-responsibility model. It is imperative that we free ourselves from the dichotomous crime or sickness models that create largely either-or situations, as well as from unworkable and contradictory crime-sickness hybrids, as with sex offenders.

New models of deviance need to be reconciled with social scientific knowledge about deviance. There is considerable evidence that economic, social, and family factors contribute to deviant behavior, and it is important to understand that the individual has only limited control over these factors. Yet it is also important, because of our understanding of human behavior, not to completely neglect its voluntary components. Thus we concur with Robert Veatch (1973) that rather than assuming that human behavior is caused by biophysiological elements ("sickness"), "it is preferable to make clear the missing categories—namely nonculpable deviancy caused psychologically, socially and culturally, for example, by lack of various forms of psychological, social, and cultural welfare" (p. 71). We need to create a "no blame" role for deviants that still holds the individual accountable for his or her action. We need to create a social role analogous to the sick role that does not assume sickness or remove responsibility and yet reconciles our understanding that there are "forces" beyond the scope of the individual that affect human behavior. For example, one can envision the conception of a "victim role"; the individual is viewed as a "victim" of life circumstances; these circumstances are known to increase the probability for certain types of "deviant" behavioral responses as well as attributions, yet because the behavior is not regarded as "determined" by the circumstances, the individual is accountable for deviant behavior. In other words, given the circumstances, the individual is accountable for the behavioral strategies chosen in a situation. Needless to say, this is a complex and sticky issue, replete with philosophical and pragmatic pitfalls. It provides an important challenge for social scientists and philosophers. We present this example only to suggest the possibility of alternatives to the medical-criminal model dichotomy. As Clarice Stoll (1968) observes, our "image of man" is central in determining our social response to deviance; we call for the development of an alternative image that reconciles societal response with the understandings of social and behavioral science.

Finally, because social control is necessary for the existence of society, we urge the development of alternative, noncriminal and nonmedical modes of social control appropriate to the new model of deviance.

## MEDICALIZING DEVIANCE: A FINAL NOTE

The potential for medicalizing deviance has increased in the past few decades. The increasing dominance of the medical profession, the discovery of subtle physiological correlates of human behavior, and the creation of medical technologies (promoted by powerful pharmaceutical and medical technology industry interests) have advanced this trend. Although we remain skeptical of the overall social benefits of medicalization and are concerned about its "darker" side, it is much too simplistic to suggest a wholesale condemnation of medicalization. Offering alcoholics medical treatment in lieu of the drunk tank is undoubtedly a more humane response to deviance; methadone maintenance allows a select group of opiate addicts to make successful adaptations to society; some schoolchildren seem to benefit from stimulant medications for hyperkinesis; and the medical discovery of child abuse may well increase therapeutic intervention. Medicalization in general has reduced societal condemnation of deviants. But these benefits do not mean these conditions are in fact diseases or that the same results could not be achieved in another manner. And even in those instances of medical "success," the social consequences indicated in this chapter are still evident.

The most difficult consequence of medicalization for us to discuss is the exclusion of evil. In part this is because we are members of a culture that has largely eliminated evil from intellectual and public discourse. But our discomfort also stems from our ambivalence about what can meaningfully be construed as evil in our society. If we are excluding evil, what exactly are we excluding? We have no difficulty depicting such conditions as pain, violence, oppression, exploitation, and abject cruelty as evil. Social scientists of various stripes have been pointing to these evils and their consequences since the dawn of social science. It is also possible for us to conceive of "organizational evils" such as corporate price fixing, false advertising (or even all advertising), promoting life-threatening automobiles, or the wholesale drugging of nursing home patients to facilitate institutional management. We also have little trouble in seeing ideologies such as imperialism, chauvinism, and racial supremacy as evils. Our difficulty comes with seeing individuals as evil. While we would not adopt a Father-Flanagan-of-Boys-Town attitude of "there's no such thing as a bad boy," our own socialization and "liberal" assumptions as well as sociological perspective make it difficult for us to conceive of any individual as "evil." As sociologists we are more likely to see people as products of their psychological and social circumstances: there may be evil social structures, ideologies, or deeds, but not evil people. Yet when we confront a Hitler, an Idi Amin, or a Stalin of the forced labor camps, it is sometimes difficult to reach any other conclusion. We note this dilemma more as clarification of our stance than as a solution. There are both evils in society and people who are "victims" to those evils. Worthwhile social scientific goals include uncovering the evils, understanding and aiding the victims, and ultimately contributing to a more humane existence for all.

## SUMMARY

In the 20th century, medicine has expanded as an institution of social control. On the most abstract level medical social control is the acceptance of a medical perspective as the dominant definition of certain phenomena. Medical social control of deviant behavior usually takes the form of medical intervention, attempting to modify deviant behavior with medical means and in the name of health. We identify three general forms of the medical social control of deviance: medical technology, medical collaboration, and medical ideology. Medical technology involves the use of pharmaceutical or surgical technologies as controls for deviance. Medical collaboration emphasizes the interwoven position of medicine in society and occurs when physicians collaborate with other authorities as information providers, gatekeepers, institutional agents, and technicians. Medical ideology as social control involves defining a behavior or condition as an illness primarily for the social and ideological benefits accrued by conceptualizing it in medical terms. Although these three "ideal types" are likely to be found in combination, they highlight the varied faces of medical social control.

There are important social consequences of medicalizing deviance. The "brighter" side of medicalization includes (1) a more humanitarian conception of deviance; (2) the extension of the sick role to deviants, minimizing blame and allowing for the conditional legitimation of a certain amount of deviance; (3) the more optimistic view of change presented by the medical model; (4) lending the prestigious mantle of the medical profession to deviance designations and treatments; and (5) the fact that medical social control is more flexible and sometimes more efficient than other controls. However, there is a "darker" side of medicalization, which includes (1) the dislocation of responsibility from the individual; (2) the assumption of the moral neutrality of medicine; (3) the problems engendered by the domination of expert control; (4) powerful medical techniques used for social control; (5) the individualization of complex social problems; (6) the depoliticization of deviant behavior; and (7) the exclusion of evil. It is this darker side that leaves us skeptical of the social benefits of medicalizing deviance.

The medicalization of deviance has become a de facto social policy. Changes in other "social policies" affect medicalization. Decarceration leads to the increasing deployment of medical social control, since it is one of the most effective social controls "in the community." Decriminalization may also increase medicalization because medicine provides an alternative social control mechanism. We postulate that if an act is decriminalized and not vindicated, its control may be transferred from the criminal justice system to the medical system. Although the therapeutic state has not become the dominant social policy, neither does it show any signs of withering away. Medicalization is also influenced by changes and trends in medicine. Medical practice is becoming increasingly specialized, technological, and bureaucratic. Society's economic investment (in terms of percentage of GNP) in medical care has nearly doubled in the past three decades. This is both an index of and incentive for medicalization. Bureaucratic medical practice removes some definitional power from the medical profession and places it in the hands of third-party payers (including the state) and hospital administrators. The number of physicians and other medical personnel will double by 1990; this may well cause further medicalization. On the other hand, the increased emphasis on self-care and individual responsibility for health, as well as the "fiscal crisis" of rapidly rising medical costs, may limit medicalization and spur demedicalization. The passage of a National Health Insurance program may have a profound effect on medicalization, although it is difficult to predict precisely what it will be. If the "punitive backlash" to perceived liberalized treatment of deviants gains strength, it may force some retreat from the medicalization of deviance.

We conclude with some brief social policy recommendations:

1. The medicalization of deviance needs to be recognized as a de facto social policy.

2. More research is needed on the extent, politics, benefits, and costs of medicalizing deviance.

3. Some form of "counterpower" to medical social control needs to be created.

4. A new model of deviance that holds people accountable for their actions but does not blame them needs to be developed, perhaps as a "victim" model. We need to be freed from the dichotomous crime or sickness models that create limiting either-or situations.

# 10 A THEORETICAL STATEMENT on the MEDICALIZATION of DEVIANCE

This chapter serves as both a conceptual summary of the various cases discussed in this book and as a theoretical statement about the medicalization of deviance in American society. In essence, we propose here a general sociological account, grounded in the historical data we have presented and drawing on common themes and patterns. The chapter offers not a formal, positivist "explanation" but rather an attempt to draw out what we perceive to be the major analytic or theoretical insights about the social and historical processes we have discussed.

In this theoretical statement we attempt to account for the rise and fall (but mostly the rise) of medical designations of deviance. Any such general sociological understanding of medicalization should also, of course, include demedicalization, although there is considerably less historical data about the latter on which to base generalizations. Thus we propose that our "theory" is neither definitive nor exhaustive but rather that it represents an attempt to specify what general lessons we may learn about the rise and dominance of, and occasional challenge to, medical definitions and controls of deviant behavior. We divide the chapter into three parts: a review of the general historical and conceptual background of medicalization, an inductive theory of medicalization, and, finally, a section containing some of our more speculative hunches and hypotheses.

## HISTORICAL AND CONCEPTUAL BACKGROUND

As is evident in the various chapters of this book, the medicalization of deviance has a long history, beginning at least as early as ancient Greece. The ideas that disease can cause deviant behavior, that deviant behavior can lead to disease, and that such conduct is itself an illness or a symptom thereof have existed in various forms for thousands of years. It is, however, only in the 19th and 20th centuries that we see medical designations of deviance become the dominant definitions of deviant behavior. We must, then, first examine the general conditions in these centuries that appear to have created an environment fertile for medicalizing deviance. Although many factors contributed to the emergence of medicine as the dominant definer of deviance, we believe the most important for the modern medicalization of deviance were the rise of rationalism, the development of determinist theories of causation that arose in the 19th century, and the growth and success of medicine in the 20th century.

The European Enlightenment of the 17th and 18th centuries nurtured the ideas of individual and collective progress. The dominance of theological definitions and explanations for human behavior, including deviance, were seriously challenged by thinkers who posited rational and scientific principles by which to understand and then govern individual behavior and society. Rousseau, Voltaire, and Cesare di

Becarria made important contributions to the new rational philosophy. The criminal in Becarria's classical criminology was depicted as a rational actor and considered to have free will (see Chapter 8); in short, to be responsible for his or her own behavior. In this view of rational action, behavior was generally seen as turning on a pleasure-pain calculus; people were believed to seek pleasure and avoid pain.

The Enlightenment also nurtured the development of science as a method for understanding the world. By the 19th century, scientific theories advanced the idea that behavior, and even society, were determined by "forces" over which individuals had little control. Classical criminology was challenged by the development and ascendance of *determinist* theories of criminality and deviance. These theories took two general forms: social (environmental) determinism and biophysiological determinism. Social determinism, such as the theories of environmental cause postulated by the American asylum superintendents (see Chapter 3), and later theories based on the work of Marx, gained considerable popularity. Toward the middle of the 19th century, biophysical theories such as that of Lombroso echoed the new discoveries of Darwin and proposed that the causes of deviance could be found in one's constitution and/or biological heritage. These determinist theories, in their many forms, became the dominant explanation of deviant conduct and persons. People were "bad" not so much because they chose to be but rather because they had no alternative; they became "objects" at the mercy of powerful social or biophysiological forces.

These determinist scientific explanations "made sense" of deviance in such a way that punishment for such conduct became somewhat less important as a strategy for controlling deviant behavior. It was considered incapable of affecting this social or biophysiological fate by which the deviant was believed to be determined. "Treatment," rather than punishment, became increasingly popular as the more humane and preferred way of controlling crime. As we have noted, this change has been called the divestment of the criminal law—the relinquishing of legal jurisdiction over many forms of traditionally "criminal" conduct—and has occurred in the United States over the past century (Kittrie, 1971).

As we pointed out in the first chapter, medicine did not become a dominant, prestigious, and successful profession until the turn of the 20th century. Medicine's own determinist theory, the germ theory of disease, became popular and dominant after about 1870 and provided medicine with some of its greatest clinical achievements. It proved to be the key that unlocked the mystery of infectious disease and provided the major perspective in terms of which physicians viewed illness. It was, however, the actual control of infectious disease (which, incidentally, had little to do directly with the discovery of the germ theory [Dubos, 1959]), along with the consolidation and monopolization of medical organization and practice about the turn of the century that enabled the medical profession to achieve a position of social and professional dominance.

Many analysts and students of Western society have suggested the great importance of certain major historical transformations in shaping the nature and contours of modern society. These various developments are used commonly to account for a broad range of other social and cultural changes. The list is somewhat standard and includes industrialization, the decline of religion, the demise of the extended family, the loss of traditional authority, increased geographical mobility, the development of technology, the professionalization of society, and the increased value of humanitarianism. Medicalization, too, has been explained at least in part by reference to some of these historic shifts. One difficulty with such explanation is that it often provides only limited understanding of how in fact a certain change in practice or policy took place. Saying, for example, that medicalization is caused by the professionalization of society leaves us wondering just what that might mean. These global developments that are themselves used to define modern society could be used to account for virtually any changes that followed them in time. This is not to argue that they are meaningless or that they should be ignored in attempting to understand the medicalization of deviance and its rise. Rather, we have attempted in the chapters of this book to give these abstractions a degree of life by identifying them as values used by real people making claims for a certain change, or at least by trying to define them on a more empirical level. We have tried to show that changes, even such massive ones as these, do not just happen; they must be championed, their themes invoked and defended against challenges, and renegotiated.

With this in mind, we can say that the rise of rationalism, science, and the popularity of determinist theories of deviance, as well as the professionalization and monopolization of medicine, were general social conditions that appear to have given impetus to medicalization. That is, people who championed these and related ideas tended also to support and sometimes to actively promote medicine as a way of defining and dealing with personal problems and deviant behavior. In terms of the history of ideas, medical theories of deviance grew out of the same materialist determinism that spawned the work of Darwin, Marx, and, later, Freud. And the medicalization of deviance in particular flourished in the United States. In the following discussion we explore some features of American society that have been supportive of medical theories of deviance.

## American society as fertile ground for medicalization

The medicalization of deviance has been nowhere more pervasive than in the United States. This is not to say that medicalization is unknown elsewhere; numerous instances can be cited. For example, we have alluded to the medicalization of madness and opiate addiction in Great Britain and to the 19th-century medicalization of homosexuality by German physicians and of crime by European positivist criminologists. American society, however, and especially since the late 19th century, has provided a particularly hospitable environment for the medicalization of deviance. In this discussion we point to some general cultural and organizational features of American society that have contributed to this nurturant context.

The United States, more than its European counterparts, has a strong heritage of experimentation and utopianism. Some have called America itself a "noble experiment." It has been a society regularly open to new ideas and innovative ways of doing things and solving problems. One might even suggest that the "new"—the latest and the best—has become a fetish with many Americans. In addition, the value of humanitarianism is deeply ingrained in the American ethos. Indeed, Americans have been espousing this value of humanitarianism since the Declaration of Independence, although not following it consistently as a society. But along with idealism and humanitarianism, Americans have shown a strong penchant for pragmatism and particularly for pragmatic solutions to human problems. Rather than engaging in philosophical or even scientific debate toward a more full understanding of such problems, Americans are more likely to ask, "What can be done about it?" Another dominant value used to describe life in the United States is individualism. Although all societies and social groups must strike some balance between the individual's needs and those of the collectivity, in America the balance usually is tipped in favor of the individual. Certainly in terms of solving social problems, typical solutions are nearly always those which involve intervention not in the established institutions of the society but rather in individuals' lives. Such a strategy is based on the dubious assumption that the source of the problem in question rests somehow in the person rather than in the diverse and often conflicting social and cultural environment (see Ryan, 1971a). In a general sense, the American values of experimentation, newness, humanitarianism, pragmatism, and individualism have all contributed to a nurturing crucible for medicalization, for the medical perspective on deviance contains elements of all these values.

Max Weber (1904-1905/1958) argued persuasively for the importance of the Protestant Ethic in the development of capitalism and the rationalization of Western society. He located the root of the Protestant Ethic in early Protestant asceticism, and particularly in the Calvinist doctrine of predestination. Predestination, in

Calvinist terms, meant that those who were among the "elect" and would thus be "saved" had been identified or selected by God when they were born. Nothing that one did on earth could change this divine ordination. Hard work, frugality, and thrift, however, were important values of Puritan life, and it was believed that certainly those whom God would choose would be those who lived their lives according to such desirable standards. Such conduct, if followed devoutly, also led ultimately to material success and accumulation, and although one could in no sense "work" one's way into heaven, such material achievement was believed to be a reasonably good sign that a person was one of God's chosen. No one, of course—at least none of the respectable members of the community—wanted to be considered among the damned; so Calvinists in general worked hard and accumulated much. Work, thrift, and material accumulation thus became important ends in themselves. This, according to Weber, provided the "spirit" conducive to the development of capitalism.

Mordechai Rotenberg (1978) suggests that Weber's thesis may be extended to account for the Western, and especially American, way of defining and treating deviance. He suggests that the Protestant ethic of predestination leads to a fundamental division of people into two camps: the righteous-elect and the wicked-damned. Since their selection is predetermined, there is little confidence in the possibility of change. In these terms, failure or deviance is the converse of success, as damnation is the opposite of election. Rotenberg suggests that the Protestant Ethic creates a "spirit of failure" that profoundly affects the manner in which we think about deviants and the techniques we use to treat them:

> More specifically, I have posited that just as the Protestant Ethic had a general impact on the Western world in terms of economic development and increased achievement behavior—as Weber [1904-1905/1958] and others have posited—the covert belief that deviance and failure are symptoms of an innate and irreversible state of damnation is equally pervasive in Western culture, since both tenets are traceable to Calvin's influential doctrine of predestination. (p. 23)

Rotenberg contends there is a historical link between the damnation metaphor and the contemporary medical model of deviance. He observes that the latter, which classifies people as healthy or sick, reflects the same dichotomous assumptions as do the Calvinist notions of elect and damned. Furthermore, the Protestant ethic of predestination is at least partly "responsible for the belief in man's inability to change," which underlies much of the biophysiological determinism of the medical model (Rotenberg, 1978, p. 2). One could also suggest that both the notions "damned" and "sick" focus attention on the individual's condition apart from social context and portray deviance as innate, determined, and largely irreversible. To the extent that the Protestant Ethic pervades American society (see Merton, 1957), it can be argued that it is a cultural condition conductive to the medicalization of deviance.

American society has cultivated an extraordinary faith in science, both as a way of making sense of experience and as a source of dazzling and problem-solving technology. As a way of understanding human behavior, this scientific legacy has been almost wholly positivist—it has involved adopting natural science assumptions to understand and account for the way human beings behave in the social world. As one might suspect, that has produced a good deal of misunderstanding in social science and particularly in the sociology of deviance. This positivist heritage has also been the kind of science adopted by nonsociologist officials, politicians, and bureaucrats, as well as the public at large, to define and "explain" deviant behavior. David Matza (1969) has called this the affinity model of explaining deviance—where conduct is portrayed as determined by an individual's affinity or "predisposition" to it. Such predisposition (sounding suspiciously like "predestination") is believed to be a product of the circumstances in which deviant actors find themselves and over which they have little control. Deviant actors have been seen by science as in general the product of various kinds of "forces"—not at all unlike the medical determinist theories just discussed. In short, this positivist view of social behavior and specifically deviant behavior reinforces the rigid and categorical thinking that is the heritage of the Calvinist idea of predestination. Deviants and their conduct may be explained, then, not only by God's will but by "natural laws" as well.

Science also has enabled us to do things and solve problems much more easily—more efficiently, with less effort and time. It has, in short, allowed the development of an amazing array of sophisticated technologies, including electricity, automobiles, airplanes, radio, television, computers, and space satellites. Medicine's technological achievements have been no less spectacular. Americans have been pioneers in technology and have adopted a pervasive belief in science as both "good" and essential to "progress."

Our society pays official tribute to democratic political participation and public debate. This allows for challenges to dominant viewpoints and established interests, both in and out of conventional political arenas. Challenges to criminal and medical definitions of deviance may emerge under such conditions. Since the Progressive era, however, more influence and "credibility" have been given to those designated as "experts." As Richard Hofstadter (1963) notes, "In the interests of democracy itself, the old Jacksonian suspicion of experts must be abated" (p. 197). In the rush to the dependence on various kinds of experts that we have witnessed in this century, perhaps the leading example has been the physician as the expert par excellence on matters of health and illness. Translated into less abstract terms, this means the physician has become the premier expert on personal problems, both of the body and the mind.

As we discussed in Chapter 1, the monopoly of medical practice and the development of medicine as a profession gave physicians relative independence and functional autonomy (Freidson, 1970b). The "miracles" of modern medicine and the growing status of the physician-expert brought a considerable charisma to the medical profession. At the same time, and perhaps not unrelated to this, health has become a primary value in American society. Health is used as a justification for controlling powerful corporations (e.g., through air pollution and occupational safety regulations) and as a criterion for defining activities as deviant (e.g., cigarette smoking and alcohol drinking). For some, a commitment to health has become almost a "leg up" on immortality or salvation. It is perhaps not surprising to find that in a society where such a high value is placed on health, the sick are considered "deviant" and the deviant are considered "sick." In both cases, this commitment to health serves as a justification for the treatment and control of such undesirable persons.

Finally, medicine can be highly profitable in a capitalist society. Medicalization can create new markets for products and services. This is true not only for medical practitioners but, perhaps more important, for entire industries. The pharmaceutical, health insurance, and medical technology corporations, as well as other medical industries, have achieved phenomenal growth in the past three decades. Although we make explicit connections to the pharmaceutical industry in three of our cases (madness, opiate addiction, and hyperkinesis), we contend that the profitability of medicine in American society has contributed in both specific and general ways to the medicalization of deviance.

In summary, important American values align well with the medical model of deviance. In recent years health itself has become a predominant value. American society, with its democratic system, is open to challenges of new definitions of deviance. Medical practice is independent and expansive. In a capitalist society, medicalization can create new markets and be highly profitable. In short, in American society medical conceptions of deviance have a cultural resonance both with dominant values and the organizational apparatus to promote and sustain them, creating a fertile environment for medicalization. In the following discussion we begin to develop a model of how this medicalization of deviance occurs.

## AN INDUCTIVE THEORY OF THE MEDICALIZATION OF DEVIANCE

Social conditions conducive to medicalization are alone insufficient to produce new definitions of deviance. New deviance designations do not emerge by themselves but are the product of collective enterprise and claims-making activities (Spector & Kitsuse, 1977). As we argued in Chapter 2, the process can be called "the politics of deviance designation." Throughout this book we have emphasized the socially constructed nature of deviance definitions and designations and the role of individuals, organizations, social movements, and other interests in creating and implementing them. In this section we outline an inductive theory of the medicalization of deviance grounded in the cases we have examined.* Given the variety of cases, actors, and circumstances we have discussed, it is not possible to construct a theory that accounts for all aspects of every case. We attempt rather to develop a theory of the medicalization of deviance that can be maximally generalized, yet that does not do violence to the empirical reality of our cases. In our discussion we will make note of cases that deviate or vary from the model proposed. We present our theoretical outline in two parts: a sequential model and grounded generalizations.

### A sequential model

Before our sequential model is presented, three points need to be made. First, we caution the reader to keep in mind that it is a theoretical model, and the stages delineated are not always distinct and separated clearly in practice. Second, it is important to understand what we mean by medical "deviance designation." When we say claims-makers promote a new deviance designation, we do not necessarily mean that the claim is presented in this manner, that is, by claiming that the deviant behavior is "sickness, not badness." Rather, medical claims are couched in terms that *attempt to conceptualize deviance as a medical problem* and may be presented as a medical diagnosis or etiology and/or treatment for the deviant and the deviant's behavior.

Third, our sequential model of medicalization takes as its point of departure the recent work of Malcolm Spector and John Kitsuse (1977) on the sociology of social problems (recall our discussion in Chapter 2). We use, for example, Spector and Kitsuse's concept of claim in two related yet distinct ways regarding the medicalization of deviance. First, after these authors, we consider a claim to be a medical demand, contention, or assertion, such as claiming that opiate addiction should be treated by physicians. Our second usage, going beyond this first meaning, defines claim in the metaphor of a miner engaged in prospecting land. Like the miner claiming that a portion of the land is his or her own, a medical "claim" of legitimate jurisdiction may be "staked" over a particular segment of social, personal, or even geographical "turf" as something that "belongs to" medicine and physicians as a professional group. An example of this latter use of claim would be the early 19th-century official medical control of access to and regulation of asylums in England. The first kind of claim is primarily a matter of words and images; the second more a question of "making good" such definitions by usurping or taking charge of a particular procedure or territory as medicine's own.

We propose a five-stage sequential model for the medicalization of deviance: (1) definition of behavior as deviant; (2) prospecting: medical discovery; (3) claims-making: medical and nonmedical interests; (4) legitimacy: securing medical turf; and (5) institutionalization of a medical deviance designation.

**Definition of behavior as deviant.** In nearly all the cases we examined, the behavior or activity in question was defined as deviant *before* the emergence of medical definitions. Madness, chronic drunkenness, homosexual conduct, delinquency, and criminal activities were all defined as highly undesirable before any medical writings or perspectives appeared. Prior to the Harrison Act, for example, opiate addiction was, by and large, not considered particularly deviant. The Harrison Act criminalized, and thus made deviant, opiate addiction. Opiate addiction was thus deviant prior to attempts to remedicalize it in the 1960s. Child abuse and hyperactivity are somewhat more am-

*Conrad (1976, pp. 93-97) presented an initial statement toward a theory of the medicalization of deviance based largely on his study of hyperkinesis. In it he outlines five antecedent and two contingent conditions of medicalization. Although that statement may still have some utility, the one presented here, drawing on comparative and historical data, is more broadly based and theoretically developed and modifies some of the earlier tenets.

biguous cases. Most likely, child battering, when it was so defined, was considered deviant. Yet among physicians and the general public alike it was rarely recognized or construed as such (Pfohl, 1977). This suggests that the medical discovery of child abuse was at least in part the invention of a new form of deviance. Hyperkinesis presents a similar situation. Restless, disruptive, and overactive children are surely defined as deviant in most school classrooms; yet it was the discovery and promotion of the medical label that gave shape to this vague form of deviant behavior. To recapitulate, behavior is generally defined as deviant before medical designations are proposed.* As Erich Goode (1969, p. 88) observes, negative evaluations of behavior precede explanations of it, or, put differently, explanations follow attitudes. We might suggest that medical designations of deviance reflect and give shape to commonly held definitions of deviance, rather than defining deviance anew out of whole cloth. In a sense, medical designations validate commonsense definitions of deviance. This highlights the continuity between badness and sickness designations: they are both negative moral judgments.

**Prospecting: medical discovery.** The "discovery" of a medical conception of deviant behavior is first announced in a professional medical journal (or, more rarely, in a book or at a conference). It appears in the form of a description of a new diagnosis (hyperactivity, child abuse), the proposal of a medical etiology of deviant behavior (alcoholism, homosexuality), or the report of a new medical treatment for problem behaviors (methadone, psychosurgery). Any of these may be used to promote a medical deviance designation. These articles are usually the product of the work of a limited number of physicians, generally researchers, who are specializing in the problem and who often are professional colleagues.

We call this stage "prospecting" for two reasons. First, many articles about medical conceptions and treatments of deviance are published in professional journals but never subsequently become ammunition in claims-making activities. They may be ignored, buried, or quietly refuted. Second, such articles are, by and large, formal and informational and, although they represent a viewpoint, constitute a "challenge" only in the most academic sense.

As we pointed out in earlier chapters, publication of scientific and professional articles, even in prestigious medical journals, does not assure a new deviance designation's recognition or acceptance. It needs champions and moral entrepreneurs to carry the banner and bring the new problem or definition to public attention. When this happens, the claims-making stage begins.

**Claims-making: medical and nonmedical interests.** This is a key stage in the emergence of new deviance designations. It is at this point that champions, moral entrepreneurs, and organized interests begin actively to make claims for a new deviance designation and attempt to expand the medical social control turf. Both medical and nonmedical interests engage in claims-making activities.

The medical professional interests involved in making claims for a new deviance designation usually comprise a specialized group. They are either medical researchers of a specific problem (as in stage 2) or are administratively involved in treating the deviant behavior in question. By "administratively involved" we mean that these physicians either operate a special clinic treating the behavior in question or are attached to an institution mandated to deal with the problem. These physicians are not typical of the medical profession in general, and their activities and concerns are far removed from the rank and file of medical doctors. The latter are rarely if ever involved at this stage. In fact, aside from receiving information about "important discoveries" and claims published in journals or presented at professional meetings, most physicians are completely removed from such claims-making activities.

*In the 19th-century example of abortion, summarized in Chapter 1, although *not* a case of medicalization, it appears physicians were instrumental in defining that activity as deviant. However, in the case of masturbation in Victorian times, physicians clearly medicalized commonsense deviance definitions of this activity (see Englehardt, 1974). George Becker (1978) notes that the negative and deviant definitions of "mad" genius preceded the development of the medical definitions. These cases seem to support our contentions in stage 1.

The small group of active medical claims-makers are, by and large, not organized specifically around the promotion of a new medical deviance designation but come together primarily because of their similar professional interests and viewpoints. Although medical professional claims-making may seem like an organized activity, in its early stages it is composed generally of individuals or small groups engaged in promoting the new designation. Their activites are more parallel than in concert. One type of concerted claims-making that medical champions do engage in is the organization of professional forums and conferences at which to display their claims. These include institutes, seminars, workshops, and various meetings designed to publicize and promote their views to others, especially the nonmedical personnel who deal regularly with the problem behavior. Exemplars include the Yale Center Summer School program on alcoholism and the series of National Conferences on Methadone Treatment.

This loose alliance of claims-makers with similar interests is at first primarily an intellectual or professional one, but as claims-making in and out of the profession progresses—sometimes in response to the rise of an opposition—the alliance becomes increasingly politicized. One aspect of this politicization may be an attempt to prevail on their professional organization (e.g., the American Medical Association, the American Psychiatric Association) to support their claims.* To the extent that medical claims-making *is* organized, those making claims for a deviance designation attempt to use the existing professional organizations for their own benefit (e.g., securing passage of a supportive resolution or getting the organization to issue a position statement substantiating the claim). Occasionally physicians organize themselves into special interest "caucuses" to promote their viewpoint within the professional organization, but physicians' claims-making is generally not that organized or politically overt. If the champions of a particular viewpoint are successful in convincing their professional organization to support their claims, the professional society itself becomes an important force for staking a claim.

Professional investigatory committees are often established to evaluate the claims about a new deviance designation. Professional societies establish such committees in response to its member-champions requesting that the organization support a particular claim or in response to outside criticism and public pressure to take a professional stand on the issue. Sometimes these committees are initiated at government request and organized under the auspices of an agency such as the Department of Health, Education and Welfare (e.g., in 1970 for hyperkinesis and 1975 for psychosurgery). The people chosen to serve on these investigative committees are designated "experts" on the subject and not infrequently include those most active in claims-making activities. The investigatory committee's report, regardless of whether it was professionally or bureaucratically initiated, is often supportive to the new deviance designation (with qualifications) and becomes important ammunition in the promotion of the new medical claim.

The activities of nonmedical claims-makers are more overt. Usually drawing on already-made professional medical claims, nonmedical champions and vested interests play an important role in the promotion of new medical deviance designations. Nonmedical claims-making groups in the cases we have examined include corporations (e.g., the pharmaceutical companies), professional and lay organizations (e.g., the Association for Children with Learning Disabilities, the National Council on Alcoholism), government bureaucracies, (e.g., Department of Health, Education and Welfare), and self-help groups (e.g., Alcoholics Anonymous). These groups, in different ways, promote new designations by engaging in publicity campaigns, lobbying in legislatures, and supporting litigation and judicial challenges. These organizations are generally already in existence, and either publicize or expand on the

*Occasionally the professional claims-makers may start their own organization to represent their viewpoint; for example, the American Orthopsychiatric Association to promote the medical view of crime and the American Society of Bariatric Physicians to promote a medical conception and treatment of obesity.

medical claim and become its most ardent supporters. These groups have a direct interest, be it economic, moral, administrative, or therapeutic, in the adoption of the medical perspective of deviance. They align and intertwine with medical claims and claims-makers; for example, by frequently calling on the medical champions to lend "scientific" credence to their claims.

These nonmedical claims-makers are important in establishing new deviance designations, since they initiate activity with the public, legislatures, and in court in a way that medical professionals usually do not. They are perhaps freer to promote their position and challenge their opponents, less constrained by "professional ethics" or "scientific" credibility. In short, they use the medical claims as ammunition to battle for the new deviance designation and become its foremost advocates. This allows physicians to take the more dignified role as "experts" rather than overt partisans.

Although claims-makers may use the popular media to advance their cause, publicity seems to play a less significant role in the politics of deviance designation than in the successful emergence of social problems (see Spector & Kitsuse, 1977), largely because the politicking occurs on a professional, administrative, or legislative rather than a public level.* The popular media can play a role in disseminating information or creating public pressure for a new designation of deviance (or creating a demand for a new medical treatment), but, generally speaking, this is peripheral rather than central to the political struggle. Although the media may occasionally take editorial positions supporting one designation over another, this influence appears to be limited. The media play a more significant role later in this stage and the next by "reporting" the challenges and the "victories" in the designation battle.

The supporters of a medical designation of deviance must, in most cases, appeal to the state for legitimation of their perspective. With this, the politics of deviance designation moves to the next stage.

**Legitimacy: securing medical turf.** This stage begins when proponents of the medical deviance designation launch an instrumental, as opposed to merely rhetorical, challenge to the existing deviance designation. This usually involves some type of appeal to the state, as arbiter of jurisdictional disputes and "official" legitimater of deviance designations, to recognize the medical viewpoint. The arenas of challenge, or "battlegrounds," include legislatures, special investigatory committees, federal bureaucracies, and courts. Often confrontation occurs simultaneously on a number of fronts. Some challenging deviance designations of course never reach this stage, withering in the verbal battles and challenges of stage 3. In some cases, such as homosexuality, appeals to the state play only a minor role, and the arenas of challenge lie elsewhere. In the face of active resistance, however, most medical claims-makers must seek state legitimacy.

The most common arenas of conflict are legislatures and courtrooms. Legislatures, including Congress, may hold hearings on deviance designations (in relation to proposed legislation) and hear arguments from the designation's champions and opponents. A "victory" here for the medical designation means passage of laws supportive of the medical viewpoint and not uncommonly granting medicine official jurisdiction over the question of social control (e.g., madness, child abuse, juvenile delinquency). Judicial decisions, especially from the Supreme Court, may affirm the dominance of one designation over another and, in effect, at least partially legitimize the designation (e.g., madness, opiate addiction, alcoholism). Special investigatory committees, organized by legislatures or part of the state bureaucracy, can weigh evidence and present a report more or less favorable to a deviance designation (e.g., hyperkinesis, psychosurgery). This can be seen as an "official" recognition of one viewpoint over another. In our metaphor of prospecting, it is somewhat akin to being given the "deed" to an identifiable and bounded piece of "property." Needless to say, however, such "victories" are rarely total, such "deeds" not with-

*The recent "gay rights" referenda are something of an exception, although they are not per se battles about deviance designations.

out conditions and being shared with other "owners" of the property in question. In fact, most cases involve grafting the challenging "sickness" designation onto some parts of older "badness" designations. Winning these "battles" does not necessarily mean achieving *exclusive* control or jurisdiction over the deviance in question, but medical claims, for the reasons stated earlier, have become increasingly dominant. The battles to define and redefine deviance, however, will continue.

It is important to note the connection between the rise of medical deviance designations and the state. Generally speaking, in the face of entrenched criminal definitions of deviance, the medicalization of deviance cannot occur without some type of approval by the state. The professional dominance of medicine does not extend to the authority to override existing criminal definitions of deviance; thus successful appeals to the state are necessary for legitimation. It is the state that grants medicine the right to a particular social control turf.* Medicine, in fact, may become the *agent* of social control *for* the state, as with opiate addiction and child abuse, or replace problematic parts of the state control apparatus, as with chronic drunkenness. This highlights the complex interface of medical and legal social control agencies.

When the significant battle or battles are won and medical claims-makers and their supporters achieve legitimacy for their deviance designation, we can say that a claim has been successfully staked. Although such claims are of course open to new challenges, if they become institutionalized, they are more resistant to challenge.

**Institutionalization of a medical deviance designation.** When a deviance designation is institutionalized, it reaches a state of fixity and semipermanence. The medical viewpoint has been legitimated and now becomes an accepted category in the official order. We find two general types of institutionalization: codification and bureaucratization.

When a deviance designation is codified, it becomes an accepted part of the official medical and/or legal classification system. It is written into law, supported by court decisions, or is included as an official diagnosis in official manuals such as the American Psychiatric Association's *Diagnostic and Statistical Manual*. This provides both a symbolic and instrumental acceptance of deviance as a medical category.

Bureaucratization, the creation of large-scale organizations, is another form of institutionalization. Large social control bureaucracies are constructed that in effect provide institutionalized support for medicalization. Examples include the federal agencies such as the National Institute of Mental Health and the National Institute of Alcohol Abuse and Alcoholism, special programs such as SAODAP, informational "clearing houses" such as the National Center of Child Abuse and Neglect, and, in a different way, the state mental hospital system itself. These bureaucracies support medicalization in one sense by providing research monies, technical assistance, and other institutional benefits to supporters of a particular viewpoint of deviance. On the other hand, they are bureaucratic "industries," with large budgets and many employees, that depend for their existence on the acceptance of a particular deviance designation. They become "vested interests" in every sense of the term. A designation with such a supportive bureaucracy is more securely anchored against challenges and becomes more resistant to change.

When a deviance designation is institutionalized, one could say, adopting Thomas Kuhn's (1970) terminology, it has become the reigning

---

*This is unnecessary when there is no prior criminal claim to a social control turf, as with hyperkinesis. Similarly, when a particular form of social control is only rarely deployed (e.g., arrest for homosexual behavior), the proponents of the new designation may bypass appeals to the state. It is important to remember, however, that the state maintains ultimate control over this resource of legitimacy. Indeed, medical practice is itself premised on the continued viability of this state-issued mandate. Moreover, in those cases in which there has been a distinction between "criminal" and "sickness" behavior, physicians have often adopted a position that explicitly supports the state's system of criminal categories (e.g., public homosexual behavior is against the law, as is driving under the influence of alcohol), quite aside from whether such illegal activity is thought to be a product of sickness.

paradigm for viewing deviance. It is, of course, open to new challenges, especially when anomalous data become available as ammunition for new claims-makers with a different definition or designation of deviance. In the model we present here, when new challengers begin to make their claims, we may return to stage 2 or 3 and continue to observe the politics of deviance designation.

To make one final point, in most cases of medicalization of deviance, public acceptance "lags behind" professional and bureaucratic support. The public remains more skeptical about medical designations than professionals, especially in the cases of alcoholism, opiate addiction, and homosexuality. This skepticism provides a reservoir of potential support for future challenges to medical deviance designations.

• • •

Although this sequential model proposes to explain "how" deviance is medicalized, it does not directly confront the questions of why or when. We begin to address these questions in the generalizations we have drawn from the cases presented earlier.

## Grounded generalizations

In this discussion we present five theoretical statements that could be called grounded generalizations in as much as they emerge from our analysis of the cases in Chapters 3 to 8. We offer these as propositions that seem to us to be suggested in our data.

**Medicalization and demedicalization of deviance are cyclical phenomena.** We have argued that the medicalization of deviance, as reflected in this book's title, is increasing in American society. Although we believe this represents the dominant trend, our investigation also has revealed a cyclical dimension to medicalization. In other words, the changes in deviance designations do not all flow in one direction; there is a movement back and forth between badness and sickness designations.

Let us recall a few examples. In Chapter 5 we described the change in opiate addiction from a medical problem to a crime and back again to a medical entity. In Chapter 7 we traced the definition of same-sex conduct from immorality to sickness to its symbolic demedicalization (followed, apparently, by a resurgence of an antihomosexual moral crusade). In Chapter 3 we saw a series of more subtle changes, an oscillation between "social" and "biological" emphases in medical designations of madness. Thus we can say that the movement of deviance designations has a cyclical quality.

We ought not be surprised at the fluidity between badness and sickness designations, since this ebb and flow occurs in a common sea of "immorality." As we argued earlier, to define a deviant activity as sickness leaves its negative moral evaluation intact. Because the direction of the moral evaluation of the behavior does not change—it is still disreputable and untoward—under proper circumstances sickness can be redesignated as badness. Unless a behavior or activity is vindicated and no longer defined as deviant, both medicalization and demedicalization take place on a moral, or more properly, an immoral continuum.

This ebb and flow of deviance designations, although played out in various arenas of conflict, sometimes creates jurisdictional compromises and marriages of convenience. Deviance designations may become hybrid badness-sickness amalgams, such as with opiate addicts and sexual offenders, and the social control turf is then shared or divided.

What factors spur a cyclical shift in deviance designations? It seems that medical-sickness deviance designations emerge as a dialectical response to extreme criminal-badness designations. A clear example is the reemergence of medical designations of opiate addiction at precisely the same time in the 1950s that the severest criminal penalties for addiction were passed into law. Other examples include (1) the appearance of medical designations of homosexuality during the same period in the 19th century that saw a sustained drive against homosexual conduct and (2) the recent reascendance of a "biological" model of madness after the domination of "social" definitions during the 1960s community mental health movement. Perhaps similarly, the disease concept of alcoholism emerged right after the repeal of Prohibition. The cyclical nature of deviance designations has a distinctly dynamic and dialectical quality. In short, the extreme of one designation creates fertile conditions for the challenge and emergence of counterclaims. This is related clearly to our next generalization.

**Medical designations of deviance are more often promoted as a "foil" against criminal definitions than as ends in themselves.** Since medical designations arise at an extreme point in criminalization, their emergence appears to be related to this criminalization. Medical designations have been used regularly to mollify the harshness of criminal definitions of deviants and in general as a foil against such designations.

In many of the cases examined, we found the champions of medical designations presenting their claims specifically as a critique of the dominant or ascending criminal definition. K. M. Benkert, the Hungarian physician who proposed a congenital theory of "homosexuality," argued directly against the growing legal repression and harsh punishments for homosexual behavior contained in the Prussian legal code. The mid–20th-century critics of America's criminalization and harsh treatment of opiate addicts used the medical model of addiction, especially as evidenced in the British system of addiction control, as a foil with which to attack the injustice of the criminal treatment of addicts (e.g., Lindesmith, 1947; Nyswander, 1956; Schur, 1965; Duster, 1970). The 19th-century champions of the asylum movement as well as the late 19th-century child savers used medical rhetoric to promote their causes. Time and again, medical and, perhaps especially, nonmedical reformers championed medical conceptions as a critique of harsh and punitive practices. These claims-makers often promoted medical definitions, not for their own sake as more "valid" or "true" conceptions of reality, but as "humanitarian" challenges to what they saw as excessively punitive practices.* This, of course, underlines the political nature of the medical claims, to which we have alluded many times.

**Only a small segment of the medical profession is involved in the medicalization of deviance.** In nearly all the cases examined, only a small specialized segment of the medical profession is ever involved in the politics of deviance designation and the promotion of medical definitions of deviance. Although these claims-making physicians are few in number, their participation is central and critical to successful medicalization. It is their conceptualization of the behavior or condition as a medical problem that provides the rationale and justification for medical designations of deviance, as well as supplying ammunition for claims-making battles. The nonmedical champions rely on and use these medical claims and formulations in their own claims-making activities.

The debates about deviance designations are far removed from everyday medical practice. Rank and file physicians, for the most part, are uninformed about the debates and battles and, furthermore, do not much care about them. Most of the "deviance" discussed in this book simply is not a significant part of the majority of medical practices, and, by and large, most physicians do not wish to deal with such problems.

This requires modification of such general notions as "medical imperialism" as an explanation of the medicalization of deviance. Medical imperialism, to the extent that it exists, is not usually initiated or even supported by the medical profession en masse. The nonmedical interests, be they political, economic, or "moral," aligned with a small segment of the medical profession, constitute the major claims-makers of new medical social control turfs. It is only when a medical claim is successfully staked and becomes part of standard medical practice that most physicians have much to do with it.

**When medical designations of deviance are proposed, they most likely will be based on the notion of "compulsivity."** For most cases examined, definitive and uncontestable evidence of biophysiological causation does not exist. In lieu of such evidence, or

*One reason reformers chose the medical model as a critique is because it is the only reduced-blame and nonpunitive alternative model of deviance available (recall our discussion in Chapter 9).

in addition to ambiguous organic data, some type of "compulsivity" is proposed as the cause of the deviant behavior. The notion of compulsivity is a central justification for the medical claim.

All concepts of addiction have this notion of compulsion at their core. Medical explanations of homosexuality and psychopathology, and, to a lesser degree, of hyperkinesis and child abuse, indicate the idea of compulsion in their conceptualizations.* Compulsivity denotes that the individual "cannot help it," since the behavior is caused by forces beyond his or her control. Compulsivity, in effect, removes motivation or cause from the will and locates it in the body or mind. By proposing that the behavior is caused by "forces" beyond both a person's understanding and control, and is therefore not the individual's fault, compulsivity aligns well with our sociological understanding of what constitutes sickness.

Let us explore for a moment the notion of compulsivity in a cultural context. In Western society, moderation and control are important moral values. To be immoderate, excessive, and "out of control" is to be potentially deviant, regardless of the effects of one's behavior. Extreme immoderation is viewed as irrational behavior. Our rational orientation to the world makes understanding such conduct difficult and puzzling. This quasimedical conception becomes then an explanation for the "puzzle" of immoderate and irrational conduct: the behavior is caused by a compulsion, which is itself an illness. Furthermore, compulsivity posits an explanation that is determinist, individualistic, and has a scientific aura, all consistent with the important American values discussed earlier.

Compulsivity, then, becomes a useful and significant part of medical designations of deviance, since it allows for a medical explanation without requiring conclusive evidence for organic cause. With the exception of opiate addiction, where the notion has been demystified and unmasked as rational behavior to reduce withdrawal pain, most medical claims for compulsivity have not been subjected to rigorous scientific testing. Indeed, it is not entirely clear how such a scientific "test" of the compulsion hypothesis might be constructed, given the vague and circular definitions of it that have been offered (e.g., alcoholism as a product of "loss of control").

The historical sources of compulsivity as a medical explanation for deviance are many and diverse. For example, 18th-century physician Benjamin Rush called inebriety a disease of the will; physicians in the 19th-century depicted masturbation as a compulsive disease; and Freudian theorists have composed several variations on this theme. Yet compulsivity and loss of control are *not* by themselves medical or biophysiological concepts—jurisdiction over compulsions must still be "won" by medical claims-makers.

**Medicalization and demedicalization are political and not scientific achievements.** We have mentioned the political aspects of medicalization so frequently throughout this book that it seems almost redundant to say it again here. We would like to review what this means and draw out a few additional significant points.

Medical designations of deviance that have been proposed either challenge existing claims or seek to carve out new deviance territory. While the medical claims are proposed in the name of science, they have not been in general subject to the scientific rules of evidence. Although science and medicine add prestige and authority to any claim, supporters must still engage in the contests necessary to get their claim recognized. This is always a political process. Because medical claims are couched in the language of science, yet rarely subject to empirical evaluation, scientific research can threaten as well as support medical deviance designations. With methadone maintenance, for example, early reports were highly supportive of its efficacy in treating heroin addiction; later reports, based on more rigorous research, were increasingly critical. Proponents and opponents

*Recently obesity and gambling have engendered medical explanations of compulsivity. George Becker (1978, p. 76) notes that in the 19th-century medical conceptions of the "mad" genius "the image of the creative process was to acquire a decidedly compulsive and irrational characteristic."

of deviance designations may use scientific evidence to support their claims. In such situations it is ironic to see scientific research used against medical claims that were themselves proffered in the name of science.

Let us briefly recall several examples that highlight the political nature of the medicalization and demedicalization of deviance. The 19th-century contest for the control of moral treatment and regulation of madhouses can be seen as a key "victory" for the medical conception of madness. The physicians were organized and were able to convince Parliament to support their definitions over lay definitions, although these physicians essentially had no specific or unique knowledge about or ability to treat madness. It was in every sense a "political" achievement. The modern disease concept of alcoholism was intentionally proposed by its champions at the Yale center not for its scientific validity but for its moral and political implications. The two cases of demedicalization we examine in some detail, opiate addiction in the early 20th century and homosexuality in the 1970s, underline with special clarity the political nature of deviance designations. The Harrison Act, and the subsequent challenges by the Treasury Department (supported by a variety of Supreme Court cases), successfully "defeated" the medical designation of opiate addiction. The recent American Psychiatric Association decision that homosexuality is no longer officially an "illness" was achieved in large part by the overt politicization of the issue by gay rights activists and a few psychiatric sympathizers. In our judgment, defining behavior as an illness is always a political achievement, although the actual politics are sometimes subtle or obscured and difficult to sort out.

We wish to make one final observation in this section. We were surprised at the apparently small significance of medical technique or technology in the politics of deviance designation that we have studied. Medical technology—drugs, surgery, or other medical treatments—played a relatively minor role in the cases we examined. Only for hyperactivity and the remedicalization of opiate addiction (with methadone) did technology play a dominant role in the political contest about designation. This is not to say that medical technique was not offered as evidence to support medical claims, but rather that it cannot be seen as the singular explanatory variable for medicalization that some have suggested. We believe, however, that with increasing research and reliance on medical technology, especially in the form of drugs and technological medical practice (especially surgery), technique will play an increasingly important role in the medicalization of deviance. A few medical claims for deviance based on technique were pointed out in Chapter 8, and one need not go far to include drugs and surgery for obesity and tranquilizers for everyday anxieties as additional examples. This leads us directly to study who is promoting medical technique and with what consequences (see the discussion of hunches and hypotheses later in the chapter).

### Sociologists as challengers

It seems fitting to include in this discussion a reflexive note on the role of sociologists in the politics of deviance designation. Sociologists, rather than being "objective" bystanders in the contests about deviance designation, are sometimes active participants. Not only do sociologists collect data about deviance and chronicle the claims-making activities of others, they often become active challengers in these activities. With one exception, sociologists in recent years have challenged rather than promoted medical deviance designations. Sociologists such as Alfred Lindesmith (1947), Edwin Schur (1965), and Troy Duster (1970), among others, supported the medical designation of opiate addiction against the dominant criminal designation. But in most of the other cases reviewed here—including, for example, madness (Goffman, 1961; Scheff, 1966), alcoholism (Gusfield, 1967; Schneider, 1978), child abuse (Gelles, 1973; Gil, 1970), and hyperkinesis (Conrad, 1975, 1976)—sociologists' analyses and viewpoints stand as clear challenges or at least alternatives to medical deviance designations. Although many other sociologists do adopt the medical model in their research, sociological analyses represent a consistent potential challenge to medical claims. The social and contextual nature of the sociological perspective, perhaps most especially in its interactionist and Marxian modes, is in fundamental ways opposed to the more individualist and reductionist medical perspective.

## Hunches and hypotheses: notes for further research

In this discussion we note briefly a number of "hunches and hypotheses" that emerge from our investigation of the medicalization of deviance. Although we do not presently have sufficient data to call them conclusions, these propositions are based on our analysis and are presented both as "informed" speculations and directions for further research. We separate them for the sake of clarity.

1. It appears that the medicalization of deviance increases after a failure or crisis in previous systems of social control. Although we must be somewhat cautious about generalizing, our examination reveals several instances where this occurred. In the 19th century, when asylums were becoming greatly overcrowded, the degeneration hypothesis was proposed as a medical explanation and a justification for custodial care. Following the repeal of Prohibition, which could itself be seen as a crisis in social control, the disease concept of alcoholism was proposed. As the "drinker" rather than the "drink" became the object of social control, alcoholism as a disease became an idea that attempted to justify a more humanitarian control of alcohol-related deviance. In the activist 1960s, "drugs" became a symbol for rebellious and alienated youth. By the end of the decade "hard" drug use was spreading rapidly in middle-class communities. The extant social controls—resident self-help groups and imprisonment—had had only small success and were too limited to accommodate the increasing number of addicts. A social control crisis was partly averted by "sentencing" adjudicated opiate offenders to a variety of newly created outpatient methadone maintenance clinics.

2. As a particular kind of deviance becomes a middle-class rather than solely a lower-class "problem," the probability of medicalization increases. There seems to be a historical proclivity to define deviance that is thought endemic to lower-class life as badness, but when it becomes evident that it is also a middle-class phenomenon, it is likely to be defined as sickness.* When chronic drunkenness was thought common only to the lower-class skid row alcoholic, badness designations prevailed. But as increasing research evidence and public recognition found problem drinkers in respectable middle-class homes, it became difficult to maintain the skid row image of drunkenness. As more middle-class people were defined as deviant drinkers, the notion that alcoholism is a disease increased in acceptance and popularity. Similarly, when opiate addiction left the ghetto and became a middle-class problem in the late 1960s, there was a rapid increase in its medicalization. Some existing evidence indicates that hyperactivity is a diagnosis disproportionately used for middle-class and suburban schoolchildren. Perhaps poorer inner-city children are expected to be overactive, restless, and distracted, but when suburban children behave this way, they are deemed "sick." Finally, we suggest that the medicalization of abortion resulted partly because middle-class women were among the largest recipients of abortions in the 1960s. In short, as public perceptions move from a lower-class problem to a middle-class problem, deviance designations tend to change from badness to sickness.

3. Medicalization increases directly with its economic profitability. This is a significant dimension of the medicalization of deviance that we have touched on several times in this book but have not pursued in depth. We can isolate three ways in which profitability encourages medicalization. First, medicalization can create new and profitable markets for large and powerful medical industries. As we noted in earlier chapters, the pharmaceutical corporations garnered considerable profits from the medicalization of hyperkinesis and opiate addiction and from the increased use of medications for madness. We can extend these examples to include the promotion of psychoactive drugs for everyday anxieties (Radelet, 1977b), obesity, "senility," and other human problems. The corporate profits from medicalizing deviance are yet uncalculated but un-

*We are indebted to Ralph Childers for this insight.

doubtedly enormous (based on the little data we do have available). Second, the medicalization of deviance can be a highly profitable enterprise for specialized groups of physicians. For example, in the *Newsletter* of the American Society of Bariatric Physicians (a professional organization of physicians specializing in treating obesity), advertisements appear offering bariatric practices for sale with six-figure salaries and short working hours. Third, the medicalization of deviance indirectly supports certain corporate interests. The alcoholic beverage industry, for example, vigorously supports the disease concept of alcoholism, which focuses attention on the individual drinker and away from the industry's advertising and marketing techniques. The health insurance industry is playing an increasing role in medicalization politics. The role of the corporate sector and the profitability of medicalization, only touched on here, are fertile areas for research. Although the necessary data are difficult to acquire, studies directed at a more specific understanding of the political economy of medicalizing deviance could provide an important extension to our analysis as well as evaluating the speculations presented here.

## A CONCLUDING REMARK

The medicalization of deviance is an abiding feature of contemporary American society. It will not disappear or even decrease perceptibly in this century and, indeed, is likely to expand. Medical definitions and treatments for deviance undoubtedly will continue to be proposed, and contests in the politics of deviance designation will persist. Barbara Wootton's (1963) remarks nearly two decades ago remain poignant today:

> We may well be on the brink of an age in which the power of science to influence behavior will achieve a new dimension. Yet the question of what behavior is to be influenced, and in what directions, remains, and will remain, as obstinate as ever. (p. 202)

## SUMMARY

In this chapter we presented a theoretical statement on the medicalization of deviance. It serves as a conceptual summary of our analysis and as an inductive and historical sociological explanation.

First, general historical and cultural conditions that have provided a foundation for the medicalization of deviance were reviewed. The most important factors appear to be the rise of rationalism, the development of science, the emergence of determinist and biophysiological theories of causation, and the growth and apparent success of medicine. American society has proven particularly hospitable to medicalization. The medical perspective of deviance aligns well with a number of dominant American values, including experimentation, newness, humanitarianism, pragmatism, and individualism. Furthermore, the cultural conceptions related to the Protestant Ethic, an abiding faith in science, a democratic political system, the organization and monopolization of the medical profession, and the profitability of medical treatment under capitalism are all facilitating social conditions for the medicalization of deviance. But, as we have noted numerous times, deviance designations do not emerge by themselves but rather are a product of collective enterprise and claims-making activities.

In the second part of this chapter we presented an inductive theory of the medicalization of deviance. Basing our analysis in the politics of deviance designations described in Chapter 2, we develop a sequential model of medicalization and offer five grounded generalizations. The stages are analytically distinct and describe the process of medicalization. The grounded generalizations begin to provide a sociological explanation of the medicalization of deviance.

In the final discussion in this chapter we propose three hunches or hypotheses as directions for future research: the medicalization of deviance increases after a failure or crisis in previous social control; as a particular kind of deviance becomes a middle-class rather than solely lower-class "problem," medicalization increases; and medicalization increases directly with economic profitability. We note the importance of developing an analysis of the political economy of medicalization.

Our concluding remark suggests that the medicalization of deviance will continue and is likely to expand and that the questions raised in this book will remain pertinent in the future.

# BIBLIOGRAPHY


Ackerknecht, E. H. *A short history of psychiatry*. New York: Hafner Press, 1968.

Agar, M. Going through the changes: methadone in New York City. *Hum. Organization*, 1977, *36*, 291-298 (Fall).

Agar, M. H., & Stephens. R. C. The methadone street scene: the addict's view. *Psychiatry*, 1975, *38*, 381-387.

Alcoholics Anonymous. *Alcoholics Anonymous*. New York: A. A. World Services, 1939.

Alcoholics Anonymous. *Alcoholics Anonymous comes of age*. New York: Harper & Row, Publishers, 1957.

Alcott, W. *The young man's guide*. Boston: Marvin, 1833.

Alexander, F. G., & Selesnick, S. T. *The history of psychiatry*. New York: New American Library, 1966.

Alexander, L. Medical science under dictatorship. *N. Engl. J. Med.*, 1949, *241*(2), 39-47.

Alford, R. R. The political economy of health care: dynamics without change. *Pol. Society* 1972, *2*(2), 127-164.

Allen, F. A. Raffaele Garofalo. In H. Mannheim (Ed.), *Pioneers in criminology*. Chicago: Quadrangle/The New York Times Book Co., Inc., 1960.

American Friends Service Committee. *Struggle for justice*. New York: Hill & Wang, 1971.

American Medical Association. Report of the board of trustees: hospitalization of patients with alcoholism. *J.A.M.A.*, 1956, *162*, 750.

American Medical Association. *Manual on alcoholism for physicians*. Chicago: American Medical Association, 1957.

American Medical Association. *Standard nomenclature of diseases and operations* (5th ed.). (E. T. Thompson and A. C. Hayden, Eds.) New York: McGraw-Hill Book Co., Inc., 1961.

American Medical Association. Alcoholism is a disease. *J.A.M.A.*, 1972, *222*, 699.

American Psychiatric Association. *Diagnostic and statistical manual of mental disorders* (2nd ed.). Washington, D.C.: American Psychiatric Association, 1968.

American Psychiatric Association. The mathematical curability of insanity . . . and its attack by Pliny Earle. *Hosp. Community Psychiatry*, 1976, *27*, 481.

Amir, M. & Berman, Y. Chromosomal deviation and crime. *Fed. Probation*, 1970, *34*, 55-62 (June).

Andenaes, J. Does punishment deter crime? *Crim. Law Quarterly*, 1968, *11*, 77-93.

Anderson, D. Alcohol and public opinion. *Q. J. Stud. Alcohol*, 1942, *3*, 376-392.

Anslinger, H. J., & Tompkins, W. F. *The traffic in narcotics*. New York: Funk & Wagnalls, Inc., 1953.

Arendt, H. *Eichmann in Jerusalem*. New York: Viking Press, 1963.

Ariès, P. [*Centuries of childhood: a social history of family life*] (R. Baldick, trans.). New York: Alfred A. Knopf, Inc., 1962.

Aristotle. [*History of animals of Aristotle and a treatise on physiognomy*] (T. Taylor, trans.). London: R. Wilks, 1809.

Aristotle. [*Problemata. The works of Aristotle (vol. 7)*] ( W. D. Ross, Ed.; E. S. Forster, trans.). Oxford: Clarendon Press, 1927.

Armor, D., & Klerman, G. Psychiatric treatment ideologies and professional ideology. *J. Health Soc. Behav.*, 1968, *9*, pp. 243-255.

Armor, D. J., Polich, J. M., & Stambul, H. B. *Alcoholism and treatment*. Prepared for the U.S. National Institute on Alcohol Abuse and Alcoholism. Santa Monica, Calif.: Rand Corp., 1976.

Aubert, V., & Messinger, S. L. The criminal and the sick. *Inquiry*, 1958, *1*, 137-160.

Ausubel, D. P. *Drug addiction: physiological, psychological, and sociological aspects*. New York: Random House, Inc., 1958.

Bacon, S. D. Alcoholics do not drink. *Ann. Acad. Pol. Soc. Sci.*, 1958, *315*, 55-64.

Bacon, S. D. Meeting the problems of alcohol in the U.S.A. In M. Keller and T. C. Coffey (Eds.) *Proceedings of the 28th International Congress on Alcohol and Alcoholism*. Highland Park, N.J.: Hillhouse Press, 1969.

Bacon, S. D. The problems of alcoholism in society. In D. Malikin (Ed.), *Social disability*. New York: New York University Press, 1973.

Bacon S. D. Concepts. In W. Filstead, J. Rossi, & M. Keller (Eds.), *Alcohol and alcohol problems*. Cambridge, Mass.: Ballinger Publishing Co., 1976.

Bacon, S. D. About Mark Keller on his retirement. *J. Stud. Alcohol*, 1977, *38*(7), v-x.

Bailey, D. S. *Homosexuality and the Western Christian tradition*. London: Longmans, Green & Co., 1955.

Bain, K. The physically abused child. *Pediatrics*, 1963, *31*, 895-897.

Baines, H. E., & Teeters, N. K. *New horizons in*

*criminology*. New York: Prentice-Hall, Inc., 1943.

Bateson, G., Jackson, D. D., Haley, J., & Weakland, J. Toward a theory of schizophrenia. *Behav. Sci.,* 1956, *1,* 251-264.

Bazelon, D. L. Psychiatrists and the adversary process. *Sci. Am.* 1974, *230,* 18-23 (June).

Beall, O. T., Jr. Aristotle's master piece in America: a landmark in the folklore of medicine. *William Mary Quarterly,* 1963, *20*(2), 207-222.

Becker, E. *Escape from evil*. New York: The Free Press, 1975.

Becker, G. *The mad genius controversy: a study in the sociology of deviance*. Beverly Hills, Calif.: Sage Publications, 1978.

Becker, H. S. Becoming a marijuana user. *Am. J. Sociol.,* 1953, *59,* 235-242.

Becker, H. S. *Outsiders; studies in the sociology of deviance*. New York: The Free Press of Glencoe, Inc., 1963.

Becker, H. S. Problems in the publication of field studies. In A. J. Vidich, J. Bensman & M. R. Stein (Eds.), *Reflections on community studies*. New York: John Wiley & Sons, Inc., 1964.

Becker, H. S. History, culture and subjective experience: an exploration of the social bases of drug-induced experiences. *J. Health Soc. Behav.,* 1967, *8,* 163-176. (a)

Becker, H. S. Whose side are we on? *Social Prob.,* 1967, *14,* 239-247. (b)

Becker, H. S. Labeling theory reconsidered. In *Outsiders* (2nd ed.). New York: The Free Press, 1973.

Bedau, H. A. Physical intervention to alter behavior in a punitive environment: some moral reflections on new technology. *Am. Behav. Scientist,* 1975, *18,* 657-678.

Bednar, R. I., Zalhart, P. F., Greathouse, L., & Weinberg, S. Operant conditioning principles in the treatment of learning and behavior problems with delinquent boys. *J. Counseling Psychol,,* 1970, *17,* 492-497.

Begelman, D. A. Homosexuality and the ethics of behavioral intervention. *J. Homosex.,* 1977, *2*(3), 213-219.

Belknap, I. *Human problems in a state mental hospital*. New York: McGraw-Hill Book Co., Inc., 1956.

Bell, A. P., & Weinberg, M. S. *Homosexualities: a study of diversity among men and women*. New York: Simon & Schuster, Inc., 1978.

Ben-David, J. *The scientist's role in society*. Englewood Cliffs, N.J.: Prentice-Hall, Inc., 1971.

Benedict, R. *Patterns of culture*. Boston: Houghton Mifflin Co., 1934.

Berger, P., & Luckmann, T. *The social construction of reality*. New York: Doubleday & Co., Inc., 1966.

Bergler, E. The myth of a new national disease: homosexuality and the Kinsey Report. *Psych. Quarterly,* 1948, *22,* 66-88.

Bergler, E. *Homosexuality: disease or way of life?* New York: Hill & Wang, 1956.

Bergler, E. What every physician should know about homosexuality. *Int. Rec. Med.,* 1958, *171,* 685-690.

Berman, A., & Siegal, A. Adaptive and learning skills in juvenile delinquents. *J. Learning Disabil.* 1976, *9,* 51-56.

Bieber, I. Speaking out frankly on a once taboo subject. *New York Times Mag.,* Aug. 24, 1964, pp. 74ff.

Bieber, I. A discussion of 'Homosexuality: the ethical challenge'. *J. Consult. Clin. Psychol.,* 1976, *44,* 163-166.

Bieber, I., Dain, H. J., Dince, P. R., Drellich, M. W., Rifkin, A. H., Wilbur, C. B., & Bieber, T. B. *Homosexuality: a psychoanalytic study*. New York: Basic Books, Inc., 1962.

Bingham, C. Seventeenth century attitudes toward deviant sex. *J. Interdisc. Hist.,* 1971, *1,* 447-472.

Bischoff, H. L. Physician acceptance of the disease concept of alcoholism. Unpublished master's thesis, University of Iowa, 1976.

Blaine, J., & Renault, P. Rx 3 times/week: alternative to methadone. *NIDA Research Monograph No. 8*. Springfield, Va.: National Technical Information Service, U.S. Department of Commerce, 1976.

Block, M. A. *Alcoholism: its facets and phases*. New York: The John Day Co., 1965.

Blumer, H. Social problems as collective behavior. *Social prob.,* 1971, *18,* 298-306 (Winter).

Blumgart, H. L. Caring for the patient. *N. Engl. J. Med.,* 1964, *270,* 449-456.

Bowart, W. *Operation mind control*. New York: Fontana Books, 1978.

Bowman, K. M., & Jellinek, E. M. Alcohol addiction and chronic alcoholism. *Q. J. Stud. Alcohol,* 1941, *4,* 98-176.

Boyer, P., & Nissenbaum, S. *Salem possessed: the social origins of witchcraft*. Cambridge, Mass.: Harvard University Press, 1974.

Bradley, C. A. The behavior of children receiving benzedrine. *Am. J. Psychiatry,* 1937, *94,* 577-585 (Nov.).

Brandsma, J. M. Alcoholismic dysbehaviorism revisited: a reply to Keller. *J. Stud. Alcohol,* 1977, *38,* 1838-1842.

Brecher, E. M. *Licit and illicit drugs*. Boston: Little, Brown & Co., 1972.

Breggin, P. R. Is psychosurgery on the upswing? *Hum. Events,* May 5, 1973, pp. 12ff. (a)

Breggin, P. R. The return of lobotomy and psychosurgery. Congressional Record, Feb. 24, 1972, E1602-E1612. Reprinted in Quality of health care—human experimentation, hearings before Senator Edward Kennedy's subcommittee on

Health, U.S. Senate. Washington, D.C.: U.S. Government Printing Office, 1973. (b)

Brenner, C. *An elementary textbook of psychoanalysis,* Revised ed. New York: Anchor Press, 1974.

Brill, H., & Patton, R. B. Analysis of the 1955-56 fall in New York state mental hospitals during the first year of large-scale use of tranquilizing drugs. *Am. J. Psychiatry,* 1957, *114,* 509-517.

Brill, H., & Patton, R. B. Clinical statistical analysis of population changes in New York state since the introduction of psychotropic drugs. *Am. J. Psychiatry,* 1962, *119,* 20-35.

Brown, H. *Familiar faces, hidden lives.* New York: Harcourt Brace Jovanovich, Inc., 1976.

Buckner, H. T. *Deviance, reality and change.* New York: Random House, Inc., 1971.

Bullough, V. L. *Sexual variance in society and history.* New York: John Wiley & Sons, Inc., 1976.

Bullough, V. L. Challenges to societal attitudes toward homosexuality in the late nineteenth and early twentieth centuries. *Soc. Sci. Quarterly,* 1977, *58,* 29-44.

Bullough, V., & Bullough, B. *Sin, sickness and sanity.* New York: The New American Library, 1977.

Bullough, V., & Bullough, B. Nineteenth century English homosexual teachers: the up front and back stage performance. Presented at meetings of The American Sociological Association, San Francisco, 1978.

Bullough, V. L., & Voght, M. Homosexuality and its confusion with the 'secret sin' in pre-Freudian America. *J. Hist. Med. Sci.,* 1973, *28,* 143-155 (April).

Burgess, A. *A clockwork orange.* New York: W. W. Norton & Co., Inc., Publishers, 1963.

Burnham, J. C. Medical specialists and movements toward social control in the progressive era: three examples. In J. Israel (Ed.), *Building the organizational society.* New York: The Free Press, 1972.

Butz, R. H. Intoxication and withdrawal. In J. E. Estes & M. E. Heinemann (Eds.), *Alcoholism: development, consequences, and interventions.* St. Louis: The C. V. Mosby Co., 1977.

Caffey, J. Multiple fractures in the long bones of infants suffering from chronic subdural hematoma. *Am. J. Roentgenol.,* 1946, *56,* 163-173.

Caffey, J. Traumatic lesions in growing bones other than fractures and lesions: clinical and radiological features. *Br. J. Radiol.,* 1957, *30,* 225-238.

Cahalan, D. *Problem drinkers: a national survey.* San Francisco: Jossey-Bass, Inc., Publishers, 1970.

Cahalan, D., Cisin, I. H., & Crossley, H. M. *American drinking practices.* New Brunswick, N.J.: Rutgers Center of Alcohol Studies, 1969.

Cahalan, D., & Room, R. *Problem drinking among American men.* New Brunswick, N.J.: Rutgers Center for Alcohol Studies, 1974.

Cahn, S. *The treatment of alcoholics.* New York: Oxford University Press, 1970.

Caldwell, R. G. *Red Hannah, Delaware's whipping post.* Philadelphia: University of Pennsylvania Press, 1947.

Cantwell, D. P. Natural history and prognosis in the hyperactive child syndrome. In D. Cantwell (Ed.), *The hyperactive child.* New York: Spectrum Publications, Inc., 1975.

Caplan, G. *Principles of preventive psychiatry.* New York: Basic Books, Inc., 1964.

Caplan, N., & Nelson, S. D. On being useful: the nature and consequences of psychological research on social problems. *Am. Psychologist,* 1973, *28,* 199-211.

Cartwright, F. F. *A social history of medicine.* New York: Longman, Inc., 1977.

Cartwright, S. W. Report on the diseases and physical peculiarities of the negro race. *N.O. Med. Surg. J.,* 1851, *7,* 691-715.

Cassell, E. J. Disease as an 'it': concepts of disease revealed by patients' presentation of symptoms. *Soc. Sci. Med.,* 1976, *10,* 143-146.

Caudill, W. *The psychiatric hospital as a small society.* Cambridge, Mass.: Harvard University Press, 1958.

Chafetz, M. E., Jr., & Demone, H. W. *Alcoholism and society.* New York: Oxford University Press, 1962.

Chalfant, P. Professionalization and the medicalization of deviance: the case of probation officers. *Offender Rehabilitation,* 1977, *2,* 77-85.

Chambliss, W. J. A sociological analysis of the law of vagrancy. *Social Prob.,* 1964, *12,* 67-77 (Fall).

Chambliss, W. J. Markets, profits, labor and smack. *Contemp. Crises,* 1977, *1,* 53-76.

Chang, J., & Block, J. A study of identification in male homosexuals. *J. Consult. Psychol.,* 1960, *24,* 307-310.

Charles, A. The case of Ritalin. *New Repub.,* Oct. 23, 1971, pp. 17-19.

Chavkin, S. Therapy or mind control? Congress endorses psychosurgery. *Nation,* 1976, *223,* 398-402.

Chein, I., Gerard, D. L., Lee, R. S., & Rosenfield, E. *The road to H.* New York: Basic Books, Inc., 1964.

Chorover, S. Big Brother and psychotechnology. *Psychol. Today,* 1973, *7,* 43-54 (Oct.).

Chorover, S. The pacification of the brain. In *U.S. Senate Committee of the Judiciary, Individual Rights and the Federal Role in Behavior Modification.* Washington, D.C.: U.S. Government Printing Office, 1974. (Reprinted from *Psychol. Today,* May, 1974, pp. 59-69.) (a)

Chorover, S.: Psychosurgery: a neuropsychological perspective. *Boston U. Law Rev.,* 1974, *74,* 231-248 (March). (b)

Christie, N., & Bruun, K. Alcohol problems: the conceptual framework. In M. Keller & T. Coffey (Eds.), *Proceedings of the 28th International Congress on Alcohol and Alcoholism* (Vol. 2.) Highland Park, N.J.: Hillhouse Press, 1969.

Chu, F. D., & Trotter, S. *The madness establishment*. New York: Grossman Publishers, 1974.

Church Committee. *Foreign and military intelligence* (Book I.) Washington, D.C.: U.S. Government Printing Office, 1976.

Churchill, W. *Homosexual behavior among males: a cross-cultural and cross-species investigation*. New York: Hawthorn Books, Inc., 1967.

Clark, W. B. Conceptions of alcoholism: consequences for research. *Addictive Dis.*, 1975, *1*, 395-430.

Clark, W. B., & Cahalan, D. Changes in problem drinking over a four-year span. *Addictive Behav.*, 1976, *1*, 251-259.

Clements, S. D. Task Force I: minimal brain dysfunction in children. *National Institute of Neurological Disease and Blindness Monograph No. 3*. Washington, D.C.: U.S. Department of Health, Education and Welfare, 1966.

Cloward, R. A., & Ohlin, L. E. *Delinquency and opportunity*. New York: The Free Press, 1960.

Cochran, W. G., Mosteller, F., & Tukey, J. W. *Statistical problems of the Kinsey Report*. Washington, D.C.: U.S. Government Printing Office, 1954.

Cockerham, W. E. Behavior modification for child molesters. *Corrections Mag.* Jan./Feb. 1975, 77-80.

Coe, R. M. *Sociology of medicine* (2nd ed.). New York: McGraw-Hill Book Co., 1978.

Cohen, A. K. *Delinquent boys: the culture of the gang*. New York: The Free Press of Glencoe, Inc., 1955.

Cohen, M., Howard, A., Klein, D. F., & Newfield, K. Evaluating the outcome criteria used in methadone maintenance programs. *Int. J. Addict.*, 1976, *2*, 283-294.

Cole, S. Hyperactive children: the use of stimulant drugs evaluated. *Am. J. Orthopsychiatry*, 1975, *45*, 28-37.

Coleman, E. Toward a new model of treatment of homosexuality: a review. *J. Homosex.*, 1978, *3*, 345-359.

Coleman, J., Katz, E. & Menzel, H. *Medical innovation*. Indianapolis: The Bobbs-Merrill Co., Inc., 1966.

Coleman, L. Problem kids and preventive medicine: the making of an odd couple. *Am. J. Orthopsychiatry*, 1978, *48*, 56-70.

Comfort, A. *The anxiety makers*. London: Thomas Nelson & Sons, 1967.

Conrad, P. The discovery of hyperkinesis: notes on the medicalization of deviant behavior. *Social Prob.*, 1975, *23*, 12-21 (Oct.).

Conrad, P. *Identifying hyperactive children: the medicalization of deviant behavior*. Lexington, Mass.: D. C. Heath & Co., 1976.

Conrad, P. Soviet dissidents, ideological deviance, and mental hospitalization. Presented at Midwest Sociological Society Meetings, Minneapolis, 1977.

Conrad, P. Types of medical social control. *Soc. Health Illness*, 1979, *1*, 1-11 (June).

Conrad, P. On the medicalization of deviance and social control. In David Ingelby (Ed.), *Critical psychiatry*. London: Penguin Books, 1980.

Conrad, P., & Schneider, J. W. Medicine. In J. Roucek (Ed.). *Social control for the 1980s*. Westport, Conn.: Greenwood Press, 1978.

Conrad, P., & Schneider, J. W. Implications of changing social policy for the medicalization of deviance. *Contemp. Crises*. (In press.)

Corley, M. C. Alcoholism as a stigmatizing condition. Unpublished doctoral dissertation, University of Kentucky, 1974.

Corwin, E. H. L., & Cunningham, E. V. Institutional facilities for the treatment of alcoholism. *Q. J. Stud. Alcohol*, 1944, *5*, 9-85.

Corzine, J. Personal communication, 1977.

Coulter, J. *Approaches to insanity*. New York: Halsted Press, 1973.

Crothers, T. D. Inebriety in ancient Egypt and Chaldea. *Q. J. Inebriety*, 1903, 25, *142-150*.

Crothers, T. D. A review of the history and literature of inebriety. *J. Inebriety*, 1911, *33*, 39-151.

Culliton, B. J. Psychosurgery: national commission issues surprisingly favorable report. *Science*, 1976, *194*, 299-301 (Oct. 15).

Cumming, E., & Cumming, J. *Closed ranks*. Cambridge, Mass.: Harvard University Press, 1957.

Cumming, J., & Cumming, E. *Ego and milieu*. Chicago: Aldine Publishing Co., 1966.

Currie, E. P. Crimes without criminals: witchcraft and its control in renaissance Europe. *Law Society Rev.*, 1968, *3*, 7-32 (Aug.).

Daniels, A. K. The captive professional: bureaucratic limitation in the practice of military psychiatry. *J. Health Soc. Behav.*, 1969, *10*, 255-265 (Dec.).

Dank, B. M. Coming out in the gay world. *Psychiatry*, 1971, *34*, 180-197 (May).

Davies, D. L. Normal drinking in recovered alcoholic addicts (comments by various correspondents). *Q. J. Stud. Alcohol*, 1963, *24*, 109-121, 321-332.

Davies, D. L. Definitional issues in alcoholism. In R. Tarter and A. Sugerman (Eds.), *Alcoholism*. Reading, Mass.: Addison-Wesley Publishing Co., 1976.

Davis, F. J., & Stivers, R., (Eds.). *The collective definition of deviance*. New York: The Free Press, 1975.

Davis, K. Mental hygiene and social structure. *Psychiatry*, 1938, *1*, 55-65.

Davis, N. *Sociological constructions of deviance*. Dubuque, Iowa: William C. Brown, 1975.

Davison, G. C. Homosexuality: the ethical challenge. *J. Consult. Clin. Psychol.*, 1976, *44*(2), 157-162.

Davison, G. C., & Wilson, G. T. Attitudes of behavior therapists toward homosexuality. *Behav. Ther.*, 1973, *4*, 686-696.

DeFrancis, V. Laws for mandatory reporting of child abuse cases. *State Gov.*, 1966, *39*, 8-13.

Delgado, J. M. R. *Physical control of the mind: toward a psychocivilized society*. New York: Harper & Row, Publishers, 1969.

Delong, A. R. What have we learned from psychoactive drug research with hyperactives? *Am. J. Dis. Child.*, 1972, *123*, 177-180.

Delong, J. V. The methadone habit. *N. Y. Times Mag*. March 16, 1975, pp. 16ff.

deMause, L. (Ed.). *The history of childhood*. New York: Psychohistory Press, 1974.

Deutsch, A. *The mentally ill in America*. (2nd ed.). New York: Columbia University Press, 1949.

Devereaux, G. Institutionalized homosexuality of the Mohave Indians. In Hendrik M. Ruitenbeek (Ed.), *The problem of homosexuality in modern America*. New York: E. P. Dutton & Co., Inc., 1963. (Originally published, 1937.)

Dickson, D. T. Bureaucracy and morality: an organizational perspective on a moral crusade. *Social Prob.*, 1968, *16*, 143-156 (Fall).

Dion, K. K. Physical attractiveness and evaluations of children's transgressions. *J. Personality Soc. Psychol*, 1972, *24*(2), 207-213.

Dohrenwend, B. P., & Chin-Shong, E. Social status and attitudes toward psychological disorder: the problem of tolerance of deviance. *Am. Soc. Rev.*, 1967, *32*, 417-433.

Dohrenwend, B. P., & Dohrenwend, B. S. *Social status and psychological disorder*. New York: John Wiley & Sons, Inc., 1969.

Dole, V. P., & Nyswander, M. A medical treatment for diacetylmorphine (heroin) addiction. *J.A.M.A.*, 1965, *193*, 646-650.

Dole, V. P., & Nyswander, M. Rehabilitation of heroin addicts after blockade with methadone. *N.Y. State J. Med.*, 1966, *66*, 2011-2017.

Dole, V. P., & Nyswander, M. Heroin addiction—a metabolic disease. *Arch. Intern. Med.*, 1967, *120*(1), 19-24.

Dole, V. P., & Nyswander, M. Methadone maintenance treatment: a ten-year perspective. *J.A.M.A.*, 1976, *235*, 2117-2119.

Donaldson, K. *Insanity inside out*. New York: Crown Publishers, Inc., 1976.

Dover, K. J. *Greek homosexuality*. Boston: Harvard University Press, 1978.

Dubos, R. *Mirage of health*. New York: Harper & Row, Publishers, 1959.

Dugdale, R. L. *The Jukes: a study in crime, pauperism, and heredity*. New York: G. P. Putnam's Sons, 1910.

Dumont, M. P. The politics of drugs. *Soc. Policy*, 1972, *3*(2), 32-35.

Dunham, H. W. *Social realities and community psychiatry*. New York: Human Sciences Press, 1976.

Dunham, H. W., & Weinberg, S. K. *The culture of the state mental hospital*. Detroit: Wayne State University Press, 1960.

DuPont, R. L. Profile of a heroin-addiction epidemic. *N. Engl. J. Med.*, 1971, *285*, 320-324.

Durkheim, E. *The division of labor in society*. New York: The Free Press, 1933. (Originally published, 1893.)

Durkheim, E. [*The rules of sociological method.*] (E. G. Catlin, Ed.; S. A. Solovay and J. H. Mueller, trans.). New York: The Free Press, 1938. (Originally published, 1895.)

Duster, T. *The legislation of morality*. New York: The Free Press, 1970.

Earle, C. W. The opium habit. In H. W. Morgan (Ed.), *Yesterday's addicts*. Norman, Okla.: University of Oklahoma Press, 1974. (Originally published, 1880.)

Eaton, V. G. How the opium habit is acquired. In H. W. Morgan (Ed.), *Yesterday's addicts*. Norman, Okla.: University of Oklahoma Press, 1974. (Originally published, 1880.)

Edelman, M. *Political language: words that succeed and policies that fail*. New York: Academic Press, Inc., 1977.

Ehrenreich, B., & Ehrenreich, J. *The American health empire*. New York: Random House, Inc., 1970.

Ehrenreich, B., & Ehrenreich, J. Medicine and social control. In B. R. Mandell (Ed.), *Welfare in America: controlling the "dangerous" classes*. Englewood Cliffs, N.J.: Prentice-Hall, Inc., 1975.

Ellis, A. *Homosexuality: its causes and cure*. New York: Lyle Stuart, Inc., 1965.

Ellis, H. *Studies in the psychology of sex*, (Vol. I), New York: Modern Library, 1936.

Embree, S. The State Department as moral entrepreneur: racism and imperialism as factors in the passage of the Harrison Narcotics Law. In D. F. Greenberg (Ed.), *Corrections and punishment*. Beverly Hills, Calif.: Sage Publications, Inc., 1978.

Empey, L. T. *American delinquency: its meaning and construction*. Homewood, Ill.: Dorsey Press, 1978.

Englehardt, H. T., Jr. The disease of masturbation: values and the concept of disease. *Bull. Hist. Med.*, 1974, *48*, 234-248 (Summer).

Epstein, E. J. Methadone: the forlorn hope. *Public Interest* Summer 1974, pp. 3-24.

Epstein, E. J., *Agency of fear*. New York: G. P. Putnam's Sons, 1977.

Erikson, K. T. *Wayward puritans*. New York: John Wiley & Sons, Inc., 1966.

Etzioni, A., & Remp, R. *Technological shortcuts to social change*. New York: Russell Sage Foundation, 1973.

Evans, R. B. Biological factors in male homosexuality. *Med. Aspects Hum. Sex.*, 1973, *7*(7), 12-33.

Everett, M. W., Waddell, J. O., & Heath, D. B. (Eds.). *Cross cultural approaches to the study of alcohol: an interdisciplinary perspective*. The Hague, Netherlands: Mouton, B.V., 1976.

Fabrega, H., Jr. Concepts of disease: logical features and social implications. *Perspect. Biol. Med.*, 1972, *15*, 583-616 (Summer).

Fabrega, H., & Manning, P. K. Disease, illness and deviant careers. In R. A. Scott & J. Douglas (Eds.), *Theoretical perspectives on deviance*. New York: Basic Books, Inc., 1972.

Faris, R. E. L., & Dunham, H. W. *Mental disorders in urban areas*. Chicago: University of Chicago Press, 1939.

Fieve, R. R. Lithium in psychiatry. *Int. J. Psychiatry*, 1970, *9*, 375-427.

Filene, P. G. *Him/her/self: sex roles in modern America*. New York: Harcourt Brace Jovanovich, Inc., 1974.

Finch, S. M., & Green, J. M. Orthopsychiatry in the United States. In B. Wolman (Ed.), *International encyclopedia of psychiatry, psychology, psychoanalysis, and neurology*, (Vol. 8) Birmingham, Ala.: Aesculapius Publishing Co., 1977.

Finestone, H. *Victims of change: juvenile delinquents in American society*. Westport, Conn.: Greenwood Press, Inc., 1976.

Fingarette, H. The perils of Powell: in search of a factual foundation for the 'disease concept of alcoholism'. *Harvard Law Rev.*, 1970, *83*, 793-812.

Fink, A. E. *The causes of crime: biological theories in the United States, 1800-1915*. Philadelphia: University of Pennsylvania Press, 1938.

Fontana, V. J. An insidious and disturbing medical entity. *Pub. Welfare*, 1966, *24*, 235-39.

Ford, C. S., & Beach, F. A. *Patterns of sexual behavior*. New York: Harper & Row, Publishers, 1951.

Foucault, M. *Madness and civilization*. New York: Random House, Inc. 1965.

Fowler, O. S. *Amativeness: or evils and remedies of excessive and perverted sexuality including warning and advice to the married and single* (40th ed.). New York: Fowler & Wells, 1857.

Fowlkes, M. R. Business as usual—at the state mental hospital. *Psychiatry*, 1975, *38*, 55-64.

Fox, Renée. The medicalization and demedicalization of American society. *Daedalus*, 1977, *106*, 9-22.

Fox, Richard G. The XYY offender: a modern myth? *J. Crimin. Law, Criminol., and Police Sci.*, 1971, *62* (1), 59-73.

Frank, J. *Persuasion and healing*. (Rev. ed.). New York: Schocken Books, Inc., 1974.

Freeman, W. Psychosurgery. In S. Arieti (Ed.), *American handbook of psychiatry* (Vol. 2). New York: Basic Books, Inc., 1959.

Freidson, E. *Profession of medicine*. New York: Harper & Row, Publishers Inc., 1970. (a)

Freidson, E. *Professional dominance*. Chicago: Aldine Press, 1970. (b)

Freidson, E. *Doctoring together*. New York: Elsevier North-Holland, Inc., 1975.

Freud, S. *New introductory lectures in psychoanalysis*. New York: W. W. Norton & Co., Inc., 1933.

Freud, S. The history of the psychoanalytic movement. In A. A. Brill (Ed.). The basic writings of Sigmund Freud. New York: Random House, Inc., 1938. (Originally published, 1914.)

Freud, S. Three contributions to a theory of sex. In A. A. Brill (Ed.), *The basic writings of Sigmund Freud*. New York: Random House, Inc., 1938. (Originally published, 1905).

Freud, S. [*Collected papers*, Vol. 2] (J. Riviere, trans.). New York: Basic Books, Inc., 1959.

Freud, S. [Letter to the mother of a homosexual son] In E. L. Freud (Ed.); J. Stern and T. Stern (trans.), *Letters of Sigmund Freud, 1873-1939*. New York: Basic Books, Inc., 1960. © 1960 by Sigmund Freud Copyrights Ltd., London. (Originally published, 1935.)

Freund, K. Should homosexuality arouse therapeutic concern? *J. Homosex.* 1977, *2* (3), 235-240.

Gagnon, J. & Simon, W. *Sexual deviance*. New York: Harper & Row Publishers, Inc., 1967.

Galliher, J. F., & Walker, A. The puzzle of the social origins of the Marijuana Tax Act of 1937. *Social Prob.*, 1977, *24*, 367-376 (Feb.)

Garth, J. The Americanization of 1984. In R. Quinney (Ed.), *Criminal justice in America*. Boston: Little, Brown, & Co., 1974.

Geis, G., & Block, H. *Man, crime, and society*. New York: Random House, Inc., 1967.

Gelles, R. J. Child abuse as psychopathology: a sociological critique and reformulation. *Am. J. Orthopsychiatry*, 1973, *43*, 611-621.

Gelles, R. J. The social construction of child abuse. *Am. J. Orthopsychiatry*, 1975, *45*, 363-371.

Gelles, R. J., Straus, M. A., & Steinmetz, S. K. Violence toward children in the United States. Presented at the meetings of The American Association for the Advancement of Science, 1977.

Gibbons, D. C. *Delinquent behavior*. (2nd ed.). Englewood Cliffs, N.J.: Prentice-Hall, Inc., 1976.

Gigeroff, A. *Sexual deviations in the criminal law*. Toronto: University of Toronto Press, 1968.

Gil, D. G. *Violence against children*. Cambridge, Mass.: Harvard University Press, 1970.

Gil, D. G., Sociocultural perspective on child abuse. *Child Welfare*, 1971, *50*, 389-395.

Gil, D. G. Unraveling child abuse. *Am. J. Orthopsychiatry*, 1975, *45*, 346-356.

Glatt, M. M. *The alcoholic and the help he needs*. London: Priority Press, 1970.

Glatt, M. M. *Drugs, society and man: a guide to addiction and its treatment*. New York: Halsted Press, 1974.

Glenn, N., & Weaver, C. Attitudes toward premarital, extramarital, and homosexual relations in the U.S. in the 1970s. *J. Sex Research, 15*, 1979, 108-118 (May).

Goddard, J. The medical business. *Sci. Am.*, 1973, *229*, 161-168 (Sept.).

Goffman, E. *Asylums*. Garden City, N.Y.: Anchor Press, 1961.

Goffman, E. *Stigma: notes on the management of a spoiled identity*. Englewood Cliffs, N.J.: Prentice-Hall, Inc., 1963.

Gold, R. Stop it, you're making me sick! *Am. J. Psychiatry*, 1973, *130*, 1211-1212.

Goldstein, A. On the role of chemotherapy in the treatment of heroin addiction. *Am. J. Drug Alcohol Abuse*, 1976, *2*, 279-288.

Goleman, D. Who's mentally ill? *Psychol. Today* Jan., 1978, pp. 34, 37-39, 41.

Goode, E. Marijuana and the politics of reality. *J. Health Soc. Behav.* 1969, *10*, 83-94.

Goode, E. *Drugs in American society*. New York: Alfred A. Knopf, Inc., 1972.

Goode, E. *Deviant behavior: an interactionist approach*. Englewood Cliffs, N.J.: Prentice-Hall, Inc., 1978.

Gordon, G. *Role theory and illness*. New Haven, Conn.: College and University Press, 1966.

Gordon, L. The politics of birth control, 1920-1940: the impact of professionals. *Int. J. Health Services*, 1975, *2*, 253-257.

Goring, C. B. *The English convict: a statistical study*. London: Her Majesty's Stationery Office, 1913.

Gove, W. R. Societal reaction as an explanation for mental illness: an evaluation. *Am. Soc. Rev.*, 1970, *35*, 873-884.

Gove, W. R. The labeling theory of mental illness: a reply to Scheff. *Am. Soc. Rev.*, 1975, *40*, 242-248.

Graham, S. *Lecture to young men on chastity*. (3rd ed.). Boston: George W. Light, 1837. (originally published, 1834.)

Green, R. Homosexuality as a mental illness. *Int. J. Psychiatry*, 1972, *10*(1), 77-98.

Greenberg, L. Alcohol in the body. *Sci. Am.*, 1953, *189* (24), 86-90.

Greenberg, L. Intoxication and alcoholism: physiological factors. *Ann. Am. Acad. Pol. Soc. Sci.*, 1958, *315*, 22-30.

Grinspoon, L., & Singer, S. Amphetamines in the treatment of hyperactive children. *Harvard Ed. Rev.*, 1973, *43*, 515-555.

Grob, G. N. The state hospital in mid-nineteenth–century America: a social analysis. In H. Wechsler, L. Solomon, & B. M. Kramer (Eds.), *Social psychology and mental health*. New York: Holt, Rinehart & Winston, 1970.

Gross, M. B., & Wilson, W. E. *Minimal brain dysfunction*. New York: Brunner/Mazel, Inc., 1974.

Gusfield, J. R. *Symbolic crusade*. Urbana: University of Illinois Press, 1963.

Gusfield, J. R. Moral passage: the symbolic process in the public designations of deviance. *Social Prob.* 1967, *15*, 175-188 (Fall).

Gusfield, J. R. Categories of ownership and responsibility in social issues: alcohol abuse and automobile use. *J. Drug Issues*, 1975, *5*, 285-303 (Fall).

Gussow, Z., & Tracy, G. S. Status, ideology and adaptation to stigmatized illness: a study of leprosy, *Hum. Organization*, 1968, *27*, 316-325.

Hagan, J., & Leon J. Rediscovering delinquency: social history, political ideology and the sociology of law. *Am. Soc. Rev.*, 1977, *42*, 587-598.

Halleck, S. L. *The politics of thearpy*. New York: Science House, 1971.

Halleck, S. L. Another response to 'Homosexuality: the ethical challenge'. *J. Consult. Clin. Psychol.*, 1976, *44* (2), 167-170.

Haller, J. S., Jr., & Haller, R. M. *The physician and sexuality in Victorian America*. Urbana: University of Illinois Press, 1974.

Halpert, H. P. Public opinions and attitudes about mental health. In H. Wechsler, L. Solomon, & B. M. Kramer (Eds.), *Social psychology and mental health*. New York: Holt, Rinehart & Winston, 1970.

Hampson, J. L., & Hampson, J. G. The ontogenesis of sexual behavior in man. In W. C. Young (Ed.), *Sex and internal secretions*. (Vol. 2, 3rd ed.). Baltimore: The Williams & Wilkins Co. 1961.

Hansen, C. *Witchcraft at Salem*. New York: George Braziller Inc. 1969.

Harper, R. F. *The Code of Hammurabi, King of Babylon*. London: Luzac, 1904.

Harris, M. Why men dominate women. *N. Y. Times Mag.*, Nov. 13, 1977, pp. 46ff.

Hatterer, L. J. *Changing homosexuality in the male*. New York: Dell Publishing Co., Inc., 1971.

Hawes, J. M. *Children in urban society: juvenile delinquency in nineteenth century America*. New York: Oxford University Press, 1971.

Hawkins, R. & Tiedeman, G. *The creation of deviance*. Columbus, Ohio: Charles E. Merrill Publishing Co., 1975.

Hayes, S. C., Johnson, V. S. & Cone, J. D. The marked item technique: a practical procedure for litter control. *J. Applied Behav. Anal.*, 1975, *8*, 381-386.

Healy, W. *The individual delinquent*. Boston: Little, Brown & Co., 1917.

Healy, W. *Twenty-five years of child guidance*. Studies from the Institute for Juvenile Research, Series C, No. 256. Illinois Department of Child Welfare, 1934.

Healy, W., & Bronner, A. F. *New light on delinquency and its treatment*. New Haven, Conn.: Yale University Press, 1936.

Heath, R. G. Electrical self-stimulation of the brain in man. *Am. J. Psychiatry*, 1963. *120*, 571-577.

Heath, R. G. Perspectives for biological psychiatry. *Biol. Psychiatry*, 1970, *2* (2), 81-88.

Helmer, J. *Drugs and minority oppression*. New York: The Seabury Press, Inc., 1975.

Hentoff, N. *A doctor among the addicts*. New York: Grove Press, Inc., 1969.

Hentoff, N. Drug pushing in the schools: the professionals. *Village Voice*, May 22, 1972, pp. 21-23.

Hills, S. L. Absolutist and relativist views of social deviance: toward a humanistic perspective. *Humanity Society*, 1977. *1*, 147-165.

Hirschfeld, M. Homosexuality. In V. Robinson (Ed.), *Encyclopaedia sexualis*. New York: Dingwall-Rock, 1936. (a)

Hirschfeld, M. Magnus Hirschfeld. In Victor Robinson (Ed.), *Encyclopaedia sexualis*. New York: Dingwall-Rock, 1936. (b)

Hite, C. Members elect Marmor, uphold DSM-II change. *Psychiatric News*, 1974, *9* (9), 1, 18.

Hoffman, M. *The gay world: male homosexuality and the social creation of evil*. New York: Basic Books, Inc., 1968.

Hofstadter, R. *Anti-intellectualism in American life*. New York: Random House, Inc., 1963.

Hollingshead, A., & Redlich, F. *Social class and mental illness*. New York: John Wiley & Sons, Inc., 1958.

Holzner, B. *Reality construction in society*. (Rev. ed.). Cambridge, Mass.: Schenkman Publishing Co., Inc., 1972.

Hooker, E. A preliminary analysis of group behavior of homosexuals. *J. Psychol.*, 1956, *42*, 217-225.

Hooker, E. The adjustment of male overt homosexuals. *J. Project. Techniques*, 1957, *21*, 18-31.

Hooker, E. The homosexual community. In J. Gagnon & W. Simon (Eds.), *Sexual deviance*. New York: Harper & Row Publishers, Inc., 1967., (originally published, 1961)

Hooton, E. A. *Crime and the man*. Cambridge, Mass.: Harvard University Press, 1939.

Horowitz, I. L. The politics of drugs. *Soc. Policy*, 1972, *3*(2), 36-40.

Horowitz, W. A. Insulin shock therapy. In S. Arieti (Ed.), *American handbook of psychiatry* (Vol. 2). New York: Basic Books, Inc., 1959.

Horrock, N. M. Eighty institutions used in CIA mind studies. *New York Times*, Aug. 4, 1977, p. 17. (a)

Horrock, N. M. CIA data show 14-year project on controlling human behavior. *New York Times*, July 21, 1977, p. 1. (b)

Huessy, H. Study of the prevalence and therapy of the choreatiform syndrome or hyperkinesis in rural Vermont. *Acta Paedopsychiatr.*, 1967, *34*, 130-135.

Huessy, H. Minimal brain dysfunction in children (hyperkinetic syndrome): recognition and treatment. *Drug Ther.*, 1973, *3* (9), 52-63.

Hughes, C. C., Tremblay, M., Rapoport, R. M., and Leighton, A. H. *People of cove and woodlot*. New York: Basic Books, Inc., 1960.

Hull, J. M. The opium habit [in Iowa]. In H. W. Morgan (Ed.), *Yesterday's addicts*. Norman, Okla.: University of Oklahoma Press, 1974. (Originally published, 1885.)

Humphreys, L. *Out of the closets: the sociology of homosexual liberation*. Englewood Cliffs, N.J.: Prentice-Hall, Inc., 1972.

Hunt, G. H., & Odoroff, M. E. Follow-up study of narcotic drug addicts after hospitalization. *Pub. Health Rep.*, 1962, *77*, 41-54.

Hunt, J. Rapists have big ears: genetic screening in Massachusetts. *The Real Paper*, July 4, 1973, p. 4.

Hurvitz, N. Psychotherapy as a means of social control. *J. Consult. Clin. Psychol.*, 1973, *40*, 232-239.

Illich, I. *Medical nemesis*. New York: Pantheon Books, Inc., 1976.

Inglis, B. *The forbidden game: a social history of drugs*. New York: Charles Scribner's Sons, 1975.

Jackson, D. D. A critique of the literature on the genetics of schizophrenia. In D. D. Jackson (Ed.), *The etiology of schizophrenia*. New York: Basic Books, Inc., 1960.

Jackson, D. D. Dachau for queers. In L. Richmond & G. Noguerra (Eds.), *The gay liberation book*. San Francisco: Ramparts Press, 1973.

Jacobs, P., Brunton, A. M., Melville, M., Brittain, R., & McClemont, W. Aggressive behavior, mental subnormality and the XYY male. *Nature*, 1965, *208*, 1351-1352.

Janowitz, M. Sociological theory and social control. *Am. J. Sociol.*, 1975, *81*, 82-108.

Jellinek, E. M. Establishment of diagnostic and guidance clincis for inebriates in Connecticut (Yale plan clinics). *Q. J. Stud. Alcohol*, 1943, *4*, 496-507.

Jellinek, E. M. Phases in the drinking history of alcoholics. *Q. J. Stud. Alcohol*, 1946, *7*, 1-88.

Jellinek, E. M. Phases of alcohol addiction, *Q. J. Stud. Alcohol*, 1952, *13*, 673-684.

Jellinek, E. M. *The disease concept of alcoholism*. Highland Park, N.J.: Hillhouse Press, 1960.

Jewson, N.D. The disappearance of the sick-man from medical cosmology, 1770-1870. *Sociology*. 1976, *10*, 225-244.

Johnson, B. D. Righteousness before revenue: the

forgotten moral crusade against the Indo-Chinese opium trade. *J. Drug Issues,* 1975, *5,* 304-326 (Fall).

Johnson, B. D. Social movements in the origin of a social problem: the moral passage of commercial opium trading in the nineteenth century. Presented at the meetings of The Society for the Study of Social Problems, New York, 1976.

Johnson, V. S. Behavior modification in the correctional setting. *Crim. Just. Behav.,* 1977, *4,* 397-428.

Joint Commission on Mental Illness and Health. *Action for mental health.* New York: Basic Books, Inc., 1961.

Joint Committee of the American Bar Association and the American Medical Association. *Drug addiction: crime or disease?* Bloomington, Ind.: University of Indiana Press, 1961.

Jones, M. *The therapeutic community.* New York: Basic Books, Inc., 1953.

Jones, R. W., & Helrich, A. R. Treatment of alcoholism by physicians in private practice: a national survey. *Q. J. Stud. Alcohol,* 1972, *33,* 117-131.

Kallmann, F. J. *The genetics of schizophrenia.* New York: Augustine, 1938.

Kallmann, F. J. The genetic theory of schizophrenia: an analysis of 691 schizophrenic twin index families. *Am. J. Psychiatry,* 1946, *103,* 309-322.

Kallmann, F. J. Comparative twin studies on the genetic aspects of male homosexuality. *J. Nerv. Ment. Dis.,* 1952, *115,* 283-298.

Kallmann, F. J. The genetics of mental illness. In S. Arieti (Ed.), *American handbook of psychiatry* (Vol. 1). New York: Basic Books, Inc., 1959.

Kameny, F. E. Gay is good. In R. W. Weltge (Ed.), *The same sex: an appraisal of homosexuality.* Philadelphia: United Church Press, 1969.

Kass, L. Regarding the end of medicine and the pursuit of health. *Public Interest,* 1975, *40,* 11-42 (Summer).

Katz, J. *Gay American history.* New York: Thomas Y. Crowell Co., Inc., 1976.

Kazdin, A. E., & Bootzen, R. R. The token economy: an evaluative review. *J. Appl. Behav. Anal.,* 1972, *5,* 343-372.

Keller, M. Definition of alcoholism. *Q. J. Stud. Alcohol,* 1960, *21*:125-134 (March).

Keller, M. Alcohol in health and disease: some historical perspectives. *Ann. N.Y. Acad. Sci.* 1966, *133,* 820-827.

Keller, M. The oddities of alcoholics. *Q. J. Stud. Alcohol,* 1972, *33,* 1147-1148. (a)

Keller, M. On the loss-of-control phenomenon in alcoholism. *B. J. Addict.* 1972, *67,* 153-166. (b)

Keller, M. The disease concept of alcoholism revisited. *J. Stud. Alcohol,* 1976, *37,* 1694-1717. (a)

Keller, M. Problems with alcohol: an historical perspective. In W. Filstead, J. Rossi, & M. Keller (Eds.), *Alcohol and alcohol problems.* Cambridge, Mass. Ballinger Publishing Co., 1976.

Kelman, S. The social nature of the definition of health. In V. Navarro (Ed.), *Health and medical care in the U.S.: a critical analysis.* Farmingdale, N.Y.: Baywood, 1977.

Kempe, C. H., Silverman, F. N., Steele, B. F., Droegemueller, W., & Silver, H. K. The battered-child syndrome. *J.A.M.A.,* 1962, *181,* 17-24.

Kenniston, K. How community mental health stamped out the riots (1968-1978). *Trans-action, 5* (7), 21-29, 1968.

Kenny, T. J., Clemmens, R. L. & Hudson, B. W. Characteristics of children referred for hyperactivity. *J. Pediatr.,* 1971, *78,* 618-622.

Kiev, A. *Magic, faith and healing.* New York: The Free Press, 1964.

Kinsey, A. C., Pomeroy, W. B., & Martin, C. E. *Sexual behavior in the human male.* Philadelphia: W. B. Saunders Co., 1948.

Kinsey, A. C., Pomeroy, W. B., Martin, C. E., & Gebhard, P. H. *Sexual behavior in the human female.* Philadelphia: W. B. Saunders Co., 1953.

Kirk, S. A., & Therrien, M. E. Community mental health myths and the fate of former hospitalized patients. *Psychiatry,* 1975, *38,* 209-217.

Kitsuse, J. I., & Cicourel, A. A note on the use of official statistics. *Social Probl.,* 1963, *11,* 131-139.

Kittrie, N. *The right to be different: deviance and enforced therapy.* Baltimore: Johns Hopkins University Press, 1971. Copyright The Johns Hopkins Press, 1971.

Kittrie, N. Court and sex laws: hands off? *Des Moines Tribune* April 14, 1976, p. 12.

Klapmuts, N. Children's rights. *Crime Delinquency Lit.,* 1972, *4,* 449-477.

Kleinman, P. & Lukoff, I. Methadone maintenance: modest help for a few. Unpublished manuscript, Columbia University School of Social Work, 1975.

Kleinman, P. H., Lukoff, I. F., & Kail, B. L. The magic fix: a critical analysis of methadone maintenance treatment. *Social Prob.,* 1977, *25,* 208-214 (Dec.).

Knowles, J. H. The responsibility of the individual. *Daedalus,* 1977, *106,* 57-80.

Krout, J. A. *The origins of Prohibition.* New York: Alfred A. Knopf, Inc., 1925.

Kuhn, T. S. *The structure of scientific revolutions* (2nd ed.). Chicago: University of Chicago Press, 1970.

Lacey, W. K. *The family in classical Greece.* London: Thames & Hudson Ltd., 1968.

Laing, R. D. *The divided self.* Baltimore: Penguin Books, 1965. (Originally published, 1960.)

Laing, R. D. *The politics of experience.* Baltimore: Penguin Books, 1967.

Laing, R. D., & Esterson, A. *Sanity, madness and the family.* New York: Basic Books, Inc., 1964.

Lambert, N., Sandoval, J., & Sassone, D. Prevalence of hyperactivity in elementary school children as a function of social system definers. *Am. J. Orthopsychiatry,* 1978, *48,* 446-463.

Lange, J. *Crime as destiny.* London: Allen & Unwin (Publishers) Ltd., 1931.

Langner, W. L. Infanticide: a historical survey. *Hist. Child. Quarterly: J. Psychohistory,* 1974, *1,* 353-367.

Larson, M. S. *The rise of professionalism.* Berkeley: University of California Press, 1977.

Lasch, C. Sacrificing Freud. *N.Y. Times Mag.,* Feb. 22, 1976, pp. 11, 70-72.

Lasch, C. *Haven in a heartless world.* New York: Basic Books, Inc., 1977.

Laufer, M. W., Denhoff, E., & Solomons, G. Hyperkinetic impulse disorder in children's behavior problems. *Psychosom. Med.* 1957, *19,* 38-49.

Lauritsen, J. & Thorstad, D. *The early homosexual rights movement (1864-1935).* New York: Times Change Press, 1974.

Lavater, J. K. [*Essay on Physiognomy,* Vol. 3] (T. Holcroft, trans.) London: C. Whittingham for H. D. Symonds, 1804.

Lea, H. C. *A history of the Inquisition of the Middle Ages* (Vol. 3). New York: Macmillan Publishing Co., Inc., 1911.

LEAA (Law Enforcement Assistance Administration). Institute designs armor, mini alarms. *LEAA Newsletter,* 1974, *3* (12), 3.

LEAA (Law Enforcement Assistance Administration). Super security programs in city schools cuts after hours crime *LEAA Newsletter,* 1975, *4* (10), 27, 29.

Leifer, R. Community psychiatry and social power. *Social Prob.,* 1966, *14,* 16-22.

Leifer, R. *In the name of mental health.* New York: Science House, 1969.

Leighton, A. H. *My name is legion.* New York: Basic Books, Inc., 1959.

Leighton, D. C., Harding, J. S., Macklin, D. B., Macmillan, A. M., & Leighton, A. H. *The character of danger.* New York: Basic Books, Inc., 1963.

Lemert, E. M. Paranoia and the dynamics of exclusion. *Sociometry,* 1962, *25* (1), 2-20.

Lemert, E. M. Sociocultural research on drinking. M. Keller and T. Coffey (Eds.), *Proceedings of the 28th International Congress on Alcohol and Alcoholism* (Vol. 2). Highland Park, N.J.: Hillhouse Press, 1969.

Lemert, E. M. *Human deviance, social problems and social control* (2nd ed.). Englewood Cliffs, N.J.: Prentice-Hall, 1972.

Lemkau, P. V., & Crocetti, G. M. An urban population's opinion and knowledge about mental illness, *A. J. Psychiatry,* 1962, *118,* 692-700.

Lender, M. Drunkenness as an offense in early New England: a study of Puritan attitudes. *Q. J. Stud. Alcohol,* 1973, *34,* 353-366.

Lennard, H. L., Epstein, L. J., Bernstein, A., & Ranson, D. C. *Mystification and drug misuse.* New York: Perennial Library, 1971.

Lerman, P. Delinquency and social policy: a historical perspective. *Crime Delinquency Lit..* 1977, *23,* 383-393.

Lerner, R. E. *The heresy of the free spirit in the later Middle Ages.* Berkeley: University of California Press, 1972.

Levine, H. G. The discovery of addiction: changing conceptions of habitual drunkenness in America. *J. Stud. Alcohol,* 1978, *39* (1), 143-174.

Levitt, E. E., & Klassen, A. D., Jr., Public attitudes toward homosexuality. *J. Homosex.,* 1974, *1* (1), 29-43.

Lewis, C. S. The humanitarian theory of punishment. *Res Judicatae,* 1953, *6,* 224-230.

Lex, B. W., & Meyer, R. E. Opiate receptors and opiate antagonists: progress in the "war on drugs." *J. Drug Issues,* 1977, *7,* 54-60 (Winter).

Licht, H. (a.k.a. Paul Brandt). *Sexual life in ancient Greece.* New York: Barnes & Noble Books, 1963. (Originally published in Germany, 1932.)

Lichtenstein, G. Poll finds public split on legalizing homosexual acts. *New York Times,* July 19, 1977, p. 12.

Lidz, C. W., & Walker, A. L. Therapeutic control of heroin: dedifferentiating legal and psychiatric controls. *Soc. Inquiry,* 1977, *47,* 294-321.

Lieber, C. S. The metabolism of alcohol. *Sci. Am.,* 1976, *234* (20), 25-33.

Lief, H. I. Sexual survey #4: current thinking on homosexuality. *Med. Aspects Hum. Sex.,* 1977, *11,* (11), 110-111.

Lindesmith, A. R. Dope fiend mythology. *J. Crim. Law Criminol.,* 1940, *31,* 199-208.

Lindesmith, A. R. *Opiate addiction.* Bloomington, Ind.: Principia Press, 1947.

Lindesmith, A. R. *The addict and the law.* New York: Vintage Books, 1965.

Lindesmith, A. R. *Addiction and Opiates.* Chicago: Aldine Press, 1968.

Lindesmith, A. R. A reply to McAuliffe and Gordon's A test of Lindesmith's theory of addiction. *Am. J. Sociol.,* 1975, *81,* 147-153 (July).

Lindesmith, A. & Levin, Y. The Lombrosian myth in criminology. *Am. J. Sociol.,* 1937, *42,* 653-671.

Lofland, J. *Deviance and identity.* Englewood Cliffs, N.J. Prentice-Hall, Inc., 1969.

Lombroso-Ferrero, G. *Criminal man: according to the classification of Cesare Lombroso.* Montclair, N.J.: Patterson Smith Publishing Corp., 1972, (Reprint.)

Lyman, S. *The seven deadly sins: society and evil.* New York: St. Martin's Press, Inc., 1978.

MacAndrew, C. On the notion that certain persons who are given to frequent drunkenness suffer from a disease called alcoholism. In S. C. Plog & R. B. Edgerton (Eds.), *Changing perspectives in mental illness*. New York: Holt, Rinehart & Winston, 1969.

MacAndrew, C., & Edgerton, R. B. *Drunken comportment*. Chicago: Aldine Press, 1969.

Maddox, J. F., & Bowden. C. L. Critique of success with methadone maintenance. *Am. J. Psychiatry*, 1972, *129*, :440-446.

Malinowski, B. *The sexual life of savages*. (3d ed.). London: George Routledge & Sons, 1932.

Malinowski, B. *Sex and repression in savage society*. New York: Meridian Books, 1955 (Reprint.)

Manders, D. Labelling theory and social reality: a Marxist critique. *Insurg. Sociologist*, 1975, *6*, 53-66.

Manges, M. A second report on the therapeutics of heroin. *N.Y. Med. J.*, 1900, *71*, 51-55.

Mann, H. B., & Greenspan, S. I. The identification and treatment of adult brain dysfunction. *Am. J. Psychiatry*, 1976, *133*, 1013-1017.

Mann, M. *New primer on alcoholism*. New York: Holt, Rinehart & Winston, 1958.

Manning, P. K., with Zucker, M. *The sociology of mental health and illness*. Indianapolis: The Bobbs-Merrill Co., Inc., 1976.

Mark, V., & Ervin, F. *Violence and the brain*. New York: Harper & Row Publishers, Inc., 1970.

Mark, V. H., Sweet, W. H. & Ervin, F. Role of brain disease in riots and urban violence. *J.A.M.A.*, 1967, *201*, 895.

Marmor, J. Introduction. In Judd Marmor (Ed.), *Sexual inversion: the multiple roots of homosexuality*. New York: Basic Books, Inc., 1965.

Marmor, J. Homosexuality and cultural value systems. *Am. J. Psychiatry*, 1973, *130*, 1208-1209.

Martin, D. "Sexual Perverts" is the new homosexual classification but psychiatrists let gay people rap. *Vector*, 1971, *7*, 34-35.

Martin, D. *Battered wives*. San Francisco: New Glide Publications, 1976.

Martin, D., & Lyon, P. *Lesbian/woman*. San Francisco: Glide Publications, 1972.

Martinson, R., Lipton, D., & Wilke, J. *The effectiveness of correctional treatment*. New York: Praeger Publishers, Inc., 1975.

Masters, W. H., & Johnson, V. E. *Human sexual response*. Boston: Little, Brown & Co., 1966.

Masters, W. H., & Johnson, V. E. *Homosexuality in perspective*. Boston: Little, Brown & Co., 1979.

Matza, D. *Delinquency and drift*. New York: John Wiley & Sons, Inc., 1964.

Matza, D. The disreputable poor. In N. J. Smelser & S. M. Lipset (Eds.), *Social structure and mobility in economic development*. Chicago: Aldine Press, 1966.

Matza, D. *Becoming deviant*. Englewood Cliffs, N.J.: Prentice-Hall, Inc., 1969.

Mauss, A. L. *Social problems as social movements*. Philadelphia: J. B. Lippincott Co., 1975.

May, E. Drugs without crime. *Harper's Mag.*, 1971, *243*, 60-65. (July).

McAuliffe, W. E., & Gordon, R. A. A test of Lindesmith's theory of addiction: the frequency of euphoria among long-term addicts. *Am. J. Sociol.*, 1974, *79*, 795-840.

McCaghy, C. H. *Deviant behavior: crime, conflict and interest groups*. New York: Macmillan Publishing Co., Inc., 1976.

McCleery, R. S., & Keelty, L. T. *One life–one physician: an inquiry into the medical profession's performance in self-regulation*. Washington, D.C.: Public Affairs Press, 1971.

McCoy, A. W. *The politics of heroin in Southeast Asia*. New York: Harper & Row, Publishers, 1973.

McIntosh, M. The homosexual role. *Social Prob.* 1968, *16*. 182-192 (Fall).

McKeown, T. A historical appraisal of the medical task. In G. McLachlan & T. McKeown (Eds.), *Medical history and medical care: a symposium of perspectives*. New York: Oxford University Press, 1971.

McKinlay, J. B. The changing political and economic context of the patient-physician encounter. In E. B. Gallagher (Ed.), *The doctor-patient relationship in the changing health scene*. Washington, D.C.: U.S. Government Printing Office, 1976.

McKnight, J. Professionalized service and disabiling help. In I. Illich et al., *Disabling profressions*. London: Marion Boyars Publisher Ltd., 1977.

Mead, M. *Male and female: a study of the sexes in a changing world*. New York: Wm. Morrow & Co., Inc., 1949.

Mechanic, D. *Medical sociology*. New York: The Free Press, 1968.

Mechanic, D. *Mental health and social policy*. Englewood Cliffs, N.J.: Prentice-Hall, Inc., 1969.

Mechanic, D. Health and illness in technological societies. *Hastings Center Stud.* 1973, *1*(3), 7-18.

Mechanic, D. *Politics, medicine and social science*. New York: John Wiley & Sons, Inc., 1974.

Mechanic, D. *The growth of bureaucratic medicine*. New York: Wiley-Interscience, 1976.

Melick, M. E., Steadman, H. J., & Cocozza, J. J. The medicalization of criminal behavior among mental patients. *J. Health Soc. Behav.*, 1979, *20*(3), 228-237.

Menninger, W. C. *A psychiatrist for a troubled world*. B. H. Hall (Ed.), New York: Viking Press, 1967.

Merton, R. K. *Social theory and social structure*. (Rev. ed.). New York: The Free Press of Glencoe, Inc., 1957.

Meyer, J. K. Attitudes toward mental illness in a Maryland community. *Pub. Health Rep.* 1964, *79*, 769-772.

Milan, M. A., & McKee, J. M. Behavior modification: principles and applications in corrections. *In U. S. Senate Committee on the Judiciary, Subcommittee on Constitutional Rights, Individual Rights and the Federal Role in Behavior Modification*. 93rd Congress, 2nd Session (Nov.). Washingon, D.C.: U.S. Government Printing Office, 1974.

Miller, K. S. *Managing madness*. New York: The Free Press, 1976.

Miller, M. *On being different*. New York: Random House, Inc., 1971.

Miller, R. Towards a sociology of methadone maintenance. In C. Winick (Ed.), *Sociological aspects of drug dependence*. Cleveland: CRC Press, Inc., 1974.

Mills, C. W. Situated actions and vocabularies of motive. *Am. Sociol. Rev.*, 1940, *6*, 904-913.

Mitchell, S. A. Psychodynamics, homosexuality, and the question of pathology. *Psychiatry*, 1978, *41*, 254-263 (Aug.).

Mohr, J. C. *Abortion in America*. New York: Oxford University Press, 1978.

Monachesi, E. Cesare Beccaria. *J. Crim. Law, Criminol. Police Sci.*, 1955, *46*, 439-449.

Money, J., Hampson, J., & Hampson, J. L. Imprinting and the establishment of gender role. *Am. Med. Assoc. Arch. Neurolog. Psychiatry*, 1957, *77*, 333-336.

Moran, R. Biomedical research and the politics of crime control. *Contemp. Crises*, 1978, *2*, 335-357.

Morgan, H. W. *Yesterday's addicts: American society and drug abuse, 1865-1920*. Norman, Okla.: University of Oklahoma Press, 1974.

Morris, N. *The future of imprisonment*. Chicago: University of Chicago Press, 1974.

Moss, A. Methadone's rise and fall. In P. Rock (Ed.), *Drugs and politics*. New Brunswick, N.J.: Transaction Books, 1977.

Mulford, H. A. Alcoholics, alcoholism and Iowa physicians. *J. Iowa Med. Soc.*, 1964, *54*, 623-628.

Mulford, H. A., & Miller, D. E. Measuring public acceptance of the alcoholic as a sick person. *Q. J. Stud. Alcohol*, 1964, *25*, 314-323.

Musto, D. F. *The American disease: origins of narcotic control*. New Haven, Conn.: Yale University Press, 1973.

Myerson, A. Review of mental disorders in urban areas. *Am. J. Psychiatry*, 1941, *96*, 995-997.

Nagi, S. Z. *Child maltreatment in the United States*. New York: Columbia University Press, 1977.

National Council on Alcoholism. Criteria for the diagnosis of alcoholism. *Am. J. Psychiatry*, 1972, *129*, 127-135.

National Institute of Mental Health. *Task force on homosexuality final report and background papers*. J. M. Livingood (Ed.). Rockville, Md.: National Institute of Mental Health, 1972.

Neaman, J. S. *Suggestion of the devil*. New York: Anchor Press, 1975.

Nelkin, D. *Methadone maintenance: a technological fix*. New York: George Braziller, Inc., 1973.

New York Academy of Medicine. The problem of homosexuality. *Bull. N. Y. Acad. Med.*, 1964, *40*, 576-580.

New York Academy of Medicine. The Academy's proposals. In J. A. O'Donnell & J. C. Ball. *Narcotic addiction*. New York: Harper & Row Publishers, 1966. (Originally published, 1955.)

New York Times. Mind control studies had origins in trial of Mindszanty, Aug. 2, 1977, p. 16.

Newman. R. G. Retention of patients in the New York City methadone program. *Int. J. Addict.*, 1976, *11*, 905-931.

Newsweek. The heroin plague: what can be done? *78*, 27-32 (July 5).

Newsweek. The methadone jones. *89*, 29 (Feb. 7).

Norris, J. L. Alcoholics anonymous and other self-help groups. In R. Tarter & A. Sugerman (Eds.), *Alcoholism*. Reading, Mass. Addison-Wesley Publishing Co., Inc., 1976.

Nunnally, J. S., Jr. *Popular conceptions of mental health*. New York: Holt, Rinehart & Winston, 1961.

Nyberg, K. L., & Alston, J. P. Attitudes toward homosexual behavior. *J. Homosex.*, 1976, *2* (2), 99-107.

Nyswander, M. *The drug addict as patient*. New York: Grune & Stratton, Inc., 1956.

Office of Child Development. *Report of the conference on the use of stimulant drugs in treatment of behaviorally disturbed children*. Sponsored by the Office of Child Development, Department of Health, Education and Welfare, Washington, D.C., Jan. 11-12, 1971.

Oliver, F. E. The use and abuse of opium. In H. W. Morgan (Ed.), *Yesterday's addicts*. Norman, Okla.: University of Oklahoma Press, 1974. (Originally published, 1872).

Orcutt, J. D., Cairl, R. E., & Miller, E. T. Ideologies of deviance: professional and public conceptions of alcoholism. Presented at the meetings of the Society for the Study of Social Problems, Chicago, 1977.

Overholser, W. Has chlorpromazine inaugurated a new era in mental hospitals? *J. Clin. Exper. Psychopathol.*, 1956, *17*, 197-201.

Paolucci, H. (trans.). Translator's introduction. In *On crimes and punishment* by Cesare Beccaria. New York: The Bobbs-Merrill Co., Inc., 1963.

Paré, C. M. B. Homosexuality and chromosomal sex. *J. Psychosom. Res.*, 1956, *1*, 247-251.

Paredes, A. The history of the concept of alcoholism. In R. Tarter & A. Sugerman (Eds.), *Alcoholism*. Reading, Mass.: Addison-Wesley Publishing Co., Inc., 1976.

Parry-Jones, W. L. *The trade in lunacy*. London: Routledge & Kegan Paul Ltd., 1972.

Parsons, T. *The social system*. New York: The Free Press, 1951.

Parsons, T. Definitions of illness and health in light

of American values and social structure. In E. G. Jaco (Ed.), *Patients, physicians and illness*. (2nd ed.). New York: The Free Press, 1972.

Parsons, T. The sick role and the role of the physician reconsidered. *Health Society,* 1975 *53,* 257-278 (Summer).

Pasamanick, B., Scarpitti, F. R., & Denitz, S. *Schizophrenics in the community*. New York: Appleton-Century-Crofts, 1967.

Pattison, E. M. Comment on the alcoholic game. *Q. J. Stud. Alcohol,* 1969, *30,* 953.

Pattison, E. M., Sobell, M. B., & Sobell, L. C. *Emerging concepts of alcohol dependence*. New York: Springer Verlag, 1977.

Paul, B. D. (Ed.). *Health, culture and community*. New York: Russell Sage Foundation, 1955.

Paulsen, M. G. Legal protection against child abuse. *Children,* 1966, *13,* 42-48.

Pavlov, I. P. [*Conditioned reflexes.*] (G. V. Amep, Ed.), New York: Oxford University Press, 1927.

Pelton, L. H. Child abuse and neglect: the myth of classlessness. *Am. J. Orthopsychiatry,* 1978, *48,* 608-617.

Pfohl, S. J. The 'discovery' of child abuse. *Social Prob.,* 1977, *24,* 310-323 (Feb.).

Phillips, D. L. Rejection: a possible consequence of seeking help for mental disorders. *Am. Soc. Rev.,* 1963, *28,* 963-972.

Pitts, J. Social control: the concept. In D. Sills (Ed.), *International encyclopedia of social sciences*. (Vol. 14). New York: Macmillan Publishing Co., Inc., 1968.

Pivar, D. J. *Purity crusade: sexual morality and social control 1868-1900*. Westport, Conn.: Greenwood Press, 1973.

Plato. *Symposium*. (W. R. M. Lamb, trans.). London: William Heinemann Ltd.; New York: G. P. Putnam's Sons, 1932.

Platt, A. M. *The child savers: the invention of delinquency*. Chicago: University of Chicago Press, 1969.

Platt, A. M. The triumph of benevolence: the origins of the juvenile justice system in the United States. In R. Quinney (Ed.), *Criminal justice in America*. Boston: Little, Brown & Co., 1974.

Platt, A., & Diamond, B. L. The origins of the 'right and wrong' test of criminal responsibility and its subsequent development in the United States: an historical survey. *Calif. Law Rev.,* 1966, *54:* 1227-1260.

Platt, J. J., & Labate, C. *Heroin addiction: theory, research, and treatment*. New York: John Wiley & Sons, Inc., 1976.

Ponse, B. *Identities in the lesbian world*. Westport, Conn.: Greenwood Press, 1978.

Quinney, R. A sociological theory of criminal law. In Quinney, R. (Ed.), *Crime and justice in society*. Boston: Little, Brown & Co., 1969.

Quinney, R. *The social reality of crime*. Boston: Little, Brown & Co., 1970.

Quinney, R. *Criminal justice in America: a critical understanding*. Boston: Little, Brown & Co., 1974.

Radbill, S. X. A history of child abuse and infanticide. In R. E. Helfer & C. H. Kempe (Eds.), *The battered child*. Chicago: University of Chicago Press, 1968.

Radelet, M. Medical hegemony as social control: the use of tranquilizers. Presented at the meetings of the Society for the Study of Social Problems, Chicago, 1977. (a)

Radelet, M. *Social factors influencing the medicalization of anxiety*. Unpublished doctoral dissertation, Purdue University, 1977 (b)

Rafferty, F. T. Juvenile delinquency: psychiatric view. In B. B. Wolman (Ed.), *International encyclopedia of psychiatry, psychology, psychoanalysis, and neurology* (Vol. 6). New York: Aesculapius Publishing Co., 1977.

Rainer, J. D. The genetics of man in health and illness. In S. Arieti (Ed.), *American handbook of psychiatry,* (Vol. 1), (2nd ed.). New York: Basic Books, Inc., 1974.

Ray, O. S. *Drugs, society, and human behavior*. (2nd ed.). St. Louis: The C. V. Mosby Co., 1978.

Reasons, C. E. The politics of drugs: an inquiry in the sociology of social problems. *Sociol. Q.,* 1974, *15,* 381-404 (Summer).

Reasons, C. E. The addict as criminal: perpetuation of a legend. *Crime Delinquency Lit.,* 1975, *21,* 19-27.

Redlich, F., & Kellert, S. R. Trends in American mental health. *Am. J. Psychiatry*. 1978, *135,* 22-28 (Jan.).

Reiser, S. J. *Medicine and the reign of technology*. New York: Cambridge University Press, 1978.

Reynolds, J. M. The medical institution: the death and disease-producing appendage. In L. T. Reynolds & J. M. Henslin (Eds.), *American society: a critical analysis*. New York: David McKay Co., Inc., 1973.

Ridenour, N. *Mental health in the United States*. Cambridge, Mass. Harvard University Press, 1961.

Rieff, P. *Triumph of the therapeutic*. New York: Harper & Row, Publishers, 1966.

Ries, J. K. Public acceptance of the disease concept of alcoholism. *J. Health Soc. Behav*. 1977, *18,* 338-344.

Riley, J. W., & Marden, C. F. The medical profession and the problem of alcoholism. *Q. J. Stud. Alcohol,* 1946, *7,* 240-270.

Ritzer, G. *Sociology: a multiple paradigm science*. Boston: Allyn & Bacon, Inc., 1975.

Robin, S. S., & Bosco, J. J. Ritalin for school children: the teacher's perspective. *J. School Health,* 1973, *47,* 624-628.

Robin, S. S., & Wagenfield, M. O. The community mental health worker: organizational and personal sources of role discrepancy. *J. Health Soc. Behav.,* 1977, *1,* 16-27.

Robinson, D. The alcohologist's addiction—some implications of having lost control over the disease concept of alcoholism. *Q. J. Stud, Alcohol,* 1972, *33,* 1028-1042.

Robinson, D. *From drinking to alcoholism: a sociological commentary*. New York: John Wiley & Sons, Inc., 1976.

Robinson, P. *The modernization of sex*. New York: Harper & Row, Publishers, 1976.

Roblin, R. The Boston XYY case. *Hastings Center Rep.,* 1975, *5* (4), 5-8.

Rock, P. *Drugs and politics*. New Burnswick, N.J.: Transaction Books, 1977.

Rogow, A. A. *Psychiatrists*. New York: Dell Publishing Co., Inc., 1970.

Roizen, R. Comment on the "Rand Report." *J. Stud. Alcohol,* 1977, *38,* 170-178.

Roman, P. M. Labeling theory and community psychiatry. *Psychiatry,* 1971, *34,* 378-390.

Roman, P. M. & Trice, H. M. The sick role, labelling theory and the deviant drinker. *Internat. J. Soc. Psychiatry,* 1968, *14,* 245-251.

Room, R. Drinking and disease: comment on the alcohologist's addiction. *Q. J. Stud. Alcohol,* 1972, *33,* 1049-1059.

Room, R. The Amsterdam Congress. *Drinking Drug Prac. Surveyor,* 1973, *7,* 1-6.

Room, R. Governing images and the prevention of alcohol problems. *Preventive Med.,* 1974, *3,* 11-23.

Room, R. Ambivalence as a sociological explanation: the case of cultural explanations of alcohol problems. *Am. Soc. Rev.,* 1976, *41,* 1047-1065. (a)

Room, R. Drunkenness and the law: comment on "The Uniform Alcoholism and Intoxication Treatment Act." *J. Stud. Alcohol,* 1976, *37:* 113-144. (b)

Rosen, G. *Madness in society*. New York: Harper & Row, Publishers, 1968.

Rosen, G. The evolution of social medicine. In H. E. Freeman, S. Levine, & L. Reeder (Eds.), *Handbook of medical sociology* (2nd ed.). Englewood Cliffs, N.J.: Prentice-Hall, Inc., 1972.

Rosen, G. *From medical police to social medicine*. New York: Science History Publications, 1974.

Rosenberg, C. E. The therapeutic revolution: medicine, meaning, and social change in nineteenth-century America. *Perspect. Biol. Med.,* 1977, *20,* 485-506 (Summer).

Rosenhan, D. L. On being sane in insane places. *Science,* 1973, *179,* 250-258.

Rosenthal, D. The genetics of schizophrenia. In S. Arieti (Ed.), *American handbook of psychiatry* (Vol. 3, 2nd ed.). New York: Basic Books, Inc., 1974.

Ross, E. A. *Social control*. New York: Macmillan Publishing Co., Inc., 1901.

Rotenberg, M. *Damnation and deviance: the Protestant Ethic and the spirit of failure*. New York: The Free Press, 1978.

Rothman, D. J. *The discovery of the asylum*. Boston: Little, Brown & Co., 1971.

Rothstein, W. G. *American physicians in the 19th century: from sects to science*. Baltimore: Johns Hopkins University Press, 1972.

Roucek, J. S. (Ed.). *Social control for the 1980s*. Westport, Conn., Greenwood Press, 1978.

Rush, B. An inquiry into the effects of ardent spirits upon the human body and mind. *Q. J. Stud. Alcohol,* 1943, *4,* 321-341.

Ryan, W. *Blaming the victim*. New York: Vintage Books, 1971. (a)

Ryan, W. Emotional disorder as a social problem: implication for mental health programs. *Am. J. Orthopsychiatry,* 1971, *41,* 638-645. (b)

Sagarin, E. The high personal cost of wearing a label. *Psychol. Today,* March, 1976, pp. 25-26, 30-31.

Sage, W. Crime and the clockwork lemon. *Hum. Behav.,* 1974, *3* (9), 16-25.

Sanders, W. B. *Juvenile delinquency*. New York: Praeger Publishers, Inc., 1976.

Sandoval, J., Lambert, N. M., & Yardell, W. Current medical practice and hyperactive children. *Am. J. Orthopsychiatry,* 1976, *46,* 323-334.

Sarbin. T. R. The scientific status of the mental illness metaphor. In S. G. Plog & R. B. Edgerton (Eds.), *Changing perspectives in mental illness*. New York: Holt, Rinehart & Winston, Inc., 1969.

Sarbin, T. R., & Mancuso, J. C. Failure of a moral enterprise: attitudes of the public toward mental illness. *J. Consult. Clin. Psychol.,* 1970, 2, 159-173.

Sawyer, G. I. Homosexuality: the endocrinological aspects. *Practitioner,* 1954, *172,* 374-377.

Schafer, S. *The political criminal*. New York: Macmillan Publishing Co., Inc., 1974.

Scheckenbach, A. F. Behavior modification and adult offenders. *Proceedings of the One Hundred Fourth Congress of Corrections of the American Correctional Association,* 1974, pp. 360-372.

Scheff, T. J. Decision rules, types of errors, and their consequences in medical diagnosis. *Behav. Sci.,* 1963, *8,* 97-107.

Scheff, T. J. *Being mentally ill*. Chicago. Aldine Press, 1966.

Scheff, T. J. The labelling theory of mental illness. *Am. Soc. Rev.,* 1974, *39,* 444-452.

Schmitt, B. D. The minimal brain dysfunction myth. *Am. J. Dis. Child.,* 1975, *129,* 1313-1318.

Schneider, J. W. Deviant drinking as disease: alcoholism as a social accomplishment. *Social Prob.,* 1978, *25,* 361-372.

Schrag, P., & Divoky, D. *The myth of the hyperactive child*. New York: Pantheon Books, Inc., 1975.

Schur, E. M. *Narcotic addiction in Britain and America: the impact of public policy*. Bloomington: Indiana University Press, 1962.

Schur, E. M. *Crimes without victims: deviant be-*

*havior and public policy*. Englewood Cliffs, N.J.: Prentice-Hall, Inc., 1965.

Schur, E. M. *Labeling deviant behavior*. New York: Harper & Row Publishers, 1971.

Schur, E. M. *The awareness trap*. New York: McGraw-Hill Book Co., 1976.

Schwab, G. *The challenge of the exception: an introduction to the ideas of Carl Schmitt between 1921 and 1936*. Berlin: Duncker und Humbolt, 1970.

Schwitzgebel, R. K. Electronic alternatives to imprisonment. *Lex et Sci.*, 1968. *5*(3), 99-104.

Schwitzgebel, R. K. Development and legal regulations of coercive behavior modification techniques with offenders. *National Institute of Mental Health Monograph,* 1971.

Scott, J. F. *The sex instinct: its use and dangers as affecting heredity and morals* (2nd ed.). London: Sidney Appleton, 1908.

Scott, J. M. *The white poppy*. New York: Harper & Row, Publishers, 1969.

Scull, A. Social control and the amplification of deviance. In R. A. Scott & J. D. Douglas (Eds.), *Theoretical perspectives on deviance*. New York: Basic Books, Inc., 1972.

Scull, A. From madness to mental illness: medical men as moral entrepreneurs. *Eur. J. Soc.,* 1975, *16,* 218-61.

Scull, A. *Decarceration*. Englewood Cliffs, N.J.: Prentice-Hall, Inc., 1977. (a)

Scull, A. Madness and segregative control: the rise of the insane asylum. *Social Prob.*, 1977, *24,* 337-351. (b)

Sedgwick, P. Mental illness is illness. *Salmagundi,* 1973, 196-224 (Summer-Fall).

Seeley, J. R. Alcoholism is a disease: implications for social policy. In D. J. Pittman & C. R. Snyder (Eds.), *Society, culture and drinking patterns*. New York: John Wiley & Sons, Inc., 1962.

Seevers, M. H. Psychopharmacological elements of drug dependence. *J.A.M.A.*, 1968, *206,* 1263-1266.

Seixas, F. A., Williams, K., and Eggleston, S. (Eds.). Medical consequences of alcoholism. *Ann. N.Y. Acad. Sci.,* 1975, *252*.

Seneca. Classics of the alcohol literature. Seneca's epistle LXXXIII; on drunkenness. *Q. J. Stud. Alcohol,* 1942, *3,* 302-307.

Sharp, H. C. The severing of the vasa deferentia and its relation to the neuro-psychopathic constitution. *N.Y. Med. J.*; 1902, *75,* 411-414.

Sharp, H. C. Vasectomy as a means of preventing procreation in defectives. *J.A.M.A.*, 1909, *53,* 1897-1902.

Shaw, C., & McKay, H. *Juvenile delinquency and urban areas*. Chicago: University of Chicago Press, 1942.

Shaw, J. C., & Ferris, G. N. Perverted sexual instinct. *J. Nerv. Ment. Dis.*, 1883, *10,* 185-204.

Sheldon, W. H. *Varieties of delinquent youth*. New York: Harper & Row, Publishers, 1949.

Sheldon, W. H., Stevens, S. S., & Tucker, W. B. *The varieties of human physique*. New York: Harper & Row, Publishers, 1940.

Short, J. F., Jr. Delinquency: the study of delinquency. In D. Sills (Ed.), *International encyclopedia of the social sciences* (Vol. 4). New York: Macmillan Publishing Co., Inc., 1968.

Shryock, R. H. *Medicine and society in America: 1660-1860*. Ithaca, N.Y.: Cornell University Press, 1960.

Shuval, J. T., & Antonovsky, A. Illness: a mechanism for coping with failure. *Soc. Sci. Med.*, 1973, *7,* 259-265.

Sigerist, H. E. *Civilization and disease*. Chicago: University of Chicago Press, 1943.

Sigler, M., & Osmond, H. *Models of madness, models of medicine*. New York: Macmillan Publishing Co., Inc., 1974.

Silver, L. B., Illiam, B., & Dublin, C. Child abuse laws—are they enough? *J.A.M.A.*, 1967, *199,* 65-68.

Silverman, S. Roentgen manifestations of unrecognized skeletal trauma in infants. *Am. J. Roentgenol.*, 1953, *69,* 413-426.

Silverman, M., & Lee, P. R. *Pills, profits and politics*. Berkeley: University of California Press, 1974.

Silverstein, C. Even psychiatry can profit from its past mistakes. *J. Homosex.*, 1976, *2*(2), 153-158.

Silverstein, C. Homosexuality and the ethics of behavioral intervention. *J. Homosex.*, 1977, *2*(3), 205-211.

Singer, R. Consent of the unfree. *Law Hum. Behav.*, 1977, *1*(1), 1-43.

Skinner, B. F. *Science and human behavior*. New York: Macmillan Publishing Co., Inc., 1953.

Skinner, B. F. *Beyond freedom and dignity*. New York: Alfred A. Knopf, Inc., 1971.

Smith, M. The Lilly connection: drug abuse and the medical profession. *Sci. for People,* 1978, *10,* 8-15.

Smith-Rosenberg, C. Sex as symbol in Victorian purity: an ethnohistorical analysis of Jacksonian America. In J. Demos & S. S. Boocock (Eds.), *Turning points: historical and sociological essays on the family,* supplement to *Am. J. Sociol.*, Vol. 84. Chicago: The University of Chicago Press, 1978.

Sobey, F. *The nonprofessional revolution in mental health*. New York: Columbia University Press, 1970.

Socarides, C. W. *The overt homosexual*. New York: Grune & Stratton, Inc., 1968.

Socarides, C. W. Homosexuality and medicine. *J.A.M.A.*, 1970, 1199-1202.

Socarides, C. W. Beyond sexual freedom: clinical fallout. *J. Psychother.*, 1976, *30,* 385-397 (July 3).

Socarides, C. W., Bieber, I., Bychowski, G., Gershman, H., Jacobs, T. J., Myers, W. A., Nackenson, B. L., Prescott, K. F., Rifkin, A. H., Stein, S., & Terry, J. Homosexuality in the male:

a report of a psychiatric study group. *Int. J. Psychiatry,* 1973, *11,* 460-479.

Solomon, T. History and demography of child abuse. II. *Pediatrics,* 1963, *51,* 773-776.

Sontag, S. *Illness as metaphor.* New York: Farrar, Straus & Giroux, 1978.

Sorenson, J. Biomedical innovation, uncertainty, and doctor-patient interaction. *J. Health Soc. Behav.,* 1974, *15,* 366-374 (Dec.).

Spector, M. Legitimizing homosexuality. *Society,* 1977, *14*(5), 52-56.

Spector, M., & Kitsuse, J. I. *Constructing social problems.* Menlo Park, Calif.: Benjamin Cummings Publishing Co., 1977.

Spicer, E. H. (Ed.). *Human problems in technological change.* New York: Russell Sage Foundation, 1952.

Spitzer, R. L. A proposal about homosexuality and the APA nomenclature: homosexuality as an irregular form of sexual behavior and sexual orientation disturbance as a psychiatric disorder. *Am. J. Psychiatry,* 1973, *130,* 1214-1216.

Spitzer, S. Toward a Marxian theory of deviance. *Social Prob.,* 1975, *22,* 638-651.

Srole, L., Langner, T. S., Michael, S. T., Opler, M. K., & Rennie, T. A. C. *Mental health in the metropolis.* New York: McGraw-Hill Book Co., 1962.

Stanton, A. A., & Schwartz, M. S. *The mental hospital.* New York: Basic Books, Inc., 1954.

Star, S. The public's ideas about mental illness. National Opinion Research Center, University of Chicago, 1955. (Mimeographed.)

Starkey, M. L. *The devil in Massachusetts.* New York: Alfred A. Knopf, Inc., 1949.

Starr, P. Medicine, economy and society in nineteenth-century America. *J. Soc. Hist.,* 1977, *10,* 588-607.

Steinmetz, S., & Straus, M. A. (Eds.). *Violence in the family.* New York: Harper & Row, Publishers, 1974.

Stevenson, J. Eli Lilly: death drug dealer. Department of Philosophy, Purdue University, no date. (Mimeographed.)

Stewart, M. A. Hyperactive children. *Sci. Am.,* 1970, *222,* 794-798.

Stewart, M. A., Ferris, A., Pitts, N. P., & Craig, A. G. The hyperactive child syndrome. *Am. J. Orthopsychiatry,* 1966, *36,* 861-867.

Stoll, C. S. Images of man and social control. *Soc. Forces,* 1968, *47,* 119-127 (Dec.).

Stoller, R. J. *Gender and sex: on the development of masculinity and femininity.* New York: Science House, 1968.

Straus, R. Community surveys: their aims and techniques. *Q. J. Stud. Alcohol,* 1952, *13,* 254-270.

Straus, R. Problem drinking in the perspective of social change. In W. Filstead, J. Rossi, & M. Keller (Eds.), *Alcohol and alcohol problems.* Cambridge, Mass.: Ballinger Publishing Co., 1976.

Strauss, A. A., & Lehtinen, L. E. *Psychopathology and education of the brain-injured child* (Vol. 1). New York: Grune & Stratton, Inc., 1947.

Strauss, A., Schatzman, L., Bucher, R., Ehrlich, D., & Sabshin, M. *Psychiatric ideologies and institutions.* New York: The Free Press, 1964.

Sutherland, E. H. Book reviews of Crime and the Man and The American Criminal: An Anthropological Study, Vol. 1, by E. A. Hooton. *J. Crim. Law Criminol.,* 1939, *29,* 911-914 (March-April).

Sutherland, E. H. The diffusion of sexual psychopath laws. *Am. J. Sociol.,* 1950, *56,* 142-148 (Sept.).

Swazey, J. P. *Chlorpromazine in psychiatry.* Cambridge, Mass: MIT Press, 1974.

Symonds, J. A. *Studies in sexual inversion.* Privately published, 1931.

Szasz, T. *The myth of mental illness.* New York: Hoeber-Harper, 1961.

Szasz, T. *Law, liberty and psychiatry.* New York: Macmillan Publishing Co., Inc., 1963.

Szasz, T. Legal and moral aspects of homosexuality. In J. Marmor (Ed.), *Sexual inversion: the multiple roots of homosexuality.* New York: Basic Books, Inc., 1965.

Szasz, T. *The manufacture of madness,* New York: Harper & Row, Publishers, Inc., 1970.

Szasz, T. *Ceremonial chemistry.* New York: Anchor Books, 1974.

Szasz, T. *Schizophrenia: the sacred symbol of psychiatry.* New York: Basic Books, Inc., 1976.

Szasz, T. Healing words for political madness. *The Advocate,* Dec. 28, 1977, pp. 37-40.

Szulc, T. The CIA's electric kool-aid acid test. *Psychol. Today,* Nov., 1977, pp. 92-104, 151-153.

Task Force of Children Out of School. *Suffer the children.* Boston: Massachusetts Advocacy Center, 1972.

Taylor, A. H. *American diplomacy and the narcotics traffic 1900-1939.* Durham, N.C.: Duke University Press, 1969.

Taylor, I., Walton, P., & Young, J. *The new criminology.* New York: Harper & Row Publishers, 1973.

Teal, D. *The gay militants.* New York: Stein & Day Publishers, 1971.

Temkin, O. *The falling sickness* (2nd ed.). Baltimore: Johns Hopkins University Press, 1971.

Terry, C. E., & Pellens, M. *The opium problem.* New York: Bureau of Social Hygiene, 1928.

Thio, A. *Deviant behavior.* Boston, Mass.: Houghton Mifflin Co., 1978.

Thrasher, F. M. *The gang.* Chicago: University of Chicago Press, 1936. (Originally published, 1927.)

Trice, H. M. Alcoholics Anonymous. *Ann. Am. Acad. Pol. Soc. Sci.,* 1958, *315,* 108-116.

Trice, H. M., & Roman, P. Delabeling, relabeling, and Alcoholics Anonymous. *Social Prob.,* 1970, *17,* 538-546.

Trice, H. M., & Roman, P. *Spirits and demons at work: alcohol and other drugs on the job*. Ithaca, N.Y.: New York State School of Industrial and Labor Relations, Cornell University, 1972.

Trice, H. M., & Wahl, R. J. A rank order analysis of the symptoms of alcoholism. *Q. J. Stud. Alcohol,* 1958, *19,* 636-648.

Trotter, T. Classics of the alcohol literature. An early medical view of alcohol addiction and its treatment. Dr. Thomas Trotter's "Essay, medical, philosophical and chemical, on drunkenness." *Q. J. Stud. Alcohol,* 1941, *2,* 584-591.

Twaddle, A. C., & Hessler, R. M. *A sociology of health*. St. Louis: The C. V. Mosby Co., 1977.

U.S. Department of Health, Education and Welfare. *Eighth revision international classification of diseases*. Washington, D.C.: U.S. Government Printing Office, 1968.

U.S. Department of Health, Education and Welfare. *The supply of health manpower* (Publication No. [HRA] 75-38). Washington, D.C.: U.S. Government Printing Office, 1974.

U.S. House Committee on Government Operations. *Federal involvement in the use of behavior modification drugs on grammar school children of the right to privacy inquiry: Hearing Before a Subcommittee of The Committee on Government Operations*. House of Representatives, 91st Congress, 2nd Session (Sept. 29). Washington, D.C.: U.S. Government Printing Office, 1970.

U.S. Senate Committee on the Judiciary, Subcommittee on Constitutional Rights. *Individual rights and the federal role in behavior modification*. Senate, 93rd Congress, 2nd Session. Washington, D.C.: U.S. Government Printing Office, 1974.

Vaillant, G. E. A twelve year follow-up of New York narcotic addicts. *Am. J. Psychiatry,* 1965, *122,* 729-734.

Vallentin, A. *Leonardo da Vinci*. New York: Viking Press, 1938.

Van Den Haag, E. Introduction. In R. von Krafft-Ebing, *Psychopathia sexualis*. New York: G. P. Putnam's Sons, 1965.

Vanggaard, T. *Phallos: a symbol and its history in the male world*. New York: International Universities Press, 1972. (Originally published in Denmark, 1969.)

Veatch, R. M. The medical model: its nature and problems. *Hastings Center Stud.,* 1973, *1*(3), 59-76.

Waitzkin, H., & Stoeckle, J. Information control and the micropolitics of health care: summary of an ongoing project. *Soc. Sci. Med.,* 1976, *10,* 263-276 (June).

Waitzkin, H. K., & Waterman, B. *The exploitation of illness in capitalist society*. Indianapolis: The Bobbs-Merrill Co., Inc., 1974.

Waldorf, D. *Careers in dope*. Englewood Cliffs, N.J.: Prentice-Hall, Inc., 1973.

Ware, J. *Hints to young men on the true relations of the sexes*. Boston: Tappan, Whittemore & Mason, 1879. (Originally published, 1850.)

Warren, C. A. B. *Identity and community in the gay world*. New York: John Wiley & Sons, Inc., 1974.

Warren, C. A. B., & Johnson, J. M. A critique of labeling theory from the phenomenological perspective. In R. Scott & J. Douglas (Eds.), *Theoretical perspectives on deviance*. New York: Basic Books, Inc., 1972.

Watson, J. B. *Behaviorism*. New York: W. W. Norton & Co., Inc., Publishers, 1930.

Weber, M. *The Protestant ethic and the spirit of capitalism*. New York: Charles Scribner's Sons, 1958. (Originally published, 1904-1905.)

Weinberg, G. *Society and the healthy homosexual*. New York: St. Martin's Press, Inc., 1972.

Weinberg, M. S., & Williams, C. J. *Male homosexuals: their problems and adaptations*. New York: Oxford University Press, 1974.

Weinberg, T. S. On "doing" and "being" gay; sexual behavior and homosexual self-identity. Unpublished manuscript, State University College at Buffalo, 1977.

Weiner, L., Becker, A., & Friedman, T. T. *Home treatment*. Pittsburgh: University of Pittsburgh Press, 1967.

Wender, P. *Minimal brain dysfunction in children*. New York: John Wiley & Sons, Inc., 1971.

Wertz, R. W., & Wertz, D. C. *Lying-in: a history of childbirth in America*. New York: The Free Press, 1977.

West, L. J., Doige, W. T., & Williams, R. L. An approach to the problem of homosexuality in the military service. *Am. J. Psychiatry,* 1958, *115,* 392-401.

West, L. J., & Glass, A. J. Sexual behavior and the military law. In R. Slovenko (Ed.), *Sexual behavior and the law*. Springfield, Ill.: Charles C Thomas, Publisher, 1965.

White, R. W. *The abnormal personality* (3rd ed.). New York: Ronald Press, 1964.

Wilbur, D. L. Alcoholism: an AMA view. In M. Keller & T. G. Coffey (Eds.), *Proceedings of the 28th International Congress on Alcohol and Alcoholism* (Vol. 2). Highland Park, Ill.: Hillhouse Press, 1969.

Wilkerson, A. E. *A history of the concept of alcoholism as a disease*. Unpublished doctoral dissertation, University of Pennsylvania, 1966.

Willette, R. (Ed.). Narcotic antagonists: the search for long-acting preparations. *Research Monograph No. 4*. Rockville, Md: National Institute on Drug Abuse, 1976

Williams, C. J., & Weinberg, M. S. *Homosexuals and the military: a study of less than honorable discharge,* New York: Harper & Row, Publishers, Inc., 1971.

Wilson, J. Q. *Thinking about crime*. New York: Basic Books, Inc., 1975.

Wiseman, J. P. *Stations of the lost*. Englewood Cliffs, N.J.: Prentice-Hall, Inc., 1970.

Wiseman, J. P. Sober comportment: patterns and perspectives on alcohol addiction. Unpublished manuscript, University of California, San Diego, La Jolla, Calif., 1979.

Wolf, I., Chafetz, M. E., Blane, H. T., & Hill, M. J. Social factors in the diagnosis of alcoholism. II. Attitudes of physicians. *Q. J. Stud. Alcohol,* 1965, *26,* 72-79.

Wolfenden Report. *Report of the Committee on Homosexual offenses and prostitution.* New York: Stein & Day Publishers, 1963.

Wolff, K. For a sociology of evil. *J. Soc. Issues,* 1969, *25,* 111-125.

Wolfgang, M. E. Cesare Lombroso. In H. Mannheim (Ed.), *Pioneers in criminology.* Chicago: Quadrangle Books, 1960.

Wolfgang, M. E., Figlio, R. M., & Thornberry, T. *Criminology index: research and theory in criminology in the United States, 1945-1972* (2 vols.). New York: Elsevier North-Holland, Inc., 1975.

Woolley, P. V., Jr., & Evans, W. A., Jr. Significance of skeletal lesions in infants resembling those of traumatic origin. *J.A.M.A.,* 1955, *158,* 539-543.

Wootton, B. *Social science and social pathology.* London: George Allen & Unwin, 1959.

Wootton, B. The law, the doctor, and the deviant. *Br. Med. J.,* 1963, *2,* 197-202.

World Health Organization. *Second report of Expert Committee on Mental Health, Alcoholism Subcommittee.* (World Health Organizational Tech. Rep. Series, No. 48). Aug., 1952.

World Health Organization. Expert Committee on Mental Health. (Tech. Rep. Series, No. 273). Geneva, 1964.

World Health Organization. Expert Committee on Mental Health (Tech. Rep. Series, No. 407). Geneva. 1969.

Yablonsky, L. *Synanon: the tunnel back.* Baltimore: Pelican Publishing Co., Inc., 1967.

Young, James H. *The toadstool millionaires.* Princeton, N.J.: Princeton University Press, 1961.

Young, Jock. *The drugtakers: the social meaning of drug use.* London: MacGibbon & Kee, 1971.

Zilboorg, G. *A history of medical psychology.* New York: W. W. Norton & Co., Publishers, 1941.

Zola, I. K. Medicine as an institution of social control. *Sociological Rev.,* 1972, *20,* 487-504.

Zola, I. K. In the name of health and illness: on some socio-political consequences of medical influence. *Soc. Sci. Med.,* 1975, *9,* 83-87.

Zurcher, L. A., Jr., Kirkpatrick, G., Cushing, R. G., & Bowman, C. K. The anti-pornography campaign: a symbolic crusade. *Social Prob.,* 1971, *19,* 217-238 (Fall).

# AUTHOR INDEX

**G**



**H**



**I**



**J**



**K**

# SUBJECT INDEX*



*Italicized numbers indicate illustrations. An "n" indicates information in a footnote, and a "t" indicates information in a table.

**D**

**E**



**F**



**G**



**H**

## I

## N